GOVERNING BY CONSENT

AN INTRODUCTION TO AMERICAN POLITICS

"...Governments are instituted among Men, deriving their just powers from the consent of the governed."

Declaration of Independence. July 4, 1776

Governing by Consent

AN INTRODUCTION TO AMERICAN POLITICS

SECOND EDITION

John F. Bibby
UNIVERSITY OF WISCONSIN, MILWAUKEE

CQ PRESS

CONGRESSIONAL QUARTERLY INC.
WASHINGTON, D.C.

Photo credits begin on page 664. This section is considered an extension of the copyright page.

Book design: Kachergis Book Design, Pittsboro, North Carolina
Cover photo: Telegraph Colour Lab/FPG International Corp.

LIBRARY OF CONGRESS CATALOGING-IN-PUBLICATION DATA
Bibby, John F.
    Governing by consent : an introduction to American politics / John F. Bibby.
  —2nd ed.
        p. cm.
    Includes bibliographical references and index.
    ISBN 0-87187-827-5
    1. United States — Politics and government. I. Title.
    JK 274.B54 1994
    320.473—dc20   94-32850
                                                     CIP

CONTENTS

TABLES, FIGURES, AND BOXES

Tables

Figures

Boxes

PREFACE

I N   A N   I N C R E A S I N G L Y interdependent yet fiercely nationalistic world, efforts to understand what is involved in sustaining a constitutional democracy have taken on greater importance as such nations as South Africa and the republics of Eastern Europe have started down the road toward representative government. As ones who chose this course over two hundred years ago, Americans continue to strive to strengthen their democratic political system, while encouraging others willing to undertake their own experiments with the democratic process.

With all this in mind, *Governing by Consent: An Introduction to American Politics* sets out to paint a clear, accurate portrait of the American political system by posing and seeking answers to the basic questions of governance: Who governs? How does the political process operate? Why does the political system work as it does? In what ways does the political system influence the daily lives and well-being of the American people? In my view, the principal obligation of an American government textbook is to describe and explain what actually happens in the political process so that students are able to make their own informed evaluations about their leaders, the system, and its results. With large numbers of Americans now lacking confidence in and even demonstrating contempt for politics and politicians, answers to the who, what, how, and why of the political process are particularly relevant if America's unique experience with government by the consent of the governed is to endure and retain its vitality.

Governing by Consent reflects and relies upon the best and latest political science scholarship to simplify, amplify, and demystify the intricacies of the governing process. This second edition, like the first, assumes that an introductory text can successfully present the findings of political science research without compromising the intellectual standards of scholarship.

This book does not present politics as an endless battle between the good guys and the bad guys. Instead it seeks to explain, rather than to indoctrinate, and to provide students with the tools that will enable them to reach their own conclusions about the American political system.

Each chapter of *Governing by Consent* has been revised and updated to reflect the changes brought about by the election of Democrat Bill Clinton, the first president born after World War II. In keeping with the dynamic nature of politics, analysis is provided of how changing domestic and international conditions have affected U.S. political institutions, processes, and policies. New statistics, illustrations, descriptions, and analyses of recent political events further enrich and enliven the presentation.

A full supplements package is available from the publisher. Call 202-887-6363 for information.

Organization of this Book

Governing by Consent is a comprehensive yet concise introductory text: it's straightforward, balanced presentation, relatively compact size, and reasonable price offer flexibility to instructors who want to supplement with thematic or topical material of their own choosing, while knowing that students have the benefit of a thorough guide to the American system in their textbook.

The organization of the text is traditional: legal framework—political processes—governmental institutions—public policy. The chapters were written to stand alone, however, so they can be assigned in a different sequence without jeopardizing comprehension.

Part I focuses primarily on the Constitution—the legal basis and framework for American government and politics. Under the constitutionally mandated "government of separated institutions *sharing*," the president and Congress must compete continually for authority and seek to protect their constitutional and political status.[1] This competition has gone on unabated (even though divided party control of government ended at least temporarily with the 1992 elections) as President Clinton and a Democratic Congress have sparred over health care, welfare reform, crime, gays in the military, and foreign policy. Part I completes its look at the constitutional foundations by examining federal-state relations as well as civil liberties and civil rights.

In Part II attention is turned to the *process* of governing by consent. Public opinion and the ways in which citizens' concerns become government concerns—through political participation, political parties,

1. Richard E. Neustadt, *Presidential Power and Modern Presidents* (New York: Free Press, 1990), 29

elections, interest groups, and the mass media—are analyzed. Over time and in many cultures the right to rule has often been seized by people on the basis of family, birth, religion, class, or wealth. Such claims have been challenged in modern times by the demand for greater participation in the governing process. Broadened participation requires that institutions, such as political parties, be capable of mobilizing citizens and contesting elections. As pointed out by V. O. Key, Jr.: "The political party becomes the instrument for organization of support in societies founded on the doctrine of consent of the governed. Inherent in that is the idea of popular displacement of governments and the substitution of other rulers preferred by the people."[2] Key also referred to the essential role of interest groups, another subject analyzed in Part II. Indeed, he called group interests "the animating forces in the political process" and observed that the governing process "consists in large degree in the advancement of legitimate group objectives, in the reconciliation and mediation of conflicting group ambitions, and in the restraint of group tendencies judged to be socially destructive."[3]

The book moves on in Part III to a discussion of the governing institutions: the Congress, presidency, bureaucracy, and judiciary. The relationships between each institution and the public—for example, popular support as a basis for presidential power and the impact of the political environment on the Supreme Court—are explored. The internal operations of each branch of government are analyzed as well, along with the politics of interbranch relations—how the various institutions have adapted to what Edwin Corwin has called the Constitution's "invitation to struggle."[4]

Part IV provides an overview of U.S. public policy, a framework for analyzing the stages in the policy process, and classifications of the types of policies emanating from government. Several critical questions are also addressed: Are the policies produced by the system adequate? Is the process truly democratic? Is reform of the system needed?

A unique feature of this book is the essay, "Politics Along the Potomac," which opens Part III. This feature is designed to help readers imagine and soak up the political atmosphere that so uniquely characterizes Washington, D.C. Among other things, it highlights the

2. V. O. Key, Jr., *Politics, Parties, and Pressure Groups,* 5th ed. (New York: Crowell, 1964), 199–200.

3. Ibid., 17.

4. Edwin S. Corwin, *The President: Office and Powers,* 4th ed. (New York: New York University Press, 1957), 171.

impact of Washington's permanent political community on governmental decision making—an influence that Bill Clinton acknowledged early in his presidency when he observed, "There is a sort of permanent government here, but there's also a permanent political culture.... It is my job as president to learn to make the most of that instead of letting it make the most of me."[5]

Acknowledgments

In preparing this text, many individuals contributed generously of their time, skills, and expertise. I wish to thank, while absolving from all blame, the following professional colleagues who reviewed the manuscript and provided wise counsel: Judith Baer, Lawrence Baum, Donald Baumer, Gary Bryner, Bradley Canon, Robert Carp, Allan Cigler, Timothy Conlan, M. Margaret Conway, Lawrence Dodd, Maureen Drummy, Louis Fisher, John Gates, Doris Graber, Cole Blease Graham, Jr., James Guth, William Keefe, Donald Kettl, Stephanie Greco Larson, James Lester, Michael Maggiotto, Kenneth Meier, Richard Niemi, Bruce Oppenheimer, Lawrence O'Toole, Jr., Mark Peterson, Leroy Rieselbach, Randall Ripley, Michael Robinson, David Rohde, Barbara Salmore, Robert Spitzer, Harold Stanley, Norman Thomas, Thomas Walker, Richard Watson, and Nancy Zingale.

Particularly helpful in shaping this second edition were John Clark, Stephen Craig, Daniel Franklin, William McLauchan, and Steven Shull, each of whom adopted the first edition and provided thorough analyses of how the book actually worked in the classroom. The second edition benefits from their experience and suggestions.

As was the case with the first edition, I had the great fortune to work with a highly talented, knowledgeable, and always good-humored editor, Sabra Bissette Ledent. The staff at CQ Press—Brenda Carter, Nancy Lammers, David Tarr, Ann O'Malley, Kathryn Suarez, and Kate Quinlin—have been supportive and generous with their assistance and made working on this project pleasurable. I am particularly grateful to my wife, Lucile, who has read various drafts of the book more times than she can remember. Throughout the process, her editorial judgment, common sense, support, and encouragement have been unfailing.

5. Quoted by the *Washington Post*, May 14, 1993, A11.

PART I

The Context of American Politics

1. Politics and Democracy in America

L IVING UNDER one of the world's oldest and stablest democratic governments, Americans are, in general, satisfied with their system of government and the quality of their lives. This rosy picture, however, masks periodic dissatisfaction with the country's leaders and doubts about the capacity of government to cope with societal problems. Indeed, in recent public opinion surveys 71 percent of respondents said that they were unhappy with the way things were going in the United States[1] and only 27 percent had a great deal of confidence in the people running Congress.[2]

Such survey results are not unusual. They reflect both a desire for change in government policy and skepticism about the capacity of government to remedy societal problems. Is the country seriously off track? Is government the problem or the answer? Are institutional reforms in order? How can policy change be achieved, if indeed it is needed? How can the most desirable features of the political order be preserved? Responses to these questions depend substantially on the information available about politics and government. Before people can assess the need for change or stability, identify appropriate policy alternatives, and engage in political activity that has a reasonable chance of achieving its stated goals, they need to know how politics works, how it is changing, and just what the forces of change and stability are.

Most people acquire information about how the political process operates in, at best, a rather sporadic and casual manner. They watch television newscasts when they can and catch brief news reports on the car radio. They scan the newspapers and perhaps subscribe to *Time* or *Newsweek*. But the difficulties encountered in absorbing the knowledge needed for informed political discussion and action in no way diminish the need for such knowledge. This book describes and analyzes what political scientists—those who analyze and teach about politics and government—have discovered about how American government works, why it works the way it does, and how government policy touches the well-being and life of every American.

1. *American Enterprise*, July/August 1993, 85.
2. *American Enterprise*, November/December 1993, 94.

The Nature of Politics and Government

Politics and government influence the very basics of life—a person's standard of living, freedoms, and future opportunities. The political process and the government policies that grow out of it are important because of what government can do for—and to—anyone. Government can supply financial assistance to attend college, withhold money from paychecks, provide medical care, send a person to prison, and even plunge the country into war. Anything that can affect people so dramatically requires a closer examination.

Politics

What is **politics**? As used in everyday language, "politics" conjures up all kinds of rather unsavory images. Frequently, it refers to the unseemly machinations of the ambitious and self-serving to gain personal advantage over others. Thus, to be called a "politician" is seldom intended as a compliment. Candidates for office may claim, in fact, that one of their main qualifications is that they are not politicians. Indeed, President Harry Truman once observed that "a President needs political understanding to run the government, but he may be elected without it." And in what may be one of today's most telling statements on the profession of politics, a company has even produced a board game called "Lie, Cheat, Steal: A Game of Political Power." Promotional materials describe it as "a game of political power that lets you play scrupulously fair or devilishly devious!" Generally, then, anyone accused of "playing politics" or acting out of political motivations is suspected of having something less than wholesome afoot.

But politics has its more favorable associations as well. As far back as Aristotle, it has been recognized that political activity "exists for the sake of noble actions" and that political leaders can accomplish things that are genuinely good. For example, George Washington, Thomas Jefferson, James Madison, and Alexander Hamilton played leading roles in founding the nation. Abraham Lincoln took steps to save the Union and free the slaves. And Franklin Roosevelt's leadership pulled the country through a depression and world war. Indeed, one look at American history reveals that the greatest national heroes have been politicians. Ordinary citizens as well have banded together to influence national policy for the better—the suffragists early in this century and the civil rights marchers in the 1960s are two prominent examples.

Political leaders who fight for especially noble causes—Washington,

Jefferson, Lincoln—are often elevated to the rank of statesmen in the public's mind. The label "statesmen" may even be applied to much-admired contemporary leaders, while others are relegated to the category of just being "politicians." But when all the value-laden connotations are stripped away, the essence of politics remains. It is *power*—the ability of one person to get another person to behave in a desired manner. And leaders, whether viewed as statesmen or politicians, work daily at gaining it and exercising it. Politics and the use of power, however, inevitably face *conflict* because people have different values and goals and because life's prized objectives—wealth, security, deference, safety, knowledge, and power itself—do not exist in sufficient quantities to satisfy everyone. In its most fundamental sense, then, politics is concerned with "who gets what, when, how."[3]

How well a political system works depends largely on whether society's inevitable political conflicts can be resolved and managed through negotiation, bargaining, and compromise. If such processes permit rival interests—whether groups or individuals—to get enough of what they want, those interests can continue to compete without disrupting the whole legal structure of government. Politics can therefore be viewed as a process of *conflict management.*

But there is more to politics than just keeping the lid on the simmering kettle of political conflict. Politics is also the process through which individuals and groups organize and act together to achieve social objectives—individual freedom, national security, public health and safety, economic opportunity, improved education, clean air and water. Through *collective action*, environmental and health groups, for example, successfully pressured Congress to enact clean air legislation.

When politics is thus stripped of both its negative and positive connotations and viewed in its essentials, it becomes a basic, inevitable social process involving the acquisition, retention, and exercise of power; the management of conflicts; and collective action.

Government

Government is an institution that through its actions has the ultimate authority to allocate values in society—to decide "who gets what, when, how." For example, neither the United States Chamber of Commerce nor the AFL-CIO (American Federation of Labor and Congress of Industrial Organizations) has final authority to decide on the minimum wage for workers or whether workers will be entitled to family leave from their jobs. The authority to set such policies rests with gov-

3. Harold D. Lasswell, *Politics: Who Gets What, When, How* (New York: Meridian Books, 1958).

ernment officials—with Congress to enact the legislation, the president to see that the law is carried out, and the courts to interpret it. Both the Chamber of Commerce and the AFL-CIO can try to influence congressional, presidential, and judicial decisions, but ultimately it is the government that makes the policy decisions. Government decisions are distinguished from those of other organizations by the fact that they are binding for all of society. By contrast, the decisions and policies of private organizations are enforceable within their own memberships but not beyond. Governments, moreover, have a monopoly on the legitimate use of force. The federal government, for example, can if necessary use physical force—the Federal Bureau of Investigation, federal marshals, Treasury agents, the Coast Guard, and even the military—to compel compliance. State and local governments have the state patrol, sheriff departments, and local police to enforce their laws. No other organizations in this society can legitimately use physical force.

Because government decisions are authoritative for all of society, this book is primarily concerned with the politics of government rather than that of nongovernmental organizations. We will, however, occasionally consider the internal politics of nongovernmental organizations—interest groups, political parties, the media—because these organizations have an impact on government decisions.

The Political Process: Never-Ending

When the World Series is over each October, the fans know which team is the world champion. The decision is final; the baseball season is at an end, and nothing can be done to reverse the outcome. But unlike major league baseball, the political season has no end, and no decision is really final.

The U.S. political system offers individuals, groups, interests, and parties ample opportunities to change existing government policies. Those who lose a policy struggle in one political arena always have a chance to win in another. Moreover, there is the possibility that the ongoing turnover—both voluntary and involuntary—in government officials will bring about the sought-after policy changes. The examples of ways in which government policies can be changed are many:

■ Laws enacted by Congress can be repealed and modified by a succeeding Congress.

■ Presidents can veto acts of Congress and influence how statutes are administered.

- Bureaucrats can implement laws of Congress in a manner that may or may not conform to the intent of Congress or the president.
- The courts can invalidate an act of Congress; they also can interpret it narrowly or expansively.
- The courts can nullify decisions of the president and the bureaucracy.
- Supreme Court decisions can be reversed or modified by constitutional amendments and legislation, or by the lower courts when they implement Supreme Court decisions.
- Elections can result in changes in government personnel, which in turn can cause the government to change its policies.

Those who win a legislative victory in Congress must normally be prepared to defend their victory before the administration, courts, and future Congresses. Those who initially lose the policy struggle in Congress still have a chance to regain part or all of their loss via the administration, the courts, or a future Congress. No decision is really final—that is, *all government decisions should be seen as interim or temporary.* No matter how important it seems at the time, each government decision is just one stage in an ongoing struggle over public policy.

The Politics of Democracy

Politics is found in all government systems whether they are democratic, authoritarian, or totalitarian. In this book, however, we will look primarily at a particular brand of politics: the American style of democratic politics.

The Many Meanings and Forms of Democracy

Democracy has a variety of meanings. It has been said that the Soviet bloc countries of the cold war era and some Third World nations had democratic systems of government because government decisions were allegedly made in the real interests of the people, whether or not they had an opportunity to participate in choosing their leaders. In the Greek city-states of antiquity and New England town meetings of today, democracy means direct citizen participation in government decision making. This is **direct democracy**. In the United States and most Western nations, democracy is a system of government in which officeholders acquire the power to make decisions by means of a competitive struggle for the people's vote. This is **representative democracy**.

Representative democracies come in several different forms. The United States has a **presidential system** in which a chief executive is elected independently of the national legislature. In the *parliamentary systems* of most Western European nations, the chief executive (called a prime minister, premier, or chancellor) is selected by the majority party or coalition of parties in the national legislature. Democracies also differ in how they divide power between the national government and regional governments. The United States, Canada, Australia, and Germany are organized on a *federal* basis—that is, they divide governmental power between the national government and the states. But in Britain and France all governmental authority resides with the national government. Democracies differ as well in the extent to which they provide their citizens with social welfare benefits. In Sweden, for example, the government assumes a much larger share of the responsibility for people's economic security and social welfare than is true in the United States.

Even with these significant differences among the Western democ-

Democracy requires the peaceful and orderly transfer of power through elections. Chief Justice William Rehnquist (right) administers the oath of office to incoming Democratic president Bill Clinton (left) at the Capitol on January 20, 1993, in the presence of outgoing Republican president George Bush. Standing beside Clinton are his wife, Hillary Rodham Clinton, and daughter, Chelsea.

racies, all measure up to a basic test of a democracy: *their citizens have a relatively high degree of control over what their leaders do.*[4] Citizens' efforts to influence political leaders are expected, accepted, and frequently successful. This sets Western democracies in stark contrast to such regimes as the People's Republic of China where open opposition to government policies is not permitted.

Leadership Succession
through Elections

Traditionally, one of the most vexing problems of government has been that of leadership succession to government offices.[5] In hereditary monarchies, leadership succession was handled through a sort of biological lottery—when the monarch died, the heir succeeded to the throne. Sometimes this worked well (Elizabeth I of England); at other times disaster ensued (Elizabeth's Stuart successors, James I and Charles I). In both traditional monarchies and modern-day dictatorships, succession often has been achieved through revolution, assassination, or a coup d'état.

The transfer of governmental authority without serious disruptions to the life of the state has been a long-standing problem of governance. The democratic solution to this problem is elections. Experience has shown that elections operate most effectively when (1) there is a tradition of elections and the citizens are fully familiar with the process, and (2) there is widespread agreement within society about the substance of public policy and political procedures. Fortunately, these conditions are present in the United States.

In a democracy, elections are more than a matter of filling government posts when they become vacant. Elections ensure that posts will become vacant at periodic intervals without the "messiness of beheading or the inconvenience of revolution."[6] As that distinguished scholar of American politics V. O. Key, Jr., has observed,

The democratic technique for the determination of succession is . . . combined with a method for the termination of the life of a government. An election poses the questions whether the ruling clique shall be continued in power and, if not, by whom shall it be succeeded. Democratic orders merge into a single ritual a substitute for older techniques of determining the heir

4. Fred I. Greenstein and Frank B. Feigert, *The American Party System and the American People*, 3d ed. (Englewood Cliffs, N.J.: Prentice-Hall, 1985), 2.

5. The discussion of the characteristics of democratic governments and their institutions draws heavily on the writing of V. O. Key, Jr., *Politics, Parties, and Pressure Groups*, 5th ed. (New York: Crowell, 1964), 4–11.

6. Ibid., 6.

to authority and a functional equivalent for the varieties of ways by which peoples rid themselves of unwanted rulers.[7]

Consent of the Governed

In democracies, governments derive their power from the people. This basis for governmental authority differs sharply from the older theory of the divine right of kings in which the ruler derived power from God and acted as God's temporal agent on earth. In a representative democracy, the rulers, or the government, are expected to defer to the views and interests of the ruled—that is, act with the consent of the governed. And elections are an essential way in which the government can consult with the people or their representatives and the people can express their consent to government action.

A corollary of the doctrine of government by consent of the governed is the freedom to express dissent against the actions of the government. In a democracy, there is not only the freedom to dissent, but also the expectation that protests will be heard and considered, though not necessarily heeded, and that no reprisals will be taken against the protesters. The freedom to dissent is accompanied by the right to join with others to seek redress of grievances by ousting officeholders through the electoral process.[8]

*The Politics of
Limited Objectives and
Hope for Tomorrow*

Democratic procedures operate best when there is the expectation that policy changes in the short run will be modest and relatively narrow, and there will be no wholesale changes in the economic order or the governmental system. Losers of an election need not fear being liquidated or deprived of their liberty without due process of law. They know that all concerned will be able to continue the struggle in the next election. There is, in other words, a societal consensus on the limits of the political struggle. Americans, for example, operate on the assumption that politics will continue to function within the existing constitutional order. They further assume that the economic system will be primarily a free-enterprise one. But within these areas of fundamental agreement, Americans dispute narrower issues such as the level of the minimum wage, the need to take military action in the Persian Gulf or Bosnia, appropriate sentences for convicted drug dealers, and the amounts to be spent on defense, health care, and education.

7. Ibid.   8. Ibid.

Ironically, if democracy works best when the political battles are over such limited objectives, a durable democracy holds out hope at the same time for far-reaching changes in the long run. Again, in Key's words,

The mystique of democracy nourishes a belief that the wrongs of today, persistent though they may seem, will be corrected in some remote tomorrow. Any regime that struggles for stability must implant such expectations in the minds of its people. . . . [D]emocratic doctrine seems especially adapted to encouragement of such a faith, for it contemplates an evolving system in which the dispossessed of today may hope to become the top dogs of tomorrow.[9]

The Institutions of Democracy

No single set of institutions is required for a democratic order. All Western-style democracies, however, supplement the executives, courts, and councils found in any government—nondemocratic as well as democratic—with institutions and processes that link the ruled with the rulers, permit consultation with the governed, manage succession of authority, and reconcile competing interests within society. Although the exact nature of the institutions and processes that carry out these functions varies from one representative democracy to another (the American representative democracy, of course, has its own distinctive features), most democratic orders have the following elements in common:[10]

■ *Political parties* to contest elections, mobilize public support for or opposition to the government's policies, and handle the succession of power

■ *An elected legislature* to serve as the agent and advocate of the representatives' constituents, to symbolize consultation with the governed, and to act as a conduit for the communication of approval of and dissent from official policy

■ *Electoral procedures* to express mass approval or disapproval of government policy, to set limits on the course of government policy, and to renew leaders' terms of office or dismiss them

■ *Nonparty associations and groups* (interest groups) to supplement the formal system of representation in the legislature, to communicate their members' views to government officials, and to act as a means of consultation between the governed and the governors

9. Ibid., 8.   10. Ibid., 9-11.

■ *Additional linkages between the government and its citizens* to provide supplementary means of communications through guarantees of freedom of the press, the right to petition the government for redress of grievances, and protection against official reprisals for dissent against government actions.

The Setting for American Politics

American politics functions always within the shadow of the Constitution, which sets the legal framework for the government (see Chapter 2). But by itself the Constitution does not explain America's unique brand of democracy or its stability. Other nations, especially in Latin America, have copied the U.S. constitutional system, but they have not developed stable democratic political orders. Rather, these countries are subject to occasional periods of free elections and civilian rule, followed by military coups, authoritarian rule, and instability.

Few would question that at the time of the founding, circumstances in the United States were favorable to the development of democracy. This vast subcontinent with its abundant natural resources and fertile land had had no history of feudalism, no titled aristocracy, and no monopoly of landownership by a privileged few. In the early years of settlement and nationhood, governments imposed few limitations on those seeking to improve their lots in life. For those for whom opportunities seemed limited, the vast western frontier was available for starting a new life. Indeed, the noted historian Frederick Jackson Turner observed that the frontier environment, with its cheap or free land, promoted democracy, individualism, and nationalism. But the frontier and the prospect of free land and a new life in the West did not last forever. By 1900 the western frontier was largely closed, and America was becoming an industrialized nation whose people were increasingly crowded into teeming cities. Yet despite these and more recent challenges, American democracy has shown a remarkable capacity for adaptability and durability.

The forces molding the uniquely American brand of politics involve more than geophysical conditions, accidents of history, and a remarkable constitution, although each of these has affected and continues to affect politics. American politics is also shaped by the cultural and socioeconomic environment of the nation: the values and attitudes that people have, the size and composition of the population, the distribution of wealth and income, the class structure, where people live, living patterns, and the issues that divide as well as unite the people.

The American Political Culture

Political culture refers to people's fundamental beliefs and assumptions about how government and politics should operate. Scholars have debated the content of the American political culture and have recognized that some beliefs are more strongly held by certain elements of society than by others. Most agree, however, that five beliefs are deeply rooted in the American psyche: popular sovereignty, an obligation of political participation, individual rights, individualism, and equality. These beliefs influence people's behavior, expectations, and evaluations of politicians and policies. They also impose limits on which policy alternatives can be seriously considered. A policy that violates a basic value—such as the right to own private property—does not have a realistic chance of being adopted.

The Declaration of Independence proclaims that governments derive "their just powers from the *consent of the governed*" (emphasis added). And the Preamble to the Constitution begins with the words "We the People of the United States." Embedded in these words is the belief that the people, not some hereditary monarch, are the source of governmental power. As every school child learns, Lincoln's Gettysburg address asserts that the United States is a "government of the people, by the people, and for the people." This phrase captures one of Americans' most fundamental beliefs: *popular sovereignty.* The primacy of this belief is reflected in the importance attached to periodic free elections and the role of public opinion in policy making. Government officials who can claim that they have a public mandate to act gain legitimacy for their policies.

The doctrine of popular sovereignty not only bestows the right to participate in the nation's political life but also carries with it a civic duty to participate. *Political participation* is important to Americans. Indeed, a criticism of the era of "Big Government" with its numbing bureaucracies is that these phenomena inhibit meaningful citizen participation. One of the appealing aspects of local and state governments is that they are thought to be "close to the people."

Despite their commitment to popular sovereignty and participation, Americans do have some reservations about democracy. Many fear that voters may be misled by demagogues—leaders who play on voters' prejudices, fears, and baser emotions. In addition, the value attached to strong presidential leadership is proof that people believe they may not always be capable of choosing the best policies by themselves.[11]

11. Raymond E. Wolfinger, Martin Shapiro, and Fred I. Greenstein, *Dynamics of American Politics,* 2d ed. (Englewood Cliffs, N.J.: Prentice-Hall, 1980), 102.

The Declaration of Independence and the Constitution, enshrined at the National Archives in Washington, D.C., embody fundamental principles of government that are the cornerstones of the nation's political system.

As for the widespread belief in *individual rights,* the Declaration of Independence proclaims that it is "self-evident, that all men are . . . endowed by their Creator with certain unalienable Rights, that among these are Life, Liberty and the pursuit of Happiness." "Liberty" is the right to make one's own decisions and live one's life freely without undue government restraints. The people's basic right to liberty constitutes a limitation on the power of the majority over individuals and groups. Also well-ingrained in American thinking is the belief in the fundamental right to hold private property. The commitment to private property and individual economic initiative has been so strong in the United States that socialism has made little headway, unlike in some other Western democracies. The largest share of votes ever gained by a socialist candidate for president was the 6 percent (900,369 votes) won by Eugene V. Debs in 1912. No socialist presidential candidate has ever carried a single state.

Individualism is deeply imbedded in the American culture as well. According to the Declaration of Independence, governments exist to fulfill an individual's right to "Life, Liberty and the pursuit of Happiness." When a government fails to provide these rights, it loses its reason to exist. Public opinion surveys reveal that America's individualistic commitments remain robust. For example, when asked in 1992 to assess the relative importance of various characteristics for getting ahead in life, Americans gave clear priority to three: ambition, hard work, and education. It was what "I do" that mattered—not family background, race, religion, or other factors extraneous to personal effort and commitment. Thus the public, across group lines, continues to believe in a meritocratic society. And compared to citizens of most advanced industrialized societies, Americans remain far more inclined to emphasize individual responsibility over government programs aimed at, for example, social welfare or income distribution.[12] Recognizing the pervasiveness of individualism, the United States has been more reluctant to institute national social welfare programs than most Western nations. Moreover, it spends a lower share of its national income on these programs than most industrialized nations.[13]

Even before asserting that people have "unalienable Rights," the Declaration of Independence states that "all men are created equal." In

12. Everett Carll Ladd, "Thinking about America," *Public Perspective* 4 (July/August 1993): 21.

13. Tom W. Smith, "The Polls: The Welfare State in Cross-National Perspective," *Public Opinion Quarterly* (Fall 1987): 406.

American thinking, *equality* and individual rights are closely linked—if all people are equal, they must have the same rights. Equality has several dimensions. In the Declaration of Independence, Jefferson was referring to political equality. To provide for this kind of equality, the Constitution and statutes contain provisions ensuring that all citizens of legal age have the right to vote, and the Fourteenth Amendment requires the states grant all people the "equal protection of the laws."

Many Americans also care about equality of opportunity—that is, they want to help those who are disadvantaged through race, gender, ethnicity, disability, or poverty to compete more effectively. This concern is manifested in the government's expanded role in providing the poor with money, food, housing, education, health care, and legal services. But despite a commitment to equality of opportunity, most Americans do not believe that everyone should be equally well off; rather, everyone should have a relatively equal chance to become better off than his or her neighbors. Americans are quite prepared in fact to accept large disparities in the economic status of their fellow citizens.

A commitment to equality also implies racial equality. In America, the goal of racial equality has not been met, and this failing is a source of continuing frustration, particularly for minority groups. There have been some accomplishments—barriers intended to prevent racial minorities from exercising the right to vote have been largely eliminated since the 1960s, and overt discrimination based on government statutes and rules (for example, requiring segregated schools, restaurants, and theaters) is no longer tolerated—but minorities have not yet achieved full social and economic equality in America. Moreover, there is no consensus on how to deal with the plight of racial minorities. One government-sponsored remedy, affirmative action programs, has stirred deep emotions in both its proponents and opponents. These programs seek to ensure that minorities (and women) are fairly considered for employment and college admission, and, in their most controversial form, they use procedures that give minorities a greater chance of being hired or admitted to educational institutions than their credentials alone would give them. Proponents see these programs as a way to compensate for past acts of discrimination and to give minorities a chance to live the American dream. Opponents, however, see affirmative action programs as violations of society's commitment to awarding people on the basis of merit and as reverse discrimination.

But America's inability to assure its racial minorities of equality

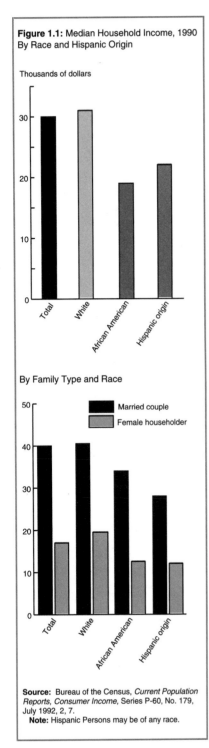

Figure 1.1: Median Household Income, 1990 By Race and Hispanic Origin

Thousands of dollars

By Family Type and Race

- Married couple
- Female householder

Source: Bureau of the Census, *Current Population Reports, Consumer Income,* Series P-60, No. 179, July 1992, 2, 7.
Note: Hispanic Persons may be of any race.

should not obscure the importance of the public's commitment to equality. The history of race relations and government civil rights policies in the United States would be much different had the American creed not included such a commitment. That commitment has been and continues to be a source of change as people are forced to confront the inconsistencies between their creed and the treatment accorded racial minorities.

The distinctive blend of beliefs and ways of thinking about politics described here gives America a unique political culture that is interwoven into the fabric of its political life and affects what public officials do and the kind of policy they produce. American politics is no less shaped by the prevailing socioeconomic conditions such as the distribution of wealth within society; the ethnic, racial, and religious composition of the population; and changes in lifestyles ranging from how Americans earn their livings to where they live.

The Socioeconomic Context of Politics

To preside over a stable democracy, a government must respond to the needs and wishes of its people. America's people are a diverse lot from all parts of the globe. They differ in their ethnic and racial backgrounds, social status, wealth, age, occupation, religious preference, lifestyle, and place of residence. Americans live in places as dissimilar as the Bronx in New York City; Midland, Texas; Minot, North Dakota; Beverly Hills, California; and Canton, Mississippi. This diversity produces myriad interests as well as conflicts within society—the raw materials of politics. In this section, we will explore the important social and economic features of American society that affect politics.

A look at the *distribution of wealth and income* in American society reveals one of that society's most important characteristics: the vast majority of Americans are not poor. In 1990 the median household income—the point that separates the upper 50 percent of families from the lower 50 percent—was $29,943 (see Figure 1.1). In the same year 13.5 percent of families had incomes that fell below the official government poverty level (see Figure 1.2). These data help to identify and explain the basic forces influencing American politics. First, a substantial proportion of people (including 22 percent of all children in 1992) are living in poverty; they are not living the American dream. As a result, there is continuing pressure on the government to develop programs that will enable the less fortunate to improve their circumstances. Second, there is a wide gap between the living standards of the average white person and that of the average African American or Hispanic. Issues of race and ethnicity, then, are inevitable factors in policy making. Third, the poor are a distinct minority in the United States. Thus, they cannot rely on the traditional weapon of the underprivileged—superior numbers—to achieve their political goals. Instead, they must make alliances with and gain the support of the nonpoor. Indeed, government programs to assist the needy must be supported by large segments of the middle class and by interests that are not poor.

As for their *national origins,* over 90 percent of the American population was born in the United States, yet except for Native Americans, the nation descended from immigrants. Until the late 1800s, immigrants came primarily from northern and western Europe, with the largest percentage from Great Britain and Ireland. The wave of "new immigration" in the late 1800s and early twentieth century was quite different, however. It was dominated by former inhabitants of eastern and southern Europe—Italians, Poles, Czechs, Slavs, Greeks, and Russian Jews. Their ethnicity tended to set them apart from native-born Americans and constituted a source of psychological identification. During the late 1920s and 1930s, these new immigrants, who were largely urban, working class, and Catholic, became politically aware and active—so much so, in fact, that their impact on politics was profound. But as the descendants of immigrants from eastern and southern Europe have become assimilated into American life and better off economically, their voting patterns have become less distinct and their traditional support of Democratic candidates is no longer assured. Like other people of European heritage, they have become less conscious of their ethnicity, with the result that their ethnicity is less relevant to them politically (see Chapter 5, Public Opinion and Participation).

An estimated 6 million legal and 2 million undocumented immigrants entered the country between 1981 and 1990 when the population grew by 22 million. This level of immigration is second only to the 8.8 million immigrants who arrived in the decade between 1901 and 1910.[14] The latest wave of immigration is dramatically changing the ethnic and racial composition of the nation. Primarily from Latin America and Asia, these new immigrants are concentrated in California, Texas, Florida, and New York. Indeed, it is expected that within the next twenty to twenty-five years, non-Hispanic whites will become a minor-

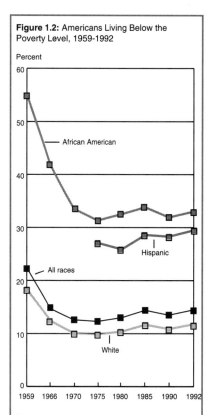

Figure 1.2: Americans Living Below the Poverty Level, 1959-1992

Source: Bureau of the Census; *Statistical Abstract of the United States: 1990* (Washington, D.C.: Government Printing Office, 1990), 420. *Statistical Abstract of the United States: 1992,* 456.
 Note: Hispanic persons may be of any race. "All races" includes those races not shown separately.

14. Bureau of the Census data reported by Barbara Vobejda, "Immigration Fueled U.S. Growth in the 1980s," *Washington Post,* Dec. 31, 1990, A1, A4.

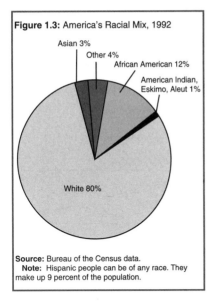

Figure 1.3: America's Racial Mix, 1992

Asian 3%
Other 4%
African American 12%
American Indian, Eskimo, Aleut 1%
White 80%

Source: Bureau of the Census data.
Note: Hispanic people can be of any race. They make up 9 percent of the population.

ity in California.[15] The influx of Asian and Latin American immigrants is transforming American politics as well. Hispanic voters, for example, are critical in states with large numbers of electoral votes such as California, Florida, New York, and Texas. And as the Hispanic American population has increased, so too has its representation in the House of Representatives (from eleven to seventeen between the 1990 and 1992 elections). With its increasing numbers, the Hispanic Caucus in the House has become evermore influential in shaping legislation, especially bills that affect immigrants.[16]

Hispanic immigrants, who can be of any race, hail from countries where Spanish is the dominant language. Because of their high immigration and birth rates, the number of Hispanic Americans is increasing rapidly—today they make up 9.0 percent of the population. Twenty-eight percent, however, live below the poverty level. A closer look at the political orientations of Hispanics reveals distinct differences. Those of Mexican and Puerto Rican heritage tend to be heavily Democratic in their voting patterns. Cuban Americans, however, who are better off economically and ardent anticommunists, tend to be Republicans.

Race is another feature of American society (Figure 1.3). African Americans, most of whom are descendants of African slaves, constitute 12 percent of the U.S. population. Unlike Europeans, for whom ethnicity has declining political relevance, African Americans are highly conscious of their ethnicity. But they have done less well economically than European immigrants, and over 31 percent live below the poverty level. African Americans tend to be concentrated in inner-city neighborhoods and poor rural areas and tend to feel the continuing effects of racial discrimination. Government policies that combat poverty and deal with civil rights issues are high on the list of political concerns for African Americans, who are a critical element of the Democratic party's electoral coalition.

According to population projections, the share of the voting age population held by African Americans and other minorities will continue to grow (Figure 1.4). It is likely, therefore, that the concerns of

15. Felicity Barringer, "Census Shows Profound Change in Racial Makeup of the Nation," *New York Times,* March 11, 1991, 1, National edition.

16. For example, the Hispanic Caucus played a critical role in defeating an unemployment benefits bill that would have severely restricted immigrant eligibility for benefits in 1993. See Martin Tolchin, "House Votes Down a Jobless-Aid Bill," *New York Times,* Oct. 15, 1993, A11, National edition.

The public agenda of the 1990s arises from changing lifestyles; shifts in the composition of the population; and concern about health care, jobs, crime, and the environment. Growing numbers of women working outside the home give salience to issues of sex discrimination, sexual harassment, and day care for children; an aging population means that increased resources will be required to care for the elderly; America's expanding need for energy poses economic and environmental challenges; and the preference of many middle-class Americans for life in the suburbs contributes to the decay of the central cities.

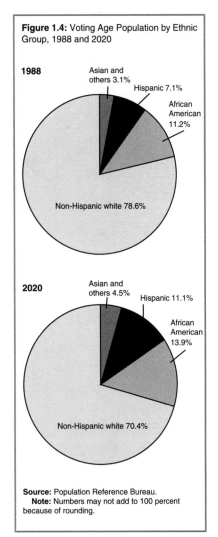

Figure 1.4: Voting Age Population by Ethnic Group, 1988 and 2020

1988

Asian and others 3.1%
Hispanic 7.1%
African American 11.2%
Non-Hispanic white 78.6%

2020

Asian and others 4.5%
Hispanic 11.1%
African American 13.9%
Non-Hispanic white 70.4%

Source: Population Reference Bureau.
  Note: Numbers may not add to 100 percent because of rounding.

these minorities will become increasingly important to political leaders. For example, in 1993 English was a foreign language for 32 million U.S. residents, including 17 million for whom Spanish was their native tongue.[17] Statistics such as these indicate that the pressures for and the controversies surrounding bilingual education are not likely to subside for decades.

Age must not be forgotten in any examination of the socioeconomic context of politics. The proportions of the population that are young, middle-aged, and elderly significantly determine the issues government must confront. As Americans have smaller families and people live longer, the population, on the whole, is aging. Thus, this growing elderly segment of the population is putting heavy pressure on the government to provide it with services, particularly pensions and health care. And, based on the population projections of the Bureau of the Census, these pressures can only be expected to intensify in coming decades. For example, 3.3 million people were over the age of eighty-five in 1993; the bureau expects this number to double to 6.5 million by 2020 and soar to 17.7 million by 2050. Even more incredibly, the number of people over 100 years of age is expected to jump from 45,000 in 1993 to over 1 million in 2050.

Generational differences are already apparent. Teenagers and those "twentysomething" are more liberal on social issues than their elders. They are more likely to favor busing for school integration, legalization of marijuana, sex education in schools, and careers for women, and be tolerant of premarital sex. Thus, advocates of a conservative social agenda for the nation may encounter opposition as younger voters assume a larger leadership role in society.

Violent clashes between Catholics and Protestants in Northern Ireland and between Christians and Muslims in Bosnia are proof that worldwide *religion* can cause bitter internal political strife as well. Fortunately, in the United States religious differences have never aroused the same kind of passions, even though substantial religious diversity exists (see Figure 1.5). Religion can, however, affect voting patterns. As we will see in Chapter 5, Protestants are predominantly Republican; Catholics have traditionally been strongly Democratic, although in the 1980s a majority voted Republican for president; and Jews have been overwhelmingly Democratic. In recent elections Protestant fundamen-

17. Bureau of the Census data reported by Felicity Barringer, "Immigration in the 80's Made English a Foreign Language for Millions," *New York Times,* April 29, 1993, A1, A10, National edition.

talists have become increasingly active in politics and have tended to support Republican candidates for president.

Although social scientists can neatly place people in a particular *social class* based on such criteria as income or occupation, most Americans are not class-conscious. Unlike Europe, which has a history of socialist parties backed by working class trade unions, the American working class has never developed either a clear sense of self-identity or an affinity for socialism as a working class ideology. After reviewing polling data on the demands that different income groups place on government, the editors of *Public Opinion* magazine concluded that there are "class differences, but no class divide."[18] Furthermore, they discovered only small differences of opinion on such issues as housing discrimination, the value of social welfare programs and public schools, the government's role in combating poverty, and the level of taxation.

American political parties draw support from voters in all social classes and at all income levels. Even so, there are differences in the extent to which the various income groups support the Republican and Democratic parties (see Chapter 5). Generally speaking, as one moves up the socioeconomic ladder, one is more likely to support the Republicans.

One of the potentially significant changes in the class composition of the United States is the emergence of a growing "new class" of college-trained professionals—engineers, computer experts, economists, research analysts, lawyers, and scientists. While political scientists are not certain about the political implications of this increasingly prominent group, its members' opinions, candidate preferences, and level of political participation will significantly affect the future of American politics.

Changing lifestyles and changes in the way people earn their livings have significant political implications as well. One of the most important changes in American society has been the growing proportion of women entering the labor force. Indeed, the Bureau of Labor Statistics reported that between 1970 and 1991 this proportion jumped from 49 percent to over 69 percent. Particularly striking is the proportion of working mothers. In 1992, 58 percent of married women with children under six years of age were in the work force and 72 percent with children six to seventeen were employed. Similar employment patterns are present among women heading single-parent families: 46 percent of women with children under six and 70 percent of those with children

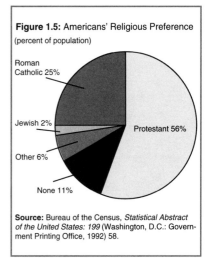

Figure 1.5: Americans' Religious Preference
(percent of population)

Roman Catholic 25%

Jewish 2%

Other 6%

None 11%

Protestant 56%

Source: Bureau of the Census, *Statistical Abstract of the United States: 199* (Washington, D.C.: Government Printing Office, 1992) 58.

18. *Public Opinion*, May/June 1987, 24–25.

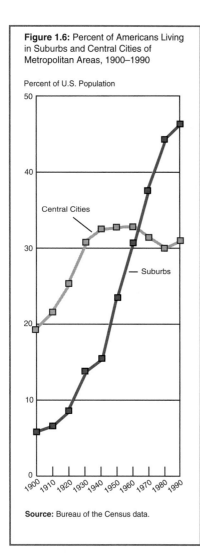

Figure 1.6: Percent of Americans Living in Suburbs and Central Cities of Metropolitan Areas, 1900–1990

Percent of U.S. Population

Source: Bureau of the Census data.

six to seventeen were working.[19] Just as the growing number of older Americans has forced politicians to pay attention to the concerns of the elderly, the dramatic upswing in the number of women in the work force also has put pressure on the government to, for example, provide day-care facilities and ensure the right to parental leave in cases of pregnancy and family illness.

Place of residence is yet another factor in America's political equation. For a large part of its history, the United States has been a predominantly rural nation with most of its citizens living on farms and in small towns. But today over three-fourths of Americans live in a metropolitan area (a central city of at least fifty thousand and its surrounding suburbs), and almost 60 percent of the nation's population resides in metropolitan areas with a population exceeding one million.

Within metropolitan areas, population growth has been concentrated in the suburbs, which in 1990 were home to almost half of the American people (see Figure 1.6). Within suburbia, one of the most striking trends has been the surge in the number of suburban or "edge" cities of over 100,000 people. In the 1980s twenty-two suburban communities swelled to 100,000 residents. These "suburban cities" are not the traditional free-standing cities because they exist in the shadow of and are partially dependent on large central cities. Suburban cities such as Plano and Irving (Dallas-Fort Worth), Texas; Scottsdale (Phoenix), Arizona; Lowell (Boston), Massachusetts; Oceanside (Los Angeles), California—reflect the way industry and retailing have sought fresh real estate away from traditional commercial areas and have brought in their wake new corridors of congestion and additional pressures on governments for services.[20]

The regional distribution of the population has changed as well. The population is growing most rapidly in the South, Southwest, and Pacific coast (especially California), while the proportion of the population living in the New England, Middle-Atlantic, midwestern, and Plains states is declining.

Such population changes have political consequences. As increasing numbers of white, middle-class Americans have migrated to the suburbs and exurbia, the central cities have become more and more occupied by the poor, African Americans, and other minorities. Another consequence of the exodus of the middle class is the shrinking of city

19. Bureau of the Census, *Population Profile of the United States: 1993* (Washington, D.C.: Government Printing Office, 1993), 24.

20. Robert Suro, "Where America Is Growing: The Suburban Cities," *New York Times,* Feb. 23, 1991, 1, 10, National edition.

tax bases; yet the proportion of city residents needing government social services has grown. It is not surprising, then, that city officials have been at the forefront of those pressing the federal government for increased assistance for urban areas and the poor.

The changing composition of the population of these central cities has its partisan implications as well. Because much of the middle class has left the central cities, few Republicans now represent central city congressional districts, which have become solidly one-party, Democratic areas. As a result, members of Congress—both white and black—from these districts are amassing congressional seniority and moving into leadership positions within the Democratic party in the House of Representatives.

The power equations in Congress also are being altered by the shifts in population among the states. For example, in 1950 California had thirty members in the House of Representatives, but the results of the 1990 census entitled it to fifty-two representatives—the largest state delegation in the House. Indeed, California now has more representatives than the thirteen Rocky Mountain and Plains states combined. New York, by contrast, saw its House representation shrink from forty-three to thirty-one between 1950 and 1990.

The electoral fortunes of the Republican and Democratic parties have felt the effect, too, of population shifts among the states. The migration of northerners carrying their Republicanism with them has contributed to a breakdown of the once solidly Democratic South. Indeed, after the 1992 elections Republicans held 38.4 percent of the region's congressional seats, and southern Republicans constituted the largest regional bloc within the House Republican party. This increase in southern Republican representation and decrease in the number of House Democrats from the South have had a significant impact on the policy orientation of both congressional parties: House Republicans have become more conservative and House Democrats more liberal.

Although America's regions are becoming more homogeneous in their political viewpoints, regional differences in political orientations continue to exist. For example, people living in the New England, Middle-Atlantic, and Pacific Coast states are, on the whole, more liberal politically than those in other regions.

The Public Policy Context

A government's policy makers are strongly influenced by the conditions and public expectations created by decisions made years earlier. As government's role in society has expanded to provide services to virtually every interest in American life, beneficiaries and their sup-porters have begun to expect that their programs will continue and perhaps grow. Farmers expect continued price supports and crop insurance; students expect loans and grants; car owners expect inter-state highways; professors expect research grants; backpackers expect wilderness areas to be preserved; the poor and their dependents expect welfare programs, food stamps, Medicaid, and housing assistance; and the list goes on. Given the constituencies of support that nearly every government program and policy develop, it is small wonder that the politicians in Washington find it difficult to make sweeping changes in government policy.

Probably the most significant of the past national policy decisions in terms of consequences for current and future government policy mak-ing have been those made about the federal budget—taxes and spend-ing. During the 1980s and early 1990s, the federal budget deficit was allowed to rise to unprecedented levels—$322 billion in fiscal year 1993. As a result of this flood of red ink, national policy making has become "fiscalized"—that is, policy proposals in both the domestic and defense areas are being judged more on how they will affect the federal budget deficit than on their merits. In the face of (1) swelling budget deficits, (2) public reluctance to support either reductions in long-familiar ser-vices or higher taxes, and (3) elected officials' fears of incurring the public's wrath for either cutting programs or raising taxes, it has become extremely difficult to advocate expanding existing programs or to propose new ones. The difficulties President Clinton encountered in gaining congressional approval by the narrowest of margins for budget legislation that included some deficit reduction, reallocation of some funds, and a limited number of new programs stand as testimony to the severe constraints under which policy makers in the 1990s must operate.

Almost all economists agree that the government's huge federal budget deficits are having adverse effects on the domestic economy and on America's position in the international economy. The budget deficits also are believed to be threatening the nation's long-term eco-nomic health. Coping with these deficits, however, requires con-fronting a series of equally unattractive policy choices: raising taxes or cutting spending. Tax increases to raise additional revenues send shiv-ers down the spines of many elected officials (Figure 1.7 shows where the federal government obtains and spends its funds). Cutting or reducing the rate of growth in existing domestic programs is an extremely difficult option as well because the largest share of the budget (50 percent) is tied up in entitlements (direct payments to individuals who meet certain criteria) for such popular programs as Social Security and Medicare, as well as such safety net programs for the poor as food stamps, Medicaid, Aid to Families with Dependent Children (welfare), and housing assistance (see Figure 1.7).

With the collapse of the threat from the Soviet Union, the Pentagon has become a prime target for budget cutters. But uncertain world conditions (of which the 1991 war in the Persian Gulf and Russia's domestic turmoil are reminders) make many Washington policy makers reluctant to tamper too severely with Department of Defense budgets. In addition, members of Congress strenuously resist military expenditure cutbacks if they think it will mean a loss of jobs in their own districts or states. Proposals, then, to close military bases or to halt production on even unneeded aircraft and weapons confront tough opposition in Congress.

Further complicating the problem of cutting expenditures is the growing share (14 percent) of the budget that must go toward paying the interest on the federal debt. As demonstrated by the prolonged and at times acrimonious conflict of 1990 between the Bush White House and Congress over taxes and spending in the 1991 budget and President Clinton's 1993 budget battle with a Congress dominated by his own party, policy making in the 1990s has been profoundly affected by what political scientist Paul Peterson has called the "new politics of deficits."[21]

It is not just in the domestic area that past policy decisions impose constraints on and influence current policy making; foreign policy decisions made long ago also affect today's decisions. For example, for over forty-five years America has provided support and leadership for the North Atlantic Treaty Organization (NATO), and it has committed U.S. ground troops to the defense of Western Europe. Indeed, a strong NATO alliance has been the cornerstone of American policy for Western Europe. But with Russia no longer seen as a military threat to Western Europe, adapting NATO policy to an increasingly united and economically vibrant European Union and to former Eastern bloc nations seeking economic and military ties to the West has proved to

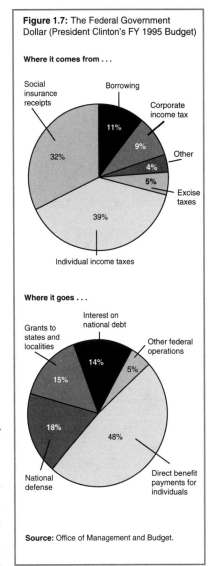

Figure 1.7: The Federal Government Dollar (President Clinton's FY 1995 Budget)

Where it comes from . . .

Social insurance receipts 32%
Borrowing 11%
Corporate income tax 9%
Other 4%
Excise taxes 5%
Individual income taxes 39%

Where it goes . . .

Interest on national debt 14%
Grants to states and localities 15%
Other federal operations 5%
National defense 18%
Direct benefit payments for individuals 48%

Source: Office of Management and Budget.

21. Paul E. Peterson, "The New Politics of Deficits," in *The New Directions in American Politics,* ed. John E. Chubb and Paul E. Peterson (Washington, D.C.: Brookings, 1985), chap. 13. Also see Gary C. Jacobson, "Deficit Cutting Politics and Congressional Elections," *Political Science Quarterly* 108 (Fall 1993): 375–402, for an analysis of how electoral politics affects and is affected by budgetary decision making.

be increasingly difficult. Similarly, the 1992 decision of the Bush administration to use the American military to provide humanitarian relief to famine-ravaged Somalia imposed on the incoming Clinton administration a number of thorny decisions about the nature and extent of U.S. military participation within the framework of U.N. policies.

The Durable and Unique American Political System

Stripped down to its basics, politics is the pursuit and exercise of power as well as the process through which society expresses and manages its conflicts. But American politics does not play itself out in a vacuum. It is affected on a daily basis by the legal structure imposed by the Constitution, society's cultural values and socioeconomic characteristics, as well as the government's past policy decisions.

Americans take pride in their creative accomplishments—their technological inventiveness which resulted in Henry Ford's Model T, bringing the automobile within reach of ordinary people, and in the electronics technology that has enabled students to have hand-held calculators; retailing inventions like the supermarket and the shopping mall; and an economic system that has produced a high standard of living for many in this country. Yet Americans rarely brag about the U.S. political system. Instead, on the Fourth of July, America's great national day, the country celebrates its creation as a new and independent nation with parades, speeches, family picnics, ball games, fireworks, and, for most people, a day off from work. But there is a certain irony that it is independence that commands so much celebration and commemoration. As British political scientist Anthony King has reminded us, achieving national independence is no great trick, especially when the colonial power is three thousand miles away, half-hearted about holding onto its colony, and internally divided.[22] After all, almost ninety nations have achieved independence since 1945.

Much more impressive is the feat of establishing a set of governmental institutions—dedicated to the principle that government should be by the consent of the governed—that are highly adaptable, liberal rather than repressive, and capable of enduring for more than two hundred years. Testimony to the political system's remarkable

22. Anthony King, "The American Polity in the 1990s," in *The New American Political System,* 2d ed., ed. Anthony King (Washington, D.C.: American Enterprise Institute, 1990), 287.

record of stability is the fact that the United States has held its elections on schedule even in the midst of a civil war, two world wars, and major economic depressions. Indeed, the American political system's record of adaptability and durability is such that if the readers of this book are still alive in one hundred years, they would be confidently looking forward to the election of the president, the entire House of Representatives, and one-third of the Senate—in 2096.

At least a partial explanation for this expectation of continuity rests with the Constitution, which provides a legal framework for America's unique and durable political system. The Constitution, therefore, is the subject of the next chapter.

For Review

1. Politics is a natural and inevitable social process through which society expresses and manages its conflicts. The political process is never-ending. Every government decision is therefore an interim one.

2. Under a democratic government, citizens have a relatively high degree of control over their leaders. All democracies, however, do not structure their governments in the same manner. The United States, for example, has a presidential system, but most Western-style democracies utilize a parliamentary form of government.

3. Democratic governments have these elements in common: guarantees of freedom of the press and speech and protection against official reprisals for dissent; political parties to contest elections and mobilize support for and opposition to the government's policies; an elected legislature; and nonparty associations and groups to supplement the formal system of representation in the legislature.

4. A nation's politics is profoundly affected by its political culture—people's fundamental beliefs and assumptions about how government and politics should operate. Among the fundamental values of the American political culture are popular sovereignty, the obligation of civic participation, individual rights, individualism, and equality.

5. The socioeconomic characteristics of the people also have significant consequences for American politics. Changes in the population's ethnic and racial composition, age distribution, places of residence and work, and lifestyle are creating new problems and demands for shifts in government policy.

6. The current policy-making process is affected by the government's past decisions as well. Today, the massive government budget deficits impose severe constraints on policy makers and make it difficult to expand existing government programs or institute new ones.

For Further Reading

Almond, Gabriel A., and Sidney Verba. *Civic Culture: Political Attitudes and Democracy in Five Nations.* Princeton, N.J.: Princeton University Press, 1963. A classic study comparing the political culture of five nations, including the United States.

Bureau of the Census. *Statistical Abstract of the United States.* Washington, D.C.; Government Printing Office, published annually. A compendium of useful information about political, economic, and social trends in the United States.

de Tocqueville, Alexis. *Democracy in America.* Translated by Philips Bradley. New York: Knopf, Vintage Books, 1945. Originally published in 1835, an important portrait of American political culture.

Dodd, Lawrence C., and Calvin Jillson, eds. *New Perspectives on American Politics.* Washington, D.C.: CQ Press, 1994. A collection of essays by leading scholars exploring such topics as how context shapes politics and how ideas and leaders reshape the context, how institutions can inhibit change, and how group tensions and competitive elections fuel change.

Huntington, Samuel P. *American Politics: The Promise of Disharmony.* Cambridge, Mass.: Harvard University Press, 1981. A fascinating analysis of America's democratic creed of liberty, equality, and hostility to authority and how it has affected the functioning of government institutions.

Lipset, Seymour Martin. *The First New Nation: The United States in Historical and Comparative Perspective.* Rev. ed. New York: Norton, 1979. An exploration of how the values of equality and achievement developed in American culture and their impact on American politics.

Ranney, Austin. *Governing: An Introduction to Political Science.* 6th ed. Englewood Cliffs, N.J.: Prentice-Hall, 1993. An informative text that presents the political process from a comparative perspective.

Schick, Allen. *The Federal Budget, 1994-95: Politics, Policy, Process.* Washington, D.C.: Brookings, 1994. An informative quide to understanding the politics and content of the Federal budget.

Shafer, Byron E. *Is America Different? A Look at American Exceptionalism.* New York: Oxford University Press, 1991. A stimulating set of essays exploring "Americaness" and its impact.

2. The Constitution

CONSTITUTIONS grant powers to public officials, distribute powers among the branches and levels of government, and impose limits on government itself. Indeed, the basic principle of **constitutional government** calls for imposing recognized and enforced limits on the government's powers.[1] Constitutions are therefore a special type of law—a law above the ordinary statutes passed by the national legislature or the orders of the chief executive—and all parts of the government are expected to abide by this higher law. In addition to outlining the basic structure and powers of the government, a country's constitution embodies the fundamental political philosophy of its citizens.

The American brand of democracy has its roots in the Constitution of the United States (see Appendix). The organization and policies of the Congress, presidency, and judiciary reflect how officials in each branch of government have interpreted their powers under that document. Serving, then, as the legal framework within which the political system functions, the Constitution has exerted a profound influence on American government for over two centuries. In this chapter, we explore the origins and basic principles of this remarkable and enduring document, as well as the processes of constitutional interpretation and change.

Origins of the American Constitution

The Constitution was written by fifty-five men gathered at a constitutional convention in Philadelphia during the summer of 1787. The document they produced was influenced, of course, by their personal philosophies of governance. It also reflected their reactions to the problems America had experienced as a colony of England and was experiencing as a newly independent nation. But to produce such a document, the Framers had to resolve through compromise the internal conflicts and divisions that existed within their own ranks.

The English Political Heritage

The Constitution of the United States, with its provisions for **limited government**, a representative legislature, and government by consent of the governed, owes much to America's English heritage. For

1. Charles H. McIlwain, *Constitutionalism: Ancient and Modern* (Ithaca, N.Y.: Cornell University Press, 1940), 23.

centuries before the writing of the Constitution in 1787, the English had been evolving and experimenting with constitutional government. As early as 1215, with the signing of the Magna Carta (the Great Charter), King John had been forced to accept limits on the monarch's powers, including the principle that extraordinary taxes could not be levied without the consent of a council of noblemen from all over his realm. This council was the forerunner of the modern British Parliament. By 1688, almost one hundred years before the convening of the Constitutional Convention in Philadelphia, the British Parliament had twice deposed kings who had sought to rule without Parliament and had violated the basic rights and liberties of English citizens. In compelling King William to agree to the Bill of Rights in 1689 as a condition to his becoming the monarch, Parliament affirmed the rights of English citizens to petition their government, to be tried by a jury of their peers, and to be free from excessive bail, fines, and cruel or unusual punishment.[2] Moreover, the English Bill of Rights banned the king from suspending laws of Parliament or interfering with free speech in the proceedings of Parliament and guaranteed frequent meetings of Parliament. Over the centuries, England also had been developing a judicial system that sought both to treat people fairly and to hold public officials to previously established rules of conduct. The English colonists carried these traditions to America and incorporated them into the governments of the thirteen original colonies. Although there were differences among the colonies in governmental structures, each had a governor, a council composed of key executive officials, an elected legislature, and a judiciary.

Until the 1770s the colonists did not consider themselves to be "Americans." Rather, they were English citizens living in the New World. Their sense of national identity only began to develop after the French and Indian War, which ended in 1763. With its victory over the French and their Indian allies, the British government sought to have the colonies share in paying for the cost of the war, which the British believed had been fought largely for the benefit of the colonists. The British also wanted the colonies to pay the costs of their own administration. The resulting taxes enacted by a parliament across the Atlantic in London created the bases for conflict between the colonies and the mother country.

2. For a concise account of the crown-parliamentary struggle that culminated in the revolution that produced the English Bill of Rights, see Stuart E. Prall, *The Bloodless Revolution: England, 1688* (Madison: University of Wisconsin Press, 1985).

The Founding of a New Nation

1763
British defeat the French in North America in the French and Indian War.

1765
Britain imposes the Stamp Act on the colonies.

1773
Britian enacts the Tea Act, and colonists in Massachusetts stage the Boston Tea Party.

1774
First Continental Congress meets in Philadelphia and asserts that the British Parliament has no authority over the colonies' internal affairs.

1775
Battles of Lexington and Concord.

1776
Second Continental Congress adopts the Declaration of Independence.

New state constitutions adopted between 1776 and 1784.

1777
Second Continental Congress adopts the Articles of Confederation.

1781
British surrender at Yorktown.

States complete ratification of the Articles of Confederation.

1786
Shays's Rebellion.

Annapolis Convention petitions the Continental Congress to call a constitutional convention.

1787
Constitutional Convention meets in Philadelphia and drafts the Constitution of the United States of America.

1787-1788
Eleven states ratify the Constitution, including the large states of New York and Virginia.

1789
First elections held under the Constitution.

The First Congress convenes, and George Washington is inaugurated the nation's first president.

North Carolina ratifies the Constitution.

1790
Rhode Island becomes the last of the thirteen original states to ratify the Constitution.

1791
Bill of Rights is ratified by the states.

The Declaration of Independence

Among the taxes imposed by the British government were the Sugar Act, which levied a duty on foreign molasses and threatened the rum trade; the Stamp Act, which imposed a tax on all legal documents, newspapers, almanacs, dice, and playing cards; and the Quartering Act, which required colonists to help support English troops by providing them with living quarters, food, and beer. From the colonists' viewpoints, however, these taxes deliberately denied them their rights as English citizens. Being such, they believed that it was their right not to be taxed except by their own elected representatives. They were, however, being taxed by the English Parliament in London where they had no representatives. Particularly distressing was the denial in the Sugar and Stamp acts of their rights as English citizens to a trial by a jury of their peers. Special courts, which operated without juries and considered the defendant guilty until proved innocent, were used to try violators of the Sugar and Stamp acts. These and other actions by the British government encouraged the colonists to see their interests as distinct from those of England, and a sense of common interest developed among them.

To protest the 1773 Tea Act, which gave a commercial advantage to England's East India Company over American traders, a band of colonists, disguised as Indians, staged the Boston Tea Party and dumped 342 chests of tea into that city's harbor. The English responded by closing the Port of Boston. American resistance to British rule then intensified, and armed hostilities broke out in nearby Lexington and Concord in 1775. But earlier, in 1774, the first Continental Congress had been convened to air the colonies' grievances, and on July 4, 1776, it approved the Declaration of Independence (see Appendix). By this act, the American colonies ended their allegiance to Great Britain.

The colonies' justification for the Revolution was set forth in the Declaration of Independence. This declaration went beyond a statement of the particular facts surrounding the eighteenth-century struggle between the British government and its colonies and alleged that the colonists' basic rights had been violated repeatedly. The enduring quality of the document results from its citation of the basic principles under which the new nation would be governed. Much of the spirit of the declaration is captured in the opening lines penned by its drafter and member of the Continental Congress, Thomas Jefferson.

We hold these truths to be self-evident, that all men are created equal, that they are endowed by their Creator with certain unalienable Rights, that among these are Life, Liberty and the pursuit of Happiness. That to secure these rights, Governments are instituted among Men, deriving their just powers from the consent of the governed.

In drafting the declaration, Jefferson drew heavily on the writings of John Locke, an English political philosopher. Locke believed that there was a natural law that bestowed on all people natural rights to life, liberty, and property. To protect these basic rights, people agree to form a government through a social compact. If a government persistently violates its citizens' natural rights, however, it then loses its legitimacy, and people have the right, in Jefferson's phrasing, "to alter or to abolish it, and to institute a new Government, laying its foundations on such principles and organizing its powers in such form, as to them shall seem most likely to effect their Safety and Happiness." In using Locke's philosophy, Jefferson articulated the basic concepts of government that are the cornerstones of the American political system: that the major purpose of government is to protect people's rights to life, liberty, and the pursuit of happiness, and that governments derive their power from the people.

Traditionally, kings have ruled by divine right, claiming that they derive their power from the Almighty and that they are acting as God's temporal agents on earth. The Declaration of Independence swept away the divine-right-of-kings rationale for governmental authority and replaced it with a new and radical doctrine—that governments derive their powers from the *consent of the governed*. The people are the source of a government's power. Over two hundred years later, the principles of the Declaration of Independence have continuing appeal and special relevance both to those groups in the United States struggling for their rights and to those people around the world asserting individual rights against authoritarian governments.

Governing the New Nation: State Constitutions

The revolutionary break with Great Britain required the thirteen former colonies to write new state constitutions to replace the colonial charters that had been granted by the Crown and that had constituted the basis for the colonial governments' authority. Power in the new post-Revolution state governments was concentrated in their legislatures. Gubernatorial and judicial authorities were reduced from their former levels in the colonial charters because these authorities had been sources of royal influence and Americans had become wary of a strong executive and judges. Under the post-Revolution state constitutions, governors were elected by the state legislatures, which also could override judicial decisions. The new state constitutions not only strengthened the legislative branch but also contained bills of rights and liberalized most property-owning and taxpaying qualifications for voting.

In framing the Constitution a decade later, the drafters drew on their experiences under the post-Revolution state constitutions. These experiences led them to conclude that the executive and judicial powers within the states were too weak to offset the tendency of each legislature to draw all power "to its impetuous vortex" and become despotic.[3] As a result, they sought in the Constitution to create a government in which the legislative, executive, and judicial branches would check each other.

3. E. M. Earle, ed., *The Federalist* (New York: Modern Library, 1937), No. 48, 322–324.

Hostility to British rule of the American colonies was inflamed by the "Boston Massacre" on March 5, 1770, when troops fired on an unruly mob of tax protesters. The incident, in which seven protesters were killed, was given a sensationalized portrayal in this engraving by Paul Revere.

Creating a National Government: The Articles of Confederation

At the national level, a union of the thirteen states was formed under a new constitution, the **Articles of Confederation,** which was ratified unanimously by the states in 1781.[4] The articles vested all powers of the national government in a one-chamber Continental Congress in which each state was entitled to one vote, regardless of the size of its population. In addition, each state paid its own delegates to the Congress and could recall them and appoint others at any time. There were no national judiciary and no national executive to coordinate the implementation of congressional policy. Important legislation required the support of nine of the thirteen states, and any amendments to the

4. A distinguished study of the articles is that by Merrill Jensen in *The Articles of Confederation* (Madison: University of Wisconsin Press, 1940).

original thirteen articles needed the unanimous approval of the states (see Figure 2.1).

Among its significant accomplishments during its eleven years (1777–1788) under the articles, the United States won its independence; made commercial treaties with European countries; created the executive departments of the Post Office, Treasury, Foreign Affairs, and War (defense); and approved the Northwest Ordinance, which established the principles that guided territorial expansion until the end of the nineteenth century. The ordinance set out the procedures for admitting new states to the Union, and it embodied the governmental principles essential for democracy, including a ban on slavery, freedom of religion, and encouragement of public education. There were, however, at least three serious weaknesses inherent in the articles that made effective governance of the Union virtually impossible.

First, *the national government was dependent on the states.* The national government created under the articles was a confederation—a "League of Friendship and Cooperation" among the several states of the Union. This meant that the national government had to exercise its authority *through the states* and could not deal directly with individual citizens. The national government, therefore, had to depend on the states to carry out many of its policies, yet it lacked the power to compel the states to comply with its statutory enactments. To raise an army and a navy, the Continental Congress had to request troops from the states, which often did not provide the required manpower. As a result, the national government could do little to combat hostile acts by foreign governments. In 1784, for example, Spain closed the lower Mississippi to foreign navigation, and Britain's King George III secretly ordered British military garrisons and trading posts to remain in the American territory west of the Appalachians. A government that could not provide for the common defense of its citizens did not inspire confidence or loyalty.

The national government's dependence on state compliance to carry out national policies also created problems in raising revenue. Because Congress could not tax individual citizens, it assessed the states. The states, however, frequently did not pay their assessments. Efforts to increase national revenues through a tax on imports revealed a further problem with the Articles of Confederation: an amendment to the articles could be implemented only by the unanimous consent of all the states. Twice, then, a single state blocked congressional efforts to amend the articles to permit taxing imports. The government under the Articles of Confederation thus lacked two essential resources required for governing: a military force and revenues.

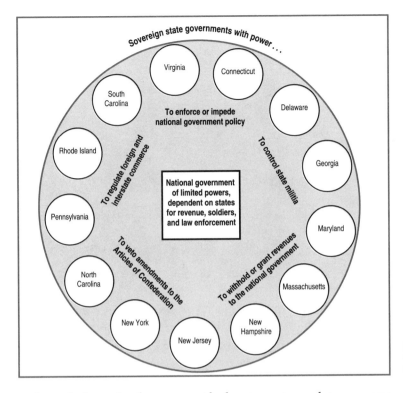

Figure 2.1: The Articles of Confederation: A "League of Friendship and Cooperation"— But Not a Strong Government

Second, *the national government had no power to regulate commerce among the states and with foreign nations.* The states, therefore, acted independently to impose tariffs and other barriers to trade with foreign countries as well as with their sister states. The result was economic chaos. The government lacked revenues it might have derived from nationally imposed tariff duties; there was no uniform commercial policy; and the states imposed restrictions on trade to protect special interests within their boundaries. Such state-imposed restrictions on interstate trade limited both the economic development of the nation and the development of a sense of a national identity.

Third, *the national government had a weak executive and judiciary.* Congress did establish executive departments presided over by secretaries, but there was no strong, unifying executive to coordinate national policy. And as there was no independent or separate national judiciary, the judicial functions of the government were carried out by the state courts. There was, however, no regularized method for dealing with disputes among the states.

But the problems of the post-Revolution period were not just problems with the national government; there were also serious problems of economic and political instability within the states. Some states failed to adopt sound measures to deal with the depressed econo-

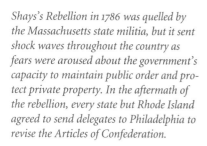

Shays's Rebellion in 1786 was quelled by the Massachusetts state militia, but it sent shock waves throughout the country as fears were aroused about the government's capacity to maintain public order and protect private property. In the aftermath of the rebellion, every state but Rhode Island agreed to send delegates to Philadelphia to revise the Articles of Confederation.

my and responded to the demands of debtors by printing excessive amounts of paper money. Such moves created inflation, which lowered the value of the currency. In Rhode Island, creditors hid from their debtors seeking to pay off debts with nearly worthless paper currency.

In those states that refused to adopt inflationary measures, debt-ridden citizens threatened with foreclosure on their farms became violent in some instances. Indeed, the militia in New Hampshire had to disperse a mob that descended on the state legislature, and in Massachusetts, crowds of angry citizens led by farmer and war veteran Daniel Shays tried to prevent courts from foreclosing on the mortgages of farmers and even sought to seize a government arsenal. This 1786 incident, known as Shays's Rebellion, was put down by the militia, but it provided an additional impetus for reform of the Articles of Confederation because it seemed to demonstrate the inherent instability of a system that vested most governmental power in the legislature and had a weak executive and judiciary.

Reforming the Articles of Confederation

The leaders of the movement to reform the articles recognized the government's inability to exercise national powers. They believed that the new nation needed a stronger national government to promote economic development and to deal with the political instability within the states. Their experience with state governments dominated by popularly elected legislatures had convinced them that stable and effective representative government required some restraint on popular rule and legislative power.

The immediate impetus for reform came out of interstate trade controversies. A conference on trade was held in Annapolis, Maryland, in 1786 under the auspices of then-retired general George Washington and James Madison, member of the Virginia House of Delegates. At the urging of Alexander Hamilton, a New York lawyer who had been agitating for constitutional reform for years, the five states represented at the Annapolis Convention petitioned the Continental Congress to call a constitutional convention. After initially ignoring this request, the Congress, in response to pressures from such states as Virginia and fears created by Shays's Rebellion, issued a call for a convention to meet in Philadelphia in 1787 for the purpose of revising the Articles of Confederation.

The Constitutional Convention: Creating a New Governmental Order

In 1787, precisely because it was fearful of a *constitutional* convention, the Continental Congress worded its call to the states carefully: the convention was for the "sole and express purpose of revising the Articles of Confederation." Thus, in deciding to draft a wholly new constitution for the United States, the delegates to the convention disregarded the mandate given to them by the Continental Congress and set about the business of creating a government strong enough to govern, while preserving individual rights and a major role for the states.

The Framers of the Constitution began their task on May 25, 1787, at the State House in Philadelphia. George Washington was unanimously chosen president of the Constitutional Convention. After four months of deliberations over a sweltering summer, delegates drafted the document known today as the Constitution of the United States. But fashioning this blueprint for American government involved lengthy debate and conflict—conflict so intense at times it was feared the convention would break up without completing its task. Reflected, then, in the Constitution are the numerous compromises required to resolve the philosophical, economic, and regional differences among the delegates; the basic principles of governance in which the writers believed; as well as their practical solutions to problems facing the new nation.[5]

5. For a discussion of the background and intellectual underpinnings of the writing of the Constitution, see Vernon L. Parrington, *Main Currents of American Thought*, vol. 1 (New York: Harcourt, Brace, 1927). Also see Clinton Rossiter, *1787: The Grand Convention* (New York: Macmillan, 1966).

The Delegates

From the beginning the convention was controversial. The revolutionary leader from Virginia Patrick Henry "smelled a rat" and, fearing that the convention would endorse the centralization of government power, stayed away from Philadelphia. Rhode Island, a center of paper money interests, even refused to send delegates. Indeed, only fifty-five of the seventy-four delegates to the Constitutional Convention actually attended. But those delegates who did convene in Philadelphia were a distinguished group of men experienced in government. There were seven former governors, thirty-nine former members of the Continental Congress, and eight persons who had helped write state constitutions. Despite their experience, they were relatively young, with an average age of forty-two.

As a group, they were also men of considerable status and wealth who had advanced beyond the positions of their fathers. Only William Few of Georgia could be considered a representative of the small farmers who constituted a majority of the free, nonslave population. The leaders of the convention included James Madison of Virginia, who at age thirty-six had served in the Continental Congress, drafted the Virginia constitution, and made a thorough study of history and political theory preparatory to the convention; Alexander Hamilton of New York, who at age thirty-one had fiercely aristocratic tendencies and strongly supported a national government with expanded authority; George Washington, the Virginia planter and general whose prestige and status lent credibility to the deliberations; Benjamin Franklin of Pennsylvania, a man of wit, experience, and charm, who helped to moderate the disputes and find bases for compromise among the conflicting factions of the convention and who at age eighty-one was the oldest delegate present; James Wilson of Pennsylvania, an attorney who played a major role in drafting sections of the Constitution relating to the presidency and executive power; and Gouverneur Morris, another Pennsylvanian, who as the head of the committee on style drafted much of the final language of the document.

The men who wrote the Constitution were the heirs to seventeenth-century English republicanism, with its opposition to monarchy, military dictatorship, and arbitrary rule, as well as its faith in representative government and belief in **popular sovereignty**—that is, that the people are the source of governmental authority.[6] Like John Locke, they

---

6. For a concise discussion of the Founders' beliefs, see Richard Hofstadter, *The American Political Tradition* (New York: Vintage Books, 1954), chap. 1.

George Washington, whose presence lent an aura of legitimacy to the proceedings, presided at the Constitutional Convention of 1787 in Philadelphia. Alexander Hamilton (seated in foreground) and James Madison (seated in front of Washington) played critical roles in arranging for the convention and in securing ratification. Madison also drafted much of the document. Eighty-one-year-old Benjamin Franklin (seated in foreground) played the role of conciliator among the convention's factions.

believed that the laws of nature entitled each person to life, liberty, and property, and that governments had as their first responsibility the protection of these rights. Because of their experiences with a powerful colonial government in London, they were fearful of concentrations of governmental power.

But for all these beliefs and fears, the writers of the Constitution had counterbalancing concerns. Like the seventeenth-century English philosopher Thomas Hobbes and the Protestant reformer and theologian John Calvin, they distrusted human nature. They saw humans as atoms of self-interest. This was more than a matter of philosophy; as practical men of affairs, the Founders had observed human nature in the marketplaces, legislative halls, and courts, and on the battlefields. Their experiences had convinced them of human frailty and caused them to be wary of what they perceived were excesses of popular rule.

The Founders believed that a sound constitution was needed to control people's natural tendencies toward evil, selfishness, and contentiousness. The writing of such a constitution, however, posed a dilemma. They believed that governments rested on the consent of the governed, who were the source of governmental authority, yet they were convinced that human beings were unchangeable creatures of self-interest. Thus, the Constitution writers feared democracy. Hamilton was quoted as saying, "Your people, sir, are a great beast." The Founders sought a government that was capable of governing—a government of expanded powers and one that could control the inherent flaws in human nature. But they did not want that government to be too strong lest it endanger the basic liberties and rights for which they had fought a revolution.

Consensus, Conflict, and Compromise

On some key constitutional provisions, the delegates quickly reached a consensus. During the first week of their deliberations, they agreed that the new government would consist of three branches—a supreme national legislature, an executive, and a judiciary—and that the national government would have powers wider than those exercised under the Articles of Confederation. The principle of representative government based on an elected legislature was accepted, while Hamilton's plan for a hereditary body like the English House of Lords was rejected. It was further agreed that the national legislature would be bicameral—consisting of two chambers. One chamber would represent the aristocracy and the other would represent the ordinary citizen. The executive branch was to consist of one person, elected, it was thought initially, by the legislature. The need for an independent national judiciary, comprised of a supreme court and lower federal courts with judges appointed for life, also was recognized.

Although the delegates quickly established a consensus on many key elements of the new government, there also were major conflicts among them as they sought to protect their states' interests. These conflicts were, however, successfully resolved through a series of compromises.

A major dispute arose over the basis on which representation in the new Congress would be apportioned among the states. The larger states favored the **Virginia Plan,** which called for a bicameral legislature with the lower house elected by the voters and the upper house chosen by the lower house from nominees submitted by the state legislatures. Representation in both houses would be based on each state's population. This plan would have assured the large and more populous states—Virginia, New York, Pennsylvania, and Massachusetts—of a majority in the legislature. The small states countered with the **New Jersey Plan.** It called for retaining the *unicameral*—single chamber—legislature in place under the Articles of Confederation in which each state had equal representation. This large-versus-small-state dispute was resolved by the Connecticut Compromise, also known as the Great Compromise. It called for a bicameral legislature with the House of Representatives elected by the voters and its membership based on each state's population and the Senate elected by the state legislatures with each state having two senators. The House of Representatives would have the power to initiate all tax legislation. This compromise reconciled the large and small states by allowing the small states to dominate the Senate, while the large states could dominate the House.

Yet another controversy about congressional representation arose over slavery. The South wanted slaves to count in a state's population when the time came to determine the number of representatives a state was entitled to have in the House of Representatives. But southern delegates to the convention did not want slaves counted in apportioning direct taxes (taxes paid directly to the national government by individual citizens) among the states. Northern delegates, however, wanted slaves counted in apportioning direct taxes but did not want them counted for purposes of determining representation. This thorny issue was settled through the Three-fifths Compromise, under which it was agreed that slaves would count as three-fifths of a person for purposes of apportioning both representation and taxes among the states.

Further conflict between the North and South arose over the power of the national government to regulate interstate and foreign commerce, including the slave trade. The North, which was developing a commercial and manufacturing economy, was anxious to have a government capable of regulating and promoting interstate and foreign commerce. Northern delegates also favored a ban on the importation of slaves. The more agrarian South, dependent on trading its commodities for imported goods, feared that a new government with extensive trade powers would harm its interests. Southern delegates also wanted the slave trade continued. This dispute was resolved through the Commerce and Slave Trade Compromise in which the North gained a strong central government with the power to regulate foreign and interstate commerce. But to protect the South's export trade, the national government was prohibited from levying any taxes on U.S. exports. Furthermore, the South was guaranteed protection against harmful trade treaties by a provision that required a two-thirds vote of the Senate to ratify treaties. Finally, to appease the slave traders and owners, Congress was banned from prohibiting the importation of slaves before 1808.

The presidency also posed a serious problem for the Founders. Initially, they had accepted the notion of having the chief executive chosen by the Congress. There was concern, however, that this method of selection would make the president subservient to Congress. In addition, the smaller states believed that a congressionally elected president would permit the larger states to control the office. Because of the distrust they had developed for the post-Revolution state legislatures, the delegates rejected selection of the president by these bodies. Their distrust of the general public also led them to reject direct popular election by the voters. The compromise solution to the presidential selection issue was the electoral college in which the president (and vice president) would be chosen by a majority of the electors. According to this plan, each state would choose, in a manner to be determined by the state legislatures, a number of electors equal to its number of representatives and senators in Congress. If no candidate received a majority of the electors' votes, the House of Representatives would then select the president from among the three candidates receiving the most electoral votes. This compromise assured the states and the Congress of a role in presidential selection yet maintained a buffer between the general public and the nation's highest executive.

Controversy over the Founders' Motives

Since Charles Beard wrote *An Economic Interpretation of the Constitution* in 1913, historians have argued over the extent to which the delegates' economic self-interest affected the content of the document. Beard made the case that, as economically advantaged citizens holding government bonds issued to fund the Revolutionary War, the Founders stood to gain from a new national government better able to pay back government bondholders.[7] More recent scholarship, however, has challenged Beard's economic interpretation of the Constitution. Although slave-owning delegates did seek to limit the national government's power over slavery, historians have demonstrated that individual economic interests did not dominate constitutional decision making and that delegates were more apt to represent their states' interests and personal beliefs.[8]

7. Charles A. Beard, *An Economic Interpretation of the Constitution* (New York: Macmillan, 1913).

8. Forrest McDonald, *We the People: The Economic Origins of the Constitution* (Chicago: University of Chicago Press, 1958); Robert E. Brown, *Charles Beard and the Constitution* (Princeton, N.J.: Princeton University Press, 1956); and Robert A. McGuire, "Constitution Making: A Rational Choice Model of the Federal Convention of 1787," *American Journal of Political Science* 32 (May 1988): 483–522.

Basic Principles of the Constitutional System

The drafters of the Constitution faced a series of complex governance problems (Table 2.1). Their goal was to create a government that derived its powers from the people, avoided potential excesses of democracy, protected individual liberties and property, had sufficient power to govern effectively, and preserved state autonomy within a strengthened union. But to devise such a government, they had to find constitutional devices that would permit reconciliation of these sometimes conflicting objectives. The combination of features in the Constitution can be viewed, therefore, as the Founders' solution to the still vexing problems of representative government.

Table 2.1 The Constitutional Balance

Problems Confronting the Drafters of the Constitution	*Constitutional Features Designed to Resolve the Problems*

Creating a government based on the consent of the governed while avoiding the evils of factions and excesses of democracy	A government of divided powers
	  • Separation of powers and checks and balances
	  • Federalism (the constitutional division of governmental powers between the national government and the states)
	  • Bicameral legislature
	An appointed judiciary
	System of direct popular elections and indirect elections

Creating a government capable of governing while preventing that government from becoming too strong and a threat to individual liberties	Granting extensive powers to the national government while imposing constitutional limits on governmental authority Dividing government powers to make it difficult for any group, faction, or temporary majority to gain control of government
Creating a union out of relatively independent states while preventing the creation of too powerful a national government and permitting state autonomy	Federal supremacy doctrine Federalism
Creating representative government while preventing the legislative excesses that characterized the post-Revolution period	Direct popular election of the House of Representatives, with indirect election of the Senate by the state legislatures Separation of powers to check the legislature Explicit limits on legislative power
Creating an executive strong enough to coordinate the operations of the government and check the legislature while preventing the executive from becoming an arbitrary ruler	Creating the office of president with specified powers Separation of powers to check executive power Election of the president for a fixed term; no hereditary executive

Figure 2.2: Constitutional Processes of Leadership Selection: The Founders' Plan

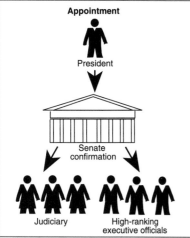

Appointment

President

Senate confirmation

Judiciary

High-ranking executive officials

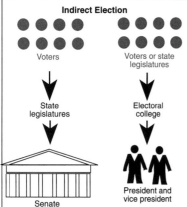

Indirect Election

Voters

Voters or state legislatures

State legislatures

Electoral college

Senate

President and vice president

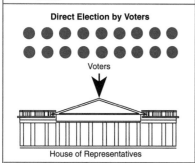

Direct Election by Voters

Voters

House of Representatives

Note: Two important changes have been made over the years in this plan. First, since 1836 the election of presidential electors by a statewide, winner-take-all popular vote has been the almost universal state practice. Second, the Seventeenth Amendment (1913) permits direct election of senators by the voters.

Popular Sovereignty and Representative Government Tempered by Indirect Election

The Founders' belief that the people should be the source of government power—popular sovereignty—is embodied in the Preamble to the Constitution, which states: "We the People of the United States, . . . do ordain and establish this Constitution for the United States of America." The commitment to popular sovereignty is reinforced in more concrete terms by the provision in Article I for direct election (by the voters) of the House of Representatives every two years.

In providing for an elected House of Representatives and a Senate chosen by the state legislatures, the Founders affirmed their commitment to representative government. They rejected monarchy (a hereditary kingship), aristocracy (rule by a hereditary elite), and direct democracy (rule by the masses).

Fears of mob rule and excessive democracy led the delegates to insulate the new government from the public through a series of indirect selection procedures (see Figure 2.2 for the Founders' system of leadership selection through a combination of direct election, indirect election, and appointment methods). The Founders believed that an indirectly elected Senate would provide a check on imprudent actions inspired by any momentary passions that might sweep through the popularly elected House of Representatives. (It was not until 1913 and ratification of the Seventeenth Amendment that all the states chose their senators through direct popular election—see Chapter 10, Congress.) The presidency was to be insulated from public opinion by its fixed four-year term of office and selection by the electoral college. Each state was free to determine how its electors would be chosen, and, until the 1830s, most states delegated this responsibility to their state legislatures rather than to the voters. To ensure the independence of the judiciary, judges were to serve life terms after being appointed by the president and confirmed by the Senate rather than be elected by the voters.

Limited Government

Like John Locke, the Framers believed that governments were instituted to protect basic individual rights. Thus, they sought to impose limits on governmental power by making explicit grants of authority to the national government. Article I, section 8, of the Constitution contains a list of powers delegated to Congress. When Congress passes legislation, it must be able to trace its authority back to this list or to powers that can be implied from these listed powers. Congress may not act just because it thinks a proposed bill is needed. The Constitution's grants of authority to Congress are, however, stated in broad, general terms—for example, Congress is empowered to pass legislation to provide for the "general Welfare" and to make laws "necessary and proper" to carry out its delegated powers. As a result, the Congress has substantial leeway in fashioning legislation.

Limitations on government also were achieved through specific prohibitions. The national government, for example, is denied the power to tax exports, and both the national government and states are banned from passing either bills of attainder (criminal punishment without benefit of a trial) or ex post facto laws (retroactive criminal statutes making something a crime that was not a crime at the time it was committed). The Bill of Rights was added later to the Constitution to provide additional and explicit limits to the national government's power (see Chapter 4, Civil Liberties and Civil Rights). The First Amendment, for example, says that "Congress shall make no law respecting an establishment of religion, or prohibiting the free exercise thereof; or abridging the freedom of speech, or of the press; or the right of the people peaceably to assemble, and to petition the Government for a redress of grievances."

Separation of Powers with Checks and Balances

A key element in the thinking of the Founders was the belief that a concentration of power leads to tyranny. They feared that some faction, group, or temporary majority might gain enough power to dominate the government and thereby threaten the basic rights of others. Thus, they divided the government's power among three separate branches of government: Congress, vested with legislative authority by Article I; the president, authorized by Article II to exercise executive powers; and the federal courts, vested with judicial power by Article III (specifically, such power is vested in "one supreme Court, and in such inferior courts as the Congress may from time to time ordain and establish").

To ensure that no one branch could dominate the government and that the government would use restraint in exercising its powers, each branch was required to share some of its powers with the other branches. Under this system of checks and balances (described in Figure 2.3), the president has the power to recommend legislation to Congress and to veto bills to indicate presidential disapproval. To check the president, Congress has authority to override presidential vetoes by a

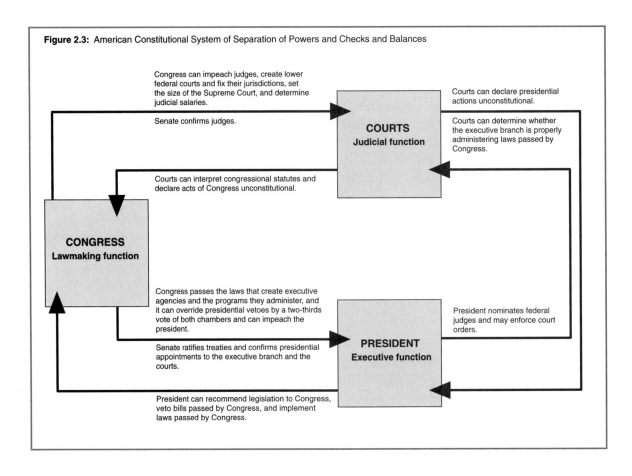

Figure 2.3: American Constitutional System of Separation of Powers and Checks and Balances

two-thirds vote, create executive agencies, impeach the president, confirm appointees to the executive and judicial branches, and ratify treaties negotiated by the president. The judiciary can check both the Congress and the president by declaring their acts unconstitutional, even though this power was not expressly granted by the Constitution. Both the Congress and president have power over the judiciary. The president nominates judges, subject to Senate confirmation, and the Congress determines the organization and jurisdiction of the federal courts. Through **separation of powers** with checks and balances, the Founders believed that they had found a constitutional device that would prevent any faction or interest that might temporarily dominate a branch of government from infringing on basic rights.

Federalism

The writers of the Constitution succeeded in extending the powers of the national government beyond those under the Articles of Confederation. Congress was now empowered to levy taxes, regulate inter-state and foreign commerce, coin money, maintain an army and navy, and provide for the common defense and general welfare. Important matters no longer required virtually the unanimous consent of all the states. Although the national government was strengthened, the states were retained as key governmental units. Actually, the Founders had little choice in this matter. The state legislatures had to ratify the draft constitution prepared by the convention in Philadelphia, and the states could hardly be expected to agree to their own demise. The Founders, therefore, created a government based on the principle of federalism. In a federal system the powers of government are constitutionally divided between the national government and the states, with each exercising significant powers. The powers of the national government were to be those enumerated—and those implied by that enumera-tion—in the Constitution, whereas the states were to exercise reserved powers, which were those not prohibited to the states (for example, the Constitution bans the states from entering into treaties or alliances with foreign countries or coining money) and those not granted to the national government. In practical terms, this division of powers has meant that today the states have the major responsibility for such gov-ernmental activities as public education, local government, intrastate highway transportation, protection of public health and safety, and family relations.

But in a system in which powers are divided between the national government and the states, it is inevitable that conflicts will arise between national and state laws. To deal with this problem, Article VI contains a federal supremacy clause, which makes the Constitution and the laws and treaties passed under it the "supreme Law of the Land." This provision means that all state laws, executive orders, and judicial decisions must conform to the Constitution, treaties, and laws of the United States, or they are invalid.

Where the Constitution draws the line between national and state governmental authority has always been both fuzzy and controversial. In the case of the Civil War, the nation's ongoing controversy over the extent of federal versus state power turned to violence as the South sought to secede from the Union. The manner in which American fed-eralism has evolved and the controversies over the extent of national versus state power are examined more closely in Chapter 3.

Judicial Review

The federal courts exercise the power of judicial review—the power to declare acts of Congress and the president unconstitutional. This principle is firmly embedded in the American constitutional system, even though there is no explicit grant of this authority to the federal courts in the Constitution. Led by Chief Justice John Marshall, the Supreme Court established the precedent for judicial review in 1803 in the case of *Marbury v. Madison* (described in more detail in Chapter 13, The Judiciary).[9] But the Court has used this power sparingly. In the fifty years after the *Marbury* decision, for example, it did not hold any federal laws unconstitutional. Judicial review is exercised only when a specific case is brought before the courts. The judiciary does not give advisory opinions to the Congress or the president.

The Struggle for Ratification

To avoid entrenched opposition within the state legislatures, the drafters provided for ratification of the new Constitution by special constitutional conventions in the states. Ratification by nine of the thirteen states was required before the Constitution could be put into effect.

The backers of the Constitution, who supported a strong national government, were called **Federalists.** James Madison, Alexander Hamilton, and John Jay, a New Yorker who later became chief justice of the United States, were leaders in this cause. Under the pen name "Publius," they anonymously wrote, published, and circulated eighty-five letters to the public that appeared in New York newspapers beginning in October 1787. Later collected to form the *Federalist Papers,* these writings, which are counted among the classics of political theory, today provide insights into how the drafters of the Constitution envisioned the new government would function. The more immediate purpose of the *Federalist Papers,* however, was to counter the arguments of the **Antifederalists,** who opposed the Constitution (see *Federalist* Nos. 10 and 51 in the Appendix).

The Antifederalists feared that the Constitution would create a national government that would endanger personal liberties and submerge the state legislatures under the supremacy of Congress.[10] They focused their fire on the absence of a bill of rights in the Constitution and the threat they believed this omission posed for basic liberties. The Federalists argued that a bill of rights was not required because the national government would be restricted to exercising the powers granted to it by the Constitution. They decided, however, to concede

9. *Marbury v. Madison,* 1 Cr. 137 (1803).

10. See Cecelia M. Kenyon, ed., *The Antifederalists* (Indianapolis: Bobbs-Merrill, 1966).

this issue in order to secure ratification of the Constitution and agreed to incorporate a bill of rights into the Constitution as its first ten amendments (see Table 2.2).

By June 21, 1788, the required nine states had ratified the Constitution but not included among them were Virginia and New York, whose support was essential if the Union was to succeed. Led by Madison in Virginia and Hamilton in New York, the Federalists late in 1788 won narrow and hard-fought victories in both states (with only a three-vote margin in New York).[11] North Carolina (1789) and Rhode Island (1790) later made ratification by the thirteen original states unanimous. The Bill of Rights was ratified on December 15, 1791.

11. For an account of Alexander Hamilton's role in securing ratification by New York, see Clinton Rossiter, *Alexander Hamilton and the Constitution* (New York: Harcourt, Brace, 1964).

Table 2.2 The First Ten Amendments to the Constitution: Bill of Rights

Amendment	Purpose
I	Guarantees freedom of religion, speech, assembly, and press, and the right of people to petition the government for redress of grievances
II	Protects the right of states to maintain a militia
III	Restricts quartering of troops in private homes
IV	Protects against "unreasonable searches and seizures"
V	Assures the right not to be deprived of "life, liberty, or property, without due process of law," including protections against double jeopardy, self-incrimination, and government seizure of property without just compensation
VI	Guarantees the right to a speedy and public trial by an impartial jury
VII	Assures the right to a jury trial in cases involving the common law (judge-made law originating in England)
VIII	Protects against excessive bail or cruel and unusual punishment
IX	Provides that people's rights are not restricted to those specified in Amendments I-VIII
X	Reiterates the Constitution's principle of federalism by providing that powers not granted to the national government nor prohibited to the states are reserved to the states and to the people

The Struggle for Ratification of the Constitution

While most of the smaller states overwhelmingly supported ratification of the Constitution (New Hampshire and Rhode Island were exceptions), strong opposition existed in the larger states whose approval was crucial for the new government's success.

Pennsylvania—Ratification was gained over stubborn opposition by a vote of 46–23 and was accompanied by a demand for a bill of rights.

Massachusetts—When the state included a demand for a bill of rights with ratification, the initial skepticism of John Hancock and Samuel Adams was overcome.

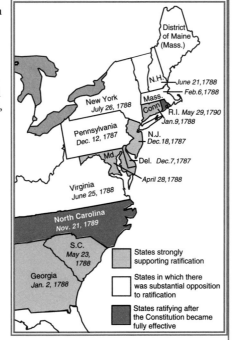

Virginia—The opposition led by George Mason and Patrick Henry was overcome by an 89–79 vote on the understanding that amendments would be added later to the Constitution.

New York—Backed by arguments in the *Federalist,* Alexander Hamilton led the fight for ratification, which was won by a narrow 30–27 vote.

Changing and Interpreting the Constitution: An Enduring Document

In 1987 the Constitution celebrated its two hundredth anniversary, an unusual record of durability for such a document. One reason for its longevity is its relative lack of detailed provisions or statutory-type language that could become quickly outmoded, necessitating frequent changes in its language through amendments. Rather, each branch of government has been able to interpret the Constitution and adapt it to changing circumstances. The records of most state constitutions have been quite different. Most are lengthy documents (averaging 27,000 words compared with 8,700 in the U.S. Constitution) heavily laden with detailed language that becomes outdated. Frequent amendment or even total revision is, then, not uncommon. Louisiana, for example, has had eleven constitutions; Georgia, ten; and South Carolina, seven. The constitution of Alabama has been amended over 513 times since 1901, and the current constitutions of eighteen states have been amended over 100 times. By contrast, the Constitution of the United States has been amended only 27 times (Table 2.3). The small number of amendments to the U.S. Constitution reflects not only the adaptability of its language to changing circumstances, but also the fact that the amending process is extremely difficult to implement.

The Formal Amending Process

The formal amending process has two stages: proposal and ratification (Figure 2.4). According to the Constitution, amendments may be proposed either by a two-thirds vote of both houses of Congress or by a constitutional convention called by Congress on petition of two-thirds of the states. Ratification is achieved by securing the approval of either three-fourths of the state legislatures or constitutional conventions held in three-fourths of the states.

Stage 1: Proposal. To date, the only method of proposal used successfully has been House and Senate approval by a two-thirds vote of resolutions proposing amendments. Congressional resolutions proposing constitutional amendments are not subject to presidential vetoes. Presidents may, however, exert substantial informal influence during congressional consideration of amendments. During the 1950s, President Dwight Eisenhower, for example, lobbied Congress forcefully and successfully to reject the so-called Bricker amendment, which would have severely limited the president's treaty-making authority.

Although the alternative method of proposal—a constitutional con-

Table 2.3 Constitutional Amendments Added after Ratification of the Bill of Rights

Amendment	Date	Purpose
Amendments Changing the Powers of the National and State Governments		
XI	1795	Removed cases in which a state was sued without its own consent from the jurisdiction of the federal courts
XIII	1865	Abolished slavery and authorized Congress to pass legislation implementing its abolition
XIV	1868	Granted citizenship to all persons born or naturalized in the United States; banned states from denying any person life, liberty, or property without due process of law; and banned states from denying any person the equal protection of the laws
XVI	1913	Empowered Congress to levy an income tax
XVIII	1919	Authorized Congress to prohibit the manufacture, sale, and transportation of liquor
XXI	1933	Repealed the Eighteenth Amendment and empowered Congress to regulate the liquor industry
Amendments Changing Government Structure		
XII	1804	Required presidential electors to vote separately for president and vice president
XX	1933	Shortened the time between a presidential election and inauguration by designating January 20 as Inauguration Day; set January 3 as the date for the opening of a new Congress
XXII	1951	Limited presidents to two full terms in office
XXV	1967	Provided for succession to the office of president in the event of death or incapacity and for filling vacancies in the office of the vice president
XXVII	1992	Banned Congress from increasing its members' salaries until after the next election
Amendments Extending the Suffrage and Power of the Voters		
XV	1870	Extended voting rights to blacks by outlawing denial of the right to vote on the basis of race, color, or previous condition of servitude
XVII	1913	Provided for the election of U.S. senators by direct popular vote instead of by the state legislatures
XIX	1920	Extended the right to vote to women
XXIII	1961	Granted voters in the District of Columbia the right to vote for president and vice president
XXIV	1964	Forbade requiring the payment of a poll tax to vote in a federal election
XXVI	1971	Extended the right to vote to eighteen-year-olds

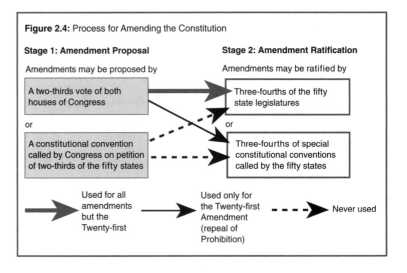

Figure 2.4: Process for Amending the Constitution

Stage 1: Amendment Proposal

Amendments may be proposed by

A two-thirds vote of both houses of Congress

or

A constitutional convention called by Congress on petition of two-thirds of the fifty states

Stage 2: Amendment Ratification

Amendments may be ratified by

Three-fourths of the fifty state legislatures

or

Three-fourths of special constitutional conventions called by the fifty states

Used for all amendments but the Twenty-first

Used only for the Twenty-first Amendment (repeal of Prohibition)

Never used

vention called by Congress on petition of two-thirds of the states—has never been used successfully, in several instances this procedure has appeared to be on the verge of implementation. For example, by 1993 thirty-two of the needed thirty-four states had petitioned Congress for a constitutional convention to propose an amendment requiring a balanced federal budget. Use of this method of proposal raises a series of important constitutional questions that have not been resolved. For example, how long can a petition from a state remain pending before Congress? Can a state rescind its petition for calling a constitutional convention as Alabama, Louisiana, and Florida have done in the case of the balanced budget amendment? Can Congress be compelled by the courts to call a constitutional convention if it fails to do so after two-thirds of the states have filed petitions? Can a constitutional convention propose amendments on topics other than those contained in the states' petitions or in the congressional call for the convention? This latter question stems from fears of a "runaway" convention that might engage in wholesale constitutional revision and mischief. Congress has therefore considered, but not yet acted on, measures that would limit constitutional conventions to the subject matter specified in the state petitions to Congress. The fact that Congress has managed thus far to adhere to the two-thirds-vote-of-Congress method of proposal reflects the national legislature's determination to maintain control of the amending process and not surrender it to a temporary convention.

Stage 2: Ratification. Congress normally specifies in its resolution proposing an amendment the length of time the states have for completing the ratification process. The customary time limit has been seven years. On occasion, however, Congress has extended the deadline, which it did in the case of the Equal Rights Amendment (ERA). In 1979 its deadline was extended three years when it became apparent that the three additional states needed for ratification would not approve the amendment within the seven-year time limit. Even with this extension, however, the ERA was not ratified. All this being said, there is no constitutional limit on the length of time an amendment can remain pending before the states for ratification. Thus, the Twenty-seventh Amendment, which prohibits Congress from raising its pay until after the next election, was sent to the states in 1789, but it did not gain the necessary three-fourths of the states needed for ratification until 1992 (202 years after it had been proposed!).

The ratification process reflects the constitutional principle of federalism by requiring three-fourths of the states to ratify proposed amendments. All amendments to the Constitution have been ratified by the state legislatures except the Twenty-first, which repealed Prohibition (a ban on the manufacture, sale, transport, and import and export of alcoholic beverages). State constitutional conventions were used to ratify this amendment because the advocates of repeal feared that a large number of state legislatures were dominated by "Drys," the advocates of Prohibition. Most states permit their legislatures to ratify amendments by a simple majority vote, although in seven states either a three-fifths or two-thirds majority is required.

Congressional Interpretation

Whenever Congress acts, it is making an interpretation of its powers under the Constitution. Article I, section 8, lists the powers of Congress in quite general terms—for example, "to regulate Commerce with foreign Nations, and among the several States." In implementing its power to regulate commerce, Congress has taken an expansive view of its authority. The commerce clause has been used to ban discrimination in places of public accommodation, to regulate working conditions, to authorize the Federal Bureau of Investigation to participate in kidnapping cases, to regulate the amount of crops farmers can plant and the prices they will receive for them, to allocate television channels and radio frequencies, to restrict monopolies and trusts, to guarantee home mortgages, to protect investor savings in banks and savings and loans—and the list goes on. Backed by court decisions endorsing broad interpretations of its constitutional powers, Congress has gradually extended its authority so that there are few aspects of American life that are safe from the long arm of Congress.

Presidential Interpretation

Like Congress, presidents also interpret the meaning of the Constitution, and in the process they have expanded significantly the scope of presidential power. The constitutional provisions in Article II state presidential powers in extremely broad terms. For example, the president is designated the "Commander in Chief of the Army and Navy" and charged with responsibility for taking "Care that the Laws be faithfully executed."

Such grants of authority, as well as those in Article I giving the president power to propose legislation and veto acts of Congress, have been used by the occupants of the White House to stretch the influence of their office. As commanders in chief of the armed forces, presidents have committed American forces to battle on foreign soil and the high seas to protect American citizens, fulfill treaty obligations, and protect American interests—all without a declaration of war by Congress. Thus through their war powers, presidents may commit the United States to a course of action that Congress will find very hard to reverse should it wish to do so.

And many presidents have used their war powers. For example, during the Civil War Abraham Lincoln suspended the writ of habeas corpus (a court order requiring government officials to bring a prisoner before a court and show cause for his or her detention), ordered a blockade of southern ports, and called up the state militia at the beginning of the war. James K. Polk's 1846 dispatch of American troops into disputed territory in what is now Texas helped to precipitate the Mexican War. In more recent times, Harry Truman supported United Nations forces after communist North Korea invaded South Korea in 1950. John Kennedy's 1962 imposition of a military blockade on Cuba to prevent the Soviets from setting up an offensive missile base was followed by the commitment of American forces to Vietnam under three presidents in the 1960s and 1970s. Finally, in the Middle East, Ronald Reagan bombed Libya in 1986 in retaliation for Libyan support of international terrorism, and in 1990 George Bush deployed ground and naval forces in the Persian Gulf region after Iraq's August invasion of Kuwait.

It is not just in the realm of foreign policy that presidents have extended their powers through constitutional interpretation. The veto power over legislation was initially used sparingly, only when presidents thought a law was either unconstitutional or technically defective. But modern presidents frequently veto legislation they find objectionable either in whole or in part. They also regularly use the threat of a presidential veto to induce Congress to pass laws more to their liking. Just as Congress has been able to extend its authority without formal amendment, presidents also have found the Constitution pliable enough to permit significant expansion of their powers.

Judicial Interpretation

The meaning of the Constitution depends heavily on how it is interpreted by the judiciary, especially the Supreme Court. In the case of *Marbury v. Madison* (1803), mentioned earlier, it was the Supreme Court that read into the Constitution the power of the courts to declare acts of Congress unconstitutional. Even though the original Constitution did not provide for judicial review, it is now a firmly established principle. It was also the Supreme Court that established the tradition of interpreting broadly the powers granted by the Constitution to Congress. In the case of *McCulloch v. Maryland* (1819), the Court established the principle of *implied powers*—that is, that Congress could do those things necessary and proper to execute its enumerated powers.[12]

Like the president and Congress, the courts are asked continually to interpret the Constitution. For example, in 1986 the Supreme Court ruled that a provision of the so-called Gramm-Rudman-Hollings budget deficit reduction law was unconstitutional. The act mandated the comptroller general, an agent of Congress, to implement budget cuts if Congress failed to meet the deficit reduction targets it had set itself by law. But because the law gave to an agency of Congress functions that were within the constitutional province of the executive branch, the Court ruled that this provision of the law violated the Constitution's separation of powers principle.[13]

The Supreme Court is also heavily involved in ongoing controversies over the meaning of the Fourteenth Amendment's guarantee that the "equal protection of the laws" will be denied to no one. In interpreting this so-called equal protection clause, the courts have banned state-supported racial discrimination in public schools and state universities, required state legislatures to create congressional and state legislative districts that are as nearly equal in population as practicable, and determined the permissible limits of affirmative action in hiring practices, government contracting procedures, and admission to institutions of higher education. Because the courts share their constitutional interpretation responsibilities with other branches of government, Charles Evans Hughes, who later became chief justice, probably

12. *McCulloch v. Maryland,* 4 Wheat. 316 (1819).
13. *Bowsher v. Synar,* 478 U.S. 714 (1986).

was exaggerating when he observed in 1907, "We are under a Constitution, but the Constitution is what the judges say it is." Few would dispute, however, that the judiciary plays a prominent role in deciding the meaning of the Constitution.[14]

Traditions and Practices

American constitutional government also has been shaped by traditions and practices that have grown up outside the formal government. For example, the Founders made no provision in the Constitution for political parties and were opposed to their development. Yet today political parties profoundly affect the governmental system in ways not envisioned by the drafters of the Constitution. National party conventions nominate presidential candidates. Presidential electors are chosen on partisan slates and almost invariably vote for their party's candidate. Moreover, candidates for the House and Senate are nominated in party primary elections, and Congress is organized on a partisan basis. Finally, presidential appointees to the federal courts are overwhelmingly of the same party as the president.

In spite of the Framers' fear of factions, interest groups have become a highly regularized part of the political process; they represent organized interests before the Congress, administration, and courts. They also have become an increasingly important and controversial source of campaign money for House and Senate candidates—especially incumbents—through their political action committees (PACs).

A Government of Divided Powers and Diverse Goals

The writers of the Constitution were not bent on creating an activist government. Rather, they wanted primarily to protect individual rights and achieve political stability. To protect individual and property rights, they created a system of limited government through a written constitution that made grants of authority to the national government and imposed prohibitions on both the national and state governments. To protect further the rights of the individual from temporary and potentially impetuous majorities, government power was divided between the national government and the states (federalism); among the legislative, executive, and judicial branches (separation of powers); and between the House and Senate (bicameralism). Different methods of selection were specified for the president (electoral college), Senate

14. For an informed analysis of the process of constitutional interpretation, see Louis Fisher, *Constitutional Dialogues: Interpretation as Political Process* (Princeton, N.J.: Princeton University Press, 1988).

(election by state legislatures), House (popular election), and judiciary (presidential appointment with confirmation by the Senate). The Framers of the Constitution did not try to design a strictly majoritarian system in which government policies would be based on the opinions of a majority of the citizenry. Rather, they sought a system that would restrain majorities and require the formation of broad coalitions and consensus for the government to act.

Indeed, the Founders' principal goals were neither equality nor democracy. As surprising as it may seem today, assuring equality was simply not one of their priorities. The Constitution even left the institution of slavery intact. Nor was there any mention of women's rights. Since 1787 and the drafting of the Constitution, however, one of the most compelling movements in American society has been the cause of political and social equality (also see Chapter 4, Civil Liberties and Civil Rights). The movement for greater equality has resulted in a series of constitutional amendments which, while not altering the fundamental structure of American government created by the Founders, has advanced the cause of equality. For example, voting rights were extended to black males (the Fifteenth Amendment outlawed denial of the right to vote on the basis of race, color, or previous condition of servitude), women (Nineteenth), residents of the District of Columbia (to vote in presidential elections, Twenty-third), and eighteen-year-olds (Twenty-sixth). And in a related area, the Seventeenth Amendment granted voters, instead of state legislators, the power to elect U.S. senators, and the Twenty-fourth Amendment abolished the poll tax as a requirement for voting in federal elections. Slavery was prohibited in 1865 by the Thirteenth Amendment, followed several years later by the Fourteenth Amendment, which prohibited the states from denying people due process of law and the equal protection of the laws.

As the Constitution enters its third century, there is little support for fundamental change in the constitutional order devised in 1787. Yet the American Constitution, like any set of governmental procedures, carries with it both costs and benefits.[15] Critics and reformers have argued that government under the Constitution is often one with divided leadership—a president from one political party and a majori-

15. For evaluations of the Constitution on the occasion of its two hundredth anniversary, see "The Constitutional Order: 1787–1987," a collection of essays published in *Public Interest* 86 (Winter 1987); Robert A. Goldwin and Art Kaufman, eds., *Separation of Powers—Does It Still Work?* (Washington, D.C.: American Enterprise Institute, 1986); and James L. Sundquist, *Constitutional Reform and Effective Government* (Washington, D.C.: Brookings, 1986).

ty in Congress from another. The result can be policy deadlocks and excessive partisan maneuvering. Even under the best of circumstances, it is argued that the American system of divided power makes it difficult for government to cope in a timely manner with societal and world problems. For example, between 1987 and 1992 Republican control of the White House and Democratic control of the Congress complicated the already formidable and intensely political task of reducing the federal budget deficit and produced policy gridlock in many areas of public concern. It is further claimed that decisive government policies are almost impossible to achieve because so many interests must be accommodated within the separation of powers system. Thus, government institutions have been frustrated in their attempts to develop a comprehensive and coherent energy policy, for example, because of conflicts between energy-producing and consuming regions, environmentalists and energy producers, pro- and antinuclear power forces, and hordes of other organized interests. Critics of the constitutional system also claim that with governmental authority so scattered, the voters find it hard to hold any group or party responsible for government policy. Popular control of government through elections is thereby frustrated.

Defenders of the constitutional order tend to stress its contributions to political stability and public consensus, as well as its protections against the possibility that any group, faction, party, or individual becomes too powerful. They acknowledge that rapid, decisive action is difficult in a system of divided powers. But they also argue that divided power and the extensive bargaining, negotiation, and compromise required for government action tend to result in policies conducive to wide public acceptance (though not necessarily support). For example, after lengthy and extensive negotiations among members of Congress, the Reagan administration, and a wide range of interest groups, a major overhaul of the federal tax code was approved in 1986. While no tax bill can be expected to win universal praise, the 1986 tax reform law was at least accepted by a diverse array of taxpayers. Similarly, in 1990 after extended negotiations, a Republican president and a Democratic Congress reached agreement on a comprehensive strengthening of the Clean Air Act, a policy field racked with intense regional, interest group, and ideological conflicts. All this bargaining, negotiation, compromise, and consensus-seeking, it is maintained, contributes to political stability.

A government of divided powers also provides citizens and groups with many possible points of access to the political process where their voices may be heard. Groups who find the Congress unresponsive can appeal to the executive and the courts. And when any of the three branches has seemed to assert power unduly, the separation of powers system has worked to restrain the overzealous.

Whatever the merits of the debate over the Constitution's strengths and weaknesses, it is a document that is widely accepted and glorified by Americans. Barring some cataclysmic event, it will not, therefore, be changed significantly in the near future. The Constitution is the legal cornerstone of American politics.

For Review

1. The Constitution reflects America's heritage as a British colony, as well as the lengthy evolution of representative government in Great Britain. Its contents also mirror the problems the young nation faced after the Revolution, the conflicts waged and the compromises offered at the Constitutional Convention of 1787, and the struggle over ratification.

2. The Constitution embodies five basic principles: popular sovereignty and representative government, tempered by indirect election; limited government; separation of powers and checks and balances; federalism; and judicial review.

3. The unusually long life and durability of the Constitution owes much to its concise yet flexible text, which has allowed Congress, the president, and the courts to interpret the Constitution in ways appropriate for changing conditions. Because the Constitution has proven so adaptable, it has not been necessary to change it frequently through formal amendment.

4. The drafters of the Constitution sought to create a government capable of governing, promoting economic development, and protecting individual rights. Since they wrote the original document, however, a movement toward greater political and social equality has resulted in a series of amendments that has advanced the cause of equality while leaving the fundamental structure of the government unaltered.

5. The Constitution, like all governmental rules and procedures, is not neutral in its impact. By dividing government power among three branches of government and between the national government and the states, it has made quick, decisive, and comprehensive policy making difficult. But at the same time, divided governmental power has provided citizens with multiple points of access to decision makers; encouraged policy making through negotiation, bargaining, and compromise; and proven resistant to authoritarian rule.

For Further Reading

Bernstein, Richard B., with Kym S. Rice. *Are We to Be a Nation? The Making of the Constitution.* Cambridge, Mass.: Harvard University Press, 1987. A spirited narrative and analysis of the Revolution, the weaknesses of the articles, and the drafting and ratification of the Constitution.

"The Constitutional Order: 1787–1987," *Public Interest* 86 (Winter 1987). A collection of essays written by leading scholars on the occasion of the Constitution's bicentennial.

Farrand, Max, ed. *The Records of the Federal Convention of 1787.* New Haven, Conn.: Yale University Press, 1913 (last reprinted in 1986). A documentary of the Constitutional Convention.

Goldwin, Robert A., and Art Kaufman, eds. *Separation of Powers—Does It Still Work?* Washington, D.C.: American Enterprise Institute, 1986. A collection of essays assessing the consequences of the Constitution's separation of powers principle.

Hamilton, Alexander, James Madison, and John Jay. *The Federalist Papers.* Available in a variety of editions. An exposition of the ideas underlying the Constitution by leading participants in the Constitutional Convention, written in support of ratification.

Lipset, Seymour Martin. *The First New Nation: The United States in Historical and Comparative Perspective.* Rev. ed. New York: Norton, 1979. A political sociologist's analysis of the impact of the values of achievement and equality on the development of the American character.

Peltason, J. W. *Understanding the Constitution.* 11th ed. New York: Holt, Rinehart, and Winston, 1988. An excellent reference guide to the meaning of the Constitution.

Rossiter, Clinton. *1787: The Grand Convention.* New York: Macmillan, 1966. A readable account of the writing of the Constitution and the struggle for ratification.

Wood, Gordon S. *The Creation of the American Republic, 1776–1787.* New York: Norton, 1972. An informative history of America's early years.

3. Federalism

T HE RELATIONSHIP OF the national government to the states and their local units of government affects virtually every American political institution from the political parties to the judiciary. It also affects many aspects of people's daily lives—the quality of the education they receive, the quality and quantity of their health care, the steps taken to protect their environment, as well as their welfare, housing, and transportation. Moreover, intergovernmental relationships influence the extent to which federal, state, and local governments pay for these services.

The national-state government relationship was of paramount concern to the writers of the Constitution. The failings of the governmental order under the Articles of Confederation stemmed in large part from the national government's weaknesses. It was subservient to the states and dependent on them for the revenues needed to perform even the most basic governmental functions such as providing for the common defense and maintaining domestic order. The national government also lacked the authority to deal effectively with the chaotic economic conditions created by each state regulating its own foreign and interstate commerce and printing its own currency. Thus, the economic development of the new nation was being strangled in a web of conflicting and confusing state laws, while the national government, bound by the Articles of Confederation, lacked the authority to respond.

The Founders' solution to these problems was to abandon the flawed system of the Articles of Confederation and create a new *federal system* that substantially strengthened the authority of the national government, yet it also reserved important powers for the states. But the American federal system is not all neat and tidy. The line between national and state powers and responsibilities is not always clear, and there are ongoing conflicts over which level of government should engage in and pay for particular kinds of activities. At the same time, however, there is a great deal of cooperation and sharing of responsibility among the various levels of government.

This chapter explores the nature of the American federal system. Specifically, it will examine the system's constitutional basis; the changes that have taken place since 1787, especially post-1960 developments; and, most important, how federalism has affected and continues to affect American government and politics.

What Is Federalism?

Federalism is a constitutional division of the powers of government between the national government and regional governments (states in the United States), with each exercising significant powers over the same people and territory. Every American, then, lives under two governmental jurisdictions: the government of the United States and the government of the state in which he or she resides. Because the national and state governments have their own officers and structures, the legislatures, governors, courts, and bureaucracies of the states are separate from those of the national government. The national and state governments do, however, share and cooperate in carrying out their functions.

A governmental order more common than federalism is one in which all governmental power is vested in a national government from which regional and local governments derive their powers. In these unitary government systems, the national government can alter or even abolish regional governments without their consent. In Britain, for example, the Conservative-dominated House of Commons abolished the Labour party-controlled Greater London Council in 1984 when the latter pursued policies sharply at odds with those of Prime Minister Margaret Thatcher. By contrast, under the American federal system, states derive their powers from the Constitution, and they cannot be abolished or have their boundaries altered by an act of Congress without their consent. Most state governments, however, are organized around the unitary principle. All local units of government—counties, cities, villages, townships, school districts—are legal creatures of the states and derive their powers from the states.

The weakest form of national government is found in a *confederation,* such as the United States under the Articles of Confederation and the southern Confederacy during the Civil War. In such a system, the states are sovereign (independent of external control) and free to join or withdraw from the nation as they choose. The national government may exercise only those powers delegated to it by the states. As a creature of the states, the national government in a confederate system must work through the states to effect domestic policies since it is not empowered to exert its authority directly upon individuals.

Why Federalism in America?

American federalism has been described as the "price of union." By introducing federalism into the Constitution, the drafters bal-

Federalism inevitably leads to clashes between the national government and the states. The national government may, however, use force to see that the Constitution and federal laws are enforced. In 1957, facing massive resistance in the South, President Dwight Eisenhower ordered federal troops to enforce desegregation of Central High School in Little Rock, Arkansas.

anced the need for a stronger national government than had existed under the Articles of Confederation with the need to maintain the states as vital instruments of self-government. Had the Founders not authorized the states to retain substantial policy-making authority, the Constitution probably would not have been ratified by the thirteen original states and there would have been no Union.

The Founders also viewed federalism as a way of preventing tyranny. Because federalism diffuses power among the national and various state governments, the Constitution writers believed that this diffusion would make it difficult for any faction, group, or party to gain control of the entire government and exercise unrestrained power. In *Federalist No. 10*, James Madison captured this argument when he observed that if "factious leaders . . . kindle a flame within their particular states," the spread of the "conflagration into other states" can be checked by national leaders.[1]

In such countries as the United States, Canada, India, Mexico, and Germany, which have wide-ranging cultural, social, religious, and economic diversity, federalism permits a sense of national identity to develop while also allowing a high degree of regional autonomy. The spirit of federalism is captured in the Latin phrase on American coins, *e pluribus unum* (out of many, one). Indeed, federalism is a means of achieving unity without uniformity. It permits the states, while abiding by the Constitution and national laws, to develop distinctive ways of organizing their governments and dealing with their citizens' concerns. For example, Nebraska operates with a unicameral (one-house) legislature; all other states have bicameral (two-house) bodies. Arkansas, New Hampshire, Vermont, and Rhode Island elect their governors for two years rather than the four years favored elsewhere. And, whereas all federal judges are nominated by the president and confirmed by the Senate, the states use a variety of judicial selection methods ranging from legislative or gubernatorial appointment, to merit commission nomination, to popular election. In addition to these differences in governmental structure, state policies vary widely. For example, Wisconsin's unique and controversial "Learnfare" program, which is designed to encourage school attendance, reduces welfare allowances to families whose children are chronically truant, and Delaware has laws so advantageous for business seeking to incorporate that the state

1. E. M. Earle, ed., *The Federalist* (New York: Modern Library, 1937), No. 10. For an informed summary of the Founders' reasons for creating a federal system in the Constitution, see Arthur N. Holcombe, *Our More Perfect Union* (Cambridge, Mass.: Harvard University Press, 1950), chaps. 1 and 2.

has become a mecca for this kind of corporate activity. In fourteen states, including New York, Michigan, Iowa, Minnesota, and Wisconsin, there is no death penalty for serious crimes, unlike in a majority of states. Finally, most states levy an income tax on wages, but, as of 1994, seven states (Alaska, Florida, Nevada, South Dakota, Texas, Washington, and Wyoming) did not.

The Constitutional Basis of Federalism

A merican federalism has its basis in the Constitution, whose provisions relate to the powers of the national government, the powers of the state governments, federal guarantees to the states, and relationships among the states (the division of powers between the national government and the states, including the restrictions on each, is shown in Table 3.1).

Table 3.1 Constitutional Allocation of Powers to the National and State Governments

EXAMPLES OF POWERS PERMITTED

NATIONAL GOVERNMENT *(Delegated, Implied, and Inherent Powers)*	NATIONAL AND STATE GOVERNMENTS *(Concurrent Powers)*	STATE GOVERNMENTS *(Reserved Powers)*
Regulate foreign and interstate commerce	Levy taxes	Regulate intrastate commerce
Coin money	Borrow money	Establish local government systems
Provide an army and navy	Spend for general welfare	Administer elections
Declare war	Establish courts	Protect the public's health, welfare, and morals
Establish federal courts below the Supreme Court	Enact and enforce laws	
Exercise powers implied from the expressed powers		
Conduct foreign relations		

EXAMPLES OF POWERS DENIED

NATIONAL GOVERNMENT	NATIONAL AND STATE GOVERNMENTS	STATE GOVERNMENTS
Violate the Bill of Rights	Enact ex post facto laws or bills of attainder	Tax imports or exports
Alter state boundaries	Grant titles of nobility	Coin money
Tax exports	Permit slavery	Enter into treaties or alliances
	Deny the right to vote on basis of race, color, previous condition of servitude, or sex	Deny people the equal protection of the laws or due process of law

Chief Justice John Marshall States the Doctrine of Implied Powers

At an early and critical stage in the development of the Constitution, the Supreme Court interpreted Article I, section 8, in a manner that vastly expanded the powers of Congress. In the case of *McCulloch v. Maryland* (1819), Chief Justice John Marshall interpreted the necessary and proper clause to give the national government *implied powers.* He wrote that

we think the sound construction of the constitution must allow to the national legislature that discretion, with respect to the means by which the powers it confers are to be carried into execution, which will enable that body to perform the high duties assigned to it, in the manner most beneficial to the people. Let the end be legitimate, let it be within the scope of the constitution, and all means which are appropriate, which are plainly adapted to that end, which are not prohibited, but consistent with the letter and spirit of the constitution, are constitutional.

Scope of the National Government's Power

Article I, section 8, of the Constitution enumerates at length the powers of the national government. Congress is empowered, for example, to lay and collect taxes, regulate foreign and interstate commerce, raise armies, maintain a navy, declare war, establish post offices, coin money, establish rules for naturalization of citizens, regulate bankruptcies, and create lower federal courts. In addition to these **delegated powers**, Article I further provides that "the Congress shall have the Power . . . to make all Laws which shall be necessary and proper for carrying into Execution the foregoing Powers, and all other Powers vested by this Constitution in the Government of the United States." This is the so-called **necessary and proper clause**, also known as the elastic clause.

Conflicts arose almost immediately after the Constitution was put into effect over the extent of federal power granted to Congress by Article I. These conflicts aligned the Federalists, who advocated a strong national government capable of encouraging commercial development and exercising discipline over the states, against the Antifederalist advocates of states' rights. In one of its most important early decisions, *McCulloch v. Maryland* (1819), the Supreme Court came down strongly on the side of those who favored interpreting constitutional grants to the national government in a broad manner.[2]

The *McCulloch* case arose over the refusal of the cashier of the United States Bank branch in Baltimore to pay a tax levied by the state of Maryland on the bank. Maryland argued that the Congress had no right to create the bank since the Constitution makes no mention of such a power in Article I. In writing the Supreme Court's opinion, Chief Justice John Marshall, an ardent Federalist, rejected Maryland's call for a strict and literal interpretation of the grant of powers to Congress in the Constitution. He noted that it was entirely reasonable for Congress to decide that it was "necessary and proper" to create a national bank in order to carry out its delegated powers to impose taxes, borrow money, and care for the property of the United States. Marshall thereby established in *McCulloch v. Maryland* the doctrine of **implied powers**, which states that the national government may exercise powers that can be reasonably implied from its delegated powers.

In later years the Supreme Court used the precedent for the doctrine of implied powers supplied by Marshall in *McCulloch* to provide the legal justification for sweeping extensions of the national govern-

2. *McCulloch v. Maryland,* 4 Wheat. 316 (1819).

ment's powers. By virtue of the implied powers doctrine, the national government has been empowered to support public schools, welfare programs, farm prices, public housing, community development, crime control, and unemployment compensation; regulate working conditions and collective bargaining; fix a minimum wage; ban discrimination in housing, places of public accommodation, and employment; and even affect highway speed limits and the legal drinking age.[3]

In the realm of foreign affairs, the national government is permitted to exercise inherent powers—powers that do not depend on constitutional grants of authority. Rather, they derive from the very existence of the national government. These inherent powers include the authority to discover and occupy territory, make treaties, and conduct foreign relations with other nations. The Supreme Court has ruled that the national government would have these powers even if the Constitution were silent on these matters because they are the powers that all national governments exercise under international law.[4]

Role and Powers of the States

As we noted in Chapter 2, the Constitution gives a special role to the states in the governmental system by guaranteeing each state equal representation in the Senate, permitting electors chosen by each state to elect the president, and requiring that three-fourths of the states ratify all constitutional amendments. The permanent bond of the states to the Union was settled once and for all by the Civil War (1861–1865). As the Supreme Court declared in a post-Civil War case, the United States is "an indestructible Union composed of indestructible states."[5]

When powers are not granted exclusively to the national government by the Constitution, the states may exercise those powers concurrently, provided there is no conflict with federal law. Among the concurrent powers of the states are the power to levy taxes, borrow money, and establish courts.

The states are authorized by the Tenth Amendment to exercise reserved powers—powers not granted to the national government and not prohibited to the states by the Constitution. But there is no specific listing of states' reserved powers in the Constitution. Thus, they consti-

3. For a concise account of how the Court used the doctrine of implied powers to greatly expand the national government's powers under the commerce clause, see C. Herman Pritchett, *The American Constitution*, 3d ed. (New York: McGraw-Hill, 1977), 194–201.

4. *United States v. Curtiss-Wright Export Corp.*, 299 U.S. 304 (1936). For a definition of inherent powers, see J. W. Peltason, *Understanding the Constitution*, 11th ed. (New York: Holt, Rinehart, and Winston, 1988), 19.

5. *Texas v. White*, 7 Wall. 700 (1869).

tute an undefined residuum of powers, including responsibility for education, intrastate commerce, local government, conduct of elections, family relations, and regulations to protect the public's health, safety, and morals.

Over the years the Supreme Court has issued different interpretations of the extent to which the Tenth Amendment protects the powers of the states from encroachment by the national government. Until the late 1930s the amendment was treated as an assertion of states' rights that severely restricted the national government's power. For example, in 1918 the Supreme Court declared a federal anti-child labor statute unconstitutional because it acted as a regulation of intrastate commerce, an area reserved to the states.[6] But the Court subsequently reversed such rulings as its 1918 child labor decision and held in 1941 that the Tenth Amendment and the reserved powers of the states imposed no limit on the national government in exercising powers granted to the Congress.[7]

Since the mid-1970s, however, the Court has shown some uncertainty about how to interpret the Tenth Amendment when federal laws are applied directly to the states. For example, in a 1976 case in which the minimum wage and maximum hours restrictions of the Fair Labor Standards Act were imposed on state and local government employees, the Court ruled that such an application of the law was unconstitutional. The grounds for this ruling were that the law impaired "the state's integrity" and "ability to function effectively in the federal system."[8] Nine years later, however, when Justice Harry Blackmun changed his position, the Court overruled its earlier decision and held by a narrow 5–4 margin that federal minimum wage and maximum hours legislation could be applied to state and local government employees.[9] But even this decision, which gave Congress extensive power through the Constitution's commerce clause to intrude on state prerogatives, was modified in 1992. In throwing out a federal law that required the states to control the disposal of low-level radioactive wastes, the Court said that Congress had exceeded its commerce clause powers and observed that the "states are neither regional offices nor administrative offices of the federal government."[10] The Court's changing interpretations of the Tenth Amendment demonstrate that the meaning of the amendment

6. *Hammer v. Dagenhart,* 247 U.S. 251 (1918).

7. *United States v. Darby Lumber Co.,* 312 U.S. 100 (1941).

8. *National League of Cities v. Usery,* 426 U.S. 833 (1976).

9. *Garcia v. San Antonio Metropolitan Transit Authority,* 469 U.S. 528 (1985).

10. *New York v. United States,* 505 U.S. _____, 112 S. Ct. 2408, 120 L. Ed. 2d 120 (1992).

and the nature of American federalism are far from settled issues. The national-state relationship of American federalism is constantly evolving. Indeed, the frequent mention in this chapter of Supreme Court decisions going back to *McCulloch v. Maryland* in 1819 brings to light an important feature of the Constitution-mandated federal system. Federalism has enlarged judicial power and influence because a system that divides power among governments requires an umpire able to resolve disputes. In the United States the courts often perform this function, making decisions that affect generations of Americans.[11]

Although the Constitution assures the states of a significant role in the governmental order, it also imposes limitations on them. Thus, they are prohibited from making treaties with foreign governments; authorizing private persons to raid and seize the shipping and commerce of enemy nations; and coining money, issuing bills of credit, or making anything but gold or silver legal tender. In addition, the states may not do any of the following without the consent of Congress: tax imports or exports; tax foreign ships; maintain troops or ships in peacetime, except for a state militia or national guard; enter into compacts or agreements with other states or foreign governments; and engage in war unless actually invaded or in imminent danger.

Obligations of the National Government to the States

In Article IV the Constitution specifies a series of obligations of the national government to the states.

In obliging the national government to *guarantee a republican form of government,* the drafters of the Constitution used the term *republican government* to distinguish the American system from either a monarchy or a direct democracy. Congress, rather than the courts, enforces this guarantee when it permits representatives and senators of a state to take their seats in the Congress.

The national government also must *protect states against foreign invasion and domestic violence.* At the request of a state for assistance, the president may send in federal troops to quell domestic violence. The president need not wait for such a request, however, to enforce federal law or court orders. For example, in 1957 President Dwight Eisenhower sent federal troops to enforce a federal court's order that Little Rock (Arkansas) Central High School be desegregated.

Finally, the Constitution specifies that to *protect states from dismemberment,* no new state may be formed from the territory of an existing

11. See Martha Derthick, "Up-to-Date in Kansas City: Reflections on American Federalism," *PS Politics and Political Science* 25 (December 1992): 672.

state, nor may a state be formed by combining two or more states, without the consent of the Congress and of the legislatures of the states concerned.

Relationships among the States

Because the operation of the federal system inevitably brings the states into contact with each other, the Constitution specifies in Article IV the obligations of the states to each other.

The **full faith and credit clause** (section 1) requires each state to honor the civil acts, judgments, and public documents of every other state. Thus, wills, contracts, and civil judgments of a state court must be enforced in the other states. The full faith and credit clause does not apply to matters of criminal law.

The **privileges and immunities clause** (section 2) prevents the states from discriminating against out-of-state residents in such matters as protection of the laws, access to the courts, and taxation. States may, however, enforce reasonable regulations to protect their citizens' health and safety through licensing requirements for doctors, dentists, lawyers, nurses, and teachers. It is also permissible for a state to increase fees for out-of-state residents wishing to enroll in state-supported universities or to buy hunting and fishing licenses.

In providing for **extradition**, Article IV, section 2, specifies that

New Hampshire's Residency Law for Lawyers Runs Afoul of the Constitution's Privileges and Immunities Clause

IN EXERCISING their powers to protect the health, welfare, and safety of their citizens, states regulate professions through licensing. As the following case illustrates, these regulations can raise constitutional issues under the privileges and immunities clause (Article IV, section 2).

In this case, Kathryn A. Piper, an attorney living four hundred yards across the Connecticut River from New Hampshire in the community of Lower Waterford, Vermont, passed the New Hampshire bar examination. New Hampshire, however, required that attorneys, in addition to passing the state bar examination, be state residents to practice law in the state courts. Thus, because Piper was not a state resident, she was not allowed to practice in New Hampshire. Attorney Piper brought suit, charging that New Hampshire's residency requirement for lawyers violated the constitutional provision that the "Citizens of each State shall be entitled to all Privileges and Immuni-

ties of Citizens in the several States." But New Hampshire argued that its residency requirement for attorneys helped maintain high standards of ethics and competency and ensured the availability of lawyers for court hearings, disciplinary matters, and public service programs.

In its ruling in the case, the U.S. Supreme Court rejected New Hampshire's claims and agreed with Piper that her rights under the privileges and immunities clause had been violated. Justice Lewis Powell wrote that the purpose of this constitutional provision was to "create a national economic union" and to prevent "economic protectionism" on the part of the states. Under this ruling, states may still require nonresidents to pass bar examinations, but they may not impose residency requirements as a prerequisite for admission to practice in state courts.

Supreme Court of New Hampshire v. Piper,
470 U.S. 274 (1985).

states are responsible for apprehending fugitives who have fled across a state line and returning them to the state having jurisdiction over the crime.

Article I, section 10, of the Constitution does permit the states to engage in cooperative arrangements by drawing up *interstate compacts* or agreements. Through such compacts, which must be approved by Congress, states may form interstate agencies and work together to solve mutual problems. Interstate compacts have been used to resolve interstate tax disputes, share higher education facilities, and administer transportation facilities. The states of New York and New Jersey, for example, jointly administer the World Trade Center and transportation facilities in the New York City metropolitan area through the Port of New York Authority. And farther west, the Western Regional Education Compact makes it possible for fifteen states to share higher education facilities, thereby sparing each the expense of operating its own medical, dental, veterinary, and other professional schools and permitting out-of-state students to pay in-state tuition.

The Ever-Changing Nature of Federal-State Relations

In the over two hundred years of America's history under the Constitution, the pattern of federal-state government relations has undergone continual change. This evolving pattern of intergovernmental relations has reflected governments' responses to the new problems faced by citizens and the shifting alignments of political power among the contending forces in society. The basic trend in federal-state relations has been away from separate and distinct areas of responsibility for national and state governments and toward shared powers and responsibilities.

Early Federalism: Separate Spheres of Federal and State Responsibility

For most of the period leading up to the Civil War, Americans had little contact with the national government; its functions were limited. It carried out foreign policy, defended the shores, delivered the mail, levied tariffs on imports, administered public lands, and supported some public works projects such as roads, canals, and harbors. Criminal justice, health, welfare, transportation, education, and regulation of business were handled largely by state and local governments.

The Civil War was a critical turning point in federal-state relations as it settled with finality the question of whether states could secede from the Union or nullify national government policies with which they disagreed. Indeed, the doctrine of federal supremacy was firmly established by the North's victory in the war. In the aftermath of the Civil War, a series of constitutional amendments—the Thirteenth, Fourteenth, and Fifteenth—were approved with the intent of protecting the rights of the newly freed black Americans. The longer-term impact of these amendments—especially the Fourteenth Amendment's ban on state actions that deny people due process of law or the equal protection of the laws—has been to give the national government the authority to invalidate state laws.[12]

Although the Civil War amendments had given the national government additional authority, the national and state governments continued until early in this century to operate in largely separate spheres of authority, in which they exercised quite separate and distinct responsibilities, without interference from the other level of government. This federal-state relationship was characterized as **dual federalism**. There were, however, a few instances of intergovernmental activity through federal land grants to the states. For example, the Morrill Act of 1862 provided the states with land grants for creating agricultural and technical colleges. America's great land-grant colleges such as Ohio State, Iowa State, Texas A&M, and Kansas State, and the agriculture schools at Cornell University and the University of Wisconsin have their origins in this legislation. Federal land grants also were made for roads, canals, and railroads, but, for the most part, the domains of the national and state governments were separate and distinct.

Expansion of Federal Economic Regulatory Activity

During the twentieth century the pressures for an expanded role for the federal government intensified. These pressures stemmed from the changed nature of American society. By the turn of the century, America had been transformed by technological and economic developments from a rural, agrarian society into an urban, industrial one. The country's population tripled between 1870 and 1920, and huge cities with populations running into the millions began to dot the nation. The corporate giants such as U.S. Steel and Standard Oil began to emerge as well. Because the societal problems created by the new industrial order were not within the power of the states to resolve, there were calls for increased governmental regulation of the economy to protect consumers and workers. For example, it was not possible for the states to cope with the monopolistic practices of huge corporate trusts, which

12. Henry J. Friendly, "Federalism Forward," *Yale Law Review* 86 (May 1977): 1020.

operated on a nationwide basis. Nor could the states effectively ensure the purity of food being consumed in cities far from where it was produced. Congress, at the urging of President Theodore Roosevelt, responded to the latter problem by passing in 1906 the Pure Food and Drug Act and the Meat Inspection Act. In response to demands for greater governmental control over business practices, federal regulatory activity continued to expand during the administration of Woodrow Wilson with the enactment of the Federal Reserve Act (1913), Federal Trade Commission Act (1914), and Clayton Anti-Trust Act (1914).

The federal government's early twentieth-century ventures into economic regulatory activity were but precursors of a much more extensive federal role that was to develop under President Franklin Roosevelt's leadership during the Great Depression of the 1930s.

The New Deal: A Tidal Wave of Federal Programs

The demand for government action to relieve the hardships created by the depression of the 1930s was intense. The Roosevelt administration responded with what has been called a "tidal wave" of federal programs (known as the **New Deal**) that permanently changed the balance of power within the American federal system.[13] President Roosevelt's New Deal policies expanded the government's economic regulatory role through the creation in 1933 of the Securities and Exchange Com-

13. Ibid., 1023.

The human misery created by the depression of the 1930s, portrayed by this massive breadline, prompted a demand for government action that resulted in President Franklin Roosevelt's New Deal, an unprecedented array of federal programs.

mission to protect investors and ensure orderly stock exchange procedures and the passage of the National Labor Relations Act in 1935 to
guarantee workers the right to organize unions and engage in collective
bargaining.

At Roosevelt's urging, Congress also enacted a series of measures
designed to provide relief and spur economic recovery. Most of these
measures involved joint action between the federal government and
the states that vastly increased the role and power of the federal government. To receive the benefits of such programs as unemployment
compensation, public housing, Aid to Families with Dependent Children, and public works projects, states were frequently required to provide administrative personnel, abide by federal regulations, and put up
some money of their own. Through the "carrot and stick" technique of
providing federal funds and programs in return for state cooperation
and adherence to federal regulations, the federal government was able
to extend its influence over the states.[14]

Further Expansion of the Federal Role in the 1960s and 1970s

During the 1960s the pattern of an expanding federal role in providing social welfare benefits was given a dramatic nudge forward by President Lyndon Johnson.[15] His administration pushed through a willing
Congress a wide array of legislation providing federal funds to the
states and localities for such purposes as cleaning up the environment,
making grants and loans to college students, providing health care to
the poor, expanding urban transit, combating crime, and improving
housing. The 1960s and 1970s were also a period in which the federal
government again increased its economic regulatory activities through
such measures as the Occupational Safety and Health Act, Consumer
Product Safety Act, Federal Coal Mine Health and Safety Act, Consumer Protection Act, and a series of environmental protection measures, including the Clean Air Amendments of 1970, Water Quality
Improvement Act, Safe Drinking Water Act, and Resource Conservation and Recovery Act.

14. James T. Patterson, *The New Deal and the States: Federalism in Transition*
(Princeton, N.J.: Princeton University Press, 1969).

15. For an account of the grant explosion of the 1960s and 1970s, see John E.
Chubb, "Federalism and the Bias for Centralization," in *The New Direction of American Politics,* ed. Chubb and Paul E. Peterson (Washington, D.C.: Brookings, 1985),
277–286.

*Federal Protection of
Civil Rights*

Federalism, which gives state governments wide leeway on many aspects of public policy, enabled the southern states in particular for much of the nation's history to engage in acts of racial discrimination—denying blacks the right to vote, maintaining separate white and black school systems, and segregating facilities of public accommodation. In the 1950s and 1960s, however, national public opinion shifted toward a position supportive of enforced civil rights, and government policy reflected this change (also see Chapter 4, Civil Liberties and Civil Rights). The federal courts took the lead in moving against racial discrimination mandated by state governments. A major judicial breakthrough in this area was the 1954 Supreme Court decision in *Brown v. Board of Education of Topeka,* which declared unconstitutional separate state-supported school systems for whites and blacks.[16] When court decisions were resisted by southern states, as they were at Central High School in Little Rock, Arkansas, and at the University of Alabama, Presidents Eisenhower and Kennedy mobilized troops and sent federal marshals to bring about state compliance with federal court orders to desegregate.

The federal role in the protection of civil rights for minorities was further expanded when Congress passed the Civil Rights Act of 1964, banning discrimination in places of public accommodation—restaurants, motels, theaters—and the Voting Rights Act of 1965, empowering the federal government to send registrars into southern states to register voters when there was a past record of racial discrimination. On these issues, the advocates of a national standard for civil rights enforced by the federal government carried the day, and the proponents of a states' rights position had to give way.

Modern Cooperative
Federalism: The
Grant-in-Aid System

The New Deal era, then, marked the end of a 150-year period during which American federalism had been characterized by the national and state governments operating in largely separate and distinct spheres of authority. With the advent of the New Deal and later extensions of the national government's role, federal-state relations began to be characterized by **cooperative federalism**—a sharing of responsibilities among the federal, state, and local governments.

16. *Brown v. Board of Education of Topeka,* 347 U.S. 483 (1954).

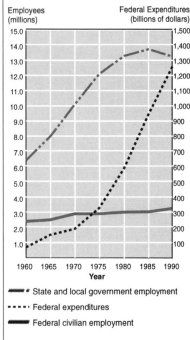

Figure 3.1: Rising Federal Expenditures and State and Local Government Employment Versus Stable Federal Employment, 1960–1990

Employees (millions)

Federal Expenditures (billions of dollars)

Year

━ ⋅ State and local government employment

⋯⋯ Federal expenditures

━━━ Federal civilian employment

Sources: Bureau of the Census, *Statistical Abstract of the United States:1978* (Washington, D.C.: Government Printing Office, 1978); and *Statistical Abstract of the United States: 1990, 1992.*

When the federal government becomes involved in a domestic policy area, it does not normally set up a federal agency—such as the U.S. Postal Service, National Park Service, or Coast Guard—to directly administer its programs. More frequently, federal policies are carried out in cooperation with state and local governments. This pattern of administering federal programs through state and local governments has meant that, even though the federal government has increased its role in society, federal employment has remained relatively stable. At the same time, however, state and local government employment has increased dramatically and constitutes over 80 percent of the civilian government work force. This growth (shown in Figure 3.1) reflects both the impact of the transfer of federal funds to the states and the resulting expansion in state and local government services.

Cooperative federalism frequently takes the form of the federal government providing money (**grants-in-aid**) to states and localities to carry out a government activity in a manner that follows federal policy guidelines but also permits some state and local flexibility in administration. As a result of this system, there are today few policy areas that are exclusively either federal, state, or local responsibilities. Rather, responsibilities are shared, and nearly all government activity, except such things as printing currency, minting coins, and maintaining the national defense, are intergovernmental in nature (Figure 3.2).[17] But even with the shared responsibilities inherent in cooperative federalism, the net effect of the growth in federal regulatory activity and the operation of domestic programs through grants to state and local governments has been a centralization of governmental decision making at the national level.[18]

The grant-in-aid system of shared federal and state and local funding, primarily state and local government administration, and federal supervision has developed and grown in this century for a variety of reasons.[19]

■ Federal grants-in-aid provide a means of meeting and coping with a societal need or problem. For example, Medicaid grants are

17. Donald F. Kettl, "The Maturing of American Federalism," in *The Costs of Federalism,* ed. Robert T. Golembiewski and Aaron Wildavsky (New Brunswick, N.J.: Transaction Books, 1984), 73.

18. See Chubb, "Federalism."

19. Deil S. Wright, *Understanding Intergovernmental Relations,* 3d ed. (Pacific Grove, Calif.: Brooks/Cole, 1988), 208–210.

used to provide the poor with health care, and mass transit grants allow cities to maintain their public transportation systems.

■ The fiscal resources and willingness of the states and localities to provide their residents with services vary tremendously. But federal grants permit all citizens, regardless of the state in which they reside, to have access to essential services.

■ Americans prefer local over federal administration of government programs, although they readily accept federal aid to state and local governments.

■ The federal income tax is the most productive government revenue raiser available. It provides the federal government with the economic underpinning required to fund an extensive grant-in-aid program.

■ Members of Congress can deliver benefits to their constituents by enacting grant-in-aid programs that channel funds to state and local governments in their districts.

■ Both Democratic and Republican presidents have found that grants-in-aid are a means of achieving their policy and political aims. Even as conservative a president as Ronald Reagan, who opposed centralization of power in the federal government, supported the requirement that states set the legal drinking age at twenty-one to qualify for federal highway funds. He also supported grants for drug enforcement, abuse prevention, and rehabilitation.

The growth in federal grant-in-aid programs since the 1930s has meant that federal funds make up a large share of the expenditures of state and local governments—indeed, ranging from 18 to over 25 percent of state and local expenditures during the 1980s (see Figure 3.3). This means, of course, that state and local governments are heavily dependent on federal grants to meet their programmatic responsibilities. Any change in federal grant policy—particularly budgetary reductions or even a slowdown in the growth of federal grant monies—can have far-reaching and painful consequences for state and local governments.

There are three principal types of grants-in-aid: (1) categorical grants, (2) project grants, and (3) block grants.[20] Each type of grant

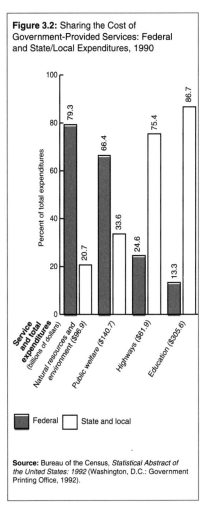

Figure 3.2: Sharing the Cost of Government-Provided Services: Federal and State/Local Expenditures, 1990

■ Federal □ State and local

Source: Bureau of the Census, *Statistical Abstract of the United States: 1992* (Washington, D.C.: Government Printing Office, 1992).

Types of Grants-in-Aid

20. For a description of different types of grants and the administrative, policy, and political implications of each, see ibid., chap. 6.

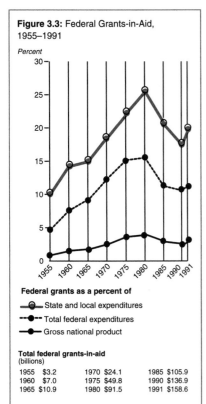

Figure 3.3: Federal Grants-in-Aid, 1955–1991

Percent

Federal grants as a percent of

—◯— State and local expenditures

--●-- Total federal expenditures

—●— Gross national product

Total federal grants-in-aid
(billions)

1955 $3.2	1970 $24.1	1985 $105.9
1960 $7.0	1975 $49.8	1990 $136.9
1965 $10.9	1980 $91.5	1991 $158.6

Sources: Advisory Commission on Intergovernmental Relations, *Significant Features of Federalism*, vol. 2 (Washington, D.C.: Advisory Commission on Intergovernmental Relations, 1991), table 24, 50; Executive Office of the President, Office of Management and Budget, *Budget of the United States Government, Fiscal Year 1993* (Washington, D.C.: Government Printing Office, 1992), table 21.3, A–438.

differs in the extent to which control over government policy resides with the federal government or state and local governments.

Categorical grants are the oldest form of federal grant-in-aid to the states and localities. These grants provide funds to state and local agencies (such as libraries, hospitals, schools, and state highway departments) for a particular category of government activity. The hundreds of categorical grants that distribute over $100 billion annually for specific programs enable the federal government to prescribe a general policy for dealing with a problem, to provide funds for that purpose, and to then turn over to state and local governments the responsibility for carrying out the policy at the grass roots. States and local governments wishing to participate in categorical grant programs are normally required to put up some of their own money (to provide some proportion of *matching funds*) and to follow federal policy guidelines in administering the program. State and local governments have some flexibility in implementing categorical grants, however. For example, Aid to Families with Dependent Children (AFDC) is a categorical grant program under which states must comply with federal guidelines to qualify for funds. It has still been possible, however, for the states to develop widely varying welfare programs under AFDC in such areas as the level of welfare benefits provided and the work (Workfare) and educational (Learnfare) requirements for receipt of benefits.

Project grants are a special form of categorical grant developed to target funds more precisely in order to better fulfill program objectives. Instead of distributing funds to the states or localities under the fixed formulas used in categorical grants, project grants provide variable levels of funding. Project grants have been used to support aid to the handicapped, to combat drug abuse, and to provide bilingual education. Applicants—which may be nongovernmental agencies, such as a local United Way agency, as well as state and local governments—submit proposals to the federal agency administering a project grant program and then compete for funding. Skill in preparation of a grant proposal and political influence in Washington—so-called grantsmanship—are often critical factors in determining how project grant funds are awarded. To enhance their abilities to influence the awarding of project grants, states, cities, and universities maintain liaison offices in Washington and try to enlist the assistance of their states' congressional delegations.

Block grants are given to the states for a general functional area of government activity (for example, job training or community development). States receiving block grants are responsible for developing a program within this general field of policy, but following federal guidelines. Block grants give the states greater policy-making discretion in developing programs to fit their specific needs than do categorical grants, which have a narrower focus and many federal conditions attached. The Partnership in Health Act of 1966, the first block grant program enacted by Congress, combined several categorical grant programs designed to combat specific illnesses. Other examples are block grants for job training of disadvantaged youth, urban mass transit, maternal and child health care, criminal justice, and community development. In 1993 block grants constituted only 7.4 percent of the total grant-in-aid funds; over 90 percent went for categorical grant programs.

The Politics of Grant-in-Aid Programs

While any description of the different types of grants may seem rather technical and uninteresting, they have in fact been the subjects of many fiercely fought political battles. Each type of grant has different consequences in terms of which level of government and which interests exert a dominant influence over government policy. Indeed, powerful alliances of interest groups, government administrators, and interested members of Congress form to generate, defend, and expand grant-in-aid programs in which they have a stake.

The differences between the Republican and Democratic parties in their approach to government are also reflected in their approaches to grant-in-aid policy. Republicans in both the White House and Congress have consistently favored decentralization of governmental decision making by reducing the number of the federal strings attached to grants-in-aid and allowing state and local governments greater discretion. In contrast, Democrats have advocated centralized decision making and a strong federal role.[21]

Categorical grants vest substantial authority in members of Congress, who by law determine the specific purposes for which the funds will be used, the amount to be spent, and the formulas used to distribute funds among states and localities. Congress also exerts influence over the federal agencies charged with developing the detailed guidelines needed to implement categorical grant programs. Thus, these grants are the predominant type of federal grant-in-aid because they provide members of Congress with a way to deliver benefits and ser-

Major highway projects within the states and the District of Columbia are heavily dependent on federal grant-in-aid funds.

21. John E. Chubb, "The Political Economy of Federalism," *American Political Science Review* 79 (December 1985): 1005.

Governments in the United States—By the Thousands		
	Number of governments	*Number of employeees (in millions)*
Federal government	1	3.103
State governments	50	4.521
Local governments	86,692	10.930
Counties	3,043	2.196
Municipalities	19,296	2.662
Townships and towns	16,666	.415
School districts	14,556	5.045
Special districts	33,131	.612
TOTAL GOVERNMENTS	86,743	18.554

Source: Bureau of the Census, *Government Units in 1992* (Washington, D.C.: Government Printing Office, 1993).

vices to their constituents by assisting state and local governments.[22] Not surprisingly, representatives and senators view providing benefits to constituents key to reelection. Moreover, the state and local agencies that receive and spend such categorical grants, the beneficiaries of the services provided through grants, and federal administrators constitute powerful interest group alliances in support of categorical grant programs.

Because block grants require that the federal grant money be spent within a general field of governmental responsibility, they give wide discretion to state authorities and shift influence away from Washington. Governors have tended to favor consolidation of categorical grants into block grants because such a policy shifts substantial decision-making power to the state governments. Of course, the current beneficiaries of categorical grant programs and members of Congress have tended to resist proposals for block grants, especially if acceptance of those proposals would mean a reduction in the amount of federal funds available for categorical grants. While categorical grants provide specific benefits to particular interests who tend to fight aggressively to maintain and enlarge such grants, block grant programs lack such zeal-

22. Chubb, "Federalism," 286. For a perceptive account of the use of grants by members of Congress to claim credit with constituents and distribute benefits, see David R. Mayhew, *Congress: The Electoral Connection* (New Haven, Conn.: Yale University Press, 1974), 129–130.

ous supporters because they cover a wide range of programs and activities and benefit a diffuse array of interests. With no single group or set of interests having a vital stake in their creation or expansion, block grants normally lack the level of political support enjoyed by categorical grants.

When President Bush proposed in his 1991 State of the Union address that $15 billion in existing categorical grant programs be converted into a large block grant to be administered by the states, the contending forces in the politics of grants-in-aid were clearly revealed. The fiscally hard-pressed governors responded favorably to the pro-spect of having additional federal funds channeled through state governments under Bush's expanded block grant proposal. Mayors, however, were apoplectic and called the president's plan an "assault on America's cities" because it meant that municipalities would no longer receive aid for targeted programs directly from the federal government through categorical grants. Rather, the cities would have to seek funds for such programs as community development (housing, street repairs, parks, child care, and shelters for battered women) from state governments, which would be administering the federal block grant. Since local governments have a long history of battling state governments for what they consider to be a fair share of state revenues, it is not surprising that their leaders reacted negatively to the Bush proposal. In contrast, in 1993 city and county officials had effusive praise for President Bill Clinton's proposed $16.3 billion economic stimulus program of grants to local governments for community development, mass transit, and summer youth employment.

The Politics of Federalism from the Nixon Years to the Clinton Presidency

Since the 1960s the functioning of American federalism has been central to domestic politics. The legacy of expanded federal programs and regulatory activity from the New Deal and Johnson administration was challenged as a series of Republican administrations— Nixon-Ford (1969–1977), Reagan (1981–1989), and Bush (1989–1993)— sought to shift policy-making responsibility away from Washington to the state capitals. The pendulum began to swing back toward a more activist federal government, however, with the election of Bill Clinton in 1992 (see Figure 3.4 for trends in federal grant-in-aid spending from 1960 to 1990).

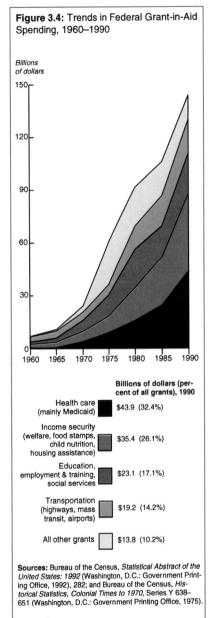

Figure 3.4: Trends in Federal Grant-in-Aid Spending, 1960–1990

Billions of dollars

Billions of dollars (percent of all grants), 1990

Health care (mainly Medicaid)	$43.9 (32.4%)
Income security (welfare, food stamps, child nutrition, housing assistance)	$35.4 (26.1%)
Education, employment & training, social services	$23.1 (17.1%)
Transportation (highways, mass transit, airports)	$19.2 (14.2%)
All other grants	$13.8 (10.2%)

Sources: Bureau of the Census, *Statistical Abstract of the United States: 1992* (Washington, D.C.: Government Printing Office, 1992), 282; and Bureau of the Census, *Historical Statistics, Colonial Times to 1970*, Series Y 638–651 (Washington, D.C.: Government Printing Office, 1975).

State and local officials regularly travel to Washington to lobby members of Congress and administration officials. Rep. Douglas Applegate (D-Ohio), right, meets with county officials from his east central Ohio district who are seeking his help in securing additional federal funds.

The Nixon Administration's Approach

When the Nixon administration took office in 1969 after a period of dramatic growth in federal grant-in-aid programs, 98 percent of all federal aid to state and local governments was in the form of categorical grants. Criticism of these grants had begun to mount, however, on the grounds that they imposed excessive administrative costs and that they distorted state and local budgetary priorities because they encouraged state and local governments to give priority to securing grants instead of making their own determinations of where there was the greatest need for governmental expenditures.

President Richard Nixon was sensitive and sympathetic to these criticisms. He believed that if decision making were decentralized so that state and local governments played a larger role, government would be more efficient and creative. He was not antigovernment, but he did distrust the federal bureaucracy and sought to weaken it by proposing general **revenue sharing** and the consolidation of categorical grants into block grants.

At Nixon's urging, Congress enacted in 1972 a program of general revenue sharing, which provided states and local governments with federal grants totaling more than $6 billion a year. Unlike other grant-in-aid programs, revenue-sharing funds could be used for whatever purpose state and local governments thought appropriate, as long as the funds were not used in a way that discriminated on the basis of race, sex, age, religion, or physical handicap. Because it gave state and local officials unprecedented flexibility in spending federal grant money, revenue sharing was enormously popular with state and local officials. But it was never popular with Congress. It tended to reduce congressional influence on grant-in-aid programs and members' capacities to claim credit for directing government benefits to particular groups of constituents and interest groups. Moreover, the federal budget deficits swelled ominously in the 1980s, sounding the death knell for Nixon's experiment in governmental decentralization via revenue sharing. It was eliminated as an economy measure in fiscal year 1987.

Along with congressional approval of revenue sharing, Nixon also succeeded in securing a block grant program for comprehensive employment and training and community development. But approval of these block grant programs by a Democratic-controlled Congress had its cost; Nixon was forced to accept increased levels of federal funding for domestic programs. Furthermore, his achievements in the block grant field were limited by Congress. It killed his grant consolidation initiatives in education, law enforcement, rural development, and transportation.[23]

Despite Nixon's reputation for budgetary penury, his presidency was a period of dramatic growth in federal domestic spending, especially in the areas of food stamps, housing supplements, and medical care for the poor.[24] The Nixon administration also presided over and contributed to an unparalleled expansion of federal regulation of state and local governments. The most dramatic of these regulatory actions was in the field of environmental protection. Under the National Environmental Policy Act of 1969, federal agencies and federal grant recipients were required to file detailed environmental impact statements before undertaking construction or other projects with environmental consequences. Even more important were the Clean Air Act amendments of 1970, which established national air quality standards to be implemented by state governments.

The Nixon administration thus sought to increase state and local power within the intergovernmental system, but, ironically, the net effect of federal actions during his presidency was quite the opposite: federal spending rose dramatically, and the federal regulatory presence became more pervasive. Despite his modest successes with block grants

23. Chubb, "Federalism," 287.

24. For an account of the Nixon administration's approach to federalism, see Timothy J. Conlan, *New Federalism: Intergovernmental Reform and Political Change from Nixon to Reagan* (Washington, D.C.: Brookings, 1988), part I.

and revenue sharing, the federal system was more centralized when he left office than when he entered.[25]

Reagan's New Federalism

Although, in response to budgetary pressures, a slowdown in federal funding for grant-in-aid programs began in the last years of the Carter administration (1977–1981), even more restrictive measures accompanied the Reagan administration (1981–1989). Like Nixon, President Ronald Reagan wanted to decentralize government decision making. In addition, and unlike Nixon, Reagan wanted to reduce government domestic spending and regulatory activity significantly. This reflected his fundamental discomfort with the modern welfare state.[26]

The most dramatic Reagan proposal was the New Federalism package that he put forward in 1982. It called for revamping the federal system by realigning federal and state government functions. In return for the federal government taking over the full cost of the increasingly expensive Medicaid program, the Reagan administration proposed that the states assume full responsibility for welfare, food stamps, and other selected grant programs. To help the states fund these new responsibilities, the federal government would turn over to the states such revenue sources as excise taxes, tobacco and alcohol taxes, and the windfall profits tax on oil production.

But Reagan's New Federalism ran into firm opposition from state and local officials who claimed that they could not fund the programs they would be assigned with the revenue sources to be available to them. Supporters of the existing categorical grant programs both inside and outside of Congress also lined up in opposition to the plan, and the New Federalism proposal died for lack of support.

Although Reagan's New Federalism proposals were never enacted, his presidency was a period of dramatic change in the operation of the American federal system. Approximately eighty categorical grants were consolidated into block grants, and several grant programs, including general revenue sharing, were eliminated. As a result, administration and policy-making responsibilities for programs once closely controlled by Washington passed to the states.

The most noteworthy impact of the Reagan years, however, was on federal spending on grant-in-aid programs. Because of federal fiscal policies enacted with presidential support in 1981, the federal government has annually run up massive budget deficits. The present-day environment for policy making, then, makes enactment of any major new domestic spending programs or the significant expansion of exist-

25. Ibid., chap. 5.   26. Ibid., 220.

ing programs all the more difficult. The large federal budget deficits also have put spending for existing grants-in-aid under heavy pressure as the executive branch and Congress have sought to limit the hemorrhaging red ink in the federal budget.

Deficit reduction measures resulted in cuts in grants-in-aid in the 1980s, both as a percentage of federal expenditures and as a percentage of state and local government expenditures (see Figure 3.3). Between 1980 and 1988, for example, federal grants-in-aid fell from 23.3 percent of federal outlays for domestic programs to 18.9 percent and from 25.8 percent of state and local expenditures to 18.2 percent. The consequences for state and local governments have been profound as they have sought to compensate for the shrinking pool of federal dollars either through cutbacks in services or increased taxes.[27]

In spite of the dramatic changes in grant-in-aid policies during the

27. For a detailed exploration of the impact of New Federalism on state and local governments, see Peter K. Eisinger and William Gormley, eds., *The Midwest Response to the New Federalism* (Madison: University of Wisconsin Press, 1988).

A Majority of the Public Wants Active Government, but It Has Doubts about the Federal Government's Ability to Solve Problems

Public opinion surveys show that in spite of the public's demand for services and government's expanding role in the federal system, Americans are highly skeptical about the capacity of government—especially the federal government—to solve problems.

Significant support for active government

Question: **Which of these statements comes closest to your view about government power today?**

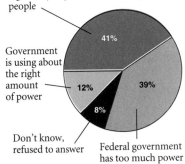

Government should use powers more vigorously to promote well-being of all people — 41%

Government is using about the right amount of power — 12%

Don't know, refused to answer — 8%

Federal government has too much power — 39%

Skepticism about government's capacity to solve problems

Question: **When the government in Washington decides to solve a problem, how much confidence do you have that the problem will actually be solved?**

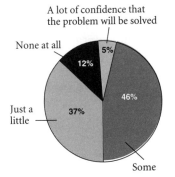

A lot of confidence that the problem will be solved — 5%

None at all — 12%

Just a little — 37%

Some — 46%

Question: **From which level of government do you feel you get the *least* for your money?**

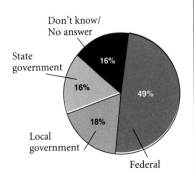

Don't know/No answer — 16%

State government — 16%

Local government — 18%

Federal — 49%

Source: Gallup Organization survey for the Advisory Commission on Intergovernmental Relations, June 23–28, 1992.

Reagan years, the net effects of the 1980s for American federalism were mixed. On the one hand, President Reagan's efforts to reduce the size and activities of the welfare state were more successful than most analysts thought possible when he took office. Yet the basic character of cooperative federalism remained intact. President Reagan may have sought major spending reductions and block grant consolidations, but Congress never abandoned categorical grants as the dominant form of federal grants-in-aid to state and local governments. Rather, it tempered proposed budget cuts in grants and resisted the Reagan administration's attempts at large-scale grant consolidation.

Just as Richard Nixon's attempts to revise the federal system had paradoxical consequences, so too did Ronald Reagan's: the public underpinnings of support for the welfare state were in some respects stronger when Reagan left office than when he entered the White House. The Reagan agenda trimmed questionable programs and seemingly answered public concerns about uncontrolled government growth. As a result, opinion surveys revealed a rebound in public confidence in the federal government and broad support for government spending.[28]

Retrenchment in Washington and a Resurgence of the States

While the Reagan administration was seeking to reduce government's role in American life, the states responded to cuts in federal grant programs by expanding their activities and levels of spending. Indeed, political commentators have stressed that it was at the state level during the late 1980s that major policy innovations were occurring. As the percentage of the federal budget devoted to grants-in-aid declined, the states devised ways—including use of their own tax revenues—to maintain higher levels of social services than would have been the case under federal budget reductions.[29] And while the Reagan administration followed a policy of deregulating the economy, many of the state governments became activists in such areas as education reform, environmental protection, plant closing restrictions, securities regulation, medical insurance, auto insurance, consumer protection, employee drug testing, family and parental leave policy, and the minimum wage.

That was not the first time that the states had played an activist role during a conservative era at the federal level. During the "Normalcy" era of the 1920s and the administrations of Presidents Warren Harding

28. Conlan, *New Federalism*, chap. 11.

29. Richard P. Nathan and Fred C. Doolittle, *Reagan and the States* (Princeton, N.J.: Princeton University Press, 1987).

and Calvin Coolidge, the states also energized the federal system by enacting child labor and unemployment insurance laws while expanding state social services.

Federal Budget Politics and Federalism during the Bush Presidency

Because of the Reagan administration's legacy of diminished grant-in-aid support for state and local governments, the Bush administration entered office in 1989 faced with pent-up demands for additional finan-

---

Major New Federal Laws Imposing Mandates on State and Local Governments, 1981-1990

TITLE OF THE LAW

Age Discrimination in Employment Act Amendments of 1986
Americans with Disabilities Act of 1990
Asbestos Hazard Emergency Response Act of 1986
Cash Management Improvement Act of 1990
Child Abuse Amendments of 1984
Civil Rights Restoration Act of 1987
Clean Air Act Amendments of 1990
Commercial Motor Vehicle Safety Act of 1986
Consolidated Omnibus Budget Reconciliation Act of 1985
Drug-Free Workplace Act of 1988
Education of the Handicapped Act Amendments of 1986
Education of the Handicapped Act Amendments of 1990
Emergency Planning and Community Right-to-Know Act of 1986
Fair Housing Act Amendments of 1988
Hazardous and Solid Waste Amendments of 1984
Handicapped Children's Protection Act of 1986
Highway Safety Amendments of 1984
Lead Contamination Control Act of 1988
Ocean Dumping Ban Act (1988)
Older Workers Benefit Protection Act of 1990
Safe Drinking Water Act Amendments of 1986
Social Security Amendments of 1983
Social Security: Fiscal 1991 Budget Reconciliation Act
Surface Transportation Assistance Act of 1982
Voting Accessibility for the Elderly and Handicapped Act (1984)
Voting Rights Act Amendments of 1982
Water Quality Act of 1987

Source: Timothy J. Conlan and David R. Beam, "Federal Mandates: The Record of Reform and Future Prospects," *Intergovernmental Perspective,* 18 (Fall, 1992), 8–9.
    Note: This inventory of twenty-seven new mandates does not include a number of costly conditions that were imposed upon state and local governments through additions to existing grant-in-aid programs for Medicaid, workfare requirements for Aid to Families with Dependent Children, and legislation increasing local government contributions to federal water projects.

cial assistance from governors, state legislators, mayors, and other local officials. The large federal budget deficit, however, effectively restrained both George Bush and the Congress from attempting to expand grant-in-aid spending. Indeed, the lengthy and often bitter budget battle of 1990 between the Republican president and Democratic-controlled Congress resulted in an agreement that put the states under intensified fiscal pressure. While not increasing grant-in-aid funds to the states, the budget for 1991 imposed additional and costly responsibilities on the states. For example, the budget legislation mandated that Medicaid coverage be expanded to cover more poor children, pregnant women, and elderly, and the states were required by Congress to pick up the tab for these expanded services without the help of additional federal funds. The federal budget agreement further compounded the states' fiscal problems by increasing federal taxes on tobacco, liquor, and luxuries. As a result, the ability of states to tax these traditional sources of state revenue was severely restricted.

Bush continued the Nixon and Reagan commitment to the decentralization of government decision making by proposing consolidation of a series of categorical grants into a $15 billion block grant program, thereby giving the states greater flexibility in using federal grants. He also proposed giving the states more leeway in spending federal highway dollars in return for the states shouldering a larger share of the total costs. With local governments opposed to both proposals and state officials vehemently against having to bear a larger share of highway costs, Bush's federalism initiatives had no chance of passage in Congress. As White House-congressional conflicts intensified in an era of divided party control of the government, policies designed to modify the federal-state relationship fell victim to policy gridlock in Washington.[30]

Federalism under Clinton: Governmental Activism Renewed

The 1992 elections ended divided government in Washington as Democrats in the White House and Congress worked harmoniously during lift-off of the Clinton administration. The new president's economic programs provided additional grants to states and localities for such activities as public works projects, temporary summer youth employment, and social services. The Clinton administration thus sought to initiate an era of increased activism by the federal govern-

30. Chuck Alston, "Call to Fuse Federal Programs Greeted Skeptically on Hill," *Congressional Quarterly Weekly Report,* March 2, 1991, 540–544.

ment and to reverse the trend of the previous twelve years during which the federal government transferred responsibility to the states.

The former Arkansas governor also promised to waive burdensome federal regulations in order to permit states to conduct their own experiments in delivering better services at lower costs. For example, he waived federal Medicaid regulations and permitted Oregon to experiment with a health care program that extended Medicaid coverage to needy recipients but at the same time limited conditions that could be treated to the 587 specified by state authorities. Clinton promised as well to oppose any new federally mandated programs for the states that did not provide the funds to pay for them.

Laws passed by Congress that impose regulatory and service responsibilities on the states without compensating federal funds have long been a sore point for state officials. Because of extremely tight federal budgets during the 1980s, Congress frequently sought to deal with societal problems by mandating that the states handle them, but without additional funding from Washington. Thus between 1980 and 1991 Congress enacted twenty-seven new mandates (including twenty in 1990) which expanded the states' responsibilities and budgetary obligations in such fields as environmental protection, assistance for the disabled, medical care for poor (Medicaid), and worker safety. Among the most expensive were Medicaid, which cost the states $38.3 billion in 1992, and environmental protection laws and primary water purification, which will force state and local governments to ante up an estimated $32 billion annually by 1995.[31] One only has to look at Ohio to see the financial pain that unfunded federal mandates can inflict on a state and its taxpayers. Between 1992 and 1995 unfunded mandates will cost the Buckeye State an estimated $1.74 billion.[32]

Clinton, like other recent presidents, has pledged to oppose any additional unfunded federal mandates placed on the states, but, to succeed, he will need to overcome the pressures that overwhelmed his predecessors, who were not able to deliver on their pledges. During their tenures both Congress and the White House responded to demands that they cope with societal needs, even though the federal budgetary cupboard was bare, by pushing additional responsibilities off on the states. In a time of continuing domestic needs and federal budget

31. Timothy J. Conlan and David R. Beam, "Federal Mandates: The Record of Reform and Future Prospects," *Intergovernmental Perspective* 18 (Fall 1992): 8–9; Michael deCourcy Hinds, "U.S. Adds Programs with Little Review of Local Burdens," *New York Times,* March 24, 1992, A1, A14, National edition.

32. "Federal Mandates: Measuring the Pain," *Governing,* November 1993, 20.

deficits, the Clinton administration and the Congress are facing the same pressures to enact unfunded mandates as did their predecessors.

Federalism, the Constitution, and Public Policy

Federalism was incorporated into the Constitution to achieve the practical governing objectives of the Founders. By dividing governmental power between the national government and the states, the drafters of the Constitution believed it would be possible to prevent any one group, faction, or party from becoming too powerful. Moreover, retaining the states as powerful governing units within the constitutional order was viewed as essential to having those same states ratify the new Constitution. The Founders believed as well that the strengthened national government created under a federal system would promote economic development, provide an improved national defense, and ensure domestic order.

The nature of the relationship between the national government and the states has changed dramatically over the last two centuries. Whereas the national government initially had little contact with its citizens, today its activities directly touch the lives of every citizen. But the development of cooperative federalism has meant that the functional lines of responsibility for government activities have become increasingly fuzzy. Moreover, with the maturing of federalism, virtually every unit of government in the United States has a major stake in seeing that it gets its slice of the federal financial pie.[33]

Decisions about which level of government will perform a particular function and how the costs of that function will be shared by federal, state, and local governments are issues over which intense battles have been and continue to be fought. These issues of federalism are important because over time different parties and interests achieve ascendancy within the federal government and within the states. And whether Democrats or Republicans, liberals or conservatives control a level of government will affect policy. Thus, the particular interests pressing for policy change in Washington or in the state capitals at any one time depend on which partisan and interest group coalition is dominant at the federal or state levels. Since the depression of the 1930s, liberal interests on domestic policy have tended to favor action by the federal government on the grounds that it was more supportive of their goals than the states. But when a conservative Republican pres-

33. Kettl, "The Maturing of American Federalism," 73–74.

ident, Ronald Reagan, was elected in 1980, the liberals began to see their policy objectives often thwarted at the national level. As a result, during the Reagan-Bush era liberal interests sought, with considerable success, to advance their objectives through governmental activism at the state level. In contrast, conservatives, who had long advocated governmental decentralization, found during the 1980s and early 1990s that with Republican administrations they could more readily push their interests through the national government. Bill Clinton's election in 1992 and continued Democratic control of Congress again reshuffled the balance of power in the federal system. Strengthened by a president who supports a more activist federal government and larger grants to states and localities to support social and regulatory programs, liberal interests in Washington, now revitalized, are working at the national level to achieve their quota. At the same time, more conservative interests are once more looking to the states. How federalism operates, therefore, is much more than just a matter of constitutional law. Decisions about the shape of federalism—which level of government will dominate policy making in a particular area of government activity and who will pay how much for that activity—go a long way toward determining who wins and loses in the American political system.

For Review

1. Federalism is a constitutional division of the powers of government between the national government and the regional governments (states), with each exercising significant powers.

2. Federalism was the "price of union"—a necessary means for creating one nation out of thirteen highly independent states.

3. Until the 1930s American federalism was characterized by the national and state governments operating in largely separate and distinct spheres of authority. But with the advent of the New Deal in the 1930s and subsequent extensions of the federal government's role, federal-state relations have been characterized by cooperative federalism, in which responsibilities are shared among the federal, state, and local governments.

4. An essential element of cooperative federalism is the grant-in-aid system, which transfers funds from the federal government to the states and localities for the purpose of carrying out federal policies. Federal grants have enabled state and local governments to expand their services but also have made them heavily dependent on the federal government for funds.

5. As federal budget deficits mounted in the 1980s and early 1990s, the federal government found itself unable to embark on new domestic grant-in-aid programs, and the states became the major policy innovators within the federal system. Nevertheless, with lawmakers feeling the pressure of budgetary deficits in Washington, grants-in-aid declined both as a per-

centage of federal budget outlays and as a source of state and local expenditures, thereby putting the states and localities under increased fiscal pressure. Although the Clinton administration has favored additional funding for federal grants, it too operates under the fiscal constraints imposed by large budget deficits.

6. Because of the expanded role of the federal government since the 1930s, the federal system of the 1990s is clearly more centralized than anything envisioned by the writers of the Constitution. Although the role of the federal government has expanded, the states have expanded their levels of activity as well and continue to play a major policy-making role in the system. Which level of government should perform which functions and how those functions should be paid for are continuing sources of conflict, however, within the American federal system.

For Further Reading

Advisory Commission on Intergovernmental Relations. *Intergovernmental Perspective.* A periodical containing timely data as well as articles of thought and opinion on the state of American federalism.

Anton, Thomas. *American Federalism and Public Policy.* Philadelphia: Temple University Press, 1989. An analysis of the political forces that determine the extent of federal and state responsibility and how the actions at one level have an impact on the other level.

Conlan, Timothy J. *New Federalism: Intergovernmental Reform and Political Change from Nixon to Reagan.* Washington, D.C.: Brookings, 1988. A detailed analysis of the often paradoxical consequences of federalism reform under two conservative presidents.

Elazar, Daniel J. *American Federalism: A View from the States.* 3d ed. New York: Harper and Row, 1984. A thoughtful consideration of the role of the states by one of the leading students of federalism.

Nathan, Richard P., and Fred C. Doolittle. *Reagan and the States.* Princeton, N.J.: Princeton University Press, 1987. An analysis of the impact of the domestic policies of the Reagan administration and the resurgence of the states as a consequence of those policies.

O'Toole, Laurence C., Jr. *American Intergovernmental Relations.* 2d ed. Washington, D.C.: CQ Press, 1993. An up-to-date collection of analyses covering various aspects of intergovernmental relations.

Rivlin, Alice M. *Reviving the American Dream.* Washington, D.C.: Brookings, 1992. An account of the confusing state of American federalism and a plan for allocating governmental functions between the national and state governments, written by an experienced Washington insider and distinguished economist.

Wright, Deil S. *Understanding Intergovernmental Relations.* 3d ed. Pacific Grove, Calif.: Brooks/Cole, 1988. A comprehensive analysis of intergovernmental relations.

4. Civil Liberties and Civil Rights

T HE DRAFTERS of the Constitution stated in its preamble that their purpose was to "establish Justice" and "secure the Blessings of Liberty to ourselves and our Posterity." But despite these intentions controversy immediately arose within the states over whether or not the new Constitution did in fact protect people's basic liberties. This controversy, as well as the desire to secure ratification of the new Constitution, resulted in the addition of a bill of rights to that document. Then, as now, people perceived a direct connection between the basic liberties guaranteed by the Bill of Rights and the existence of a free society. Although most Americans take their basic liberties and rights under the Constitution for granted, they are nevertheless repelled by television news pictures that depict the governments of China and Haiti, for example, repressing their citizens.

Despite the public's almost unanimous endorsement of basic civil liberties, these liberties have been a continual source of controversy in American political life. The issue is not whether it is desirable to have freedom of speech, the press, or assembly. Rather, controversy is created by the actual application of such straightforward language in the First Amendment as "Congress shall make no law . . . abridging the freedom of speech, or of the press; or the right of the people peaceably to assemble."

As this chapter will demonstrate, there are no absolutes in a government's civil liberties and civil rights policies. To the contrary, the actual application of the civil liberties and civil rights guaranteed in the Constitution is ever-changing, ambiguous, and delicate—and even creates controversies when highly cherished values collide. For example, what are the values of a free press versus those of protecting national security? Should the press be allowed to print documents whose release will be, in the government's opinion, a threat to national security? What are the values of a fair trial versus those of the need for public safety and order? Should a person clearly guilty of a serious crime go free because the police seized evidence without a proper search warrant? And how does one weigh the right of privacy against the need to protect an unborn human life? Does a woman have the right to an abortion, or can the government limit abortions to protect the unborn? And what are the values of providing greater economic and educational opportunities for minorities and women who have suffered from discrimina-

Even Flag Burning Is Protected Communication under the First Amendment

Who's right? Supporters of a constitutional amendment to protect the U.S. flag rallied on Capitol Hill in 1990; in 1989 Gregory Johnson helped set the American flag on fire to assert his First Amendment rights.

In 1989 the Supreme Court threw out the conviction under Texas law of Gregory Johnson, who had burned the American flag at the 1984 Republican National Convention to protest the policies of President Ronald Reagan *(Texas v. Johnson)*. In making this decision, the Court held that Johnson had been engaged in symbolic speech protected by the First Amendment. This unpopular decision unleashed demands, endorsed by President George Bush, for a constitutional amendment banning desecration of the flag. In an effort to head off such an amendment, Congress responded by passing the Flag Protection Act of 1989. This law made it a punishable offense to mutilate, deface, physically defile, burn, or trample the flag of the United States.

When people protesting passage of the law burned the U.S. flag in Washington, D.C., in 1989, they were arrested for violating the Flag Protection Act. While noting in *U.S. v. Haggerty,* 110 S.Ct. 2404 (1990),that the defendants' desecration of the flag had been "deeply offensive to many," the Supreme Court reasserted its view that "[i]f there is a bedrock principle underlying the First Amendment, it is that the Government may not prohibit the expression of an idea simply because society finds the idea itself offensive or disagreeable." It concluded by saying, "Punishing desecration of the flag dilutes the very freedom that makes this emblem so revered, and worth revering."

tion versus treating all people equally before the law? Does past government and societal discrimination justify **affirmative action** programs that provide special opportunities for minorities and women? These are the kinds of issues that the Supreme Court is forced to confront when applying the Constitution to specific cases.

Because they involve conflicts over cherished values, civil liberties and civil rights issues are not only complicated but also highly contentious. For example, when the Supreme Court declared in 1989 that burning the American flag was a constitutionally protected form of free expression and subsequently pronounced a law banning desecration of the flag unconstitutional, a major political controversy was created. It pitted President George Bush, who advocated a constitutional amendment protecting the flag, against Democratic congressional leaders and such groups as the American Civil Liberties Union.

Civil Rights and Civil Liberties—What's the Difference?

Many people think *civil rights* and *civil liberties* mean about the same thing—their meanings are distinctly different.

On December 1, 1955, Rosa Parks refused to relinquish her seat to a white person and move to the back of a Montgomery, Alabama, bus. Her arrest and trial sparked a bus boycott, one of the first organized civil rights protests in the South.

A "bugged" telephone. Court opinions evolved on whether eavesdropping constituted an unreasonable search as such devices became more sophisticated.

Civil rights refers to a concept of being free from discrimination when engaging in public activities, such as voting, or participating in other aspects of civic life; using public transportation or other public accommodations; buying or renting a home; or looking for or working in a job. In the United States since the end of the Civil War, the term *civil rights* has referred in particular to the effort to eliminate racial discrimination against African Americans.

Civil liberties has been defined as claims of right that a citizen can assert against the government. Most of the civil liberties Americans enjoy today are embodied in the Bill of Rights. These include the freedoms of expression guaranteed by the First Amendment; the Fourth Amendment protection against unreasonable searches and seizures; and the rights in criminal and civil trials set out in the Fifth, Sixth, Seventh, and Eighth amendments.

Undeniably all Americans have a big stake in the policy decisions made about their civil liberties and civil rights. **Civil liberties** provide constitutional and legal protection from governmental interference. They include the basic freedoms that are considered essential to a free society such as freedom of speech, the press, assembly, and religion—the freedoms guaranteed by the First Amendment. Civil liberties also include guarantees of **procedural due process** or fairness (for example, the right to a lawyer in a criminal trial or protection from unreasonable searches and seizures) when the government seeks to deny a person life, liberty, or property. In contrast to civil liberties, **civil rights** encompass the government's responsibilities and policies to achieve greater equality among the citizens. Major concerns of civil rights policy makers have been to remove the barriers created by racial, gender, and disability discrimination. Recently other groups—for example, homosexuals and the elderly—also have sought governmental protection of their civil rights.

Nationalizing the Bill of Rights

Initially the Bill of Rights was interpreted by the Supreme Court (*Barron v. Baltimore,* 1833[1]) to apply only to the national government and not to the states. As a result, basic rights protected against violation by the national government were not protected from violations by state governments. Beginning in the 1920s, however, the Supreme Court began to interpret the Fourteenth Amendment in a manner that protected people from state infringement on most of the rights guaranteed by the Bill of Rights. According to the Fourteenth Amendment, no *state* shall "deprive any person of life, liberty, or property, without due process of law."[2] The Supreme Court interpreted this to include most of the rights protected by the Bill of Rights. The Court thereby engaged in **selective incorporation** of the Bill of Rights into the Constitution (see Table 4.1).

It began by declaring in *Gitlow v. New York* (1925) that freedom of speech and freedom of the press were protected from state infringement[3] and gradually extended Fourteenth Amendment protection to most of the guarantees in the Bill of Rights of a fair trial. Today all the provisions of the Bill of Rights apply to the states except the right to bear arms and have a militia (Second Amendment), the protection against quartering troops in private homes (Third Amendment), the right to a grand jury indictment (Fifth Amendment), the right to a trial by jury in civil cases (Seventh Amendment), and the protection against excessive bail and fines (Eighth Amendment). The present Supreme Court appears unlikely to adopt a "total incorporation" theory of the Fourteenth Amendment. Rather, it has adopted a case-

1. *Barron v. Baltimore,* 7 Peters 243 (1833).

2. The nationalization of the Bill of Rights through interpretation of the Fourteenth Amendment's due process clause is described by Richard C. Cortner, *The Supreme Court and the Second Bill of Rights: The Fourteenth Amendment and the Nationalization of Civil Liberties* (Madison: University of Wisconsin Press, 1981).

3. *Gitlow v. New York,* 268 U.S. 652 (1925).

Table 4.1 Selective Incorporation of the Bill of Rights into the Fourteenth Amendment

Amendment and Right Incorporated	Supreme Court Decision
FIRST	
Free speech	*Gitlow v. New York* (1925)
Free press	*Near v. Minnesota* (1931)
Peaceable assembly	*DeJonge v. Oregon* (1937)
Free exercise of religion	*Cantwell v. Connecticut* (1940)
No establishment of religion	*Everson v. Board of Education* (1947)
FOURTH	
No unreasonable searches and seizures	*Wolf v. Colorado* (1949)
Exclusionary rule	*Mapp v. Ohio* (1961)
FIFTH	
Protection from self-incrimination	*Mallory v. Hogan* (1964)
Protection from double jeopardy	*Benton v. Maryland* (1969)
SIXTH	
Right to counsel in capital cases	*Powell v. Alabama* (1932)
Right to know nature of accusations	*Cole v. Arkansas* (1948)
Right to public trial	*In re Oliver* (1948)
Right to counsel in noncapital felony cases	*Gideon v. Wainwright* (1963)
Right to confront accusers	*Pointer v. Texas* (1965)
Right to an impartial jury	*Parker v. Gladden* (1966)
Right to speedy trial	*Klopfer v. North Carolina* (1967)
Right to jury trial in felony cases	*Duncan v. Louisiana* (1968)
Right to counsel in all cases involving jail terms	*Argersinger v. Hamlin* (1972)
EIGHTH	
Protection from cruel and unusual punishment	*Robinson v. California* (1962)

by-case approach to determining whether defendants have received a fair trial.

First Amendment Freedoms

The rights to freedom of speech, the press, assembly, and religion contained in the First Amendment are, in the words of Justice Benjamin Cardozo (*Palko v. Connecticut*, 1937), "the very essence of ordered liberty. . . . [They are the] 'fundamental principles of liberty and justice which lie at the base of all our civil and political institutions.'"[4] But the essential character of the basic civil liberties has not made their application to specific circumstances any less difficult or controversial. Freedom of speech, as the following discussion demonstrates, can clash with other closely held values.

4. *Palko v. Connecticut*, 302 U.S. 319 (1937).

Freedom of Expression

In protecting freedom of expression, the First Amendment specifies that Congress may not impose restrictions on the rights of the people and the press to speak out or on the right of the people to gather peacefully and to petition the government when they feel they have been wronged. Without these freedoms governments cannot be responsive to the needs of the citizenry and free elections become impossible. Freedom of expression is, therefore, more than a personal right to say what one wishes. One also has the right to hear conflicting views, to conclude what is truth and what is not as ideas clash in the free marketplace, and to organize with fellow citizens to influence government policy. Freedom of expression is an essential cornerstone of and prerequisite for a democratic order.

In spite of the need to maintain a free marketplace of ideas, the Supreme Court has not interpreted the First Amendment to mean there are no limits on freedom of expression. Libelous and slanderous statements may be penalized. Obscenity and child pornography do not enjoy constitutional protection, nor do "fighting" words—words uttered in circumstances that by their utterance injure or provoke acts of violence. Justice Oliver Wendell Holmes observed, for example, that no one has a right to cry "Fire!" in a crowded theater.[5] The onerous task of developing doctrines that distinguish between constitutional and unconstitutional limitations on freedom of expression has fallen largely to the Supreme Court. The doctrines used by the Court have changed over time in response to changing national and world conditions.

One of the best-known doctrines has been the "clear and present danger" test developed in 1919 when the Court was confronted with a case in which a man had been arrested for distributing leaflets urging young men to resist the draft during World War I. According to the Court, in deciding such cases it had to take into account the circumstances in which the seemingly dangerous speech occurred. Speech could be restricted only if the words used created "a clear and present danger" that they would bring about substantive evils that Congress had a right to prevent.[6] The clear and present danger test thus stressed the likelihood and proximity of the threat posed by the speech in question. The burden of proof rested with the government; it had to show that freedom of expression constituted a serious and immediate threat to society.

5. *Schenck v. United States,* 249 U.S. 47 (1919).
6. Ibid., at 52.

In 1925 the Court modified the clear and present danger test and adopted a "bad tendency" test, which permitted restrictions on speech deemed to have a tendency to lead to illegal acts. The bad tendency test made it significantly less difficult for the government to justify limitations on speech. By the 1940s, however, the Court had adopted a much tougher standard for judging the constitutionality of restrictions on free expression: the preferred position doctrine. This doctrine holds that the rights of free expression are so crucial to a democratic order as to be in a preferred position. It is therefore assumed that restrictions on political speech are unconstitutional unless the government can demonstrate that the speech constitutes an imminent and serious threat to create a substantive evil.

When the values of national security and freedom of expression have seemed to collide, the Court has been confronted with particularly troublesome decisions. In 1940, with World War II looming on the horizon, Congress passed the Smith Act, which made it a crime to knowingly advocate, advise, teach about, or print or distribute written material advocating the overthrow of the U.S. government. It also made it illegal to knowingly become a member of a group advocating the overthrow of the government. In the context of the cold war that followed World War II, when the threats of Soviet espionage and aggression seemed real to most Americans, eleven of the top American Communist party leaders were arrested and convicted of violating the Smith Act. And in *Dennis v. United States* (1951), the Supreme Court upheld their convictions. On the basis of their activities and membership in the Communist party, the Court maintained that the government was justified in restricting the communist leaders' rights to freedom of speech. Using a rather relaxed version of the clear and present danger test, the Court upheld the Communists' convictions under the Smith Act by emphasizing the gravity of the evil to be prevented (in this case the overthrow of the government) and discounting the likelihood of the evil actually occurring.[7] Since the *Dennis* decision, the Court has greatly restricted the scope of the Smith Act. Mere membership and statements of belief have ceased to be a basis for prosecution, as opposed to advocacy of imminent action that is likely to produce unlawful acts.

Today the Court essentially adheres to the preferred position doctrine and maintains a high level of skepticism about any restrictions on expression, particularly on political speech—whether spoken, written, or portrayed through pictures and demonstrations. It is therefore pos-

7. *Dennis v. United States,* 341 U.S. 494 (1951) at 510–511.

Government Support of the Arts and Freedom of Expression

Partial funding by the National Endowment for the Arts of an exhibit of Robert Mapplethorpe's homoerotic photographs stirred intense controversy and debate over the government's role in supporting the arts.

Controversies over freedom of expression extend well beyond court decisions. One focal point in the clash between upholding freedom of expression and maintaining standards of public decency has been the National Endowment for the Arts (NEA), a government agency that supports financially the visual and performing arts.

In 1989 the NEA became embroiled in bitter disputes over its partial funding of art exhibitions by Robert Mapplethorpe and Andres Serrano. Particularly offensive to critics were Mapplethorpe's explicit homoerotic photos and Serrano's picture of a crucifix in a jar of urine. Congress responded by passing legislation banning the NEA from using taxpayers' dollars to fund "obscene, sadomasochistic, and homoerotic" art. The arts community charged that such restrictions were acts of censorship and a threat to the freedom of expression.

In 1990 a compromise eased the statutory restrictions on the NEA by empowering the endowment's chairman, John E. Frohnmayer, to take action to ensure that grants were made on the basis of "general standards of decency and respect for the diverse beliefs and values of the American people." The controversy flared anew, however, during the 1992 presidential primaries when President George Bush's Republican challenger, Patrick Buchanan, charged that through the NEA the Bush administration had invented "tax dollars in pornographic and blasphemous art." As these examples illustrate, the issue of the government's appropriate role in encouraging the arts remains unresolved and is likely to remain so as long as Americans have differing standards of decency and artists seek to express themselves on controversial topics.

sible to hold meetings, rallies, or demonstrations in support of virtually any cause without political speech being restricted. For example, in 1992 the Supreme Court declared unconstitutional a St. Paul "hate speech" ordinance making it a crime to engage in speech or behavior likely to arouse "anger or alarm" on the basis of "race, color, creed, religion, or gender."[8] Even demonstrations that burn or desecrate the American flag, however distasteful these acts may be to most Americans, are constitutionally protected. The changing doctrines adopted by the Supreme Court during the twentieth century, however, are testimony to the fact that the First Amendment rights of freedom of

8. *R. A. V. v. St. Paul, Minnesota,* 505 U.S. ___, 112 S.Ct. 2538, 120 L.Ed. 2d 305 (1992). The Court has, however, upheld so-called hate crime statutes that impose harsher sentences on criminals who select their victims on the basis of race, religion, or other personal characteristics. In upholding hate crime statutes, the Court has emphasized that these statutes punished conduct and not expression as in the St. Paul case; see *Wisconsin v. Mitchell,* 508 U.S. ___, 113 S.Ct. 2194, 124 L.Ed. 2d 436 (1993).

expression are not absolute and that the principle of free expression must be applied constantly to specific and diverse circumstances.

Freedom of the Press

Like freedom of speech, an unfettered press is considered a prerequisite for democracy. While it cannot be doubted that the media play an essential role in keeping people informed about the pursuits of the president, Congress, and the courts, it is also true that the media are in a position to exercise great influence on public opinion and government policy. As a result, periodic attempts are made to muzzle the press—attempts that inevitably provoke controversy and pose thorny issues, particularly in times of war. During the Persian Gulf War of 1991, for example, the U.S. military severely limited media access to the battle zone by utilizing a "pool" system. Under this arrangement, small groups of tightly controlled correspondents accompanying U.S. troops in Kuwait and Iraq reported back to their more than seven hundred colleagues confined to bases in Saudi Arabia. In addition, press reports were censored. The Pentagon defended these restrictions as essential for effective prosecution of the war and for protection of the lives of American military personnel. Reporters and media representatives objected loudly and strenuously, claiming that the public was not being permitted to see and hear the full story of what their military forces were doing in the Middle East, one of the world's more volatile and dangerous regions. The media's objections, however, did not change the Pentagon's policy, and the public showed little concern about the media's complaints. Because the issues raised by the Persian Gulf War about freedom of the press are not new, they demonstrate the long-standing effort to reinterpret the First Amendment.

Prior Restraint. Although the government did restrict reporters' abilities to report battle-front news during the Persian Gulf War, the courts generally have taken a tough line against such government attempts at **prior restraint** as censorship and preventing the publication of information that the government finds objectionable.[9] The Supreme Court's hostility to prior censorship by the government was made clear in the 1971 *Pentagon Papers* case in which the U.S. attorney general sought a court injunction against publication by the *New York Times, Washington Post,* and other newspapers of classified Pentagon documents relating to American involvement in the Vietnam War.[10]

9. Freedom of the press, including freedom from prior censorship, was incorporated into the Fourteenth Amendment in *Near v. Minnesota,* 283 U.S. 697 (1931).

10. *New York Times Co. v. United States,* 403 U.S. 713 (1971). For an account of the *Pentagon Papers* controversy, see Anthony Lewis, *Make No Law* (New York: Random House, 1991).

The Court, however, held that the government had failed to demonstrate that publication of the documents would cause immediate and specific damage to national security.

Freedom of the press means not only that the government may not engage in prior censorship but also that it may not dictate the content or form of what the press prints. Indeed, the Supreme Court has held that a command by the government to print specific material collides with the First Amendment. Thus, when Florida passed a law that forced publishers to give free space to people who had been criticized in the pages of a newspaper, the Supreme Court voided the law, thereby extending constitutional protection to the editorial judgments of newspaper writers.[11]

Libel. Even though virtually all prior censorship is banned, people are not without legal recourse against the press. Citizens can sue the media for libel when they can demonstrate that what was published was false and that the publisher knew it was false or published it without regard to whether or not it was true. Public figures, such as politicians, have a more difficult time obtaining libel judgments against the media than do private citizens. Since 1964 and *New York Times v. Sullivan,* the Supreme Court has held that public figures lose some of their rights to privacy by virtue of their positions and, therefore, must prove not only that what was published about them was false and defamatory, but also that it was published with "reckless disregard" for the truth.[12] This test has made it extremely hard for public figures to win libel cases against the media. The Court's restrictive attitude toward permitting public figures to win libel judgments stems from its concern that burdensome libel laws could stifle valued public debate.

Obscenity. Obscene materials do not enjoy constitutional protection. But, because people's views on what constitutes obscenity vary widely, it has been difficult to develop workable definitions of obscenity for use by law enforcement officials. The definition of obscenity developed by a majority of the Supreme Court in 1973 involves a three-part test:[13]

1. Would an average person applying the contemporary standards of a particular community find that the work taken as a whole appeals to prurient interests?

2. When taken as a whole, does the work lack serious literary, artistic, political, or scientific value?

11. *Miami Herald Publishing Co. v. Tornillo,* 418 U.S. 241 (1974).
12. *The New York Times v. Sullivan,* 376 U.S. 254 (1964).
13. *Miller v. California,* 413 U.S. 15 (1973).

3. Does the work depict or describe sexual conduct in a patently offensive way?

In devising these tests for obscenity, the Court indicated that although the same standards did not have to be applied in every community, it did not intend for local enforcement officials and juries to have carte blanche in determining what constituted obscene material. Indeed, anti-obscenity laws must define specifically what constitutes obscenity in a manner that avoids vague language; vaguely drawn obscenity statutes provide no guidance to booksellers and theater managers of what could constitute a violation of the law. In addition, sellers of allegedly obscene materials must be shown to have knowingly offered such materials for sale. It is not enough merely to have obscene material in one's possession. Although the Court has explicitly denied constitutional protection to obscene material, developing statutes and then prosecuting offenders within the confines of the First Amendment have proven to be no easy task.

The conflicts between the advocates of freedom of artistic and political expression and the various groups anxious to protect the public, especially the more vulnerable members of society, are continuing and serious. For example, women's groups have sought to restrict hard-core sex publications on the grounds that they degrade women and encourage violence against women.[14] A particularly troubling issue is the access of children to sexually oriented material in print, movies, television, and records. Amid public outcries against child abuse, sexual harassment, and crime, the congressional committees with jurisdiction over legislation regulating the television industry have pressured the television networks and cable companies to curb sex and violence in their programming. Tipper Gore, a concerned mother and the wife of Vice President Albert Gore, Jr., has received widespread publicity (both highly critical and favorable) by advocating that, to protect children, warning labels be placed on records containing sexually explicit lyrics. Some civil liberties advocates and the record industry charge that such actions amount to censorship and would have the effect of limiting the rights of adults. These conflicts, then, over obscenity and freedom of the press are not likely to go away because they involve prized, but often clashing, values.

Shield Laws for the Press. Another controversial area of freedom of

---

14. On the issues raised by the women's movement about pornography, see Donald A. Downs, *The New Politics of Pornography: The First Amendment's Encounter with a Dilemma* (Chicago: University of Chicago Press, 1989); and Catharine MacKinnon, *Only Words* (Cambridge, Mass.: Harvard University Press, 1993).

the press is whether reporters having knowledge of criminal activities should be required to testify during criminal trials and divulge the sources of their information. Those who favor requiring reporters to testify argue that reporters are not exempt from the obligations of citizenship imposed on all Americans. But press groups have urged legislatures to adopt shield laws that would prevent reporters from being compelled to divulge their sources. Reporters claim that their sources will dry up and that they will not be able to gain access to vital news if their sources can be revealed in a court of law. Thus far the courts have not granted reporters the right to withhold information in criminal prosecutions, and, as a result, some reporters have gone to jail rather than reveal their information sources.

Freedom of Religion

The First Amendment guarantees religious freedom in two ways: through the **establishment of religion clause**, which bans the establishment of an official state-sanctioned religion and erects a "wall of separation" between church and state, and through the **free exercise of religion clause**, which protects people's right to practice their religion. As with the rights of free speech and a free press, neither clause has been interpreted in absolute terms. For example, in spite of the so-called establishment clause, the government is not totally separated from religion. The House and Senate have official chaplains, who open each session with prayer, and the military has chaplains on the payroll as well. Similarly, the free exercise clause does not exempt a person from obeying otherwise nondiscriminatory laws such as those banning

When Allegheny County, Pennsylvania, erected on public property a holiday display that included a nativity scene and a combined Christmas tree and menorah display, the Supreme Court ruled in County of Allegheny v. ACLU, Greater Pittsburgh Chapter *(1989) that the crèche violated the separation of church and state doctrine, but that the combined display did not.*

the practice of polygamy (having two or more spouses at the same time) or requiring parents to provide medical care for their children.

The relationship between the government and religion is complex and often controversial because it involves balancing the constitutional mandate for religious freedom and separation of church and state against America's deep religious heritage and the commitment that many have to their faiths. It is therefore inevitable that issues involving the relationship of the government to church organizations and religious practices would enter the political arena. For example, should parents, who on religious grounds do not believe in medicine, be required to immunize their children? Is it a violation of the establishment clause to permit prayer in public schools or to use tax funds to pay for textbooks used in nonreligious classes in parochial schools? These and other vexing, and sometimes emotional, issues confront anyone seeking to determine the appropriate relationship of the government to religion.

Establishment of Religion. The drafters of the Constitution clearly wanted to prevent the creation of a state-sponsored and state-supported religion such as the Church of England. Today, however, issues of church-state relations are raised by the more indirect involvement of the government in religion.[15] For example, in 1947 the Supreme Court was confronted with an establishment of religion case when the constitutionality of a New Jersey law providing free bus transportation to children attending parochial schools was challenged *(Everson v. Board of Education).*[16] While stating that the government should not be involved in the affairs of religious organizations, the Court upheld New Jersey's law on the grounds that it provided aid to students rather than to religious organizations. Similar reasoning has been applied to permit governmental support of school lunches and nonsecular textbooks for children attending parochial schools.

Since 1971 and the case of *Lemon v. Kurtzman,* the Supreme Court has used a three-part test to determine whether government involvement in religion violates the establishment clause. A law is said not to violate the establishment clause if (1) it has a secular rather than a religious purpose; (2) its actual effect is neutral—neither promoting nor

15. For a detailed discussion of the establishment of religion clause, see Leonard W. Levy, *The Establishment Clause: Religion and the First Amendment* (New York: Macmillan, 1986); and Robert A. Goldwin and Art Kaufman, eds., *How Does the Constitution Protect Religious Freedom?* (New York: University Press of America, 1988).

16. *Everson v. Board of Education,* 330 U.S. 1 (1947).

inhibiting religion; and (3) it does not cause excessive government involvement in religion.[17] Using the *Lemon* test, the Court has declared unconstitutional state sponsorship and encouragement of religion through such means as a nondenominational prayer at the opening of the school day and a devotional Bible reading. State bans on teaching the theory of evolution, which offends the religious sensitivities of some fundamentalist Protestants, also have been declared unconstitutional. Government-sponsored religious displays—such as nativity scenes at Christmas—are permitted when done in a secular holiday context, but displays of the crèche in a manner that suggests state support for a particular religion have been declared to be in violation of the First Amendment. And while clergy-led prayers at public school graduation ceremonies are prohibited, student-led prayers are allowed.

A particularly complex area is state financial aid to parochial schools. In applying the *Lemon* test on a case-by-case basis, the Court has held that states may not subsidize the salaries of parochial schoolteachers, even when they teach only nonreligious subjects. Nor may states pay for counseling, audiovisual equipment, field trips, or maintenance of facilities in parochial schools. The Court has permitted, however, state financial assistance to pay for textbooks, lunches, transportation to and from school, diagnostic tests, and remedial assistance. Tax deductions and credits by parents for the cost of tuition at nonpublic schools also have been permitted.

In 1993 the Court threw out a New York State law that permitted after-school use of public school buildings by community groups but banned their use for any religious purpose. In banning the use of a Long Island school for a program on child rearing from a "Christian perspective," school authorities had, according to the Court, unconstitutionally discriminated against the expression of certain views on the basis of content.[18]

As these examples demonstrate, the "wall of separation" between church and state so strongly advocated by Thomas Jefferson can be penetrated. A government that is actively involved in the lives of its citizens inevitably interacts with religious organizations. The Supreme Court's policy has tended to be one of accommodating constitutional guarantees to religious traditions and practices. But as long as the government remains a powerful force in society and the nation becomes

17. *Lemon v. Kurtzman*, 403 U.S. 602 (1971).
18. *Lamb's Chapel v. Center Moriches School District*, 508 U.S. ___, 113 S.Ct. 2141, 124 L.Ed. 2d 352 (1993).

more diverse in its religious faiths and practices, controversy about interpretation of the establishment of religion clause will continue.

Free Exercise of Religion. The free exercise clause of the First Amendment, which prohibits the federal government from interfering in people's right to practice their religion, has been incorporated by the Supreme Court into the Fourteenth Amendment for protection against state infringement. People have an absolute right to believe whatever they wish. The government therefore cannot compel a particular religious belief or penalize people because of their beliefs or lack of religious faith.

But the right of people to *practice* their religion freely has been interpreted by the courts in a less absolute manner than the right of people to *believe* as they see fit. For example, the Supreme Court has allowed the states to impose restrictions on certain religious practices (such as the use of illegal hallucinogenic drugs) as long as such restrictions advance a valid state purpose and are not enacted to inhibit religious freedom.[19] Yet the Court has been highly protective of the rights of various religious groups. Thus, a state law requiring a flag salute in public schools was declared unconstitutional because Jehovah's Witnesses claimed it conflicted with their faith's prohibition on the worship of graven images. Nor can Jehovah's Witnesses, contrary to their religious beliefs, be required to display on their New Hampshire license plates the state motto, "Live Free or Die." And Amish parents cannot be required to send their children to school after the eighth grade. The Court has upheld other legislation, however, including Sunday closing laws for businesses, compulsory vaccination of children, bans on polygamy, bans by the military on such religious headgear as the Jewish yarmulke, and requirements that the Amish collect and pay Social Security taxes on their employees, even though some religious groups have asserted that these laws interfere with their free practice of religion.

Freedom of Assembly and Association

The right of people to assemble peaceably, including demonstrations, parades, and other types of symbolic speech, is constitutionally protected. But this protection does not extend to incitements to vio-

---

19. In 1993 Congress enacted a religious freedom statute that sought to impose on the courts a severer test for judging laws that incidently restrict a person's religious freedom. Under the new statute, such laws would have to be shown to serve a compelling government interest in a way that posed the lightest possible burden on religious freedom.

lence. Thus, the Supreme Court ruled in 1994 that the federal antirack-
eteering law could be used against people engaged in violence and
intimidation against abortion clinics *(NOW v. Scheidler)*. Nor are governmental entities helpless in dealing with the problems associated
with crowd control—such as blocked highways and sidewalks or the
disruption of such public facilities as schools or courthouses. Reasonable regulations governing the time, place, and manner of demonstrations, for example, have been permitted by the courts, as well as the
arrest of protesters who deliberately made noise that disrupted the
peace and good order of a school.[20] Such restrictions, however, cannot
be applied in a discriminatory manner.

The courts have been particularly protective of people's rights of
assembly on or in such public property as parks, sidewalks, squares,
and buildings. But there is no constitutional right of assembly on private property. The owners of shopping centers, for example, may
restrict the distribution of political campaign materials and financial
solicitations. Yet the Supreme Court has allowed state and local governments to require shopping centers to permit political activities that
do not interfere with business.

The Supreme Court also has ruled that the right to freedom of
assembly, along with the right to freedom of speech, implies a right to
freedom of association. This means that people are free to associate
with whom they please and to form organizations espousing diverse
causes as long as such organizations do not constitute an immediate
threat to society. Thus, people have a constitutional right to form
political parties as well as religious, charitable, social, ethnic, and racial
organizations.

The Right to Privacy

Although the Constitution does not state explicitly that people have
a right to privacy, the Supreme Court has determined that the
First Amendment, taken together with the Third, Fourth, Fifth, Ninth,
and Fourteenth amendments, provides the basis for this right. The
Third Amendment bans quartering troops in private homes; the
Fourth Amendment protects against unreasonable searches and seizures; the Fifth and Fourteenth amendments provide protection
against being deprived of liberty without due process of law; and the
Ninth Amendment specifies that the enumeration of rights in the Constitution does not imply that other natural rights have been abandoned.

20. *Grayned v. Rockford,* 408 U.S. 104 (1972).

Abortion foes and pro-choice advocates confront each other while trying to influence Washington policy makers through mass demonstrations.

The most significant Court decisions relating to the right to privacy have dealt with sexual relations and reproduction. In 1965 *(Griswold v. Connecticut)* the Supreme Court declared unconstitutional a Connecticut law that made it a crime for married or unmarried couples to use birth control devices or medication. The same law also made it illegal to provide a person with birth control information. The Court, then, considered marital relations so personal and intimate a matter as to be "within the penumbra of special guarantees of the Bill of Rights."[21]

By far the most controversial application of the right of privacy has been to abortion. In *Roe v. Wade* (1973) the Supreme Court held that a woman has the right to an abortion during the first three months (or first trimester) of pregnancy and that for a state to interfere with that right violates her right to privacy.[22] But the Court did permit reasonable regulation of abortions during the second trimester, and during the third trimester, when life outside the womb is possible, state prohibitions on abortion were permitted. The *Roe* decision, involving as it did the highly emotional issue of a woman's right to control her own body and the right of the unborn fetus to life, set off a highly charged controversy.

As the membership of the Court became more conservative during the 1980s, it became more tolerant of state restrictions on a woman's right to an abortion during the first trimester. In *Webster v. Reproductive Health Services* (1989) it held that a state can prohibit the use of state resources in performing abortions and that reasonable state regulations can be imposed to ensure that abortions are not carried out once the fetus is viable.[23]

In 1992, amid indications that it was on the verge of overturning *Roe v. Wade,* the Court, by a narrow 5–4 margin, reaffirmed but significantly recast the *Roe* decision establishing abortion as a fundamental right.[24] In upholding most of the provisions of a Pennsylvania statute, the Court's majority held that state regulations of abortion might be permitted if they did not impose an "undue burden" on a woman seeking an abortion by placing "substantial obstacles" in her path. Among the regulations that met this test were those that required doctors to advise women of the risks of and alternatives to abortion, those that imposed a twenty-four-hour waiting period before performance

21. *Griswold v. Connecticut,* 381 U.S. 479 (1965).
22. *Roe v. Wade,* 410 U.S. 113 (1973).
23. *Webster v. Reproductive Health Services,* 492 .U. S. 490. (1989).
24. *Planned Parenthood of Southeastern Pennsylvania v. Casey,* 505 U.S. _____, 120 L.Ed. 2d 305 (1992).

of an abortion, and those that required women under age eighteen to have the consent of one parent or a judge. The Court did, however, strike down the requirement that married women notify their husbands of their intention to undergo an abortion. According to the justices, women fearing physical harm from their husbands "are likely to be deterred from procuring an abortion as surely as if [the state] had outlawed abortion in all cases."

Although the Pennsylvania case did reaffirm *Roe,* it has not diminished the controversy. The Court's somewhat imprecise standard for upholding restrictions on abortion has stirred activists on both sides of the issue. Freedom-of-choice advocates are seeking statutory protection for abortion both in Congress and in state legislatures, while abortion opponents are trying to tighten the restrictions on abortion. Involving, as it does, a clash of deeply held values, the abortion controversy does not end with Supreme Court pronouncements.

The Bill of Rights and Criminal Proceedings

The authors of the Bill of Rights were all too familiar with governments that arbitrarily deprived people of life, liberty, and property. Therefore, they included in that document detailed guarantees of procedural due process or fairness to people accused of criminal wrongdoing. These guarantees include the Fourth Amendment's prohibition against "unreasonable searches and seizures," the Fifth Amendment's prohibition against double jeopardy (trying a person twice for the same offense) and protection of defendants from self-incrimination, the Sixth Amendment's guarantee of trial by jury and the right to an attorney, and the Eighth Amendment's interdiction against "cruel and unusual punishments." Although these protections initially were intended to apply only to the federal government, they are now applicable to the states through the doctrine of selective incorporation.

In applying these amendments to specific cases, the judicial system is often confronted with the delicate issue of balancing the rights of the accused with society's need for order and protection. A question that arises time and again in procedural due process cases is whether to let a guilty person go free because law enforcement officials failed to observe the procedural guarantees of the Bill of Rights. Under the leadership of Chief Justice Earl Warren, the Supreme Court moved in the 1960s to define more clearly and extend the rights of the accused. These efforts sparked praise from civil liberties advocates and sharp criticism from those who believed the Court was unduly hampering law enforcement. From the 1970s to the 1990s the Burger and Rehnquist Courts did narrow some of the Warren Court doctrines, but for the most part they maintained the guarantees enunciated during the Warren era.

Protection from Unreasonable
Searches and Seizures

The Fourth Amendment protects a person's privacy in guaranteeing security from unreasonable searches and seizures. Under most circumstances, it requires that a judge issue a search warrant authorizing law officers to search for and seize evidence of criminal activity. But warrants can be issued only when there is *probable cause* to believe that the search will produce criminal evidence. In 1914 the Supreme Court adopted the **exclusionary rule,** which barred evidence seized illegally from being used in a criminal trial,[25] and in 1961 *(Mapp v. Ohio)* the Warren Court made this rule applicable to state as well as to federal criminal proceedings through the Fourteenth Amendment's **due process clause.**[26] This decision stirred criticism of the Court on the grounds that criminals could be set free on procedural technicalities. The rationale of the Court, however, was that law enforcement officials should have no incentive to obtain evidence illegally in order to obtain convictions.

Since 1969 the Burger and Rehnquist Courts have narrowed significantly the application of the exclusionary rule. Under the doctrine of "objective good faith" adopted by the Court in 1984, when the police seize evidence with a search warrant that was obtained in objective good faith that the warrant was valid, the evidence is admissible in a trial even if it is later demonstrated that the warrant contained a technical flaw that made the search illegal. The Court has further weakened the exclusionary rule through the doctrines of "inevitable discovery" and "independent evidence." These doctrines mean that evidence that otherwise would have been seized illegally may be introduced into a trial if it might have been discovered "inevitably," or if a search warrant is obtained after the fact on the basis of "independent evidence." Clearly, then, in balancing the rights of the accused with society's interest in convicting lawbreakers, the Court has weakened the exclusionary rule substantially.

The Fourth Amendment also offers protection from warrantless police searches in places where a person has a legitimate right to expect

25. *Weeks v. United States,* 232 U.S. 383 (1914).
26. *Mapp v. Ohio,* 367 U.S. 643 (1961).

privacy, including his or her home, office, hotel room, desk, or file cabinets. But the same Fourth Amendment protection does not extend to all places where a person has a legitimate right to be. Thus, the Court has permitted stopping and searching automobiles when there is probable cause to believe that the car is carrying something illegal. There are, however, limits on the police's authority to search cars. For example, if the police stop a car that they believe is carrying illegal aliens, they are not then authorized to search containers or suitcases for drugs. But the police are permitted to stop cars for traffic offenses and conduct a full search of the driver. And in what other private areas are law enforcement officials allowed or not allowed to delve? Owners of fenced or open fields on which marijuana is growing do not enjoy Fourth Amendment protection, but the Court has held that police may not tap phones without a court order.

Protection from
Self-incrimination

According to the Fifth Amendment, no person shall "be compelled in any criminal case to be a witness against himself." Initially the courts interpreted this amendment to be protection against the requirement that defendants testify in their own criminal trials, and judges banned prosecuting attorneys from commenting on the fact that a defendant had chosen not to testify. Not all self-incrimination occurs in the courtroom under cross-examination, however. After taking suspects into custody, police may fail to inform them of their constitutional rights and subject them to third-degree tactics to coerce confessions.

In an effort to put an end to such practices, the Warren Court took the position in the landmark case of *Miranda v. Arizona* (1966) that police custody is inherently threatening and that confessions obtained during custody can be admitted as evidence only if subjects have been (1) advised of their constitutional right to remain silent, (2) warned that what they say may be used against them in a trial, (3) informed of the right to have an attorney paid for by the state if they cannot afford one and to have that attorney present during interrogation, and (4) told of the right to terminate the interrogation at any time.[27] Failure by law enforcement authorities to abide by these *Miranda* rules can result in the courts excluding as evidence the statements made by a suspect.

Many law enforcement officials and politicians, including Richard Nixon in his 1968 presidential campaign, severely criticized the *Miran-*

---

27. *Miranda v. Arizona,* 384 U.S. 436 (1966). For an account of the decision and the controversy it created, see Liva Baker, *Miranda: Crime, Law and Politics* (New York: Atheneum, 1983).

PD 47
Rev. 8/73

METROPOLITAN POLICE DEPARTMENT
WARNING AS TO YOUR RIGHTS

You are under arrest. Before we ask you any questions, you must understand what your rights are.

You have the right to remain silent. You are not required to say anything to us at any time or to answer any questions. Anything you say can be used against you in court.

You have the right to talk to a lawyer for advice before we question you and to have him with you during questioning.

If you cannot afford a lawyer and want one, a lawyer will be provided for you.

If you want to answer questions now without a lawyer present you will still have the right to stop answering at any time. You also have the right to stop answering at any time until you talk to a lawyer.

WAIVER

1. Have you read or had read to you the warning as to your rights? _____

2. Do you understand these rights? _____

3. Do you wish to answer any questions? _____

4. Are you willing to answer questions without having an attorney present? _____

5. Signature of defendant on line below.

_____

6. Time_____   Date _____

7. Signature of Officer _____

8. Signature of Witness_____

As a result of the Supreme Court's ruling in Miranda v. Arizona *(1966), police officers now carry "Miranda cards" so that they can inform suspects of their constitutional rights prior to any custodial interrogation.*

da decision for handcuffing the police and undermining law and order. With their more conservative memberships in the 1970s through the early 1990s, the Burger and Rehnquist Courts narrowed the scope of the *Miranda* decision. The Burger Court ruled that statements made without the *Miranda* warnings being given could still be admitted as evidence in order to contest the credibility of a defendant's testimony. For example, if statements made by a defendant in court contradict statements made without a prior *Miranda* warning, prosecutors may use the earlier statements to challenge the credibility of the defendant's court testimony. Further limits on the *Miranda* decision occurred in 1984, when the Court held that the *Miranda* warning need not be given if public safety is threatened. In 1991 the Court even went so far as to rule that the use of a coerced confession in a trial does not automatically invalidate a conviction if it can be shown that other evidence, obtained independently of the coerced confession, was also introduced at the trial and was adequate to sustain a guilty verdict.[28] In 1990, however, the Court reiterated the importance of protection against self-incrimination when it held in *Minnick v. Mississippi* that suspects held in custody who ask to consult a lawyer when police try to interrogate them may not be approached later for questioning when their lawyers are not present.[29]

As with the exclusionary rule, the Court's policy on self-incrimination is not fixed, and the seemingly explicit meaning of the constitutional language is not absolute. The broad extensions of rights

28. *Arizona v. Fulminante*, 499 U.S. 279 (1991).
29. *Minnick v. Mississippi*, 498 U.S 146 (1990).

designed to preserve a defendant's presumption of innocence, introduced in the 1960s under the Warren Court, have met with powerful opposition from those concerned about the government's obligation to protect public safety. In balancing these highly prized values, the Burger and Rehnquist Courts have tended to tilt the balance in the direction of public safety needs.

Right to an Attorney

Lawyers have a saying that "he who defends himself has a fool for a client." This adage is testimony to the accused's need for an attorney if there is to be any hope for a fair trial. Such a need is explicitly recognized by the Sixth Amendment, which specifies that defendants in criminal trials have the right to the "Assistance of Counsel." The right to counsel was first incorporated into the Fourteenth Amendment in the case of the Scottsboro boys in 1932. In this case nine young black defendants were charged with raping two white women in Alabama. Noting that this case involved a capital crime (one punishable by death), the Supreme Court ruled that the defendants—who were poor, illiterate teenagers—were entitled to an attorney paid for by the state.[30]

In the 1963 case of *Gideon v. Wainwright* the Warren Court extended the right to an attorney to any poor state defendant charged with a felony (a serious criminal offense punishable by death or imprisonment, depending on the gravity of the offense). In this case Clarence Gideon sent a handwritten petition to the Supreme Court from his Florida prison cell claiming that his five-year prison sentence was unconstitutional because he had been too poor to hire an attorney and had been required to defend himself at his trial. The Court agreed that his constitutional right to counsel had been denied.[31] In a new trial, at which he was provided with counsel, Gideon was acquitted. The Court's *Gideon* decision has been responsible for the development and growth of public defender programs within the states.

In the 1970s the Burger Court extended the right of indigent defendants to counsel to include misdemeanor offenses that would result in a jail sentence. But the Court has not required states to provide counsel to poor defendants in civil cases involving the custody of children or the loss of property.

---

30. *Powell v. Alabama,* 287 U.S. 45 (1932).

31. *Gideon v. Wainwright,* 372 U.S. 335 (1963). For an engrossing and complete account of the *Gideon* case, see Anthony Lewis, *Gideon's Trumpet* (New York: Random House, 1964).

Lawyers in Criminal Courts: Necessities, Not Luxuries

Clarence Earl Gideon

During the 1960s the Supreme Court was actively involved in extending the protection of the Bill of Rights to defendants in state courts. A dramatic example of this protection was evident in the 1963 case of *Gideon v. Wainwright,* involving Clarence Earl Gideon, an indigent, who after being denied a court-appointed attorney, tried to defend himself against a charge of breaking into a Florida pool hall. The Supreme Court ruled that by denying Gideon an attorney, Florida had violated the due process clause of the Fourteenth Amendment, which requires that all persons charged with serious crimes be provided with the aid of an attorney. Justice Hugo Black explained the reasoning of the Court:

"[R]eason and reflection require us to recognize that in our adversary system of criminal justice, any person haled into court, who is too poor to hire a lawyer, cannot be assured a fair trial unless counsel is provided for him. This seems to us to be an obvious truth. . . . Lawyers to prosecute are everywhere deemed essential to protect the public's interest in an orderly society. . . . That government hires lawyers to prosecute and defendants who have the money hire lawyers to defend are the strongest indications of the widespread belief that lawyers in criminal courts are necessities, not luxuries." (*Gideon v. Wainwright,* 372 U.S. 335 at 343-344, 1963)

Protection from Excessive Bail,
Excessive Fines, and Cruel and
Unusual Punishment

According to the Eighth Amendment, "Excessive bail shall not be required, nor excessive fines imposed, nor cruel and unusual punishments inflicted." Because the bail provision of the Eighth Amendment has not been incorporated into the Fourteenth Amendment, state judges can set bail at high levels to keep the accused in jail until a trial has been concluded. Such a measure is a type of preventive detention. Critics of this practice point out that the defendants in such cases, who under the American system of justice are presumed to be innocent until proven guilty, are subject to all the indignities of prison life before being convicted, and, indeed, they may ultimately be acquitted. But the proponents of preventive detention defend it as a reasonable way to protect the public from dangerous criminals and to prevent the accused from jumping bail. In 1984 Congress enacted the Bail Reform Act, which authorized the use of preventive detention through the denial of bail in federal court cases in which the judge determines that the defendant is a threat to public safety (for example, the defendants in the 1993 World Trade Center bombing in New York City).

For the first time in 1993 the Supreme Court set a constitutional limit on the government's power to seize the homes, businesses, and other property of criminals and suspects by invoking the Eighth Amendment's prohibition on "excessive fines." It ruled in the case of a North Dakota man who had had his business and mobile home seized after selling two grams of cocaine that there had to be some relationship between the gravity of the crime and the property seized.[32]

The Eighth Amendment ban on cruel and unusual punishment raises the question of the meaning of "cruel and unusual." As society's standards for judging cruelty have changed, the meaning of the phrase has evolved. But the amendment clearly bans the torture practices that were condemned by English common law when the Bill of Rights was drafted. In addition, the federal courts have ruled that such conditions in state prisons as excessive crowding, improper diets, poor sanitation, or denials of needed medical care are violations of the Eighth Amendment. On rare occasions the Supreme Court also has ruled that the severity of the punishment was out of proportion to the seriousness of the offense. But the Court has been reluctant to second-guess legislative decisions in this area and has upheld a forty-year sentence and a

32. *Austin v. United States*, 509 U.S. ___, 113 S.Ct. 2801, 125 L.Ed. 2d 488 (1993).

$20,000 fine for the crime of intending to distribute nine ounces of marijuana. Yet in a related area the Supreme Court ruled in the 1962 case of *Robinson v. California* that a state law making it a crime to be a drug addict violated the constitutional protection against cruel and unusual punishment because the law made it a crime for a person to have an illness.[33]

Most contemporary controversies have revolved around the death penalty. Now-retired justice William Brennan, Jr., and the late justice Thurgood Marshall considered the death penalty to be a cruel and unusual punishment as did Justice Harry Blackmun. The majority of the Court, however, has not accepted this view. While permitting the death penalty when a person kills, intends to kill, or tries to kill another person, the Court has placed limits on the use of this severest of all punishments. When imposed in an arbitrary and discriminatory manner (as was true in a 1972 case in Georgia, where juries had such wide discretion that racial bias entered the process), the death penalty has been considered cruel and unusual punishment. But statistics showing that blacks convicted of murdering whites have a greater chance of receiving a death sentence than whites convicted of killing blacks have not been considered sufficient evidence of a violation of the Eighth Amendment.[34] The Rehnquist Court also has restricted multiple appeals by persons sentenced to death and prohibited appeals by third parties when the convicted person did not wish to have an appeal go forward.[35] As long as it has been shown that the accused had a fair trial and was convicted under a valid death penalty law, the Court has declined to throw out a conviction.

Civil Rights: The Quest for Equality

The Declaration of Independence includes Thomas Jefferson's affirmation that the new nation would be based on the principle of equality: "We hold these truths to be self-evident, that all men are created equal." The Constitution of 1787, however, did not guarantee that the government would treat all citizens equally. It was not until 1868 that equality gained a formal place in the Constitution with the ratification of the Fourteenth Amendment, which provides that "no state shall deny any person the *equal protection of the laws*" (emphasis added). This amendment was intended to protect the newly freed

33. *Robinson v. California,* 370 U.S. 660 (1962).
34. *McCleskey v. Kemp,* 481 U.S. 279 (1987).
35. *Whitemore v. Arkansas,* 495 U.S. 149 (1990).

slaves from state acts of discrimination (unequal treatment of people based on such arbitrary classifications as race), and the federal government was given enforcement authority. With its broad language, however, the **equal protection clause** has over time come to be interpreted as banning government acts of discrimination based on gender, religion, or national origin, as well as those based on race. Although the Fourteenth Amendment does not prohibit discrimination by private citizens, it does ban private acts of discrimination when supported by government actions (for example, state court enforcement of real estate deed restrictions that prohibit the sale of property to nonwhites).

Equality is a broadly accepted part of the American creed, but it has several dimensions, some of which are a source of continuing debate.[36] The least controversial is the notion of *equality under the law,* which asserts that the government should treat everyone the same and not make arbitrary distinctions among people based on such criteria as race, sex, national origin, or religion. For some Americans, however, equality has a more expansive meaning. It can encompass *equality of opportunity*—that all people should have the same chance in life regardless of the color of their skin, sex, national origin, or religion. Most Americans accept the notion that the government should provide some minimum standard of living and education so that people can compete and achieve a better life for themselves and their children. The most controversial conception of equality is *equality of outcomes*— that equality exists when all people share the benefits of society regardless of race, sex, national origin, or religion. Advocates of equality of outcomes have endorsed preferential treatment in education and hiring for disadvantaged groups to compensate for past acts of discrimination or deprivation. But such affirmative action policies have created sharp divisions within society as America continues to debate the meaning of its commitment to equality.

Racial Equality

To combat the discriminatory laws (called black codes) passed by southern states after the Civil War, a series of constitutional amendments protecting the rights of black Americans were proposed and ratified in the years after the war. The Thirteenth Amendment (1865) banned slavery and involuntary servitude; the Fourteenth Amendment (1868) contained guarantees of "equal protection" and "due process of law" and declared blacks to be citizens of the United States and the states in which they resided; and the Fifteenth Amendment (1870)

36. See Sidney Verba and Gary Orren, *Equality in America: The View from the Top* (Cambridge, Mass.: Harvard University Press, 1985).

guaranteed that the right to vote could not be abridged on the basis of race or previous condition of servitude. In addition, Congress passed a series of civil rights laws, including the Civil Rights Act of 1875, which banned discrimination in places of public accommodation such as hotels and restaurants as well as in jury service.[37]

Rise of Jim Crow Laws and the "Separate but Equal" Doctrine. From the 1870s through the 1940s the rights that these federal actions were intended to protect were gradually eroded. The Supreme Court narrowed the applicability of federal civil rights legislation, and racist state legislatures passed so-called Jim Crow laws requiring segregation of blacks and whites in schools, parks, restrooms, transportation facilities, and other places of public accommodation. So that blacks could not challenge segregation via the ballot box, they were effectively disenfranchised. One means of disenfranchisement used by southern states was the "poll tax," a head tax a citizen was required to pay in order to vote. These taxes hit poor blacks particularly hard, especially since normally there was a provision for payment of back taxes before voting for the first time. Literacy tests also were adopted as a qualification for voting. These tests were often administered in a discriminatory manner that effectively prevented blacks from registering to vote. To further insulate the electoral process from black influence, southern states instituted what they called a **white primary**, which excluded blacks from the primary elections of the dominant party in the region, the Democratic party.

The Supreme Court gave constitutional status to the Jim Crow system in 1896 when it stated in the case of *Plessy v. Ferguson* that segregation did not violate the equal protection clause.[38] The case arose when Homer Plessy, who was seven-eighths white, appealed his conviction for having violated Louisiana's segregation laws by sitting in a "whites only" railroad car. In upholding Plessy's conviction, the Court adopted the **separate but equal doctrine**, which held that government-enforced segregation of the races was constitutional as long as the facilities for blacks and whites were equal. With this constitutional endorsement of segregation, Jim Crow laws proliferated, notably in education at both the elementary and secondary levels and in universities.[39]

Blacks were clearly relegated to second-class citizenship and, even worse, were subjected to intimidation and violence if they sought to

The Fourteenth Amendment, ratified in 1868, was intended to protect the civil rights of former slaves. However, it was not until ninety-six years later with the passage of the Civil Rights Act of 1964 that racial segregation in places of public accommodation, as in this bus station, was made unlawful.

37. This act was later declared unconstitutional by the Supreme Court. See *Civil Rights Cases,* 100 U.S. 3 (1883).

38. *Plessy v. Ferguson,* 163 U.S. 537 (1896).

39. For a thorough account of segregation, see C. Vann Woodward, *The Strange Career of Jim Crow,* 2d rev. ed. (New York: Oxford University Press, 1966).

assert their rights to equality under the law. Ku Klux Klan cross burnings, beatings, and vigilante lynchings were used to enforce the system of segregation by private means.

Brown v. Board of Education of Topeka and the Desegregation of Public Education. In the 1930s the Supreme Court, under prodding from cases brought before it through the efforts of the National Association for the Advancement of Colored People (NAACP), began to cast a more critical eye on segregation. For example, the Court began to enforce the requirement that facilities for blacks and whites actually be equal, and in a series of cases it required that blacks be admitted to state university law schools since no comparable legal education was available elsewhere for blacks.[40] It also declared the white primary to be a violation of the Fifteenth Amendment because a party primary is an integral part of the electoral process.[41]

The real revolution in Court policy toward government-enforced segregation occurred in 1954 in the case of *Brown v. Board of Education of Topeka.* In this case Oliver Brown, on behalf of his eight-year-old daughter, Linda, challenged Topeka's school segregation policy, which was permitted under Kansas law. Since the black and white schools of the city were presumed to be equal, the Court was not able to decide the case by determining whether the two school systems were in fact equal. Rather, it had to confront the issue of segregation per se and decide its constitutionality. In a unanimous decision the Court threw out the old doctrine of "separate but equal," pointing out that in public education 'the doctrine of `separate but equal' has no place. Separate educational facilities are inherently unequal."[42] This case was followed by an enforcement decision that recognized the difficulty of achieving integrated schools and called for desegregation to occur "with all deliberate speed."[43]

Integration of southern school systems did not occur voluntarily. It required the filing of numerous lawsuits seeking federal court orders to desegregate. At times, southern opposition to court orders to desegregate public schools was both massive and violent. In 1957 in Little

40. See *Missouri ex rel. Gaines v. Canada,* 305 U.S. 337 (1938); *McLaurin v. Oklahoma State Regents for Higher Education,* 339 U.S. 637 (1950); and *Sweatt v. Painter,* 339 U.S. 629 (1950).

41. *Smith v. Allwright,* 321 U.S. 649 (1944).

42. *Brown v. Board of Education of Topeka,* 347 U.S. 483 (1954). For an account of the events leading up to the *Brown* case, see Richard Kluger, *Simple Justice: The History of Brown v. Board of Education and Black America's Struggle for Equality* (New York: Knopf, 1976).

43. *Brown v. Board of Education of Topeka,* 349 U.S. 294 (1955).

The Birth and Death of "Separate but Equal"

Pictured on the steps of the Supreme Court are the National Association for the Advancement of Colored People (NAACP) Legal Defense Fund lawyers who argued the school segregation cases that resulted in the 1954 Brown v. Board of Education *decision declaring segregated schools unconstitutional. Fourth from the right is Special Counsel Thurgood Marshall, who went on to become the first African American to serve on the Supreme Court.*

Although the preamble to the Declaration of Independence proclaims the equality of all people, the drafters of the Constitution, in deference to the slave-holding South, omitted a definition of equality and permitted slavery to continue. The Civil War and the constitutional amendments that followed the war—especially the Fourteenth, which banned the states from denying any person the "equal protection of the laws"—sought to correct that omission. But in 1896 the Supreme Court delivered a mighty blow to racial equality in the case of *Plessy v. Ferguson* (163 U.S. 537, 1896). In this case the Court held that a Louisiana law requiring "equal but separate accommodations" on public transportation was constitutional. In reconciling state-enforced segregation with the Fourteenth Amendment's equal protection clause, the Court adopted the infamous "separate but equal" formula—that is, state-enforced segregation was to be permitted so long as the facilities for blacks and whites were equal. Justice Henry Brown sought to justify the Court's position by saying that

in the nature of things [the Fourteenth Amendment] could not have been intended to abolish distinctions based upon color, or to enforce social, as distinguished from political equality, or a commingling of the two races upon terms unsatisfactory to either.

In protest to this line of constitutional interpretation, Justice John Marshall Harlan dissented, saying that "our Constitution is colorblind and neither knows nor tolerates classes among citizens." It was not until fifty-eight years later that Harlan's principles of equality were embraced by the Supreme Court and the law was brought into closer conformity with the ideals of the Declaration of Independence. In *Brown v. Board of Education of Topeka* (347 U.S. 483, 1954) the Court ruled that state-enforced segregation was unconstitutional. The case concerned young Linda Brown, who because of Kansas state law and local segregation rules was required to travel a mile outside her neighborhood to attend a segregated black school. In 1950, when her father sought to enter her in the white school closer to their home, he was refused. The National Association for the Advancement of Colored People (NAACP) took up Linda's cause and carried her case to the Supreme Court. A unanimous Supreme Court led by Chief Justice Earl Warren explicitly reversed the *Plessy* decision. The chief justice stated, "We conclude that in the field of public education the doctrine of 'separate but equal' has no place. Separate educational facilities are inherently unequal."

In the years since Linda Brown's father, with the assistance of the NAACP, successfully challenged the "separate but equal" doctrine, the federal government has been embroiled in one controversy after another over how to combat discrimination by state and local governments, school boards, and some private sector employers.

Rock, Arkansas, Gov. Orval Faubus used National Guard troops to block black students from entering Central High School. A federal court, however, ordered desegregation to continue and the guard to be withdrawn. President Dwight Eisenhower then sent in U.S. Army troops to protect the black students from harassment by white mobs. Indeed, the various tactics used by southern states to postpone the inevitable desegregation of their school systems were so effective that a decade after the *Brown* decision, schools in the eleven states of the old Confederacy remained overwhelmingly segregated. Finally, the Supreme Court lost its patience with delays. In 1969 it stated that "[t]he time for mere 'deliberate speed' has run out.... Delays in desegregating school systems are no longer tolerable." The Court then demanded that every school district terminate dual school systems.[44]

The Civil Rights Movement and the Civil Rights Act of 1964. As the desegregation of public schools proceeded slowly ("with all deliberate speed") in the face of white southern opposition during the 1950s and early 1960s, the civil rights movement gathered momentum as blacks demonstrated against centuries of injustice. Lunch-counter sit-ins protesting segregated eating facilities, bus boycotts protesting requirements that blacks sit at the back of buses, a massive march on Washington to dramatize support for federal civil rights legislation, and marches for voting rights captured public attention, and whites became increasingly aware of the gap between the American creed of equality and the reality of the black experience. As the civil rights movement, led by the Reverend Martin Luther King Jr., made headway, pressure mounted in Congress for passage of civil rights legislation.[45] A major legislative breakthrough occurred with the passage of the Civil Rights Act of 1964, which banned racial discrimination in places of public accommodation. It also authorized the Department of Justice to enter into the integration battle by filing desegregation suits. Moreover, the law required that federal funds be cut off when any person shall "on the basis of race, color, or national origin be subjected to discrimination under any program or activity receiving federal financial assistance." Since public schools received federal financial assistance, the act provided the government with a powerful weapon to require desegregation. Through the combined enforcement activities of the Office of

44. *Alexander v. Holmes Board of Education,* 396 U.S. 19 (1969).

45. For an account of the civil rights movement, see Taylor Branch, *Parting the Waters: America in the King Years 1954-63* (New York: Simon and Schuster, 1988); and on the congressional politics of major civil rights laws, see Gary Orfield, *Congressional Power: Congress and Social Change* (New York: Harcourt Brace Jovanovich, 1975).

Civil Rights in the Department of Health, Education and Welfare and the Justice Department, school desegregation proceeded rapidly so that by 1972 the number of blacks in the South attending all-black schools had dropped to 9 percent.

School Integration in the North. The problems of school desegregation in the North proved even more difficult than those in the South. The Fourteenth Amendment bans *governmental* acts of discrimination—that is, **de jure segregation.** In the South, then, where segregat-

Major Civil Rights Legislation

Date	Act	Major Provisions
1875	Civil Rights Act	Bans discrimination in places of public accommodation (declared unconstitutional in 1883)
1957	Civil Rights Act	Makes it a federal crime to prevent a person from voting in a federal election
1963	Equal Pay Act	Bans wage discrimination based on race, sex, color, religion, or national origin
1964	Civil Rights Act	Bans discrimination in places of public accommodation Authorizes Justice Department to bring school integration suits Bans discrimination in federally funded programs Bans racial-and gender-based discrimination in private employment
1965	Voting Rights Act	In states and counties with literacy tests or where less than 50 percent of the population was registered to vote on November 1, 1964 —Federal registrars could register voters and ensure that those registered could exercise their right to vote —Any changes in voting laws must be approved by the attorney general or the U.S. District Court for the District of Columbia
1967	Age Discrimination Act	Bans discriminatory employment practices based on age
1968	Civil Rights Act, Title VIII	Bans racial discrimination in sale or rental of housing
1972	Higher Education Act, Title IX	Forbids discrimination based on sex by universities and colleges receiving federal aid
1974	Equal Credit Opportunity Act	Bans discrimination in granting credit based on sex, marital status, race, age, or receiving public assistance
1974	Housing and Community Development Act	Bans housing discrimination based on sex
1988	Civil Rights Restoration Act	Bans discrimination on the basis of race, sex, age, or physical disability by any part of an organization that receives federal aid
1990	Americans with Disabilities Act	Bans discrimination in employment, transportation, public accommodations, and telecommunications against persons with physical or mental disabilities
1991	Civil Rights Act	Counters a series of Supreme Court decisions that had made it difficult for employees to bring lawsuits charging employers with hiring bias, and for the first time allows victims of harassment and intentional discrimination based on sex, religion, or disability to seek limited damages from their employers

ed schools stemmed from state laws that mandated dual school systems for blacks and whites, the courts could order the schools to be integrated. But in the North, state laws did not require segregated schools; such schools largely resulted from residential housing patterns—that is, **de facto segregation** based on practices, not state laws. Thus, to order the integration of northern schools the federal courts had to demonstrate that segregation stemmed from government actions that violated the equal protection clause. When prior government actions did indeed result in racial imbalances in the schools, the Supreme Court held in 1971 that federal judges could order that remedial actions be taken to redress the imbalances. This frequently meant busing children to distant schools—a highly controversial and politically explosive issue in many communities.[46]

Today in most metropolitan areas the existence of separate central city and suburban school districts, as well as demographic patterns, work against racial integration of the schools. Expanding African American and Hispanic populations in city centers coupled with white migration to the suburbs have created central city schools dominated by minority students and largely white suburban schools. In these situations the busing of children within only the central city school district is unlikely to create racially balanced schools. Thus, the Supreme Court has held that cross-district busing is an appropriate remedy if it can be demonstrated that school district lines have been defined in a discriminatory manner.[47] But when government involvement in creating and operating segregated school systems cannot be demonstrated, as the Court stated in a case involving the Detroit area, federal judges may not order cross-district busing to achieve racial balance in the schools.[48] In interpreting the Fourteenth Amendment's equal protection clause to mean that proof of government actions that achieve or perpetuate segregation is needed to enforce desegregation, the Supreme Court has significantly limited the extent to which school integration can be achieved through judicial action.

Federal Legislation to Combat Discrimination in Public Accommodations, Employment, and Housing. The Civil Rights Act of 1964 stands as one of the most significant and lasting achievements of the civil rights movement. It contains provisions designed to eliminate private acts of

46. For an absorbing account of how school busing to achieve racial integration affected three families in Boston, see J. Anthony Lukas, *Common Ground: A Turbulent Decade in the Lives of Three American Families* (New York: Knopf, 1985).

47. *Swann v. Charlotte-Mecklenburg County Board of Education,* 402 U.S. 1 (1971).

48. *Milliken v. Bradley,* 418 U.S. 717 (1974).

Blacks and Whites in America: Progress, Problems, and Differences

Question: Compared to ten years ago, do you think blacks in America are a lot better off, a little better off, about the same, a little worse off, or a lot worse off?

Compared to ten years ago, I think blacks in America are . . .

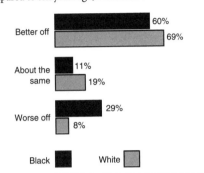

Question: Over the course of the past five years, do you feel that race relations between blacks and whites have gotten better, gotten worse, or stayed about the same?

Over the past five years, race relations have . . .

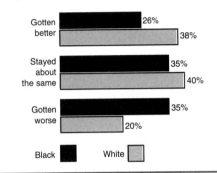

Source: Survey by Peter Hart and Robert Teeter for NBC News/*Wall Street Journal*, July 6-10, 1990; reported in *American Enterprise*, September/October 1991, 82.

Question: Do you think the United States currently has enough federal laws and regulations aimed at reducing racial, religious, and sexual discrimination, or does the Congress need to pass additional laws and regulations aimed at reducing this type of discrimination?

The United States currently has enough laws and regulations aimed at reducing racial, religious, and sexual discrimination.

Question: Do you think blacks and other minorities should or should not receive hiring preference to make up for past discrimination against them?

Blacks and minorities should receive hiring preference to make up for past discrimination.

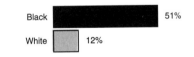

Source: Survey by the Gallup Organization, June 13-16, 1991; reported in *American Enterprise*, September/October 1991, 82.

Source: Survey by Peter Hart and Robert Teeter for NBC News/*Wall Street Journal*, June 22-25, 1991; reported in *American Enterprise*, September/October 1991, 82.

discrimination that are not covered by the Fourteenth Amendment. The act's ban on discrimination based on race, religion, or national origin in places of public accommodation is derived from the commerce clause in Article I of the Constitution, which gives Congress the power to regulate foreign and interstate commerce. Because of vigorous enforcement of the act, persons of color are no longer denied access to such public facilities as hotels, restaurants, theaters, service stations, and sports arenas.

The Civil Rights Act of 1964 also sought to combat discrimination

Table 4.2 African American Elected Officials: Steady Growth, 1970–1992

	1970	1975	1980	1985	1990	1992
Members of Congress and state legislatures	179	299	326	407	440	499
County and city officials	719	1,885	2,871	3,689	4,481	4,557
Judges, sheriffs, and other law enforcement officials	213	387	534	685	769	847
State education officials, college and school boards	368	951	1,232	1,531	1,695	1,614
TOTAL	1,479	3,522	4,963	6,312	7,335	7,517

Source: Bureau of the Census, *Statistical Abstract of the United States: 1993* (Washington, D.C.: Government Printing Office, 1993), 280.

in employment by banning businesses and unions involved in interstate commerce and employing fifteen or more workers from discriminating in their employment practices on the basis of race, color, religion, national origin, or sex. Since 1964 the same protection has been extended to the handicapped, armed services veterans, and people over forty years of age.

The effectiveness of Congress's efforts to combat workplace discrimination was limited in the 1980s by nine Supreme Court decisions that restricted the ability of workers to challenge racially biased employment practices. After a lengthy struggle between President George Bush and congressional Democrats over whether legislation designed to counter these Court decisions would impose racial hiring quotas, the president and Congress reached agreement on the Civil Rights Act of 1991. This act removed Court-imposed impediments to seeking relief from racially biased employee practices (see Table 4.2).

In 1968 Congress passed the Fair Housing Act, which, as amended in 1988, banned discrimination in housing offered for sale or rent. Small rooming and apartment houses in which the owner maintains a residence, private clubs and religious organizations providing housing for their members, and homeowners selling their property without a real estate agent are exempt from the law's coverage, however.

The history of antidiscrimination efforts in the post-World War II years demonstrates that getting Congress to pass legislation is only the first step in an ongoing process. Good faith compliance by individuals and private organizations as well as supportive governmental institutions to implement the laws are also needed.

Sexual Equality

Women have long been subjected to discriminatory actions by governments and private organizations. Indeed, it was not until 1920 and ratification of the Nineteenth Amendment that women were guaranteed the right to vote throughout the United States. Nevertheless, educational and employment opportunities, access to credit, and wages and salaries for women continued to be severely restricted. Even into the 1960s, for example, some school districts maintained separate salary schedules for women and men and paid women less than men.

As women entered the work force in larger numbers in the 1960s and the women's movement gained strength, public and government policy became more sensitive to discrimination based on sex. The Supreme Court began the process of striking down gender-oriented statutes in 1971 when it declared unconstitutional an Idaho law requiring that men be given preference when hiring individuals to administer estates.[49] This law and others that distinguished between women and men on an unreasonable basis have been declared in violation of the Fourteenth Amendment's equal protection clause. But this is not to say that the courts have banned all legislation that makes distinctions between the sexes. Male-only registration for the draft, for example, has gained Supreme Court approval. And, although women have often been assigned hazardous military duty, as during the 1991 Persian Gulf War, the armed services traditionally have restricted the participation of women in combat. Recently, however, the Pentagon has eased those restrictions in response to pressures from Congress and women's groups, and the combat roles of women have been expanded to include service on warships and in combat aircraft.

In an effort to correct the inequity in paying women at a lower rate than men for the same work, Congress passed in 1963 the Equal Pay Act. It requires that those who do the same work be paid the same without regard to race, color, religion, national origin, or sex. This legislation did nothing, however, to remove the barriers to employment that had tended to confine women to traditionally female occupations—teaching, nursing, and clerical work. The way was opened for increased employment opportunities for women by the inclusion in the Civil Rights Act of 1964 of Title VII, which prohibited employment discrimination based on sex. Interestingly, this provision was proposed by the leader of the southern anti-integration forces in Congress, Rep. Howard Smith (D-Va.). Smith believed that by adding what he considered to be an outrageous amendment to the Civil Rights Act, the entire

49. *Reed v. Reed,* 404 U.S. 71 (1971).

The role of women in the military is undergoing major changes in areas that were long the exclusive domain of men.

bill would be defeated. But his ploy failed, and the entire bill, including his anti-sex discrimination amendment, passed. After several years during which its enforcement proved difficult, Title VII became an effective weapon in gaining employment opportunities for women and in forcing companies to cease discriminatory pay policies.

As the drive for equal opportunities for women intensified, Congress enacted Title IX of the Higher Education Act of 1972. This act forbids discrimination on the basis of sex by colleges and universities receiving federal aid. Since Title IX carries the sanction of a cutoff in federal aid, it has provided a powerful incentive against gender-based discrimination.

Also in the early 1970s the women's movement, led by the National Organization for Women (NOW), pressed for adoption of a constitutional amendment that read: "Equality of rights under the law shall not be denied or abridged by the United States or by any State on account of sex." Congress responded in 1972 by approving the so-called Equal Rights Amendment (ERA) by the necessary two-thirds vote and sending it on to the states for ratification. But the ERA fell three states short of the thirty-eight needed for ratification and died on June 30, 1982, the extended deadline for ratification set by Congress. In the ratification struggle, feminist groups confronted antifeminist organizations led by conservative activist Phyllis Schafly, who insisted, among other things, that the ERA would guarantee a woman's right to an abortion. She therefore sought to enlist the support of right-to-life groups in opposing the amendment.[50] Although the ERA was defeated, sixteen states have equal rights amendments in their state constitutions, and most of the protections sought by advocates of the amendment have been achieved by judicial and legislative means.

Other Claims to Equality: Gays, Disabled, Elderly, Voters

Although gays and lesbians have become increasingly militant in fighting discrimination and asserting claims to equality, to date the Supreme Court has not determined the rights of homosexuals under the equal protection clause. In 1986, however, the Court ruled that there is no constitutional right to engage in homosexual sodomy, and therefore it upheld a Georgia law that made sodomy a crime. Laws have been passed by various states and localities granting antidiscrimi-

50. For an account of the ERA battle, see Jane Mansbridge, *Why We Lost ERA* (Chicago: University of Chicago Press, 1986). Also see Gilbert Y. Steiner, *Constitutional Inequality: The Political Fortunes of the Equal Rights Amendment* (Washington, D.C.: Brookings, 1986).

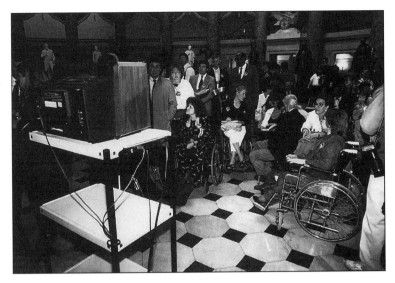

In the Capitol's Statuary Hall, advocates of the Americans with Disabilities Act of 1990 watch House debate and demonstrate their support for this major piece of civil rights legislation.

nation rights to gays and lesbians. Gays rights issues, however, continue to create intense heat as the controversy over President Clinton's proposal to lift the ban on gays and lesbians in the military has demonstrated.

In seeking protection for the disabled, Congress in 1990 passed overwhelmingly the Americans with Disabilities Act, the most sweeping piece of antidiscrimination legislation since the Civil Rights Act of 1964. It requires that (1) businesses with twenty-five workers or more adapt their physical plants to accommodate disabled employees; (2) new buses, trains, and subway cars be accessible to people in wheelchairs; (3) renovated or new hotels, retail stores, and restaurants be accessible to people in wheelchairs and that existing barriers be removed where it is "readily achievable"; and (4) telephone companies provide within three years relay services that would allow the hearing-impaired or voice-impaired possessing special telephones to place and receive calls from ordinary telephones.

With their relatively high levels of voter turnout and political activity, Americans aged sixty-five and over are an influential segment of the total population, of which they constitute approximately 12 percent. Congress responded to older Americans' concerns about age discrimination in the workplace by enacting the Age Discrimination Act of 1967. Unless age is essential to job performance, the act prohibits employers from giving preference to younger workers in hiring, firing, or benefits. Congress also has banned mandatory retirements at age seventy in most occupations.

Voters, too, have claimed equality. The equal protection clause has been used to advance equality of representation—that is, to have each person's vote count the same as that of every other person. It is not possible to adhere to a strict one person, one vote standard under the Constitution because of the provision for equal representation for each state in the Senate. But the federal courts have used the equal protection clause to prevent the states from engaging in gerrymandering—drawing congressional, state legislative, judicial, and municipal election district boundaries in a manner that violates the one person, one vote principle or discriminates against particular groups in society (see Chapter 10, Congress, for a discussion of the role of the courts in preventing gerrymandering).

Affirmative Action

The principle stated by Supreme Court Justice John Marshall Harlan in his famous dissent in *Plessy v. Ferguson* that the "Constitution is colorblind" and that the government should prevent acts of discrimination has gained wide acceptance since the 1960s. Advocates for more rapid progress toward equality for disadvantaged groups have argued, however, that it is not enough for the government to be neutral and prohibit acts of discrimination. It also should take positive steps (affirmative action) to achieve equality of outcomes for the victims of past acts of discrimination. For example, employers have been required to advertise job openings widely and to advise applicants that they are "equal opportunity employers." These requirements are intended to break up "old boy" hiring networks and prevent discriminatory hiring practices by making the application process open to all. Much more controversial are government programs based on explicit racial and gender distinctions, which give preference in government contracting, university admissions, or employment to minorities and women, even if the individuals themselves have not been personally discriminated against. Proponents of such programs believe that they are essential to overcoming sexism and racism in society and achieving real progress toward equality for women and minorities. Opponents consider these affirmative action programs to be *reverse discrimination,* which is banned by the equal protection clause and the Civil Rights Act of 1964.

The constitutionality of affirmative action programs based on racial and sexual classifications was first confronted by the Supreme Court in the case of Allan Bakke, a white male applicant to the University of California at Davis Medical School. Although qualified for admission, Bakke was rejected and minority applicants with lower grades and interview ratings were admitted under a special program designed to overcome underrepresentation of minorities in the student body. Bakke then claimed reverse discrimination and denial of equal protection under the Constitution. In 1978 the Supreme Court agreed with Bakke and declared the University of California at Davis admission system unconstitutional.[51] It found the university's quota system for admissions to be unreasonable. The Court, however, did not ban all affirmative action programs and held that race could be considered along with other factors in university admissions procedures.

After *Bakke,* the Court further restricted affirmative action programs that imposed strict quotas in the absence of proof of past records of discrimination. Thus in a Richmond, Virginia, case in 1989, the Court held as unconstitutional a city affirmative action plan that required 30 percent of all city contracts to be awarded to minority contractors.[52] In ruling against Richmond's program, the Court indicated that racially based measures would be subjected to strict judicial scrutiny and that to be upheld they would have to be designed carefully to deal with demonstrated past acts of discrimination.

Despite its recent rather skeptical attitude toward some state and local government affirmative action programs, the Court has been more tolerant of race-conscious programs mandated by Congress. In 1980, for example, it upheld a federal public works project that reserved 10 percent of its funds for minority contractors.[53] And in a 1990 decision that surprised many Court watchers, a narrow 5–4 majority of justices upheld a Federal Communications Commission (FCC) program that made minority ownership a special consideration in granting new station licenses and in buying stations that were in danger of losing their licenses. The FCC program was not designed to rectify past acts of discrimination but rather was aimed at promoting minority ownership in the future. The decision of the Court in the FCC case has been interpreted by constitutional lawyers as signaling a green light for federally initiated affirmative action programs.[54]

Controversy also has arisen over implementation of provisions in the 1982 Voting Rights Act designed to assure African Americans and

51. *University of California Regents v. Bakke,* 438 U.S. 265 (1978). Also see Allen P. Sindler, *Bakke, DeFunis, and Minority Admissions: The Quest for Equality* (New York: Longman, 1978).

52. *City of Richmond v. J. A. Croson Co.,* 488 U.S. 469 (1989).

53. *Fullilove v. Klutznick,* 448 U.S. 448 (1980).

54. See the analysis of the FCC decision by Linda Greenhouse, "Justices Bolster Race Preferences at Federal Level," *New York Times,* June 28, 1990, A1, A12, National edition; and Neil A. Lewis, "Ruling on Minority Broadcasting Seen as Aiding Affirmative Action," *New York Times,* July 4, 1990, 8Y, National edition.

North Carolina's 1st and 12th Districts, the Voting Rights Act, and the Supreme Court

The 1st and 12th congressional districts of North Carolina were responses to the Voting Rights Act of 1982 as the state sought to create two minority-majority districts in the congressional redistricting that followed the 1990 census. In *Shaw v. Reno, Attorney General* (1993) the Supreme Court ruled that oddly shaped districts designed to provide a minority majority may constitute grounds for a constitutional challenge under the Fourteenth Amendment's equal protection clause. But the Court also stated that North Carolina's congressional district map might pass constitutional muster if it could be demonstrated that the map was "narrowly tailored to further a compelling governmental interest."

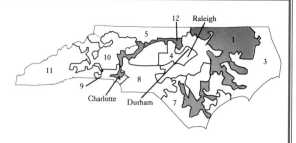

	1st District	12th District
Voting-age population (1990)	399,949	410,871
Percent minority	54	54
Percent African American	53	53
Representative elected in 1992	Eva Clayton (Dem.)	Melvin Watt (Dem.)

other minorities of greater representation in Congress. The act requires states to create majority-minority congressional districts when it is feasible. To comply with the act, North Carolina, after the 1990 census, created two minority-majority districts, including the ribbon-like 12th District of 160 miles that winds through ten counties and is in some places no wider than Interstate 85. But in a narrow 5–4 decision, the Supreme Court held that such "bizarre" districts may unconstitutionally violate the rights of white voters and that states must demonstrate a "compelling interest" in having drawn them in disregard of the traditional districting standards of compactness and contiguity.[55] Justice Sandra Day O'Connor, writing for the Court majority, asserted that by creating legislative districts for people of the same race, North Carolina had engaged in actions that bore "an uncomfortable resemblance to political apartheid." African American members of Congress and civil rights leaders were highly critical of the decision and considered it a setback for the civil rights movement.

The narrow division and sharp disagreements among Supreme Court justices on affirmative action cases mirror the divisiveness of this issue within the public. Only the most reactionary would suggest that no programs are needed to assist minorities in achieving greater economic equality. But whether race- or gender-conscious remedies are appropriate, constitutional, or effective is a source of continuing debate.

55. *Shaw v. Reno, Attorney General,* 509 U.S. ___, 113 S.Ct. 2816, 125 L.Ed. 511 (1993).

Civil Liberties and Civil
Rights, the Constitution,
and Politics

The principles of basic civil liberties, procedural rights, and equality
are enshrined in the Constitution. The language of the Constitution, however, requires application and interpretation. Much of this
responsibility has fallen to the Supreme Court, which, since the 1930s,
has taken on the role of protecting and expanding the liberties and
rights of Americans. But in spite of the simple and straightforward language of the Constitution, Bill of Rights, and such amendments as the
Fourteenth, Americans' civil liberties and civil rights under the Constitution appear to be anything but absolute. Indeed, most government
decision making in this field reflects a balancing of the competing
claims of deeply held traditional values. As a result, civil liberties and
civil rights issues often create emotionally charged controversies such
as those over abortion, prayer in school, flag burning as free speech,
and affirmative action. It is not surprising, therefore, that the nature
and scope of constitutionally protected liberties and rights have
changed over time and will continue to change in response to changing
political conditions—shifts in public thinking, membership changes in
the courts, and congressional and presidential decision making.

For Review

1. The Bill of Rights was added to the Constitution to protect individual
rights from encroachment by the federal government. Since the 1920s the
Fourteenth Amendment's due process clause has been interpreted to include
most of the protections guaranteed in the Bill of Rights and to prevent the
states from infringing on those rights. This process is known as "selective
incorporation." While most of the basic rights—such as freedom of speech,
religion, the press, and assembly—have been incorporated into the Fourteenth Amendment, a few of the rights included in the Bill of Rights do not
apply to the states (for example, indictment by a grand jury).

2. The rights conferred by the Constitution are not absolute, and the
extent of protection afforded by the Constitution has varied over time
depending on political conditions, including the composition of the
Supreme Court. The Court, however, has played a major role, particularly in
the twentieth century, in guaranteeing individual rights and liberties.

3. Controversies over civil rights issues normally occur when cherished
values appear to come into conflict—for example, the right of freedom of
the press versus the need for national security or the right of a person to a
fair trial.

4. With the Supreme Court's abandonment of the separate but equal doctrine in 1954 and the rise of the civil rights and women's movements, the federal government has leaned toward policies aimed at tearing down the barriers represented by racial and other forms of discrimination. These policies, however, continue to stir major controversies within society as illustrated by the ongoing debate over affirmative action programs.

5. Ultimately, the nature of the rights and liberties enjoyed by Americans is determined through the political process.

For Further Reading

Abraham, Henry. *Freedom and the Court.* 5th ed. New York: Oxford University Press, 1988. A survey of judicial decisions on civil liberties.

Alderman, Ellen, and Caroline Kennedy. *In Our Defense: The Bill of Rights in Action.* New York: Morrow, 1991. A series of case studies dealing with Bill of Rights controversies.

Branch, Taylor, *Parting of the Waters: America in the King Years, 1954-1963,* New York: Simon and Schu;ster, 1988. An account of the civil rights movement.

Bullock, Charles S., III, and Charles M. Lamb, eds. *Implementation of Civil Rights Policy.* Monterey, Calif.: Brooks/Cole, 1984. Analyses of the implementation of federal civil rights legislation in the areas of voting, housing, education, and employment.

Carter, Stephen. *Reflections of an Affirmative Action Baby,* New York: Basic Books, 1991. Reflections on affirmative action by an African American attorney.

Cortner, Richard C. *The Supreme Court and the Second Bill of Rights: The Fourteenth Amendment and the Nationalization of Civil Liberties.* Madison: University of Wisconsin Press, 1981. A comprehensive account of the process of incorporating the Bill of Rights into the Fourteenth Amendment.

Faludi, Susan. *Backlash: The Undeclared War against Women.* New York: Crown, 1991. A critical account of society's treatment of women and its response to the women's movement.

Goldstein, Leslie Friedman, *Contemorary Cases in Women's Rights.* Madison: University of Wisconsin Press, 1994. A collection of leading court decisions on women's rights with commentary and interpretation.

Kluger, Richard. *Simple Justice: The History of Brown v. Board of Education and Black America's Struggle for Equality.* New York: Knopf, 1976. An account of the struggle for racial equality with emphasis on the 1954 landmark school desegregation case.

Lewis, Anthony. *Gideon's Trumpet.* New York: Random House, 1964. A detailed account of the Supreme Court's decision to extend the right to counsel to noncapital cases.

Lukas, J. Anthony. *Common Ground.* New York: Knopf, 1985. An account of families affected by the forced busing controversy in Boston.

PART II

Political Participation and Mobilizing Political Influence

5. Public Opinion and
Participation

BECAUSE AMERICAN-STYLE DEMOCRACY is built on the assumption that the people are the source of all governmental authority, public opinion figures prominently in American politicking and policy making. The Framers of the Constitution acknowledged a role for public opinion by calling for popular election of the House of Representatives. Their confidence in the public's ability to decide government policy, however, was not sufficient for them to create a strictly majoritarian democracy. As noted in Chapter 2, the Framers sought instead to create a government that was somewhat insulated from the popular passions of the day through a series of constitutional devices that included separation of powers, checks and balances, indirect election of senators, election of the president by an electoral college, and a judiciary appointed for life.

As the Framers envisioned, the government does not necessarily run the country on the basis of the public's preferences. Indeed, American government institutions—the Congress, president, and courts—frequently differ in how and to what extent they respond to public sentiments. Public opinion is nonetheless an important ingredient of American politics. People's opinions influence their political behavior—whether and how they vote, which political party they support, which interest groups they join, whether they contribute money to a cause or candidate, whether they run for public office. The behavior of public officials, who periodically must face the voters in elections, is also affected by public opinion. For example, when members of Congress find their constituents strongly supportive of the president, they, too, tend to back the chief executive's policies.

Public officials not only take public opinion into account when framing public policy but also try to shape it. For example, President Franklin Roosevelt, through his "fireside chat" radio addresses in the depths of the depression and World War II, and President Ronald Reagan, through television and radio addresses in the 1980s, used their communications skills to strengthen their presidencies.

Because public opinion has such far-reaching consequences for the governing process, this chapter explores the nature of public opinion, how it is measured and shaped, as well as its impact on policy making. The depth and breadth of public influence, however, involve more than citizens just having opinions on public policy issues; they also must act on the basis of their opinions. Government decisions are affected by who actually participates in the political process and by the nature and extent of that participation. Thus, public participation, another essential ingredient of a democratic order, is the focal point of this chapter as well.

What Is Public Opinion?

The term **public opinion** is invoked almost daily in political discourse: "Public Opinion Demands All-out War on Crime!" "Public Opinion Opposes Casino Gambling!" "Public Opinion Supports Increased Federal Funding for AIDs Research!" But invocations of the public's views offer little information about the nature of public opinion. What is the meaning of this concept? *Public opinion* is people's attitudes on an issue or question. Students of political science are particularly concerned about political public opinion—what people think about the issues surrounding politics and government. Such issues are always changing, however, depending on events and circumstances. For example, in the 1950s abortion was rarely high on the list of people's major concerns. But in the 1980s and 1990s heightened concerns about the rights of women and the unborn elevated abortion's position, and it became a highly divisive issue within society.

The General Public and Issue Publics

Public opinion is often viewed as a semiorganic entity that goes through a process of deliberation before reaching a collective decision on an issue. Indeed, the formation of public opinion is likened to the traditional New England town meeting. But large nation-states such as the United States do not operate through national town meetings that discuss, debate, and decide public issues. It is the rare issue that attracts the attention of a majority, let alone all, of the adults in this country. It is seldom, then, that the *general public*—the adult population—takes an interest in an issue.

For most issues the public consists of just those people who are affected by or aware of the issue. There are in fact many publics, each created by an issue that generates interest. These **issue publics** exist for the whole range of public issues—taxes and spending, law and order, health care, welfare, civil rights, education, relations with the republics of the former Soviet Union, the environment. A person can be part of many different issue publics simultaneously.

Public Opinion Polling

Americans are confronted, and often surprised, daily by polling statistics that tell them what they, the public, think about an assortment of public issues. Indeed, public opinion polls themselves are big business in modern-day American politics and corporate life.

Polls are conducted by commercial organizations that sell the results of their work to clients—newspapers, corporations, interest groups—anxious to know the public's thinking. The Gallup, Roper, Harris, and Yankelovich organizations are the best known of the nation's pollsters. Campaign consultants engage in opinion polling as well for their political clients. In fact, few serious candidates for a major elected office undertake campaigns without the advice of pollsters. Major newspapers, news magazines, and television networks also do extensive polling, and the results are a regular feature of their coverage. Even academic institutions, such as the Center for Political Studies (CPS) at the University of Michigan, survey opinion regularly in an effort to develop a database for theoretical explanations of human behavior. Political scientists utilize all of these sources in their work and rely heavily on the CPS studies of voting behavior.

Surveying the Public: A New Science. Knowledge of public opinion has been advanced tremendously by the development in the twentieth century of scientific public opinion surveys or polls. Before scientific polling, it was almost impossible to measure public sentiment reliably.

Most polling organizations rely on telephone polls rather than in-person interviews because they are more economical. Since most American households now have telephones, this survey method does not significantly distort polling results. The recent increased reluctance of people to be interviewed over the phone, however, is worrisome to public opinion analysts. One form of in-person interviewing that has figured more and more in election day surveys is *exit polling*—surveying voters as they leave the polling place about how they voted.

Pollsters normally interview between one thousand and two thousand people in a national survey. But how can such a small group of respondents accurately reflect the views of an entire nation? The answer: it cannot unless the people being interviewed constitute a representative sample of the population whose opinion is being sought. To create such a sample, pollsters use a **probability sampling** procedure in which every person in the population being surveyed has the same chance of being chosen for an interview as everyone else.

A classic example of a nonrepresentative sample that resulted in a distorted picture of public opinion was the 1936 *Literary Digest* poll

BLOOM COUNTY
by Berke Breathed

that predicted that Kansas governor Alfred Landon would win over President Franklin Roosevelt in the presidential election. The *Digest*'s sample had been selected from phone books and automobile registrations, overlooking the fact that in the depths of the depression people with phones and cars were only a fraction of the electorate and certainly not a cross section of American voters.

Drawing a probability sample is a technical matter for which reasonably reliable methodologies have now been developed. All responsible polling organizations take great care to determine that they have a representative sample of the population they are studying. Preelection polls pose special problems for pollsters because not all of the eligible voters will actually vote on election day. Thus, a poll that reports the preferences of all eligible voters presents a potentially inaccurate prediction of the election outcome. To deal with this problem, polling organizations try to interview those people who are most likely to vote.

Most polling organizations rely on *random-digit-dialing* to overcome the problems associated with unlisted telephone numbers—30 percent or more in some areas. Random-digit-dialing typically involves using a computer random-number generator or table of random numbers to select the last four digits of the phone numbers to be called after the area codes and exchanges (the first three digits of a seven-digit phone number) in the area to be surveyed have been identified.

Survey interviews can last from a few minutes to as long as an hour, depending on the amount of information being sought. Most questions are *closed-ended*—that is, the respondent chooses from a predetermined set of possible answers, thereby enhancing the comparability of the responses. A small number of questions may be *open-ended*.

Here respondents are allowed to answer questions in their own words. Open-ended questions may elicit subtle distinctions in people's opinions, but they substantially complicate interpretation and analysis of interview data.

Particular care must be taken that the wording of questions does not bias or influence respondents' answers, which would affect the results of the poll. For example, a 1992 *New York Times*/CBS poll asked respondents: "Are we spending too much, too little, or about the right amount on *assistance to the poor?*" Only 13 percent said that they were spending "too much." But when *"welfare"* was substituted for "assistance to the poor," 44 percent said they were spending "too much."[1]

Accuracy of Polls. As polling techniques have improved, the accuracy of polls has improved. The Gallup poll, for example, has had an average deviation from the actual winning vote in the nine presidential elections since 1960 of only 2.0 percentage points (see Table 5.1). Inaccurate polls might stem from a **sampling error**—the degree to which the sample can be expected to vary from the total population being studied. National surveys typically have a sampling error of about 4 percent. This means that if 55 percent of the respondents prefer the Republican candidate, the actual value is likely to be in the range of 51 to 59 percent (55 percent plus or minus 4 percent).[2] Inaccurate poll results also might stem from a faulty questionnaire, sloppy interview procedures, and mistakes in interpreting and analyzing survey responses. An analytical error, for example, occurred in the Gallup poll's final estimate of the 1992 presidential vote because of the unprecedented independent candidacy of Ross Perot, who received equal status with the major party nominees in the presidential debates and had a record advertising budget. Based on the past performance of independent candidates, the Gallup organization decided to allocate none of the undecided voters to Perot. As a result, Gallup overestimated Clinton's vote by almost 6 percentage points.[3]

This example demonstrates that it is hazardous to predict on the basis of polls what the public's opinions or behavior will be at some time in the future; the public's views can change dramatically in a short period of time. For example, President Clinton's public approval rating dropped from 58 to 37 percent (minus 21 points) in the Gallup poll between January and June of his first year in office, but by December it

1. *New York Times,* July 5, 1992, 1, National edition.
2. Herbert Asher, *Polling and the Public: What Every Citizen Should Know,* 2d ed. (Washington, D.C.: CQ Press, 1992), 58–66.
3. *Gallup Poll Monthly,* November 1992, 33.

Table 5.1 Accuracy of Gallup Poll in Presidential Elections, 1960–1992 (*percent of votes cast*)

Year	Final Gallup Survey		Election Results		Deviation
	Percentage	Candidate selected	Percentage	President elected	
1960	51.0	Kennedy	50.1	Kennedy	+0.9
1964	64.0	Johnson	61.3	Johnson	+2.7
1968	43.0	Nixon	43.5	Nixon	−0.5
1972	62.0	Nixon	61.8	Nixon	+0.2
1976	48.0	Carter	50.0	Carter	−2.0
1980	47.0	Reagan	50.8	Reagan	−3.8
1984	59.0	Reagan	59.1	Reagan	−0.1
1988	56.0	Bush	53.9	Bush	+2.1
1992	49.0	Clinton	43.2	Clinton	+5.8

Source: *Gallup Poll Monthly,* November 1992, 33.

had climbed up to 54 percent.[4] A poll is only a snapshot of opinions at the time it was taken, and its validity cannot be extended into time.

Dimensions of Public Opinion

In 1989 members of the House of Representatives voted to reject a 50 percent raise in their own pay. Underpaid compared with individuals in the private sector, they nevertheless bowed to public opposition to the salary boost. Why did they turn down what a government panel and many political commentators saw as a justified raise? The answer: an overwhelming proportion of the public was strongly opposed, and elected officials take the direction, intensity, and other dimensions of public opinion into account in their decision making.

The *direction* of public opinion is simply whether people view an issue or action favorably or unfavorably. Surveys of public opinion can provide information on the yes-no dimension: how people align themselves on such issues as the death penalty, affirmative action, abortion, implementation of an energy tax to reduce the budget deficit, or aid for Russia.

A related and critical aspect of public opinion is the *distribution,* or extent, of agreement or consensus on an issue, with opinions clustering on one side or the other of the yes-no dimension. Like the congressional pay raise controversy, some issues evoke high levels of agreement. Other issues are highly divisive (see the examples in Figure 5.1). When a high level of consensus exists on an issue, government policy

4. Gallup poll surveys, reported in *American Enterprise,* May/June 1993, 91; September/October 1993, 104; and January/February 1994, 83.

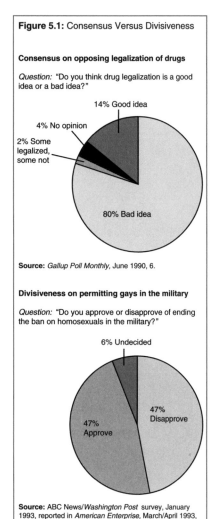

Figure 5.1: Consensus Versus Divisiveness

Consensus on opposing legalization of drugs

Question: "Do you think drug legalization is a good idea or a bad idea?"

14% Good idea

4% No opinion

2% Some legalized, some not

80% Bad idea

Source: *Gallup Poll Monthly,* June 1990, 6.

Divisiveness on permitting gays in the military

Question: "Do you approve or disapprove of ending the ban on homosexuals in the military?"

6% Undecided

47% Disapprove

47% Approve

Source: ABC News/*Washington Post* survey, January 1993, reported in *American Enterprise,* March/April 1993, 83.

makers usually find it wise to follow public opinion. For example, when crime became a prime concern in 1993 and the Gallup poll showed that 88 percent of the public was in favor of imposing a waiting period for the purchase of a handgun, Congress finally overcame its long-standing reluctance to offend the pro-gun lobby and by wide margins in both chambers enacted the long-delayed Brady bill. Named for former presidential press secretary James Brady, who was permanently disabled by a handgun bullet during the 1981 attempt to assassinate Ronald Reagan, this legislation requires a five-day waiting period for the purchase of a handgun.

When opinions divide and the public's feelings are strong, outcomes are less certain. Thus, when Bill Clinton proposed in the first days of his presidency to implement a campaign pledge to lift the ban on homosexuals in the military, he created a firestorm of controversy that revealed a deeply divided public (see Figure 5.1). Stands were adamantly taken—87 percent of those opposed to his policy felt strongly about the issue as did 63 percent of those in support of his policy. Based, then, on the public's response and the opposition of senior military personnel and such influential senators as Armed Services Committee chairman Sam Nunn (D-Ga.), Clinton was forced to back down and settle for modestly revised policy under which homosexual conduct would still be prohibited, but recruits would no longer be asked if they were gay.

The *saliency,* or importance, of an issue is another dimension of public opinion. People differ in the extent to which they find an issue salient. For National Rifle Association (NRA) members, for example, gun control is extremely salient. In the same way, retired people care more about cost-of-living adjustments to Social Security benefits than do working parents, who find tax deductions for child care expenses more important than do retirees. For the public as a whole the saliency of issues changes over time. Thus, at the beginning of the Reagan administration in 1981 the Gallup poll reported that 72 percent of Americans believed inflation to be the most important problem facing the nation, but by 1988, when the inflation rate was down to 4.1 percent from 13.5 percent, only 2 percent of the people gave it such importance.[5]

The *intensity* of public opinion can vary as well—people may feel strongly about some issues and not so strongly about others (such issues as abortion, which involve moral questions, are likely to generate

5. Gallup poll data, reported in *Public Opinion,* July/August 1988, 34–35.

At a 1993 Capitol Hill news conference designed to gain public support for the Brady gun control bill, Rep. Charles Schumer (D-N.Y.) and Sarah and James Brady announce the introduction of the bill. While serving as presidential press secretary, Brady was disabled by a handgun bullet during an attempted assassination of President Ronald Reagan.

the most impassioned opinions).[6] Those who feel strongly about an issue are more likely to act on their sentiments and participate in the political process than those whose views are weakly held. The impact of public opinion is, then, influenced by the strength of commitment people give to a cause, with the result that small but energetic minorities often have an influence well out of proportion to their numbers. Understanding the intensity with which people hold and act on their opinions helps to explain why policy positions opposed by a majority of the people can become public policy. For example, polls show that at least two-thirds of the public support tougher gun control legislation.[7] But deeply committed opponents, led by the National Rifle Association, have blocked most new bills (with the exception of the Brady bill) that would strengthen gun control laws and have even succeeded in weakening previously passed laws. The NRA efforts have included advertising campaigns, campaign contributions, and aggressive lobbying, with their members deluging members of Congress with mail against gun control. By contrast, people favoring tougher gun laws have generally not felt strongly enough about the issue to act on their convictions.

A final dimension of public opinion is its *stability*—the public's

6. Robert E. Lane and David O. Sears, *Public Opinion* (Englewood Cliffs, N.J.: Prentice-Hall, 1964), 9.

7. Gallup surveys, reported in *American Enterprise*, July/August 1991, 79.

opinion on an issue can change over time, occasionally with amazing rapidity. For example, President George Bush's public approval ratings were a roller coaster ride. His rating dropped 23 percentage points in the fall of 1990 from 76 to 53 percent after he reneged on his "Read my lips, no new taxes" campaign pledge and negotiated a budget compromise with congressional Democrats. But in the aftermath of victory in the 1991 Persian Gulf War, he rebounded to a record 89 percent approval rating, which proceeded to fall precipitously to 33 percent by August 1992 as the public's anxiety over the state of the economy grew.[8] Similarly, America stopped embracing an isolationist foreign policy in one day on December 7, 1941, when the Japanese bombed Pearl Harbor. Although these examples suggest a high level of volatility in public opinion, studies show that American opinion on many issues exhibits a substantial level of stability and that change in public attitudes tends to occur gradually.[9] Thus, since 1972 the public has overwhelmingly supported allowing a woman to have an abortion when there is a strong chance of a serious birth defect or when the pregnancy stems from rape. At the same time, a majority of Americans have consistently opposed permitting abortions sought when, for example, a married woman does not want any more children.[10]

Another aspect of the stability dimension is that a public once divided on an issue can over time achieve a high level of agreement. For example, in 1942 only 30 percent of whites said that they thought white and black students should go to the same schools. Yet by 1984, 90 percent of whites said that they accepted integrated schools. Analysis of these data, however, showed that whites were not monolithic in their racial attitudes. Differences in attitudes stemmed from people's diverse social backgrounds and life experiences.[11] An exploration of public opinion, therefore, must consider **political socialization**—the learning process through which people acquire political attitudes.

8. Gallup surveys, reported in *American Enterprise*, November/December 1990, 92, and March/April 1991, 91; and *Washington Post*, Aug. 17, 1992, A11.

9. Benjamin I. Page and Robert Y. Shapiro, "Changes in American Policy Preferences, 1935-1979," *Public Opinion Quarterly* 46 (Spring 1982): 24-42; and James A. Stimson, *Public Opinion in America: Moods, Cycles, and Swings* (Boulder, Colo.: Westview Press, 1991).

10. National Opinion Research Center data, reported in *American Enterprise*, July/August 1990, 103.

11. Tom W. Smith and Paul B. Sheatsley, "American Attitudes toward Race Relations," *Public Opinion*, November/December 1984, 15, 51-53.

Acquiring Political Attitudes: Political Socialization

As people go through life they acquire an awareness of, facts about, and values related to politics. Much of this process of political socialization is incidental as, for example, children observe, listen to, and imitate their parents. Although early childhood is important in shaping such basic attitudes as attachment to one's country and feelings toward government and authority, political socialization is a life-long process. Among the agents of political socialization are the family, schools, peers, the mass media, and leaders.

Childhood Socialization

The impact of the family on political attitudes is profound. It is the family that first interprets the world for a child and, presumably, acquaints that child with certain moral, religious, social, economic, and political values. Moreover, when parents are interested in politics, this interest tends to be passed on to their children.[12]

Parents also often pass on to their children a political attitude that is important in understanding political behavior: party identification—a feeling of attachment to and sympathy for a political party. As early as the third grade children frequently think of themselves as Democrats or Republicans. Family influence on party identification is greatest when both parents agree on their partisan preference. When the father and mother do not agree, mothers are likely to have a greater influence than fathers (reflecting the traditional tendency of mothers to spend more time with children than fathers). Although the maternal influence is present for both boys and girls, it is especially strong on the daughters of college-educated, politically active mothers.[13]

The parental influence on a child's party identification is strong, but research indicates that this influence decreases as children get older and are subjected to influences outside the family. Children, however, are more likely to change from partisans to independents than they are to go through a conversion process and affiliate with the other party.

12. W. Russell Neuman, *The Paradox of Mass Politics: Knowledge and Opinion in the American Electorate* (Cambridge, Mass.: Harvard University Press, 1986), 113–114.

13. M. Kent Jennings and Kenneth P. Langton, "Mothers versus Fathers: The Foundations of Political Orientations among Young Americans," *Journal of Politics* 31 (May 1969): 329–358. Important studies of children's political socialization include those by Fred I. Greenstein, *Children and Politics* (New Haven, Conn.: Yale University Press, 1965); and Robert D. Hess and Judith V. Torney, *The Development of Political Attitudes in Children* (Chicago: Aldine, 1967).

When the conversion does occur, it normally can be attributed to economic issues.[14] Parents' influence on their child's party identification is strengthened when it is reinforced, or at least not contradicted, by the messages received from other participants in the child's environment such as friends or neighbors.[15]

Political learning occurs in the schools as well. Schools normally do not make a conscious effort to promote a preference for a political party or a specific viewpoint on issues. Rather, they tend to present children with the facts about their country and its political system and, in the process, foster patriotism and support for the institutions of government. The picture presented of American government in the early grades is beneficent and positive, with the president often viewed as a benevolent leader. Although the high schools continue the process of political education through American history and civics courses, such courses have been found to have only a modest influence on students' political interest, tolerance for differing opinions, trust in government, or inclination to participate in politics.[16]

Adolescents' almost slavish conformity in their clothing and hairstyles, as well as their musical tastes, is strong evidence of the impact that peer pressure, too, has on young people's attitudes and behavior. This influence is more limited, however, in the realm of political attitudes. One of the factors contributing to the only modest influence that peers have on adolescent political attitudes is the relatively low salience of politics to adolescents' lives. It has little to do with their day-to-day concerns or their status in the peer group.[17]

Politics is apt to take on greater relevance at the college level where peer pressures can have a big impact on students' political attitudes. In his classic study of peer group influence, Theodore Newcombe examined the political attitudes of women attending Bennington College, an

14. Russell J. Dalton, "Reassessing Parental Socialization: Indicator Unreliability versus Generational Transfer," *American Political Science Review* 74 (June 1980): 421–431.

15. Robert C. Luskin, John P. McIver, and Edward G. Carmines, "Issues and the Transmission of Partisanship," *American Journal of Political Science* 33 (May 1989): 440–458. Also see Richard G. Niemi and M. Kent Jennings, "Issues and Inheritance in the Formation of Party Identification," *American Journal of Political Science* 35 (November 1991): 970–988.

16. Kenneth P. Langton and M. Kent Jennings, "Political Socialization and the High School Civics Curriculum in the United States," *American Political Science Review* 62 (September 1968): 852–877.

17. M. Kent Jennings and Richard G. Niemi, *The Political Character of Adolescence* (Princeton, N.J.: Princeton University Press, 1974), 243.

In an effort to reach young voters through television, their preferred communications medium, both Gov. Bill Clinton and President George Bush campaigned on MTV during 1992.

exclusive liberal arts college in Vermont, in the 1930s. These students' political attitudes were affected significantly by Bennington's politically liberal culture. Indeed, during their years there many of the women students became a great deal more liberal than their generally well-to-do and conservative parents. Twenty-five years later in a follow-up study Newcombe found that Bennington alumnae retained the liberalism of their college days because it was reinforced by their spouses and adult peers.[18]

The mass media—television, newspapers, magazines, radio—are another influential agent of political socialization. Teachers, especially, rely heavily on the media for the information and values they transmit to their students. Outside the classroom children's direct exposure to the media is extensive. In winter, children from ages two to eleven log an average thirty-one hours a week watching television, and average high school graduates spend fifteen thousand hours watching television compared with eleven thousand hours in the classroom. The media's impact, then, is substantial. When asked to identify sources of

18. Theodore M. Newcombe, *Persistence and Social Change: Bennington College and Its Students after Twenty-five Years* (New York: Wiley, 1967); and Duane F. Alwin, Ronald L. Cohen, and Theodore M. Newcombe, *Political Attitudes over the Life Span: The Bennington Women after Fifty Years* (Madison: University of Wisconsin Press, 1991).

information on which they base their attitudes, high school students mention the mass media more often than families, teachers, friends, or personal experiences. According to media analyst Doris Graber, young people who are heavy users of the media show greater understanding and support for basic American values, such as freedom of speech and the right to equal and fair treatment, than children who are light media users (see Chapter 9 for a more detailed look at the role of the media in American politics).[19]

Adult Socialization

The shaping of basic political beliefs, values, and attitudes does not stop with graduation from high school or college. But the influences that were the most prominent in youth—parents, school, childhood peers—recede and are replaced by daily events and experiences, the mass media, political leaders, and new peer groups such as coworkers, neighbors, friends, and fellow church and club members.

As people grow older their politically relevant experiences abound. They encounter the Internal Revenue Service, military recruiting, government-influenced mortgage rates, Social Security and Medicare, and economic setbacks. The impressions gained from these experiences and interactions with peers continue to shape people's political attitudes. The daily hardships of the depression of the 1930s, for example, caused people to change their views about the role of government. Unlike in earlier times, they now expected the government to manage the economy and provide social services. Likewise, over fifty years later people's assessment of their own and the nation's well-being played critical roles in the electoral victories of Ronald Reagan (1980) and Bill Clinton (1992) over Democrat Jimmy Carter and Republican George Bush, incumbent presidents who were held accountable by the voters for economic hard times.

Personal experiences, however, are quite limited compared to the range of politically relevant experiences that are provided by the mass media. Throughout adulthood, as in childhood, people consume the media in massive doses: in a day the average adult spends more than four hours in front of a television, over two hours listening to a radio, and eighteen to forty-five minutes reading a newspaper. As a result, much of what the average person learns about politics is absorbed from both the media's factual news programs and its fictional sitcoms

19. The impact of the media on childhood socialization is ably summarized by Doris A. Graber, *Mass Media and American Politics,* 4th ed. (Washington, D.C.: CQ Press, 1993), 204–206.

and soap operas. As for the latter, viewers of soap operas may well conclude that most politicians are crooked—since most shown on such programs are.[20]

Media news coverage is a major force in shaping the people's perceptions of reality. For example, the public's perception that the economy was in desperate straits during the 1992 presidential election campaign was a major factor in Bill Clinton's defeat of President George Bush. Interestingly, however, objective economic data showed that the economy was beginning to grow, though sluggishly, in late 1991 and more robustly in 1992. Yet content analysis revealed that news coverage of the economy by ABC, CBS, and NBC was overwhelmingly (96 percent) negative and pessimistic in the July-September quarter of 1992. Public opinion analyst Everett Carll Ladd has concluded that this almost uninterrupted stream of negative press reports and commentary on the nation's economy was the "most important political event of the 1992 campaign." He stresses, however, that this kind of reporting was not caused by some media plot to elect Bill Clinton but rather by the coming together of three elements: journalists feeling closer to the stands of Democrats than those of Republicans; a sense that after twelve years the Republicans and their economic policies had become an old, tired news story; and the fact that "the economy in shambles" was an inherently more interesting story than "some problems, but also many economic strengths."[21]

People's attitudes are affected as well by the actions and statements of political leaders, particularly the president. One of the most dramatic changes in public opinion began in the early 1970s when President Richard Nixon, a man whose entire public career had been built on staunch anticommunism, began the process of normalizing diplomatic relations with the communist government of the People's Republic of China. Virtually overnight, American opinion changed from that of overwhelming opposition to that of heightened tolerance toward and interest in the communist government on mainland China. The actions of successive presidents to strengthen diplomatic, economic, and cultural ties with China continued to garner widespread public support until June 1989 when the communist government brutally repressed pro-democracy demonstrations.

Presidential leadership of public opinion is most effective when the

20. Ibid., 206–207.

21. Everett Carll Ladd, "The 1992 Vote for President Clinton: Another Brittle Mandate?" *Political Science Quarterly* 108 (Spring 1993): 1–28.

president is riding a crest of popularity. During times of declining popular support, however, the president finds it difficult to sway the public. Even as effective a communicator as Ronald Reagan could not—as his popularity fell during the 1982 recession—muster support for a constitutional amendment that permitted prayer in the public schools.[22]

Social Groups and Political Opinions

No two Americans have identical political socialization experiences. People with similar social backgrounds, however, are apt to share some political opinions, which are likely to differ from the views of people with different backgrounds. Differences in education, income or class, ethnicity, race, religion, region, and gender can produce distinctive political orientations.

Education

Education increases people's interest in and understanding of politics and affects the political attitudes that they develop. College graduates, on the one hand, profess greater support for civil liberties and have more tolerant racial attitudes than people who attended but did not graduate from college.[23] The better-educated also are more likely to support environmental protection measures, space research, and affirmative action hiring programs for women and minorities. But, on the other hand, the more highly educated appear to be less supportive of extending the government's role in providing social services. They also are less likely to back such conservative social policy agenda items as permitting prayer in the public schools or banning abortion counseling (see Table 5.2).

Income and Social Class

Income and social class affect people's views on a range of issues. Those in the higher-income bracket—as opposed to lower-income earners—are somewhat more supportive of racial and sexual equality, tolerant of diverse views, internationalist in foreign affairs, and conservative on social welfare issues. The higher education level characteristic of the well-to-do appears to be a major factor in their liberalism on noneconomic issues; income affects their views on social welfare is-

22. Benjamin I. Page, Robert Y. Shapiro, and Glenn R. Dempsey, "What Moves Public Opinion?" *American Political Science Review* 81 (March 1987): 37.

23. On the effect of education on support for civil liberties, see Herbert McClosky and Alida Brill, *Dimensions of Tolerance: What Americans Believe about Civil Liberties* (New York: Russell Sage Foundation, 1983), 250–251, 370–371, 420–422.

Table 5.2 Level of Education and Public Opinion (*percent*)

Opinion	College Degree	Less Than College Degree	High School Graduate	Did Not Complete High School
Favor allowing women in the military to take combat jobs	62	59	58	33
Favor allowing gays to serve in the military	60	50	50	30
Favor allowing doctors/health care workers at federally funded clinics to discuss abortion with patients as a family planning option	76	72	60	45
Favor prayer in public schools	57	64	77	77
Favor increased government spending for food programs for low-income families	36	44	45	53

Sources: First three issues: *Gallup Poll Monthly*, November 1992, 21; remaining issues: *Gallup Report*, No. 274, July 1988, 5–17.

sues.[24] In contrast to the situations found in many Western nations, class-based differences do not greatly divide American society. For example, a recent nine-nation study revealed that in spite of great income disparities in the United States, only 29 percent of Americans supported the notion that it is government's responsibility to reduce the differences between those at the upper and lower ends of the income scale. In contrast, income redistribution was supported by 82 percent of the respondents in Italy, 65 percent in the Netherlands, and 64 percent in Great Britain (see Figure 5.2).

Ethnicity and Race

America is frequently called a nation of immigrants, and with each new wave of immigration the mix of nationalities becomes more varied. Most of the earliest settlers came from England, Scotland, and Wales, followed by those from Ireland, Germany, and Scandinavia. During the late nineteenth and early twentieth centuries, immigrants from eastern and southern Europe—Poles, Italians, Russians—predominated. The cultural and religious differences between immigrants

24. For a summary of the relationship between class and political opinions, see Robert S. Erikson, Norman R. Luttbeg, and Kent L. Tedin, *American Public Opinion*, 4th ed. (New York: Macmillan, 1991), 168–176.

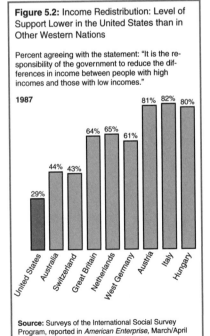

Figure 5.2: Income Redistribution: Level of Support Lower in the United States than in Other Western Nations

Percent agreeing with the statement: "It is the responsibility of the government to reduce the differences in income between people with high incomes and those with low incomes."

1987

United States 29%
Australia 44%
Switzerland 43%
Great Britain 64%
Netherlands 65%
West Germany 61%
Austria 81%
Italy 82%
Hungary 80%

Source: Surveys of the International Social Survey Program, reported in *American Enterprise*, March/April 1990, 113.

with eastern and southern European backgrounds and those of English heritage have been a basis for political division within the United States. For example, immigrants from eastern and southern Europe provided essential support for the New Deal Democratic coalition forged by President Franklin Roosevelt in the 1930s, and those of British heritage traditionally have constituted an important base of Republican voting strength.

Although differences in voting patterns among voters of European heritage are still detectable, these differences are diminishing as these older immigrant groups become assimilated into American society. Public opinion surveys do show modest differences in thinking, however, among European ethnic groups on issues of government responsibility for health care, improved living standards for the poor, and a more equitable distribution of income. For example, persons with British ancestry are less likely to support government social welfare programs than those with southern and eastern European roots.[25]

The current tide of immigrants from Spanish-speaking (Hispanic) countries in this hemisphere—particularly Mexico and Central America—and from Asia is showing distinctive political attitudes and partisan preferences as well. Reflecting the relatively less well-off economic positions of these "new ethnics," Mexican-Americans, for example, are more highly supportive of extending government services and of the Democratic party than are the "old ethnics" from eastern and southern Europe. The political attitudes of Mexican-Americans also differ from those of another Hispanic group, the Cuban-Americans, who, with their fierce anticommunist stance and generally higher standard of living, are predominantly Republican.

African Americans constitute the country's largest racial minority (over 12 percent) with other nonwhites (Asians and Native Americans) making up approximately 3 percent. Both African Americans and Asians are expanding segments of the population. According to numerous surveys conducted by the National Opinion Research Center, African Americans and other racial minorities tend to have some political attitudes in common. But in contrast to older European ethnics and Hispanics, African Americans are more likely to believe that government should assume a larger responsibility for solving the country's problems, helping the poor, reducing income differences between rich and poor, and providing health care.

25. For a survey of attitudes by ethnic groups, see *Public Opinion*, October/November 1984, 26–27.

Religion

America is a predominantly Protestant nation with 56 percent professing a Protestant religious preference, followed by Catholics, 25 percent; Jewish, 2 percent; other religions, 6 percent; and no religious preference, 11 percent. Some of the differences in attitudes and partisan preferences found among people of various religious faiths can be traced to historic causes. Most Catholic immigrants, for example, arrived in the United States at a time when Protestants and Republicans dominated the nation's political and economic life. This fact, as well as the limited discrimination to which Catholics were once subjected, has left traces of liberal and pro-Democratic sentiment among Catholics. The 1928 election also helped to forge an electoral bond between Catholics and the Democratic party. In that year the Democratic governor of New York, Al Smith, became the first Catholic to be a major party presidential nominee. The unique history of Jews as a persecuted minority also has had an impact on their political views; centuries of antisemitism have tended to drive them in a liberal direction, especially on civil liberties issues.

Doctrinal differences among religions have political relevance as well. The Catholic church has taken a strong stand against abortion and birth control, and the emphasis Protestants place on individual responsibility for one's economic and spiritual well-being may predispose them toward conservative positions on economic issues. Fundamentalist Protestants show a particularly conservative orientation. They overwhelmingly favor prayer in public schools and oppose abortion.

One of the most striking recent developments about religion and politics is the close relationship between frequency of church attendance and partisan choice. According to the 1992 election data, among whites Republicans fare much better with the "churched" portion of the electorate than with the "less churched" and "unchurched" (Table 5.3). African Americans, including regular churchgoers, however, are overwhelmingly Democratic, as are Jewish voters.

Region

Regional differences of opinion have been periodic sources of conflict since the earliest days of the American political system.[26] The Civil War was the most dramatic instance in American history of issues

26. For a detailed analysis of sectional conflicts in American politics, see Richard F. Bensel, *Sectionalism and American Political Development, 1880–1980* (Madison: University of Wisconsin Press, 1984).

Table 5.3 The "Churched" and the "Unchurched": Church Attendance and Partisan Preferences, 1992 *(percent)*

	Percent of Electorate	Voted for			Party Identification		
		Clinton(D)	Bush (R)	Perot (I)	Dem.	Rep.	Ind.
White Protestants who attend church each week	17	27	59	14	26	50	24
White Protestants who do not attend church each week	20	39	37	23	34	42	24
White Catholics who attend church each week	11	39	41	20	42	32	26
White Catholics who do not attend church each week	12	44	33	24	40	33	26
All whites	85	39	40	20	34	38	28
African Americans who attend church each week	4	85	9	6	79	7	13
All African Americans	10	83	10	7	75	8	17
Jews	3	80	11	9	65	13	21
Religion: "None"	6	59	19	22	40	18	42

Source: Voter Research and Surveys, reported in *Public Perspective*, March/April 1993, 9. Reprinted by courtesy of *The Public Perspective* magazine, a publication of the Roper Center for Public Opinion Research, Storrs, Conn.

aligning one region against another, and that war and its aftermath left their marks on American politics for over a century. After the war, small-town, white Protestant, middle-class conservatives, who might otherwise have been Republicans, created a one-party Democratic stronghold in the South. But, as the memories of the Civil War faded, northerners migrated to the South, and the region's per capita income disadvantages began to diminish after World War II, the partisanship of whites changed and some of the distinctiveness of southern attitudes receded. Southerners, however, continue to hold more conservative views on most issues than people from other regions. They are more likely to consider themselves conservatives, to trust the Republicans to deal with the country's most important problems, to oppose abortion, to favor prayer in the public schools, to oppose homosexual relations, and to support defense expenditures.[27] Liberalism on social issues tends to be bicoastal, with New England and the Pacific Coast standing out as being the most supportive of women's rights, the right to an abortion, and other issues on the social agenda. The East is also more liberal on economic issues. On civil rights the South is more conservative than the rest of the nation.

Although the unique histories and cultures of the states have an impact on the political outlooks of their residents, powerful forces in American society are undermining these regional influences. For

27. Regional attitudes on a range of social and foreign policy issues are summarized in *Public Opinion*, January/February 1988, 28–29; and Erikson et al., *American Public Opinion*, 194–198.

example, the mobility of Americans (approximately 20 percent move each year) is diluting the homogeneity of regional populations, and the national media, which have made their way into living rooms across the country, are diminishing the uniqueness of regional influences.[28]

Gender

Because men and women go through differing processes of political socialization even though they may share common racial, social class, ethnic, and religious backgrounds, they do not have the same attitudes about some issues. The most frequently noted difference in attitude has been toward the Democratic party: in the 1980s and in 1992 a higher proportion of women than men supported Democratic candidates. As a result, the term *gender gap* entered the political vocabulary. Women are less apt than men to be supportive of military expenditures and the use of force in international affairs and are more apt to be supportive of gun control and social welfare spending.[29] Not all issues, however, are gender-sensitive. On the questions of increased spending for education and family leave legislation, no significant gender differences emerge (see Table 5.4).

Table 5.4 Differences in the Political Opinions of Male and Female Registered Voters (*percent*)

Opinion	Males	Females
Favor increased spending for the U.S. space program	34	17
Support increased government spending to improve medical and health care for Americans generally	64	70
Support increased government spending for food programs for low-income families	40	47
Support increased government spending to improve the quality of public education	65	67
Favor requiring companies to allow employees twelve weeks of unpaid leave for a new baby or a serious illness in the family	74	77
Believe Anita Hill's charge of sexual harassment against Supreme Court nominee Clarence Thomas	39	46
Approve of U.S. having gone to war against Iraq	84	68
Voted for Bill Clinton	41	45

Sources: *Gallup Report*, No. 274, July 1988, 5–8; *Gallup Poll Monthly*, November 1992, 21; October 1992, 35; ABC News/*Washington Post* poll, January 16, 1991, reported in *American Enterprise*, March/April 1991, 86; and Voter Research and Surveys exit polls.

28. For a summary of research findings on the impact of geography on political views, see Erikson et al., *American Public Opinion*, 194–198; on the impact of individual state political cultures, see Robert S. Erikson, John P. McIver, and Gerald C. Wright, "State Political Culture and Public Opinion," *American Political Science Review* 81 (September 1987): 797–814.

29. For a concise consideration of gender and political opinions, see Erikson et al., *American Public Opinion*, 198–201.

Political Ideology in America

This chapter began with a look at the forces that shape the values and differences of opinion that exist among various demographic groups in American society. But what are the beliefs that structure people's political thinking? Such an organized and coherent set of attitudes about government and public policy is known as a **political ideology**. In America, people with a liberal ideology traditionally have supported a strong national government that actively promotes social welfare and equality and intervenes to regulate the economy. Conservatives, by contrast, have believed that government should have a limited role in regulating the economy and providing social services. They have stressed that people are primarily responsible for their own welfare.

Ideological Self-identification

Americans' descriptions of their own ideological positions changed relatively little from the 1970s to the 1990s (see Figure 5.3). Although there was some growth of conservative sentiment in the 1980s, the proportions of the public considering themselves liberal, moderate, and conservative tended to remain stable, with moderates consistently constituting the largest category. The significance of such ideological self-identification data is limited, however, because many people do not understand the meaning of the categories. For example, some self-identified conservatives are supportive of such "liberal" policies as increased federal spending for health, the elderly, and education.[30]

Dimensions of Liberalism and Conservatism

A further difficulty in determining the meaning of people's ideological self-identification stems from the way in which political discourse has changed since the 1950s. During the 1950s and until the mid-1960s **liberalism** and **conservatism** pertained primarily to a single dimension of public policy—the scope of government involvement in the economy and society. Since the 1960s, however, this traditional distinction between liberalism and conservatism has been overlaid with additional policy dimensions. In foreign policy, for example, conservatism is now equated with supporting military expenditures, showing a

30. For an early confirmation of Americans' tendencies to view themselves as conservatives in the abstract but to be liberal regarding specific policies, see Lloyd Free and Hadley Cantril, *The Political Beliefs of Americans* (New York: Simon and Schuster, 1968), chap. 3.

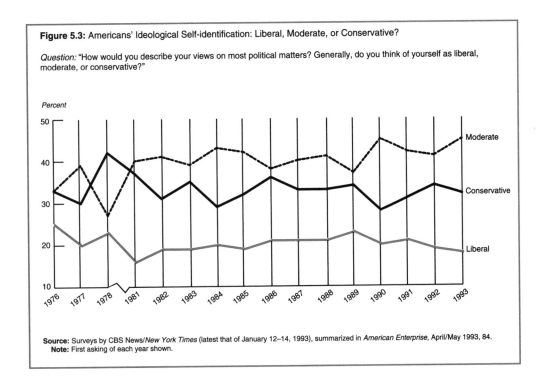

Figure 5.3: Americans' Ideological Self-identification: Liberal, Moderate, or Conservative?

Question: "How would you describe your views on most political matters? Generally, do you think of yourself as liberal, moderate, or conservative?"

Source: Surveys by CBS News/*New York Times* (latest that of January 12–14, 1993), summarized in *American Enterprise*, April/May 1993, 84.
Note: First asking of each year shown.

greater willingness to use military force in international affairs, and giving the president the primary role in formulating policy in international affairs. By contrast, liberalism is equated with giving less priority to military expenditures, exhibiting greater reluctance to use military power, and giving Congress a substantial role in the shaping of foreign policy. There is also a social policy dimension to use of the terms *liberalism* and *conservatism*. On so-called lifestyle issues—abortion, law and order, prayer in the public schools, women's rights, gay rights, pornography—conservatives show a greater willingness to permit government intervention to regulate human conduct than do liberals.[31]

This multidimensional nature of liberalism and conservatism in current political discourse, then, makes it increasingly difficult for people to place themselves accurately on a liberal-conservative continuum. It also means that a person might take a traditionally liberal position on issues relating to the government's social welfare responsibilities, yet at the same time support such conservative lifestyle positions as advo-

31. A discussion of how the meanings of liberalism and conservatism have changed since the 1950s is included in Herbert A. Asher, *Presidential Elections and American Politics: Voters, Candidates, and Campaigns since 1952*, 5th ed. (Pacific Grove, Calif.: Brooks/Cole, 1992), 24–28.

cating prayer in the public schools, taking a hard line on law and order, and opposing abortion. Indeed, it was just such lifestyle issues that gave more recent Republican presidential candidates Richard Nixon, Ronald Reagan, and George Bush an opening wedge with which to split off traditional Democratic voters from their party. In 1992, however, the Republicans' attempt to place "lifestyle" issues within the context of "family values" proved much less effective in motivating Democrats to defect from their party because of people's anxiety over the state of the economy.

Extent of Ideological Thinking in America

Although students of public opinion have engaged in a lively debate about the extent of the ideological thinking of the American public, the evidence indicates that the level of ideological thinking among Americans is not high. In 1992, for example, self-identified liberals split their votes among Democrat Bill Clinton (68 percent), Republican George Bush (14 percent), and independent Ross Perot (18 percent), while 18 percent of conservatives voted for Clinton, 64 percent for Bush, and 18 percent for Perot. In 1988 only 18 percent of the voters used such terms as *liberal* or *conservative* in evaluating candidates and issues; the number was even lower—12 percent—in 1956.[32] But surveys done in the 1960s and 1970s found a higher level of ideological awareness among Americans. Thus, the voters' use of ideology-based evaluations of presidential candidates and parties hit levels of 27 percent in 1964, 26 percent in 1968, and 22 percent in 1972.[33]

The reasons for this rise in ideological thinking are not altogether clear, but it is likely that the high-voltage political environment of the 1960s and 1970s had an impact. The 1964, 1968, and 1972 elections took place in the super-charged and often polarizing atmosphere of civil rights demonstrations, urban riots, and the Vietnam War. Moreover, these elections were characterized by sharp policy differences between the presidential candidates. For example, the 1964 Republican nominee, conservative senator Barry Goldwater (Ariz.), offered Americans "a choice not an echo" as he campaigned against a committed liberal Democrat, President Lyndon Johnson. Not all public opinion analysts, however, are prepared to acknowledge that Americans became more ideological in the 1960s and 1970s. Some skeptics believe that reworded

---

32. Angus Campbell et al., *The American Voter* (New York: Wiley, 1960), chap. 10.
33. The research of John C. Pierce and Paul R. Hagner is summarized in Asher, *Presidential Elections and American Politics*, 109.

survey questions were responsible for the findings of an increased incidence of ideological thinking.[34]

This controversy among students of public opinion is just one more indication of the complexity and changing nature of public opinion. Although some analysts claim that ideological thinking has been on the rise, the thrust of political science research is that most Americans do not view politics from an ideological perspective. To the extent that they do, however, education is a contributing factor.[35] An education helps people better understand political issues and government's role in society and thus the links between issues.

Although most Americans do not view politics ideologically and are more likely to consider an issue from the perspective of individual or group self-interest, it is important to distinguish between the mass public and *political elites*—individuals active and influential in political decision making. Candidates, for example, are more likely than the average citizen to have coherent views on current political affairs. They also are more likely to rely on ideological criteria in evaluating issues and political events.

Analysts have discovered as well that, in their political ideologies, political activists are less moderate than the rank-and-file voters. This difference is revealed by a comparison of the ideologies of the delegates to national conventions and those of the rank-and-file voters. According to Figure 5.4, not only is there a major "ideology gap" between Republican and Democratic national convention delegates, but Republican delegates are considerably more conservative than rank-and-file Republicans, and Democratic delegates are more liberal than their party's voters.[36] This, of course, has implications for presidential nominating politics. Republican presidential aspirants must demonstrate their conservative credentials to have a chance of being nominated. Thus,

34. W. Lance Bennett, *Public Opinion in American Politics* (New York: Harcourt, 1980), 48–56; Christopher H. Achen, "Mass Attitudes and the Survey Response," *American Political Science Review* 69 (December 1975): 1218–1231; and John L. Sullivan, James E. Pierson, and George E. Marcus, "Ideological Constraint in the Mass Public," *American Journal of Political Science* 22 (May 1978): 233–249.

35. Norman H. Nie, Sidney Verba, and John R. Petrocik, *The Changing American Voter* (Cambridge, Mass.: Harvard University Press, 1976), 121.

36. For an analysis of mass-elite differences and linkages, see Warren E. Miller, *Without Consent: Mass-Elite Linkages in Presidential Politics* (Lexington: University of Kentucky Press, 1988). The divergent policy orientations of Republican versus Democratic campaign workers and county chairs is analyzed by John M. Bruce, John A. Clark, and John H. Kessel, "Advocacy Politics in Presidential Politics," *American Political Science Review* 85 (December 1991): 1089–1105.

even George Bush, an incumbent president, was forced to stress conservative themes in 1992 while fending off the right-wing challenge of Pat Buchanan. And Democratic candidates for presidential nominations must certify their liberal bona fides. This was true even for Bill Clinton, who while proclaiming himself to be a "new kind of Democrat" also made it a point to cultivate support among liberal constituencies (such as organized labor, feminists, African Americans, and gays and lesbians) with substantial influence over the nominating process.

Ideology and the American Political Process

The functioning of American politics is profoundly influenced by the scant attention most people pay to ideological concerns and their failure to divide themselves neatly into distinct liberal or conservative groups. Instead of a situation in which liberals and conservatives stand united against each other, people tend to fall into either the liberal or conservative camp depending on the domestic or foreign policy issue at stake. Economically liberal auto workers, for example, may fight business interests on such issues as raising the minimum wage or requiring health insurance for workers. Later, however, they may find themselves arm in arm with the "Big Three" auto makers in jointly opposing tougher government clean air standards for auto emissions because they believe these standards pose an economic threat to American auto manufacturers. Thus, people who are at odds on one issue today may find themselves allied on another issue tomorrow, making it difficult for cumulative antagonisms to build up through a series of confrontations. The overlapping and inconsistent belief systems that characterize the American public, therefore, reduce the intensity of political conflict. At the same time, however, these overlapping belief systems make it hard to form political alliances based on common attitudes. This in turn contributes to the government's frequent difficulty in reaching policy decisions.[37]

The public's lack of ideological perspectives on many issues also has meant that it often settles for the easier route of simple party allegiance (discussed more fully in Chapter 7, Elections, Campaigns, and Voters). Party allegiance is an important component of the political thought process for many voters and a basis for their election day decisions.

37. See the discussion of the inconsistent nature of Americans' political opinions and the implications of this phenomenon for American politics in V. O. Key, Jr., *Public Opinion and American Democracy* (New York: Knopf, 1961), chap. 7.

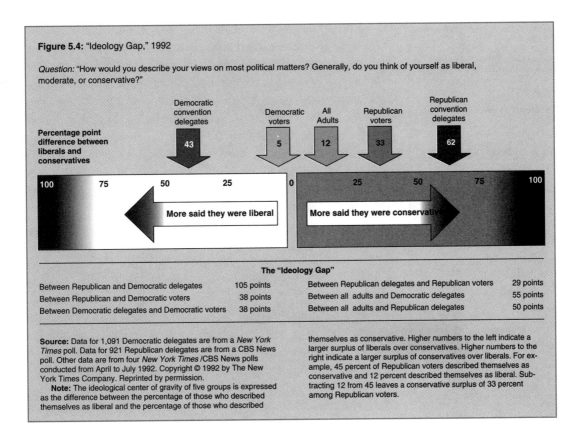

Figure 5.4: "Ideology Gap," 1992

Question: "How would you describe your views on most political matters? Generally, do you think of yourself as liberal, moderate, or conservative?"

The "Ideology Gap"

Between Republican and Democratic delegates	105 points		Between Republican delegates and Republican voters	29 points
Between Republican and Democratic voters	38 points		Between all adults and Democratic delegates	55 points
Between Democratic delegates and Democratic voters	38 points		Between all adults and Republican delegates	50 points

Source: Data for 1,091 Democratic delegates are from a *New York Times* poll. Data for 921 Republican delegates are from a CBS News poll. Other data are from four *New York Times* /CBS News polls conducted from April to July 1992. Copyright © 1992 by The New York Times Company. Reprinted by permission.
   Note: The ideological center of gravity of five groups is expressed as the difference between the percentage of those who described themselves as liberal and the percentage of those who described themselves as conservative. Higher numbers to the left indicate a larger surplus of liberals over conservatives. Higher numbers to the right indicate a larger surplus of conservatives over liberals. For example, 45 percent of Republican voters described themselves as conservative and 12 percent described themselves as liberal. Subtracting 12 from 45 leaves a conservative surplus of 33 percent among Republican voters.

Public Trust in Government

Although no government can expect to welcome the trust of all its citizens, there is general agreement that some (usually unspecified) level of trust is required to gain voluntary compliance with either existing or new policies. Thus, when trust is high, the government can put new policies into place, as in the 1960s when a number of social welfare programs (for example, Medicare, federal aid to education, the War on Poverty) were implemented as a part of President Lyndon Johnson's Great Society agenda. Since the mid-1960s, however, the public's trust in its social institutions has declined, with Congress, in particular, having suffered a loss in public confidence (see Figure 5.5). Indeed, in the early 1990s fewer Americans had confidence in the institutions that help to form the foundation of the American political system than at any time in over two decades.

The reasons for this decline in trust include dissatisfaction with the government's handling of such controversial issues as the civil rights movement, the Vietnam War, and the economy as well as such scan-

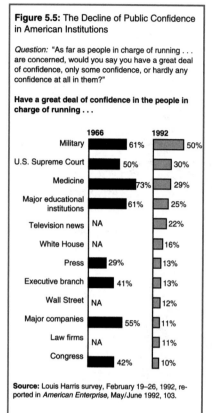

Figure 5.5: The Decline of Public Confidence in American Institutions

Question: "As far as people in charge of running . . . are concerned, would you say you have a great deal of confidence, only some confidence, or hardly any confidence at all in them?"

Have a great deal of confidence in the people in charge of running . . .

	1966	1992
Military	61%	50%
U.S. Supreme Court	50%	30%
Medicine	73%	29%
Major educational institutions	61%	25%
Television news	NA	22%
White House	NA	16%
Press	29%	13%
Executive branch	41%	13%
Wall Street	NA	12%
Major companies	55%	11%
Law firms	NA	11%
Congress	42%	10%

Source: Louis Harris survey, February 19–26, 1992, reported in *American Enterprise,* May/June 1992, 103.

dals as Watergate in the 1970s or the Iran-contra affair in the 1980s. There is also evidence that public trust in government responds strongly to evaluations of incumbent officeholders' performances.[38]

While the evidence of declining trust in government is strong, its significance is less apparent. Some believe lack of trust is a threat to the established order and holds the potential for radical change, extralegal behavior, and realignment of voters' partisan preferences. On the other side are those who make a distinction between lack of confidence in public officeholders and lack of faith in the governmental system. They point out that trust wanes when political leaders appear to have failed. Political scientist Jack Citrin has commented that

political systems, like baseball teams, have slumps and winning streaks. Having recently endured a succession of losing seasons, Americans boo the home team when it takes the field. But fans are often fickle; victories quickly elicit cheers. And to most fans what matters is whether the home team wins or loses, not how it plays the game.[39]

This rather optimistic use of a baseball analogy does not erase the fact that public trust and confidence in government have continued to decline. With America facing an array of seemingly intractable problems—massive budget deficits, modest job growth, rising costs and inadequate coverage in health care, violent crimes, an unstable postcold war international order—it does not appear that there are many easy wins in the offing for public officials. No significant upturn in public trust, then, is likely in the near future.

Public Opinion and Government Policy

P ublic opinion has its most obvious impact on government decision making through elections. In the United States, elections are usually held to vote for candidates for public office and not for specific policies, except in those states (such as California) that permit voters to enact laws through initiative and referendum. Clear electoral mandates from the voters are rare in American politics because candidates take stands on scores of issues and thus collect voters for different and even conflicting reasons; elections are seldom dominated or decided by just one or two issues. Moreover, the candidates' positions on salient issues

38. Paul R. Abramson and Ada W. Finifter, "On the Meaning of Political Trust: New Evidence from Items Introduced in 1978," *American Journal of Political Science* 63 (May 1981): 297–306.

39. Jack Citrin, "The Political Relevance of Trust in Government," *American Political Science Review* 68 (September 1974): 987.

are not always clear, nor are their positions necessarily in opposition to each other.

But even if it is hard to discern a clear policy mandate from the voters on election day, a verdict on the past performances of incumbent officeholders is frequently rendered. Indeed, the public can affect the general direction of government policy by changing the people and parties in control of government institutions. In the 1992 election, for example, the public gave a negative verdict on President George Bush's handling of the economy and on divided party control of the government.[40] But in rejecting Bush and replacing him with Bill Clinton, the public did not necessarily signal its approval of Clinton's policy proposals. It did, however, indicate that it was prepared to give him a chance to solve the nation's problems, and Clinton's Democratic administration had a policy agenda of governmental activism that was markedly different from that of its Republican predecessor.

Public opinion can determine not only who governs but also the context within which political leaders must act. Thus, periodic swings in the general disposition of Americans—changes in their policy *mood*—provide the setting for and affect government policy making. These shifts in the public's overall mood normally precede eras of governmental policy change and serve as the basis of support for such change. The liberal winds that began blowing during the latter 1950s, then, provided the basis for the governmental activism that characterized the Kennedy-Johnson era of the 1960s. But these breezes died down in the mid-1970s as Americans became increasingly conservative in their general disposition toward government's role in society. Indeed, this conservative policy mood was already in place *before* Ronald Reagan, the most conservative president since Herbert Hoover, took office and initiated policies designed to restrict the role of government.

Another policy swing in the public policy mood in the mid-1980s to the early 1990s deviled the presidency of George Bush. The idea of "liberalism" remained unpopular, but the electorate was expressing more liberal policy preferences and demanding change. Bush, however, was in no position to meet these expectations. He was elected in 1988 in large part because of his ties to the popular Reagan presidency. Even if he had been so inclined, Bush could have hardly turned away from the Reagan policies that he had supported as a loyal vice president. The

40. The postelection analysis in the *New York Times* noted it was an "election whose results rang with a cry for change but offered no specific mandate." *New York Times*, Nov. 5, 1992, A1, National edition. Also see Ladd, "The 1992 Vote for President Clinton," 1–28.

public's policy mood, which was characterized by a belief that the country was headed in the wrong direction, diminished support for his administration and created a major obstacle to his reelection.[41]

Public opinion has its greatest impact on policy when people have clear preferences and feel strongly about an issue. A study by political scientist Alan Monroe found that on issues particularly important to the public, government policy and public opinion were in agreement over two-thirds of the time.[42] Research also has demonstrated that government policy moves in the direction of a change in public opinion 87 percent of the time when the shift in public opinion on salient issues is substantial and not temporary.[43] One of the most striking examples of the impact of public opinion on national policy was the congressional pay raise controversy of 1989. Overwhelming and vehement public opposition caused a reluctant Congress to reject the 50 percent salary increase proposed by a bipartisan, blue-ribbon commission and endorsed by Presidents Reagan and Bush.

There are, of course, instances when public opinion and government policy are not consistent. Such inconsistencies may stem from the influence of well-organized and energetic interest groups (also see Chapter 8, Interest Groups). For example, a popular majority favored tougher clean air laws throughout the 1980s, yet Congress was unable to enact such legislation. This inaction reflected the ability of auto makers, utilities, several unions, and key legislators to mobilize opposition to clean air bills. Inconsistencies between public opinion and government policy also occur when the public cares little about an issue. Polls have shown repeatedly, for example, that Americans favor abolishing the electoral college system for electing the president, but this issue is not high on their list of concerns. As a result, the likelihood of Congress proposing a constitutional amendment to abolish the electoral college seems remote.

Public opinion does, then, influence public policy in the United States, but only through a complicated and often indirect process. It takes more than a majority of the public registering its approval or disapproval in a poll to affect policy. People's policy preferences are translated into government policy only when individuals act on opinions— that is, when they actually participate in politics.

41. On electoral impact of swings in the public's policy moods, see Stimson, *Public Opinion in America*, chap. 5.

42. Alan D. Monroe, "Consistency between Public Preferences and National Policy Decisions," *American Politics Quarterly* 7 (January 1979): 3–21.

43. Benjamin I. Page and Robert Y. Shapiro, "Effect of Public Opinion on Policy," *American Political Science Review* 77 (March 1983): 175–190.

Citizen Participation in Politics

For most Americans political participation simply means exercising their right to vote. But many other avenues of participation are available, requiring a higher level of political involvement. For example, millions open their checkbooks each year and contribute to the Republican and Democratic parties, preferred candidates, or interest groups such as Planned Parenthood, the Sierra Club, or the American Conservative Union. Thousands work on campaigns, distributing campaign literature, staffing phone banks, and putting up lawn signs. Parents work through their local parent-teacher associations to improve schools; environmentalists support the Wilderness Society or the Nature Conservancy to protect wilderness areas from development; and doctors join the American Medical Association to have their say about health policy. Concerned citizens contact their representatives, senators, and local officials to express their views on such issues as gun control, abortion, or Social Security. Unusually committed persons take part in demonstrations—for gay rights, the homeless, and women's rights, as well as against rising property taxes or higher university tuitions. Some citizens try to make their protests especially dramatic by participating in such illegal acts as damaging research facilities to protest scientific research using animals or blocking entrances and even physically attacking workers at abortion clinics.

There are, then, abundant opportunities for political participation,

Each year thousands of Americans seek to gain publicity for their causes and influence government policy through marches and demonstrations. Advocates of lifting the ban on gays in the military paraded in Washington, D.C., while the president, the Pentagon, and Congress were deciding this issue in 1993.

Table 5.5 Participation Rates in Political Activities, 1987

Activity	Percent Participating
Voted regularly in presidential elections	58
Voted always in local elections	35
Persuaded others how to vote	47
Worked actively for party or candidate	26
Attended a political meeting or rally	19
Contributed only to party or candidate	23
Joined a political club	4
Worked with others on a local problem	34
Participated in a community problem-solving organization	34
Formed a group to solve a local problem	14
Contacted a local official about an issue	24
Contacted a state or national official about an issue	22

Source: Adapted from Norman H. Nie, et al., "Participation in America: Continuity and Change" (Paper presented at the annual meeting of the Midwest Political Science Association, Chicago, April 14–16, 1988), table 1.

but most Americans are not consumed by an overwhelming interest in politics.[44] Job and family responsibilities, friends, and recreational activities have a much higher priority than politics for the average citizen.

Extent of Political Participation

Ironically, the United States, with its open and participatory political culture, ranks below most Western democracies in its rate of voter turnout in elections (the causes and consequences of voter turnout are considered in Chapter 7). A comparative study of voter turnout in the 1980s revealed that America's average voter turnout rate of 53 percent was at least 20 percentage points below those for elections to the national legislatures in Denmark, Germany, Greece, Israel, Italy, Norway, Sweden, and the United Kingdom.[45] But Americans are more likely to join and work in community organizations than the citizens of other countries.[46]

Beyond voting, which involves only registering and getting to the polls on election day, almost three-quarters of the U.S. adult population participates in at least one political activity (for example, contributing money to candidates; attending campaign rallies; joining an organization concerned with a local, state, or national issue; or contacting government officials), and a majority participates in at least two political activities. Among their political undertakings, Americans are drawn more to community organizations than to party or campaign work (see Table 5.5).

What Influences a Person's Level of Participation?

People's levels of political participation are affected by their social and economic status, age, political beliefs and attitudes, and the influence of any groups to which they belong (see Figure 5.6).

Men and women with higher *social and economic status*—whether

44. For a landmark study of participation, see Sidney Verba and Norman H. Nie, *Participation in America: Political Democracy and Social Equality* (New York: Harper and Row, 1972). For a more recent survey, see M. Margaret Conway, *Political Participation in the United States,* 2d ed. (Washington, D.C.: CQ Press, 1991).

45. Ruy A. Teixeira, *The Disappearing American Voter* (Washington, D.C.: Brookings, 1992), 8. Also see the analysis of America's relatively low voter turnout rates in G. Bingham Powell, "American Voting Turnout in Comparative Perspective," *American Political Science Review* 80 (March 1987): 17–43.

46. Norman H. Nie and Sidney Verba, "Political Participation," in *Handbook of Political Science,* ed. Fred I. Greenstein and Nelson W. Polsby (Reading, Mass.: Addison-Wesley, 1975), 4: 24–25.

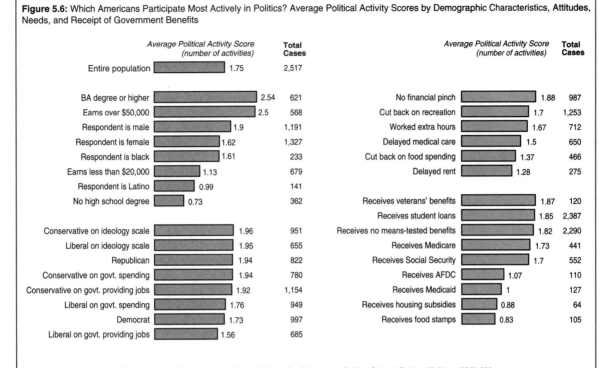

Figure 5.6: Which Americans Participate Most Actively in Politics? Average Political Activity Scores by Demographic Characteristics, Attitudes, Needs, and Receipt of Government Benefits

	Average Political Activity Score (number of activities)	Total Cases
Entire population	1.75	2,517
BA degree or higher	2.54	621
Earns over $50,000	2.5	568
Respondent is male	1.9	1,191
Respondent is female	1.62	1,327
Respondent is black	1.61	233
Earns less than $20,000	1.13	679
Respondent is Latino	0.99	141
No high school degree	0.73	362
Conservative on ideology scale	1.96	951
Liberal on ideology scale	1.95	655
Republican	1.94	822
Conservative on govt. spending	1.94	780
Conservative on govt. providing jobs	1.92	1,154
Liberal on govt. spending	1.76	949
Democrat	1.73	997
Liberal on govt. providing jobs	1.56	685

	Average Political Activity Score (number of activities)	Total Cases
No financial pinch	1.88	987
Cut back on recreation	1.7	1,253
Worked extra hours	1.67	712
Delayed medical care	1.5	650
Cut back on food spending	1.37	466
Delayed rent	1.28	275
Receives veterans' benefits	1.87	120
Receives student loans	1.85	2,387
Receives no means-tested benefits	1.82	2,290
Receives Medicare	1.73	441
Receives Social Security	1.7	552
Receives AFDC	1.07	110
Receives Medicaid	1	127
Receives housing subsidies	0.88	64
Receives food stamps	0.83	105

Source: Sidney Verba et al., "Citizen Activity: Who Participates? What Do They Say?" *American Political Science Review* 87 (June 1993): 306.
Note: Political activities included voting; working for a candidate; contributing to a candidate; contacting candidates, elected officials, and nonelected officials; participating in a protest or demonstration; attending a local government meeting; serving in a unit of local government; and informal involvement in community issues and activities.

measured by level of education, income, occupation, or government benefits received—participate more actively in politics than those with lower social and economic status.[47] Education, however, is the single most important socioeconomic characteristic determining political participation. The better educated are more likely to understand how the political process works, to be aware of how the machinations of government might affect their lives, to move in social environments in which politics is discussed, and to be subjected to social pressures to participate. In addition, education helps people to acquire the skills necessary to participate.

Age affects participation as well. Young people are less likely to vote and engage in election-related activities than middle-aged and older citizens, but they are more likely than their elders to take part in

47. Verba and Nie, *Participation in America*, 125. For a survey of the impact of social and economic characteristics on participation, see Conway, *Political Participation*, 15–40.

unconventional forms of political participation such as protest demonstrations.

In the past, significant differences in political participation were related to *gender and race,* with women and blacks lagging behind men and whites. Today, however, the differences between men and women have diminished.[48] And the gap between white and black participation rates has been narrowed as the right of African Americans to vote has been protected, educational attainment and economic mobility have been enhanced, and black political awareness has increased. Black participation rates are now similar to those of whites, when differences between the races in educational attainment and socioeconomic status are taken into consideration.

Political participation is affected as well by people's *political beliefs and attitudes.* Among the attitudes related to participation are a sense of civic duty (a feeling of obligation to participate), an interest in politics, a sense of political efficacy (a feeling of personal political effectiveness), and a sense of party identification.[49] These attitudes are indicators of whether or not a person is predisposed to participate in politics, but, aside from party identification, they do not indicate which issues or candidates will receive that person's attention. In addition to such long-term attitudes as ideology and party identification, short-term influences—the salient issues of the day and the qualities of particular candidates—have an impact on the nature of participation as well. Thus, in the period leading up to Senate ratification of the 1988 treaty reducing the number of U.S. and Soviet intermediate-range nuclear missiles (INF treaty), a liberal activist might have campaigned actively for a nuclear freeze. But as the nuclear issue declined in salience after ratification of the treaty, the same activist might have turned to a domestic concern such as the well-publicized plight of the homeless.

Group affiliations and *social involvement* also affect the extent of people's participation in politics. Indeed, an active social life provides the politically relevant information and social expectations that motivate political action. One of the most influential social involvements is the workplace, where people spend almost half of their waking hours and where they are bound to coworkers by common interests and

48. Interestingly, women are less likely than men to seek to persuade people how they should vote. See Ronald B. Rapoport, "The Sex Gap in Political Persuading: Where the 'Structuring Principle' Works," *American Journal of Political Science* 25 (February 1981): 32–48.

49. For a summary of the psychological components of participation, see Conway, *Political Participation,* 41–68. Also see Verba and Nie, *Participation in America.*

friendship. In fact, political leaders frequently try to stimulate participation in politics by contacting workers through their places of employment—for example, candidates might shake hands at a factory gate, and employers might suggest that employees contact government officials to urge support for policies that will benefit the company and preserve jobs. The employed are therefore more likely to have written their member of Congress than are the unemployed.

Outside the workplace, voluntary social involvement in clubs, interest groups, and associations also works to increase the likelihood of participation in politics. When seeking to mobilize public support for such activities as a letter-writing campaign to Congress, political activists target organized groups for their appeals.[50]

All this points to the fact that political participation is greatly affected by the *mobilization strategies of political leaders.* For example, the outpouring of letters opposed to the North American Free Trade Agreement (NAFTA) that rained down on Congress in 1993 was precipitated to a large extent by union leaders exhorting their members to contact the appropriate representatives and senators.

Conventional and Unconventional Forms of Political Participation

The distinction between conventional and unconventional forms of participation is a hard one to make. Conventional participation comprises such traditionally accepted activities as voting, assisting with campaigns, contributing campaign funds, running for office, working in community organizations and interest groups, and making one's views known to public officials. Unconventional participation is more unusual, often dramatic, outside the normal government channels, and sometimes even illegal. Among the less conventional kinds of activities are demonstrations, protests, civil disobedience, and, occasionally, violence.

Conventional Activities. Other than voting, the most common form of political activity is persuading others how to vote (see Table 5.5); almost half of the public engages in this pastime. Other forms of campaign activity—such as contributing money, working for a candidate, attending political meetings, or belonging to political clubs—are popular only with a much smaller group of political activists. Level of cam-

---

50. On how personal characteristics, social involvements, and leaders' mobilization strategies affect participation, see Steven J. Rosenstone and John Mark Hansen, *Mobilization, Participation, and Democracy in America* (New York: Macmillan, 1993), chap. 4.

paign involvement is strongly related to such basic political orientations as a person's interest in and attention to politics, sense of party identification, and belief that participation contributes to community welfare.[51]

As important as elections are in a democracy, politics is more than elections; it also includes efforts to influence government officials between elections—especially those efforts made by interest groups (considered in detail in Chapter 8). Most Americans belong to some kind of organized group that tries regularly to shape government policy. A labor union or manufacturers' trade association, for example, may seek protection against Japanese imports through trade legislation; churches may advocate enactment of civil rights laws; Planned Parenthood may work hard to block the appointment of a Supreme Court nominee whose views on abortion law it opposes; or a neighborhood association may try to obtain a higher level of police protection and city services. Unlike campaign activity, community involvement is not closely associated with a strong sense of partisan identification. Rather, it stems from people's interest in politics and their concern about the overall welfare of the community.[52]

Another conventional form of political participation is contacting government officials. In contrast to the fixed schedules of voting and campaign activities and the largely controlled lists of issues raised in campaigns, the timing, content, and targets of citizen-initiated contacts with government officials are determined by individuals themselves or by the leaders of the organized groups to which they belong. Interestingly, while voter turnout has been declining since 1960, the number of citizens contacting public officials has been increasing.[53] Communications advances such as electronic mail enable interest groups to contact their members almost instantaneously and urge them to write, phone, or fax their representative or senator. The result can be an avalanche of communications pouring into a legislator's office. As with other forms of political participation, people with more prestigious occupations, higher incomes, and better educations are most apt to contact public officials and to be active in other ways.

Unconventional Activities. Protest marches, demonstrations, and acts of civil disobedience—refusing to obey the law on the grounds

51. Nie and Verba, "Political Participation," 17–20.

52. Ibid., 20–21.

53. Richard A. Brody, "The Puzzle of Political Participation in America," in *The New American Political System,* ed. Anthony King (Washington, D.C.: American Enterprise Institute, 1978), 317.

that it is immoral—have been used throughout U.S. history as means of political expression, publicity, and citizen mobilization. The AIDS activists, pro-life and pro-choice demonstrators, antiviolence crusaders, gay rights advocates, and the pro- and anti-gun control protagonists of the 1990s are following in the tradition of the patriots who dumped tea in Boston Harbor, the abolitionists before the Civil War, the suffragists at the turn of the century, and the civil rights marchers in the 1960s.

Unconventional political activity often attracts a deluge of media attention. Indeed, one reason participants find protest activities worth the cost and effort is the media's tendency to cover these events—farmers using their tractors to block traffic in Washington to protest low prices for their products; a candlelight procession to urge an end to urban crime and violence; erection of a tent city in Lafayette Park across the street from the White House to dramatize the plight of the homeless. However dramatic such activities may be, it is useful to remember that only a tiny fraction of the public participates in such protests and that the issue at stake by and large determines the social backgrounds and ideological orientations of the protesters. For example, activists who chain themselves to trees to prevent logging or lie down in front of bulldozers to prevent development are dedicated environmentalists; protestors blocking access to abortion clinics have a deep commitment to their cause; and men and women staging sit-ins in college presidents' offices to protest tuition hikes are college students. There is not, therefore, a cadre of active protesters that moves from issue to issue.

Protests require a high level of commitment. Only those who are deeply stirred by an issue (and, in reality, only a fraction of these people) are likely to take the protest route.[54] The most likely participants are people who feel a sense of distrust of the political system, but who also have a sense of political efficacy—the belief that they can have an impact on politics.[55] The mobilization of such individuals to participate in protests usually falls to organized groups—for example, right-to-life groups might organize the picketing of abortion clinics; gun control groups might mass their followers at the Capitol to show support for restrictions on handguns; or Mothers Against Drunk Driving (MADD) might hold vigils to dramatize the death toll caused by intoxicated drivers.

54. Ibid., 316–317.
55. Stephen C. Craig and Michael A. Magiotto, "Political Discontent and Political Action," *Journal of Politics* 43 (May 1981): 514–522.

Although Americans are normally unmoved by unconventional political action, under some circumstances it can be most effective. The civil rights demonstrations of the 1960s—bus boycotts, lunch-counter sit-ins, and marches for voting rights—helped to mold public opinion and build broad support for civil rights and voting rights legislation. These demonstrations dramatized, where more conventional political activity had failed, the extent to which American society was not yet living up to its creed of equality. But protest activity that does not strike a responsive chord with the public and that does not have the organized support of a group to back it up is not likely to succeed.

The Question of Representation and Equality of Political Participation

This discussion of political participation has revealed that the level of participation among Americans varies significantly, depending on their demographic characteristics, economic needs, attitudes, and the government benefits they receive (Figure 5.6). Those who are college educated, relatively affluent, and ideologically liberal or conservative are more likely to participate than the disadvantaged. Research also has shown that these disparities become even greater as people move beyond the most common political act of voting to activities that are somewhat more complicated—making financial contributions, joining organizations, conveying information, and exerting pressure.

Some activists share the views of the disadvantaged and less active and act as their surrogates or spokespersons in the political arena. The effectiveness of such surrogates for the disadvantaged, however, is diminished by the fact that these usually liberal activists have other issues on their policy agendas besides the concerns of the poor. These aspects of the differences in participation of the advantaged and disadvantaged raise serious questions about the extent to which government officials are hearing messages from the public that are reasonably representative and the extent to which the American beliefs in political equality are actually being realized.[56]

Public Opinion, Participation, and Governing

This chapter has examined the nature of public opinion as well as the forces that shape people's political thinking. Public opinion is

56. Sidney Verba et al., "Citizen Activity: Who Participates? What Do They Say?" *American Political Science Review* 87 (June 1993): 303–318.

important because it is the basis for the political action or participation of citizens. But understanding how the American government works and the role of citizens in that government requires moving beyond the realm of public opinion and participation to explore in more detail how people connect with their government. Thus, the intermediary groups and processes—political parties, interest groups, and elections—through which citizens channel their views to their government are the focus of the upcoming chapters.

For Review

1. Public opinion is people's attitudes on an issue or question. It can be measured with a relatively high degree of accuracy by using scientific polling techniques that include interviewing carefully selected samples of the population.

2. To understand the nature of public opinion on an issue, one must understand the various dimensions of public opinion: direction, distribution, saliency, intensity, and stability.

3. Political socialization is the process through which people acquire an awareness of, the facts about, and the values concerning politics. It is a life-long process. Among the agents of political socialization are the family, schools, peers, and the mass media.

4. Political attitudes vary in America, depending on such socioeconomic characteristics as education, income/class, ethnicity and race, religion, region, and gender.

5. A political ideology is an organized, coherent set of attitudes on government and public policy. Liberal and conservative ideologies have taken on a multidimensional character, reflecting not only the traditional concern for government's role in society but also social and foreign policy concerns. Most Americans do not approach politics from an ideological perspective.

6. Public opinion has its greatest impact on governmental decision making when people feel strongly about clear-cut preferences. Although government policy tends to coincide with public opinion, this may not always be the case, particularly when a well-organized interest group intervenes or public apathy is evident.

7. Most Americans are not highly interested or intensely involved in politics. Level of involvement is strongly influenced by one's social and economic status, level of education, political attitudes such as party identification and political efficacy, and group affiliations.

For Further Reading

American Enterprise. A bimonthly magazine published by the American Enterprise Institute in Washington, D.C., featuring summaries of public opinion surveys in each issue.

Asher, Herbert. *Polling and the Public: What Every Citizen Should Know.* 2d ed. Washington, D.C.: CQ Press, 1992. A citizen's guide to understanding public opinion polling.

Conway, M. Margaret. *Political Participation in the United States.* 2d ed. Washington, D.C.: CQ Press, 1991. A concise survey of political science research on participation.

Dalton, Russell J. *Citizen Politics in Western Democracies.* Chatham, N.J.: Chatham House, 1988. A comparative study of public opinion and its role in the United States and three European democracies.

Erikson, Robert S., Norman R. Luttbeg, and Kent L. Tedin. *American Public Opinion.* 4th ed. New York: Macmillan, 1991. A comprehensive text on public opinion.

Huntington, Samuel P. *American Politics: The Promise of Disharmony.* Cambridge, Mass.: Harvard University Press, 1981. A provocative analysis of the impact of underlying American values on political reform and foreign policy.

Jennings, M. Kent, and Richard G. Niemi. *Generations and Politics: A Panel Study of Young Adults and Their Parents.* Princeton, N.J.: Princeton University Press, 1981. A longitudinal study of the political socialization of young people and their parents.

Moore, Stanley W., James Lare, and Kenneth A. Wagner. *A Child's Political World.* New York: Praeger, 1988. A longitudinal study of children's political learning starting with kindergarten.

Page, Benjamin I., and Robert Y. Shapiro. *The Rational Public: Fifty Years of Trends in Americans' Policy Preferences.* Chicago: University of Chicago Press, 1992. A review of survey findings showing the public to be rational and relatively stable in its views.

Rosenstone, Steven J., and John Mark Hansen. *Mobilization, Participation, and Democracy in America.* New York: Macmillan, 1993. An analysis that demonstrates the impact of political leaders' mobilization strategies on participation.

Verba, Sidney, and Norman H. Nie. *Participation in America: Political Democracy and Social Equality.* New York: Harper and Row, 1972. A benchmark study of political participation in the United States.

6. Political Parties

POLITICAL PARTIES were not part of the Founders' plan for America. Indeed, James Madison warned in the *Federalist* against the "mischiefs of faction," and the first president, George Washington, used his "Farewell Address" to caution that a spirit of party is divisive, "foments occasionally riot and insurrection," and "opens the doors to foreign influence and corruption." Yet wherever free elections have been conducted on a regular basis at the national and regional levels, political parties have been part of that process. They have developed as suffrage has been extended and the need has arisen for organizations that can mobilize voters. Because the United States was one of the first nations to extend voting rights to all free men, it also was one of the first to develop political parties.

Even though parties are an integral part of American-style democracy and two-thirds of voters consider themselves either Democrats or Republicans, people tend to be suspicious of such groups. In 1992, 82 percent of the respondents in a *Washington Post* poll agreed with the statement that "both political parties are pretty much out of touch with the American people." Surveys also have shown broad support for the proposition that "it would be better if in all elections we put no party labels on the ballot," and only 29 percent disagreed with the statement that "parties do more to confuse the issues than to provide a clear choice on issues."[1] Reflecting the public's distrust, the federal and especially state governments have placed stringent regulatory restrictions on parties. The state statutes, for example, limit party campaign expenditures, specify party nominating procedures, and frequently stipulate how parties must organize themselves and elect their officers.

What Is a Political Party and What Does It Do?

Although political parties are a fixture of the political process, political commentators have found them difficult to define. In 1770 Edmund Burke, the English parliamentarian and philosopher, defined a **political party** by stressing the common ideology of its members: "Party is a body of men united, for promoting by their endeavors the national interest, upon some particular principle in which they are all

1. *Washington Post*, July 8, 1992, A1; Jack Dennis, "Public Support for the Party System, 1964–1984" (Paper presented at the annual meeting of the American Political Science Association, Washington, D.C., August 28–31, 1986).

agreed."[2] But Burke's conception of parties has little relevance to today's Republican and Democratic parties. Both include in their ranks conservatives, moderates, and liberals. As Speaker of the House of Representatives Thomas ("Tip") O'Neill (D-Mass.) once remarked about his party, "We Democrats are all under one tent. In any other country we'd be five splinter parties."

Political scientist Leon Epstein has provided a definition of *political party* that is well adapted to the American experience: "Any group, however loosely organized, seeking to elect governmental officeholders under a given label."[3] The essential elements of this definition are that, first, political parties are preoccupied with *contesting elections* and, second, only parties run candidates *under their own labels.* Epstein's conception of parties takes into account the absence of ideological and policy unity that characterizes American political parties. It also accommodates the many different kinds of party organizations found in the United States—for example, the patronage-based and centrally controlled machine of the late mayor Richard Daley in Chicago, the well-financed suburban operations such as the Nassau County (Long Island, New York) Republicans, the ideological Democratic reformers in Los Angeles and New York, the professionally staffed headquarters of the Republican and Democratic national committees, and the poorly funded and understaffed local party committees in hundreds of communities.

Analysts have found political parties difficult to define because of their complex, overlapping social structures, which have these components: (1) *the party in the electorate:* voters who identify with, vote for, or register a preference for a particular party; (2) *the party organization:* party officers, committee members, paid staff, and volunteer workers; and (3) *the party in government:* government officeholders of a party and a party's nominees for office.[4] Each of these elements is an essential component of a political party, but none by itself constitutes the whole of a party. Within a party are found the most weakly committed voter, the dedicated party worker, the paid professional staffer, and even, perhaps, the president of the United States.

2. Edmund Burke, "Thoughts on the Cause of the Present Discontents," in *The Works of Edmund Burke* (Boston: Little, Brown, 1871), 151.

3. Leon D. Epstein, *Political Parties in Western Democracies* (New York: Praeger, 1967), 9. Also see Joseph A. Schlesinger, "The New American Political Party," *American Political Science Review* 79 (December 1985): 1152–1169.

4. This tripartite conception of American political parties was developed by V. O. Key, Jr., *Politics, Parties, and Pressure Groups,* 5th ed. (New York: Crowell, 1964), 163–164. Also see Paul Allen Beck and Frank J. Sorauf, *Party Politics in America,* 7th ed. (New York: HarperCollins, 1992), 10–13.

Act as an Intermediary between Citizens and Their Government

Parties serve as linkages or intermediaries between citizens and their government. They bring the scattered elements of the public together to define objectives, support candidates, and achieve common goals through government policy. The parties' role as linkages between the citizens and their government was held so important by political scientist E. E. Schattschneider that he observed in his 1944 classic study, "Political parties created democracy and modern democracy is unthinkable save in terms of parties."[5] More recently, political scientist Samuel Huntington concluded after a multi-nation study that parties organize participation, bring together different groups in society, and "serve as a link between social forces and the governments."[6] Parties, of course, are not the only intermediary institutions in the political system. They must compete for influence with interest groups, political action committees (committees established by business groups, ideological groups, and unions to distribute money to candidates), and the mass media. But even if Schattschneider and Huntington may have overstated the role of parties, it is evident that parties are involved in every aspect of government. After all, it is men and women elected as Democrats and Republicans who make the laws and decide whether and at what level government benefits should be available to the poor, elderly, veterans, students, farmers, businesses, and local governments. It is also Democrats and Republicans who determine who will pay how much for these benefits through taxes, as well as whether or not Americans will be sent into war.

Nominate Candidates

The **nomination** of candidates—determining which candidates' names will appear on the general election ballot—is a critical phase in the electoral process. Indeed, the nomination is, for candidates, a hurdle that must be crossed for election to public office. For all practical purposes, the nominating process also restricts the voters' choices on election day to the candidates of the Republican and Democratic parties, except in those rare instances when a strong independent, like Ross Perot in 1992, emerges.

Party nominating procedures narrow the field of candidates. Without a party nomination, it is virtually impossible to win major elective

---

5. E. E. Schattschneider, *Party Government* (New York: Holt, Rinehart, and Winston, 1944), 10.

6. Samuel Huntington, *Political Order in Changing Societies* (New Haven, Conn.: Yale University Press, 1980), 91.

office. In fact, since the emergence of modern parties in 1800, every president has been a major party nominee. Between 1978 and 1994 members of Congress were either Republicans or Democrats except for Bernard Sanders (Vt.), an independent who was first elected to the House in 1990. And since 1942 only three persons (two in 1990—Lowell Weicker in Connecticut and Walter Hickel in Alaska) have been elected governor as an independent. At the same time, however, nomination procedures in the United States permit broad voter participation, making it difficult for party leaders to control the nomination process.

Contest Elections and Mobilize Voters

Parties and their candidates contest elections by mobilizing the electorate. Although they must contend with broad cultural diversity, rapid social change, competing interests, and simultaneous elections in fifty states and thousands of communities, the two major parties have been remarkably successful in channeling the vote and dominating electoral competition. But voters have been less guided by partisan commitments since the 1970s than they were in earlier years.[7] This is reflected in the tendency of many voters to engage in **ticket splitting**— for example, electing Republican presidents while voting Democratic in congressional elections.

Organize the Government

To carry out their responsibilities, the institutions of government must have leaders, procedural rules, and divisions of labor. Most such institutions are organized along party lines. Congress, for example, is organized on a partisan basis. Because Democrats held a majority of the seats in the House and Senate after the 1992 elections, they controlled the institution's most powerful leadership positions. Members of Congress also tend to be guided by party positions when casting their votes on the floors of the House and Senate. The executive branch is organized in a partisan manner as well. Presidential appointees— department secretaries and assistant secretaries, White House staff, and agency heads—are almost exclusively members of the president's party.

When different parties control the executive and legislative branches, as has often been the case since 1968, the institutional rivalries created by the separation of powers system are intensified. For example, executive-congressional conflicts during the 1980s and 1990s were worsened by Republican control of the White House and Democratic control of Congress. But when the same party controls both branches,

---

7. See Martin P. Wattenberg, *The Rise of Candidate Centered Politics: Presidential Elections of the 1980s* (Cambridge, Mass.: Harvard University Press, 1991), 36–39.

Following their victories in the 1992 elections, it was the responsibility of the Democrats to organize both the executive and legislative branches. President Clinton participates in a Capitol Hill press briefing with his party's congressional leaders, Senate Majority Leader George Mitchell (center) and Speaker of the House Thomas Foley (right). Vice President Al Gore is at the far left.

the prospects for presidential-congressional cooperation are enhanced. Partisanship can thus help bridge the separation of powers. President Bill Clinton has found, however, that his fellow Democrats in Congress are not always the most reliable allies. The congressional wings of both parties are composed of relatively independent politicians who give first priority to taking care of their own reelection needs and their constitutents' interests. Serving the interests of even a president from their own party is seldom their foremost concern.

Act as an Agent of Public Accountability

Parties contribute to democracy by providing voters with a means of holding public officials accountable for their actions. The political world within which the average citizen must function is incredibly complex—multiple and interrelated issues, political power divided by separation of powers and federalism, and a lengthy election day ballot that includes candidates from the president to the county registrar of deeds. Making informed choices under these conditions, then, is almost mind-boggling. Fortunately, a lengthy, in-depth study of politics is not a prerequisite for making rational electoral choices; political parties provide the voter with a few simple criteria that help to make election day decision making manageable.

For one thing, parties simplify voters' choices on election day by structuring the election into a contest between Democrats and Republicans. The voters, then, can vote for the candidates from the party they feel best represents their viewpoints. Voters also may use their ballots to hold elected officials accountable for how well the government is working. With all elected officials wearing a party label—a political brand name—the voters are in a position to assign blame or credit for the state of the Union to the party that controls the government. Elected officials' fears of being held responsible for adversity and their desires to be credited for good times tend to make them responsive to society's needs. But without political party labels, it would be much more difficult to achieve public accountability through elections.

All this being said, this means of using the ballot box to control government leaders is indirect and imperfect. Elections do not tell elected officials what specific policies the voters favor. Rather, they provide an opportunity to register a general reaction to a party's stewardship in office or the general direction of future policy. When the Democrats in 1980 and the Republicans in 1992 were forced to vacate the White House, the voters were not telling the respective new presidents what specific policies they should follow. They were instead expressing their dissatisfaction with the incumbent parties' performances and giving the new administrations a chance to deal with the country's most pressing problems.

Manage Conflicts in Society

In a society composed of people and groups with different goals, interests, and values, conflict is inevitable. But when conflict gets out of hand, it can make living conditions intolerable. A stable democratic order, then, requires some means of managing and resolving the conflicts that arise.

In going about the business of winning elections by fashioning broad-based voter coalitions, political parties help to manage societal conflict in America even though such coalitions inevitably contain contentious elements. For example, the **New Deal Democratic coalition** forged by President Franklin Roosevelt in the 1930s comprised southern white Protestants, northern urban Catholics, blue-collar workers, Jews, and blacks. Yet in spite of this variety, the party's leadership was able to work out intracoalition compromises that allowed it to dominate American elections from the 1930s into the 1970s. Similarly, the Republican coalitions that elected Ronald Reagan and George Bush in the 1980s included such unlikely partners as well-educated northern suburbanites and southern fundamentalist Protestants. As for President Bill Clinton in the 1990s, he quickly discovered that to fashion a domestic program he would have to bargain and compromise with the Democrats' contending factions, which include African Americans, northern white liberals, and southern/border state white moderates and conservatives. These examples demonstrate, then, that by settling some of society's conflicts *within the parties,* American political parties have helped to manage conflict, thereby contributing to political stability.

The Party Struggle in America

Despite the Founders' forecast that the establishment of political parties would have dire consequences for the new Republic, parties quickly became an institutionalized part of the political process. By the 1830s presidential candidates were nominated by party conventions, presidents were selected by partisan slates of presidential electors, and Congress was organized on a partisan basis. The United States has had five **party systems**—different eras of partisan politics characterized by their own unique alignment of voters, patterns of control over the national government, and policy orientations. Except for the initial alignment of voters during the first party system, each party system began with a **realignment**—a significant shift in the partisanship of the electorate and in the underlying bases of the parties' electoral support. The history of party conflict described in the following pages reveals the durability of political parties in spite of public misgivings about their influence, frequently inhospitable federal and state regulations, and changing social and economic conditions (see Table 6.1).[8]

The First Party System, 1789–1824

Although the government under the Constitution did not begin with organized political parties, they came into being in its early days when conflicts arose between the congressional followers of Secretary of the Treasury Alexander Hamilton and those of Secretary of State Thomas Jefferson in the Washington administration. It was the followers of Jefferson who first sought to expand their activities beyond the halls of Congress. Organizing at the state and local levels, they ran candidates for Congress and the electoral college under the banner of the Democratic-Republican party. Reluctantly, the Federalist supporters of Hamilton and President John Adams (1797–1801) followed the Jeffersonian example of local political organizing to influence elections.

Federalists supported a strong national government capable of protecting and stimulating business development. Thus, they were strongest in the commercial centers of the Northeast and along the seaboard and among well-to-do business and tradespeople. They also tended to favor England and oppose the revolutionary government in

8. An excellent short summary of party history is found in Key, *Politics, Parties, and Pressure Groups,* 166–198. For more detailed accounts, see Everett Carll Ladd, *American Political Parties: Social Change and Political Response* (New York: Norton, 1970); and A. James Reichley, ed., *The Life of the Parties: A History of American Political Parties* (New York: Free Press, 1992).

Table 6.1 American Party Systems

Party System	Years	Major Parties	Characteristics and Major Events
FIRST	1789–1824	Federalist Democratic-Republican	Political parties emerge in 1790s. War of 1812. Democratic-Republicans dominate, 1800–1824.
SECOND	1828–1854	Democratic Whig	Factional conflicts develop within Democratic party, 1828–1836. Whigs emerge as opposition to Democrats in 1830s. Two-party competition results, with the Democrats stronger electorally. Sectional conflicts between North and South intensify and create schisms within Democratic and Whig parties.
THIRD	1856–1896	Democratic Republican	Republican party emerges as major opposition to Democrats in 1850s. Lincoln elected in 1860; Civil War and Reconstruction follow. Republicans dominate, 1864–1874; two-party competition characterizes 1874–1896. Agrarian unrest surfaces; Populist party contests 1892 election.
FOURTH	1896–1932	Democratic Republican	Republicans dominate, 1896–1910. Progressive movement develops; Progressives split away from GOP and run Theodore Roosevelt for president, but Democrat Woodrow Wilson is elected. South becomes solidly Democratic. World War I and Normalcy of 1920s. Republicans dominate nationally, 1920–1928.
FIFTH	1932–	Democratic Republican	Great Depression of 1930s, World War II. New Deal Democratic coalition forms; Democrats dominate electorally in 1930s and 1940s. Korean and Vietnam wars. After 1950s Democratic electoral coalition is weakened, especially among southern whites; the rise of candidate-centered politics and split-ticket voting; Republican domination of the presidency and Democratic control of Congress create an era of divided government; Democrats regain presidency in 1992.

France. Jefferson's Democratic-Republicans drew their support from the less well-to-do elements and were defenders of agrarian interests. They feared a strong national government that supported business development. In foreign policy they tended to favor France over England.

In the election of 1800 the Democratic-Republicans won an overwhelming victory, and the Federalists then went into a steady decline. As the party of the elite elements of society, the Federalists had failed to adapt to the more democratic style of politics that was emerging in the early decades of the nineteenth century as the right to vote was extended to all white males.[9]

9. For accounts of the early development of political parties in the United States, see William Nisbet Chambers, *Political Parties in a New Nation* (New York: Oxford University Press, 1963); and Richard Hofstadter, *The Idea of a Party System: The Rise of Legitimate Opposition in the United States* (Berkeley: University of California Press, 1969).

The Second Party System, 1828–1854

In 1828 Andrew Jackson, running as a Democrat, defeated President John Quincy Adams and then was reelected in 1832. The forces opposed to Jackson had coalesced by 1834 to form the Whig party. Thereafter for two decades the Democrats and the Whigs engaged in bitter electoral struggles in all regions of the country. Both created state and local party organizations and ran full slates of candidates for public office. In this atmosphere of party competition voters began to think of themselves as Democrats or Whigs, yet throughout this period the Democrats were the dominant party, with the minority Whigs winning presidential elections only when they nominated such military heroes as William Henry Harrison in 1840 and Zachary Taylor in 1848.

Both parties were broad electoral coalitions that sought to balance the interests of farmers, manufacturers, and merchants; the native-born and immigrants; and Protestants and Catholics. The Whigs attracted proportionally more support from manufacturing and trading interests, planters, and old Protestant stock, and the Democrats did best among western farmers, newly enfranchised voters, immigrants, and Catholics.

During the second party system national conventions became the standard method for nominating presidential candidates and writing party platforms. Before the 1830s presidential candidates had been nominated by their parties' members of Congress, the congressional caucuses.

Racial and slavery issues became increasingly divisive during the 1850s and split both the Democrats and Whigs along a North-South axis. Neither party was capable of resolving this sectional conflict, and America entered its third party system era with the emergence of the Republican party.

The Third Party System, 1856–1896

Between 1854 and 1860 the electorate went through a major **realignment.** The Whigs dissolved; the Democrats split into northern and southern factions; and the Republican party—made up of abolitionists, Free-Soilers (an 1848 third-party movement opposed to the extension of slavery to the newly acquired territories in the West), and dissident northern Whigs and Democrats—emerged. In 1860 Abraham Lincoln, a former Whig, captured the presidency for the new Republican party, and the period 1864–1874 was one of Republican electoral dominance.

The electoral base of the Republican party (also known as the "Grand Old Party" or GOP) was in the North, where for decades after the Civil War it effectively campaigned using the emotional symbols of the war: the Union, emancipation, and the martyred president. The GOP's dominant electoral coalition comprised diverse interests— Union veterans, farmers, northern business interests, and working people in the cities.

The Civil War and the Reconstruction policies of the Republicans alienated that party from the South, which became strongly Democratic. The Democratic party also gained the support of both the scattered elements of the business community through its commitment to free trade and the new and largely Catholic immigrant groups in the cities.

After 1874 and the end of Reconstruction in the South the Democrats and Republicans began to compete on a more even basis and alternated control of the presidency and Congress up until 1896. Overall, however, the post-Civil War era was a period of Republican dominance of the national government and of sectional conflict between the southern-based Democrats and the northern-based Republicans.

The Fourth Party System, 1896–1932

America was transformed socially and economically in the second half of the nineteenth century. Urbanization created cities with populations of over one million; transcontinental railroads spanned the nation; mammoth corporations such as Standard Oil and U.S. Steel emerged; and waves of immigrants from non-English-speaking nations reached American shores. The social dislocations and discontent caused by these social changes reverberated through the political system and spawned third-party protest movements. The most significant was the People's (Populist) party of 1892, whose platform of agrarian radicalism called for an income tax, nationalization of railroads and telephone/telegraph companies, and inflation through unlimited coinage of silver. The popular unrest demonstrated by the 1892 election set the stage for the capture of the Democratic party in 1896 by the Populist movement.

The election of 1896, which found the Democrats nominating a prairie Populist, William Jennings Bryan, and the Republicans selecting as their candidate a traditional conservative, William McKinley, was a watershed in American political history. Running on a platform of "Prosperity—Sound Money—Good Markets and Employment for Labor—A Full Dinner Pail," McKinley was elected with the support of business classes who were scared by Bryan's populism. Working people

After failing to win the Republican presidential nomination in 1912, former president Theodore Roosevelt ran on his own "Bull Moose" Progressive ticket. This split the Republican vote between Roosevelt and President William Howard Taft and contributed to Democrat Woodrow Wilson's election to the presidency.

in the cities also supported McKinley because they believed that the Republican policy of a high protective tariff would shield their jobs.

The political landscape was transformed by the 1896 election. The Republican electoral coalition, which had been weakened after 1874, gained an infusion of voters, especially among urban residents in the Northeast. The Democrats were severely weakened in much of the North and were forced to rely on their southern base. Thus, the fourth party system of 1896–1932 was dominated by the Republicans, except when a split within the GOP permitted Democrat Woodrow Wilson to win the presidency in 1912 and gain reelection in 1916.

The Fifth Party System, 1932–?

In 1929, the first year of Republican Herbert Hoover's administration, the stock market crashed, signaling the beginning of the Great Depression of the 1930s which left about a quarter of the work force unemployed. The once-dominant Republicans were crushed in the elections of 1932 and 1936 as the electorate realigned itself and the nation entered a long period of Democratic ascendancy. Indeed, the new president, Franklin Roosevelt, had the support of his remarkably diverse New Deal Democratic coalition (southern whites, Catholics, blacks, union households, and Jews), and his leadership of the nation during World War II strengthened support for the Democratic party as well.

But by the 1950s the New Deal Democratic coalition had begun to show signs of strain as Republican Dwight Eisenhower won the presidency in 1952 and 1956. Although the electoral alignments of the 1930s were still visible, the erosion of the Democrats' electoral base intensified from the late 1960s into the 1980s, especially among white southerners. At the same time, however, black voters came to constitute a larger and loyal component of the Democratic coalition.

The weakening of the New Deal Democratic coalition and Republican domination of the presidency during the 1970s and 1980s fueled speculation that America was on the verge of another of its periodic electoral realignments and that the fifth party system was coming to an end. An examination of the evidence, however, indicates that a major realignment has not yet occurred: there continue to be more Democratic than Republican identifiers among the voters, although the Democratic margin declined in the 1980s (see Table 7.4). In spite of GOP successes in presidential elections, the Democrats have continued to dominate the Congress, governorships, and state legislatures, and there has been no major shift in the policy orientation of the voters, who remain basically middle-of-the-road. Although no realignment has occurred comparable to those of the 1860s and 1930s when the compelling issues of slavery and the depression tore at the fabric of American politics and caused wholesale shifts in voter partisanship, the nature of the party system has changed significantly. Electoral **dealignment** has occurred as many voters, viewing parties as less relevant, have opted to become independents. Politics also has become increasingly candidate-centered rather than party-centered as candidates organize and run their own campaigns quite independently of their parties and voters engage in split-ticket voting (voting for candidates of different parties).[10]

10. See Wattenberg, *Rise of Candidate Centered Politics;* Paul Allen Beck, "Incomplete Realignment: The Reagan Legacy for Parties and Elections," in *The Reagan Legacy and Performance,* ed. Charles O. Jones (Chatham, N.J.: Chatham House, 1988), 145–171; Thomas E. Cavanagh and James L. Sundquist, "The New Two-Party System," in *The New Directions in American Politics,* ed. John E. Chubb and Paul E. Peterson (Washington, D.C.: Brookings, 1985), 33–68; and Everett Carll Ladd, "The 1988 Elections: Continuation of the Post–New Deal System," *Political Science Quarterly* 104 (Spring 1989): 1–18.

Interparty Competition

The nature of the competition among political parties has varied significantly over time. Between 1800 and 1990 three distinct patterns characterized interparty competition. The first, *balanced two-party competition,* was evident in the Democratic-Whig confrontations of 1836–1854 and in the Republican-Democratic struggles since World War II. The second, *sustained one-party dominance* of national politics, characterized the Republican era of 1896–1910 and the Democratic New Deal period of 1932–1946. And the third, *intraparty factionalism and pluralism,* describes the factional battles between progressive and conservative Republicans from 1910 to 1912 and the multiparty politics of the 1850s and early Civil War years.[11] Interestingly, all three types of electoral competition have existed in this century, but the years since World War II have constituted the longest stretch of sustained balanced interparty competition in American history.

Over 130 Years of Republican-Democratic Electoral Dominance

One of the most remarkable features of the history of American political parties has been the way two parties—the Democrats and Republicans—have dominated electoral politics since 1856. Indeed, this record of two-party durability and electoral dominance is unmatched in the world's democracies. The two parties have survived demoralizing defeats and adapted to the dislocations in society caused by a civil war, two world wars, depressions, waves of immigrants, industrialization, urbanization, suburbanization, and a communications revolution.

Among the reasons for the Democratic and Republican parties' amazing record of durability is their *capacity to absorb protest.*[12] Although third-party protest movements have flowered periodically, they usually have withered as their causes and supporters have been incorporated into the major parties. Thus, the 1892 Populists were absorbed into the Democratic party in 1896, and Theodore Roosevelt's "Bull Moose" Progressives of 1912 moved back into the GOP in 1916. The direct primary method of nominating candidates is one of the reasons parties are able to absorb protest. This uniquely American method of nomination takes the power over nominations out of the hands of party leaders and permits voters to select their party's nominees. As a

11. Samuel J. Eldersveld, *Political Parties in American Society* (New York: Basic Books, 1982), 35–36.

12. Ibid., 40–41.

result, dissidents can work *within* the established parties to achieve their goals instead of having to form third parties.[13]

The electoral dominance of the Republican and Democratic parties has been further enhanced by election procedures that work to the disadvantage of third parties. Members of the Congress and most state legislators are elected from single-member districts under a winner-take-all system—whoever receives a plurality of the vote is the winner. This is in contrast to proportional representation systems in which parties win a share of the seats in the legislature directly proportionate to their share of the popular vote. Thus, if party A receives 40 percent of the popular vote, party B gets 30 percent, party C 20 percent, and party D 10 percent, party A would be entitled to 40 percent of the seats in the legislature; party B would be entitled to 30 percent; and so on. Under proportional representation, parties have little incentive to form broad coalitions since they are virtually assured of some representation in the legislature. But under America's winner-take-all system of single-member districts, only two parties normally have a reasonable chance of victory; third or minor parties are condemned to perpetual defeat. As a result, there is an incentive in countries using single-member constituencies to form broadly based parties capable of winning pluralities in legislative districts.

The electoral college system for choosing presidents also discourages the development of strong third parties. To be elected president, a candidate must receive an absolute majority of the electoral votes—an almost impossible feat for a minor party. In addition, states' electoral votes are allocated on a winner-take-all basis—that is, the candidate receiving a plurality of a state's popular votes receives all of its electoral votes. Like the single-member district system, this winner-take-all system works to the disadvantage of minor parties.

Democratic-Republican electoral dominance also has been sustained by the parties' *ideological pragmatism*. Rather than adhere to a strict ideology, both parties have shifted their policy orientations in response to changing conditions. The Democrats have gone from populism in 1896, to conservatism in 1904, to Woodrow Wilson's New Freedom progressivism in 1912, to New Deal liberalism in the 1930s and 1940s, to Jimmy Carter's moderation in the 1970s, to Walter Mondale's and Michael Dukakis's liberalism in the 1980s, and to Bill Clinton's "new kind of Democrat" centrist campaign in 1992. The Republicans have shown similar flexibility: McKinley-style conservatism in the

13. Leon D. Epstein, *Political Parties in the American Mold* (Madison: University of Wisconsin Press, 1986), 131–133, 243–245.

1890s, Theodore Roosevelt progressivism at the turn of the century, "normalcy" (business domination of government and a retreat into isolationism) in the 1920s, Eisenhower's mild brand of domestic conservatism and foreign policy internationalism in the 1950s, and Reagan-Bush conservatism in the 1980s.

Finally, the parties have demonstrated *coalitional flexibility*—an ability to attract voters from all segments of society, even those normally thought to support the opposition. In 1988, for example, Republicans showed a capacity to win a majority of Catholics and 42 percent of union household voters even though these groups generally are thought to be in the Democratic camp. And in 1992 Democratic presidential nominee Bill Clinton ran only 2 percentage points behind George Bush among voters in the $50,000–$74,999 income bracket— a group that normally delivers healthy pluralities to the GOP.[14] Party coalitions thus are not static. As political scientist Samuel Eldersveld has observed, "The history of American parties is one of breakup, modification, and reconstruction of socioeconomic coalitions."[15]

*Two-Party Competition:
More than Meets the Eye*

With the Republicans and Democrats dominating the political landscape, the phrase "American two-party system" accurately describes the overall pattern of electoral competition. But it also masks a great deal of variation in the nature and extent of interparty competition. Most statewide elections—contests for a state's electoral votes as well as its senatorial and gubernatorial elections—tend to be confrontations between the Republicans and Democrats. A large proportion of congressional (House) districts, however, are safe havens for one party. In the 1980s an average of 71 House seats (16 percent) went uncontested by one of the major parties, and in 1992 the average House incumbent won by a comfortable 64 percent of the vote. Elections for some state officials also often lack authentic **two-party competition.** Either uncontested elections or an absence of meaningful interparty competition is commonplace in state legislative elections, especially in the traditional Democratic strongholds of the South and in big-city districts or in traditionally Republican-dominated states like New Hampshire. Races for state constitutional offices such as attorney general and secretary of state also are frequently not competitive. For example, in 1992 in the South only half of the contests for these types of offices were genuinely competitive.

14. Exit poll data, reported in the *New York Times,* Nov. 5, 1992, B9, National edition.

15. Eldersveld, *Political Parties in American Society,* 42.

Comparative state studies have shown that socioeconomic diversity within a state's population contributes to two-party competition.[16] A socially diverse population provides a basis for differences over government policy and allows both parties to build up support among selected groups. The changeover of the South from a one-party Democratic region to one characterized by increased interparty competition, especially in statewide elections, illustrates what happens when a society becomes more diverse. Until the 1950s the southern electorate was relatively homogeneous, sharing common ethnic, religious, and economic characteristics. Indeed, it was overwhelmingly white (blacks had been disenfranchised), Anglo-Saxon, and Protestant. The economy of the South was primarily agrarian, and its people tended to live in rural areas and small towns. Such homogeneity, therefore, offered little basis for the development of two parties. Real two-party competition did not come to the region until industrialization, unionization, urbanization, the enfranchisement of blacks, and the immigration of northerners created divisions within society that enabled the Republicans to gain a basis of support.

Third and Minor Parties: At Times a Critical Impact

Although American politics is dominated by two major parties, third parties have at times had a critical impact on the nation's history (see Table 6.2).[17] For example, the new Republican party of the 1850s helped to focus the national debate on the slavery issue. Indeed, its election victory in 1860 precipitated the Civil War. The Republican party also was a factor in the dissolution of the Whig party.

Unlike the Republicans, most third parties do not become major parties. They can, however, affect election outcomes and electoral alignments. Most third parties in this century have been **splinter parties**—offshoots of the major parties—which formed to protest the policies of their parent party's dominant faction. Theodore Roosevelt's 1912 Progressive ("Bull Moose") party, for example, was born because of a split in the GOP. As a result, the Republican vote was divided in the 1912 election, and Democrat Woodrow Wilson was elected president with less than a majority of the popular vote. In 1968 Alabama's

16. See Sarah McCally Morehouse, *State Politics and Policy* (New York: Holt, Rinehart, and Winston, 1981), chap. 2.

17. For an analysis of how third parties emerge and why people vote for their candidates, see Steven J. Rosenstone, Roy L. Behr, and Edward H. Lazarus, *Third Parties in America: Citizen Response to Major Party Failure* (Princeton, N.J.: Princeton University Press, 1984). Also see J. David Gillespie, *Politics at the Periphery: Third Parties in Two-Party America* (Columbia: University of South Carolina Press, 1993).

Table 6.2 Fate of Third Parties and Independent Candidates

Year	Third Party	Percent of Popular Vote for President	No. of Electoral Votes	Status in Next Election
1832	Anti-Masonic	7.8	7	Endorsed Whig candidate
1848	Free-Soil	10.1	0	Received 4.9% of vote
1856	American (Know-Nothing)	21.5	8	Party dissolved
	Republican	33.1	114	Won presidency
1860	Southern Democrat	18.1	72	Party dissolved
	Constitutional Union	12.6	39	Party dissolved
1892	Populist	8.5	22	Endorsed Democratic candidate
1912	Progressive (T. Roosevelt)	27.4	88	Returned to Republican party
	Socialist	6.0	0	Received 3.2% of vote
1924	Progressive (R. La Follette)	16.6	13	Returned to Republican party
1948	States' Rights Democratic	2.4	39	Party dissolved
	Progressive (H. Wallace)	2.4	0	Received 0.23% of vote
1968	American Independent (G. Wallace)	13.5	46	Received 1.4% of vote
1980	John B. Anderson	7.1	0	Did not run
1992	H. Ross Perot	18.9	0	

Source: Congressional Quarterly, *Guide to U.S. Elections,* 2d ed. (Washington, D.C.: Congressional Quarterly Inc., 1985); *Congressional Quarterly Weekly Report,* January 30, 1993, 233.

Democratic governor George Wallace ran on the American Independent ticket. His populist, antiestablishment, and hawkish military policies won 13 percent of the vote, siphoned off votes from both the Republican and Democratic candidates, and contributed to one of the closest presidential elections in the twentieth century.

In addition to major third-party movements, there occasionally have been important independent (nonparty) candidacies. The most recent and significant was Texas billionaire Ross Perot's independent run for the presidency in 1992. Perot won 18.9 percent of the popular vote—the highest percentage for an independent or third party since Theodore Roosevelt netted 27.4 percent in 1912. Perot's unusually well-funded and publicized campaign won him equal status with the Republican and Democratic nominees in the presidential debates. There and elsewhere on the campaign trail, he played a big role in arousing public concern about the federal budget deficit and forced the major party candidates to confront this issue more head-on than they had in the past. But, like independent candidate John Anderson in 1980, Perot found that his support was not sufficiently concentrated to win him a single electoral vote.

Strong third-party movements or major independent candidates are normally a sign of widespread discontent within the country. This was certainly true of the Populists in 1892, the La Follette Progressives in 1923 (Wisconsin senator Robert La Follette, its founder, ran for the presidency in 1924, losing to Republican Calvin Coolidge), Wallace's American Independent party in 1968, and Perot's 1992 campaign. Faced with such evidence of social unrest, at least one of the highly adaptive major parties normally has sought to accommodate the protest group within its ranks (for example, the Democrats adopted the Populist program in 1896).[18]

Some minor parties such as the Socialists and Libertarians are characterized by strong policy or ideological orientations. Their goals are not to win elections; rather, they use the electoral process to publicize their cause in the hope that eventually some of their policies will be adopted by the major parties.

Characteristics of American Parties

The American party system shares many traits with those in other Western democracies. These include long-established parties; a limited number of major parties; electoral alignments organized around national issues; and class-, religious-, and regionally based patterns of electoral support. But the American party system encompasses a particular combination of characteristics that makes it distinctive.

Decentralized Power Structure

Power within American parties is fragmented and scattered among thousands of elected and party officials at the national, state, and local levels. American parties thus are not hierarchical or centralized organizations. And elected officials, including the president, as well as party officers, such as the national chairs, do not have the power to order fellow party officials about. Of the factors contributing to the decentralized power structure of American parties, two factors—separation of powers and federalism—are constitutionally mandated. Two other factors—party nominating procedures and campaign practices—originate within the parties themselves.

Bases of the Party Power Structure. In countries with a **parliamentary system** such as Great Britain, the chief executive or prime minister is chosen by the majority party or a coalition of parties in the national legislature. If the legislators of the prime minister's party fail to sup-

18. For a discussion of the role of third parties in electoral realignments in American history, see Walter Dean Burnham, *Critical Elections and the Mainsprings of American Politics* (New York: Norton, 1970), 27–33.

American Political Parties since 1789

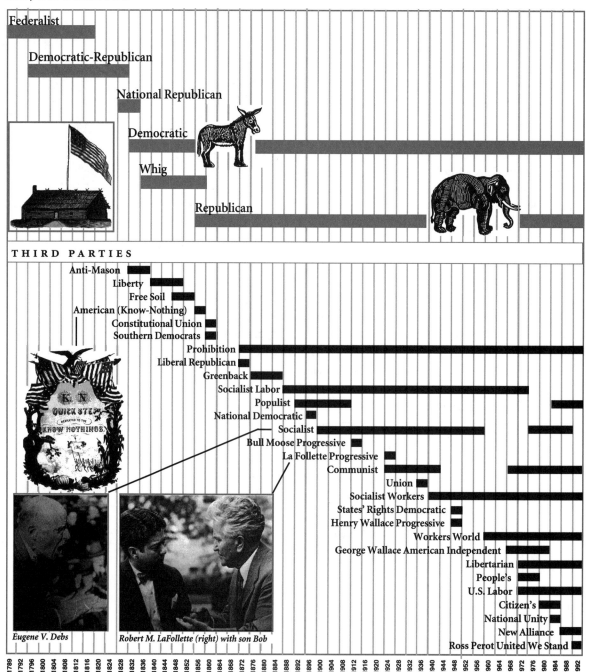

MAJOR PARTIES

Federalist

Democratic-Republican

National Republican

Democratic

Whig

Republican

THIRD PARTIES

Anti-Mason
Liberty
Free Soil
American (Know-Nothing)
Constitutional Union
Southern Democrats
Prohibition
Liberal Republican
Greenback
Socialist Labor
Populist
National Democratic
Socialist
Bull Moose Progressive
La Follette Progressive
Communist
Union
Socialist Workers
States' Rights Democratic
Henry Wallace Progressive
Workers World
George Wallace American Independent
Libertarian
People's
U.S. Labor
Citizen's
National Unity
New Alliance
Ross Perot United We Stand

Eugene V. Debs

Robert M. LaFollette (right) with son Bob

1789 1792 1796 1800 1804 1808 1812 1816 1820 1824 1828 1832 1836 1840 1844 1848 1852 1856 1860 1864 1868 1872 1876 1880 1884 1888 1892 1896 1900 1904 1908 1912 1916 1920 1924 1928 1932 1936 1940 1944 1948 1952 1956 1960 1964 1968 1972 1976 1980 1984 1988 1992

port their leader's policies, new parliamentary elections may be called or a new prime minister and cabinet may be appointed. Thus, in a parliamentary system party members in the legislature and in the executive have an incentive to remain united.

Under America's separation of powers principle, however, members of the president's party in Congress may oppose presidential policies without risking either having to stand immediately for reelection or forcing the resignation of the president and the cabinet. Operating on a different election schedule than the president and running in separate constituencies, members of Congress have an incentive to look after their own reelection needs first; support for their party's president is secondary. The separation of powers principle is embedded as well in state constitutions and its party-fragmenting effects are therefore present at the state level.

In creating a wide array of government units and elected officials, federalism, too, has contributed to the decentralization of power in political parties. Parties must organize not only to win the presidency but also to win offices in the thousands of constituencies found in the fifty states. Each of these election districts has its own party organization, elected officials, and candidate organizations. Frequently, the interests and priorities of these state and local politicians are quite different from those of their party's national leadership. For example, when the Democratic leader in New York City's Bronx was asked whether he was concerned about the outcome of the presidential election, he responded: "It [presidential politics] doesn't affect our life one bit. National politics—President and such—are too far removed from the bread and butter things that matter to local leaders and mayors and governors. The local leader cares about a senior citizen center, a local concern."[19] Thus, by creating thousands of distinct party organizations and separately elected state and local officials, the American brand of federalism has made centralized control of the parties virtually impossible.

The decentralizing effects of separation of powers and federalism are reinforced by the manner in which nominations are made and elections are conducted. As noted earlier, party nominations for state, local, and congressional offices are made through a system of popular elections (direct primaries). Because in this way the voters, not the party leaders, control the nominating process, the candidates build personal—not party—organizations to compete in the primaries. Knowing, then, that it is their personal campaign efforts and organiza-

19. Maurice Carroll, "For Once, a Primary Unites a Party," *New York Times,* March 25, 1984, 6E, National edition.

tions that win primary elections, elected officials rarely feel a strong sense of obligation to their party organization.

Indeed, electoral survival requires building a personal organization and not depending on popular presidents or a party organization to carry one to victory. Individual candidates are responsible for raising their own campaign war chests. Armed with adequate financing, a candidate can then secure the other resources essential to a campaign—media experts, pollsters, computer specialists, direct-mail specialists, accountants, lawyers, campaign managers, and consultants. With candidates largely on their own in securing the needed campaign resources, it is not surprising that they emerge from elections believing that the party's role in their victory was minor and that they can operate quite independently of party leaders.

A Countertrend. Although American parties remain decentralized institutions, important countertrends should be noted. Since the 1970s the national organizations of both major political parties have been strengthened significantly. The Democratic National Committee (DNC), backed by Supreme Court rulings, has aggressively asserted its authority over its state affiliates in matters pertaining to the selection of delegates to the **national nominating conventions**. The DNC requires, for example, that all delegation selection procedures used in the states conform with national party rules. Failure to conform can result in a state's delegation not being seated at the convention.

Both the national Democratic and Republican organizations, especially the Republicans, have developed highly efficient fund-raising operations. With millions of dollars to spend, the national parties have been able to provide financial and technical assistance to state-level candidates and party organizations. In doing so, the national party has gained increased influence over party organizations at the state level.[20]

Broad-based Electoral Support

In some parts of the world partisan attachments closely parallel social and economic divisions within society—Catholics versus Protestants, Christians versus Moslems, rich versus poor, workers versus management, city versus countryside, immigrants versus the native-born. When political and socioeconomic splits coincide, political con-

20. See John F. Bibby, "Party Renewal in the Republican Party," in *Party Renewal in America: Theory and Practice,* ed. Gerald M. Pomper (New York: Praeger, 1980), 102–115; Paul S. Herrnson, "The Revitalization of National Party Organizations," in *The Parties Respond: Changes in the American Party System,* 2d ed., ed. L. Sandy Maisell (Boulder, Colo.: Westview Press, 1994), 45–68; and Herrnson, *Party Campaigning in the 1980s* (Cambridge, Mass.: Harvard University Press, 1988).

flicts tend to be intense, sustained, and even violent. The tragic histories of Northern Ireland and Lebanon illustrate this pattern.

In sharp contrast, American political parties are coalition-type parties that can count on significant levels of support from virtually every
major socioeconomic group. While both parties can anticipate some
support from most social groups, there are important differences in
the levels of support provided by various voter groups (see Table 6.3).[21]
Moreover, the composition of the Republican and Democratic electoral coalitions has changed since the 1950s. The Republican party has
become more southern and white, while the Democratic party has
become distinctly less southern, with African Americans and Hispanics
constituting a growing share of its adherents (Table 6.3).[22]

Table 6.3 Profile of Democratic and Republican Electoral Coalitions since the 1950s *(percent)*

	1950s	1960s	1970s	1980	1984	1988	1992
DEMOCRATIC PARTY IDENTIFIERS							
White Protestants	18	20	17	16	17	15	17
Catholics	14	16	17	14	14	14	13
Northern union households	22	16	19	17	16	14	12
White southerners	31	26	23	23	22	23	19
Jews	4	4	3	5	3	4	4
African Americans	9	13	16	18	17	22	22
Hispanics	1	2	2	3	7	5	11
All others	2	2	3	4	5	3	2
TOTAL	100	100	100	100	100	100	100
REPUBLICAN PARTY IDENTIFIERS							
White Protestants	51	50	43	37	38	37	38
Catholics	10	12	12	14	14	16	15
Northern union households	16	11	14	16	12	12	11
White southerners	15	21	23	22	25	25	23
Jews	1	1	1	1	1	2	1
African Americans	5	2	2	3	2	4	3
Hispanics	0	–	1	2	4	2	7
All others	2	3	3	5	5	3	3
TOTAL	100	100	100	100	100	100	100

Source: John R. Petrocik, "Issues and Agendas: Electoral Coalitions in the 1988 Election" (Paper presented at the annual meeting of the American Political Science Association, Atlanta, August 31–September 3, 1989); 1992 data provided by Petrocik.

21. A comprehensive analysis of party electoral coalitions is found in John R.
Petrocik, *Party Coalitions: Realignments and the Decline of the New Deal Party System*
(Chicago: University of Chicago Press, 1981).

22. For an analysis of the changing voting patterns of socioeconomic groups, see
Ladd, "The 1988 Elections."

As noted in Chapter 5, differences in income and class, religion, race and ethnicity, and gender produce distinctive political orientations and thus patterns of support for political parties. More specifically, low-wage earners, union members, and blue-collar workers traditionally have supported the Democratic party, whereas professional, business, and managerial types have tilted toward the Republicans. In general, as income, level of education, and occupational status rise, the tendency to support Republicans increases (see Table 6.4). But these general tendencies should not obscure the fact that both parties receive significant support from the other party's core support groups—for example, in the 1988 presidential election Democrats received 40 percent of the professional and managerial vote, and Republicans received 42 percent of the union household vote.

Religion traditionally has provided a basis for partisan alignments in the United States. Since the New Deal era of the 1930s Catholics and Jews (overwhelmingly) have tended to be Democrats and white Protestants have tended to be Republicans. (Among Catholics the tendency to vote Democratic declined in the 1980s, with the Republicans gaining a plurality among these voters. And, unlike other social groups, Jews tend to vote Democratic regardless of their socioeconomic status.) Moreover, since 1980 an increasingly significant component of the GOP has been white fundamentalists or evangelical Christians, who voted 61 percent Republican in the three-way 1992 presidential race.

The influences of race and ethnicity on partisan choices are fairly clear-cut as well. Although from the post-Civil War era until the 1930s blacks supported Republicans as the party of emancipation, they have been overwhelmingly Democratic in recent decades (averaging 87 percent in the 1980s). The shift to the Democrats began during the depression of the 1930s and was accelerated by the 1964 election campaign, during which the Republican presidential nominee, Sen. Barry Goldwater (Ariz.), opposed major civil rights legislation proposed by President Lyndon Johnson. Hispanic voters have a definite but less pronounced tendency to support the Democratic party. Cuban-Americans, however, many of whom have achieved economic prosperity and are adamantly anticommunist, show strong pro-Republican tendencies. Asian Americans are a smaller, but rapidly expanding, element of the population. The politically active among the new Asian immigrants have tended to be disproportionally drawn from the professional and educated classes; they voted 55 percent Republican in 1992. Interestingly, as African Americans, Hispanics, and Asians are emerging as the critically important voter groups of the 1990s, the political

Table 6.4 Voting Patterns of Demographic Groups, 1988 and 1992 Presidential Elections

		Percent of Party Vote					1992
		1988		1992			
Percent of 1992		Rep.	Dem.	Rep.	Dem.	Ind.	Rep./Dem. Advantage
	Total vote	53	45	38	43	19	+5 D
46	Men	57	41	38	41	21	+3 D
54	Women	50	49	37	46	17	+9 D
87	Whites	59	40	41	39	20	+2 R
8	African Americans	12	86	11	82	7	+71 D
3	Hispanics	30	69	25	62	14	+ 37 D
1	Asians	52	39	55	29	16	+26 R
65	Married	57	42	40	40	20	———
35	Unmarried	46	53	33	49	18	+16D
22	18–29 years old	52	47	34	44	22	+10 D
38	30–44 years old	54	45	38	42	20	+4 D
24	45–59 years old	57	42	40	41	19	+1 D
16	60 and older	50	49	38	50	12	+12 D
6	Not a high school graduate	43	56	28	55	17	+27 D
25	High school graduate	50	49	36	43	20	+7 D
29	Some college education	57	42	37	42	21	+5 D
40	College graduate or more	56	43	39	44	18	+5 D
24	College graduate	62	37	41	40	19	+1 R
16	Postgraduate education	50	48	36	49	15	+13 D
49	White Protestant	66	33	46	33	21	+13 R
27	Catholic	52	47	36	44	20	+8 D
4	Jewish	35	64	12	78	10	+66 D
17	White born-again Christian	81	18	61	23	15	+38 R
19	Union household	42	57	24	55	21	+31 D
14	Family income under $15,000	37	62	23	59	18	+36 D
24	$15,000–$29,999	49	50	35	45	20	+10 D
30	$30,000–$49,999	56	44	38	41	21	+3 D
20	$50,000–$74,999	56	42	42	40	18	+2 R
13	$75,000 and over	62	37	48	36	16	+12 R
24	From the East	50	49	35	47	18	+12 D
27	From the Midwest	52	47	37	42	21	+5 D
30	From the South	58	41	43	42	16	+1 R
20	From the West	52	46	34	44	22	+10 D
11	First-time voters	51	47	30	48	22	+18 D

Sources: 1988: *New York Times*/CBS poll, reported in *New York Times*, Nov. 10, 1988, 18Y, National Edition, copyright © 1988 by the New York Times Company. Reprinted by permission. (Percentages for Asians: *Los Angeles Times* exit poll, reported in *Public Opinion*, January/February 1989, 32); 1992: Voter Research and Surveys exit polls.

influence of European ethnic groups is declining. With the assimilation of such groups into American society, their voting patterns have become less distinct.

Until the 1980s gender was not a basis for political divisions in the United States. In the presidential elections since 1980, however, there has been a consistent "gender gap": women have consistently voted more Democratic than men. For example, 1992 exit polls revealed that women gave Clinton a 9 percentage point margin; men favored him by only 3 points. Among women with four or more years of college, Clinton's margin climbed to 18 percentage points, and among those with graduate training it jumped to 25 points. The establishment of gender differences in the contemporary party system reflects the fact that since the 1960s women have encountered new types of problems as they have entered the work force in expanded numbers and as the number of single-parent, female-headed households has increased. In the process, family status also has become a variable influencing voting behavior. Thus, in 1992 married voters narrowly favored Bush, while those who were single, divorced or separated, and widowed all strongly backed Clinton by approximately 20 percentage points.[23]

Nonprogrammatic Policy Orientation

American political parties have an interest in influencing government policy, but they are not highly programmatic in their orientation, nor is their approach to policy guided by a social theory to which the party is expected to adhere—an approach that has been used by European labor and socialist parties. American party positions on issues tend to be adopted to meet immediate problems or electoral circumstances, not to achieve long-range goals. Thus, in 1992 Clinton strategists sought to use the Democratic platform to appeal to middle-class moderates who had deserted the Democratic party in the 1980s. The platform that was adopted by the Clinton-dominated national convention was therefore clearly more centrist than any Democratic platform since 1972. And to project an image of party unity, the platform was kept unusually short; it was more a statement of broad principles than a list of policy proposals. By contrast, the 1992 GOP platform-writing process was used by party strategists to solidify President Bush's weak-

23. Everett Carll Ladd, "The 1992 Vote for President Clinton: Another Brittle Mandate?" *Political Science Quarterly,* 108 (Spring 1993): 6. Also see Mary E. Bendyma and Celinda Lake, "Gender and Voting in the 1992 Presidential Election," in *The Year of the Woman: Myths and Realities,* ed. Elizabeth Adell Cook, Sue Thomas, and Clyde Wilcox (Boulder, Colo.: Westview Press, 1994), 237–254.

Table 6.5 Comparison of Selected Planks in the Republican and Democratic Platforms, 1992

Plank	Republican Party	Democratic Party
Taxes, budget, deficit	Would oppose any attempt to increase taxes, cap growth of non-Social Security entitlements, cut capital gains tax, adopt line-item veto, reduce personal exemption by $500.	Would generate more revenues through economic growth, control health care costs, make rich pay their fair share of taxes, reduce taxes on middle class.
Abortion	Reaffirms support of right-to-life amendment; opposes use of public funds for abortions.	Supports the right to choose, consistent with *Roe v. Wade,* regardless of ability to pay.
Gay rights	Supports continued ban on homosexuals in military as a matter of good order and discipline.	Would extend civil rights protection to gay men and lesbians, and end Defense Department discrimination.
Trade	Supports North American Free Trade Agreement (NAFTA) while sensitive to possible effects on regional markets.	Would advance NAFTA but include protections for legitimate concerns with the environment, safety and health standards.
Campaign finance	Opposes public financing of campaigns; would eliminate PACs.	Would limit overall campaign spending and role of PACs.
D.C. statehood	Opposes D.C. statehood.	Supports D.C. statehood.
Family leave	Supports parental leave negotiated between employer and employee.	Supports requiring unpaid leave for workers caring for ill children or relatives.
Environment	Would apply market-based solutions to environmental problems; opposes transfer of control of environmental policy outside the U.S.	Would protect old-growth forests, provide "no net loss" of wetlands, sign biodiversity treaty.

ened position with the most conservative elements of the Republican electoral coalition. Neither major party, in fact, has a clear image of the type of society it wishes to foster, and neither is committed to either unfettered capitalism or socialism.

With their broad-based electoral coalitions, moreover, it is difficult for political parties to adopt highly ideological and consistent policy positions. They must appeal to both labor and management, farmers and consumers, central city and suburban dwellers, Catholics and Protestants, homeowners and renters, whites, Hispanics, African Americans, and Asians. Even if their diverse followings permitted a strongly ideological approach to politics, political parties would find it difficult to achieve the internal unity needed to enact their programs because of their decentralized character.

Although their nonprogrammatic approach to public policy makes them moderate or centrist rather than doctrinaire extremists of the

Left or Right, the Republican and Democratic parties differ considerably in their policy orientations. Republicans, for example, tend to be less supportive of economic planning, redistribution of wealth, and social welfare benefits than Democrats (see Table 6.5 for a comparison of the 1992 party platforms).

Party Organization

The primary task of party organizations is winning elections. Parties are, therefore, organized around geographic election districts, beginning with the local unit of election administration (called a precinct in most states) and ascending through city/village/town committees, county committees, legislative district committees, congressional district committees, state central committees, and the national committee. The relationship of one level of committee to another is not hierarchical—that is, higher-level committees do not have control over those at a lower level. Rather, the party organizational structure is a series of layers (see Figure 6.1).[24] Each layer concentrates on the election campaign in its jurisdiction but also may cooperate in running campaigns at a higher level, such as those for governor or president. Each stratum of the party is more or less autonomous in its operations. A midwestern Republican state party chairman ("chair" is the designation used by the Democratic party) captured the essence of party organization when he described his relationship with the county party chairmen: "At best we are a loose confederation. I have no jurisdiction over county chairmen. I'd have resented a state chairman telling me what to do when I was county chairman."[25]

National Party Organizations

The national party organizations reflect the decentralized character of American parties. The Republican and Democratic national organizations both consist of a series of largely autonomous organizations: the national committee, the congressional campaign committee, and the senatorial campaign committee. Each committee has a separate membership and a specific set of elections on which it concentrates its activities.

National Committees. The highest governing authorities of the two major parties are their national conventions, which meet every four years to nominate presidential candidates and adopt party platforms and rules. During the long intervals between conventions, the national affairs of the parties are managed by their national committees: the

24. See Eldersveld, *Political Parties in American Society,* 133–136.
25. Interview conducted by the author as part of a National Science Foundation-funded study of state parties.

Republican National Committee (RNC) and the Democratic National Committee (DNC).

Each national committee is composed of representatives of state party organizations, as well as representatives of various voter groups and such elected officials as members of Congress, state legislators, and governors. Because the national committees are large bodies (the RNC has 162 members, and the DNC has a variable roster of slightly over 400 members) which meet only a few times a year, the real work of the committees is carried out by their national chairs and headquarters staff.

The national chair is formally elected by the national committee. For the party of the president (the "in-party"), however, the president actually makes the selection. In 1993 President Clinton designated his campaign manager, David Wilhelm, to be DNC chair. In-party chairs usually operate in strict accordance with White House directives and have little freedom of action. "Out-party" leaders are normally chosen in contested elections as various party factions seek to gain control of the national committee. Because they are not beholden to the White House, out-party chairs have more leeway and can have a greater impact than in-party leaders on their party's image and level of organizational activity.

National committees arrange for and manage national conventions, raise funds, carry out research, provide financial and technical assistance to state parties and candidates, and conduct polling and public relations. Through their highly successful direct-mail programs for soliciting small contributions and their efforts to gain large contributions, the national committees have been able to raise huge campaign war chests. In the 1991–1992 election cycle, for example, the RNC reported receipts of $85.4 million and the DNC receipts of $65.8 million.

With its superior fund-raising capacity, the RNC is a much more important campaign resource for assisting GOP candidates and state parties than is the DNC for its candidates and state affiliates. Under the leadership of chairs Paul Kirk (1985–1989) and Ronald Brown (1989–1993), the DNC narrowed its fund-raising gap with the RNC and significantly expanded its services to candidates and state parties.[26]

Senatorial and Congressional Campaign Committees. The Republican and Democratic senatorial and congressional campaign committees are composed of incumbent senators and representatives whose func-

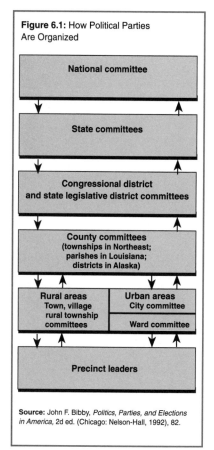

Figure 6.1: How Political Parties Are Organized

National committee

State committees

Congressional district and state legislative district committees

County committees (townships in Northeast; parishes in Louisiana; districts in Alaska)

Rural areas Town, village rural township committees | Urban areas City committee / Ward committee

Precinct leaders

Source: John F. Bibby, *Politics, Parties, and Elections in America,* 2d ed. (Chicago: Nelson-Hall, 1992), 82.

26. Herrnson, "The Revitalization of National Party Organizations"; and Reichley, *Life of the Parties,* chap. 18.

tion is to elect fellow partisans to Congress. Each committee has a professional staff that recruits candidates, raises campaign funds, and provides technical assistance to candidates. Like the national committees, the Republican congressional and senatorial committees have greater fund-raising capacities than their Democratic counterparts. In the 1991–1992 election cycle these Republican committees raised $107 million and the Democratic committees raised $37 million.[27]

In addition to their direct support of congressional and senatorial candidates, these committees transfer funds to state and local parties for use in party-building and get-out-the-vote activities that indirectly assist candidates vying for seats on Capitol Hill.

State Committees

Each state has both a Republican and a Democratic state central committee. The memberships of these committees are determined by state law and party rules. Committee members frequently represent congressional districts, legislative districts, or counties, as well as such auxiliary groups as the Young Democrats or the Federation of Republican Women. The size of central committees varies from approximately twenty in Iowa to over a thousand in California. Because of the size and periodic meeting schedules of these committees, their leadership normally falls to the state's party chairs and the headquarters staffs.

In the decades before the 1960s state parties commonly had neither a permanent headquarters nor a paid, full-time staff. Over the past two decades, however, state parties have operated out of permanent headquarters, and their professional staffs have dealt with fund-raising, research, public relations, and the provision of technical assistance to candidates and local party organizations. Just as Republican national party organizations are stronger than their Democratic counterparts, Republican state organizations tend to be stronger than Democratic state parties.[28] For example, the Florida state Republican organization operates a high-tech headquarters crammed with computer hardware, telephone banks, and printing facilities, and has a budget in excess of $6 million.

Counterparts of the senatorial and congressional campaign committees exist at the state level. State legislative campaign committees, composed of incumbent legislators who provide support for their parties' candidates, have become increasingly important in state politics.

27. Federal Election Commission data.

28. For a detailed consideration of state party organizations, see Cornelius P. Cotter et al., *Party Organizations in American Politics* (New York: Praeger, 1984). Also see John F. Bibby, "State Party Organizations: Coping and Adapting," in Maisel, *Parties Respond*, 21–44.

Indeed, in some states they are a more significant source of support for legislative candidates than the regular state central committees.[29]

County and Local Committees

When people think of local party organizations, they often envision a traditional urban machine, something like that once run by Mayor Richard Daley of Chicago. By dispensing 35,000 patronage jobs and other government favors to its supporters, Daley's Democratic machine maintained a hierarchically organized network of ward and precinct captains capable of mobilizing voters on election day. But such organizations are fast fading from the political landscape and are far from typical.[30]

Most county and local party organizations operate without a headquarters, using volunteer leaders and workers. Their activities are highly cyclical and concentrated during campaign periods. While normally short-handed, underfunded, and hardly models of professionalism or efficiency, local parties do manage to carry off many kinds of campaign activities—distributing campaign literature, raising funds, and getting out the vote.[31]

Unofficial Party Groups

The formal and legally recognized party organizations just described are supplemented by allied interest groups, unofficial party groups, and campaign consultants who work within the parties and constitute an element of their organizational strength. Organized labor, for example, has traditionally engaged in major get-out-the-vote drives in behalf of Democratic candidates and has coordinated many of its activities with the official units of the Democratic party. In quite a few states teachers' unions are one of the most important campaign resources available to Democratic candidates. And some business organizations have been a ready source of help to the GOP.

Because American political parties are coalitions of diverse and competing interests, elected officials, and factions, there is constant maneuvering for advantage within the parties. To achieve heightened

29. See Anthony Gierzynski, *Legislative Campaign Committees in the American States* (Lexington: University of Kentucky Press, 1992).

30. For a discussion of the decline of the Chicago Democratic organization and other urban machines, see Beck and Sorauf, *Party Politics in America*, 83–91.

31. The organizational status of local parties is analyzed utilizing a national survey in James L. Gibson et al., "Whither the Local Parties," *American Journal of Political Science* 29 (February 1985): 139–160; and James L. Gibson, John P. Frendries, and Laura L. Vertz, "Party Dynamics in the 1980s: Change in County Party Organizational Strength, 1980–1984," *American Journal of Political Science* 33 (February 1989): 67–90.

influence over party policy and presidential nominations, like-minded elected officials and party activists often form their own organizations. A prominent and influential example of this kind of organization is the Democratic Leadership Council (DLC), which was formed in 1985 by moderate and conservative Democrats and led by then-Arkansas governor Bill Clinton and Senators Sam Nunn (Ga.), Charles Robb (Va.), and John Breaux (La.). Convinced that the party needed a more moderate image if it was to ever regain the White House, the DLC worked through the 1980s and early 1990s to move the party toward the political center. To help it in this effort, the DLC created its own Washington "think tank," the Progressive Policy Institute, to issue policy papers. All this could not be done, however, without stirring controversy within the Democratic ranks and facing competition from such liberal groups as Jesse Jackson's Rainbow Coalition.

On the Republican side, the Republican Mainstream Committee headed by Rep. James Leach (Iowa), the Ripon Society led by former Vermont representative Peter Smith, and the National Republican Coalition for Choice chaired by Mary Crisp, a former RNC official, seek to combat what their members see as their party's drift too far to the Right. Empower America, led by former Reagan-Bush cabinet members William Bennett, Jack Kemp, and Jeane Kirkpatrick, carries the conservative torch. Such conservatively oriented think tanks as the American Enterprise Institute and Heritage Foundation work primarily with GOP elected officials.

Party activists also create unofficial organizations designed to augment the resources of the regular party structure. For example, the Forum for International Policy is a foreign policy and rapid-response group headed by former Bush administration officials, including National Security Adviser Brent Scowcroft, CIA Director Robert Gates, and Trade Representative Carla Hills.

In addition to these informal organizations, the Republican and Democratic parties each have a stable of political consultants and pollsters who constitute a basic party resource. Many are considered so essential that they are kept on retainer by the RNC or DNC. For example, among President Clinton's trusted political advisers are campaign consultants James Carville and Paul Begala, and pollster Stan Greenberg.

Nominations for Congressional and State Offices

On election day a voter essentially chooses between the Republican and Democratic candidates because, as noted earlier, only the nominees of the two major parties have a realistic chance of being elected. The functioning of American democracy is, then, dramatically affected by the Republicans' and Democrats' nominating decisions.

The Rise of the Direct Primary

In most Western democracies nominations are the responsibility of the party organizations; the ordinary voters play no role in the process. The American practice is quite different. Most candidates for congressional and state offices are nominated via a direct primary in which the voters pick the nominees who will represent each party.[32]

In the nineteenth century, nominations were made by each party organization meeting in a **caucus** or convention. These procedures fell into disrepute early in this century, however, because of allegations of corrupt boss rule, and the direct primary spread across the country as a reform designed to give ordinary voters a voice in choosing party nominees. Another reason for introducing the direct primary was the absence of real interparty competition after the 1890s in the solidly Democratic South and in GOP-dominated areas of the North. Primary elections provided a way for the voters to participate in the electoral choice that in one-party areas was most important—the selection of the dominant party's candidate.[33]

Types of Direct Primaries

Primaries operate quite differently from state to state because each state regulates by statute how primaries are to be conducted for congressional and state candidates. Most states use a form of **closed primary,** which restricts participation in the primaries to people who either register as party affiliates or declare publicly the party primary in which they wish to participate. Advocates of a mandatory public declaration of party preference before voting in a primary believe that party nominations should be made by party adherents and that the process should not be contaminated by people who are either members of the opposition party or independents.

32. Several states such as New York and Virginia give parties the option of using party conventions to nominate candidates.

33. On the development of the direct primary and its consequences, see Key, *Politics, Parties, and Pressure Groups,* chap. 14; and Epstein, *Political Parties in the American Mold,* chap. 6.

A minority of the states choose their candidates without requiring public declarations of party preference. In the nine states using an **open primary** procedure, voters decide in the secrecy of the polling booth in which party's primary they wish to vote. They may vote in only one party's primary, but the party primary in which they voted is secret. The open primary permits wider participation in the nominating process. Its critics argue that it also encourages **crossover voting**— voting in the primary of the party to which the voter does not belong. In open primary states voters tend to participate in the party primary with the hottest contests.

Alaska and Washington operate a wide-open primary—a **blanket primary**—which permits citizens to vote in more than one party's primary by switching back and forth between parties from office to office, provided they vote for only one candidate per office.

Under Louisiana's unique "nonpartisan" primary, all candidates for each office, regardless of party affiliation, are listed on the primary ballot. If a candidate receives a majority of the vote, that candidate is automatically elected. If no candidate receives a majority, the top two finishers run against each other in the general election.

In most states the candidate who receives the most votes (a plurality) wins the primary and is given a place on the general election ballot. In nine of the southern and border states, however, a candidate is required to win a majority of the primary vote to qualify as the party nominee on the general election ballot. If no candidate receives a majority of the votes in the primary, a **runoff primary** is held between the top two finishers. This practice developed in the South earlier in this century when there was no meaningful Republican competition in the general election. Winning the Democratic primary, therefore, was the equivalent of being elected.[34]

Consequences of the Direct Primary

Weakening the control of the party over nominations was the intended consequence of the direct primary, and it succeeded. Party organizations now rarely have enough influence to control the outcome of primary elections. They often recruit candidates for primaries, discourage others from running, and provide support for preferred candidates, but ultimately it is the primary voters who pick party nom-

34. For an analysis of the impact of runoff primaries and the issue of whether they discriminate against African American candidates, see Charles S. Bullock III and Loch K. Johnson, *Runoff Elections in the United States* (Knoxville: University of Tennessee Press, 1991).

inees. Without control over nominations, parties lack the power to discipline maverick officeholders by denying them a nomination and a place on the general election ballot.

The reformers who urged adoption of the direct primary envisaged high levels of voter turnout in primary elections, but low voter turnout has been the reality. In northern states only about 30 percent of the eligible electorate participates in primaries. Participation had been higher in the South because its one-party Democratic traditions made the Democratic primary the real election in the region. But as Republican electoral strength has grown and turned many general elections into real interparty contests, primary turnout as a proportion of the general election vote has fallen.[35]

The sponsors of the direct primary expected as well substantial competition in such contests, but the advantages that incumbents carry into campaigns tend to discourage serious opposition in the primaries. In fact, for most incumbents the primary is like the common cold—a nuisance but unlikely to be fatal. Over 90 percent of all incumbent governors, senators, and representatives gain renomination. When no incumbent is seeking renomination—an open seat—the primary may resemble a battlefield, especially in the party with the best prospects for winning the general election.

Presidential Nominations

Presidential nominees of the Republican and Democratic parties are formally nominated by national conventions held in the summers of presidential election years. These conventions, which are the culmination of a long season of campaigning, are composed of delegates representing the fifty states, the District of Columbia, Puerto Rico, and the territories.[36]

Methods of Delegate Selection

National convention delegates are chosen within each state under procedures spelled out in state laws or state party rules. Because each state legislature or party organization devises its own delegate selection procedures, the exact procedures of the states vary widely. But in cases in which statutes or party rules violate national party rules, the nation-

35. Larry J. Sabato, *Goodbye to Goodtime Charlie: The American Governorship Transformed,* 2d ed. (Washington, D.C.: CQ Press, 1983), 124.

36. For an informed critique of the presidential nominating process and various proposals for change, see Leon D. Epstein, "Presidential Nominations since Party Reform," *American Review of Politics* 14 (Summer 1993): 149–162.

al party reigns supreme and the national convention may refuse to seat the offending state's delegation.

The national Democratic party has been particularly active in developing, revising, and vigorously enforcing its complicated delegate rules. As a result, it has come into periodic conflict with state party organizations whose delegate selection procedures were found to be in violation of national party rules. The most prominent case involved Wisconsin's use of an open presidential primary to select its delegates—a procedure contrary to a national Democratic rule banning this type of presidential primary. Strict enforcement of this rule meant that Democrats in Wisconsin—which had the oldest presidential primary law in the nation (enacted in 1903)—were forced in 1984 to abandon their traditional open presidential primary and use a system of party caucuses to select convention delegates. Seeking to avoid such intraparty conflicts, the national party changed its rules after 1984 and granted Wisconsin and Montana exemptions from the ban on open primaries. The national Republican party's delegate selection rules are much more lenient than those of the Democrats and give the state parties wide latitude in devising delegate selection procedures.[37]

Three principal methods of selecting national convention delegates are used (Figure 6.2). They are (1) the presidential primary, (2) state party caucuses and conventions, and (3) for the Democrats only, automatic selection based on a person's status as a party or elected officeholder.

Presidential Primaries. A **presidential primary** is an election in which the voters of a state have the opportunity to cast a ballot in favor of a preferred candidate for their party's presidential nomination or for delegates pledged to support that candidate. In 1992 approximately 80 percent of the Republican delegates and two-thirds of the Democratic delegates were chosen through presidential primaries. It is therefore essential that presidential contenders contest virtually all of the primaries, which are held from February to June in presidential election years.

Presidential primaries have an importance that extends beyond the number of delegates at stake. Primary outcomes reveal to party leaders, the media, and the public a candidate's popularity, electability, and campaign momentum. Thus, it is particularly important that candidates do well in the early primaries—most notably in New Hamp-

37. For a thorough analysis of delegate selection procedures and their impact on national conventions, see Byron E. Shafer, *Bifurcated Politics: Evolution and Reform in the National Party Convention* (Cambridge, Mass.: Harvard University Press, 1988).

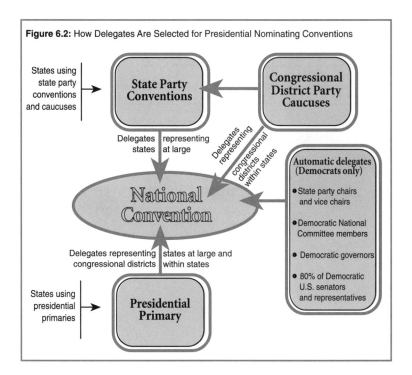

Figure 6.2: How Delegates Are Selected for Presidential Nominating Conventions

States using state party conventions and caucuses → State Party Conventions

Congressional District Party Caucuses

Delegates representing states at large

Delegates representing congressional districts within states

National Convention

Automatic delegates (Democrats only)
- State party chairs and vice chairs
- Democratic National Committee members
- Democratic governors
- 80% of Democratic U.S. senators and representatives

Delegates representing states at large and congressional districts within states

States using presidential primaries → Presidential Primary

shire's first-in-the-nation primary and on "Super Tuesday" three weeks later when most southern states and several northern and western states hold their primaries and caucuses.

But to do well in the presidential primaries and to compete ably for a majority of the national convention delegates at stake, candidates must be extremely well organized on a nationwide basis and well financed. It is not surprising, then, that Republican George Bush and Democrat Bill Clinton, the candidates who had both the strongest organizations and superior financing, succeeded in winning their parties' nominations in 1992 (Table 6.6). Indeed, since 1980 every Democratic and Republican presidential nominee has led his party's candidates in fund-raising as of December 31 of the year before the presidential election.[38]

Organizational and financial strength becomes especially important after the New Hampshire primary, which features "retail politics"— direct selling of the candidates through extensive personal contact with voters. After that primary the nominating terrain changes dramatically and becomes an exercise in "wholesale politics"—reaching the mass electorate in a number of states simultaneously. In successive weeks

38. Mark Shields, "High-Stakes Presidential Poker," *Washington Post,* Feb. 6, 1994, C7.

Table 6.6 Presidential Primary Results, 1992

	No. of Primaries on Ballot	No. of Primaries Won	Total Vote	Percent	Best Showing (Percent)
DEMOCRATS					
Bill Clinton (Ark.)	39	32	10,471,965	51.89	Puerto Rico (95.6)
Jerry Brown (Calif.)	39	2	4,023,373	19.94	Calif. (40.2)
Paul Tsongas (Mass.)	35	4	3,644,543	18.06	Mass. (66.3)
"Uncommitted"	25	0	779,895	3.86	Idaho (29.1)
Bob Kerrey (Neb.)	30	1	317,939	1.58	S.D. (40.2)
Tom Harkin (Iowa)	30	0	280,324	1.39	S.D. (25.2)
Others, scattered write-ins	—	1[a]	661,934	3.29	—
REPUBLICANS					
George Bush (Texas)	39	39	9,512,142	73.03	Puerto Rico (99.2)
Pat Buchanan (Va.)	36	0	2,912,156	22.36	N.H. (37.4)
"Uncommitted"	18	0	290,118	2.23	S.D. (30.7)
David Duke (La.)	16	0	119,942	0.92	Miss. (10.6)
Ross Perot (Texas)	0	0	56,136	0.43	Wash. (19.6)
Others, scattered write-ins	—	0	135,330	1.04	—

Source: *Congressional Quarterly Weekly Report,* July 4, 1992, 71; August 8, 1992, 67.
   Note : a. None of the major Democratic candidates entered the North Dakota primary, which was won by Ross Perot with write-in votes.

during March and April states in every region hold primaries or caucuses to select their national convention delegates. Only an organization that is well-financed and effective across the country can succeed under these circumstances. In the 1992 Democratic nomination contest Clinton had a major organizational and financial advantage over his principal rival, former Massachusetts senator Paul Tsongas. The *Washington Post*'s respected national politics reporter David Broder noted that after its New Hampshire primary victory Tsongas's campaign

illustrated the problems of a fledgling candidacy that has suddenly exceeded its own expectations and been flung into a national contest for which it was organizationally ill-prepared. . . . A cottage industry—a few young aides helping one man hand out autographed copies of his campaign manifesto—suddenly had to transform itself into a mass-market operation ready to compete across the country.[39]

With the Tsongas campaign not equipped to campaign effectively on a nationwide scale, Clinton defeated him in eight of ten states on

39. David S. Broder, "Tsongas Forced to Play Organizational Catch-Up," *Washington Post,* March 8, 1992, A19.

Self-Nomination: Running for President as an Independent

Is it possible to become a serious presidential candidate without going through the grueling process of seeking a Republican or Democratic nomination? Yes, one can nominate oneself and run as an independent as John Anderson did in 1980 and Ross Perot did in 1992.

But if the truth be told, getting on the ballot as an independent is an arduous, labor-intensive, expensive undertaking. Unlike the Republican and Democratic presidential nominees, independent candidates are not automatically placed on the ballots of the fifty states and the District of Columbia. Instead, they must qualify for a place on the ballot by complying with the often-demanding laws of each state. At a minimum this involves collecting the signatures of thousands of registered voters on a petition. But when campaign workers and money have to be devoted to this daunting task, an independent candidate's ability to cam-

paign and gain public visibility can be substantially reduced, as the underfunded 1980 campaign of John Anderson discovered.

Ross Perot, however, did not have this problem. By August 1992 the Texas billionaire had spent $17.5 million of his own money on his campaign, including $4 million on petition drives after his announcement in July during the Democratic convention that he was withdrawing from the race. In New York State alone he spent $1 million on his petition drive, which required the services of over eighty paid employees (mostly imported from his Dallas headquarters) as well as temporary workers from a number of employment agencies. At just one agency Perot spent nearly $110,000.

Winning a presidential nomination at the Republican or Democratic national conventions, then, requires huge financial and organizational resources, but so too does

self-nomination by a prominent and influential independent candidate.

Source: Steven A. Holmes, "Perot Ponders Reentering Presidential Campaign," *New York Times*, Sept. 24, 1992, A12, National edition.

Super Tuesday and delivered knockout blows in the Illinois and Michigan primaries a week later.

State Party Caucuses and Conventions. In states using the caucus and convention system of delegate selection, the process normally starts with party meetings at the local level (for example, at the precinct or county level). These local meetings select people to represent the local party at congressional district caucuses and state conventions. Those attending the congressional district caucuses select delegates to represent their congressional districts at the national convention; the state convention selects national convention delegates to represent the state at large.

This progression of party meetings involves a relatively small proportion of the electorate. Those attending party caucuses tend to be party activists and enthusiastic supporters of the presidential candidates. Thus, the candidates who do best in the caucus states are those who have strong organizations capable of mobilizing supporters to attend the meetings (Bush for the Republicans and Clinton for the Democrats in 1992), and who instill passionate support among their loyalists (Jesse Jackson for the Democrats and Pat Robertson for the Republicans in 1988).[40]

Automatic Delegates. In an effort to encourage greater involvement by their elected and party officials, the Democrats began in 1984 to give these leaders **automatic delegate** status. In 1992 the 772 so-called super-delegates included 80 percent of the Democratic members of the Senate and House, Democratic governors, members of the Democratic National Committee, and the state party chairs and vice chairs. The impact of these automatic delegates has been rather limited because they have overwhelmingly supported the front-running candidates and thus have provided additional delegates for the apparent winners of the primaries (Walter Mondale in 1984, Michael Dukakis in 1988, and Bill Clinton in 1992). The Republicans do not have any automatic delegates. Republican party and elected officials must be selected through the normal primary or caucus processes.

Stages in the Nominating Process

Gaining a major party nomination is often an almost full-time, four-year undertaking. Because it is such an all-consuming activity, it is difficult for politicians who have major government responsibilities to enter the contest. Aside from incumbents, the major contestants for presidential nominations have been either out of office—former governor Jimmy Carter in 1976, former governor Ronald Reagan in 1980, former vice president Walter Mondale in 1984, and Jesse Jackson in 1984 and 1988—or elected officials with sufficiently limited leadership responsibilities to permit full-time campaigning—Sen. Gary Hart (D-Colo.) in 1984 and Sen. Albert Gore (D-Tenn.) and Vice President George Bush in 1988. Governors of small to medium-sized states have been able to combine presidential campaigning with their governing duties, as the successful 1992 campaign of Arkansas governor Bill Clin-

40. Rhodes Cook and Dave Kaplan, "In 1988, Caucuses Have Been the Place for Political Passion," *Congressional Quarterly Weekly Report,* June 4, 1988, 1523–1527; and Barbara Norrander, "Nomination Choices: Caucus and Primary Outcomes, 1976–88," *American Journal of Political Science* 37 (May 1993): 343–364.

Former Massachusetts senator Paul Tsongas (left photo) won the 1992 Democratic presidential primary in New Hampshire and conservative television commentator Pat Buchanan dealt President George Bush a severe blow by winning 37 percent of the Republican vote. But when the nomination campaigns moved from the personalized, "retail politics" of New Hampshire to the media intensive, "wholesale politics" of the later multistate primaries, Tsongas and Buchanan collapsed before the organizational and financial muscle of the Clinton and Bush campaigns.

ton illustrates. New York governor Mario Cuomo, however, cited his state responsibilities as a reason for not making a presidential bid in 1992. The marathon struggle that such contestants must confront for the nomination can be divided into a series of stages.[41]

Stage One: Building a Base of Support and Entering Preliminary Contests. The planning and preparation for a nomination campaign normally begin shortly after a presidential election with the recruitment of an experienced campaign staff. Candidates also customarily create political action committees (PACs) and tax-exempt foundations to help to fund their preliminary campaign activities.[42] These activities include crisscrossing the nation to speak to state party meetings, congressional candidate fund-raisers, trade associations, unions, and college groups. Because Iowa and New Hampshire hold the earliest delegate selection events, the itineraries of the candidates normally include a concentration of stopovers in these states. Well-publicized trips abroad to confer with foreign leaders are yet another standard part of the process of becoming a nationally known leader.

In the year of the midterm congressional and state elections (for example, 1986, 1990, 1994), the pace of campaigning normally picks up. The candidates blanket the country to appear at events in support of

41. A summary of 1992 presidential nominating politics is found in Michael Nelson, ed., *The Elections of 1992* (Washington, D.C.: CQ Press, 1993), chap. 2. For a more complete description of the stages in the presidential nomination process, see John F. Bibby, *Politics, Parties, and Elections in America,* 2d ed. (Chicago: Nelson-Hall, 1992), chap. 6.

42. For an example of the use of presidential candidate political action committees, see Dan Morgan, "PACs Stretching Election Law Limits," *Washington Post,* Feb. 5, 1988, A1, A10.

their party's congressional and state candidates and in the process to gain the backing of key party leaders and elected officials.

Following the midterm elections the candidates begin to enlarge and perfect their campaign staffs and to concentrate their campaign efforts on the states holding early primaries and caucuses. These also are days of candidate testing as the national media begin to pay closer attention to the activities, issue positions, backgrounds, and personalities of the candidates. Revelations of past indiscretions or recent errors in judgment can damage a campaign beyond repair as the news media have become increasingly aggressive in investigating the private lives of candidates. Gary Hart, the early Democratic front-runner in the 1988 race, saw his nomination drive collapse within a month of its formal opening when revelations of his extramarital adventures with an attractive model on a yacht named *Monkey Business* created a storm of publicity.

In the year before the national conventions the candidates are brought into face-to-face contests during candidate debates and straw polls conducted at state party gatherings. In 1992 there was a proliferation of candidate debates in which Democratic contenders sought to establish a national identity and demonstrate credibility as potential presidents. As for the straw polls, a good showing is extremely important in the early stages of a campaign because strong poll results encourage financial contributions and help in recruiting campaign workers.

Stage Two: Competing in Early Primaries and Caucuses. The early events in the delegate selection process have a significance that goes well beyond the number of convention delegates at stake. The Iowa caucuses, New Hampshire primary, and Super Tuesday primaries and caucuses follow one another in quick succession in February and March of presidential election years. By weeding out the weaker candidates, these events narrow the field of candidates. The early contests also provide the more successful candidates with campaign momentum—standing in the polls, campaign contributions, and volunteer workers—which helps them to sustain their campaigns during the long grind of primaries and caucuses that stretch from February to June. In 1992, for example, a strong second-place finish to native New Englander Paul Tsongas's win in the New Hampshire primary revived Bill Clinton's campaign, which had been thrown off track by widely publicized rumors of womanizing. At the same time, the weak showings of Senators Tom Harkin (Iowa) and Bob Kerrey (Neb.) foreshadowed their rapid demise as serious contenders for the nomination. When Clinton followed up his New Hampshire comeback (he dubbed himself the "comeback kid") with impressive victories three weeks later on Super Tuesday, the Tsongas campaign was on the ropes and near collapse. That left only the maverick, the antiestablishment former governor of California, Jerry Brown, as a potential obstacle to Clinton's becoming the Democratic nominee.

In 1996 the early primaries will take on even greater importance because of intensified "front-loading"—the scheduling early in the primary season of primaries that select large blocs of delegates. In March 1996 a series of major primaries will follow in quick succession after Super Tuesday. On the third Tuesday of the month the large midwestern states of Illinois, Michigan, and Ohio will hold their primaries, and one week later the delegate-rich California primary will be held. With its major contests in the South, Midwest, and California, the last three weeks of March 1996 will constitute a virtual national primary that could well decide the presidential nomination.

Throughout the primary season, but especially during the early primaries, the news media play an important role in interpreting the meaning of primary outcomes. The media determine winners and losers—which candidates made strong or stronger-than-expected showings and which candidates did less well than expected. President Bush's campaign, for example, received a severe jolt when conservative columnist and TV talk show participant Pat Buchanan, who attacked the president in an often bitter and derisive manner (calling the president "King George"), received 37 percent of the vote in the New Hampshire primary and held the incumbent president to 53 percent. Buchanan's marshaling of a sizable protest vote was widely interpreted as a forbidding sign of weakness for Bush, even though Buchanan was not seen as a serious contender for the GOP nomination.

Stage Three: Competing in Later Primaries and Caucuses. After the March primaries and caucuses the serious contenders left in the race try to sustain their early momentum and win the maximum number of delegates. In the later primaries and caucuses the front-runner does not have to win all or even most of the contests, but he or she must continue to gain a significant share of the delegates being contested. Jimmy Carter in 1976 and Walter Mondale in 1984, for example, failed to win a majority in the later primaries, but their strong showings in the early primaries and their abilities to win a significant portion of the delegates in the later primaries, even in states they did not carry, enabled them to gather a majority of the convention delegates.

In the 1992 Democratic contest, Bill Clinton, after knocking Tsongas out of the race, smashed Jerry Brown's chances on April 7 in the New

York, Wisconsin, and Kansas primaries, and from then on was on an unstoppable course toward the nomination. And after losing the Republican primaries in these states by huge margins (his best showing was 14.8 percent in Wisconsin), Buchanan virtually conceded to Bush by telling reporters that only "celestial intervention" could prevent the president's renomination.

Because candidates' organizations run slates of candidates for delegate positions in both the primary and caucus states and amass pledges of support from delegates as they are chosen, it is usually apparent before the end of the primary and caucus season in June which candidate will have sufficient delegate strength to be the nominee of the national convention. It was, therefore, certain in the weeks before the 1992 Republican and Democratic conventions that George Bush and Bill Clinton would be the nominees of their respective parties (a summary of 1992 presidential primary results is provided in Table 6.6).

Stage Four: Confirming the Nomination at the National Convention. National nominating conventions are not deliberative bodies whose delegates carefully weigh the merits of the various candidates before casting their votes on the presidential nomination roll call.[43] To the contrary, the vast majority of the delegates have already announced and pledged their support to a candidate. It is their function to ratify and legitimize the decisions that have been made in the presidential primaries and caucuses across the nation. As for its other duties, the convention adopts the party platform and makes rules governing party operations for the next four years.

The principal significance of the national convention is that it kicks off the presidential election campaign. It is an opportunity for the party to showcase its presidential nominee while it has the attention of the television networks and to establish campaign themes for the fall campaign. As David Broder has commented:

Convention week is important, not because it marks the end of the nominating period, but because it is the start of the general election. It is the time when most voters take their first serious look at the candidates and their parties and begin to focus on the choice they will make in November.[44]

Conventions also are places for working out the compromises that will unify the party for the upcoming campaign. The winning faction can make concessions to the losers on key provisions in the platform, on party rules, and on the people who will run the campaign. In 1988

43. On the role of the modern-day convention, see Shafer, *Bifurcated Politics.*
44. David S. Broder, "A Chance to Be 'Presidential,'" *Washington Post,* July 15, 1984, A8.

Conventions kick off the presidential election campaigns. These carefully scripted television productions are designed to gain favorable media coverage and create enthusiasm among party loyalists. At the 1992 GOP convention, President and Mrs. Bush along with Vice President and Mrs. Quayle give the traditional clasped hands signal to their supporters.

the Dukakis organization made concessions to Jesse Jackson in each of these areas in an effort to enlist his enthusiastic support of Dukakis in the general election.

Particularly important for party unity is the selection of a vice-presidential nominee. Presidential nominees usually select their vice-presidential running mates from a faction of the party different than their own. Such choices are aimed at unifying the party for the campaign and adding vote-getting appeal to the ticket. In 1988, for example, Governor Dukakis picked Sen. Lloyd Bentsen (D-Texas), a prominent member of the moderate wing of the Democratic party, to be his vice-presidential candidate. George Bush's surprising selection of youthful senator Dan Quayle (R-Ind.) was done with an eye toward reassuring conservative activists and appealing to younger voters. Bill Clinton's selection of Sen. Al Gore seemed at first surprising because he was so like Clinton in age, region, religion and ethnicity, and ideology. The choice of Gore, however, was meant to highlight Clinton's theme of change: the Democratic ticket would be of a different generation than either Bush or Ross Perot.[45] And a second southerner on the ticket, it was hoped, would enhance Democratic prospects in a region that had been a base of GOP electoral strength in the 1980s. In addition, Gore was a Vietnam veteran, and his strong support from the environmental community shored up potential Clinton vulnerabilities.

Although the outcome of convention nomination contests are normally known well in advance of the event, conventions are seldom dull affairs. The front-running candidates usually continue to court the delegates to ensure their eventual nomination. The underdog candidates

45. See Nelson, *Elections of 1992*, 52.

Table 6.7 Postconvention "Bounce":
1960–1992
(percent of points gained)

| Year/ | Candidate's Party | |
Candidates	Dem.	Rep.
1992 Clinton vs. Bush	+16	+5
1988 Dukakis vs. Bush	+7	+6
1984 Mondale vs. Reagan	+9	+4
1980 Carter vs. Reagan	+10	+8
1976 Carter vs. Ford	+9	+5
1972 McGovern vs. Nixon	±0	+7
1968 Humphrey vs. Nixon	+2	+5
1964 Johnson vs. Goldwater	+3	+5
1960 Kennedy vs. Nixon	+6	+14
Average, 1960–1988:	+5.7	+6.7

Source: *Gallup Poll Monthly,* August 1992, 25.

frequently seek test votes on issues that, on the surface, appear to be matters of fairness or ideology rather than contests between the candidates for the nomination. Such issues include convention rules, platform planks, and the seating of delegates whose status is being challenged on legal grounds. The underdog candidates hope to use such issues to cast doubt on the strength of the front-runner and to demonstrate their own support among the delegates. An example of this strategy occurred at the 1980 Democratic convention when Sen. Edward Kennedy (D-Mass.) was seeking to derail President Jimmy Carter's bid for renomination. The Kennedy forces sought a rules change that would have freed delegates from their pledges of candidate support made at the time they were selected, enabling them to vote for whomever they chose on the nomination roll call. When Carter handily defeated this Kennedy tactic, it was clear to all that Carter would be renominated, and Kennedy withdrew from the contest. These fights over rules, the platform, and delegate seating (credentials) are the most crucial events of a convention. Their outcomes foreshadow who will win the convention's nomination.

After the conventions the presidential nominees normally receive a "bounce" in the polls—the result of intense media attention and the careful staging for television. The 16 percentage point "bounce" for the Clinton campaign after the 1992 Democratic convention set a Gallup poll record and gave Clinton the lead in the polls over President Bush, who received a much more average postconvention "bump" in the polls of 5 percent (see Table 6.7).

Clinton's big postconvention bounce in the polls stemmed from two factors. First, the skillfully orchestrated Democratic convention conveyed an unusually positive image of the party and its nominee. Second, midway through the convention Ross Perot announced his withdrawal from the presidential race and threw in some kind words about the Democrats. Perot's withdrawal (which turned out to be only temporary) left a large bloc of voters open to Democratic appeals at a time when the media spotlight was focused on the Democratic nominee, Bill Clinton.

Financing Presidential Nomination Campaigns

The disclosures of campaign finance irregularities made during the Watergate investigations of the Nixon presidency culminated in passage of major reform legislation, the Federal Election Campaign Act (FECA) amendments of 1974. This law has dramatically changed the financing of presidential nomination campaigns so that it is no longer possible to fund such campaigns by relying on a few large contributors or "fat cats." Strict contribution limits have been imposed: $1,000 for individuals and $5,000 for political action committees. Candidates must raise funds through broad-based efforts that rely on small and medium-sized contributions.

One of FECA's most significant innovations is a provision making it possible for major party candidates to receive **federal matching funds**. Under this system the Federal Election Commission (FEC) will match private contributions in amounts up to $250 with federal funds. To be eligible for federal matching funds, candidates must raise at least $5,000 through individual contributions (not to exceed $250 each) in each of at least twenty states; abide by a nationwide spending limit which is adjusted before each presidential campaign for inflation (in 1992 the limit was $27.6 million); abide by individual state spending limits based on a formula of 16 cents plus an inflation factor per eligible voter; and disclose all contributions and expenditures of $200 or more.

The FECA reforms have not made money less important in presidential nominations than it was before 1974, but the rules of the game for raising it are now different. Without adequate private contributions to generate matching funds, campaigns can quickly run out of gas and stall as Tom Harkin, Bob Kerrey, Paul Tsongas, and Pat Buchanan discovered in 1992.

An additional consequence of FECA has been a requirement that candidates impose tightfisted budgetary control over their campaigns in every state. But the task of staying within the national and individual state spending limits is complicated by three factors: (1) the total of all state spending limits is greater than the national spending ceiling; (2) the state spending limits do not take into account whether a state chooses its delegates by primary or by caucus (primary campaigns are much more expensive); and (3) state spending limits are based on the number of eligible voters in the state and not on the state's strategic importance (the spending limit for New Hampshire's first-in-the-nation primary is the same as that for Guam's caucus!). Presidential nomination campaigns are, therefore, characterized by centralized control exercised by the candidates' national headquarters.

American Political
Parties: Unrivaled Record
of Durability

American political parties, while sharing many characteristics with the parties found in other Western democracies, are still quite distinct. They tend to be weaker organizationally and to have less influence over party nominations because of the direct primary. Not based on a mass dues-paying membership, American parties also show a distinct lack of internal unity, and they have a nonprogrammatic or nonpolicy-oriented approach to politics.

Despite the handicaps under which they have been forced to operate, American parties have demonstrated an unrivaled record of durability. Indeed, the same two parties have dominated electoral politics since 1856. Among the handicaps the Republican and Democratic parties have surmounted are the Constitution's provisions for separation of power and federalism which fragment the parties, such reforms as the direct primary, and hostile public attitudes toward parties and party leaders. Yet through a civil war, depressions, world wars, waves of immigration, scandals, and technological and social change, the parties have survived. They have melded diverse elements of society into their ranks and sought to compromise and reconcile their differences, achieving a remarkable record of durability and adaptability. This being said, it was only a decade ago that some scholars and commentators were lamenting the passing of parties as viable participants in the political process. As this chapter has demonstrated, however, the uniquely American style of political party is still very much alive and is showing at the national level unprecedented strength as a fund-raising and campaign support agency.

Parties also help citizens exercise indirect control over their government. In the American system candidates for major national and state offices—incumbents and challengers—must wear party labels. This simplifies the voter's choice. These labels also make it possible for voters to force some accountability on elected officials. The party in control of the government—especially the executive branch—is usually held accountable for the state of the Union during its tenure in office. And because public officials like to keep their jobs and parties want to control the White House and Congress, both have an incentive to deal with and even anticipate societal problems. They do this out of fear that the voters will throw them out if domestic and foreign conditions deteriorate, as well as in the hope that they will be rewarded by the voters for their successes in office. Parties may not be a perfect mechanism for ensuring public accountability by elected officials, but they are the most broadly based institution found in democracies for mobilizing voters and for peaceably replacing the "ins" with the "outs."

For Review

1. Parties are complex social structures composed of the party in the electorate, the party organization, and the party in the government. They developed in the United States as suffrage was extended and the need for institutions to mobilize voters developed.

2. Parties serve as linkages between citizens and their government and perform such functions as nominating candidates, contesting elections, serving as agents for holding public officials accountable for their actions, and managing societal conflicts.

3. The two-party competitive model accurately describes the electoral competition for president and many state elections. Below the state level, however, the ideal of meaningful two-party competition often goes unrealized.

4. American political parties are characterized by decentralized power structures, broad-based electoral support, and relatively nonprogrammatic policy orientations.

5. Nominations for state and congressional offices are made via the direct primary, which severely weakens party organization control over the nomination process and encourages candidates to rely on personal campaign organizations.

6. Presidential nominations are made formally by national conventions. Party organizations do not control presidential nominations, and candidates form personal campaign organizations. The crucial events in the nomination process are presidential primaries.

For Further Reading

Beck, Paul Allen, and Frank J. Sorauf. *Party Politics in America.* 7th ed. New York: HarperCollins, 1992. A comprehensive text on political parties.

Bibby, John F. *Politics, Parties, and Elections in America.* 2d ed. Chicago: Nelson-Hall, 1992. A concise account of the functioning of parties in the electoral and governmental processes.

Epstein, Leon D. *Political Parties in the American Mold.* Madison: University of Wisconsin Press, 1986. An analysis of American political parties that considers their distinctive characteristics, development, durability, and adaptability.

Grimshaw, William J. *Bitter Fruit: Black Politics and the Chicago Machine.* Chicago: University of Chicago Press, 1992. An in-depth examination of one of the most vexing relationships in American politics.

Herrnson, Paul S. *Party Campaigning in the 1980s.* Cambridge, Mass.: Harvard University Press, 1988. An analysis of the expanding electoral role of national party committees.

Jewell, Malcolm E. *Parties and Primaries: Nominating State Governors.* New York: Praeger, 1984. The most complete account of the operation of direct primaries available.

Key, V. O., Jr. *Politics, Parties, and Pressure Groups.* 5th ed. New York: Crowell, 1964. A classic text written by the leading twentieth-century student of American political parties.

Maisel, L. Sandy, ed. *The Parties Respond: Changes in the American Party System.* 2d ed. Boulder, Colo.: Westview Press, 1994. A collection of essays by leading scholars describing changes in party organizations, the party in government, and the party in the electorate.

Rae, Nicol G. *The Decline and Fall of the Liberal Republicans.* New York: Oxford University Press, 1989.

———.*Southern Democrats.* New York: Oxford University Press, 1994.

Reichley, A. James, ed. *The Life of the Parties: A History of American Political Parties.* New York: Free Press, 1992. An up-to-date history of parties with data and commentary on their current status.

Shafer, Byron E. *Bifurcated Politics: Evolution and Reform in the National Party Convention.* Cambridge, Mass.: Harvard University Press, 1988. A comprehensive analysis of changes in presidential nominating politics.

Wayne, Stephen J. *The Road to the White House 1992.* New York: St. Martin's Press, 1992. A comprehensive treatment of presidential nomination and election politics.

7. Elections, Campaigns, and Voters

B Y C A S T I N G their votes in elections, Americans make their most important collective decisions. They determine who will lead their government—who will decide when and where to use military force, what taxes to impose, what services to provide, and how to regulate the economy and social relations. Moreover, voters can demonstrate with their election day choices their displeasure as well as their satisfaction with the state of the Union, with the performance of public officials, and with how their own lives are going. By either terminating or renewing leaders' leases to government offices, the voters can hold public officials accountable for their actions and indirectly affect government policy.

Periodic free elections are democracy's solution to the problem that has plagued government regimes for ages: how to arrange a peaceful succession to government posts and an end to the life of a government without having to rely on a *coup d'état*, execution, or revolution. Americans have the opportunity to participate in elections more frequently and for more offices than the citizens of most democracies. They vote for their president, senator, representative, governor, state legislator, and a host of other state and local officials. They vote in presidential years and midterm years, in general elections and primaries, and on referendums.

This chapter explores the American electoral process—the formal rules that govern how elections are conducted, the nature of campaigns (especially presidential campaigns), the behavior of the voters, and the meaning and significance of elections (elections for congressional seats are considered in Chapter 10, Congress).

How America Conducts Its Elections

Under America's federal system, the responsibility for regulating elections is shared by the national and state governments. The states make many of the important decisions about how elections will be conducted, including who is eligible to vote, what regulations are applied to political parties, how elections are administered, and how votes are counted. The federal government's role is largely one of setting the times for federal elections, preventing discrimination in the exercise of the right to vote (also known as **suffrage** or **franchise**), and regulating campaign finance in federal elections.

The Right to Vote

Suffrage qualifications are set by the states, subject to constraints imposed by the Constitution and Congress. Congress, for example, has used its constitutional power to regulate the "Times, Places and Manner of holding Elections" for federal officials (1) to set a uniform date across the country for the election of representatives, senators, and presidential electors, (2) to set age requirements for voting in federal elections, and (3) to require states to make voter registration easier.

Extending the Right to Vote. When the Constitution was ratified, the states placed severe restrictions on the right to vote by demanding that voters meet certain property-owning or tax-paying requirements. As a result, the eligible electorate was confined to adult white males with property, leaving an estimated three-quarters of adult males not eligible to vote. But by the 1830s the states had largely abolished economic qualifications for voting so the United States could claim that it had universal white manhood suffrage. This easing of restrictions, of course, still left large portions of the adult population—including women and blacks—unable to cast their votes.

In the continuing struggle to make the right to vote a reality for all adult citizens, the states have ratified constitutional amendments and Congress has passed legislation aimed at eliminating state-imposed barriers to voting. The Fourteenth and Fifteenth amendments forbid the states from imposing unreasonable and racially based qualifications; the Nineteenth Amendment capped the long battle for women's suffrage; the Twenty-fourth Amendment bans denial of the right to vote because of failure to pay a state-imposed poll tax; and the Twenty-sixth Amendment forbids denying the right to vote to eighteen-year-olds.

But as described in Chapter 4, states found ways to prevent blacks from participating in the electoral process even after ratification of the Fourteenth and Fifteenth amendments. Eventually, however, the heightened public concern in the early 1960s about civil rights issues, as well as the use of violence and intimidation in the South to prevent black voter registration drives, led to passage of the Voting Rights Act of 1965. This law suspended literacy tests in all states and counties in which less than 50 percent of the voting age population was registered to vote in 1964 and authorized federal registrars to register voters and supervise elections in these areas. To prevent manipulation of election laws to disenfranchise blacks, officials in these states were required to gain Department of Justice approval for all election law changes.

The enfranchisement of black voters has had a dramatic effect on

Supporters of women's suffrage campaigning for the Nineteenth Amendment.

American politics. In 1965 there were only a few hundred black elected officials; by 1992 there were almost eight thousand. With their greatly expanded numbers and their overwhelming support for Democratic candidates, the African American electorate has become a critical voting bloc within the Democratic electoral coalition (see Chapter 6, Political Parties). This same electorate also played an important role in enabling Jesse Jackson to become the first member of his race to compete seriously for the presidential nomination.

Voter Registration. Although constrained by constitutional and congressionally enacted restrictions, the states play a major role in regulating and administering elections. Their most important regulations apply to voter registration. Even though justified as a means of preventing fraud (for example, when people vote more than once or a voter uses the name of someone deceased) and protecting the integrity of elections (some states impose restrictions on voting by convicted felons, aliens, and the mentally incompetent), registration requirements also can work to depress voter **turnout**.[1] These requirements vary widely among the states, with the most lenient states permitting

1. See Raymond E. Wolfinger and Steven J. Rosenstone, "The Effect of Registration Laws on Voter Turnout," *American Political Science Review* 72 (March 1978): 22–48; and Ruy A. Teixeira, *The Disappearing American Voter* (Washington, D.C.: Brookings, 1992), chap. 4.

voters to register at the polls on election day and the stricter states requiring would-be voters to register in person at such government buildings as a courthouse or city hall. Among the world's democracies the United States is unique in that here individual citizens are responsible for getting themselves registered. In most democracies the government assumes responsibility for voter registration.

In 1993, after much partisan wrangling, Congress enacted the so-called Motor Voter bill, which requires states to make registration easier. Starting in 1995, states must implement procedures for registration by mail, as well as for registration of applicants for driver's licenses and the clients of public assistance agencies, agencies serving the disabled, and other agencies to be selected by the states. Election administration—printing ballots, providing polling places and poll workers, setting hours the polls will be open, counting ballots, certifying outcomes, providing for recounts, and regulating campaign practices on election days—is largely the responsibility of state and local governments.

Types of Ballots. States also determine the type of ballot to be used. Either of two basic ballot forms is usually found in U.S. polling booths. Twenty-one states use the *party column ballot,* which arranges the names of the candidates so that all those from one party are in one column or row. In this way the voter can cast a vote for one party's candidates by simply marking an "X" at the top of the party's column or by pulling a lever on the voting machine. The party column ballot encourages straight-ticket voting. The *office bloc ballot,* used in twenty-nine states, arranges the names of candidates according to the office they are seeking. This ballot tends to discourage straight party line voting and encourages candidates to campaign as individuals rather than as part of a party slate.

The Electoral College

When Americans were choosing among George Bush, Bill Clinton, and Ross Perot on November 3, 1992, they were actually voting for slates of presidential electors who would cast their states' electoral votes for a president and vice president. American presidents are elected through an indirect system that relies on electoral votes, not popular votes (also see Chapter 2, The Constitution).

To be elected president, a candidate must receive an absolute majority (270) of the 538 votes in the electoral college, where each state's electoral votes equal its total number of senators and representatives. Thus, California with two senators and fifty-two representatives has fifty-four electoral votes, and Delaware with two senators and one representative has three. The District of Columbia, which was granted the right to vote for president by the Twenty-third Amendment, has three electoral votes.

A winner-take-all system is used to determine which presidential candidate will win the electoral votes of a state—that is, whichever candidate receives the most popular votes (a plurality) receives that state's entire complement of electoral votes.[2] In 1992, then, all of Ohio's twenty-one electoral votes went to Bill Clinton, who received 90,671 more votes (40.2 percent) than George Bush (38.3 percent) out of the almost 5,000,000 votes cast.

In the event no candidate receives the 270 electoral votes required for election, the election is thrown into the newly elected House of Representatives, which chooses from among the three candidates who received the largest number of electoral votes. In making its selection, the House votes by state delegation, with each state having one vote and with a majority of states required to elect a president.[3] When no vice-presidential candidate has a majority in the electoral college, the Senate chooses one of the two candidates having the largest number of electoral votes. Unlike members of the House, senators vote as individuals, not as part of a state delegation. A majority of the total Senate membership is required to elect a vice president.

Because of the winner-take-all system for deciding which candidate will receive a state's electoral votes, the big states, in terms of population, take on critical significance in electing presidents. This is true even though sparsely populated states such as North and South Dakota have more electoral votes than a population-based system of electoral vote apportionment would entitle them. For example, a vote cast in California holds the potential of determining which candidate will win that state's fifty-four electoral votes. By contrast, a vote cast in South Dakota influences only which candidate will win three electoral votes. The ten most populous states control 257 out of the 270 electoral votes needed to elect a president, and the thirteen least populous states have only forty-six electoral votes—fewer than the largest state, California (the map in Figure 7.1 shows the relative importance of each state's

2. The only exceptions to the winner-take-all rule are Maine and Nebraska, which allocate their electoral votes on the basis of two electoral votes to the candidate who receives a statewide plurality and one electoral vote to the winning candidate in each of the state's congressional districts.

3. The House has selected a president only twice (after the elections of 1800 and 1824), before the United States developed a stable two-party system.

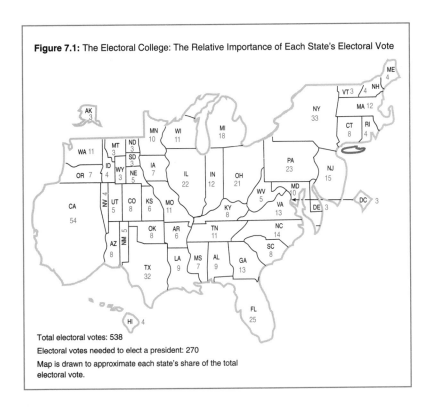

Figure 7.1: The Electoral College: The Relative Importance of Each State's Electoral Vote

Total electoral votes: 538

Electoral votes needed to elect a president: 270

Map is drawn to approximate each state's share of the total electoral vote.

electoral votes). In these circumstances it is not surprising that presidential candidates normally concentrate their campaign efforts on winning as many of the most thickly populated states as possible.

A persistent criticism leveled at the electoral college is that a candidate can win a plurality of the popular vote and still not be elected president because of failure to gain an electoral college majority. This happened in 1824, 1876, and 1888. Thus, would-be presidents Andrew Jackson (1824), Samuel J. Tilden (1876), and Grover Cleveland (1888)— each of whom received a plurality of the popular vote—found their aspirations dashed when they failed to receive a majority of the electoral college vote (happily for Jackson and Cleveland, they succeeded in occupying the White House after their second runs for the office). Normally, however, the electoral college system exaggerates the popular vote winner's margin of victory (see Figure 7.2). In the cliffhanger election of 1960, for example, John Kennedy received 49.7 percent of the popular vote, but his electoral vote percentage was a more comfortable 56.4 percent. Similarly, in 1992 Bill Clinton gained 43 percent of the popular vote but won 68.7 percent of the electoral votes. The reason for this pattern: the winning candidate normally carries a number

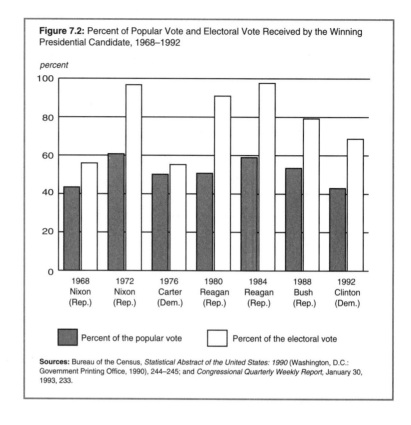

Figure 7.2: Percent of Popular Vote and Electoral Vote Received by the Winning Presidential Candidate, 1968–1992

Sources: Bureau of the Census, *Statistical Abstract of the United States: 1990* (Washington, D.C.: Government Printing Office, 1990), 244–245; and *Congressional Quarterly Weekly Report,* January 30, 1993, 233.

of states by narrow margins and, because of the winner-take-all system, collects all of those states' electoral votes. Since newly elected presidents usually have substantial majorities in the electoral college, they can then claim electoral mandates from the voters even though their popular vote pluralities may have been relatively modest.

Although it has not happened in over a hundred years, the possibility of a person being elected who did not receive a popular vote plurality bothers many Americans because it seems to violate democratic principles. As a result, calls are heard periodically for a constitutional amendment that provides for direct popular election of the president. Defenders of the electoral college believe that the current system has worked reasonably well and see potential risks in moving to direct election. One of those risks is that splinter parties would be encouraged to run candidates in the popular election, thereby altering the character of the party system. Opponents of change also are concerned that campaigns would be conducted differently; candidates would have an even greater incentive to run national media-oriented campaigns that pay little attention to voters on a state-by-state basis.[4] All this being said, because in recent history there has been no instance in which a popular vote winner failed to win a majority of the electoral college, attempts to revise the procedure for electing the president have received little sustained effort. Indeed, proponents of change have failed to muster the two-thirds majorities needed in Congress to propose a constitutional amendment.

The Campaign: Electing a President

Election campaigns play a crucial role in the struggle for political power in the United States. But to succeed, campaigns must be run by well-managed organizations, using well-thought-out strategies. In spite of their importance, campaign organizations are highly transitory structures. Presidential campaign organizations, which spend millions of dollars and enlist thousands of people, are erected quickly to contest the election and then disbanded even more rapidly whether the candidate has won or lost.

Traditionally, presidential campaigns have kicked off formally around Labor Day after the July and August national conventions. For example, Democratic presidential nominees have frequently started their campaigns with massive rallies in Cadillac Square in Detroit. As was noted in Chapter 6, however, the real opening of the general election campaigns occurs at the national conventions where each party tries to present its candidate to the television audience in the most positive manner possible. In 1992 neither party waited for the traditional Labor Day opening of the campaign. Democratic presidential nominee Bill Clinton and his running mate Al Gore hit the road with a bus tour of middle America, during which their lead in the polls over President Bush climbed to 20 percentage points. Not to be left behind, President Bush also set out on the campaign trail immediately after his party's national convention.

Campaign strategies can have a big effect on election outcomes. During the 1988 presidential campaign Democrat Michael Dukakis saw

4. For a discussion of the issues involved in electoral college reform, see Nelson W. Polsby and Aaron Wildavsky, *Presidential Elections: Contemporary Strategies of American Electoral Politics*, 8th ed. (New York: Free Press, 1992), 307–317. Also see Neal R. Pierce and Lawrence D. Longley, *The People's President*, rev. ed. (New Haven, Conn.: Yale University Press, 1981); and Wallace S. Sayre and Judith H. Parris, *Voting for President: The Electoral College and the American Political System* (Washington, D.C.: Brookings, 1970).

his lead in the polls over Republican George Bush go from a 17 percentage point advantage in July to a 5 percentage point deficit in November. Analysts attributed Dukakis's slide in part to his inability to respond effectively to an aggressive Republican media attack that portrayed him as a liberal sympathetic to criminals, unconcerned about the victims of crime, and unappreciative of the need for a strong defense. By contrast, in 1992 the Clinton-Gore campaign was given high marks for its portrayal of the ticket as centrist in policy orientation and for effectively focusing on people's concern about the economy. At its campaign command post in Little Rock a simple reminder was tacked to the wall—"It's the economy, stupid!"—lest anyone be tempted to push less-salient issues. To its regret, the Bush organization was unable to develop a campaign message that resonated with the electorate and diverted it from economic worries.[5]

When the Voter Decides

Most voters make up their minds well before election day. In the presidential elections from 1960 to 1988, over 60 percent of the voters, on average, made up their minds before or during the national conventions. But in 1992 a sizable portion (42 percent) of those surveyed as they left their polling places said they had made their decisions only in the last two weeks of the campaign (see Figure 7.3). Was Perot a factor in this late decision making? In fact, his voters were twice as likely as Clinton or Bush voters to have made their choice in the last three days of the campaign.[6] Although most voters make their presidential voting decisions early, late deciders can swing the electoral votes of key states, which are often won by margins of less than 5 percent of the vote. For example, in 1992 Bill Clinton carried eleven states (106 electoral votes) by a margin of less than 5 percent so that a late surge of support for his opponents could conceivably have reversed the election outcome. Can anyone doubt, then, that campaigns and how they are organized do make a difference?[7]

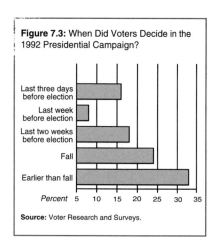

Figure 7.3: When Did Voters Decide in the 1992 Presidential Campaign?

Last three days before election

Last week before election

Last two weeks before election

Fall

Earlier than fall

Percent   5   10   15   20   25   30   35

Source: Voter Research and Surveys.

5. Clinton and Bush campaign strategies and tactics are analyzed by Paul J. Quirk and Jon K. Dalager, "The Election: A 'New Democrat' and a New Kind of Presidential Campaign," in *The Elections of 1992*, ed. Michael Nelson (Washington, D.C.: CQ Press, 1993), chap. 3; and by F. Christopher Arterton, "Campaign '92: Strategies and Tactics," in *The Election of 1992: Reports and Interpretations,* ed. Gerald M. Pomper (Chatham, N.J.: Chatham House, 1993), chap. 3.

6. Data derived from exit polls conducted by Voter Research and Surveys, reported in *American Enterprise,* January/February 1993, 106.

7. For a comprehensive consideration of campaign strategy, see Stephen A. Salmore and Barbara G. Salmore, *Candidates, Parties, and Campaigns: Electoral Politics in America,* 2d ed. (Washington, D.C.: CQ Press, 1989).

Organizing and Running
the Campaign

According to journalist Theodore White, a presidential campaign "starts with a candidate, a handful of men, a theme and a plan. By November of election year it has enlisted hundreds of thousands of volunteers, politicians, state staffs, national staffs, media specialists and has become an enterprise."[8] Creating a presidential campaign organization is indeed a mammoth undertaking, requiring establishment of a headquarters and recruitment of a staff of experienced, savvy professionals capable of developing and implementing a campaign plan and mobilizing thousands of campaign volunteers.[9]

Staffing the Campaign Operation. In a sharp departure from presidential campaigns of the 1980s when the Democrats were at an organizational disadvantage, the 1992 Republican reelection effort on behalf of George Bush suffered from organizational weaknesses. For one thing, many of the people who had directed the successful 1988 campaign were no longer there to make the calls: strategist Lee Atwater had died; media guru Roger Ailes was doing commercial advertising; and campaign chairman James Baker was secretary of state and only took over direction of the reelection campaign in late August 1992, when it already was in serious trouble. The new team recruited for 1992 was afflicted with organizational bickering and unable to develop a theme and consistent focus for the campaign.

In contrast to the organizational problems in the GOP camp, the Clinton campaign team was cohesive and disciplined, with a competitive edge that had been honed during the presidential primaries. Many of its leaders (top strategist James Carville and media consultants Frank Greer and Mandy Grunwald) had sharpened their skills in southern elections and, in the process, had mastered the art of rebutting conservative attacks—unlike the Dukakis campaign in 1988. Clinton's staff also included experienced Washington hands, such as campaign chairman Mickey Kantor and communications director George Stephanopoulos. Carville's "war room" personnel reveled in their reputations as "tough Democrats" as they scanned the news wire services and satellite feeds for attacks on their candidates, priding themselves

8. Michael P. Riccards, *A Republic, If You Can Keep It: The Foundation of the American Presidency, 1700-1800* (New York: Greenwood Press, 1987), 101.

9. For a discussion of campaign organizations and the development of strategy, see John H. Kessel, *Presidential Campaign Politics,* 4th ed. (Pacific Grove, Calif.: Brooks/Cole, 1992), chaps. 3 and 4.

on the speed of their responses (all the while, of course, firing off their own first strikes).[10]

Developing Campaign Themes and Issues. Effective campaign themes embody the declared political and policy commitments of the candidates in ways that appeal to public support. The themes and issues developed by campaigns reflect the records and experience of the candidates, their objectives and those of their supporters, and the campaign organization's assessments of current political conditions. In 1980, for example, as inflation and interest rates reached double-digit levels, unemployment soared, and people felt frustrated by the Carter administration's inability to free American hostages captured when Iran seized the U.S. Embassy in Teheran, Ronald Reagan asked the voters to "Vote Republican for a change!" and pledged to lower taxes, cut domestic spending, and increase military expenditures. Twenty years earlier, when the American economy was in a slump and Americans were worrying at the height of the cold war about the adequacy of the country's defenses, Democrat John Kennedy had promised to "get the country going again" and to erase the alleged "missile gap" by bolstering defense capabilities.

In 1992 the Clinton campaign focused its rhetoric on the theme of change and emphasized the two issues—the economy and health care—of foremost concern to voters. To gain the support of moderates and independents who had voted for the Republicans throughout the 1980s, the campaign proclaimed that Clinton was a "new kind of Democrat" who would "end welfare as we have known it." Clinton's major weakness was the issue of his character. During the primaries the character issue had nearly torpedoed his candidacy as rumors and charges surfaced of extramarital affairs, marijuana use while an Oxford student, and draft evasion. Fortunately for Clinton these allegations occurred early enough in the primary campaign to seem stale by the time of the general election even though the Republicans continued to exploit the character issue.

With large segments of the electorate believing that the country was on the wrong track and worrying about the economy, the Bush campaign was put on the defensive. It tried a series of different campaign themes: an economic plan for American renewal; an attack, à la Harry Truman in 1948, on a "do nothing" Congress controlled by liberal Democrats; exploitation of Clinton's vulnerabilities on the character

10. Robin Toner, "This Year It's the Democrats Who Run on GOP Tactics," *New York Times,* Aug. 9, 1992, 16, National edition.

While "Keep Cool with Coolidge" posters, banners, and buttons may have gotten the message across in 1924, today candidates rely on television advertising, such as George Bush's use of this image of his opponent in 1988.

and trust issue; and an assault on Clinton's record as governor of Arkansas in the areas of taxation, crime, civil rights, the environment, and education (a tactic that had worked successfully against another Democratic governor, Michael Dukakis, in 1988). But in the context of 1992, with the voters riveted on the economy and the need for change, none of the various themes tried by the Bush campaign were received warmly by the voters.

Bush, as the incumbent president, also was damaged by the themes hammered at relentlessly by independent candidate Ross Perot. During his first period of candidacy Perot attacked the Washington establishment for its corruption by lobbyists and political action committees and for its remoteness from average Americans. When he later resumed his candidacy Perot focused on the dangers posed by the mounting federal budget deficit, which he claimed resulted from a failure of leadership in Washington. Perot maintained that only someone from outside the system with a strong record of business leadership could clean up the "mess in Washington."[11]

Getting the Message Across. In this telecommunications age, coordination of the various elements of a campaign—public opinion polling, media advertising, candidate appearances, and use of the free media—is essential to get the candidate's message out to the voters. In 1988 the Bush campaign had been unusually well disciplined at this task and more experienced than the Dukakis organization. Polls were taken every night of the campaign with the results available for campaign chairman James Baker's daily 7:30 A.M. senior staff meeting. At these

11. See Arterton, "Campaign '92"; and Quirk and Dalager, "The Election."

meetings polling data were reviewed, and campaign activities, including candidate appearances, were carefully planned for each day and week to stress the campaign message of the day or week. Media consultants even inserted snappy lines into Bush's speeches—tested in advance, of course—to ensure that they were included as "sound bites" on TV news programs. To complete the media package, television commercials were designed to back up the chosen message. The Bush campaign also sought to limit news conferences with reporters, lest the free-wheeling and often adversarial nature of these sessions resulted in messages being communicated to the voters that differed from those in the campaign plan. The campaign was thus designed to exert maximum control over what the voters would see and hear about the candidate on television, the people's most important and trusted source of news.

The 1992 campaigns used many of these time-tested techniques and added some innovative ones to get their messages across to the public.[12] In seeking favorable free coverage from the national news media, the Clinton organization took full advantage of the media's distaste for the attack style of campaigning that they felt had excessively dominated the 1988 campaign. With the national press corps continually looking for distortions in the charges leveled by one candidate against another, the Clinton campaign adopted a strategy of reacting quickly to attacks from the Republicans. If a staff response promptly faxed to the media did not do the job, Clinton himself frequently responded in person, in the process gaining extensive media coverage and blunting the GOP charges.

The Clinton campaign also tried to use the local television news more fully by providing local reporters in pivotal media markets with access to the candidate through satellite feeds. From one location the candidate often did five to six interviews for local evening news programs. Using the local media had the added advantage of bypassing the national press corps with its often critical "gotcha" style of journalism. And local reporters, because they were less familiar with the details of national policy, were more likely to allow the candidate to get his message out without journalistic tinkering. Going one step further, Clinton's organization did its own filming of its candidate's campaign appearances and then sent the footage via satellite feeds to local stations for use on news programs.

12. For an excellent account of the media strategies of the candidates in 1992, see Arterton, "Campaign '92."

After independent candidate Ross Perot demonstrated the effectiveness of campaigning via television talk shows and even announced his presidential candidacy on "Larry King Live," Bill Clinton (enthusiastically) and George Bush (reluctantly) also appeared on the programs of King (above) and other talk show hosts.

One of the most distinctive features of 1992 was the "talk-show campaign." Ross Perot was the first to discover that this format was an effective way to bypass national political reporters and speak directly to the public. His campaign quite literally began on "Larry King Live" where Perot said that, after the New Hampshire primary, he would run if "volunteers" put his name on the ballot. Clinton was the first of the major party candidates to follow the Perot example and exploit the talk shows with appearances on such nontraditional candidate forums as MTV, "Larry King Live," and ESPN as well as the Arsenio Hall and Phil Donahue shows. The early morning network broadcasts such as "Today" and "Good Morning America" even brought the candidates to the nation's breakfast tables. President Bush at first resisted participating in what he characterized as these "weird talk shows," but he too eventually followed the trend.

Unlike the tough questions posed by national political reporters about campaign tactics, polls, and inconsistencies in policy positions, the less-confrontational questions posed on talk shows concerned how the candidates would solve the problems on the minds of callers or members of the studio audience. This kind of forum, in which Clinton was highly effective, gave him an opportunity to reach voters on subjects they cared about without having his message "stepped on" by reporters. The talk show campaign of 1992, then, reflected the increasingly fragmented nature of the news media, which are no longer so heavily dominated by the three major networks as they were even as recently as the 1980s. To be sure, future candidates will continue to utilize the nontraditional television news formats. Indeed, in adopting a "continuous campaign" strategy after taking over the White House, both President Clinton and Vice President Gore have made extensive use of television call-in shows and town hall meetings to promote the president's programs.

Another media innovation of 1992 was the "infomercial," pioneered and paid for by independent candidate Ross Perot. Shunning the traditional thirty-second spot, Perot featured on his lengthy (thirty-minute) infomercials a blizzard of charts and graphs, accompanied by folksy Perot commentary on such issues as the federal budget deficit. These unconventional advertisements garnered surprisingly high audience penetration, boosted Perot's candidacy, and heightened interest in fiscal issues.

Using the Incumbency Advantage. It is impossible for anyone in American political life to match the publicity and symbolic advantages of an incumbent president. The office carries with it symbols of the nation and of power—the presidential seal, the Oval Office with its massive desk and flags of the military services bedecked with battle ribbons, *Air Force One,* and the strains of "Hail to the Chief," which is played for ceremonial occasions. In truth, no challenger can match the presidential aura that surrounds each incumbent. Just by carrying out their official duties, presidents are able to transcend the appearance of mere politicians campaigning for office; rather, they appear to be servants of the people—all the people. As one example, President Reagan's 1984 visit to the Normandy beaches of France to celebrate the fortieth anniversary of D-Day (the Allied invasion of Europe during World War II) provided him with a dramatic and emotional setting for television coverage on the eve of his 1984 reelection campaign. Less dramatic, but nonetheless effective, are bill-signing ceremonies and gatherings in the White House Rose Garden to honor foreign dignitaries, Super Bowl champions, and astronauts. A further advantage of incumbency is the ability of an administration to make policy decisions that will help win support for the incumbent president's party— for example, approving contracts for military procurement or public works projects in states considered essential for an electoral college majority.

Incumbent presidents and vice presidents—George Bush, for example—are in a position to claim credit for the good things that happened during their administrations. Presidents Dwight Eisenhower and Ronald Reagan, as well as Vice President Bush, all ran on themes of peace and prosperity. But when the economy turns sour and international affairs go against American interests, it is the president who stands alone, exposed and accountable. It does not matter that presidents cannot control all aspects of domestic and foreign affairs. The defeats of Presidents Jimmy Carter in 1980 and Bush in 1992 can be attributed primarily to their being held accountable for the troubled state of the economy.

Participating in Televised Debates. Televised debates now go hand in hand with presidential elections. For nonincumbent and underdog candidates, such debates are potentially advantageous because they place these candidates on an equal footing with a president, vice president, or front-running candidate. On an unadorned stage, the candidates stand alone as equals before the television audience, poised to answer the questions to come. Not only are presidents and vice presidents robbed of the aura of the White House, but their claims of superior experience can be quickly eroded during the debate by challengers who are credible and clever—which most are.

Because the news media give prime-time coverage to debates, candidates tend to see them as the make-or-break events of the campaign.[13] In fact, extended negotiations among campaign managers over the format of the debates are usually the rule—all aimed, of course, at preventing the opposition from gaining any procedural advantage. Wrangling over the number, timing, and format of the presidential debates in 1992 lasted until late September, with incumbent president Bush unenthusiastic about debating Clinton, who was generally considered more articulate and practiced in the debate format. In addition, Bush strategist James Baker believed that, in general, voters' decision making becomes "frozen" as they await the televised matchup. Baker hoped that by delaying an agreement on the debates, the Bush campaign could narrow Clinton's lead. It was, however, acknowledged that the debates were inevitable since now they are an institutionalized part of presidential elections.

The negotiations resulted in a series of debates that were helpful to Clinton's candidacy. Perot was allowed to participate because both Bush and Clinton anticipated that his presence would help their candidacies—Bush hoped that Perot would cut into Clinton's lead, and Clinton expected Perot to attack Bush's record on the economy and thereby reinforce a Clinton campaign theme—but Clinton's expectation proved closer to the mark than Bush's hope. The candidates

---

13. Social scientists disagree about the impact of presidential debates. See John G. Geer, "The Effects of Presidential Debates on the Electorate's Preference for Candidates," *American Politics Quarterly* 16 (October 1988): 486–501; and Mack C. Shelley and Hwarng-Du Hwang, "The Mass Media and Public Opinion Polls in the 1988 Presidential Election," *American Politics Quarterly* 19 (1991): 59–79.

The combatants in the 1992 presidential race, Ross Perot (left), George Bush, and Bill Clinton, shake hands after sparring in a free wheeling debate that included questions from the audience.

agreed to three different debate formats: questioning by a panel of reporters; a candidates' discussion led by a sole moderator; and questioning by an audience of undecided voters. The audience participation format proved especially advantageous to Clinton who had gained experience and skill in responding to audiences through his appearances on talk shows.

The actual impact of the debates was mixed. Polls showed that viewers picked Clinton as either the winner or co-winner with Perot in all three debates. Thus, Clinton did what he had to do: he held his own against the president and maintained his front-runner position. As for Perot, the debates gave legitimacy to his candidacy—and his standing in the *New York Times*/CBS poll went from 10 percent before the first debate to 17 percent after the third debate. Interestingly, Bush too seemed to have benefited from the debates even though he was not seen as the winner of any them. He apparently was able to reassure wavering Republicans, thereby cutting Clinton's lead from 13 percentage points before the first debate to 5 points after the final debate.[14] The Gallup poll reported that only 12 percent of the viewers questioned said that the last debate had changed their vote; 86 percent remained

14. Poll results of the debates are summarized by Quirk and Dalager, "The Election," 73.

unmoved.[15] As in the past, then, debates are more likely to reinforce support for candidates than to change voting intentions.

Dealing with the Political Geography of the Electoral College. Because electoral, not popular, votes determine the winner, presidential elections are in reality fifty-one separate contests for the electoral votes of each state and the District of Columbia. The candidates' campaign organizations must, therefore, devise strategies and allocate their campaign resources among the states in a way that will produce a majority in the electoral college. During the 1980s Republican strength in the South and states west of the Mississippi resulted in what was called the GOP "lock" on the electoral college. This base of electoral support (approximately 140 electoral votes strong) had enabled such Republican candidates as George Bush in 1988 to focus their campaign resources on key competitive states (for example, Ohio, New Jersey, Missouri, Michigan, and Illinois) that had large blocs of electoral votes. By winning these states GOP candidates in the 1980s were able to roll up large electoral vote majorities. Indeed, in 1988 the Democratic presidential contender, Michael Dukakis, was forced to virtually write off these regions. With most southern and western electoral votes out of reach, Democrats faced the nearly impossible task of having to carry practically all the competitive states of the Northeast and Midwest.

The GOP lock on the electoral college, however, was not as secure as it appeared at first glance (see Figure 7.4). In 1988 Bush carried fourteen states in which he received 55 percent or less of the popular vote. Included on this list were states rich in electoral votes: California, Pennsylvania, Illinois, and Ohio. Picking the so-called GOP lock on the electoral college, therefore, was feasible for the Democrats in 1992, provided there was a national swing of voter sentiment away from the Republican candidate.

And that is precisely what happened in 1992. With Bush's popular vote falling from 53 percent in 1988 to 37 percent in 1992, states that had been narrowly Republican fell into the Democratic column. The national swing toward the Democrats resulted in even southern and western states in which Clinton's campaign had made a special effort going Democratic (Louisiana, Georgia, Tennessee, Colorado, and New Mexico). The electoral college lock was shattered. With 43 percent of the popular vote in a three-way contest, Clinton won 370 electoral votes (69 percent); Bush with 37 percent of the popular vote won 168 electoral votes (31 percent); and Perot was shut out of the electoral col-

15. *Gallup Poll Monthly,* October 1992, 20.

Figure 7.4: Electoral Votes by State, 1988 and 1992

1988: A Republican "lock" on the electoral college?

Carried by Democrats (Dukakis)   Carried by Republicans (Bush)

Note: Dukakis received 3 electoral votes from the District of Columbia

1992: Democrats pick the Republican electoral college "lock."

Carried by Democrats (Clinton)   Carried by Republicans (Bush)

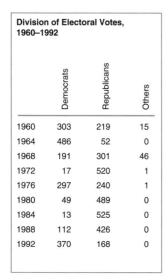

Division of Electoral Votes, 1960–1992			
	Democrats	Republicans	Others
1960	303	219	15
1964	486	52	0
1968	191	301	46
1972	17	520	1
1976	297	240	1
1980	49	489	0
1984	13	525	0
1988	112	426	0
1992	370	168	0

lege. There was some continuity in the electoral college results, however, as the Republicans won seven of the eleven states of the Confederacy, dominated the Plains states, and won four of the eight Rocky Mountain states (see Figure 7.4).

In devising its winning electoral college strategy, the Clinton campaign focused its energies on thirty-two states with 376 electoral votes. In an attempt to force Bush to defend his own territory, Clinton-Gore bus trips were even scheduled into two states, Florida and Texas, considered out of reach for the Democrats.

Financing Presidential Elections

A credible presidential campaign costs a lot of money. Money purchases a headquarters, staff, consultants, pollsters, advertising, research, and jet travel. Paying for campaigns has always been a troublesome aspect of the electoral process, and today that is particularly true. The expense of television time and new technologies—computer-based analyses of voting behavior and nightly telephone polls tracking candidate support levels—have caused the costs of campaigns to escalate dramatically. Moreover, the candidates and their parties differ in their abilities to raise campaign funds from private sources. But of even greater concern is the possibility that in the eagerness of the candidates to fill their campaign coffers, the government process may be corrupted by large contributors seeking access to and influence with government officials.

Faced with unprecedented levels of spending by President Nixon's 1972 Committee to Re-elect the President and charges of improprieties in the raising of those funds, Congress enacted in 1974 a major campaign finance reform act. The 1974 amendments to the Federal Election Campaign Act (FECA) seek to relieve presidential candidates of the need to spend time raising money, provide the public with information about the sources of campaign funds, limit the role of a few large contributors and interest groups in funding campaigns, and reduce the role of money in elections.

The most important provision of the act affecting presidential elections pertains to public funding of campaigns.[16] Major party presidential candidates may elect to accept federal funding for their campaigns. But candidates accepting public funding ($55.2 million in 1992) must

16. For an analysis of the operation of public funding in presidential elections, see Frank J. Sorauf, *Money in American Elections* (Glenview, Ill.: Scott, Foresman, 1988), chap. 7; and his *Inside Campaign Finance* (New Haven, Conn.: Yale University Press, 1992), 133–146.

Current Laws Regulating Presidential Campaign Finance

The following provisions regulating presidential campaign finance are listed in order of the progress of the nomination and general election campaigns.

■ Federal regulation. The Federal Election Commission (FEC) is the federal agency responsible for enforcement of campaign laws.

■ Disclosure. Presidential candidates must file regular reports with the FEC listing campaign contributions and expenditures. Donors of $200 or more must be listed in the reports. Any organization spending more than $5,000 on campaigns must establish formal political action committees. Candidates must establish a single organization for their campaigns. State parties must report expenditures that are allocatable to federal elections.

■ Political Action Committees (PACs). Corporations and labor unions may establish separate units to promote political ends and not be in violation of federal prohibitions on direct contributions.

■ Taxpayer checkoff. Citizens may indicate on their tax forms that they would like $1 ($2 for joint filings) of their tax money to be put into the Presidential Election Campaign Fund. This fund has been used to help finance nomination and general election campaigns.

■ Matching funds during primaries. Candidates may receive federal matching funds if they raise at least $100,000 in twenty or more states. Each of those states must contribute a total of at least $5,000 to the candidate in individual donations of $250 or less.

■ Limits on contributions. Citizens may contribute only $1,000 to each primary or general election campaign, a total of $25,000 to federal candidates overall, and $20,000 to committees of national parties. Candidates may spend only $50,000 of their own or their family's money on their campaigns if they accept federal funding. Multicandidate committees—most commonly PACs—may contribute only $5,000 per candidate and $15,000 to committees of the national parties.

■ Federal funding of national conventions. The parties receive funding for their summer conventions.

■ Spending limits. Candidates receiving federal matching funds may spend limited amounts during the nomination season and other limited amounts in each of the states (state limits are determined by population).

■ Federal funding of general election campaigns. The federal government offers the nominees of the major parties equal sums of money for the general election campaign. Candidates who accept the money may not raise or use additional campaign funds. The figure was $55.2 million in 1992; the amount has been adjusted each election year according to the inflation rate.

---

agree not to accept or spend any additional campaign funds other than up to $50,000 of their own personal money. The national committees of the parties also are limited in the amount ($10.3 million in 1992) they can spend to support their presidential nominees.

Since 1976 when the 1974 FECA amendments went into effect, every Republican and Democratic presidential nominee has accepted public funding for his campaign. In practice, however, FECA has not been effective in limiting the cost of campaigns or the role of nonpublic funds in presidential elections because the parties have taken full advantage of a 1979 amendment to FECA designed to encourage grassroots, volunteer involvement in campaigns. The amendment permits state and local parties to spend without limit on "party-building" activities—voter registration and turnout drives as well as such volunteer activities as party rallies, distributing bumper stickers, and putting up yard signs. Using this provision to get around the contribution and expenditure limits of the FECA, the national party organizations have collected massive amounts of money, often from large contributors in amounts of $100,000, which is then channeled to state and local party organizations for mainly get-out-the-vote activities supportive of presidential campaigns. Funds raised, channeled, and spent in this manner outside the restrictions of the FECA are called "soft money." The magnitude of the soft money flowing into campaigns has escalated rapidly since 1980 as national party-designed get-out-the-vote drives operating within the states have become an integral part of presidential campaigns. In 1992 the Democratic National Committee spent $30 million in soft money and the Republican National Committee $36 million. This constituted a $21 million increase in national committee soft money expenditures over the 1988 election.[17]

In addition to these party expenditures, private groups and individuals are permitted to make *independent expenditures* in support of the candidates of their choice—but without the collusion of the candidate's campaign organization. The Supreme Court has ruled that the First Amendment protects such expenditures and that the provisions in the FECA that sought to limit these expenditures were unconstitutional.[18]

Voter Turnout in Elections

Although elections are the underpinning of a democratic order, only a relatively small percentage of Americans actually take advantage of their right to vote.[19] Reversing a downward trend of thirty-two years, the 1992 presidential election saw 55.9 percent of the voting age population cast ballots (Figure 7.5). Voter turnout is even lower in midterm elections for the House of Representatives and Senate. In the 1990 midterm elections, for example, just one-third of the eligible voters went to the polls (see Figure 7.5).

With their saturation media coverage and complex strategies, presidential campaigns bombard voters with stimuli to vote. Midterm elections, however, tend to have much less media coverage and, in many

17. On "soft money," see Beth Donovan, "Much Maligned 'Soft Money' Is Precious to Both Parties," *Congressional Quarterly Weekly Report*, May 15, 1993, 1195–1200; and Sorauf, *Inside Campaign Finance*, 146–152.

18. *Federal Election Commission v. National Conservative Political Action Committee*, 470 U.S. 480 (1985).

19. Though now somewhat dated, the most thorough study of voter turnout in America is that by Raymond E. Wolfinger and Steven J. Rosenstone, *Who Votes?* (New Haven, Conn.: Yale University Press, 1980).

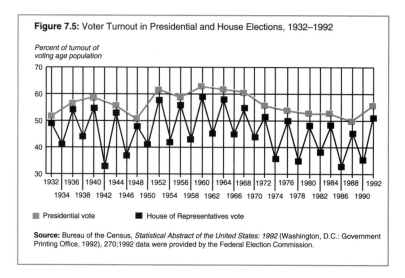

Figure 7.5: Voter Turnout in Presidential and House Elections, 1932–1992

*Percent of turnout of
voting age population*

■ Presidential vote   ■ House of Representatives vote

Source: Bureau of the Census, *Statistical Abstract of the United States: 1992* (Washington, D.C.: Government Printing Office, 1992), 270;1992 data were provided by the Federal Election Commission.

congressional districts, lackluster contests when the incumbent representative is largely unchallenged. Voter disinterest and lower turnout than in presidential contests are the result. Since 1952 the falloff in turnout from each presidential election to the next midterm election has averaged -18 percent.

The states vary widely in their rates of voter turnout—in 1992 Maine had a 72 percent turnout and Georgia only a 39 percent turnout (see Figure 7.6). These widely different rates can be attributed to three factors, the first of which is a combination of *levels of interparty competition, intensity of campaigning, and voter mobilization efforts.* When there is genuine electoral competition between the Republicans and Democrats and an intense campaign effort on the part of candidates, parties, and interest groups to reach the voters within a state, voter participation is increased.[20] A second factor is *state voter registration requirements,* which differ greatly by state. North Dakota has no voter registration; Maine, Minnesota, and Wisconsin permit election day registration at the polls; and eleven states had "motor voter" programs in 1992 that allowed people to register automatically to vote when they renewed or applied for a driver's license (federal law requires all states to have "motor voter" registration by 1995). The third factor affecting state voter turnout is the *composition of a state's electorate,* which also

20. Samuel C. Patterson and Gregory A. Caldeira, "Getting Out the Vote: Participation in Gubernatorial Elections," *American Political Science Review* 77 (September 1983): 675–689; and Gregory A. Caldeira, Samuel C. Patterson, and Gregory A. Markko, "The Mobilization of Voters in Congressional Elections," *Journal of Politics* 47 (May 1985): 498–509.

Figure 7.6: Where They Voted . . . and Where They Did Not
(1992 presidential election turnout as percent of voting age population)

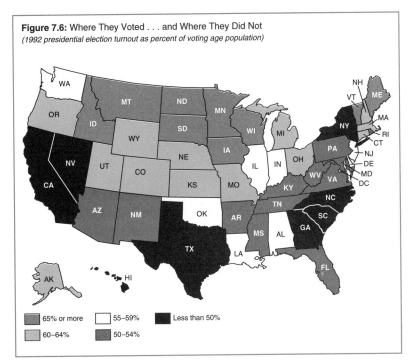

65% or more   55–59%   Less than 50%
60–64%   50–54%

	1992 Turnout Rate (% of voting age population)	Change, 1988–1982 (percentage points)
NATIONAL	55.9	+4.8
1. Maine	72	+11
2. Minnesota	71	+5
3. Montana	70	+7
4. Wisconsin	69	+8
5. North Dakota	68	+6
6. Vermont	68	+10
7. Idaho	66	+8
8. South Dakota	66	+6
9. Iowa	65	+7
10. Alaska	64	+8
11. Connecticut	64	+6
12. Colorado	63	+7
13. New Hampshire	63	+8
14. Utah	63	+2
15. Missouri	62	+7
16. Oregon	62	+5
17. Kansas	61	+7
18. Michigan	61	+7
19. Nebraska	61	+5
20. Wyoming	61	+8
21. District of Columbia	60	+19
22. Massachusetts	60	+2
23. Ohio	60	+5
24. Illinois	59	+6
25. Louisiana	59	+7
26. Oklahoma	59	+10
27. Washington	59	+5
28. Alabama	55	+9
29. Delaware	55	+5
30. Indiana	55	+2
31. New Jersey	55	+2
32. Kentucky	54	+6
33. Pennsylvania	54	+5
34. Rhode Island	54	+1
35. Arkansas	53	+5
36. Virginia	53	+5
37. Arizona	52	+5
38. Mississippi	52	+7
39. Tennessee	52	+7
40. Maryland	51	+2
41. New Mexico	51	+2
42. Florida	50	+5
43. West Virginia	50	+3
44. North Carolina	49	+4
45. California	48	+1
46. Nevada	48	+4
47. New York	48	0
48. Texas	48	+2
49. Georgia	46	+7
50. South Carolina	45	+6
51. Hawaii	42	-1

Sources: Federal Election Commission and Bureau of the Census data.

varies from state to state. Characteristics associated with high levels of turnout are a high income, a high-status occupation, educational achievement, and being middle-aged, Jewish or Catholic, and white.

Who Votes? Personal Characteristics of Voters and Nonvoters

Age and education are the two personal characteristics most closely related to voter turnout. Young people tend to have the lowest rates of turnout (see Table 7.1). In the 1992 presidential election only 38.5 percent of eighteen- to twenty-year-olds reported that they had voted, compared with 70.0 percent of those between ages forty-five and sixty-four. Registration requirements, attending college away from home, military service, and residential mobility all create obstacles to election day participation by the young.

Although the turnout rates of various age groups differ significantly, by age thirty-five most people vote at least occasionally. Only a small proportion of the middle-aged population are habitual nonvoters, and, of the total electorate, less than 5 percent almost never vote.[21]

21. William H. Flanigan and Nancy H. Zingale, *Political Behavior of the American Electorate,* 8th ed. (Washington, D.C.: CQ Press, 1994), 41–45.

Table 7.1 Voter Participation in 1992

	% Who Reported Voting
White	64
African American	54
Hispanic origin	29
Male	60
Female	62
Age	
18–20	39
21–24	46
25–34	53
35–44	64
45–64	70
65 and older	70
Employed	64
Unemployed	46
Not in labor force	59
School years completed	
8 years or less	35
4 years of high school	58
1–3 years of college	69
4 years or more of college	81

Source: Bureau of the Census, *Statistical Abstract of the United States: 1993* (Washington, D.C.: Government Printing Office, 1993), 283.

Education is the most important personal characteristic affecting turnout: the higher one's level of education, the greater the likelihood of voting. Better-educated people are likely to recognize how politics affects their lives and the things they care about, to be interested in politics, and to be skilled in dealing with registration requirements. Higher levels of education also are associated with higher incomes and greater social prestige. When education is held constant, however, income has little impact on voter turnout.

Racial groups also differ in their turnout rates. African Americans have lower turnout levels than whites, but African Americans vote more frequently than Hispanics. These turnout rates tend to reflect the generally lower levels of education of these minorities. Turnout rates among African Americans have risen steadily as discriminatory barriers to their voting have been outlawed and determined efforts to mobilize these voters have continued. As a result, the African American vote has become a critical factor in determining the outcome of some elections, especially for Democratic candidates because African Americans tend to be overwhelmingly Democratic.

In the past women had lower rates of turnout than men because until 1920 and ratification of the Nineteenth Amendment giving them the vote, their participation in politics had been neither widely accepted nor encouraged. Today, however, women report slightly higher rates of turnout than men.

Partisan Implications of Turnout Patterns

Because people who rank relatively high in socioeconomic status and educational attainment, who are middle-aged, and who are white have the highest turnout rates, more Republicans are likely to go to the polls than Democrats. Is it surprising then that get-out-the-vote campaigns and efforts to increase turnout through easing of registration requirements have been a standard Democratic electoral strategy? Increased voter turnout does not necessarily benefit the Democrats, however. In the 1988 presidential election nonvoters probably held down Bush's margin in the popular vote. A 1989 *New York Times*/CBS survey showed that nonvoters preferred Bush by a 50–34 margin.[22] But when turnout swelled by 13 million in 1992, the Democrats and Ross Perot benefited. First-time voters accounted for 11 percent of the ballots and went strongly Democratic, giving Clinton 48 percent, Bush 30 percent, and

22. *New York Times*/CBS poll, reported in *Congressional Quarterly Weekly Report,* January 21, 1989, 138. Also see James DeNardo, "Turnout and the Vote: The Joke's on the Democrats," *American Political Science Review* 74 (June 1980): 406–420.

Perot 22 percent. In exit polls 15 percent of Perot voters indicated that they would not have voted had their candidate not been on the ballot.

Is Nonvoting a Social Disease?

Nonvoting is not primarily a matter of voter registration holding down turnout. Rather, it is caused by personal attitudes—a lack of interest, a low sense of civic duty, a feeling that elections are not important, and weak attachments to a political party (see Table 7.2).

With a voter turnout rate at just over 50 percent, well below those of most Western democracies, is the American Republic healthy? Any comparison with other democratic systems, however, must take into account how most nations compute their turnout rates: based on the percentage of registered voters who actually cast ballots on election day. In the United States, which does not have uniform national registration requirements and the federal government does not assume responsibility for registering voters, turnout rates are normally based on the percentage of the voting age population. These different methods of calculation mean that other nations consistently show much higher turnout rates than the United States. Although it must be recognized that a higher proportion of the citizens of other democracies are registered, a quite respectable 87 percent of registered Americans turn out to vote.[23]

23. David Glass, Peverill Squire, and Raymond Wolfinger, "Voter Turnout: An International Comparison," *Public Opinion,* December/January 1984, 52. For a more complete comparative analysis of voter turnout, see Ivor Crewe, "Electoral Participation," in *Democracy at the Polls,* ed. David Butler, Howard R. Penniman, and Austin Ranney (Washington, D.C.: American Enterprise Institute, 1981), 216–262.

Table 7.2 Personal Attitudes and Voter Turnout *(percent agreeing)*

Attitude	Likely Voters	People Who Do Not Vote Regularly
I'm aligned with a political party.	88	54
There are important differences between the parties.	85	65
I'd feel guilty if I didn't vote.	71	31
Politics and government are so complicated that I can't understand them.	50	77
People like me have no say in what government does.	32	57
It's a waste of time to vote.	12	41

Source: Jeff Alderman, ABC News Poll, Survey 0080, June 29–July 13, 1983.

But all this raises a disturbing question: Do Americans' relatively low turnout rates distort the will of the people? To date, there is no convincing evidence that turnout rates are distorting the public's policy and candidate preferences in elections. In general, nonvoters have candidate preferences much like those of voters.[24] Analyses of presidential elections held between 1964 and 1988 by political sociologist Ruy Teixeira reveal that if all the eligible citizens had actually voted in those elections, the outcomes would have remained the same (see Table 7.3). This does not mean that nonvoting never makes a difference in election outcomes. But it does mean that relatively unusual conditions must be met for turnout to play a determining role in election outcomes. For example, the election must be close to begin with because of partisan balance or other circumstances; a very large turnout increase can be generated; and a large group of nonvoters with heavily lopsided candidate preferences is available for mobilization. Although they are not apt to be present too often, such conditions—and turnout—probably determined the outcome when Chicago elected its first African American mayor, Harold Washington, in 1983. In that election African Americans voted overwhelmingly (99 percent) for Washington, and their historically low turnout rate swelled by 30 percent.[25]

Voter turnout rates provide only a limited perspective on the electoral and more general political participation within a society. As noted in Chapter 5, there is more to political participation than casting a ballot, and Americans tend to have higher rates of nonvoting participation in politics than the citizens of most democracies. Nor do turnout rates reflect the amount of electing—frequency of elections, the range of offices, and type of electoral decisions—that can take place in a country. Thus, although Americans have a turnout rate below those of most other democracies, they do not necessarily do less voting than other citizens; in fact, they probably do more. Americans' relatively low rates of turnout also may reflect general satisfaction with the political order and a belief that the next election will not bring major

---

24. See John R. Petrocik, "Voter Turnout and Electoral Preference: The Anomalous Reagan Elections," in *Elections in America*, ed. Kay Schlozman (Boston: Unwin Hyman, 1987), 261–292.

25. Teixeira, *Disappearing American Voter*, 94–97. On the turnout and the 1988 and 1992 elections, see Paul R. Abramson, John H. Aldrich, and David W. Rohde, *Change and Continuity in the 1988 Elections*, rev. ed. (Washington, D.C.: CQ Press, 1991), 108–113; as well as Abramson et al., *Change and Continuity in the 1992 Elections* (Washington, D.C.: CQ Press, 1994).

Table 7.3 What If There Were an Election and Everyone Came? Self-reported Preferences of Voters and Nonvoters in Presidential Elections, 1964–1988

Vote or Preference	Nonvoters	Voters	Voters and Nonvoters
1964			
Democratic vote or preference	79.7	67.4	70.0
Republican vote or preference	20.3	32.4	29.9
Other vote or preference	0	0.2	0.1
1968			
Democratic vote or preference	44.6	40.9	41.7
Republican vote or preference	40.4	47.6	46.0
Other vote or preference	15.0	11.5	12.2
1980			
Democratic vote or preference	46.8	39.4	41.1
Republican vote or preference	45.1	50.8	49.5
Other vote or preference	8.2	9.8	9.4
1984			
Democratic vote or preference	38.6	41.4	40.8
Republican vote or preference	61.2	57.7	58.4
Other vote or preference	0.3	0.9	0.8
1988			
Democratic vote or preference	44.4	46.6	46.0
Republican vote or preference	54.3	52.3	52.8
Other vote or preference	1.3	1.2	1.2

Source: Ruy A. Teixeira, *The Disappearing American Voter* (Washington, D.C.: Brookings, 1992), 96.

Note: The National Election Study (NES) did not ascertain the presidential preference of nonvoters in 1972 and 1976.

and threatening changes since both the Republican and Democratic parties espouse essentially middle-of-the-road policies.

Although nonvoting in America is perhaps less worrisome than it might appear at first glance, reasons for concern still exist. With the educated, more well-to-do, and influential having the highest turnout rates, universal suffrage does not provide the kind of counterweight to power and wealth once envisioned by the advocates of universal suffrage.[26] A high incidence of nonvoting also can threaten the legitimacy of democratic government. As fewer and fewer people vote, there is the danger that people will withdraw their support from the government as the principle of government by the consent of the governed is called into question.

26. See Crewe, "Electoral Participation," 261–262.

The Voter's Choice on Election Day

Voters' choices on election day reflect their long-held attitudes and beliefs as well as such short-term transitory influences as current issues and **candidate images**. The impacts of these long- and short-term influences on the voter vary from election to election.

The Impact of Partisanship

The most important and enduring influence on voters' choices is their *party identification*—a feeling of attachment and sympathy toward a political party.[27] Party identification is considered a long-term, stable influence on voter choice because it is not normally subject to sudden shifts from one election to the next.[28]

Political scientists measure party identification by surveying voters with such questions as "Generally speaking, do you think of yourself as a Republican, Democrat, or independent?" The strength of voters' commitments to a party and the party leanings of independents have been probed as well. These surveys were the basis for the development of a seven-point scale of partisanship, ranging from strong Democrats through independents to strong Republicans. According to this scale, from 1952 to 1992 between two-thirds and three-fourths of the electorate identified with either the Republican or Democratic parties (Table 7.4), but Democrats have held a consistent advantage over Republicans in terms of party identification. This advantage narrowed, however, during the 1980s but left the Democrats with a modest advantage in the early 1990s.

For strong partisans the pull of their commitment to the Republican or Democratic party is substantial, and their rate of defection to the opposition is low. Strong Republicans in particular show a high level of party loyalty in presidential elections. For those with weaker partisan commitments, short-term influences such as issues and candidate appeal take on greater importance and can cause a substantial proportion of such voters to defect from their party on election day. In 1980, 1984, and 1988, for example, over 25 percent of weak Democrats failed to support their party's presidential candidate,[29] making it possi-

---

27. A classic explanation of the concept of party identification is found in Angus Campbell et al., *The American Voter* (New York: Wiley, 1960), 121–128.

28. For a summary of research on the stability of party identification, see Herbert B. Asher, *Presidential Elections and American Politics: Voters, Candidates and Issues since 1952*, 5th ed. (Chicago: Dorsey, 1992), 69–78.

29. For data on defection rates by strong and weak partisan identifiers as well as those leaning toward one or the other of the parties, see Asher, *Presidential Elections*

Table 7.4 Party Identification in the United States, 1952–1992 *(percent)*

	1952	*1956*	*1960*	*1964*	*1968*	*1972*	*1976*	*1980*	*1982*	*1984*	*1988*	*1992*
Strong Democrats	22	21	20	27	20	15	15	18	20	17	17	17
Weak Democrats	25	23	25	25	25	26	25	23	24	20	18	18
Independent (leaning) Democrats	10	6	6	9	10	11	12	11	11	11	12	14
Independent	5	9	10	8	11	13	15	13	11	11	11	12
Independent (leaning) Republicans	7	8	7	6	9	11	10	10	8	12	13	13
Weak Republicans	14	14	14	14	15	13	14	14	14	15	14	15
Strong Republicans	14	15	16	11	10	10	9	9	10	12	14	11
Apolitical	3	4	3	1	1	1	1	2	2	2	2	1
TOTAL	100	100	101	101	101	100	101	100	100	100	101	101

Source: National Election Study surveys.
Note: Some totals do not add up to 100 because of rounding.

ble for Republicans to win recent presidential elections even though they have fewer party identifiers than the Democrats. But most partisans do vote for their party's presidential candidates. In 1988 a *New York Times*/CBS exit poll reported that 91 percent of all Republicans and 82 percent of all Democrats voted for their parties' presidential tickets.[30] But in the three-way contest for the presidency in 1992 among Clinton, Bush, and Perot, partisan defections were higher than usual, and for the first time since 1964 the Republican defection rate was higher than that of the Democrats: 81 percent of Democrats voted for their party's nominee, while 72 percent of Republicans stayed with their party.[31]

The tendency of both strong and weak partisans to support their parties' nominees is more pronounced in elections below the presidential level. At the presidential level, weakly committed voters, bombarded with saturation news coverage and a deluge of campaign advertising, may be influenced to defect from their party by a particularly salient issue or appealing candidate. But at the level of House races, with their relative lack of publicity and low-visibility campaigns, weak

---

and American Politics, 85–88; and Flanigan and Zingale, *Political Behavior of the American Electorate,* 69.

30. *New York Times,* Nov. 10, 1988, 18Y, National edition.

31. National Election Study (NES) data. NES is conducted under the supervision of a panel of social scientists and provides historical and recent data on voting behavior. NES data are available from the Inter-University Consortium for Political and Social Research at the University of Michigan.

partisans are more likely to vote in accord with their party identification because less information is available to them.

More Independents? One of the most notable changes in the partisanship of the electorate has been the increase in the proportion of voters labeling themselves independents. This trend was especially strong from the 1960s through the mid-1970s and was most noticeable among young voters who did not align themselves with a party as quickly as older generations had. Thus, the increased proportion of independents in the electorate has stemmed mainly from a large influx of new voters—so-called baby boomers who came of voting age in the 1960s and 1970s—and not from partisans adopting the independent label.[32] The tendency of voters to declare themselves independents leveled off after the mid-1970s, and in the 1980s partisanship showed a modest resurgence among voters. Even so, the current number of independents is high compared with the number found in the 1950s.

Some political observers have suggested that the increased proportion of the voters declaring themselves independents has caused a high level of volatility in election outcomes and even provides the basis for the emergence of a major third party. Not too much significance, however, should be read into the fact that a large share of the voters consider themselves to be independents. Independents are not a homogeneous bloc. Instead, they are three quite distinct groups—Republican leaners, Democratic leaners, and pure independents—with the latter by far the smallest group. Moreover, these three groups behave quite differently in the voting booth. Most self-proclaimed independents are not uncommitted but are in fact closet Democrats and Republicans who generally are more loyal to their party than are weak partisans. Only the pure independents exhibit substantial volatility from one election to the next. Indeed, they vote in a manner that tends to reflect in an exaggerated way the election outcome. For example, in 1980 Ronald Reagan had a 5:4 advantage over President Jimmy Carter in the total popular vote but had a 3:1 (66 to 22 percent) advantage among pure independents.[33]

Ticket Splitting and Candidate-Centered Politics. Although studies of voting behavior consistently demonstrate that party identification is the single most important determinant of voter choice, there is also evidence that partisanship's influence has lessened in recent decades.

32. Warren E. Miller and Teresa E. Levitin, *Leadership and Change: Presidential Elections from 1952-1976* (Boston: Winthrop, 1976), 250-251.

33. Bruce E. Keith et al., *The Myth of the Independent Voter* (Berkeley: University of California Press, 1992), 64.

Candidate-centered Politics and the Growth of Split-ticket Voting

Although partisanship is a powerful influence on people's election day choices, candidates increasingly seek votes on the basis of their personal image and record rather than as the nominees of the Republican and Democratic parties. In this environment of candiate-centered rather than party-centered politics, large numbers of voters are splitting their tickets when voting for president and U.S. representative by voting for one party's nominee for president and the other party's candidate for the House.

Among the consequences of ticket splitting are divided party control of the government and high proportions of incumbent House members winning reelection.

Year	Number of districts*	House districts with split results for president and House		Divided or united party control of presidency and House
		Number	Percent	
1900	295	10	3.4	united
1916	333	35	10.5	united
1932	355	50	14.1	united
1948	422	90	21.3	united
1952	435	84	19.3	united
1956	435	130	29.9	divided
1960	437	114	26.1	united
1964	435	145	33.3	united
1968	435	139	32.0	divided
1972	435	192	44.1	divided
1976	435	124	28.5	united
1980	435	143	32.8	divided
1984	435	190	43.7	divided
1988	435	148	34.0	divided
1992	435	100	23.0	united

Source: Thomas E. Mann, Norman J. Ornstein, and Michael J. Malbin, *Vital Statistics on Congress, 1993-1994* (Washington, D.C.: Congressional Quarterly Inc., 1994), 64.

* Before 1952 complete data are not available for every congressional district.

The incidence of ticket splitting—voting for candidates of different parties instead of voting a straight party ticket—has increased. Earlier in this century ticket splitting was much rarer—in 1920, for example, only 3.2 percent of the congressional districts had split outcomes compared with 45 percent in 1984, 34 percent in 1988, and 23 percent in 1992.[34] To a large degree the high incidence of split-ticket voting in presidential and House elections reflects the pull of incumbency in House races because incumbents are normally better known, evaluated favorably, well funded, and facing weak challengers.

Split-ticket voting is further encouraged by the trend in this century away from party-centered campaigns in which the party organizations controlled nominations, ran campaigns, and appealed to the voters on the basis of partisanship. Modern-day campaigns—especially presidential ones—tend to be *candidate centered* and media oriented. Today's candidates are no longer dependent on the organizational resources of their parties. Through television, candidates can establish

34. For data on ticket splitting, see Norman J. Ornstein, Thomas E. Mann, and Michael J. Malbin, *Vital Statistics on Congress, 1993-1994* (Washington, D.C.: Congressional Quarterly Inc., 1994), 64; Martin P. Wattenberg, *The Rise of Candidate Centered Politics: Presidential Elections of the 1980s* (Cambridge, Mass.: Harvard University Press, 1991), 38.

contact with voters without relying on party organizations. In addition, candidates can create their own campaign organizations by hiring consultants who specialize in all the techniques—direct mail, polling, placement of television ads, appeals to various voter groups—of modern campaigning. Then, with a personal organization and through extensive use of the media, particularly television, candidates can sell themselves, not their parties, to the voters. They can even deemphasize their party ties when it is advantageous. Such candidate-centered campaigning reinforces attitudes about the candidates, but it does little to reinforce partisan commitments among the electors and can render party affiliation a less powerful influence on many voters. Voters do see differences between the Republican and Democratic parties, but issues and evaluations of the candidates themselves are looming larger in their decisions.

The Role of Candidate Image

A candidate's image—personality, physical appearance, style, and background—figures heavily in the media coverage accompanying presidential campaigns. Candidates with a favorable public image can contribute significantly to their party's vote on election day. Dwight Eisenhower, whose personal appeal transcended partisanship, was a classic example of a candidate whose image added substantially to his total vote. His status as a hero of World War II and his personal qualities—sincerity, sense of duty, commitment to family, religious devotion, and sheer likableness—all of which were captured in the slogan "I like Ike," caused heavy Democratic defections to the Republican party in 1952 and again in 1956. Candidate images also played a role in the 1992 election. In the context of public worries over the state of the economy, exit polls revealed that the candidate's qualities that mattered most to voters were "will bring about change" (favored Clinton over Bush 67 to 5 percent) and "cares about people like me" (favored Clinton over Bush 64 to 11 percent). Bush's most positive qualities were his experience and his ability to handle a crisis.[35]

Voters also are influenced by negative perceptions of candidates. In both 1984 and 1988 Democratic nominees were hurt by such perceptions. In 1984, for example, Ronald Reagan benefited from public perceptions of the Democratic nominee, Walter Mondale, as "a weak leader," "a big spender," and "tied to special interests."[36] When asked as they left the polls in 1988 what they liked least about the candidates, Bush voters most often said that Dukakis was too liberal, indicating

35. Voter Research and Surveys exit polls.
36. ABC News poll, year-end wrap-up, 1984.

that the Bush campaign's efforts to define Dukakis in ideological terms were successful. Interestingly, in response to the same question Dukakis supporters said that Bush ran a dirty campaign.[37]

Since 1952, with the exception of the 1964 contest (Lyndon Johnson versus Barry Goldwater) and the 1992 election, the Republicans have been helped more than the Democrats by the public's evaluation of their presidential candidates. In the 1980 election between President Jimmy Carter and Ronald Reagan, however, there was a general lack of enthusiasm for both candidates, and candidate images had a negligible effect on the election.[38]

The Impact of Issues

Classical democratic theory assigns issues a prominent role in voters' decisions. Nevertheless, issues normally follow party identification and candidate image in importance of influence on the voter. Early systematic research in the 1940s and 1950s found that issues had scant influence on how voters arrived at a decision.[39] But these findings have been questioned by more recent research, which used improved methodologies and took into account the relatively calm politics of the 1950s compared to the more turbulent and divisive decades of the sixties, seventies, and eighties. According to this research, issues are now a more important basis for determining voters' choices than in the 1950s.[40] Some aspects of human behavior, however, work to reduce the impact of issues.

The widespread ignorance of voters about issues and candidates' positions on them works against issue-based voting. This is especially true of foreign policy matters, which voters often find little related to their own lives. So-called issue voting is further diminished by some voters projecting their personal issue positions onto their preferred candidates, regardless of those candidates' actual issue positions. In 1968, for example, both hawks and doves on America's military involvement in Vietnam were found among the supporters of Richard Nixon and his Democratic opponent Hubert Humphrey. Since the candidates were less than explicit about their Vietnam policies, voters

37. *National Journal,* November 12, 1988, 2854.

38. Asher, *Presidential Elections and American Politics,* 176–177.

39. See Bernard Berelson, Paul Lazarsfeld, and William McPhee, *Voting* (Chicago: University of Chicago Press, 1954); and Campbell et al., *American Voter.*

40. For a summary of research on the extent of issue influence on voter choice, see Asher, *Presidential Elections and American Politics,* chap. 4. An important study in demonstrating the heightened significance of issues was that by Norman Nie, Sidney Verba, and John R. Petrocik, *The Changing American Voter* (Cambridge, Mass.: Harvard University Press, 1976).

who saw a difference between them on this issue were responding to their own wishes and not engaging in issue voting.[41] It is also possible for voters to adopt issue positions because their preferred candidate has taken that position.

An issue has an impact on voter choice only when (1) voters are informed and concerned about the issue; (2) candidates take distinguishable stands on the issue; and (3) voters perceive how the candidate stands in relation to their own concerns. In the 1972 presidential contest between Republican Richard Nixon and Democrat George McGovern, issues clearly had an impact. On eleven of fourteen issues studied the voters felt closer to Nixon than to McGovern, and there was a close correlation between people's perceptions of where the candidates stood on the issues and the candidate for whom they voted. Only on issues related to the environment and urban unrest did McGovern appear to be closer to citizens' positions, whereas Nixon was viewed as closer to voters' preferences on such issues as the Vietnam War, marijuana, desegregation, and campus unrest.[42]

To base their voting on issues, voters must have information about candidates' policy positions. Such information is available quickly and easily when candidates and parties take distinct positions on issues and campaign on the basis of those positions. But the candidates and parties do not always offer clear-cut policy alternatives the way they did in the Nixon-McGovern contest. With most voters tending to be moderate or centrist in their orientations and with each party composed of people with diverse viewpoints, there may be little incentive for candidates to take strongly opposing stands. They may, therefore, straddle issues and make issue-based voting difficult for the average citizen.

Voters' decisions are made easier when an incumbent is seeking reelection. Having had an opportunity to judge the candidate's performance, voters can render a verdict on his or her behavior in office. This process of electoral decision making is called retrospective voting.[43] In 1980 and 1992 voters issued negative verdicts on the performances of presidential incumbents Jimmy Carter and George Bush, each of whom saw their public support plummet as economic problems overwhelmed their administrations. By contrast, in 1984 Ronald Reagan's

41. Benjamin I. Page and Richard A. Brody, "Policy Voting and the Electoral Process: The Vietnam Issue," *American Political Science Review* 66 (September 1972): 987.

42. Arthur H. Miller et al., "A Majority Party in Disarray: Policy Polarization in the 1972 Election," *American Political Science Review* 70 (September 1976): 753–778.

43. See Morris P. Fiorina, *Retrospective Voting in America* (New Haven, Conn.: Yale University Press, 1981).

performance was judged favorably on the whole, and he rolled to a landslide victory. And in 1988, even though no incumbent was on the ballot, Vice President Bush clearly benefited from the public perception that President Reagan had performed well and that Bush would stay the course. Nonetheless, evaluations of the Reagan presidency were less favorable than in 1984, and the vote was therefore closer.[44]

The Meaning of Elections

E lections do make a difference. Not only do they periodically change the government's leadership, but they also can lead to significant changes in public policy. For example, the 1964 Democratic landslide that extended Lyndon Johnson's White House tenure and greatly strengthened Democratic majorities in the House and Senate enabled the president to gain congressional approval for a wide range of social welfare legislation, including Medicare, Medicaid, and the War on Poverty. Similarly, Ronald Reagan's election in 1980 resulted in a reordering of governmental priorities as the share of funds allocated to the military was increased, the rate of growth in domestic social spending was restricted, income tax rates were reduced, the budget deficit was allowed to grow, the government embarked on a policy of deregulating the economy, and the Supreme Court became more conservative as a result of three Reagan appointees.[45] And the 1993 return of a Democrat to the White House after twelve years of Republican control signaled renewed governmental activism under the Clinton administration.

Since most presidents try to keep their campaign commitments to the voters who elected them,[46] elections often are seen as the process through which voters register their policy preferences and direct the course of government. But do election results really reveal the policy preferences of the voters? Do elections provide the winners with clear-cut mandates for specific policy decisions? This look at the forces influencing voter choice certainly suggests that there are limits to how much elections reflect the voters' views on specific issues. For many, the decision in the voting booth is determined by party identification

44. Abramson et al., *Change and Continuity in the 1988 Elections,* 195.

45. The Reagan presidency's impact on domestic and foreign policy is summarized in *The Reagan Legacy: Promise and Performance,* ed. Charles O. Jones (Chatham, N.J.: Chatham House, 1988), chaps. 7 and 8.

46. See Gerald M. Pomper and Susan S. Lederman, *Election in America: Control and Influence in Democratic Politics,* 2d ed. (New York: Longman, 1980); and Jeff Fishel, *Presidents and Promises: From Campaign Pledge to Presidential Performance* (Washington, D.C.: CQ Press, 1985).

The 1992 Election: The Passing of Divided Government

For the fifth time since World War II a divided government consisting of a Republican president and at least one congressional chamber controlled by the Democrats faced the voters for reelection in 1992.[1] Three times (1956, 1972, and 1984) the citizens had registered their approval of this governmental arrangement as they gave GOP presidents landslide victories and returned incumbents of both parties to the House and Senate in overwhelming numbers. The 1976 contest, however, was a *disapproval election* that ended Republican Gerald Ford's presidency and brought Democrat Jimmy Carter to the White House. The 1992 election was even more decisively a disapproval one as an incumbent president was rejected, substantial numbers of incumbent representatives (110) and senators (12) were replaced either voluntarily via retirement or through electoral defeat, and divided partisan control of government ceased. It was an example of voters engaging in *retrospective voting*—assessing divided government and rendering in this instance a negative verdict. The extent of voter dissatisfaction was unusually high. A Gallup poll in June 1992 revealed that 84 percent of the public was "dissatisfied with the way things are going in the United States at this time." Even 66 percent of Bush supporters shared this assessment.[2]

Voters were demanding change, but it was almost impossible for President Bush either to project the image of change or to be the agent of change. He had served eight years as the loyal vice president of Ronald Reagan and was elected in his own right largely because he was closely identified in the public's mind with Reagan and was expected to continue Reagan's policies. Bush, therefore, had only a limited opportunity to put his own stamp on the presidency by installing a new team or taking his administration in new policy directions. And like Herbert Hoover, the only other Republican president in this century to follow a two-term president of his own party, Bush was defeated when economic discontent boiled over.

By defeating Bush, Bill Clinton became the third challenger in the last five presidential elections to defeat an incumbent. This record of incumbent defeats reflects the importance of voter verdicts on administration performance, public concern about America's future, and the fragile nature of a president's hold on popular support.

The 1992 election thus marked the passing, at least temporarily, of an extended period of divided government and the transfer of power to the post-World War II, baby-boomer generation. The politics of a Republican White House blaming a Democratic Congress for the ills of the nation and a Democratic Congress returning the charge was no longer feasible after the 1992 elections. But one-party control of the legislative and executive branches does not necessarily ensure smooth and cooperative poli-

Figure 7.7: Party Control of the Presidency and Congress, 1969–1994

	Presidency	Senate	House
1969–70	Nixon–Rep.	DEMOCRATIC	DEMOCRATIC
1971–72	Nixon–Rep.	DEMOCRATIC	DEMOCRATIC
1973–74	Nixon-Ford–Rep.	DEMOCRATIC	DEMOCRATIC
1975–76	Ford–Rep.	DEMOCRATIC	DEMOCRATIC
1977–78	Carter–Dem.	DEMOCRATIC	DEMOCRATIC
1979–80	Carter–Dem.	DEMOCRATIC	DEMOCRATIC
1981–82	Reagan–Rep.	REPUBLICAN	DEMOCRATIC
1983–84	Reagan–Rep.	REPUBLICAN	DEMOCRATIC
1985–86	Reagan–Rep.	REPUBLICAN	DEMOCRATIC
1987–88	Reagan–Rep.	DEMOCRATIC	DEMOCRATIC
1989–90	Bush–Rep.	DEMOCRATIC	DEMOCRATIC
1991–92	Bush–Rep.	DEMOCRATIC	DEMOCRATIC
1993–94	Clinton–Dem.	DEMOCRATIC	DEMOCRATIC

Total Divided Party Control:	20 years
Total Single Party Control:	6 years

cy making. Just out of the starting gate, the Clinton administration encountered congressional opposition to its domestic programs and was forced to modify its proposals. These difficulties stemmed not so much from united Republican opposition but from the contending factions of the Democratic party.

Without a doubt, the Clinton-Gore administration took office facing problems of daunting proportions: an uncertain economy, a massive federal budget deficit, a mounting foreign trade debt, and a post-cold war international scene characterized by instability and intensified ethnic strife. In seeking to cope with these problems, the administration operates in an environment of shared powers not only with Congress but also with the other world leaders. Presidents can influence both an independent-minded Congress and world leaders but cannot control or dictate to them. Yet by virtue of the voters' decision in 1992, governing responsibility and accountability for the state of the Union rest with President Clinton and the Democratic party. Therefore, when the voters in 1996 are again asked to render their verdict on governmental performance, for the first time in sixteen years they will not be judging a divided government but one controlled by a single party.

1. In 1948 a divided government consisting of a Democratic president, Harry Truman, and a Republican Congress stood for reelection. In that election the Democrats retained the presidency and regained control of Congress.

2. Gallup survey, June 12–14, 1992, reported in *American Enterprise*, September/October 1992, 95.

and generalized notions that one party or the other is best for peace or jobs. Still others vote on the basis of candidate image, and many base their votes on a general retrospective judgment of an incumbent party's performance in office. Only a minority engage in issue- or policy-based voting.

Elections, then, are rarely mandates from the voters on specific issues, and often the message conveyed is quite murky.[47] This was certainly the case in 1992. As R. W. Apple, Jr., noted in the *New York Times,* it was an "election whose results rang with a cry for change but offered no specific mandate."[48] The Republicans were forced to vacate the White House as 62 percent of the voters cast ballots against the administration of George Bush. But Bill Clinton, with 43 percent of the vote, became the fourth post-World War II president to receive less than a popular majority. Change without a clear policy mandate was also apparent in the 1992 congressional elections. While there was a massive 25 percent turnover in the membership of the House of Representatives, the chamber's partisan makeup looked pretty much as it had before the election.

Other factors over and above the mixed results of elections for the president, House, and Senate make discernment of clear policy mandates from elections difficult. For example, with so many issues and so many different voter groups involved in a presidential election, candidates tend to collect voters for different, and even conflicting, reasons. Furthermore, candidates do not always indicate clearly what their policies will be once elected. John Kennedy's promise to "get the country going again," for example, was vague enough to cover a wide range of voters' hopes and gave little indication of the policies he intended to follow to achieve economic growth.

Even when candidates are clear about their intentions, the voters may base their decisions on other grounds. Thus, in 1980 Reagan was forthcoming with specific proposals in the fields of taxation, government expenditures, and national security policy. Public opinion surveys, however, revealed that the voters did not base their decisions on the conservative policies advocated by candidate Reagan. Rather, the election was primarily a referendum on the performance of the Carter administration, particularly its handling of the economy.

47. For a more detailed consideration of why elections are seldom mandates to public officials, see Polsby and Wildavsky, *Presidential Elections,* 322–328. The Polsby and Wildavsky argument is similar to that found in Robert A. Dahl, *A Preface to Democratic Theory* (Chicago: University of Chicago Press, 1956).

48. R. W. Apple, Jr., "Clinton, Savoring Victory, Starts to Size Up the Job Ahead," *New York Times,* Nov. 5, 1992, A1, National edition.

American elections, then, are seldom referendums on specific issues; they decide which of two competing political parties will control government institutions. The relationship between election outcomes and public policy is, to be sure, subtle and indirect. Political scientists Nelson Polsby and Aaron Wildavsky have described the electoral process in the following manner:

Two teams of politicians, one in office, the other seeking office, both attempt to get enough votes to win elections. In order to win, they go to various groups of voters and, by offering to pursue policies favored by these groups, or by suggesting policies they might come to favor, hope to attract their votes. If there were only one office-seeking team, their incentive to respond to the policy preferences of the groups in the population would diminish; if there were many such teams, the chances that any one of them could achieve a sufficient number of backers to govern would diminish. Hence the two-party system is . . . a kind of compromise between the goals of responsiveness and effectiveness.[49]

Because elections give elected officials only limited guidance in divining the public's policy preferences, these officials have considerable leeway in devising government policies. Future elections, however, always carry the threat of involuntary retirement for those who fail to anticipate the voters' reactions to their decisions. Just the thought of the political activists—opposition leaders, potential challengers, and interest group leaders—poised to criticize an elected offficial's decisions and campaign for his or her defeat creates powerful incentives for elected officials to stay in touch with the voters.[50]

49. Polsby and Wildavsky, *Presidential Elections*, 323.

50. On how citizens exert indirect control over elected officials who want to keep their jobs, see R. Douglas Arnold, *The Logic of Congressional Action* (New Haven, Conn.: Yale University Press, 1990).

For Review

1. Elections are regulated by both the federal and state governments. The federal government is engaged primarily in protecting people from discrimination in their exercise of the right to vote, regulating campaign finance in elections for federal office, and setting uniform dates for federal elections. The states regulate voter registration and the administration of elections.

2. To be elected president, a candidate must receive a majority of the electoral college vote. A state's electoral votes are allocated to candidates on a winner-take-all basis in which the candidate who gains a plurality of the popular vote receives the state's full complement of electoral votes. Because of the winner-take-all feature, candidates concentrate their campaign efforts

on states with large blocs of electoral votes and on states where the race is tightly contested.

3. The Federal Election Campaign Act provides public funding for presidential candidates who agree to accept no private contributions to their campaigns. The law's expenditure limits have been breached, however, by both parties channeling funds to state and local party committees for use in party-building activities that aid presidential campaigns.

4. The turnout of eligible voters is approximately 50 percent in presidential elections and normally less than 40 percent in midterm elections. Voter turnout is affected by such social characteristics as age and education, registration requirements, the amount of publicity a campaign receives, the competitiveness of the election, and personal attitudes such as party identification.

5. Voter choice on election day is influenced by the interaction of party identification, a long-term influence, and more short-term forces such as issues and candidate image.

6. Elections seldom provide winning candidates with mandates to pursue specific policies once in office. The voters do, however, exert an indirect influence over elected officials, who seek to ward off defeat at the polls by determining the public's policy preferences and anticipating the voters' reactions to policy decisions.

For Further Reading

Abramson, Paul, John H. Aldrich, and David W. Rohde, *Change and Continuity in the 1992 Elections*. Washington, D.C.: CQ Press, 1994. An analysis of the 1992 elections demonstrating the interaction of partisanship, candidates, issues, and presidential performance on voter choice.

Asher, Herbert B. *Presidential Elections and American Politics: Voters, Candidates and Issues since 1952*. 5th ed. Pacific Grove, Calif.: Brooks/Cole, 1992. An analysis of presidential elections between 1952 and 1988.

Flanigan, William H., and Nancy H. Zingale. *Political Behavior of the American Electorate*. 8th ed. Washington, D.C.: CQ Press, 1994. A concise consideration of voter turnout, determinants of voter choice, and the social bases of partisanship.

Guide to U.S. Elections. 3d ed. Washington, D.C.: Congressional Quarterly Inc., 1994. An authoritative compendium of election statistics, along with brief accounts of American electoral history.

Keith, Bruce, et al. *The Myth of the Independent Voter*. Berkeley: University of California Press, 1992. A convincing challenge to the notion that a growing army of independents is threatening the two-party system.

Kessel, John H. *Presidential Campaign Politics*. 4th ed. Pacific Grove, Calif.: Brooks/Cole, 1992. An analysis of presidential campaign organizations, strategies, and the determinants of citizen choice.

Nelson, Michael, ed. *The Elections of 1992.* Washington, D.C.: CQ Press, 1993. A collection of essays by leading scholars on the various aspects of the 1992 election.

Sorauf, Frank J. *Inside Campaign Finance.* New Haven, Conn.: Yale University Press, 1992. An account of how and why campaign finance works as it does, with suggestions for reform.

Teixeira, Ruy A. *The Disappearing American Voter.* Washington, D.C.: Brookings, 1992. An analysis of the reasons for and consequences of low voter turnout in the United States.

Wattenberg, Martin P. *The Rise of Candidate Centered Politics: Presidential Elections of the 1980s.* Cambridge, Mass.: Harvard University Press, 1991. An argument, based on survey data, that parties have declined and that American politics is increasingly candidate centered.

West, Darrell M. *Air Wars: Television Advertising in Election Campaigns, 1952-1992.* Washington, D.C.: CQ Press, 1993. A study of the role of television advertising in campaigns and its impact on voters, the news media, and the political system.

8. Interest Groups

FEW ASPECTS of American politics arouse more suspicion and righteous indignation than the activities of interest groups and their agents—so-called lobbyists. These "special interests" are perceived as having a self-serving, sometimes corrupt, disregard for the interest of the general public. *Time* magazine captured this sentiment in a cover story, "Influence Peddling: Lobbyists Swarm over Capitol Hill."

The hallway is known as Gucci Gulch after the expensive Italian shoes they wear. At tax-writing time, the Washington lobbyists line up by the hundreds in the corridor outside the House Ways and Means Committee room, ever vigilant against the attempt of lawmakers to close their prized loopholes. Over near the House and Senate chambers, Congressmen must run a gauntlet of lobbyists who sometimes express their views on legislation by pointing their thumbs up or down. . . . Senator John Danforth . . . could be seen on the Capitol steps trying to wrench his hand from the grip of a lobbyist. . . . The Senator, an ordained Episcopal minister, rolled his eyes heavenward and mumbled, "Save me from these people."[1]

Although Americans are suspicious of interest groups, they also are world-class organizers of such groups. This tendency was noted as far back as the 1830s by Alexis de Tocqueville, the astute French observer who wrote *Democracy in America,* a classic commentary on American society in its formative years.[2] Even de Tocqueville probably would be amazed at the extent of interest group proliferation in present-day Washington. Indeed, Congressional Quarterly's *Washington Information Directory* uses up almost eight hundred pages just listing major government offices and the organizations that have a stake in their policies.

The widespread public disapproval and fear of group activities that exist side by side with broad public participation in interest groups reflect the public's ambivalence toward interest groups in general. Many people object to some groups' policy goals, fearing that through such groups the well connected, well organized, and well off will exert undue influence over government institutions. Yet at the same time people can be firm, fervent supporters of the groups to which they

1. *Time,* March 3, 1986, 26.
2. Alexis de Tocqueville, *Democracy in America,* ed. Richard D. Heffner (New York: New American Library, 1956), 102. For evidence of the extensive group affiliations by Americans, see Frank R. Baumgartner and Jack L. Walker, "Survey Research and Membership in Voluntary Associations," *American Journal of Political Science* 32 (November 1988): 908–928.

Lobbyists jam the hallway outside a closed House committee meeting and wait for a chance to buttonhole representatives and gain information about the committee's deliberations.

themselves belong. The self-described citizens' organization Common Cause exemplifies this ambivalence. This organization has pushed aggressively for measures that would reduce the role of interest groups in the government process. Yet Common Cause itself is an influential participant in the interest group system with thousands of members and a professional staff in Washington.

Whether condemned as special interests or cherished as a special way in which citizens can have their say in politics, interest groups are an integral part of the American political process. This chapter examines the nature and scope of interest groups in America, the determinants of a group's clout, the techniques groups use to exert influence, and the issues raised by the prominent role they play in the American system.

What Are Interest Groups?

"An interest group is an organized body of individuals who share some goals and who try to influence public policy."[3] The key elements of this definition are "organized" and "influence public policy." Thus, the National Association of Manufacturers (NAM),

3. Jeffrey M. Berry, *The Interest Group Society,* 2d ed. (Glenview, Ill.: Scott Foresman/Little, Brown, 1989), 4.

the National Association for the Advancement of Colored People (NAACP), the AFL-CIO, and the American Farm Bureau Federation (AFBF) are organized groups seeking to influence government policy. But manufacturers, African Americans, workers, and farmers are not interest groups; being unorganized, they are interests and potential interest groups.

Not all interest group activity is carried on by such huge groups as the AFL-CIO or AFBF. Some organizations consist merely of a small staff backed by financial patrons. For example, the Media Access Project is a public interest law firm concerned about the public's access to government information. In addition, there are the so-called hired guns—Washington lawyers, public relations consultants, and lobbyists—who, for a fee, try to influence government policy for their clients.

As the opening quotation from *Time* suggests, much of the media coverage of interest group activities is critical in nature. Yet it is important not to lose sight of the essential functions these groups perform: they are one way in which people who share the same attitudes or interests can be represented informally. Specialized interests in society are drawn to such organizations as the American Council for the Blind, the Association of Flight Attendants, the American Symphony Orchestra League, and the National Association of Securities Dealers. Because such groups often deal with issues that affect too few people to attract the attention of the political parties, or with issues too specialized and technical to attract media attention, it can be said that the group system of informal representation supplements the formal system of geographic area representation used in Congress. In their representational roles, interest groups provide policy makers with specialized information that otherwise might not be readily available. Interest groups also are an avenue for more effective political participation than is likely to be achieved by a lone person picketing on the sidewalk in front of the White House.

The Diversity of Organized Interests

One glance at the building directory of one of the office buildings that line K or M streets in Northwest Washington just a few blocks from the White House demonstrates dramatically the wide range of organized interests that are riding herd on national politics. The thousands of organizations, corporations, law firms, and political consultants listed in such directories reflect the incredible diversity of American interests.

Groups with a direct economic stake in government policy (such as the National Association of Broadcasters) as well as organizations not motivated by material gain (such as the Children's Defense Fund) operate in a permanent state of mobilization on the scene in Washington, poised to advance or defend their organization's interests. According to political scientist David Truman, organized groups become involved in politics and inevitably gravitate toward Washington and the federal government when they find their own resources inadequate to deal with a problem.[4] Government assistance in solving their problems or achieving their objectives is their goal. Even business organizations, which often espouse a philosophy of minimal government interference in economic markets, troop to Washington for assistance when times are difficult and they feel threatened. Thus as Congress responded to consumer complaints about rising cable rates and poor service by considering legislation to regulate cable television, the National Cable Television Association, National Association of Broadcasters, Motion Picture Association of America, and Association of Independent Television Stations engaged in a high-stakes lobbying war over the rules governing how money (over $50 billion annually) would flow among the creators and distributors of television programs.

Lobbying organizations, which seek to influence government decision makers, are concentrated on 16th and K Streets, N.W., a few blocks north of the White House.

But organized interests do not reserve their big guns just for the federal government; on occasion, they also react (mostly negatively) to the objectives of another interest group. Indeed, one group's actions to advance its interests are likely to trigger a defensive response from those who would be disadvantaged by the new policy, causing a spiraling level of interest group activity. For example, when the Clinton administration proposed an energy tax as a part of its budget package in 1993, the president of the National Association of Manufacturers, Jerry Jasinowski, organized the American Energy Alliance, a broad-based coalition of adversely affected groups, to fight the tax. The NAM-led alliance included 1,650 organizations ranging from such peak associations as the American Farm Bureau Federation, to such major corporations as Goodyear, Gillette, and Coors, to hundreds of small businesses and local chambers of commerce. These groups mobilized their members to bombard Capitol Hill with letters and faxes opposing the energy tax, while their lobbyists, armed with reams of information, pounded on the doors of members of Congress.[5] President Clinton's

4. The concept of interest groups inevitably gravitating toward the government is developed in one of the classic books in the field, David B. Truman's *The Governmental Process* (New York: Knopf, 1951), chap. 3.

5. Agis Salpukas, "Going for the Kill on the Energy Tax Plan," *New York Times,* June 6, 1993, 17, National edition.

In a State of Permanent Mobilization: The Growth and Extent of Washington's Interest Group Community

■ The number of interest group representatives grew from 4,000 in 1977 to more than 14,500 in 1991.

■ More than four thousand corporations retain representatives in Washington.

■ Thirty-two hundred associations have their headquarters in Washington.

■ Associations with annual payrolls in excess of $15 million employ eighty thousand people in Washington and constitute the capital's third largest employer. Only government and tourism employ more people.

■ In 1965 only 45 out-of-town law firms had set up offices in the nation's capital. By 1983 the number had grown to 247 and in just ten years, between 1973 and 1983, the size of the District of Columbia Bar tripled from 10,925 to over 37,000 attorneys.

Source: Mark P. Petracca, "The Rediscovery of Interest Group Politics," in *The Politics of Interests: Interest Groups Transformed*, ed. Mark P. Petracca (Boulder, Colo.: Westview Press, 1992), 14. Reprinted by permission of Westview Press.

proposal for sweeping changes in the health care system also activated a massive array of organized interests—over 1,100 according to a tally by the White House.[6]

Since the 1960s there has been a virtual explosion in the number and diversity of interest groups operating in Washington. As the scope of government activities has grown, more and more groups have recognized the benefits of having a presence in the nation's capital. The composition of the interest group system has changed as well. The traditional farm, union, professional, and business groups must now compete with a vast array of citizens' groups organized around an idea or cause and having no occupational basis for membership. In addition, individual corporations, states, cities, counties, and universities have gravitated toward Washington to advance or protect interests that can be dramatically affected by government policy. This being said, however, business, union, and professional groups—organizations based on economic self-interest—are among the most prominent and durable of the interests seeking to influence government policy.

Economic Interests

Business-oriented groups dominate the interest group universe. The largest of these are the so-called peak business organizations that seek to represent general business interests. These include the U.S. Chamber of Commerce, the National Association of Manufacturers, and the Business Roundtable. NAM is composed of large manufacturing concerns, and the Business Roundtable comprises approximately two hundred of the nation's largest companies—for example, IBM, General Motors, GTE, and Shell Oil.

The more specialized business groups are called trade associations, composed of companies in the same line of business. Trade associations range from the American Bankers Association with its thirteen thousand member banks to the much smaller International Association of Refrigerated Warehouses and the Pet Food Institute.

Individual corporations also try to influence policy making. Over eight hundred have Washington offices, and those without an office frequently hire a law firm or lobbyist to look out for their interests.[7] In a sense, corporations have multiple representation in Washington: their own corporate representation as well as the resources of such

6. David S. Broder, "Gridlock Begins at Home," *Washington Post*, Jan. 23, 1994, C2.

7. A listing of corporate offices in Washington is found in the *National Journal*'s annual publication *The Capital Source: The Who's Who, What, Where in Washington*.

groups as the U.S. Chamber of Commerce and the trade associations to which they belong. In fact, large corporations engaged in several lines of business can belong to over twenty lobbying organizations.

Labor unions have a larger base of individual members than do business organizations. The largest and most influential union is the AFL-CIO, a confederation of such operating unions as the United Steel Workers, United Auto Workers, and United Brotherhood of Carpenters and Joiners of America. (Not all unions are affiliated with the AFL-CIO; the highly politicized National Education Association, a union of teachers, operates independently of the AFL-CIO, as do various railroad employee unions.) The AFL-CIO's political involvement extends beyond bread-and-butter union issues such as the minimum wage and occupational safety and health to include what the federation considers to be the social justice concerns of working people—civil rights, health care, and Social Security. Member unions are likely to focus their political activities on issues dear to their members. The postal workers' union, for example, is primarily concerned with wages, work rules, and retirement benefits for government workers.

As the industrial sector of the economy has declined since the 1950s so have the memberships of the longtime AFL-CIO unions representing industrial and building trades workers. In the 1950s the auto workers', steel workers', and carpenters' unions were the nation's largest. Today they have been replaced by such white-collar and service sector unions as the Teamsters and the American Federation of State, County, and Municipal Employees.

The agricultural sector, another economic interest, is organized to reflect general farm interests as well as those of specific commodity producers. The largest of the general farm interest groups is the American Farm Bureau Federation, composed of state farm bureau federations representing approximately three million farm families. AFBF tends to represent the larger, more efficient producers and to support a relatively conservative political agenda. On many issues it is opposed by the politically weaker National Farmers Organization and National Farmers Union, who represent the dwindling number of small producers. Major powers in agricultural policy making are the organizations that promote the interests of specific commodity growers and processors—for example, the National Peanut Council, Tobacco Institute, National Association of Wheat Growers, and such agri-business corporations as Ralston Purina, Cargill, and Archer-Daniels-Midland.

Finally, professional associations represent many of the individuals whose occupations demand technical training and expertise. Political

---

Partial Listing of Organizations to Which General Electric Belongs

- Peak business associations: U.S. Chamber of Commerce, National Association of Manufacturers, Business Roundtable
- Export trade associations: Council of the Americas, Business Group on the Export Administration Act, Coalition for Employment through Exports
- Nuclear power trade associations: American Nuclear Energy Council, Atomic Industrial Forum, American Nuclear Society, U.S. Committee for Energy Awareness
- Taxes and finance groups and trade associations: The Carlton Group, American Council for Capital Formation, Tax Foundation, American Financial Services Association, American Equipment Leasing Association
- Medical equipment and electronics trade associations: National Electrical Manufacturers Association, Health Industries Manufacturers Association, Electronics Industries Association, American Electronics Association
- Defense and aircraft trade associations: Aerospace Industries Association of America, American Helicopter Society, American Defense Preparedness Association, National Security Industries Association

Source: "Organizations to Which General Electric Belongs," *Washington Post*, April 13, 1985, A12. Copyright © 1985 by the *Washington Post*. Reprinted with Permission.

involvement is greatest among those professional groups heavily regulated by government or dependent on government for financing. Examples of such groups are the American Bar Association and the American Medical Association.

Nonprofit Organizations

Unlike private sector groups that advance the interests of those engaged in profit-making enterprises or have occupational prerequisites for membership, nonprofit organizations represent the interests of people not as wage earners, stockholders, or producers, but as citizens, consumers, and taxpayers, or as the elderly, disadvantaged, handicapped, and minorities.[8] Membership in these organizations is open to all regardless of professional or organizational affiliations. Many of these organizations—particularly advocates for consumers, the environment, minorities, and the poor—are commonly called **public interest groups,** although their "public interest" label has stirred the resentment of those who oppose them and have a different conception of public interest.[9]

The range of interests spanned by nonprofit groups is quite broad. Some groups voice the concerns of citizens, consumers, women, minorities, and environmentalists; others crusade for single issues such as the right to life and gun control; and still others are ideologues of the Left and Right. One of the most prominent and influential of the public interest groups is Common Cause. It has called for government reforms in such areas as campaign finance, lobbying, government ethics, congressional organization, and voter registration.[10] Public interest groups also have taken up the causes of the environment (Sierra Club and National Wildlife Federation), women's rights (National Organization for Women), civil rights (NAACP), and those unable to present their own case to the government such as children (Children's Defense Fund). The broad ideological concerns of liberals and conservatives have found outlets in the interest group system as well. For those with a liberal policy orientation, there is the Americans for Democratic Action, and for conservatives, there is the American Conservative Union.

Religious organizations have long played a prominent role in poli-

8. A typology of interest groups is provided by Jack L. Walker, "Origins and Maintenance of Interest Groups in America," *American Political Science Review* 77 (June 1983): 392–394.

9. For a comprehensive and insightful study of public interest groups, see Jeffrey M. Berry, *Lobbying for the People: The Political Behavior of Public Interest Groups* (Princeton, N.J.: Princeton University Press, 1977).

10. For a detailed analysis of Common Cause, see Andrew S. McFarland, *Common Cause: Lobbying in the Public Interest* (Chatham, N.J.: Chatham House, 1984).

tics. In earlier eras Protestant groups led the struggle for the abolition of slavery and for Prohibition. More recently church organizations were in the forefront of the civil rights and anti-Vietnam War movements. The National Council of Churches and its mainline Protestant denominations—such as the Methodists, Presbyterians, and Episcopalians—have generally adopted liberal policy positions. Opposing them have been the fundamentalist Christian groups such as the Christian Coalition led by evangelist Pat Robertson. The National Council of Churches and right-wing Christians, for example, clashed over the nomination of Judge Robert Bork, an outspoken conservative, to the Supreme Court in 1987.

The principal Catholic organizations that lobby the government are the U.S. Catholic Conference and the National Conference of Bishops. These organizations strongly oppose abortion but have taken generally more liberal stands on such issues as welfare, civil rights, regulating business, and arms control. The policy clashes among the wide array of church organizations have led one analyst of these politically active groups to note that they were speaking with "dissonant voices" and "not praying together."[11]

Government Interests

Because the federal government is a critical source of funds for state and local governments, as well as their major regulator, these governments have been no less eager than other groups to have organized representation in Washington. Thus, nearly all of the states have federal liaison offices, and many cities, counties, and state universities as well have their own Washington offices or law firms or lobbyists representing them. Major associations representing the government sector include the National Governors' Association, the National Association of Counties, and the U.S. Conference of Mayors.

Given America's prominent role in world affairs, even foreign governments have joined the fray of interest group politics in an effort to influence U.S. public policy. Some of this activity is carried out by foreign ambassadors and their staffs, but, increasingly, high-priced Washington lobbyists and law firms are acting on behalf of their foreign government clients. This is a highly controversial practice, however, because critics claim that these representatives of foreign interests are using their skills for purposes that may run counter to the interests of the United States.[12] Not all interest group activity in behalf of foreign

11. Kirk Victor, "Not Praying Together," *National Journal*, October 10, 1987, 2546.

12. See Kirk Victor, "Risky Representation," *National Journal*, December 12, 1987, 3132–3137.

countries is initiated by their governments or hired agents in Washington. Some nations have home-grown support organizations. For example, Israel has benefited from having an aggressive, politically savvy, and well-financed organization of Americans, the American Israel Public Affairs Committee, devoted to protecting its interests.

*Diversity, Conflicts,
and Alliances among Groups*

The sweeping range of interests making up the interest group system is suggested by the preceding categories of groups. What is less apparent from such descriptions is the lack of unity among groups that on the surface seem to represent similar interests. It is, for example, frequently impossible to cite a business position on a particular issue because within the organizations representing business interests great diversity exists, possibly leading to intergroup conflicts. In one such instance, by calling for a major overhaul of the tax code, the 1986 tax reform act caused a sharp split among business interests. With major corporations and business organizations found on both sides of the issue, depending on how the new tax code would affect their operations, business was unable to present a united front and maximize its influence in shaping the legislation. Fearful of being hit with higher taxes, Chase Manhattan, Ford, Exxon, AT&T, DuPont, Inland Steel, and various trade associations worked to defeat the bill. Squared off on the other side was another constellation of business interests that would see its taxes reduced under the proposed law. Included in this group were the U.S. Chamber of Commerce and corporate giants General Mills, IBM, Philip Morris, Levi Strauss, and Pepsico.[13]

The environmental movement also has had difficulty maintaining a united front (Table 8.1). In 1993 environmentalists were divided over whether the North American Free Trade Agreement (NAFTA) would weaken environmental and health standards in the United States. Supporting NAFTA were the big Washington- and New York-based groups, which have shown a willingness to compromise to increase their influence at the highest levels in Washington. By contrast, such grass-roots groups as Greenpeace and the Sierra Club, which are generally disdainful of tactics that involve compromise, fought vigorously against congressional approval of the agreement.[14]

Organized medicine does not speak with one voice as well. The

13. Jeffrey H. Birnbaum, "Business's Schisms over Tax Overhaul Reflects the Divide-and-Conquer Strategy of Proponents," *Wall Street Journal,* Dec. 5, 1985, 64.

14. Keith Schneider, "Environmentalists Fight Each Other over Trade Accord," *New York Times,* Sept. 10, 1993, A1, A10, National edition.

American Medical Association (AMA), with its 292,000 physician members, has seen its influence undermined by rivalries among medical specialists. Thus, in 1993 when President Clinton proposed a major restructuring of health care in the United States, he sought to take advantage of these schisms by following a strategy of divide and conquer among physicians who might have been expected to oppose the plan's provisions designed to bring down health care costs. The president's plan carefully promoted certain types of doctors at the expense of others by seeking to chop specialists' fees while giving primary care physicians and internists raises—or at least promising that their incomes would not fall. As a result, the AMA, dominated by medical specialists, objected to the plan, whereas the American College of Physicians, representing internists, backed it. Splits also developed within the health insurance industry. The Health Insurance Association of America (HIAA), representing small and medium-sized insurance companies, feared that the president's plan would force its member firms to withdraw from the health insurance business. HIAA, therefore, attacked the president's plan in a series of television advertisements. Because the Clinton plan enabled the "big five" insurance companies such as Aetna and Prudential to continue in the health insurance business, these large firms distanced themselves from HIAA by forming the Alliance for Managed Competition, which embraced health care reform without endorsing all the elements of the Clinton plan.[15]

The level of intergroup conflict depends on the policy issue at stake. For example, the role of government in agriculture tends to create a high level of conflict among the major farm interest groups as the American Farm Bureau Federation tries to limit government involvement in the agriculture sector and the National Farmers Union promotes government regulation and assistance. Energy and health care issues, however, are somewhat less likely to generate conflicts among business groups operating in these fields. As for labor unions, they tend to stick together and generally develop supportive relationships.[16]

In their efforts to influence government policy, groups frequently form alliances and work cooperatively on selected issues. One of the oldest and most prominent alliances is the Leadership Conference on Civil Rights, composed of approximately 150 African American, labor, religious, Hispanic, Asian American, women's, and senior citizens'

Table 8.1 Divided They Stand: Unity Problems within the Environmental Community on the North American Free Trade Agreement (NAFTA)

For NAFTA

National Wildlife Federation
Conservation International
Natural Resources Defense Council
World Wildlife Federation
National Audubon Society
Environmental Defense Fund

Against NAFTA

Public Citizen
Sierra Club
Friends of the Earth
Greenpeace
Earth Island Institute
Public Interest Research Group
Rainforest Action Network
American Society for the Prevention of Cruelty to Animals
American Humane Society

Source: *New York Times*, Sept. 16, 1993, A10, National edition. Copyright © 1993 by the New York Times Company. Reprinted by permission.

---

15. Jeffrey H. Birnbaum, "Clinton Health Package Has a Little Something for Just Enough Factions to Splinter the Opposition," *Wall Street Journal*, Sept. 23, 1993, A20; and Julie Kosterlitz, "Itching for a Fight?" *National Journal*, January 15, 1994, 106–110.

16. Robert H. Salisbury et al., "Who Works with Whom? Interest Group Alliances and Opposition," *American Political Science Review* 81 (December 1987): 1217–1234.

organizations. Since its founding in 1950, this group has been at the forefront of issues involving minorities, women, the handicapped, and the poor. Other coalitions are more short-lived and dissolve when the issue of immediate concern is resolved. For example, the American Energy Alliance formed to combat President Clinton's energy tax did not become a permanent organization.

Why Interest Groups Organize

Interest groups form around people's shared attitudes and interests. One compelling basis for organization is a common economic interest such as those shared by farmers, teachers, manufacturers, doctors, factory workers, and realtors. Other bases for organizing include a common ethnic heritage, race, religion, recreational interest, ideology, or concern about a specific issue such as gun control, environmental protection, abortion, hunger, or civil rights. People frequently resort to creating a formal organization and trying to influence the government when they find their positions threatened or their goals unfulfilled. Thus, farmers organized in the face of agricultural depressions; workers formed unions to achieve decent wages and working conditions; businesses organized in the earliest days of the Republic to gain the protection of tariffs; and veterans formed such groups as the Society of Cincinnati, Grand Army of the Republic, American Legion, and Vietnam Veterans of America to secure government benefits to compensate for the hardships caused by serving the nation in time of war. Even independent-minded college students have periodically organized to oppose hikes in tuition.

America's society, culture, Constitution, and party system have all created a favorable climate for the proliferation of interest groups.[17] Groups develop when there are substantial differences and disagreements among a society's citizens, and since this nation's birth these conditions have abounded. In the post-Revolution period, for example, conflicts arose between debtor and creditor classes and between commercial interests in the North and agrarian interests in the South. As the nation expanded from ocean to ocean, sources of division and conflict were introduced when immigrants from diverse racial, ethnic, and religious backgrounds had to be accommodated, an industrialized economy became the rule, and massive metropolitan areas began to dot the landscape.

17. Allan J. Cigler and Burdett A. Loomis, *Interest Group Politics,* 2d ed. (Washington, D.C.: CQ Press, 1986), 5–6.

By providing a way for people to advance their own interests or the causes in which they believe, interest groups help Americans to satisfy their need for personal achievement and the value they attach to individualism. Likewise, by guaranteeing freedom of speech, association, and the right to petition the government for redress of grievances, the U.S. Constitution has made its contribution to a favorable environment for interest group formation. The structure of the governmental system has encouraged group proliferation as well. Confronted with a highly decentralized government produced by the principles of separation of powers and federalism, groups must be capable of influencing the three branches of the federal government as well as state and local governments.[18] And the large number of points—especially local ones—at which citizens can influence public policy probably contributes to Americans' sense of political effectiveness and proclivity to join groups.[19]

The decentralized and undisciplined nature of the American political party system also has proven a favorable setting for interest group activity. The inability of the parties to control their own elected officials has created a power vacuum in the decision-making process that has been readily filled by interest groups.

Effects of Societal Complexity and Disturbances

David Truman has concluded that interest groups develop and proliferate naturally as society becomes more diverse and economic specialization emerges.[20] Farm organizations, for example, developed only after the Civil War when agriculture became commercialized and farmers began increasingly to specialize in growing particular commodities.[21] The interests of the various commodity producers then began to vary as well—among wheat, cotton, beef, corn, hog, sugar, and tobacco producers.

It also has been suggested that interest groups develop when disturbances threaten certain interests or provide them with opportunities to improve their positions. The American Agriculture Movement, for example, whose tractorcades of angry farmers tied up traffic in downtown Washington, D.C., in 1979, was the response of small farmers to

18. See Truman, *Governmental Process,* 519.

19. See Gabriel Almond and Sidney Verba, *The Civic Culture* (Boston: Little, Brown, 1976), chaps. 8 and 10.

20. Truman, *Governmental Process,* chap. 3.

21. Robert H. Salisbury, "An Exchange Theory of Interest Groups," *Midwest Journal of Political Science* 13 (February 1969): 3–4.

Falling prices for farm commodities pro-voked angry farmers to form the American Agriculture Movement. In 1979, its mem-bers drove their tractors to Washington—and tied up traffic—to draw lawmakers' attention to their plight.

low farm prices in the 1970s. The National Association of Manufactur-ers was formed to take advantage of opportunities for developing for-eign trade, but it grew and prospered by responding to the emergence of organized labor as a political force. The interest group system is thus believed to go through waves of group mobilization and countermobi-lization.[22]

Personal Motivations

While there are many examples of groups forming because of indi-viduals' shared and specialized interests, there also are examples of groups not forming even though circumstances would seem to require it. The poor, for example, are not organized into interest groups even though they share a common plight. Nor have racial and gender dis-crimination led most African Americans and women to join interest groups. Political scientists have begun to believe, therefore, that any explanations of group development require attention to personal moti-vations.

According to economist Mancur Olson, the free-rider problem is a major barrier to people joining groups that serve their interests.[23] Olson has contended that rational people—the free riders—recognize that the "collective" benefits (safer cars, cleaner air, improved Social Security benefits, and such) of an interest group's activities are avail-able to group members and nonmembers alike. Nonmembers, then, can receive the benefits of a group's activities without paying the costs

22. Truman, *Governmental Process*, chap. 3.

23. Mancur Olson, *The Logic of Collective Action* (Cambridge, Mass.: Harvard University Press, 1965).

(dues, time, effort) of formal group membership. Thus, the efforts of the American Lung Association to pass tougher clean air legislation in 1990 made the benefits of cleaner air available to all Americans even though most did nothing to assist the association.

To overcome the free-rider problem, many groups provide their members with "selective" benefits—benefits available only to group members. For example, the American Association of Retired Persons (AARP), the country's largest interest group in terms of membership, provides members with such selective benefits as low-cost prescription drugs, discount travel fares, health insurance, and its slick monthly magazine, *Modern Maturity.*

Three incentives or motivations are usually behind an individual's decision to actually join a group: material, solidary, and expressive.[24] Material incentives are tangible rewards that have economic value. Thus, an important basis for joining a union, business group, professional association, or farm organization is the promise of economic benefits—better prices for corn, higher wages, larger corporate profits, and such—that will flow from the group's activities.

Not everyone joins a group to gain material rewards; there also are solidary incentives—the rewards of companionship, fraternity, status, and pleasure that come from associating with people with whom one shares a common bond. One of the benefits of the American Legion, for example, is the fellowship derived from sharing common wartime and other military experiences. Nationality, racial, and religious organizations all provide their members with solidary benefits.

Expressive (also known as purposive) incentives also induce people to join groups. These incentives are the intangible rewards that come from working for a cause that is thought to be right and just, even though no personal gain is to be had from it. Members of environmental groups, such as the Wilderness Society or Sierra Club, gain these benefits from their organizations, as do members of the League of Women Voters, Planned Parenthood, and Common Cause. Such ideological groups as the liberal People for the American Way or the Right-leaning Young Americans for Freedom also have memberships based on expressive incentives.

Material, solidary, and expressive incentives should not be viewed as mutually exclusive; membership in a group may indeed produce all three types of benefits. For example, members of the American Legion

24. See Peter Clark and James Q. Wilson, "Incentive Systems: A Theory of Organizations," *Administrative Science Quarterly* 6 (September 1961): 126–166; and James Q. Wilson, *Political Organizations* (New York: Basic Books, 1973).

Founder and president Marian Wright Edelman of the Children's Defense Fund, an advocacy group for poor and minority youth, at a Capitol Hill rally for child care legislation.

may enjoy the comradeship of fellow veterans, gain the legion's assistance in securing benefits from the Department of Veterans Affairs, and derive satisfaction from belonging to an organization that lobbies for a strong national defense.

Organizational Entrepreneurs

Examples abound of leaders who felt strongly about issues or a cause and were willing to risk investing their time and personal resources in the formation of an interest group.[25] The nation's leading advocacy group for poor and minority children, the Children's Defense Fund, was founded because of the determined efforts of Marian Wright Edelman and now operates with an annual budget of over $12 million. Its chairs have included First Lady Hillary Rodham Clinton and Health and Human Services Secretary Donna Shalala. Similarly, Common Cause owes its existence to the vision and determination of its founder, former secretary of health, education, and welfare John Gardner. Ralph Nader, the consumer advocate who heads a number of consumer, health, and environmental organizations, is a particularly striking case of individual commitment and organizational entrepreneurship. With the over $300,000 he received from General Motors in settlement of his infringement-of-privacy charge against the company for hiring private detectives to dig up information about him, Nader was able to form a series of consumer rights organizations that gave impetus to the consumer movement in the 1970s.

Entrepreneurs like Nader and Gardner have been aided in their organizational efforts by advances in communications technology such as computerized direct-mail solicitation. Using such technology, group leaders can reach large target audiences with appeals designed to enlist members and financial contributions.

Sponsors

The National Council on Aging, a group founded to champion the expansion of senior citizens centers across the country, relied in its early years primarily on Ford and other private foundation grants for funding. And the militant National Welfare Rights Organization, which flourished briefly in the 1970s, received large contributions from Singer and Sears Roebuck heirs. Organization and maintenance of an interest group often require a patron or sponsors who will provide financial backing. An early 1980s survey by Jack Walker revealed that 34 percent of occupational groups and 89 percent of citizens' groups used

25. See Salisbury, "An Exchange Theory of Interest Groups."

financial aid from outside sources to start their operations.[26] Indeed, some organizations unable to overcome the free-rider problem have had to rely on sponsors—individuals, foundations, government in the form of grants, and other interest groups—rather than a membership to sustain them. It is estimated that sponsors and patrons provide public interest groups with over 40 percent of their annual income. Some groups have no members at all and are staff operations working out of a Washington headquarters.[27]

The government itself can be an important force in the creation of interest groups. Early in this century the federal and state governments promoted the development of the American Farm Bureau Federation and provided encouragement and financial support for local Farm Bureau organizations so that they could help county extension agents in their work with farm families. Interest groups also form when major new legislation creates a clientele for government services. For example, more than half of the groups representing the elderly were formed after 1965, the year in which Medicare and the Older Americans Act were passed by Congress. Similarly, the numbers of education, transportation, environmental, and women's[28] groups have ballooned as a result of government action or support. In providing this assistance to groups, the federal government is seeking their help in publicizing and supporting its programs.[29] Thus, interest groups may be the offshoots as well as the roots of public policy.

Determinants of Group Influence

Interest groups can affect government policy by providing public officials with what they need to keep their jobs: public support, election campaign assistance, and information. With their abilities to mobilize people, groups can help to supply (or withhold) the votes a legislator needs to gain and stay in office. Groups also can help to fill campaign coffers, as well as to gather the reliable facts that public officials need to make informed decisions. Although interest groups are not decision makers' only sources of information, members of Congress, for example, are reluctant to act without at least having the

26. Walker, "Origins and Maintenance of Interest Groups," 397.

27. See Jack L. Walker, *Mobilizing Political Interests in America* (Ann Arbor: University of Michigan Press, 1992); and Berry, *Lobbying for the People*, 28.

28. For information on how government resources were used to help build the women's movement, see Georgia Duerst-Lahti, "The Government's Role in Building the Women's Movement," *Political Science Quarterly* 104 (Summer 1989): 249–268.

29. Walker, "Origins and Maintenance of Interest Groups," 401–403.

perspectives of the groups affected on an issue. Thus when considering changes in banking regulatory statutes during the 1980s, Congress eagerly sought the views of various segments of the banking industry. And during the periodic debates on renewing the Clean Air Act, Congress has consistently solicited information from the auto industry about its ability to manufacture cars at a reasonable price that meet the government-mandated standards for auto exhaust emissions.

But interest groups are not equal in their abilities to influence government policy. While it is exceedingly difficult to measure group influence, it is possible to identify the factors that affect the potential power of a group. These factors include group characteristics such as membership and financial resources, the various effects of how the government itself is organized, and the structure of the conflict in a particular controversy.

Membership

The advantages of being a huge organization—such as the American Association of Retired Persons (thirty-four million elderly members; its Washington headquarters even has its own ZIP Code), the National Education Association (two million teachers), or the National Rifle Association (three million gun owners)—are likewise huge. Representatives and senators are unlikely to ignore the views of a group that has millions of informed, interested members back in their home districts or states. Moreover, a large dues-paying membership can provide the financial resources often required to sway government policy making.

But a large membership has a disadvantage as well: internal unity problems. A group whose members are split on an issue is not apt to be an effective force. A good example of such unity problems is the American Bankers Association (ABA). Disagreements between the big banks, which pay most of ABA's expenses, and the small, independent banks, which provide the ABA with grass-roots influence, have substantially weakened the group's clout. Presenting a unified front on issues has been an acute problem as well for the giant U.S. Chamber of Commerce. As one business lobbyist noted, "With its breadth of members, the Chamber has trouble finding consensus on anything except labor-management issues."[30]

When the members of an organization are deeply committed to that organization and its objectives, its capacity to exert influence is enhanced. As members of Congress know, people who feel strongly about an issue are likely to cast their votes and mobilize other voters based on the way their representatives and senators dealt with that issue. Not sur-

30. Burt Solomon, "Measuring Clout," *National Journal*, July 4, 1987, 1711.

prisingly, then, legislators frequently try to avoid antagonizing such fervent groups. This helps to explain how a group like the National Rifle Association, which is fiercely opposed to gun control, has managed to block gun-control legislation even though polls show that a majority of the public favors restricting handguns. A similar forcefulness of commitment has made the Independent Insurance Agents of America an effective force. Individual agents have shown a willingness to travel to Washington and aggressively lobby representatives and senators. In a colorful and disapproving description of the group in action, the leader of a rival organization recounted how these agents "regularly swarm Capitol Hill. They can almost be like rabid dogs."[31]

When a group's membership tends to be concentrated in particular districts or states (for example, the concentrations of dairy farmers in Wisconsin, Minnesota, Vermont, and upstate New York), the members of Congress representing those constituencies are usually particularly sensitive to these groups' interests. A membership dispersed across many states and congressional districts can be advantageous as well. When a group's membership blankets virtually every state and district in the nation and is, moreover, politically assertive, representatives and senators sit up and listen. Such groups include the National Education Association (NEA), the National Rifle Association, and the National Association of Realtors.

The prestige and status of a group's members also affect its ability to influence government policy makers. Groups whose members belong to prestigious professions or have achieved status in their chosen professions normally gain access to decision makers—that is, a hearing for their point of view in a nonhostile environment—with relative ease. Physicians, attorneys, and bankers, for example, can expect at least an opportunity to state their positions before government officials. But for such groups as students or migrant workers access may be more difficult.

Financial and Leadership Resources

The tools of governmental influence—experienced lobbyists, up-to-date communications equipment, a research staff—do not come free.[32] They cost money, giving those groups with substantial financial resources a hefty advantage over poorer groups. Such groups as the U.S.

31. Ibid., 1707.

32. The sources of group funds and the differences among groups in their funding sources are described in Mark A. Peterson and Jack L. Walker, "Interest Group Responses to a Partisan Change," in Cigler and Loomis, *Interest Group Politics*, 162–182.

In addition to the traditional economic interest groups, Washington now has a wide array of "public interest" groups. One of the most resourceful organizers and skillful practitioners of advocacy group politics is Ralph Nader (left), shown joining forces with the leader of Citizens for Congressional Reform in an effort to publicize and kill a congressional pay raise bill.

Chamber of Commerce, AFL-CIO, Teamsters, and NEA are financially very well off and even have their own office buildings near either the Capitol or White House. Groups with adequate funding can hire the most skilled, best-connected Washington operatives, conduct sophisticated research, undertake public relations and media campaigns, contribute financially to campaigns, and stir up blizzards of mail from constituents, all to fall on the desks of government decision makers.

Although it is always better to have plenty of financial resources than be without them, lack of money is not necessarily a fatal liability for interest groups. Skill in generating publicity, a dedicated staff, effective research, and a strong commitment, for example, have made Ralph Nader's organizations highly effective in spite of their only modest revenues. Even poorly financed, low-status groups, if clever enough, can grab the public's attention for a cause. The late Mitch Snyder, an advocate for the homeless, used demonstrations—including encampments in Lafayette Park across from the White House—to dramatize the plight of people living on the streets and thereby succeeded in attracting the attention of Congress.

Indeed, no small part of some groups' clout has been attributed to shrewd leadership. Jack Valenti, head of the Washington outpost of the Motion Picture Association of America (MPAA) for over twenty-five years, uses his organization's best asset—Hollywood glamour—to influence members of Congress: "He arranges Hollywood fund-raisers, lends celebrities to Members' campaigns and invites Members and spouses to the MPAA's plush little theater in Washington to watch films before they are released."[33]

In addition to using a group's resources skillfully to influence the

33. Solomon, "Measuring Clout," 1708.

powers that be, a group leader must be able to maintain the organization—gain and hold members, raise money, and fire up member commitment to the group's goals. Group leaders spend a great deal of their time, therefore, just trying to keep the group afloat and avoiding internal rifts.

*Organization of
the Government Itself*

Governmental structures, procedures, and rules are not neutral in their impacts on interest groups. Some groups benefit and others suffer from the way in which the government is structured and decisions are made.[34] The lengthy, complicated process involved in getting a bill approved by the Congress, with its many opportunities for delay and obstruction, works to the defensive advantage of groups opposed to policy changes. The congressional committee system also has its advantages for selected interests. The House and Senate agriculture committees, for example, tend to be composed of members from commodity-producing regions. They are therefore more responsive to producer interests than to the more general consumer interests.

The constitutional mandate that each state shall have two senators has important consequences for interest group access. Agricultural and mining interests, which are concentrated in the sparsely populated Plains and Rocky Mountain states, derive an advantage from having the same number of senators responsive to their concerns as the more thickly populated states like California. Federalism also has implications for group access. Groups with minimal influence at the federal level may find state governments more responsive. For example, with Republicans controlling the White House and the Senate for six of the eight years of the Reagan administration, organized labor had few policy victories at the national level in the 1980s. But with the Democrats in control of most governorships and state legislatures, it had notable successes at the state level when it came to, for example, raising the state minimum wage.

It is because changes in governmental rules and procedures could help some interests and damage some others that the battles over rules changes are often so pitched. Maritime interests, for example, waged a fierce battle in the 1970s to prevent a House reform committee from abolishing the Merchant Marine and Fisheries Committee, the membership of which was drawn from coastal constituencies and was supportive of the maritime industry.

34. For a classic statement of the impact of governmental structure on group access, see Truman, *Governmental Process*, 322–332.

The Structure of the Conflict

Interest group influence is also affected by the structure of the conflict in a particular controversy. Groups gain leverage when they are supported by congressional party leaders whom rank-and-file members of Congress do not wish to alienate or antagonize. But the effectiveness of organized pressure on members of Congress is apt to be severely limited if it is confronted by opposing pressure, especially pressure that is highly visible and involves a sizable number of attentive constituents. Enactment of clean air legislation, for example, has proven so tortuous and racked with delay because environmental and health interests have had to confront the auto industry, its unions, and midwestern public utilities, each of which has been capable of mobilizing members' constituents.[35] Related to this, interest groups are likely to have greater influence on narrow amendments to bills than on an entire piece of legislation. Specific and technical amendments do not normally attract broad opposition because their impact is generally narrower than that of an entire bill, and on discrete amendments members of Congress are more likely to be dependent on the information provided by an interest group.

The Tactics of Influence

Interest groups have at their disposal an arsenal of tactics and techniques for use in pressuring representatives, senators, bureaucrats, and presidents. The technique or combination of methods selected depends largely on the nature of the group, its resources, which branch or level of government is making the decision, and whether the group is seeking to initiate a policy change or defend an existing policy.

Lobbying

A *lobbyist* acts as an agent of an interest to influence legislative or administrative government decisions. The term goes back to the early 1800s when favor-seekers jammed the lobbies, cloakrooms, and hallways of legislatures. Initially, these hallway denizens were called "lobby agents," a designation that was shortened to lobbyists in the 1830s. Although the term lobbying was not yet in vogue when the Constitution was written, the right to lobby was made explicit by its First Amendment, which provides that "Congress shall make no law . . .

35. On the importance of the structure of the conflict, see John T. Tierney, "Organized Interests and the Nation's Capital," in *The Politics of Interests: Interest Groups Transformed*, ed. Mark P. Petracca (Boulder, Colo.: Westview Press, 1992), 216–218. The battles over clean air legislation are told in a concise and dramatic manner by Richard E. Cohen, *Washington at Work: Back Rooms and Clean Air* (New York: Macmillan, 1992).

Superlobbyist Thomas Hale Boggs, Jr.

Among Washington's over 14,500 hired hands in the lobbying trade, there is an elite corps of superlobbyists. They include Charles Walker, a former deputy secretary of the Treasury; Bill Timmons, White House director of congressional relations under Richard Nixon; Stuart Eizenstadt, policy adviser to President Jimmy Carter; Frank Mankiewicz, former aide to Robert Kennedy and George McGovern; and Anne Wexler and Nancy Reynolds, a bipartisan team that served as aides to Carter and Reagan. Among these superlobbyists, Thomas Hale Boggs, Jr., rates as one of the city's most influential, skilled, and financially successful (with an annual income of over $1 million).

Tommy Boggs was born into a political family—he was the son of the late House majority leader Hale Boggs (D-La.) and former representative Lindy Boggs (D-La.). He is also the brother of National Public Radio and ABC News reporter Cokie Roberts. His legal skills, political savvy, understanding of Capitol Hill, and ability to raise campaign funds (Boggs and his wife contributed $45,000 of their own money to federal candidates and political committees in 1991–1992) for the people he seeks to influence are legendary. One

colleague commented that "he has the best understanding of the Hill and how it works of anyone I have ever seen—and that includes a great many of the Members themselves."

Boggs heads Patton, Boggs, and Blow, a 180-member law and lobbying firm that in 1991 had a gross income of $49.5 million. Its client list includes big trade associations—American Association of Newspaper Publishers, Association of Trial Lawyers, National Cable Television Association, National Association of Retail Druggists, National Machine Tool Builders Association, National Soft Drink Association, and National Association of Life Underwriters; major American companies—Northwestern Mutual Life Insurance Com-

pany, New York Life Insurance Company, and Nutri/Systems Inc.; U.S. subsidiaries of big Japanese companies—Nakajima USA, Nakamichi USA, and NEC Electronics; and foreign governments.

Clients pay Boggs for his brains, experience, and knowledge of the policy process. Among his successes in the lobbying arena, he helped to engineer passage of the Chrysler bailout bill that established guaranteed government loans for the company and saved it from bankruptcy; assisted the newspaper publishers in fighting off the regional telephone companies ("baby Bells") in a high-stakes battle over the electronic information business; and worked with the Association of Trial Lawyers to defeat a bill that would have established federal product liability standards.

Patton, Boggs, and Blow has prospered under Republican and Democratic administrations alike and is well positioned to maintain its standing under the Clinton administration because of its excellent connections to Democratic leaders. A former partner in the Boggs firm, Ronald Brown, was appointed Clinton's secretary of commerce.

Source: W. John Moore, "The Gravy Train," *National Journal*, October 10, 1992, 2294–2298.

Lobbying by representatives of special interest groups is not a new phenomenon. This reproduction from Harpers Weekly *portrays lobbyists outside the House of Representatives seeking to influence House action on the Civil Rights Act of 1866.*

abridging . . . the right of the people . . . to petition the Government for a redress of grievances."

About three-quarters of the over 14,500 lobbyists in Washington work as officers and other employees of interest groups. The rest are attorneys or consultants, who represent clients and in return receive a fee or retainer. But lobbyists, who need support to do their jobs, constitute only a small fraction of the interest group work force in Washington. It has been estimated that eighty thousand people work in Washington for associations seeking to influence government policy.[36]

Lobbying Congress. In *direct lobbying* interest group representatives meet personally with government officials to inform them about and persuade them to accept their groups' positions. This method of exerting influence is most readily available to groups that have sufficient status and political standing to gain access to policy makers, as well as the financial resources to hire skilled Washington insiders who understand the inner workings of Congress and the executive branch.

Members of Congress are usually willing to meet with lobbyists because the interest groups they represent often have the expertise and specialized knowledge members need to make informed decisions on legislative issues. This information is presented formally at congressional committee hearings or informally (and usually more effectively) in private meetings with legislators and their staffs. Normally missing from lobbyist-legislator meetings are such threats as "If you don't support us on this bill, we'll see that you're defeated in the next election!" To the contrary, lobbyists try to maintain good relations even when members of Congress oppose them on a key issue. Interest group representatives understand that politics is an ongoing process; the member whose support they cannot win today may be supportive tomorrow on a different issue.[37]

It is just because most interest groups are interested in influencing representatives and senators on a range of issues over an extended period of time that lobbyists guard their reputations as providers of reliable, specialized information. It may be possible to peddle misleading information while seeking to influence a congressional decision and even have some impact, but such a technique is not a passport to long-

36. Mark P. Petracca, "The Rediscovery of Interest Group Politics," in Petracca, *Politics of Interests,* 14.

37. For an informed consideration of how the ongoing nature of the political process in Congress affects interest group politics, see Raymond A. Bauer, Ithiel de Sola Pool, and Lewis A. Dexter, *American Business and Public Policy* (New York: Atherton, 1963), part V.

term influence in Washington. Career politicians have long memories when it comes to those who caused them political embarrassment.

In seeking to influence congressional decision making, interest groups follow a strategy of lobbying both their legislative allies and those predisposed to vote against them. Friendly legislators are lobbied to counter the efforts of opposing groups, while likely congressional opponents are provided with information that it is hoped will cause them to have a change of heart.[38] Often the relationship between lobbyist and legislator is that of allies working cooperatively to achieve a legislative objective important to both. Interest groups can help draft bills and amendments and line up support and provide strategic advice as well. Members, in turn, often have indispensable insider information on the political situation within Congress. Representatives and senators may even lobby interest groups to take up an issue, a situation described by a Democratic House member:

> I find myself arguing with an interest group . . . to get them turned on to go to work on some other members. I had a couple of people in my office this afternoon. They're involved in something that's key in my committee, and they were of the opinion that a couple of Democratic colleagues on that committee were with them on this issue. I knew the guys had taken a walk [not voted] on a key vote, and we lost by two votes. . . . I told them that and laid out for them the record of what had happened and urged them to go focus on what I thought ought to be an appropriate target. You do get into that occasionally . . . so they'll go to work where they're going to be effective. They can be an ally.[39]

When a major issue is at stake, legislators can exert heavy reverse lobbying pressure on their interest group allies. For example, during hearings in 1994 before a House committee, the U.S. Chamber of Commerce, in response to an intense lobbying campaign by House Republicans, reversed its earlier position on a key provision in President Clinton's health care proposal.[40]

Because elected officials ignore the sentiments of the voters at their own peril, an effective technique called *grass-roots lobbying*—mobilizing constituents to contact their representative and senators—is often used in conjunction with direct in-person lobbying. With its strategy

38. David Austin-Smith and John R. Wright, "Counteractive Lobbying," *American Journal of Political Science* 38 (February 1994): 25–44.

39. John F. Bibby, ed., *Congress Off the Record: The Candid Analyses of Seven Members* (Washington, D.C.: American Enterprise Institute, 1983), 35.

40. Spencer Rich and Ann Devroy, "Chamber of Commerce Opposes Clinton Health Plan," *Washington Post*, Feb. 4, 1994, A12.

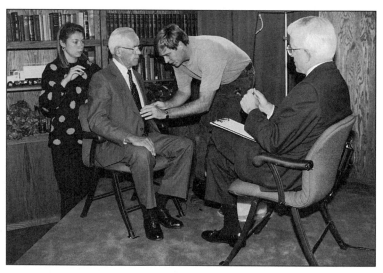

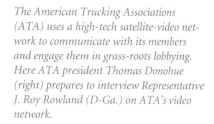

The American Trucking Associations (ATA) uses a high-tech satellite-video network to communicate with its members and engage them in grass-roots lobbying. Here ATA president Thomas Donohue (right) prepares to interview Representative J. Roy Rowland (D-Ga.) on ATA's video network.

of calling on constituents to bury their legislators under an avalanche of mail, telegrams, faxes, and phone calls, grass-roots lobbying is not a new technique, but it has become feasible for more groups (as well as more efficient and economical) with the development of advanced computer and communications technologies. In legislative warfare the mobilization of grass-roots outrage has become a rather commonplace weapon in which some Washington political operatives now specialize. Detractors, however, describe the tactic as one of creating "non-spontaneous outrage" or engaging in "astroturf lobbying."[41] When an interest group sends out a "legislative alert" to its members across the country advising them of a crucial vote in Congress and asking them to contact their representative or senators immediately, the result can be a flood of communications to Capitol Hill. But not all groups can use grass-roots lobbying; it requires a sizable membership concerned enough about an issue to contact their representatives, as well as the funds to finance a mass mailing to the membership.

Members of the House have even attested to the effectiveness of constituency pressures mobilized by interest groups:

[The] most effective lobbyists are the ones back home. I think hospital cost containment got beat not by anybody here in Washington lobbying heavily. It got beat by people who were on boards of directors of various community hospitals back home who personally wrote you a letter or called you on the phone or stopped by to see you.

41. Robin Toner, "Gold Rush Fever Grips Capital as Health Care Struggle Begins," *New York Times,* March 13, 1994, 10, National edition.

The Chrysler bailout bill [was] . . . a classic piece of work in terms of mobilizing local support. . . . I just got hammered on that one. . . . When a Chrysler dealer walks in from your home town area and says, "If I go down, it involves this number of mechanics, this number of local people, and these jobs"—that has a real impact. . . . That's a radically different quality of information [than that] from a $300,000-a-year lawyer sitting in your office.[42]

Members of Congress, of course, cannot help but recognize mail inspired by an interest group, but their responses are not always the ones a grass-roots campaign is looking for. This does not mean, however, that grass-roots lobbying has no impact. It tells legislators that an interest group feels strongly enough about an issue to mount a major constituent contact operation. They should, therefore, give that issue their thoughtful consideration so that they can account to their constituents for their final decision. Grass-roots lobbying does not necessarily tell members of Congress what to do, but it does tell them they will have to take some action on the issue. As a Senate aide noted, "If senators think that AARP [American Association of Retired Persons] is going to send a letter on an issue to everybody in their state 65 years and older, they sit up and take notice."[43]

Lobbying the Executive. Most discussions of lobbying emphasize interest group efforts to influence Congress. Indeed, efforts to lobby the legislative branch are highly visible. A tourist visiting Capitol Hill might spot lobbyists testifying before congressional committees, patrolling the hallways outside the House chamber, or cornering a senator for an informal talk outside a committee room. The visibility of congressional lobbying, however, should not obscure the fact that the executive branch (indeed, any place in government where policy decisions are made) also is a target for lobbyists—executive branch operations may be less visible, but they are not less important.

Even the White House is not out of reach of the long arms of interest groups. Many groups, particularly those that supported the president in the last election, seek to influence appointments to executive posts as well as policy decisions through their contacts with key White House staffers. Because interest groups are such important players in Washington politics, specific White House personnel maintain contact with interest group leaders and keep the president and senior presidential aides advised of their concerns and activities. Like members of

42. Bibby, *Congress Off the Record,* 34.
43. Quoted by Michael Weisskopf, "Shaking the Telephone Tree at the Grass Roots," *Washington Post,* June 6, 1992, A9.

Congress, the White House also tries to mobilize interest groups to support its policies. For example, in early 1994 President Clinton, First Lady Hillary Rodham Clinton, and senior White House officials put a full court press on corporate chief executives in an unsuccessful effort to win the Business Roundtable's support for the administration's health care proposal. Twenty Roundtable CEOs were lobbied personally by the president and first lady at the White House, and another group met with Clinton's top aides.[44] During the Ford administration the interest group contact function was formally recognized through creation of the Office of Public Liaison within the White House.[45]

The "Revolving Door." One means of gaining access to Washington policy makers is to hire as lobbyists former officers of the executive and legislative branches who have insider knowledge of how a congressional committee, department, or agency operates, as well as personal ties with its personnel. Washington has scores of ex-lawmakers who now lobby their former colleagues. Similarly, former executive branch officials often find highly lucrative employment as lobbyists after leaving government service. Defense contractors, for example, commonly hire as their Washington operatives former officials of the Department of Defense, and industries regulated by the Federal Trade Commission, Securities and Exchange Commission, and Federal Communications Commission frequently hire former agency staff personnel. (Critics refer to this practice of trading on insider knowledge and personal contacts as *influence peddling.*)

One of the most prominent examples of cashing in on one's ties to high-ranking government offices was Michael Deaver, President Reagan's deputy chief of staff during his first term. Until questions about the propriety of Deaver exploiting his access to the White House created a storm of adverse publicity and he was charged with perjuring himself before a congressional committee, Deaver's lobbying firm had picked up six-figure retainers from such major clients as CBS, TWA, and the governments of Singapore and Canada.

Although it is impossible to assess with any accuracy the impact of lobbying by ex-government officials, both the Congress and executive

44. Dana Priest and Ann Devroy, "Business Group Splits with Clinton," *Washington Post,* Feb. 3, 1994, A1, A13.

45. For an account of White House-interest group relations, see Mark A. Peterson, "The Presidency and Organized Interests: White House Patterns of Interest Group Liaison," *American Political Science Review* 86 (September 1992): 612–624; and Joseph A. Pika, "Opening Doors for Kindred Souls: The White House Office of Public Liaison," in *Interest Group Politics,* ed. Allan J. Cigler and Burdett A. Loomis, 3d ed. (Washington, D.C.: CQ Press, 1991), chap. 13.

branch have moved, in response to demands for ethics reform, to impose restrictions on the "revolving door" from government to business. In 1989 Congress prohibited former lawmakers from lobbying Congress or representing foreign interests for one year after leaving office. The law, however, gives ex-lawmakers ample leeway because it does not prevent them from lobbying the executive branch, plotting strategy, and advising others who directly contact members of Congress. A move has been made as well toward strengthening restrictions on lobbying by former officials of the executive branch. A 1993 executive order bars former senior officials from lobbying the federal agency in which they worked for five years (the old limit had been one year) after leaving government employment.

Political Action Committees

Because elected officials cannot wage credible election campaigns without money, interest groups are often willing to provide campaign cash. The chosen vehicle for these financial contributions is the **political action committee** or PAC. The Federal Election Campaign Act (FECA) amendments of 1971 and 1974 allow a political committee created by an interest group to solicit funds for distribution to candidates. According to the act, corporate PACs are exempt from the general rule against campaign expenditures by corporations or federally insured financial institutions such as banks and savings and loan associations. These PACs can use corporate funds to offset the cost of setting up a PAC and can solicit voluntary contributions from stockholders, administrative personnel, and their families. Labor unions and trade associations also are given the right by the FECA to solicit campaign funds from their members. Independent PACs abound as well, composed of like-minded people interested in promoting a particular ideology or policy position—for example, the National Abortion Rights Action League PAC, Emily's List (supports women candidates), the National Right to Life Committee, the National Congressional Club (a conservative PAC formed by supporters of Sen. Jesse Helms, R-N.C.), and the liberal National Committee for an Effective Congress. PACs must comply with federal regulations calling for regular reports of receipts and with expenditure limits on contributions to candidates of $5,000 per election.

Before the 1960s PACs were largely a labor union phenomenon led by the AFL-CIO's Committee on Political Education (COPE), although the American Medical Association and National Association of Manufacturers also operated PACs. Changes in the FECA in the 1970s resulted in a massive increase in the number of PACs, especially those

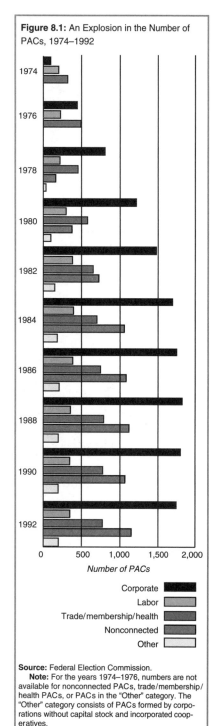

Figure 8.1: An Explosion in the Number of PACs, 1974–1992

Number of PACs

Corporate
Labor
Trade/membership/health
Nonconnected
Other

Source: Federal Election Commission.
Note: For the years 1974–1976, numbers are not available for nonconnected PACs, trade/membership/health PACs, or PACs in the "Other" category. The "Other" category consists of PACs formed by corporations without capital stock and incorporated cooperatives.

Table 8.2 PAC Contributions to Winning House and Senate Campaigns, 1975–1992

Election Cycle	Senate Campaigns		House Campaigns	
	Amount (millions of dollars)	% of Total Receipts	Amount (millions of dollars)	% of Total Receipts
1975–1976	3.1	14.8	10.9	25.6
1977–1978	6.0	14.0	17.0	28.3
1979–1980	10.2	24.5	27.0	31.4
1981–1982	15.6	22.0	42.7	34.7
1983–1984	20.0	19.8	59.5	41.1
1985–1986	28.4	26.6	72.8	42.2
1987–1988	31.8	26.1	86.4	45.1
1989–1990	31.3	25.8	91.5	46.4
1991–1992	31.8	26.7	97.2	41.7

Source: Federal Election Commission.

sponsored by corporations and trade associations (see Figure 8.1). As the number of PACs has increased, their role in funding election campaigns has expanded as well (Table 8.2). Individual contributors are still the largest source of campaign money, but PACs constituted 40 percent of the total receipts of House candidates in 1991–1992 and over a quarter of total Senate campaign funds.

In their allocations of funds PACs show a strong preference for incumbents. In fact, almost three-quarters of PAC contributions to House and Senate candidates in the 1991–1992 election cycle went to incumbents, and only a little over 10 percent was given to candidates challenging incumbents; the balance went to open-seat campaigns in which no incumbent was running (Table 8.3 and Figure 8.2). Incumbency also affects the shares of PAC money received by Republican and Democratic candidates. In 1991–1992 the Democrats, with more congressional incumbents than the Republicans, received $114.3 million— or 64 percent of all PAC contributions—compared with $63.8 million for the Republicans (Table 8.3).

PACs representing different interests show distinctive contribution patterns. Labor PACs give almost exclusively to Democrats (95.2 percent of their 1991–1992 contributions), and business PACs, although often thought to favor Republicans, follow a strategy of giving to incumbents. Thus, in the 1991–1992 election cycle Democrats received 54 percent of corporate and trade association PAC money. Because ideological PACs want to influence the policy orientation of the Congress as a whole, they frequently contribute to challengers and open-seat races.

Table 8.3 PAC Contributions to House and Senate Candidates, 1991–1992 Election Cycle

PAC Contributions to	Amount (millions of dollars)	% of Total PAC Contributions
All incumbents	126.3	71.7
All challengers	21.5	11.7
All open-seat candidates	31.4	16.7
TOTAL	179.2	100.1[a]
REPUBLICANS		
House candidates	41.6	23.4
Senate candidates	22.2	12.5
TOTAL	63.8	35.9
DEMOCRATS		
House candidates	85.4	48.0
Senate candidates	28.9	16.2
TOTAL	114.3	64.2

Source: Federal Election Commission.
  Note: Minor parties not included.
  [a] Does not add up to 100 because of rounding.

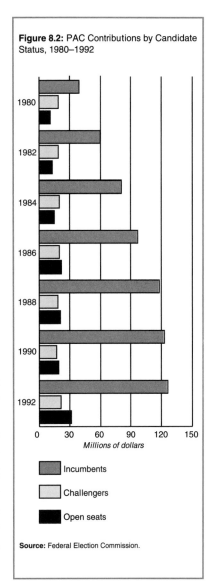

Figure 8.2: PAC Contributions by Candidate Status, 1980–1992

Millions of dollars

Incumbents
Challengers
Open seats

Source: Federal Election Commission.

Even with the significant exceptions such as the labor PACs, most PACs are *not* trying to shape election outcomes by following a strategy of, first, contributing only to candidates who support their groups' issue positions and, second, of intervening only when the race is close enough to be affected by the infusion of additional cash. Rather, by contributing primarily to incumbents, most of whom have strong reelection prospects, PACs tend to follow a strategy designed to win them access to Congress. They operate on the belief, borne of practical experience, that campaign contributions "grease the skids" and help their lobbyists in presenting their groups' positions to congressional decision makers. The impact of their access gained from PAC contributions, however, tends to vary, depending on the nature of the issue.

PAC contributions and follow-up lobbying by an interest group are apt to have their greatest impacts on issues that are highly technical and attract little public attention, such as amendments to the tax code. But when issues generate media attention, competing forces—ideological concerns, party and White House pressures, and constituency interests—impinge on legislators and weaken the impacts of interest groups and their PACs. The impact of PAC contributions on public policy making is a matter of lively public debate. Some journalists and public interest groups believe PAC contributions have a pervasive influence, which is creating what one PAC critic has called "the best Congress money can buy."[46] Common Cause and other public interest groups have sought to ban PAC contributions altogether. The analyses of political scientists, however, find much less evidence of PAC contributions affecting congressional votes than many journalists and public interest groups believe.[47]

Electioneering

Campaign funds are not the only kind of campaign assistance interest groups make available to candidates; mass membership organizations can even mobilize their members to vote for and work in behalf of preferred candidates. Organized labor, for example, operates phone banks during election campaigns, contacting union households to get out the vote for union-endorsed candidates (almost exclusively Democrats). But efforts by group leaders to mobilize their memberships to support a particular candidate may meet with only limited success. Group members often have other commitments and beliefs that conflict with those of the group, and they may, therefore, not vote in accordance with the official position of their leaders. Indeed, in spite of organized labor's vigorous support of Democratic presidential nominee Bill Clinton, 45 percent of voters in union households cast their ballots instead for either his Republican opponent, George Bush, or independent Ross Perot.

Few groups have the resources or personnel to operate phone banks like those of the AFL-CIO, but all organizations are themselves communications systems that can be used to help preferred candidates. Informal communications channels within firms can pass the word from senior to junior executives that the leadership is supporting a particular candidate or party. Newsletters and other publications can shower candidates with favorable publicity and make their mailing lists available to campaign organizations. Invitations to speak at group meetings and conventions may be forthcoming as well for favored candidates.

Interest groups may even take the more extreme measure of reach-

46. See Philip M. Stern, *The Best Congress Money Can Buy* (New York: Pantheon Books, 1988).

47. For a discussion of the PAC vote-buying controversy, see Larry J. Sabato, *PAC Power: Inside the World of Political Action Committees* (New York: Norton, 1984), 132–140; John R. Wright, "PACs, Contributions, and Roll Calls," *American Political Science Review* 79 (June 1985): 400–414; Janet M. Grenzke, "PACs and the Congressional Supermarket: The Currency Is Complex," *American Journal of Political Science* 33 (February 1989): 1–24; and John R. Wright, "Contributions, Lobbying, and Committee Voting in the U.S. House of Representatives," *American Political Science Review* 84 (June 1990): 417–438.

ing beyond their membership and publicizing the record—often in a negative manner—of a public official. Environmental Action, for example, periodically announces the names of its "Dirty Dozen," incumbent members of Congress who, in its view, have the worst records on environmental issues. And interest groups, particularly such large and well-financed organizations as the American Medical Association PAC and the realtors' PAC, have engaged in independent expenditures either to bolster the campaigns of supportive members of Congress or to defeat those who have opposed them. In the 1991–1992 election cycle PACs contributed $6.4 million in independent expenditures to House and Senate races.

Shaping Public Opinion

Few can doubt that public support adds strength to an interest group's lobbying and other efforts to influence government policy. Corporations, unions, and nonprofit sector groups often supplement their lobbying and PAC activities with media advertising. This technique is especially evident when an interest group believes its political influence as well as its public image could benefit from a little polishing. Perhaps no group is better at this than the National Rifle Association, which tries to offset criticism of its intense opposition to gun control legislation by using the likes of gun-toting movie stars in television spots and former presidents like Franklin Roosevelt with a rifle in hand in newspaper ads.

Citizens' organizations reliant on broad public support resort to media advertising as well. Handgun Control, Incorporated, for example, used media advertising extensively in its drive to gain congressional approval for the Brady bill, which requires a five-day waiting period for handgun purchases. The bill was named for former presidential press secretary James Brady, who was permanently disabled in the 1981 assassination attempt against President Reagan. As part of its media campaign, Handgun Control effectively utilized Brady and his wife, Sarah, for news program interviews. In 1993 rising public awareness of the carnage in the nation's streets led to House and Senate approval of the Brady bill.

Advertising campaigns have their limits, however. Because they are expensive and only a small fraction of the population is likely to even view or read the advertisements, they are an option only for such well-established, well-heeled groups as corporations, trade associations, and unions.

Direct marketing via mail and telephone—targeting past and potential supporters with an appeal to join a group, contact public officials, and contribute money to a group—is another means of mobilizing mass support for a cause.[48] One large-scale practitioner of this method is right-wing organizer Richard Viguerie, who claims to have the addresses of millions of conservative voters on file in his northern Virginia office.

Not all techniques for shaping public opinion to affect public policy are costly. For example, "outsider" organizations that lack close ties with friendly members of Congress and administrative agencies often simply release information calculated to raise eyebrows and rate a story on the evening news. A skilled user of this technique is Ralph Nader. His exposés of government and corporate insensitivity to threatened public health and safety have helped to build support for stronger consumer, workplace safety, and environmental protection legislation. Nader and other leading nonestablishment organizations have found the revelations leaked to them by so-called **whistle-blowers** particularly helpful. Acting out of either sympathy for a group's goals or disillusionment with the actions of an agency, whistle-blowers are employees of the government or private sector who reveal inside information. For example, advocates of reduced military spending and procurement reform have periodically publicized leaks from within the Pentagon about cost overruns—such as $1,000 toilet seats—to dramatize their arguments. This information is then used by an interest group to generate publicity for its position on an issue.

When the more conventional techniques for exerting group influence do not produce the desired results or are not available to a group because of limited resources or lack of access to public officials, groups may resort to demonstrations and protests—such as picketing and marching—to express their frustration and outrage over government policy and to attract public and media attention. For example, after the Supreme Court's highly controversial 1989 decision in *Webster v. Reproductive Health Services,* which permitted state regulation of abortion, a Washington protest march coordinated by the National Organization for Women (NOW) attracted 300,000 protesters and extensive media coverage. Similarly, groups opposed to abortion rights have demonstrated periodically—including attempts to block and close down abortion clinics—to dramatize their opposition to abortion and attract publicity for their cause.

Not all demonstrations and protests are orchestrated and planned

48. For an account of the use and impact of direct marketing, see R. Kenneth Godwin, *One Billion Dollars of Influence: The Direct Marketing of Politics* (Chatham, N.J.: Chatham House, 1988).

by organizing groups; they may arise spontaneously out of frustration. This was certainly the situation in the South during the 1960s with the early civil rights demonstrations. In one case a handful of young black men initiated lunch-counter sit-ins, and in Montgomery, Alabama, a bus boycott started when Rosa Parks refused to accept racial discrimination and sit in the back of a bus. These acts of protest were then used by the Reverend Martin Luther King, Jr., and such civil rights groups as the NAACP to mobilize public support for the cause of racial equality.

The use of demonstrations and protests as a tool for exerting influence has a major drawback, however: they are hard to sustain over an extended period of time. Yet a prolonged effort is normally required to affect government policy because the policy-making process is lengthy and complicated, with most policy changes occurring in increments. One of the remarkable features of the civil rights movement of the 1960s was its ability to sustain a high level of activity and public visibility. Only through this accomplishment was it able to achieve in turn such major legislation as the Civil Rights Act of 1964 and the Voting Rights Act of 1965.

Going to Court

With its vast powers to interpret and enforce the Constitution and laws, the judicial branch, like the Congress and executive, has been used by interest groups to shape policies to their liking. The most common method of lobbying the Supreme Court is via *amicus curiae* or "friend of the court" briefs—formal statements filed with the Court to argue in support of a litigant and a particular legal doctrine.[49] Interest groups also bring or sponsor litigation—test cases—aimed at challenging existing laws or government practices. This important avenue for advancing the goals of public interest groups is favored particularly by organizations who have been unsuccessful in their efforts to influence either Congress or the executive branch. But such litigation requires access to capable attorneys either through in-house counsel or the assistance of outside lawyers. And in using the courts to shape government policy, a group must select test cases with care so that, first, the chances of winning a favorable decision are enhanced and, second, the courts will have to rule on the specific question of law the group is contesting.

When directed by a skilled attorney, bringing test cases to the courts can be an effective means for achieving group policy objectives as Supreme Court Justice Ruth Bader Ginsburg demonstrated in the 1970s when she was a lawyer for the Women's Rights Project of the American Civil Liberties Union.

49. On the use of *amicus curiae* briefs and litigation to influence the Supreme Court, see Karen O'Connor and Bryant Scott McFall, "Conservative Interest Groups Litigation in the Reagan Era and Beyond," in Petracca, *Politics of Interests,* 263–284; and Gregory A. Caldeira and John R. Wright, "Amici Curiae before the Court: Who Parties, When and How Much?" *Journal of Politics* 52 (August 1990): 782–806.

One of the most important and far-reaching instances in which a group used litigation to promote its interests involved the National Association for the Advancement of Colored People. The NAACP and its legal staff supported the lawsuit, *Brown v. Board of Education of Topeka* (1954), that resulted in the Supreme Court declaring school segregation unconstitutional. Similarly, during the 1970s the Women's Rights Project of the American Civil Liberties Union under the direction of Ruth Bader Ginsburg (later President Clinton's first nominee to the Supreme Court) systematically brought a series of cases to the Supreme Court in an effort to convince the justices that gender was a suspect classification that required strict scrutiny under the equal protection clause of the Fourteenth Amendment. Other groups, including environmental, consumer, business, religious, and conservative organizations, also have used court cases to shape policy.

Court decisions can be swayed in indirect ways as well, such as by trying to influence the selection of judges. These indirect techniques of influence over court policy are covered in Chapter 13, which describes the politics of the judiciary.

Policy Making, Group Representation, and Regulation

Although interest group activities have received more media attention in recent years, lobbyists are hardly a new phenomenon in the nation's capital. The number and diversity of interests represented have increased greatly, however, since the 1960s. Well-established economic interests—business, farm, labor, and professional groups—must now compete not only among themselves but also with newly mobilized nonprofit organizations representing the interests of minorities, consumers, women, environmentalists, and the disadvantaged, among others.

All this has meant that policy making is dominated less now than in the early 1960s and before by tight little subgovernments or **iron triangles**, composed of cooperating and allied interest groups, congressional committees, and executive agency bureaus. During the earlier era a subgovernment could virtually control specific areas of public policy such as sugar import quotas, milk marketing, water projects, and public works projects. Today, with the proliferation of nonprofit groups, the notion of policy making through cozy arrangements among a few select interest groups, congressional committees, and agency bureaus fails to capture the complexity of the process. Policy making increas-

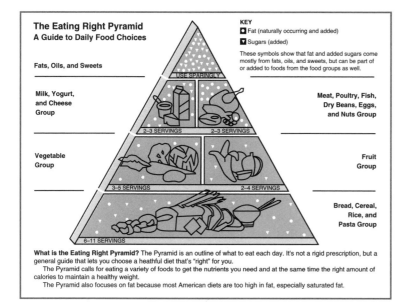

When the U.S. Department of Agriculture prepared the "Eating Right Pyramid" in 1991 to help educate the public about nutrition and health, a fierce controversy erupted among the diverse interests concerned with nutrition policy. Ranchers and the dairy industry demanded that the pyramid be withdrawn, while consumer and health groups joined the fray to defend the diagram.

ingly involves not so much iron triangles as it does loose, highly flexible, and web-like **issue networks,** composed of varied and competing interest groups (both profit- and nonprofit-oriented), policy experts, academicians, consultants, executive department personnel, and members of Congress and their staffs.[50]

Almost nowhere have the breakup of the cozy iron triangle and its replacement by a more complex issue network been more evident than in agriculture—a policy domain once dominated by a small cadre of farm state legislators, Department of Agriculture officials, and major farm interest group representatives. This tripartite alliance was so powerful that agriculture policy was portrayed as being outside the control of or intervention by the Congress or White House. But as the components of food and fiber production have become more fragmented and specialized, farms have become larger and more capital-intensive, and agriculture has been forced to operate in an international competitive market affected by food surpluses, government trade policies, and budget deficits, the interests concerned with agriculture policy have become much more complex and conflictual. The old iron triangle has been supplemented by specific commodity producer and processor organizations, which have proliferated and become as active as such general organizations as the American Farm Bureau Federation, huge

50. On issue networks, see Hugh Heclo, "Issue Networks and the Executive Establishment," in *The New American Political System,* ed. Anthony King (Washington, D.C.: American Enterprise Institute, 1978), chap. 3.

agribusiness organizations, protest groups asserting the anxieties of smaller producers, and consumer and environmental groups, among others. The executive branch agencies vitally interested in agriculture policy also have expanded beyond the Department of Agriculture to include the White House, Office of Management and Budget, and the Office of the U.S. Trade Representative. The cozy iron triangle that once dominated farm policy has ceased to exist, and policy is now shaped by a much broader array of forces.[51]

The emergence of issue networks like the one operating in the field of agriculture has made policy making much more complicated and less predictable than in the past. It also has heightened the level of conflict in American politics because of the ideological differences between commercial interests and the newly developed citizens' groups attempting to achieve broad policy objectives.[52] (See Chapter 12 for more discussion of "iron triangles" and issue networks.)

How Representative Is the Interest Group System?

The increased diversity of interest groups, the expanded role of public interest groups, and the diminished capacity of iron triangles to dominate selected areas of policy have not resolved the concern that many feel about the representativeness of the interest group system. Participation in group politics has its costs: time away from work, family, and recreation, and the expense of attending meetings, contacting government officials, and communicating with group members. Not everyone, therefore, is able to participate equally in the interest group system. Not surprisingly, studies show that interest group participation is more prevalent among better-educated and up-scale Americans than among the less well-to-do.[53] Because data on interest groups with Washington offices or representatives show a heavy preponderance of economic groups (Table 8.4), it has been suggested that the interest group "chorus sings with a strong upper-class accent."[54]

51. For an account of the development of the agriculture policy issue network, see William P. Browne, "Policy and Interests: Instability and Change in a Classic Issue Subsystem," in Cigler and Loomis, *Interest Group Politics*, 2d ed., chap. 10.

52. Thomas I. Gais, Mark A. Peterson, and Jack L. Walker, "Interest Groups, Iron Triangles and Representative Institutions in American National Government," *British Journal of Political Science* 14 (April 1984): 161–185; and William P. Browne and Won K. Paik, "Beyond the Domain: Recasting Network Politics in the Postreform Congress," *American Journal of Political Science* 37 (November 1993): 1054–1078.

53. Kay Lehman Schlozman and John T. Tierney, *Organized Interests and American Democracy* (New York: Harper and Row, 1986), chap. 4.

54. E. E. Schattschneider, *The Semi-Sovereign People* (New York: Holt, Rinehart and Winston, 1960), 35.

This apparent class bias of the interest group system is counterbalanced in part by the existence and increasing activity of groups that act as advocates for the poor or for more general interests—consumers, taxpayers, and environmentalists. But many issues do not pit the rich against the poor—for example, most foreign policy issues or the struggles over water rights between California and its neighboring states. Nor are all elements of the poor in agreement—for example, the young poor have scant interest in Medicare and Social Security, but these are prime concerns of the elderly poor. It is even possible for powerful economic interests to benefit from and support programs designed to help the poor. Agribusiness benefits from the food stamp program; health care professionals and hospitals benefit from Medicare and Medicaid. The influence of major economic interests may be diminished, however, by disagreements among them. Such is the case with the continuing battles over government regulatory policy, which pit banks against savings and loan associations.

Although there are limits on the effectiveness of economic interest groups and advocates for the disadvantaged do exist, the fact remains that groups anchored in economic self-interest do have certain advantages. They are relatively permanent, have substantial resources, and normally can develop working relationships with policy makers. Public interest groups must rely more heavily on their abilities to mobilize and sustain public support and interest—more difficult tasks than using insider lobbying techniques and making campaign contributions. In politics, as in other aspects of life, it is still better to be well off than poor. The group struggle in America, however, is a process open to all who wish to participate.

Regulation

Concern about the undue influence of special interest groups on the political process has led Congress to enact regulatory legislation. Regulation of interest groups, however, is limited by their protection under the Constitution's First Amendment guarantees of freedom of speech, press, assembly, and the right to petition the government for redress of grievances.

Under the Federal Regulation of Lobbying Act passed in 1946, groups and individuals seeking to influence legislation are required to register with the clerk of the House and the secretary of the Senate and to file quarterly financial statements. As it has been interpreted, however, the act has little practical impact. The Supreme Court has held that the law applies only to groups or individuals involved in direct lobbying and

Table 8.4 Interest Group Representation in Washington

	% of Total Groups Having a Washington Office	% of Total Groups Retaining a Lobbyist or Having a Washington Office
Corporation	20.6	45.7
Trade association	30.6	17.9
Foreign business	0.5	6.5
Professional association	14.8	6.9
Union	3.3	1.7
Citizens' group	8.7	4.1
Civil rights, minorities	1.7	1.3
Social welfare and poor	1.3	0.6
Elderly, women, handicapped	2.5	1.1
Government units	1.4	4.2
Others	14.6	8.2
TOTAL	100.0	100.0
	(N = 2,810)	(N = 6,601)

Source: Adapted from *Organized Interests and American Democracy* by Kay Lehman Schlozman and John T. Tierney. Copyright © 1986 by Kay Lehman Schlozman and John T. Tierney. Reprinted by permission of HarperCollins Publishers.

whose "principal purpose" is lobbying. As a result, not all groups register, and grass-roots lobbying is not covered by the law. In addition, it does not apply to attempts to influence the executive branch.

There is broad support for the notion that the public is entitled to more information than the current law permits about the activities of interest groups. But proposals to strengthen the reporting and disclosure provisions of the law have raised serious issues. Disclosure of groups' contributors has been opposed by consumer, environmental, and civil rights groups on the grounds that such information could expose such contributors to intimidation. It also has been recommended that interest groups file detailed reports on their activities and contacts with public officials. These proposals would impose particularly heavy burdens on small and modestly financed groups, which have claimed that all the red tape would impair their effectiveness.

Interest Groups, Government, and the Public Interest

Interest groups are a natural development in a free society characterized by socioeconomic diversity, and they gravitate toward the government as its power enables them to achieve goals that they cannot secure with their own resources. Because groups supplement the geographic representation system of Congress and are a means of mobilizing citizens to influence their government, they are essential linkages between the people and the government and their activities are constitutionally protected. But intergroup competition, lack of internal unity, and the competition of other political forces such as political parties and the mass media limit the capacity of interest groups to gain all their policy objectives.

For all their contributions to the political system, however, interest groups continue to stir unease in Americans. Even though interest group membership is widespread, there is concern that the public interest is being trampled by the stampede of interest groups to Washington. Most question whether the net effect of interest group pulling and hauling necessarily results in what is best for the nation as a whole. There is also worry about the inherent biases in the interest group system because not all interests have the same capacities for influencing the government; middle- and upper-class interests appear to have an advantage. It is for this reason that political scientists stress the role of political parties as America's most broadly based counterweight to interest group influence. The influence of interest groups also can be limited by the force and persuasiveness of an idea or symbolically appealing cause such as clean air or tax reform. Indeed, a review of the big policy battles of the last quarter century—over environmental protection, workplace safety, tax reform, transportation deregulation, and consumer protection—demonstrates that powerful economic interests have not been able to dictate policy outcomes in Washington. Interest group politics, then, has been supplemented by a "politics of ideas"[55]—a politics in which the mass media often play an active and influential role in molding and disseminating the ideas that affect public policy making. The media are the subject of the next chapter.

55. See John T. Tierney, "Organized Interests in the Nation's Capital," in Petracca, *Politics of Interests,* 216; and Paul R. Schulman, "The Politics of 'Ideational Policy,'" *Journal of Politics* 50 (1988): 263–291.

For Review

1. An interest group is an organized body of people with shared goals who try to influence government policy. Interest group activity is protected by the Constitution.

2. American society contains a vast array of interest groups which have grown dramatically in number since the 1960s. With their growth has come a change in the composition of the interest group universe. Traditional occupational groups have been supplemented by an increase in citizens' (public) interest groups and lobbying operations sponsored by corporations and state and local government bodies. Moreover, policy making now takes place in an often more complex and conflictual group environment than in the recent past.

3. The influence of individual interest groups depends on such factors as the nature of a group's membership, its financial and leadership resources, its prestige and status, and government structure, rules, and procedures.

4. Groups try to influence any branch or level of government that they believe will respond to their concerns. The tactics used by interest groups to influence government policy include direct and grass-roots lobbying, PAC contributions and other forms of electoral support, efforts to shape public opinion, demonstrations, protests, and litigation.

5. The interest group system supplements the formal and geographic system of congressional representation by providing citizens with an informal means of influencing government. Not all Americans are equally represented, however, by the interest group system. Although every American is free to organize and participate in interest group activity, the people most likely to participate are the better educated and those with financial resources.

For Further Reading

Berry, Jeffrey M. *The Interest Group Society.* 2d ed. Glenview, Ill.: Scott, Foresman, 1989. An overview of the formation and maintenance of groups as well as their activities in the political arena.

Birnbaum, Jeffrey H. *The Lobbyists: How Influence Peddlers Get Their Way in Washington.* New York: Times Books, 1992. A reporter's inside and often critical look at Washington lobbying.

Cigler, Allan J., and Burdett A. Loomis, eds. *Interest Group Politics.* 3d ed. Washington, D.C.: CQ Press, 1991. A collection of original studies detailing the tactics of groups.

Heinz, John P., Edward O. Laumann, Robert L. Nelson, and Robert H. Salisbury. *The Hollow Core: Private Interests and National Policy Making.* Cambridge: Harvard University Press, 1993. A data rich analysis of interest groups in the policy making process that reveals the porous and diffuse nature of policy networks and the uncertainty of policy outcomes.

McFarland, Andrew S. *Common Cause: Lobbying in the Public Interest.* Chatham, N.J.: Chatham House, 1984. The most thoroughgoing analysis of the internal politics and lobbying tactics of a unique and influential public interest group.

Moe, Terry M. *The Organization of Interests: Incentives and the Internal Dynamics of Political Interest Groups.* Chicago: University of Chicago Press, 1980. An analysis of the internal dynamics of farm and business organizations.

Olson, Mancur, Jr. *The Logic of Collective Action.* New York: Schocken, 1968. An analysis of the free-rider problem and how shared interests are not sufficient for groups to organize and maintain themselves.

Petracca, Mark P., ed. *The Politics of Interests: Interest Groups Transformed.* Boulder, Colo.: Westview Press, 1992. A collection of essays by leading scholars on the changing nature, activities, and impact of interest groups.

Schlozman, Kay Lehman, and John T. Tierney. *Organized Interests and American Democracy.* New York: Harper and Row, 1986. An analysis of group formation, internal dynamics, and strategies of influence.

Truman, David B. *The Governmental Process.* New York: Knopf, 1951. A classic treatment of the group basis of politics.

9. The Mass Media

I N   T H E   1992 presidential election campaign only a tiny fraction of the voters actually met or saw the Republican and Democratic nominees, George Bush and Bill Clinton, or the independent candidate, Ross Perot. Most of what people knew about these men was absorbed from watching television or reading about them in newspapers and news magazines. In fact, news stories from all of these sources are an important part of how Americans perceive what is happening politically in the world around them, whether it be crime in one's own community, congressional deliberations on health care reform proposals, or conflict in the Middle East. These shared political experiences constitute a basis for public opinion and the coming together of people for political action.

The term **news media** refers to the diverse array of national and local newspapers, weekly and monthly news magazines, television networks and stations, and radio stations. Within this broad complex of news outlets there are the more narrowly defined and influential national media consisting of the major television networks, the Public Broadcasting Service (PBS), and the three newspapers specializing in national political news—the *New York Times, Washington Post,* and *Wall Street Journal.* These national media are especially influential because they are watched or read by the country's political leaders, as well as by journalists themselves. This chapter deals primarily with this powerful national segment of the news media.

The news media act as intermediaries between the people and their government institutions. And like political parties and interest groups and their members, the media can spur their viewers and readers to become active politically in ways that will affect the inner workings of the government. Although the extent of the media's influence has not been determined conclusively, it is widely accepted that they played a significant role in shaping public opinion about the Vietnam War and even swayed the Vietnam policies of news-obsessive president Lyndon Johnson.[1] Public support for American military involvement fell after intense, ongoing television coverage, which featured graphic pictures of the deaths, atrocities, and destruction caused by the war. Television also helped antiwar leaders to win respectability by simply giving them coverage. President Johnson attached so much importance to the role of

1. Doris A. Graber, *Mass Media and American Politics,* 4th ed. (Washington, D.C.: CQ Press, 1993), 293–294.

President Ronald Reagan's Hollywood training made him an unusually effective communicator, and his presidency relied heavily on television presentations to gain public support for its programs.

the media that he concluded there was no hope of regaining public support for the war after trusted and respected CBS anchorman Walter Cronkite editorialized against Johnson's Vietnam policy. This led *New York Times* reporter David Halberstam to observe, "It was the first time in history a war had been declared over by an anchorman."[2]

Unlike in the Vietnam days, media coverage also can increase public support for government policy. For example, the steady flow of almost exclusively positive news accounts of the Persian Gulf War—U.S.-made Patriot missiles downing Iraqi Scud missiles, "smart" bombs hitting their targets, well-trained military personnel performing their missions efficiently, and a charismatic commander, Gen. Norman Schwartzkopf, providing televised briefings—moved a nation initially divided about going to war to give its overwhelming support to President Bush's decision to use force to drive Iraqi invaders from Kuwait.

Because they recognize the importance of the media's effects on public opinion, political leaders regularly try to influence the content of news coverage. For their part, the media are able to raise issues that political leaders would prefer to keep out of the limelight. It was the enterprising journalism of two *Washington Post* reporters, for example, that played a critical role in revealing President Richard Nixon's role in covering up the 1972 break-in at the Democratic National Headquarters in the Watergate complex and led to his eventual resignation from the presidency. And it was the news media's airing of allegations of marital infidelity and draft evasion early in the contest for the 1992

2. David Halberstam, *The Powers That Be* (New York: Knopf, 1979), 514.

Table 9.1 Americans' News Consumption

Percent Who Regularly

Watch news on TV regularly	74
Less than 15 minutes yesterday	4
15–29 minutes yesterday	8
30–59 minutes yesterday	15
60 minutes or more	25
Read a daily newspaper	54
Read a metropolitan paper	20
New York Times or	
Los Angeles Times	6
USA Today	5
Wall Street Journal	3
Listen to news on radio regularly	53
Less than 15 minutes yesterday	22
15–29 minutes yesterday	12
30–59 minutes yesterday	9
60 minutes or more	10
Read news magazines such as	
Time, U.S. News, or *Newsweek*	18
Read personality magazines such as	
People or *US*	8
Read business magazines such as	
Fortune or *Forbes*	5
Read magazines such as	
Atlantic Monthly, Harpers,	
or *New Yorker*	2

Source: "The American Media," Times Mirror Center for the People and the Press, July 15, 1990.

Democratic presidential nomination that nearly sunk Bill Clinton's candidacy. The media have affected Bill Clinton's presidency in a major way as well. During late 1993 and 1994 the media appeared mesmerized by the Clintons' involvement in an early 1970s Arkansas real estate deal, dubbed "Whitewater," and charges of a White House coverup. As a result, an independent counsel was appointed to investigate the affair, a senior White House aide was forced to resign, White House aides were required to testify before a grand jury, congressional hearings investigating the affair were held, and the president, first lady, and their staffs found themselves diverted from policy matters.

In these days in which the average high school student spends more time in front of a television screen than in school, and adults are spending half their leisure time watching television (on average four hours a day) or reading newspapers and magazines, the potential political influence of the media is obviously substantial (Table 9.1). This chapter, then, probes the nature of the media and their influence on public opinion, elections, and government institutions. The starting point for this analysis is a look at the media's evolution as well as the government's regulatory policies for the media.

The Coming of Age of the Mass Media

Today's multidimensional print and electronic media are vastly different from the highly partisan, exclusively print media that existed when the government under the Constitution began. The character of the twentieth-century media reflects the interaction of social changes, technological advances, government policies, and the attitudes of Americans toward both the media and the government.

From a Party Press to a Popular Press

In the early days of the Republic, political factions and later political parties founded and controlled newspapers to convey their own interpretations of political events to the reading public. The *Gazette of the United States* gave the Federalist view of public affairs, and the opposing Jeffersonian interpretation was found in the *National Gazette*. Party leaders even used public funds to subsidize their papers. Indeed, when he became president, Thomas Jefferson began to help to support the *National Intelligencer,* his administration's party organ, by awarding it contracts to print government documents.

Perhaps more than any other single event the Civil War brought about major changes in journalism. The war created a popular appetite

Newspaper stories that extolled and exaggerated his exploits as leader of the Rough Riders in Cuba during the Spanish-American War made Theodore Roosevelt a celebrity at home and advanced his political career.

for news, which editors scurried to fill. In the North alone over five hundred correspondents covered the war. Of these, sixty represented the *New York Herald,* which spent more than $1 million on coverage. Although war coverage was hampered by erratic mail and telegraph service, government censorship, and inexperienced correspondents, the war established war correspondence as an essential brand of reporting and significantly expanded journalism's horizons.

By the mid-1880s technological advances and societal changes had made it possible for newspaper publishers to establish profitable enterprises based on mass readership. Industrialization, immigration, and urbanization, as well as rising literacy rates, had created mass audiences for newspapers in America's cities. Mass readership, in turn, attracted advertising that paid the cost of printing and enabled publishers to turn a profit. Later, technological advances such as high-speed presses made it possible to print thousands of papers and sell them at low cost—often for only a penny a copy. The invention of the telegraph in 1844 enabled the national news to be cabled immediately from Washington to all parts of the country.

The popular press that emerged in the nineteenth century was often highly partisan, but its partisanship stemmed from the orientations of its publishers and not from its sponsorship by various political parties. The papers of the late 1800s and early 1900s often engaged in sensationalism, vulgarity, and sleazy reporting—also called **yellow journalism** for the Yellow Kid, a comic-strip character in the *New York World*. One of the most notorious examples of sensationalism occurred when William Randolph Hearst's *New York Journal* found itself locked in a circulation battle with Joseph Pulitzer's *New York World*. Both papers sent reporters and illustrators to Cuba in 1897 with orders to provide lurid details of Spanish atrocities against the Cuban people. When Frederic Remington, the noted artist and illustrator, sent a cable to Hearst in New York requesting permission to return to the United States because "everything is quiet. . . . There will be no war," Hearst responded, "Please remain. You furnish the pictures and I'll furnish the war." The newsmen obliged—frequently with only casual regard for accuracy—and provided American readers with a steady stream of stories depicting Spanish mistreatment of Cubans. This form of yellow journalism stoked the fires of public indignation against Spain and provided public support for the Spanish-American War of 1898.

Also during this era mass-circulation magazines of opinion—*Collier's, McClure's, Scribner's,* and *Cosmopolitan*—emerged. Their investigative reporting, which President Theodore Roosevelt called **muckraking,** exposed the seamy side of American government and business—corrupt urban political machines, special-interest influence in the Senate, and corporate misconduct that threatened public health and safety. The muckraking tradition and its accompanying suspicion of politicians are still very much alive today in American journalism as CBS's popular and long-running investigative program "60 Minutes" demonstrates.

The Media in the Twentieth Century

The communications industry has changed dramatically in this century. Yellow journalism has been largely replaced by more professional news-gathering standards, and the mass media now encompass a staggering assortment of both print and electronic outlets: over 9,100 newspapers (of which 18 percent are published on a daily basis), 11,000 periodicals, 10,000 radio stations, 1,200 television stations, and 7,800 cable systems. But while Americans are served by a wide array of news sources, the communications industry itself has become increasingly centralized in terms of ownership and control, largely as a result of economic forces. Because worldwide news gathering and program production for television are extremely expensive (on average each story broadcast on the "NBC Nightly News" costs $63,000!),[3] only large-scale

3. Graber, *Mass Media and American Politics,* 50.

enterprises are able to generate the revenue required to provide Americans with the range and quality of media fare they have come to expect.

Journalistic Professionalism. In the twentieth century journalists began to adhere to professional norms calling for factual accuracy and objectivity. This movement toward professionalism was aided by the establishment of university schools of journalism. Journalistic independence took root in this heightened professionalism as well; reporters believed themselves independent of politicians, whose actions were to be reported accurately, fully, and fairly, and of their colleagues on the business side of the media, whose interference with news content was not to be tolerated.

Newspapers. Newspapers, like most other forms of media, are profit-making enterprises whose ownership is increasingly concentrated in the hands of large chains such as Gannett, Thompson, Cox, Scripps Howard, Knight-Ridder, Times Mirror, and the Tribune Company. Although more than sixteen hundred papers publish on a daily basis, 68 percent of these papers (boasting 78 percent of total circulation) are controlled by national and regional chains. Thus, with the fourteen largest chains accounting for nearly half (63 million papers) of the total daily newspaper circulation in the United States, a large share of the news read by Americans each day is screened by the people who work for these giant firms. These chains do permit their individual papers to enjoy editorial page autonomy, but these papers tend to be more uniform in their political endorsements than the independently owned papers.[4] The trend toward concentration within the industry has been exacerbated by the decline in the number of daily papers. Intense competition and rising costs have forced smaller papers to cease operation and left many cities such as Cleveland and Columbus with only one daily newspaper.

Even though ownership and control of the industry have become increasingly concentrated, individual papers still have a strong local orientation—after all, newspaper readers want to know what their state and local governments are up to, and it is impossible for the national media to cover state and local politics. Most papers therefore devote a large proportion of their news space to state and local politics. Even the Washington bureaus of the newspaper chains and the large city dailies have a local orientation. The job of the reporters for such papers as the *Denver Post* or *Milwaukee Journal* is to get the local or state angle on Washington events. It is not their job to cover the big national news stories. That task is left up to the national-circulation papers as well as

4. Ibid., 44.

Radio's potential for mobilizing public support for presidential policies was demonstrated by President Franklin Roosevelt, who is shown delivering one of his "fireside chats" to the American people during the Great Depression.

the Associated Press (AP) and United Press International (UPI) wire services.

National-circulation papers that are not primarily local or regional in their orientation include the *New York Times, Washington Post, Wall Street Journal, Los Angeles Times,* and *USA Today.* These papers are important sources of information not just for ordinary citizens but also for Washington decision makers. Political leaders even communicate with each other by making statements and taking actions that are reported in the national press. Other segments of the news industry rely on these papers as well. Reporters, editors, and producers in local newsrooms and editorial offices across the country read the national press to identify newsworthy events and trends. Television news executives, in particular, having only limited air time available to them, use the national newspapers to help them to decide what to cover. Indeed, the professional standing of such leading national newspapers as the *New York Times* and *Washington Post* is so great that there is a tendency for other journalists to follow their interpretations and presentations. Stories that appear in these trend-setting papers often reappear on network and local newscasts and are circulated by wire services to local papers across the country. This process is known as pack journalism. The various components of the mass media focus their attention on the same topics, which leads to homogeneity in the news supply even though the number and diversity of news outlets are expanding.[5]

5. Ibid., 48; and Stephen Ansolabehere, Roy Behr, and Shanto Iyengar, *The Media Game: American Politics in the Television Age* (New York: Macmillan, 1993), 54–55.

Periodicals. Periodicals are an important part of the print media. The mass-circulation news weeklies—*Time, Newsweek,* and *U.S. News and World Report*—tend to provide a more interpretative slant on the news than newspapers and may reflect the opinions of reporters and editors. More clearly journals of opinion are such periodicals as the conservative *National Review* and the liberal *Nation* and *New Yorker.* Periodical publishing also includes highly specialized publications for trade and professional associations as well as for people with particular lifestyles, ethnic and religious backgrounds, and recreational interests. The American Association of Retired Persons, for example, sends *Modern Maturity* and other publications to 27 million households to update its members on government policies affecting the elderly, and *Golf Digest* keeps its readers apprised of how changes in the tax code will affect country club members.

Radio and Television. The mass communications industry was transformed from an exclusively print medium into a more complex print and electronic enterprise with the advent of radio in the 1920s and television after World War II. Radio and then television made possible instantaneous coverage of public affairs and gave political leaders unprecedented opportunities to speak directly to the American people. One of the first to utilize radio skillfully was President Franklin Roosevelt, whose "fireside chats" from the White House hearth to the living rooms of millions demonstrated radio's potential for swaying public opinion.

Television added a visual dimension to the electronic media that enhanced their impact. With 98 percent of American homes having a television set, which is on in the average home about seven hours a day, television has become the public's primary source of news (see Figure 9.1). According to the Roper Organization, not only is television the principal news source for 65 percent of the public, but it also is the source that Americans trust most. More than any other medium, television has close-up, intimate qualities. Confirming this, a 1988 survey found that in a case of conflicting news reports, 49 percent of those surveyed said they would believe the television report; in contrast, the believability score for newspapers was 21 percent; magazines, 7 percent; and radio, 6 percent.[6]

The extent of television viewing varies by gender, age, and income. Except for sporting events, women tend to watch more television than men—the average per minute audience of prime-time network broad-

6. Survey by the Roper Organization for the Television Information Office, November 1988, reported in *American Enterprise,* July/August 1990, 96.

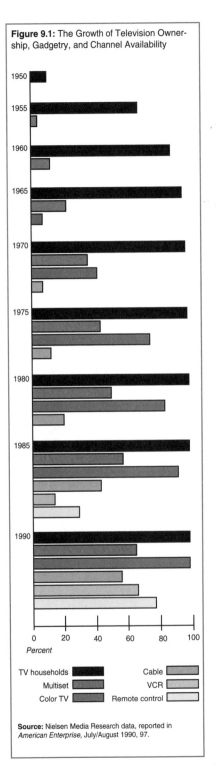

Figure 9.1: The Growth of Television Ownership, Gadgetry, and Channel Availability

Percent

TV households   Cable
Multiset   VCR
Color TV   Remote control

Source: Nielsen Media Research data, reported in *American Enterprise,* July/August 1990, 97.

casts is 9.8 million women and 7.4 million men. Viewership increases with age. Teenagers watch on average 22 hours a week; 18–34-year-olds, 26.5 hours a week; 35–54-year-olds, 30 hours a week; and those 55 and over, 39 hours a week. TV viewing is also affected by household income: households with incomes below $30,000 watch an average 53 hours a week, while those with incomes of $60,000 or more watch an average 46 hours a week.[7] The less well educated are more likely to rely on television as their sole source of political information than are the better educated, who are apt to supplement television with print information sources.

Because of the high cost of television technology and personnel, television is even more centralized than newspaper publishing. In fact, the industry is dominated by three major commercial networks—ABC, CBS, and NBC. The drawing power of the commercial networks is enormous: approximately thirty million households tune into one of the three network evening news programs on weekdays. The networks not only supply 65 percent of the programming shown by their local affiliates (each network has over two hundred affiliates) but also own stations in the nation's largest media markets—New York, Los Angeles, and Chicago—as well as in Washington, D.C., Philadelphia, Detroit, St. Louis, and San Francisco.

Competition for the Networks and the Rise of Cable Television. In spite of combined revenues of $10 billion in 1990, the networks' longtime dominance of the television industry has been weakened in recent years. Two networks were acquired by conglomerates (NBC by General Electric and ABC by Capital Cities Communications), which have subjected the networks' news divisions to unprecedented fiscal discipline: budgets have been slashed, staffs reduced, and news bureaus closed. The networks' principal problem, however, is a shrinking audience share, which has affected their bottom line. This decline stems from the stiff competition from cable television, serving 52 million households in 1990, and the Fox network owned by media baron Rupert Murdoch (see Figure 9.1). A major player is the Cable News Network (CNN), which, with its all-news format, relays its programs to over 50 million homes in the United States and 200 million viewers in more than one hundred other countries.[8] CNN was a particularly important news source (even at the Pentagon!) during the Persian Gulf War of 1991. There is also competition from the over three hundred public television

7. Data on demographic group viewing patterns are found in Ansolabehere et al., *Media Game,* 13–14; and *American Enterprise,* July/August 1990, 98.
8. Graber, *Mass Media and American Politics,* 363.

Since 1979, C-SPAN (the Cable Satellite Public Affairs Network) has made gavel-to-gavel coverage of proceedings in the House of Representatives available to more than 60 million households in fifty states. C-SPAN also provides coverage of the Senate.

stations, which receive programming and financial assistance from the federally funded Corporation for Public Broadcasting. All in all, in the 1980–1981 season the ABC-CBS-NBC aggregate audience share was 85 percent of viewers, but by 1990–1991 it had fallen to 62.4 percent.

Technological advances are undermining the position of the networks as well. Minicams and satellite transmissions are making local television stations less dependent on the network news organizations. Even major national news stories such as the New Hampshire primary, congressional hearings, or presidential visits to disaster areas, are within the reaches of local broadcasters. At the international level plans are also being developed by the British Broadcasting Corporation (BBC), as well as by other European and Japanese broadcasters, to develop global networks via satellite.[9] Finally, viewers have the option of using videocassette recorders (in 62 million households in 1990) to do their own programming.

All these developments mean that America is moving away from a broadcast era in which television signals were transmitted over the air to the wireless home receivers of a massive, heterogeneous audience. Rather, the television industry is rapidly entering an age of **narrowcasting** in which television signals are transmitted by air or direct wires to people's homes and are aimed at smaller, more narrowly defined, and more homogeneous audiences. Some viewers, then, can push their

9. See Ansolabehere et al., *Media Game,* 26–28; and Jeffrey B. Abramson, F. Christopher Arterton, and Gary R. Orren, *The Electronic Commonwealth* (New York: Basic Books, 1988), chap. 2.

remote-control buttons and choose from over sixty programming options to find the one compatible with their interests and political tastes. Some choose programming devoid of political content such as ESPN sports coverage, the Home Shopper's Network, or an old movie on a VCR; others select a channel that stresses a particular point of view such as one of the Christian broadcasting channels; and still others choose public affairs programming on CNN or C-SPAN (the Cable-Satellite Public Affairs Network, which relays the proceedings of both the House and Senate) or a prime-time investigative program on NBC. Media analyst Austin Ranney has speculated about the consequences of this new type of communications cafeteria:

> In the era of narrowcasting, people who are already highly politicized are likely to become even more so. . . . A certain amount of channel hopping will yield an even higher proportion than formerly of the kind of politics they find congenial. . . . People who are not very politicized—which is most Americans—. . . are likely to become even less so. This . . . is likely to make political interest groups even less inclined and less able to make coalitions, and to make mass publics even less concerned about whether they do.[10]

Wire Services. Newspapers and radio and television news depend heavily on wire services for a huge share of all but their local news stories. Ninety-nine percent of the daily news sources in the United States utilize the services of the two largest wire services, AP and UPI.[11] Major national newspapers such as the *New York Times, Washington Post, Los Angeles Times,* and *Chicago Tribune* also operate wire services. Wire service news stories may be used verbatim or rewritten by client papers and radio and television stations.

Ownership and Regulation of the Media

In the United States most forms of media are privately owned, profit-making businesses. As such, they operate under less government control than the media in, for example, France, Israel, and Sweden, where the national governments own and operate the major television channels. The ever-widening control of the American media by large corporate enterprises has taken several forms: *multiple ownership* of several media of the same type; *crossmedia ownership*—ownership of a combination of different types of media (Capital Cities/ABC, for exam-

10. Austin Ranney, "Broadcasting, Narrowcasting, and Politics," in *The New American Political System,* 2d ed., ed. Anthony King (Washington, D.C.: American Enterprise Institute, 1990), 201.

11. Graber, *Mass Media and American Politics,* 47.

ple, owns in addition to ABC a cable network, seven television stations, nineteen radio stations, nine daily newspapers, forty weekly newspapers, and a number of magazines); and *conglomerates*—ownership of media and other enterprises unrelated to communications (General Electric, for example, owns NBC in addition to its various manufacturing and service enterprises).[12]

FCC Regulation of the Electronic Media

Because the concentration of print media ownership has generally stopped short of violating antitrust laws, the print media are largely unregulated. Government regulation impinges much more directly, however, on the operation of the radio and television industries. The airwaves are a national resource, and only a limited number of radio and television frequencies are available. To avoid chaos, therefore, the Federal Communications Commission (FCC) licenses stations. FCC regulations fall into three categories: (1) rules limiting the number of stations controlled by a single organization; (2) rules calling for examination of the goals and performances of stations as part of their periodic licensing; and (3) rules guaranteeing fair treatment of individuals.[13]

By using its licensing power to limit the number of television stations owned by a single organization, the FCC is able to prevent high concentrations of ownership and assure the public of diverse sources of information. Thus, FCC rules state that an owner can acquire no more than one AM and FM radio station or more than one television station within the same media market. Limits also are placed on the total number of stations one owner may hold: not more than twelve AM radio stations, twelve FM radio stations, and twelve television stations. In actual practice the FCC rarely uses its power to refuse a station's license renewal application in an effort to reduce ownership concentration.

Radio and television stations are required by law to "serve the public interest, convenience, and necessity." This rather vague standard gives the FCC little guidance in determining whether to renew a station's license other than to review the mix of programs presented, the proportion of public service offerings, and the inclusion of programs for selected groups. But the agency does not try to scrutinize the contents of programs in any detail. With its limited staff, the FCC has been neither inclined nor able to rigorously define and enforce rules on programming for the public interest.

12. Ibid., 41.

13. The categories of FCC regulations are adapted from Graber, *Mass Media and American Politics*, 51.

To ensure that the airwaves are used fairly by broadcasters, the FCC implements equal time and right-of-rebuttal rules. Under the **equal time rule,** a station that gives or sells time to one candidate for a specific office must make the same opportunity available to other candidates for the same office. But the rule does not apply to regular news programs, most talk shows, and debates between candidates. The *right-of-rebuttal* rule requires stations to make their facilities available to any person who has been assailed on radio or television for purposes of rebutting the criticism.

Until 1987 radio and television stations were required to comply with the **fairness doctrine,** which required stations to give opposing views reasonable time if a controversial public issue was discussed on the air. This rule had a long history of controversy and litigation. Broadcasters were highly critical of the fairness doctrine, claiming that it actually worked against presentation of different viewpoints on issues of public policy. Indeed, they pointed out that the fairness doctrine actually encouraged stations to avoid controversial programming for fear of having to give free air time to opposing viewpoints. There also was evidence that under the fairness doctrine the media, wishing to comply with the doctrine and not risk nonrenewal of their licenses, assumed that every political issue had two sides and only two sides—a rather dubious assumption. In answer to this interpretation, CBS correspondent Bill Plante observed, "If you have somebody who's calling the president an idiot, you then almost have to have somebody who's saying, 'Well, no, he's not, he's a great statesman.'"[14] In the atmosphere of deregulation that characterized the Reagan administration, such arguments received a sympathetic hearing and the FCC abandoned the fairness doctrine. Congressional pressures and potential litigation, however, have encouraged broadcasters to permit the airing of opposing viewpoints, and the broadcast of rebuttals after presidential, gubernatorial, and mayoral addresses dealing with major public issues is now commonplace.[15]

Generally the FCC regulates the electronic media with a light hand. With its vague statutory mandate and small staff, as well as its constant buffeting by conflicting industry, congressional, and administration pressures, the agency has earned the reputation of a benign regulator.

14. Quoted by Michael J. Robinson and Margaret A. Sheehan, *Over the Wire and on TV: CBS and UPI in Campaign '80* (New York: Russell Sage Foundation, 1983), 61. Also see Austin Ranney, *Channels of Power: The Impact of Television on American Politics* (New York: Basic Books, 1983), 48–50.

15. Graber, *Mass Media and American Politics,* 69.

Even so, the broadcasting industry is vulnerable to government pressures in a way that the print industry is not. Radio and TV station licenses are not granted on a permanent basis and must be renewed every five years. Although nonrenewal is rare, the absence of a clear standard for determining whether a station has used the airwaves in a responsible manner makes the industry extremely uneasy and sensitive to the political winds blowing through the FCC and Congress.

Access to Government Information

As described in Chapter 4, the First Amendment's guarantee of freedom of the press has been interpreted as a virtual ban on government acts of prior censorship. Freedom of the press, however, is of limited value if the press does not have access to information about how the government is going about its business. In gaining such access the press has been strengthened by the 1966 Freedom of Information Act, which gives the media a strong legal basis for forcing government officials to release documents that they might prefer to keep under wraps. To prevent the release of government documents the government is required by law to demonstrate that public access to them will be harmful to the country—such as by damaging national security. The impact of the act has been limited, however, because application procedures are burdensome and most reporters tend to cover current events rather than dig into government files to report on past government actions. Nevertheless, the act has revealed some newsworthy happenings such as the involvement of American troops in the 1968 My Lai massacre of civilians in Vietnam, Central Intelligence Agency (CIA) involvement in the overthrow of Chilean president Salvador Allende in 1973, and government failures to protect the public from unsafe nuclear reactors, contaminated drinking water, and ineffective drugs.

Disagreements over just where the government should draw the line in providing the media with information almost always arise during military operations and when national security is a concern. For example, during the 1983 invasion of the small Caribbean island of Grenada where a Cuban-backed government was in control, the Reagan administration restricted the media's access to the island. Then-secretary of state George Shultz justified the restriction, recalling that

[during World War II] reporters were involved [in military operations] all along. And on the whole, they were on our side. These days, in the adversary journalism that's been developed, it seems as though the reporters are always against us and so they're always seeking to report something that's going to screw things up. And when you're trying to conduct a military operation, you don't need that.[16]

The working press was so enraged by the Pentagon's restrictions on news coverage of the Grenada invasion that later a new set of guidelines for press coverage of military actions was developed by the Department of Defense. In 1991 the controversy flared anew, however, during the early stages of the war against Iraq in the Persian Gulf. The U.S. military exercised tight control by withholding information about the extent and impact of coalition bombing, limiting press access to combat areas, and restricting interviews with troops and returning pilots. Some journalists complained that these restrictions prevented accurate reporting of the war and left the public without adequate information to assess its progress. But the military justified its actions on the grounds that they were essential to prevent the inadvertent disclosure of battle plans to the enemy and to protect the lives of combat personnel.

All this being said, government leaders are generally sensitive to the issue of media access because they rely on the media for public visibility. They then are reluctant to stir up alienation among the press corps.

The Issue of Media Bias

The media are constantly under fire about their designations of what is and is not newsworthy and their fairness and objectivity in reporting the news. News reporters are subject to two kinds of bias. The first is political bias—unbalanced or slanted news coverage of issues, candidates, or political parties stemming from a reporter's personal attitudes. The second is structural bias—an orientation toward news coverage and content that stems from the nature of the communications industry and the news-gathering process.[17]

Thunder on the Right and Thunder on the Left: Political Bias

Conservatives often accuse the media of having a liberal bias. In a blistering attack in 1969 former vice president Spiro Agnew singled out "the effete Eastern liberal press"—a "tiny and enclosed fraternity of privileged men, elected by no one"—for undermining public support for the Nixon administration and its policies.[18] The political Right's continuing concern about liberal bias was reflected as well in the 1980s

16. Quoted by David S. Broder, *Behind the Front Page: A Candid Look at How the News Is Made* (New York: Simon and Schuster, 1987), 305.

17. Ranney, *Channels of Power*, 35–36.

18. Quoted by Ranney, ibid., 32.

Campaign 1992: Negative Coverage of Bush, But Was It Media Bias?

The Center for Media and Public Affairs analyzed every evaluation of the presidential candidates made by a voter, party official, or policy expert who was interviewed on ABC, CBS, and NBC newscasts between Labor Day and election day. As is shown below, the evening news programs showed a greater tendency to carry negative comments about George Bush than about Bill Clinton or Ross Perot.

Percent of All Remarks by Persons Interviewed on ABC, CBS, and NBC Evening News Programs that Were Negative

Negative remarks included those on such things as candidates' abilities to govern, proposals, and actions. They did not include remarks on the "horse race"—for example, the candidates' standings in the polls or how the campaign was going.

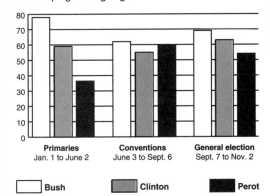

Source: Center for Media and Public Affairs, reported in *New York Times*, Nov. 22, 1992, E3, National edition. Copyright © 1993 by The New York Times Company. Reprinted by permission.

But can this be attributed to media bias? While there is a general consensus that news coverage on the whole helped Clinton, journalists and academic observers disagree about whether or not bias played a role.

Most journalists deny that any bias was involved. They assert that candidates acquire negative coverage the hard way: they earn it. Accordingly, Al Hunt, the *Wall Street Journal*'s Washington bureau chief, observed that "it's guaranteed that if an incumbent president is running behind, his people will blame the messenger. This is totally predictable. Anyone who thinks George Bush has gotten tougher press than Bill Clinton this year has been doing a great imitation of Rip Van Winkle." And since press coverage was criticized by Republicans, Democrats, and Ross Perot, NBC News anchor Tom Brokaw suggests that "bias, like beauty, is most often in the eye of the beholder."

Eleanor Clift of *Newsweek*, however, has suggested that "the press . . . [was] willing to cut Clinton some slack be-cause they like[d] him and what he . . . [had] to say." And Strobe Talbott, editor-at-large for *Time* and long-time friend of Clinton, advised his readers, "I've been prepared to acknowledge the bias of friendship the first time Clinton's name appeared under my byline."[1]

In 1992 the media's tendency to focus on the problems of the economy meant that Bush, as the incumbent, was inevitably in for a lot of critical coverage. Political scientist Everett Carll Ladd has commented that "an uninterrupted stream of negative press reports and commentary on the economy that left much of the nation in a state of bewilderment and frustration" was "the most important political event of the 1992 campaign."[2]

1. *National Journal*, October 3, 1992, 2245-2247.
2. Everett Carll Ladd, "The 1992 Vote for President Clinton," *Political Science Quarterly* 108 (Spring 1993): 20-21.

campaign by Sen. Jesse Helms (R-N.C.) to have conservatives gain control of CBS by buying up its stock.

Conservatives and Republicans are not the only ones to question the objectivity of the media. The political Left has voiced its doubts as well. President Jimmy Carter's press secretary, Jody Powell, argued that reporters are harder on Democratic presidents than on Republican presidents.[19] Other media-watchers have charged that the media are

19. Jody Powell, *The Other Side of the Story: An Insider's View of the Carter Administration* (New York: William Morrow, 1984).

biased against liberal and radical leaders and their causes. According to this argument, the media are owned by profit-motivated businesspeople who find it in their interest to use their influence to maintain the status quo. It is charged therefore that the media fail to report antiestablishment ideas and movements and use entertainment—sitcoms, cop shows, and sports—to prevent the public from questioning and challenging mainstream politics.[20]

Journalists' Personal Attitudes. Conservatives often base their charges of media bias on surveys that consistently reveal that journalists are more liberal in their attitudes than the general public or other college-educated professionals. Liberalism, a preference for an internationalist foreign policy, caution about military intervention, and suspicion about the ethics of big government and big business are especially pronounced among the most elite and influential in the national media.[21] In a 1992 survey the 44 percent of journalists with a Democratic party identification far outnumbered those who considered themselves Republicans (16 percent).[22] This preference for the Democrats is also reflected in surveys that since 1964 have shown a substantial majority of journalists favoring Democratic presidential nominees. While revealing the political orientation of people in the news business, these data do not prove that newspeople are guilty of biased reporting. To prove bias it must be demonstrated that journalists act in accordance with their ideological or partisan orientations.

Do the Media Give a Partisan or Ideological Slant to the News? The most thorough studies of possible media bias have been analyses of television coverage of presidential campaigns. Media researcher Michael Robinson and his associates concluded after an exhaustive study of television's coverage of presidential campaigns that there was no continuing or consistent partisan or candidate bias. Nor did the selection of stories to be covered reveal a consistent bias.[23] As political scien-

20. The leftist critique of the media is summarized by Ranney, *Channels of Power,* 39–42. Also see Robert Cirino, *Don't Blame the People* (New York: Random House, 1972); and Nicholas Johnson, *How to Talk to Your Television Set* (Boston: Atlantic-Little, Brown, 1970).

21. See S. Robert Lichter, Stanley Rothman, and Linda S. Lichter, *The Media Elite: America's New Powerbrokers* (New York: Adler and Adler, 1986); G. Cleveland Wilhoit and David H. Weaver, *The American Journalist: A Portrait of U.S. News People and Their Work* (Bloomington: Indiana University Press, 1991); and Graber, *Mass Media in American Politics,* 104–107.

22. William Glaberson, "More Reporters Leaning Democratic, Study Says," *New York Times,* Nov. 18, 1992, A13, National edition.

23. Michael J. Robinson, "Just How Liberal Is the News? 1980 Revisited," *Public Opinion,* February/March 1983, 55–66. Also see Robinson and Sheehan, *Over the Wire*

tist James Q. Wilson has noted, "Ideology exists, but reporters, though liberals, are not ideologues, and ideology can be combated by public pressure."[24]

A variety of forces work against political bias in the media. One counterforce against potential liberal bias stemming from reporters' political views is the generally more conservative political orientation of the owners, managers, and editors who direct the flow of the news by deciding which events will be covered and how stories will be handled.[25]

Both the economics and professional norms of the industry also work against political bias by either management or reporters. Unlike the media owners of an earlier era, today's owners and managers generally believe that it is their responsibility to provide their readers or viewers with information, not to indoctrinate them. But there are other compelling reasons why they do not dictate news content and tone of coverage to their correspondents. Media owners are interested in the profits produced when there is a large audience for their product. They do not want to alienate readers or viewers by offering them biased news coverage.

The increasing level of professionalism found in the newsroom reduces publisher/owner-induced bias as well. Professional reporters tend to be independent-minded and unlikely to accept owners' political dictates. For example, David Broder of the *Washington Post* has observed that had his paper's management bowed to pressure from the Nixon administration to call off the investigation of the 1972 Watergate scandal, "it would have caused a newsroom rebellion that might have damaged the *Post*'s credibility far more than any political or commercial pressure from the administration."[26]

Journalism's professional norms also have a disciplinary impact on reporters. One moves up in the profession by demonstrating reporting skills, not ideological purity. To climb to a prominent position with a television network or national newspaper, a reporter must undergo a long and demanding process of peer assessment and screening. As Michael Robinson has observed, "If you show much ideological bias in network journalism . . . you're going to be out of a job because there are

---

and on TV. A study of the 1972 campaign also found an absence of ideological and partisan bias; see C. Richard Hoffstetter, *Bias in the News* (Columbus: Ohio State University Press, 1976).

24. James Q. Wilson, "Stage Struck," *New Republic*, June 21, 1993, 33.

25. William Schneider and I. A. Lewis, "Views on the News," *Public Opinion*, August/September 1985, 8.

26. Broder, *Behind the Front Page*, 325.

bigger questions here to be resolved at the network level than whether you can as a journalist express your point of view."[27]

The Antipolitician Bias. Most social scientists and journalists reject the charge that the media exhibit ideological or partisan bias in news coverage. Media analysts, however, believe that reporters have a skeptical and even cynical attitude toward politics and politicians and that these feelings are reflected in their news coverage.

Reporters tend to view politics as a game in which one side wins and the other loses, not as a process for resolving conflicts or distributing values within society. Politicians are viewed as players whose basic motives are simple enough: to win elections and to hold power.[28] The muckraking tradition is still strong among journalists. Their working hypothesis is that politicians are suspect; therefore, the journalist's job is to ferret out wrongdoing, strip politicians of their disguises, debunk their claims, and pierce their rhetoric. The media's skeptical and often adversarial attitude toward politicians has been defended on the grounds that it serves the public interest by keeping people informed about what is really happening, by raising troublesome issues that politicians might prefer to ignore, and by preventing abuses of power. The media serve as the public's watch dog, it is claimed. Some political scientists, however, see potential adverse consequences stemming from the media's generally antipolitician orientation. Since the 1960s, for example, public trust in government institutions has declined. This decline has multiple sources—among others, the divisiveness of the Vietnam War, the Watergate scandal, and double-digit inflation during the 1970s; the Iran-contra affair of the 1980s; and the revelations of House members bouncing checks and not paying their House restaurant tabs in the 1990s. Austin Ranney believes that television's portrayal of politics has been a contributing factor as well.[29]

Structural Bias

The nature of the communications industry and the processes of news gathering have introduced a number of well-verified structural biases into news coverage.

Deciding What Is News. The masthead of the *New York Times* pro-

27. Michael J. Robinson, quoted from an interview taped by the Department of Governmental Affairs, University of Wisconsin-Madison, July 1987.

28. See Ranney, *Channels of Power,* 58–61; and Edward Jay Epstein, *The News from Nowhere* (New York: Random House, 1973), 215.

29. Ranney, *Channels of Power,* 74–79. Also see Michael J. Robinson, "American Political Legitimacy in an Era of Electronic Journalism," in *Television as a Social Force,* ed. Douglass Cater and Richard Adler (New York: Praeger, 1975), 113–114; Epstein, *News from Nowhere,* 215–217; and Wilson, "Stage Struck," 33, 36.

claims that the paper contains "All the News That's Fit to Print." But even as complete a paper as the *Times* cannot fulfill this goal. There is simply too much happening in the world, and more stories are filed by reporters than can be carried in either the print or electronic media. Thus, within all news organizations there are gatekeepers—city editors, national news editors, editors-in-chief, film editors, executive producers—who decide what is printed in the papers and aired on television and radio. Their decisions about what is news determine to a significant extent the pictures of reality that Americans carry around in their heads.

The primary criterion used by newspeople in selecting news stories is their audience appeal—not their political impact, educational value, or social purpose. Other criteria are whether the story concerns violence, conflict, disaster, or scandal; whether it involves a familiar person or situation (one reason the Kennedy family has provided much fodder for news stories); whether it is a story close to home (newspapers and local television and radio stations devote roughly three-fourths of their coverage to local events); and whether it is timely and novel.[30]

What gets reported also is affected by accessibility—the feasibility and cost of covering an event or issue. For example, it is both convenient and relatively inexpensive for ABC News to rely on officials in Washington for their stories, in contrast to the difficulties and expense involved in covering ethnic strife between Armenia and Azerbaijan.

News organizations also tend to select stories that are appropriate or a good "fit" for the particular medium and audience. Thus, the print and television media have different standards for what is appropriate. Network television prefers fast-moving, colorful stories with good visuals—for example, a line of police cars following O. J. Simpson on a bizarre sixty-mile trek over the Los Angeles freeways following the 1994 murder of his ex-wife and her friend. But this kind of story would not have been of major interest to the *Wall Street Journal,* which emphasizes business news and more in-depth coverage of issues. Similarly, the needs of national and local television are quite different. For local stations the weather is a major component of their newscasts. But national news programs ignore the weather except when a section of the country is particularly hard-hit, as was the case when floods overran the Midwest in the summer of 1993.[31]

30. These criteria were identified by Graber, *Mass Media and American Politics,* 116–120.

31. On the criteria of accessibility and appropriateness, see Ansolabehere et al., *Media Game,* 51.

Table 9.2 Network Television News Characteristics

Story Length (seconds)	%	Picture Exposure (seconds)	%	Number of Pictures	%
Less than 60	29	1–10	47	1–4	38
60–179	47	11–20	29	5–10	13
180–299	16	21–30	12	11–20	26
300+	8	31+	13	21–54	23

Source: Doris A. Graber, *Mass Media and American Politics,* 4th ed. (Washington, D.C.: CQ Press, 1993), 228. Author's research based on a sample of 149 news stories from early evening newscasts on ABC, CBS, and NBC.

With such criteria being used to select news stories, it is inevitable that the media are giving the public a world view that is incomplete, simplified, and a bit distorted. But this is not the result of some conscious plot or conspiracy on the part of the media's gatekeepers or reporters. Rather, distortion is introduced in the effort to create a sizable audience for the media's product.

Time and Space Constraints. The totality and complexity of the human experience, and of politics in particular, just cannot be captured in a half-hour telecast or a page of national news. For television, the public's most important news source, time limitations and powerful commercial dictates have spurred it to become a "headline news service," providing something equivalent to the headline and first and second paragraphs of a newspaper story.

Television news tends to be presented in episodic bits that depict public issues in terms of concrete events or the experiences of specific individuals (for example, a presidential news conference, the plight of a flood-stricken family, or the arrest of terrorist bombers)—see Table 9.2 on the length of TV news stories. This kind of on-the-scene coverage is frequently fast-paced and visually compelling (that is, "good pictures"). But with its emphasis on episodic coverage, TV news has little time for thematic presentations that provide background information and indepth analyses of complex issues such as the Middle East peace process, health care reform, fiscal policy, or conflicts between loggers and environmentalists in the Northwest. Nor do the networks, always concerned about their audience rating, have much commercial incentive to provide backgrounder-type programming. Backgrounders are normal-

In an attempt to appeal to a mobile television generation, the national daily USA Today *relies on concise reporting, information graphics, color photographs, and organized layouts to help readers find and follow stories.*

ly characterized by "talking heads" and therefore lack the compelling visuals of episodic stories.[32]

With in-depth analyses largely precluded from their programs, news editors and producers have recognized the benefits of presenting news stories as part of a larger, ongoing story. In the early 1980s such a continuity theme was the "Reagan Revolution." And in the 1990s it has been the legacy of problems created by 1980s policies and solutions to unemployment. An extremely important part of television production is therefore the selecting, editing, and interpreting of material so that thirty-second and two-minute sound bites will make sense to the viewer. Unless continuity and meaning can be established quickly, viewer interest may be lost.[33]

The print media, of course, must undergo the same process, but they are not subject to the same tight time/space constraints as television and can cover a wider range of events and give more play to their context. But even in the newspaper business a tremendous pressure is on to be concise and to give only bare-bones coverage to public affairs. The successful national daily *USA Today* illustrates this pattern.

Reliance on Politicians as News Sources. Whenever the media must depend heavily on political leaders for information, the content and

32. Ibid., 50–51.
33. Ranney, *Channels of Power*, 46–47.

tone of news stories are bound to be affected. Reporters are naturally reluctant to alienate the powerful news sources with whom they must deal on a day-to-day basis. They also are vulnerable to manipulation by political leaders, who may try to co-opt them through exclusive stories, background briefings, regular access, or friendly gestures.

Politicians also try to shape the flow of news. This is particularly true of presidents because their political influence depends heavily on the support they receive from the American people. Thus, one of the responsibilities of David Gergen, a former director of communications to President Reagan, when he joined the Clinton White House staff in the summer of 1993 was to improve its press relations and the ability of the president to get his message out to the public. Soon after coming on board Gergen arranged for Clinton's first news conference in the East Room—an event that featured charts (much as Reagan had done) designed to defend the president's economic program. Gergen also made fuller use of the White House pressroom for advocacy by dispatching there Secretary of the Treasury Lloyd Bentsen and Budget Director Leon Panetta to push the president's economic package; set up a speech at Northeastern University in Boston and a radio address that sought to shift the debate over the president's program from a struggle between the White House and congressional Democrats to a fight between Clinton and the Republicans; and reopened the press secretary's office area to reporters. An admiring colleague noted, "He knows when an issue's ripening and how to stage things to get our sound bites and message across."[34]

Is There Media Bias?

Although the issue of media bias is normally posed in partisan or ideological terms, social science studies provide little support for a consistent pattern of media bias favoring particular parties, candidates, or issues. There is, in other words, no conspiracy afoot to manipulate public opinion to bring it into conformity with that of the professionals who work for the media. There are, however, structural forces inherent in the communications industry and in news gathering that substantially affect the news content. Decisions by the media about what constitutes news, for example, determine in part what information reaches the public. But as revealed in the next section, it is important to keep in mind that the media play a larger role in conveying information than they do in shaping attitudes and opinions. Many who gain information from the media use it as a point of departure for formulating their own

34. Fred Barnes, "Whirling Gergen," *New Republic,* June 19 and 26, 1993, 10–12.

opinions. And some readers and viewers either reject or ignore any opinions and attitudes conveyed explicitly or implicitly by the media.[35]

The Impact of the Media on Politics

Although it is widely accepted that the media profoundly affect people's attitudes and the operation of the political system, attempts to establish a direct link between media coverage and people's attitudes and government action have proven difficult and controversial. Two presidential commissions, for example, have produced contradictory conclusions about the impact of sexual stimuli in the media on the incidence of deviant behavior such as rape or child abuse. The assessment of the media's impact that follows examines its bearing on public opinion, the public agenda, and the electoral process.

Do the Media Affect Public Attitudes?

The media are a major source of information and news for Americans, yet in spite of their heavy exposure to the media, people remain relatively uninformed about political events.[36] In July 1993, for example, a *New York Times*/CBS poll revealed that 49 percent of Americans had not heard anything about the North American Free Trade Agreement (NAFTA) even though it had been a major issue in the 1992 presidential election, a favorite target of Ross Perot after the election, and the subject of a steady stream of news stories for over a year. Moreover, once president, Clinton had frequently endorsed NAFTA, whereas a number of labor unions had mobilized to defeat the agreement, opposed by business groups intent on seeing it implemented.[37] How can public ignorance of politics continue to thrive with such widespread coverage? Is it possible that the media have no influence on the public and politics?

The impact of television, radio, newspapers, and the like on public attitudes is limited by people's selective exposure and attention to them. Viewers, listeners, and readers tend to avoid information that upsets their peace of mind, offends their political and social tastes, or conflicts with information, attitudes, and feelings they already have. In addition, many people watch the television news, for example, while doing other things such as preparing dinner, caring for children—or

35. Ibid., 212–216; and Doris A. Graber, *Processing the News: How People Tame the Information Tide,* 2d ed. (New York: Longman, 1988), 90–93.

36. L. Harmon Zeigler and William Haltom, "More Bad News about the News," *Public Opinion,* May/June 1989, 50–52.

37. Keith Bradsher, "Free Trade Pact Is Still a Mystery to Many in U.S.," *New York Times,* July 12, 1993, A1, C3, National edition.

even reading the newspaper! These distractions can diminish the media's impact. An individual's lack of interest in politics also may limit the media's capacity to influence his or her opinion as does the distrust of the media that exists among some elements of society. Some whites, police, and union members view the media with a jaundiced eye because they believe the media tend to improperly cast the police as oppressors of the disadvantaged and the unions as corrupt and barriers to economic progress.

How the media present the news can diminish its impact as well. Television news programs bombard viewers with fifteen to eighteen news stories—unconnected snippets of three minutes or less—in half an hour. The public is thus given more news than it can handle. Furthermore, much of the news is touted as being important, but it actually may be quite trivial. The net effect can be numbness and boredom.[38]

But even with these limitations, the media are capable of moving public opinion. For example, public approval of the president is highly volatile and has been found to be related to whether the news media are reporting stories that are favorable or unfavorable to the president.[39] In a study that compared changes in public opinion on eighty domestic and foreign issues with the positions taken by a variety of information sources—television news commentators, interest groups, the president, and political parties—researchers found that television news commentators were capable of moving public opinion by as much as 4 percentage points.[40] Similarly, the ups and downs of the public's evaluations of presidents are affected by cues provided by the media. The greater the coverage accorded to presidential critics, the more the president's popularity is apt to drop. Thus, President Bush's popularity surged during the Gulf War of 1991 while congressional Democrats were silent. But when criticism picked up later in the year and was reported in the media, Bush's popular support began to decline.[41]

Finally, just the way in which the media present issues also can affect the public's thinking. People's explanations for the causes of such national problems as poverty, unemployment, and terrorism have been

38. Graber, *Mass Media and American Politics,* 212–229.

39. Richard A. Brody and Benjamin I. Page, "The Impact of Events on Presidential Popularity: The Johnson and Nixon Administrations," in *Perspectives on the Presidency,* ed. Aaron Wildavsky (Boston: Little, Brown, 1975), 136–148.

40. Benjamin I. Page, Robert Y. Shapiro, and Glenn R. Dempsey, "What Moves Public Opinion?" *American Political Science Review* 81 (March 1987): 23–43.

41. Research of Richard Brody, "Crisis, War, and Public Opinion: The Media and Public Support for the President in Two Phases of the Confrontation in the Persian Gulf," reported in Ansolabehere et al., *Media Game,* 200–201.

shown to be related to how these issues were depicted on television. Moreover, people's explanations for these problems affect their assessments of presidential performance. Those who attributed poverty to the poor being insufficiently motivated were more likely to give a favorable assessment of presidential performance than those who viewed the primary cause of the problem as government policies or societal trends.[42]

The Media as Agenda Setter

According to some political scientists, the media play a particularly big role in determining which issues are put on the **public agenda**—the issues of concern to the public and worthy of government attention. By covering some events, problems, and issues and ignoring others the news media help to determine the priority Americans give to various issues.[43] The importance the media attach to a story is communicated through such cues as banner headlines, front page placement, lead story placement on television, and frequent, repeated coverage. For example, repetitious and often lead story coverage of the American hostages in Iran during the last year of the Carter administration helped to keep the hostage issue on the public's front burner. As Bernard Cohen has observed, "The press is significantly more than a purveyor of information and opinion. It may not be successful in telling its readers what to think, but it is stunningly successful in telling its readers what to think *about*."[44]

Political leaders follow the news closely, especially that provided by the major television networks and such national papers as the *New York Times, Washington Post,* and *Wall Street Journal.* Indeed, the president and senior White House aides receive a daily summary of the news and how it was covered by the major media outlets. Issues worthy of the attention of these outlets often find their way onto the public agenda. For example, the coverage accorded by the media in 1992 to the starvation and anarchy in Somalia pushed this problem onto the public agenda and helped to prompt the U.S. government, in conjunction with the United Nations, to embark on a humanitarian program to provide food and to restore civil order.

But while the media may set a policy agenda, the public does not

42. Shanto Iyengar, "Television News and Citizens' Explanations of National Affairs," *American Political Science Review* 81 (September 1987): 815–831.

43. See Graber, *Mass Media and American Politics,* 182–190, 216–217; and Shanto Iyengar and Donald R. Kinder, *News That Matters: TV and American Opinion* (Chicago: University of Chicago Press, 1987).

44. Bernard Cohen, *The Press and Foreign Policy* (Princeton, N.J.: Princeton University Press, 1963), 13.

necessarily follow it slavishly. Past and current experiences, discussions with friends and family, and independent reasoning also have an impact on people's political priorities. Media guidance tends to apply most to issues not yet subject to widespread discussion or to issues beyond people's personal experiences.

Media Coverage of Elections

Because media coverage is essential in a campaign for a major office, campaigns are structured to generate maximum media visibility and present the candidate in a positive light (also see Chapter 7, Elections, Campaigns, and Voters). National nominating conventions are now programmed for national television and their sessions scheduled for broadcast during prime evening viewing hours. Political parties use their ready access to the media during the conventions to showcase their candidates and kick off the general election campaigns. After the conventions media events are staged regularly to gain media attention and get a minute or two on evening news programs.

President Ronald Reagan's campaign managers in 1984 were particularly adept at creating settings for campaign events that evoked positive images of the president. Lesley Stahl of CBS News reported that after the network aired a piece in which she gave a particularly biting commentary about Reagan avoiding serious discussion of issues, she actually got a call from Michael Deaver, Reagan's media adviser, saying he loved the piece. A surprised Stahl asked how he could love such a critical news story. Deaver replied, "Haven't you figured it out yet? The public doesn't pay attention to what you say. They just look at the pictures." Later, when Stahl replayed the tapes with the sound turned off, she realized that she had prepared a "magnificent montage of Reagan in a series of wonderful, upbeat scenes, with flags, balloons, children, and adoring supporters—virtually an unpaid commercial."[45] In addition to television's quest for "good visuals," other patterns characterize media coverage of elections, such as emphasizing slogans, the "horse race," and "campaign issues."

The rhetoric of candidates is filled with references to substantive domestic and foreign policy issues. In 1992, for example, Bill Clinton campaigned on themes of economic growth and health care reform; George Bush stressed continuity; and Perot emphasized reducing the budget deficit. Their stump speeches were finely tuned to embody policy positions. Reporters, however, do not find the policy statements of the candidates particularly newsworthy. They prefer clear-cut issues that neatly divide the candidates, provoke controversy, seem to rest on prin-

45. Broder, *Behind the Front Page*, 181–182.

ciple, and can be stated in simple terms. It has been argued, for example, that a turning point in the 1988 presidential campaign occurred when Bush recognized that serious discussion would not carry him far in news coverage and that a dramatic phrase like "Read my lips—no new taxes!" was needed. And in 1992 candidate Bill Clinton used shorthand phrases to relate to voter concerns about jobs and welfare as he promised to "grow the economy" and "end welfare as we know it." Candidates' issue positions tend to become newsworthy only after they have assumed a stylized, slogan-like form.[46] The television networks, by the way, do not accord presidential candidates much air time for statements—slogan or no slogan. Between 1968 and 1992 the average length of a statement made by a presidential candidate on the evening news broadcasts fell from forty-two seconds to less than nine seconds.[47] In campaigns for state and congressional offices, local stations also severely restrict the air time devoted to the statements of candidates.

In its emphasis on the "horse race" aspects of the campaign, election coverage tends to resemble that used for sporting events. The stress on who's ahead, who's behind, who's gaining, who's falling back, and candidate strategies reflects the public's relatively low level of interest in issues, offset by the media's efforts to provide drama and generate interest in and an audience for their product.

The media focus as well on "campaign issues"—concerns about how the campaigns are being run, the performances of the candidates and their staffs, and the personal qualities of the candidates. In 1984, for example, 40 percent of television news coverage focused on campaign issues: Reagan's age, his lack of availability to the press, his ties to fundamentalist preachers, and the family finances of Democratic vice-presidential candidate Geraldine Ferraro.[48]

The tendency toward coverage of campaign issues was particularly marked in 1992, when a highly critical tone characterized the reports on campaign advertising. As politicians have turned increasingly to a strategy of attack advertising, ad-watch reporting has become a standard feature of campaign coverage. In fact, in the process of assessing the veracity of campaign advertising, reporters have taken on the role traditionally assigned to the traveling "truth squads" of the opposition party. As advocates, candidates, not surprisingly, tend to slant the facts

46. Thomas E. Patterson, "The Press and Its Missed Assignment," in *The Elections of 1988*, ed. Michael Nelson (Washington, D.C.: CQ Press, 1989), 101–102.

47. Data of Kiku Adatto, reported by Wilson, "Stage Struck," 30–31.

48. Maura Clancey and Michael J. Robinson, "General Election Coverage: Part I," in *The Mass Media in Campaign '84*, ed. Michael J. Robinson and Austin Ranney (Washington, D.C.: American Enterprise Institute, 1985), 29–30.

30-Second Politics

Candidate: PRESIDENT BUSH

Contest:	Georgia primary
Producer:	Mike Murphy, Don Sipple, and Alex Castellanos
Time:	30 seconds

Audio: When Pat Buchanan attacks President Bush, remember: Two networks found him guilty of false and misleading advertising. And Buchanan's record? He opposed Operation Desert Storm. His isolationism threatens thousands of Georgia jobs. And he even said women are less equipped psychologically to succeed in the workplace. Pat Buchanan. Isolationist. Wrong on the economy. Wrong on Desert Storm. Wrong for America.

Background: This counterattack ad attempts to neutralize Buchanan's negative barrage by citing the verdicts of NBC and CNN. Encouraged by research showing that Buchanan scares some women voters, it also unearths a damaging 1983 Buchanan column about women. But the ad is blatantly misleading in flashing on the screen a claim that Buchanan would threaten 164,000 Georgia jobs. This assumes that Buchanan's tough talk on trade would somehow jeopardize every last dollar of Georgia's $7.2 billion in annual exports. Bush spokeswoman Torie Clarke defends the charge by saying Buchanan would "put up a protectionist wall around this country and shut down trade."

Source: © 1992, The Washington Post. Reprinted with permission.

The 1992 presidential primary and general election campaigns featured ad-watch journalism as the media sought to inform voters about the accuracy of the candidates' 30-second television advertisements. Above is a Washington Post *analysis of an ad used by the George Bush campaign that is critical of Bush's opponent in the Georgia presidential primary, Pat Buchanan.*

and arguments to suit their own needs. But reporters, being inherently suspicious of politicians, are quick to point out that this type of advertising smacks of misleading distortion.

In the 1992 campaign, to demonstrate their objectivity, reporters were critical of both the Clinton and Bush ads.[49] Indeed, ad-watch journalism appears to have forced politicians to contemplate the veracity of their ads and to provide documentation for their claims because they knew the accuracy of their ads would be challenged. But ad-watch journalism did not stop attack advertising or give voters much in the way of additional perspective with which to view ads.[50] Media critics contend that the emphasis on the horse race and campaign issues, especially by television, tends to trivialize elections. According to political scientist James Q. Wilson, instead of "carefully summarizing the candidates' views and analyzing the fit between those views and the facts of some policy issue," political reporters have become "theater critics," commenting on the image-making efforts of the candidates and their managers. He goes on to assert that by emphasizing the theatricality of campaigns, the media have given campaign managers even more incentive to stage theatrical events for the cameras.[51]

Finally, in covering campaigns reporters often add a "spin" to their stories, giving the story a tone or embellishing the facts. Content analysis of campaign reports reveals which candidates tend to be favored or disadvantaged by reporters' spins.[52] The emphasis on economic woes in 1992 news reports was damaging to the incumbent president, George Bush, but earlier, in 1988, the media spin favored Bush. Analyses of *Time* and *Newsweek* election coverage revealed that in 1988 the coverage of George Bush was initially negative (a *Newsweek* cover story even featured his alleged "wimp" image) and then became positive after he emerged from President Reagan's shadow at the Republican convention. By contrast, Michael Dukakis's early press coverage was generally positive, but then it took a negative turn as news reports zeroed in on his icy personality and his problems in becoming a credible candidate when his popularity began to slip and he fell behind Bush in the polls

49. For analysis of how the media cover campaign advertising, see Darrell M. West, *Air Wars: Television Advertising in Election Campaigns, 1952-1992* (Washington, D.C.: CQ Inc., 1993), chap. 4.

50. F. Christopher Arterton, "Campaign '92: Strategies and Tactics of the Candidates," in *The Election of 1992: Reports and Interpretations,* ed. Gerald M. Pomper (Chatham, N.J.: Chatham House, 1993), 100-101.

51. Wilson, "Stage Struck," 31-32.

52. See, for example, the analysis of "spin" in the 1984 presidential campaign by Clancey and Robinson, "General Election Coverage: Part I," 31-35.

(see Figure 9.2). The changing nature of candidate coverage in 1988 raises the intriguing, but as yet unresolved, question of whether journalists' evaluations of candidates reflect voters' assessments or actually influence voters' perceptions.[53]

Impact of the Media on the Voters

In the 1940s, before the introduction of television into political campaigning, the media apparently had little impact on voters' decisions. Researchers believed that the media mainly *reinforced* the partisan loyalties or predispositions of voters. Although the capacity of the media to reinforce people's attitudes is important, reinforcement implies that there were initial predispositions to be strengthened and that these predispositions were often partisan loyalties.[54] As Chapter 7 revealed, however, partisan considerations are less important in guiding voter choices today than in the 1940s and 1950s, presenting fewer opportunities for the media, through their coverage of candidates and campaigns, to reinforce voters' partisan inclinations. With voters now showing weaker attachments to parties, could it be that the media have a greater potential to affect voter choice?

Like the classic studies of the 1940s, however, contemporary research has found that the media have little effect on voter preference. In particular, studies have demonstrated that regular viewing of network news has no effect on voters' awareness of candidates, yet viewing of political commercials is associated with higher voter awareness of candidates' issue stances. The simple explanation for the difference in issue awareness associated with viewing network news versus paid advertisements is that political commercials contain more information about the issues than nightly news programs.[55]

The tendency noted in Chapter 7 of approximately two-thirds of voters to decide on their choice for president by the close of the national conventions and before the general election campaign officially begins further limits the impact of media coverage of the general election on voter choice. In close elections, however, media coverage that sways even a small percentage of voters can be crucial.

The real importance of the media is not in changing people's votes.

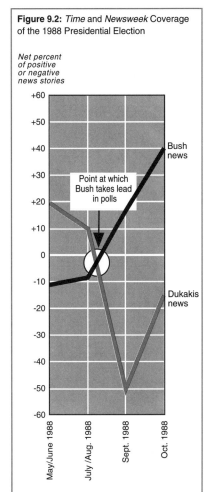

Figure 9.2: *Time* and *Newsweek* Coverage of the 1988 Presidential Election

Net percent of positive or negative news stories

Source: Thomas E. Patterson, "The Press and Its Missed Assignment," in *The Elections of 1988*, ed. Michael Nelson (Washington, D.C.: CQ Press, 1989), 107.
  Note: "Bush news" and "Dukakis news" figures are the differences between the percentage of positive and percentage of negative news references to Bush and Dukakis, respectively, for the time period indicated.

53. Patterson, "The Press and Its Missed Assignment," 105–106.

54. See Bernard Berelson, Paul Lazarsfeld, and William McPhee, *Voting* (Chicago: University of Chicago Press, 1954).

55. Research on the impact of the media on voter choice is ably summarized by Herbert B. Asher, *Presidential Elections and American Politics,* 5th ed. (Pacific Grove, Calif.: Brooks/Cole, 1992), 251–259; and by Graber, *Mass Media and American Politics,* 275–281.

Rather, long before the formal campaigning begins, media interpretations of the significance of issues can shape the political and emotional context of an election. The media also can shape and reinforce people's predispositions toward candidates.[56] For example, the many Democrats who decided early in 1972 that they would not support their party's nominee, George McGovern, did so based on information and images conveyed to them by the media. Walter Mondale, the 1984 Democratic nominee, was hurt by preconvention news stories portraying him as dominated by special interests.[57]

The role of the media in setting the agenda for an election and in framing responsibility for the state of the Union was demonstrated in 1991 and 1992. During the Persian Gulf War Americans were distracted from domestic concerns as they watched with fascination the war unfolding in the Middle East. The prominent play given to defense and foreign policy concerns by the media meant that for this period the most important criterion for evaluating the president was his performance in foreign affairs. In this context of military success President Bush was accorded high marks.[58] But after the war, when media coverage emphasized economic adversity at home and policy gridlock in Washington, the criteria for evaluation shifted to domestic concerns and the president was evaluated harshly. The content and emphasis of news reporting thus are significant because they help to create the context within which voters' choices are made.

Paid Media

Following the 1968 presidential campaign, Joe McGinnis published a best-seller, *The Selling of the President,* which was based on the thesis that it was possible to buy the presidency with television ads—after all, he claimed, winner Richard Nixon had fooled the public through slick advertising. The McGinnis thesis rapidly found its fans, especially among supporters of losing presidential candidates. Political scientists, however, have not uncovered convincing evidence that paid media advertising has a significant effect on voter choice in presidential elections. Nor does the level of spending on commercials appear to affect voters in presidential elections. In a study of the 1988 presidential campaign, media expert Michael Robinson and his associates compared the Bush campaign's week-by-week paid media buys with the candidate's standing in the polls and found no significant correlations.[59]

56. Graber, *Mass Media and American Politics,* 280.

57. Asher, *Presidential Elections and American Politics,* 253.

58. Ansolabehere et al., *Media Game,* 148.

59. Michael Robinson, Clyde Wilcox, and Paul Marshall, "The Presidency: Not for Sale," *Public Opinion,* March/April 1989, 49–53.

The ability of the paid media to raise the visibility of a candidate and permit relatively unknown candidates to build support among the electorate is not relevant in a presidential election where both candidates receive extensive news media coverage. But in elections that receive little press attention, paid media can be important. Media expenditures by challengers for House seats, for example, enable them to be better known and to compete with the generally more visible and familiar congressional incumbents. Indeed, such expenditures, the largest share of which goes for advertising, are related to the percentage of the vote received by House challengers. Thus, as challengers' expenditures increase, their share of the vote also goes up.

Interestingly, paid advertising seems to be most effective in campaigns for and against ballot propositions—lawmaking by popular referendums, which is permitted in some states (most noticeably California). When party identification is not a factor, no candidates are on hand to provide a human embodiment of policy directions, and public knowledge of the issues is at its usual low level, political advertising can have a maximum influence. In these circumstances ads can effectively portray the nature and consequences of the proposition and help to crystallize public opinion.[60]

The Media and Government Institutions

The news media cover more aspects of politics than just electoral campaigns; government institutions, public officials, and the processes of decision making are fair game as well. No matter which branch of the government the media happen to be covering, tension inevitably arises between public officials and reporters. Reporters are out to get the real story on what is going on in the government, but political leaders frequently find that reporters' quests for stories serve neither their career interests nor the causes they support. Conflict also arises when public officials try to use or manipulate the media to gain the public support needed to stay in office and implement many policies. The media, however, see themselves as an independent force and not as a willing helpmate of politicians.

Conflicts between public officials and reporters intensified after the events of the 1960s and 1970s. During the Vietnam War and the Watergate crisis, reporters felt that they had been misled and lied to by Presidents Johnson and Nixon. This led to a breakdown of trust between reporters and public officials, with the result that the media challenged

60. Graber, *Mass Media and American Politics*, 353.

the statements, explanations, and actions of public officials more vigorously than in the past, and public officials became distrustful of reporters and reluctant to provide the media with access to information.

Although tension in the media-public official relationship is greater now than in the pre-Vietnam War/Watergate era, reporters and public officials find that they have to cooperate. Reporters need access to public officials if they are to get the information necessary to produce news stories. At the same time, public officials need the media if they are to get their messages out to the public. Neither media personnel nor politicians, however, want to feel used or abused by the other.

The Media and the Presidency

Although presidents are at the center of the government, they cannot know fully what is happening within their administrations, the nation, or the world without the media. Thus, in fulfilling one of their critical functions the media help to keep the chief executive informed of current events. The role of the media also extends to providing information about the major concerns of the public, helping to convey presidential messages to the country, and maintaining public visibility for presidents.

The president's personal image, the nature and effectiveness of administration policies, and presidential behavior are all heavily influenced by the saturation media coverage the president inevitably receives as head of the executive branch and the nation's most powerful public official. Indeed, the power of the White House has been enhanced by the unremitting attention the media give its occupant. Everything the president does, from meeting with world leaders to eyeing a Big Mac after jogging, is covered extensively. Media coverage, however, tends to emphasize not the substantive issues with which the president is dealing or the consequences of presidential decisions but rather the politics of a situation: the battles among contending forces or the president's ability to handle a delicate situation. For example, coverage of the Clinton administration during its first year in office emphasized its struggles with a Democratic Congress over economic/budget issues and gays in the military. And as the president entered his second year in office, the media were almost obsessed with botched White House efforts at damage control in handling of the Whitewater affair, a complicated Arkansas real estate deal involving the Clintons.

Former White House staffer James Fallows has attributed reporters' tendencies to focus on the politics of the White House rather than on

THE PRESIDENCY, THE PRESS, AND NEWS MANAGEMENT

EACH PRESIDENT has had his troubles with the press. . . . We have a photograph of FDR in our press room which is inscribed to the White House reporters from their "devoted victim." "When the press stops abusing me, I'll know I'm in the wrong pew," said Truman. "Reading more and enjoying it less," said Kennedy. What LBJ said is unprintable. . . . Once when the press walked in the Cabinet room for a picture taking, Nixon looked up at the press and said, "It's only coincidental that we're talking about pollution when the press walks in." Carter always seemed to be saying, "Lord, forgive them for they know not what they do." As for Reagan, well, it's like being in those silent movies. He thinks we should be seen and not heard.

Helen Thomas, senior White House reporter, United Press International

THE WHOLE BUSINESS is so influenced by network television. . . . 100 million people across this country get all their news from network television. So the visual is extremely important. . . . That visual is as critical as what we're saying. . . .

If you only get your message across in 30 or 40 seconds on the evening news, then it's important that you restate that message in as many ways as you can. . . . We plot out a decent story or theme for every day. . . .

Michael Deaver, White House deputy chief of staff, 1981–1985

THEY DON'T NEED US as long as they capture our cameras.

Sam Donaldson, ABC News White House correspondent

FROM THE Eisenhower administration to Ronald Reagan's, the White House propaganda machine has become an increasingly effective instrument of presidential will and presidential purpose. . . . It has enhanced the power of the Communicator-in-chief as against that of other institutions of government. . . .

Managing the news and public opinion was recognized by the . . . administration as such a central part of running the presidency that it had to become a major part of the workday of senior policy aides.

David S. Broder, *Washington Post* reporter and columnist

THE EXPECTATIONS for a long honeymoon (or indeed a honeymoon at all, which the President [Clinton] bemoaned missing . . .) may have derived from his conceptions about Washington reporters.

Because many of them are of the same generation as the President and are widely believed to be Democrats and politically liberal, there may have been some belief among the President's staff that the press would be on their side. "I think they're surprised that being adversarial is more important than being liberal," said William Kristol, who was chief of staff for Vice President Dan Quayle.

William Glaberson, *New York Times* reporter

Sources: David S. Broder, *Behind the Front Page: A Candid Look at How the News Is Made* (New York: Simon and Schuster, 1987), 178–195. Helen Thomas quote was originally printed in Kenneth W. Thompson, *The White House Press on the Presidency* (Lanham, Md.: University Press of America, 1983), 41. Glaberson quote taken from article by him, "The Capital Press vs. the President: Fair Coverage or Unreined Adversity?" *New York Times,* June 17, 1993, A11, National edition.

the substance of decisions to the fact that reporters feel more comfortable and competent dealing with political conflicts than with policy. He notes that White House reporters are particularly attracted to scandal, internal White House dissension, political blunders or gaffes, and the business of winning elections and gaining points in opinion polls.[61]

In a similar vein Austin Ranney has observed that:

61. James Fallows, "The Presidency and the Press," in *The Presidency and the Political System*, 3d ed., ed. Michael Nelson (Washington, D.C.: CQ Press, 1990), 317–318.

no television correspondent or anchorman has ever received an Emmy or Peabody or even a promotion for a series of broadcasts focusing on what a marvelous job a president (or any other elected official) is doing. Those rewards go to newspeople who expose moral lapses, lies, and policy failures of public officials, and the president is the biggest game of all in the perennial hunt.[62]

Presidents and their staffs try to overcome these tendencies of the media by "managing the news"—staging media events, controlling the flow of information, and communicating directly with the public via televised speeches, interviews, and press conferences from the White House.[63] Using one of its more controversial techniques, the Reagan White House restricted media access to the president by rarely holding press conferences and forcing reporters to shout their questions over the roar of helicopter motors on the South Lawn of the White House. By contrast, President Bush used the opposite technique. He held frequent news conferences, engaged in spontaneous exchanges with reporters, schmoozed with journalists, invited them to White House barbecues, and sent reporters handwritten notes.

The Clinton White House initially sought to tightly control access to White House personnel, only to receive generally critical press coverage for its efforts. After communications guru David Gergen joined the Clinton senior staff in the summer of 1993, efforts were mounted to provide access to influential members of the national media. Thus, the day before the president presented his health care proposal to Congress in September 1993, he and Mrs. Clinton lunched with and gave "exclusive" interviews to such mandarins of print journalism as David Broder of the *Washington Post*, R. W. Apple of the *New York Times,* and Gerald Seib of the *Wall Street Journal.* It was an effort to use the media to frame public debate on health care reform. As Seib noted, the White House is a "powerful message machine. They have the ability to influence what people in the press say, just by letting them in the doors."[64]

The most striking feature of the Clinton White House's media strategy has been its heavy use of the "new news" outlets to supplement the traditional or "old news" outlets—national newspapers, television net-

62. Ranney, *Channels of Power,* 141.

63. See Samuel Kernell, *Going Public: New Strategies of Presidential Leadership,* 2d ed. (Washington, D.C.: CQ Press, 1993); and John Anthony Maltese, *Spin Control: The White House Office of Communications and the Management of Presidential News* (Chapel Hill: University of North Carolina Press, 1992).

64. Edwin Diamond, Ruth Gurevitch, and Robert Silverman, "Using the Old and New Media to Sell Clinton's Programs to the Public," *National Journal,* November 20, 1993, 2792.

The Clinton administration has made unprecedented use of alternative or "new news" outlets to get its message out to the public. To dramatize wasteful tests on government-issue products, Vice President Al Gore shatters an ashtray on David Letterman's "Late Night" show.

works, and news magazines—that have mediated between politicians and the public for decades. The "new news" includes call-in shows, electronic town meetings, White House briefings for talk show hosts, 800 telephone numbers, narrowcast cable TV, and satellite hook-up interviews with local (not national) reporters. It is an attempt to go directly to the public and win support rather than relying primarily on the traditional and often critical national media to present and interpret the administration's message to the public.[65] Although it has the advantage of bypassing the national media, the "new news" strategy does carry the risk of intensifying the inherently critical and adversarial nature of the White House press corps—a mainstay of the "old news."

No administration, however, can completely manage the news. Reporters have too many alternative sources of information; their goals and those of an administration are not necessarily the same; and the norms of the profession dictate that reporters keep some distance between themselves and the subjects they cover. Thus, in spite of the widely held belief that most members of the Washington press corps are liberal and Democratic, the Clinton White House was frustrated and at times angry at a national media that had little good to say about the administration during its first six months in office. This critical tone reached its zenith in June 1993 when *Time*'s cover pictured a diminutive president under the massive title "The Incredible Shrinking President."[66]

Through its media management strategies, then, the White House

65. "Old News Locked Out," *Economist*, April 24, 1993, 32.
66. *Time*, June 7, 1993.

No other political leader can compete with the president for publicity. The media's saturation coverage of the presidency even extends to the pets of the first family like Chelsea Clinton's cat, Socks.

can have a major impact on which news stories make it onto the evening news programs and how those stories are interpreted. But the tone of the coverage is likely to reflect the media's interest in the politics of the situation and their desire not to appear as propaganda agents for the president. Media coverage also can bring to the public's attention issues that administrations would rather keep off the front pages. Media probing and prodding into the 1972 Watergate scandal, for example, played a major role in forcing President Nixon's resignation. Likewise, in 1986–1987 the media's thirst for more details on the Iran-contra affair (so-called because the administration used surreptitious arms sales to Iran and other means to support the Nicaraguan contras) caused the Reagan administration severe embarrassment. And President Clinton's popularity fell in 1993 when the press gave extensive and highly critical attention to his alleged $200 haircut by a Hollywood hairstylist and to the White House travel office affair in which his staff was accused of cronyism and using the FBI for political purposes. And when the media became awash with critical stories on the Whitewater affair in 1994, the White House was forced into a defensive mode that made it difficult to direct its activities toward achieving public policy objectives.

Public support is critical to a strong and successful presidency (also see Chapter 11). Direct appeals for public support via television can help a president to build that support, but this approach is seldom enough to sustain support. Perceptions of a presidency are affected by media coverage that cannot be controlled by any president. Successful administrations, then, must be able to explain and defend their actions to sensible people in the media. When they have difficulty doing so, the president is likely to suffer a severe setback as President Reagan found after the media revealed the Iran-contra affair in 1986.

The Media and Congress

Media coverage of the executive branch has a focal point—the president. But Congress, with its 535 members, hundreds of committees and subcommittees, platoons of leaders, and lengthy and complicated decision-making processes, has no such focal point. Except for the final stages of decision making on the floors of the House and Senate or an unusually dramatic congressional hearing, congressional proceedings are not very interesting television fare. Yet, even though the president often seems to dominate the news, Congress and the president are accorded roughly equal coverage. Probably to Congress's dismay, however, congressional activity in shaping public policy is often treated as if it were part of the work of the executive branch.

The nature of the reporting on Congress depends in part on whether the national or the local and regional media are involved. The national media tend to cover the big, dramatic stories of nationwide importance such as a resolution authorizing military action against Iraq, Senate confirmation of Supreme Court nominees, conflicts between the president and Congress, investigations, and scandals. These media, especially television, are particularly attracted to congressional hearings and investigations like the 1991 Senate hearings into Professor Anita Hill's charges of sexual harassment against Supreme Court nominee Clarence Thomas because they provide drama and confrontation. The nuts-and-bolts work of Congress—such as shepherding bills through the Senate and House and negotiating complicated compromises—is largely ignored by the national media. National media correspondents tend to treat Congress in a tough, skeptical, hard-nosed, and frequently cynical manner. Veteran television broadcaster David Brinkley, for example, once remarked during an evening newscast that "it was widely believed that it would take Congress 30 days to make instant coffee." One consequence of this type of coverage is a generally negative image of Congress as an institution.[67]

In a more positive vein, national media publicity can catapult a member of Congress into prominence and contention for a presidential nomination as it did for Senators Estes Kefauver, Hubert Humphrey,

67. Michael J. Robinson, "Three Faces of Congressional Media," in *The New Congress*, ed. Thomas E. Mann and Norman J. Ornstein (Washington, D.C.: American Enterprise Institute, 1981), 73–75.

John Kennedy, Lyndon Johnson, and Robert Dole. The media also provide senators and representatives with a means of mobilizing national constituencies to back legislation they are supporting. For example, Sen. Jesse Helms (R-N.C.) has used media attention to create a personal following for a series of conservative policies, and during the 1980s Sen. Bill Bradley (D-N.J.) gained national attention for his role in the sweeping reform of the tax code.

For members not trying to use national publicity as a springboard to the presidency or for legislative purposes, the local and regional media are more important. Reporters for local and regional media outlets do not cover the big national news stories or Congress as an institution. Rather, they concentrate on their home state's congressional delegation. Because these delegations are an essential part of the local and regional reporters' beats in getting the local angle on Washington events, coverage of them is normally rather "soft" and seldom as critical in tone as the coverage accorded Congress by the national media.

With the national media dealing with Congress in a generally harsh manner and the local and regional media treating congressional incumbents relatively well, the net media effect is one of conveying a negative impression of the institution while presenting its individual members in a favorable light to their constituents. This dual pattern of congressional coverage helps to explain why Americans seem to like their representatives in Congress and consistently reelect them but do not hold Congress as an institution in high regard.[68]

Also handy for strengthening the positions of individual members of Congress with their constituents are the in-house congressional media. Using their franking privilege (free mailings) and computerized printing, members of Congress can run sophisticated direct-mail operations to maintain contact with the people back home. Members also are provided with the personnel and facilities needed to produce broadcast and print material for use by the media. Indeed, recording studios are available for members who wish to produce radio and videotapes for distribution to media outlets in their constituencies. Some senators and representatives even produce television shows that are aired regularly on local stations. Finally, each member has at least one press aide responsible for media relations and for supervising the preparation and release of materials to the media.

68. Robinson, "Three Faces," 93. Also see Timothy C. Cook, *Making Laws and Making News* (Washington, D.C.: Brookings, 1989), chap. 4.

In addition to the television studios provided to members of Congress in House and Senate office buildings, state-of-the-art facilities such as those of the Republican National Committee are also available to legislators and other party leaders.

The Media and the Judiciary

Media coverage of the Supreme Court is usually limited to informing the public and government officials about selected newsworthy decisions. The Court in turn uses the media to gauge the public's reaction to and acceptance of its decisions. Of the three branches of government, however, the judiciary gets the least (and the most superficial) coverage.[69] Supreme Court justices receive substantial publicity at the time of their appointments, but little personal publicity is forthcoming after they go on the bench. Justices rarely grant press interviews, and they keep conventional politics at arm's length.

Information about the Court is largely restricted to the formal decisions handed down by the justices, who conduct their business in an atmosphere cloaked in secrecy, tradition, legalese, and solemnity. These practices tend to insulate the Court from the day-to-day hassle of politics and protect judicial independence and influence. Media coverage of the Court, therefore, focuses almost entirely on major controversial decisions such as those about school prayer, abortion, affirmative action, or legislative redistricting. Other decisions tend to receive only cursory media attention or are ignored altogether.

Although decisions like the 1954 school desegregation case of *Brown v. Board of Education of Topeka* can have consequences that reverberate through the political system for decades, a variety of factors hold down extensive media coverage of the Supreme Court. These include the

69. Graber, *Mass Media and American Politics,* 329–331. Also see David M. O'Brien, *Storm Center: The Supreme Court in American Politics,* 3d ed. (New York: Norton, 1993), 351–357.

Specialists in legal affairs such as National Public Radio's Nina Totenberg are unusual in broadcast news organizations. Totenberg, who is known for her in-depth coverage of the Supreme Court, broke the story of alleged sexual harassment charges by Anita Hill against Supreme Court nominee Clarence Thomas that led to Thomas's controversial confirmation hearings before the Senate Judiciary Committee in 1991.

Court's ability to control the flow of information to the media about its internal operations; the complexity of the subject matter, which does not lend itself to exciting sound bites or headlines; the large volume of cases decided each year; the understaffed Supreme Court beat; and the need for reporters covering the Court to have more specialized training than reporters covering the Congress or White House. The job of covering the Supreme Court is further complicated by the fact that reporters receive little assistance from the Court in interpreting the meaning and significance of decisions. Justices do not grant interviews to discuss their decisions, nor do they indulge in the practice of leaking confidential information to the media. This contrasts sharply with the executive and legislative branches where officials are usually anxious to provide reporters with background information and the rationales for their actions. Because news about the Court is gathered under such conditions, coverage of its decisions may be not only limited but also inaccurate and misleading.

The Media and Governing

The media link citizens to their government by helping to shape public opinion, by giving public officials a channel of communication to citizens, and by influencing the behavior of political leaders. In providing common experiences and depicting common concerns, the media also help to unite Americans, but they divide Americans as well by bringing into the nation's living rooms the controversies that are brewing daily in society.

The media can have a profound influence on public perceptions of governmental institutions and leaders. But because television news tends to be negative and to focus on the problems and shortcomings of government, it may distance people from their government instead of bringing them closer to it. Indeed, public trust in government has declined during the television age.

Austin Ranney has suggested several additional consequences that the mass media, particularly television, might have for the governing process.[70] First, through its instantaneous coverage of events and preference for neat, clear-cut decisions and fast results, television tends to compress the time elected officials have to get programs off the ground and get results in dealing with the nation's problems. Because of their expectations of fast results and their tendencies to treat politics like a sporting event, many newscasters lean toward keeping score and dra-

70. Ranney, *Channels of Power,* 124–147.

matizing short-term changes in such indicators as inflation and unemployment rates.

Second, the media may reduce the policy options available to leaders by publicizing proposals in the early stages of consideration. When the spotlight of news coverage focuses on a policy option in the early stages of its development, the publicity may raise a storm of controversy that effectively precludes further consideration of the policy option.

And third, by highlighting the activities of politicians who offer simple solutions and take extreme and uncompromising stands, the media weaken the coalition builders who make governmental action possible. Governance involves negotiation, compromise, and the knitting together of coalitions of diverse interests. These processes are complicated, it is thought, by the media's tendency to cover those participants who offer dramatic and controversial proposals and assume a confrontational stance toward their opponents.

Political science research has not produced definitive conclusions about the impact of the media on the governmental process. But informed suggestions about that impact, such as those just noted, serve as a reminder that the messages received each day from the media continually affect how the political system operates.

For Review

1. As a major source of political information, the media, particularly television, help to shape the public's perceptions of reality. These perceptions, in turn, constitute a basis for the public's political activity. As intermediaries between the people and their government, the media are then able to mobilize citizens to take political action and influence the behavior of government officials.

2. The various kinds of print and electronic media approach public affairs in different ways. The American people rely on and trust television more than the other kinds of media, but the dominance and influence of the major television networks have been reduced by cable networks, videocassette recorders, and other technological advances.

3. Among the most important decisions journalists make is what constitutes news. What should be aired on television and printed in the papers? The standards for newsworthiness include audience appeal and impact, uniqueness, and timeliness. The nature of media coverage also is affected by time and space constraints and the accessibility of news sources.

4. The media have a strong voice in deciding which issues will be placed on the public agenda, but when the media cover election campaigns, they tend to focus on the "horse race" aspects of the contest and not on substantive issues.

5. Political leaders and newspeople are mutually dependent. Politicians rely on the media to provide them with information and to convey their

messages to the public. The media in turn rely heavily on public officials for the information on which to base their reporting. The relationship is characterized by tension, however, as politicians seek to use the media to achieve their objectives and the media seek to perform their news-gathering functions.

For Further Reading

Ansolabehere, Stephen, Roy Behr, and Shanto Iyengar. *The Media Game: American Politics in the Television Age.* New York: Macmillan, 1993. An informative account of the nature of the media and their impact on American politics based on up-to-date media research.

Broder, David S. *Behind the Front Page: A Candid Look at How the News Is Made.* New York: Simon and Schuster, 1987. A description and critique of how reporters cover political news by one of journalism's most respected and insightful reporters.

Graber, Doris A. *Mass Media and American Politics.* 4th ed. Washington, D.C.: CQ Press, 1993. A thorough account of how the media cover political events and their impact.

Iyengar, Shanto, and Donald R. Kinder. *News That Matters: TV and American Opinion.* Chicago: University of Chicago Press, 1987. A report on experimental research assessing the impact of television news on opinion.

Lichter, S. Robert, Stanley Rothman, and Linda S. Lichter. *The Media Elite: America's New Powerbrokers.* New York: Adler and Adler, 1986. An analysis of survey research findings about the political and social values of journalists.

Maltese, John Anthony. *Spin Control: The White House Office of Communications and the Management of Presidential News.* Chapel Hill: University of North Carolina Press, 1992. An account of how presidents seek to manage the news, from Nixon through Bush.

Mann, Thomas E., and Norman J. Ornstein, eds. *Congress, the Press, and the Public.* Washington, D.C.: Brookings, 1994. Experts on Congress and the media examine coverage of Congress, attitudes of media personnel toward Congress, and how members of Congress present themselves and their institution to the public.

Patterson, Thomas E. *Out of Order.* New York: Knopf, 1993. An analysis of the media's role in presidential campaigns which argues that they are ill-equipped to give order and direction to campaigns and are an unreliable guide for voter choice.

Ranney, Austin. *Channels of Power: The Impact of Television on American Politics.* New York: Basic Books, 1983. An analysis of how the media do their jobs and their impact on the public, elections, and the governing process.

PART III

Governmental Institutions

POLITICS ALONG THE POTOMAC

Washington, D.C., is the center of national policy making and a magnet for all those who wish to influence, have a say in, or report on that process. It is a city that mirrors the American people and their politics. Yet it is also unique among American cities; in no other are politics so all-consuming, the political stakes so high, or the players more skilled. With a professional political community that numbers in the thousands, Washington has a special impact on the U.S. political system.

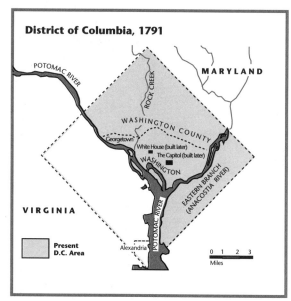

District of Columbia, 1791

POTOMAC RIVER

MARYLAND

ROCK CREEK

WASHINGTON COUNTY

Georgetown

White House (built later)

The Capitol (built later)

WASHINGTON

EASTERN BRANCH (ANACOSTIA RIVER)

VIRGINIA

POTOMAC RIVER

Present D.C. Area

Alexandria

0 1 2 3
Miles

Congress created the District of Columbia in 1790 from land along the Potomac River that was given to the United States by the states of Maryland and Virginia. The Virginia portion of the District (Arlington County and the city of Alexandria) was ceded back to Virginia in 1846.

Spearheading the District of Columbia's drive for statehood and full voting rights in Congress is its "shadow senator," the Reverend Jesse Jackson (center). Jackson, a contender for the Democratic presidential nomination in 1984 and 1988, is shown here using his persuasive powers on Rep. Henry Gonzalez (D-Tex.), chair of the House Banking Committee.

A Federal City with Its Roots in a Maryland-Virginia Wilderness

Unlike all other American cities, Washington is not located within state boundaries and is not subject to state laws and regulations. Rather, the District of Columbia, on the banks of the Potomac River, is a *federal city,* carved out of the surrounding states of Maryland and Virginia (see map of the District of Columbia). As a federal city, the district falls under the jurisdiction of Congress, which created its system of local government. The federal government is the district's largest landowner, but, in lieu of paying property taxes, Congress appropriates substantial sums (more than $600 million annually) to help fund the city government's activities.

The district's status as a federal city is not without controversy, however. Since it is not a state of the Union, Washington residents lack representation with full voting rights in Congress, although they do have an offcial delegate to the House of Representatives. In fact, advocates of statehood for the district assert that Washington is America's "last colony." In an effort to advance the cause of statehood, the district recently elected two "shadow senators," the Reverend Jesse Jackson and Florence Pendleton, to lobby for statehood from those unofficial posts. Proponents of retaining the district's current federal city status stress that since Washington is the seat of government for all the people of the United States, it requires congressional supervision.

Unlike such world-famous European capitals as Paris, London, and Rome, whose political preeminence evolved from their positions as centers of commerce and culture, America's seat of government was created where there was no existing metropolis. Georgetown (now a chic shopping and residential section of Washington) was a small port city just below the falls of the Potomac; the National Mall area between what is now the Capitol and the Washington Monument was a swamp drained by Tiber Creek; and Jenkins Hill (now Capitol Hill) was undeveloped.

In 1791 President George Washington, himself a former surveyor, commissioned visionary French engineer and architect Pierre Charles L'Enfant to plan the city. L'Enfant dreamed of transforming this wilderness plot into a monumental city of grand avenues and stately buildings. In keeping with the Constitution's separation of powers principle, however, L'Enfant and Washington proposed a city with no central focus of activity; the legislative, executive, and judicial branches were to be separated by considerable distances to avoid confrontation and yet to share routes of communication and be "seemingly connected," in L'Enfant's words.[1] Although battered by land speculators and altered by generations of political leaders, L'Enfant's basic plan for the city has been retained to this day.

With its massive government buildings, green expanses of the Mall and Rock Creek Park, memorials to the famous (and not so famous), wide thoroughfares like Pennsylvania and Constitution avenues, traffic circles with tiny parks at their centers, and a regulation forbidding construction of any building higher than the Capitol, the Washington of today has a distinguished and appealing character. Also adding to Washington's uniqueness is L'Enfant's quadrant system—NE, SE, SW, NW—and street grid (alphabetical streets run east-west and numbered streets run north-south).

One important change in L'Enfant's plan is particularly noteworthy because it speaks volumes about how the capital city's geography and architecture reflect American values. In his original plan L'Enfant included a "great church of national purpose" to be built on a site near the Capitol. Proponents of church-state separation, however, found another location for the Washington Cathedral (the world's only Gothic cathedral to be completed in the twentieth century) in Northwest Washington on Mount St. Alban, the highest point in the city, miles from the Capitol.

Washington, which was named such to honor the first president, was for most of its history a rather sleepy southern city. Although it is not well known, the District of Columbia is located sixty miles south of the Mason-Dixon line and, like the rest of the South, practiced racial segregation until the 1950s. Even into the early twentieth cen-

---

1. Quoted by James Sterling Young, *The Washington Community, 1800–1828* (New York: Harcourt, Brace and World, 1966), 3. Young provides one of the most complete and insightful studies of the Washington community in the formative days of the Republic.

Before Washington became a fast-paced center of world politics and Pennsylvania Avenue, the grand avenue linking the White House and Capitol, became a thoroughfare lined with massive federal buildings, the nation's capital was a quiet and segregated southern city. The great mall stretching from the Capitol to the Potomac River was a malaria-infested swamp where cattle grazed. Sheep groomed the White House lawn. It was not until air-conditioning provided relief from the humid heat of summer that Washington ceased to be considered a hardship post by foreign diplomats.

In laying out the original plans for Washington, Maj. Pierre L'Enfant envisioned "a great church of national purpose" to be built on a site near the Capitol. Proponents of church-state separation, however, prevailed and the National Cathedral was located on Mount St. Alban in Washington's Northwest quadrant. Although presidents and other national leaders have participated in its religious services, the cathedral plays no official role in American public life and receives no federal funds.

Linked by Pennsylvania Avenue, the Capitol and the White House are the focal points of central Washington, D.C.

tury sheep manicured the White House lawn. And before air-conditioning and ready cures for malaria, Washington was considered a hardship post by foreign diplomats.

Today, however, the Washington area is a booming metropolis of over 3.9 million people, about 607,000 of whom actually live in the District of Columbia. The area's phenomenal growth (its population grew by 20.7 percent between 1980 and 1990), prosperity, and international prominence have coincided with the federal government's increased responsibilities for social services and economic regulation, as well as America's assumption of a leadership role in world affairs. In the process Washington has become the world capital for news and information, politics, and diplomacy. It also has developed a vibrant cultural life and is becoming a commercial center.

This sprawling metropolitan area revolves around the action occurring in the major geographic sectors of the city (identified in the map of central Washington).

Capitol Hill

The Capitol, with its imposing landmark dome, reflects the checks and balances devised by the drafters of the Constitution. The House and Senate occupy separate wings of the building. Surrounding the Capitol (which has no "behind"—only two "fronts," East and West) are the massive House and Senate office buildings named for

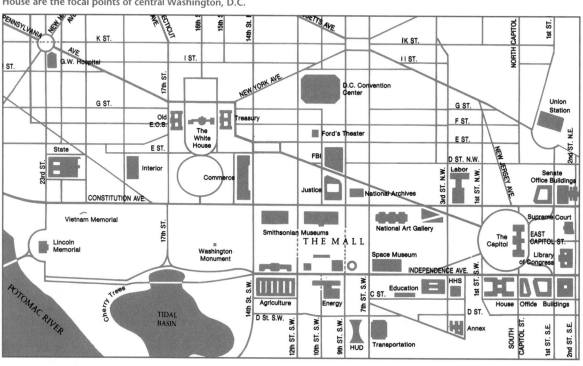

The Washington Monument stands tall amid cherry trees, which were a gift from the city of Tokyo and planted in 1912.

The Lincoln Memorial contains thirty-six columns, the number of states in the Union at the time Lincoln was assassinated.

three famous Speakers of the House—Joseph Cannon (R-Ill.), Nicholas Longworth (R-Ohio), and Sam Rayburn (D-Texas)—and three respected senators—Richard Russell (D-Ga.), Everett Dirksen (R-Ill.), and Philip Hart (D-Mich.). The growth of congressional staff since the 1970s has been so great that House staffers have spilled over into two annexes, buildings named for former Speaker Thomas ("Tip") O'Neill (D-Mass.) and former minority leader and president Gerald Ford (R-Mich.). On the other side of Capitol Hill, the Senate annex in the old Immigration Building accommodates Senate staff and the Capitol Police, Congress's own police force. Also nearby are the Botanic Garden, Library of Congress, Supreme Court, the headquarters of the Republican and Democratic national committees, a smattering of offices for lobbyists and "think tanks" (nonprofit public policy research centers), and an increasingly gentrified residential area of townhouses.

The Mall

Extending westward from the Capitol all the way to the Potomac River is the Mall, a green parkway on which are located two of the city's most famous landmarks, the Lincoln and Washington memorials. Between these landmarks in a tastefully landscaped grove of trees is the simple but stirring Vietnam Veterans Memorial—a low wall of black marble on which are inscribed the names of all the American men and women who are missing in action or who died in that conflict. The Mall is also home to a series of museums, including the Smithsonian Institution's

The memorial to Thomas Jefferson—author of the Declaration of Independence and third president of the United States—is situated along the south bank of the Tidal Basin.

The names of the men and women who are missing in action or who lost their lives in Southeast Asia are memorialized at the Vietnam Veterans Memorial. Here, President Clinton looks for the name of a high school classmate who died in the war.

In Washington, where ideas and policy research have a major impact on decision making, the Library of Congress is a valued information source. Begun with books in Thomas Jefferson's personal collection the library was housed initially in the Capitol (top photo is of the library at the Capitol in the 1880s). The majestic Great Hall (bottom) symbolizes the library's importance to Washington and the nation's research and cultural activities.

National Gallery of Art, Air and Space Museum, and Museum of American History. These attractions make the Mall a mecca for tourists, particularly in the spring, when the Japanese cherry trees that line the Tidal Basin adjacent to the Mall are in bloom.

The Federal Triangle

Bounded on the north by Pennsylvania Avenue, the east by Sixth Street, the south by Constitution Avenue, and the west by the Ellipse behind the White House, the Federal Triangle is the site of thirteen limestone buildings that include the Departments of Commerce and Justice, Federal Bureau of Investigation, Federal Trade Commission, Internal Revenue Service, and National Archives. Close by on Pennsylvania Avenue amid government buildings stands the new and architecturally distinct Canadian embassy, the neighbor to the north's bid for prominence in Washington. The Federal Triangle is also home to the beautifully restored Old Post Office Pavilion, which houses a few federal agencies such as the National Endowment for the Arts and a collection of shops and restaurants.

Independence Avenue Area

Across the Mall from the Federal Triangle is another complex of executive agencies that includes the National Aeronautics and Space Administration, U.S. Information Agency, U.S. Postal Service, as well as the Departments of Agriculture, Energy, Health and Human Services, Housing and Urban Development, and Transportation.

Downtown

The White House, an attractive but not overly elegant dwelling appropriate for an elected chief executive, is this section's focal point. Next door is the magnificent, but inefficient, Old Executive Office Building, a French Second Empire structure, which accommodates many of the president's key aides. In the immediate neighborhood are found the Departments of the Treasury and Interior, the World Bank, the American Red Cross, and the offices of trade associations, unions, and all manner of interest groups, lobbyists, consultants, law firms, and think tanks. Indeed, the high-rent area around K and M streets in downtown Washington is so crammed with the offices of lobbyists, lawyers, and consultants that it is sometimes referred to as "Lobby, Inc."

From the steps of the U.S. Capitol the distinctive architecture of the buildings on the Mall is clearly evident. On the left is the "Castle" of the Smithsonian Institution, completed in 1855; at center are the Washington Monument and the Grecian temple-like Lincoln Memorial; and on the right is the Smithsonian's Museum of Natural History.

Embassy Row

Northwest of downtown along Massachusetts and Connecticut avenues and the adjoining tree-lined streets are the frequently lavish embassies of foreign governments.

Foggy Bottom

The Department of State, a massive building with a commanding view of the Potomac, is located in what was once a low-lying, swampy, and often foggy section of the city. Each summer foreign diplomats are invited to the State Department's elegant, antique-filled, top-floor reception areas to view the massive July Fourth fireworks display at the Tidal Basin and Mall.

Close to the State Department and bordering the Potomac River is the Kennedy Center for the Performing Arts, a memorial to the late president and home of the National Symphony. Also overlooking the river is the Watergate complex of shops, offices, a hotel, and apartments that was the site of the infamous 1972 break-in that ultimately ended the presidency of Richard Nixon. The Watergate is also the residence of many prominent Wash-

Pictured here is the Greek embassy on Embassy Row.

367

Arlington Cemetery is the final resting place for more than two hundred thousand veterans representing every war the United States has fought.

In the 1990s, special privileges extended to public officials have become increasingly controversial and none is more so than VIP reserved parking close by the terminal at Washington's National Airport. However, this is a "perk" that members of Congress, most of whom fly home to meet constituents several times a month, are prepared to defend no matter how many critical editorials it generates.

The Pentagon, said to be the world's largest office building, is the only U.S. government departmental headquarters outside the District of Columbia.

ingtonians, including Supreme Court Justice Ruth Bader Ginsburg, Senate Minority Leader Robert Dole (R-Kan.), and Elizabeth Hanford Dole, president of the American Red Cross.

The Pentagon, Arlington National Cemetery, and National Airport

Across the Potomac in Virginia lies Arlington National Cemetery with its precise rows of memorials to bravery and sacrifice. In addition to offering panoramic views of the nation's capital, the cemetery is the site of the family home of Confederate general Robert E. Lee. Adjacent to Arlington National Cemetery is the focal point of the country's defense establishment, the massive five-sided Pentagon building—headquarters of the Department of Defense. To provide busy politicians with ready access to air transportation, National Airport is located on the Potomac just a short drive from the White House and the Capitol.

The Other Washington

The sections of Washington just described are the ones frequented by tourists and the ones that serve as the backdrop for the events and people making the news. But in this city of movers and shakers, monumental buildings, and stately homes, there is another Washington. Largely out of the public eye, it provides disquieting examples of the problems afflicting inner cities across the country: poverty, drug abuse, high crime rates, substandard housing, and inadequate schools. Indeed, in poor and predominantly African American neighborhoods the problem of young people dealing in drugs and guns became so severe in 1993 that Mayor Sharon Pratt Kelly asked Presi-

Away from the monumental buildings, broad tree-lined avenues, plush office buildings, and stately embassies is the "Other Washington," where the inhabitants do not share in the general affluence of the nation's capital.

dent Bill Clinton for authority to call up the National Guard to help in policing the city. Although he denied the mayor's request, the president did endorse legislation that would give the D.C. mayor the authority to call out the National Guard. In doing so, he handed over to Congress the politically touchy issue of how much independent power the mayor of the nation's capital should have.[2]

2. B. Drummond Ayres, "Clinton Denies Washington's Request to Use Guard," *New York Times,* Oct. 26, 1993, A8, National edition.

A One-Industry Town

Like any city, Washington has many faces, and the face one sees is to a large degree in the eye of the beholder. The casual tourist mainly sees the awesome government buildings and monuments. But *Washington Post* columnist Haynes Johnson sees Washington as a reflection of the nation. According to this over thirty-year veteran of the city, "Washington *is* America, quintessentially, indisputably a mirror of all the country's strengths and weaknesses."[3] But other observers see it as a city atypical of America. They note Washington's affluence—it has the highest per capita household income of any metropolitan area in the country. Moreover, the Washington area is almost recession-proof because the federal government and related interests maintain such high employment levels. Washington area residents as a group also are better educated than the inhabitants of other metropolitan areas. But above all, its residents are more politicized and attuned to national politics than other Americans. In a nationally televised address, President Jimmy Carter, who remained a Washington outsider even after his election, called Washington an island, cut off and isolated from the concerns of ordinary Americans. His successors have been no less critical. Ronald Reagan complained about the "puzzle palaces along the Potomac" of "Disneyland East," and just before leaving office he assailed the alliances of members of Congress, the media, and special interests for thwarting his policies, which he claimed the public supported.[4]

There is, however, one aspect of the city few would dispute. It is a one-industry town and that industry is politics. Washington is not America's economic or cultural center; it is the political center of the nation. Washington's preoccupation with politics and politicians was noted critically by President Clinton when he responded to a reporter's

President Jimmy Carter and his aides, even after four years in Washington, considered themselves outsiders. Carter's successor, Ronald Reagan, also raised political capital by railing against "the Washington establishment." In this photo, Carter is chatting with his closest advisers and fellow Georgians Jody Powell (left) and Hamilton Jordan (right).

Posing in his Washington office—adorned with photographs of friends in high places—is Paul A. Equale, lobbyist for the Independent Insurance Agents of America.

3. Haynes Johnson, "The Capital of Success," *Washington Post Magazine,* February 2, 1986, 44.

4. Bill McAllister, "Reagan Assails 'Washington Colony' as Out of Touch," *Washington Post,* Dec. 14, 1988, A4.

request for an assessment of the culture of Washington. After almost one hundred days in office, the president observed that

the culture of Washington is too dominated by what happens to politicians instead of what happens to the people, and too much into the day-to-day gamesmanship of politics: who's up, who's down, who's not. . . . [I]t puts an enormous extra burden on the process of change because it's hard, basically, to keep what's really at stake in mind.[5]

The manifestations of the city's obsession with things political are everywhere. For example, the office walls of Washington's political community are covered with row after row of "power pictures"—autographed photographs of the office's occupant with prominent politicians. These "walls of fame" are collected over the years and are adjusted to mirror shifting loyalties and changes in the balance of power within Congress and the administration. The significance of this Washington tradition has been described by an insider:

It's an anthropological signal to your visitors of . . . what your station in life is. . . . It's a sign of what fires you've walked through . . . and what potentates you've touched. It's a way of letting your visitors know who you are, establishing a parentage and a peerage much more interesting than the Green Book [Washington's social registry] or Burke's peerage.[6]

Social standing in Washington is not based on wealth or good bloodlines; it is based on political standing. The nature of the social life of the political community has been captured by *New York Times* correspondent Lynn Roselli:

Looks, charm, wealth, intellect—they alone count for little in Washington. Power is all. What really matters is: Whom do you know? What have you done? And what can you do for me? Guests don't get invited out in Washington because they've got twinkly blue eyes. . . . Nobody among the 2,500 men and women who make up the inner village of political-social Washington goes anywhere just for fun. "It's really a continuation of a day's work," says . . . a veteran hostess.[7]

With social standing dependent on political position, election to the Senate or appointment to a key White House post can elevate a person's status overnight. But politics is as uncertain as ever, and in Washington a fall from social grace can be just as rapid.

The sheer number of politically motivated social events

to which public officials are invited is staggering—up to one hundred or more a week for White House officials and members of Congress. Every evening between 5:30 and 8:00 dozens of receptions are held in hotels and office buildings to which members of Congress, lobbyists, and administration officials are invited. Most of these events are sponsored by businesses or interest groups.

Because social events so frequently have a primarily political/business function, Washingtonians develop strategies for holding and attending events. In fact, the intimidating number of nightly receptions has spawned a bizarre ritual called the "drop by": "In just 20 minutes, a skilled Congressman can arrive, seek out a few key individuals [such as home state constituents, interest group leaders, or administration officials], pump their hands and then depart, perhaps even grabbing a snack on the way out."[8] And a thirty-year-old rising public relations man hires a driver so he can make it to three receptions a night. Without a driver such an attendance rate would be impossible because parking in downtown Washington is rarely available between 5:30 and 8:00 P.M.[9]

On the diplomatic circuit, British ambassador Anthony Acland was known for giving "closely focused" dinners at his residence and for not "wasting taxpayers' money on unusable guests."[10] Sondra Gotlieb, the somewhat irreverent wife of a recent Canadian ambassador, was noted for her glamorous parties and skill in promoting her country's interests. She operated using a similarly utilitarian social code: "We invite *jobs* [people holding influential positions], not individuals. Our purpose is to promote our country. We don't spend the taxpayers' money for the neighbors."[11]

For Washington's political leadership, social life is an extension of business as people relate to each other in terms of position and title and exchange implicit *quid pro quos.* Hedrick Smith, an insightful chronicler of life "inside the Beltway" (the interstate highway encircling the city), has noted that at dinners and informal gatherings

5. "Excerpts from Interview with President Clinton," *Washington Post,* May 14, 1993, A11.
6. Elizabeth Kastor, "The Walls of Fame," *Washington Post,* Aug. 18, 1987, D1.
7. Lynn Roselli, "A Capital Game of Power," *New York Times Magazine,* January 4, 1981, 18.

8. Lynn Roselli, "Good Eating and Good Politicking (in 20 Minutes)," *New York Times,* Aug. 17, 1981.
9. See Walt Harrington, "The Education of David Carmen," *Washington Post Magazine,* February 28, 1988, 13–19, 35–37.
10. "Washington: The Silk Tie and Hairy Chest," *Economist,* December 24, 1988, 19.
11. Quoted by Sandra McElwaine, "Take 'My Wife of'—Please," *Regardie's,* October 1985, 42.

journalists turn to officials and politicians for stories; politicians trade for favorable mention. Lobbyists need politicians for legislation, and the politicians need lobbyists for money and votes. Of course, there are times of levity and humor, but the underlying transactions of the political bazaar sap most occasions of serendipity.[12]

In the same vein, diplomatic hostess Sondra Gotlieb wrote, "People will go to an embassy party if they think they might see someone they have missed during the day. . . . Powerful Jobs come to parties to trade information with other Powerful Jobs they hadn't made contact with during the day."[13]

In this environment it is small wonder that the cynics enjoy quoting President Harry Truman, who said, "If you want a friend in Washington, buy a dog." Similarly, Hedrick Smith, after years of observing the capital's political culture, concluded that despite their back-slapping gregariousness, Washington politicians tend to be "a lonely crowd, making few deep friendships because almost every relationship is tainted by the calculus of power. How will this help me?"[14]

Although Washington's political community finds the contacts made and the information gathered at social events helpful in their continuing struggle for influence and advancement, the social pressures do take their toll. The highly politicized nature of Washington life means that there is almost no respite from one's political work. Family life can be particularly hard-hit by the pressures of the Washington environment.[15]

Washington's preoccupation with politics is also reflected in its hunger for news. Information is power, and Washingtonians are anxious for the latest. In no other city does a single corner (Connecticut Avenue and K Street, N.W.) have twenty-five newspaper vending machines. As the *New Yorker*'s Elizabeth Drew noted:

Washingtonians do not live like other people. On Sunday, when other people are hiking, sailing or doing nothing, many Washingtonians are earnestly going through their thick Sunday papers and watching "Meet the Press" and "Face the Nation." Washingtonians do this even when there is little going on.[16]

Receptions, like this one at the Austrian embassy, are considered part of the job for Washington's political leadership—a place to make contacts, discuss business informally, and even practice the art of persuasion. (From the left) Ambassador Helmut Tuerk and his wife chat with James Cardinal Hickey at the embassy.

On Pennsylvania Avenue between the Capitol and the White House, Canada has erected a distinctive new embassy in an effort to gain stature among the foreign governments seeking to influence American policy makers.

12. Hedrick Smith, *The Power Game: How Washington Works* (New York: Random House, 1988), 110.

13. Sondra Gotlieb, *Wife of . . .* (Washington, D.C.: Acropolis Books, 1985), 28.

14. Smith, *Power Game,* 92.

15. For an informed account of the impact of Washington on politicians' marriages, see Myra MacPherson, *The Power Lovers: An Intimate Look at Politicians and Their Marriages* (New York: Putnam, 1975).

16. Elizabeth Drew, *Washington Journal* (New York: Random House, 1975), 23.

Sunday interview shows are consumed and analyzed by Washingtonians while beyond the Beltway most Americans enjoy a day of rest and relaxation. Dan Quayle (left) is shown here with Tim Russert (center), moderator of "Meet the Press," and panelist Al Hunt of the *Wall Street Journal.*

The Washington community's hunger for news is demonstrated by this phalanx of newspaper vending machines on a downtown street corner.

The Sunday process of soaking up the news shows now goes on for hours. Viewers tape the competing network programs on their VCRs and watch them back to back.

Washington's preoccupation with politics also has made it a mecca for think tanks. In 1993 the *Capital Source,* a reliable Washington directory, listed ninety-six think tanks. These competing and politically savvy public policy research centers reflect a wide variety of policy interests and ideological perspectives. For example, a number of moderate to liberal think tanks had a significant impact on Bill Clinton's issue positions in the 1992 campaign and later the policies of his administration. The moderate, pro-Democratic Progressive Policy Institute helped to shape the policy positions of the campaign, and its leaders served as senior domestic policy advisers on the administration's transition team after the 1992 election. The liberal Economic Policy Institute, one of whose founders was Clinton transition leader and Secretary of Labor Robert Reich, claimed credit for Clinton framing the government spending debate in terms of "investment." And Judith Feder of the Urban Institute headed Clinton's health care policy transition team.[17] The more scholarly Brookings Institution—called a Democratic "government in exile" during the Reagan-Bush years by conservative critics, even though it employs both Democrats and Republicans—also has been a source of ideas and personnel for the Clinton administration. For example, Alice M. Rivlin, a Brookings economist, was appointed director of the Office of Management and Budget by the president.

On the political Right the Heritage Foundation is widely acknowledged to have provided the Reagan administration with much of its policy agenda. The foundation now supplies ammunition to conservatives as they seek to shoot down policies of the Clinton administration and the Democratic Congress. The more scholarly and moderately conservative American Enterprise Institute provided policy initiatives and staffing for the Reagan and Bush administrations. There are also policy enterprises on the political Left, most notably the Institute for Policy Studies.

The existence of almost one hundred think tanks in Washington reflects the tremendous market among the political leadership for alternative public policy ideas, critiques of existing policy, and insights into future events.[18]

17. David Von Drehle, "With Friends in High Places, Democratic Think Tank Bids for Glory," *Washington Post,* Dec. 7, 1992, A17.

18. For an informed discussion of think tanks, see James A. Smith, *The Idea Brokers: Think Tanks and the Rise of the New Policy Elite* (New York: Free Press, 1993); and David M. Ricci, *The Transformation of American Politics: The New Washington and the Rise of Think Tanks* (New Haven, Conn.: Yale University Press, 1993).

When President Clinton reorganized his staff in June 1994, he sought the assistance of experienced and politically savvy members of Washington's permanent political community. His choice to be director of the Office of Management and Budget (OMB) was economist Alice Rivlin, who since earning her doctorate at Radcliffe College has moved back and forth between economic posts in government and outside: Brookings Institution economist (1957–1975); a stint as the first director of the Congressional Budget Office; back to Brookings (1983–1992) and teaching at George Mason University; deputy OMB director (1992–1994); and OMB director (1994–).

Importance of Image Making in Washington's Political Culture

Careful observers of the nation's capital such as *New York Times* reporter Michael Kelly believe that its political culture has become dominated by "people professionally involved in creating public images of elected officials." They hold various jobs as pollsters, news media consultants, campaign strategists, advertising producers, political scientists, reporters, columnists, and media commentators.

Concern about the president's image is so strong at the White House, according to Kelly, that

what a President (or Presidential candidate) says or does must always be calculated for its effect on his image, plotted as points along the arc of his ideal persona, a construct largely determined by what the pollsters say the people regard as ideal at the moment. Since the news media will trumpet the slightest deviation from the ideal as evidence of a flawed presidency, the marketing of the President and his politics must be the primary concern of a White House, and campaigning must be a permanent feature of governance.

This preoccupation with public imagery and putting the right "spin" on the news is revealed in the language of Washington insiders.

The day is composed, not of hours or minutes, but *news cycles.* In each cycle, *senior White House officials* speaking *on background*

define the *line of the day.* The line is echoed and amplified *outside the Beltway,* to *real people,* who live *out there,* by the President's *surrogates,* whose appearances create *actualities* (on radio) and *talking heads* (on television). During the *roll-out* of a new policy, the President, coached by his *handlers* and working from *talking points* and *briefing books* churned out by *war room* aides, may permit his own head to talk. There are various ways in which he might do this, ranging from the simplest *photo op* to a *one on one* with a media *big foot,* to the more elaborately orchestrated *media big hit* (perhaps an *impromptu* with real people) to a full fledged spectacle of a *town hall.*

The line, a subunit of the Administration's thematic *message,* is reinforced by *leaks* and *plants* and *massaged* through *care and feeding* of the press. It is adjusted by *spin patrol* and corrected through *damage control* when *mistakes are made* or *gaffes* are committed that take attention *off-message* and create a dreaded *feeding frenzy.* Reaction to the line is an important part of the cycle, and it comes primarily from Congressional leaders of both parties, the strange-sounding *biparts,* whose staff-written utterances are often delivered directly to *media outlets* via *fax attacks.* The result of all this activity passes through a *media filter,* where it is cut into tiny, easily digestible *sound bites* and fed to . . . *pundits,* who deliver the ultimate product of the entire process, a new piece of *conventional wisdom.*

Source: Michael Kelly, "David Gergen, Master of the Game," *New York Times Magazine,* October 31, 1993, 64, 67.

Just Who Makes Up Washington's Political Community?

Although Washington is hardly a typical American city, it is not an island unto itself. The leadership of the Washington community consists mainly of people who hail from someplace else. Even middle-aged residents who raised their children in Washington often do not think of themselves as Washingtonians. Rather, they view themselves as transplanted Texans, Wisconsinites, Georgians, Arkansans, and Californians. Unlike other cities, this highly permeable community "regularly accords automatic, immediate, and unshakable top status to someone from out of town, even if that someone's [Jimmy Carter's or Ronald Reagan's] public conversation

Two of Washington's most experienced and best-connected insiders are Republican James A. Baker III (right) and Democrat Vernon E. Jordan. They are shown here conferring at the White House during the transition from the Bush to the Clinton administration. Baker was President Bush's chief of staff and Jordan headed Clinton's transition team.

consists mainly of unpleasant statements about the community and attacks on its oldest inhabitants."[19]

Washington's political community is a large collection of people who came to Washington specifically to practice politics—presidents and their staffs, members of Congress and their aides, people who direct the major government departments and agencies, the upper levels of the permanent bureaucracy, career military personnel, judges and their clerks and assistants, foreign diplomats, interest group representatives, think tank associates, media personnel, and politically oriented lawyers. With every election a new group of outsiders, in Nelson Polsby's words, "floats into Washington on the political tide and is deposited in one or another organization . . . most of which contain strata from previous administrations."[20] Washington can, therefore, be viewed geologically. It contains strata of people who came to town around the same time and remained to build up networks of friendship, alliance, and enmity dating back to the Eisenhower, Kennedy, Johnson, Nixon, Ford, Carter, Reagan, or Bush years. Indeed, many of these people caught "Potomac Fever"—an addiction to wielding power, being close to power, or feeling that one is at the center of things. When

their president departed the White House, they were defeated for reelection, or their patron lost his or her position of power, most stayed on in Washington. They became lobbyists, lawyers, and consultants, seeking to remain part of the action. These geological networks, then, interconnect with networks of people who must deal with each other because they share a common policy interest (for example, health, trade, housing, urban transit, or national security policy), though not necessarily a common point of view. There also are political networks based on people's states of origin.

Providing an element of continuity in the Washington political community are the so-called in-and-outers. When the political leaders with whom they are affiliated are in office, then they are in; they help to staff the White House and key departmental posts. But when those to whom they have access are out of office, then they too are out and they return to their law firms, consultantships, think tanks, interest groups, and congressional staff positions. Thus, Clinton administration officials who are also Democratic Washington insiders—Secretary of Commerce Ron Brown, Trade Representative Mickey Kantor, and Deputy National Security Adviser Samuel Berger, among others—earned their livings as lawyer-lobbyists while the Republicans held sway in the White House during the 1980s and early 1990s. And when the Democrats regained the presidency in 1992, it was the Republican in-and-outers who moved their places of business to law offices, consulting firms, and friendly think tanks.

Washington also has its sages. These are the senior members of the community who over the years have earned its respect—people such as columnist David Broder of the *Washington Post;* lawyers Robert Strauss, Leonard Garment, Howard Baker, Lloyd Cutler, Harry McPherson, and William Rogers; former defense secretary Melvin Laird; lobbyist Charles Walker; pollster Peter Hart; and former presidential economic advisers Herbert Stein and Charles Schultze. These elders are known for their straight talk and sound advice. Their analyses of complex problems, assessments of political leaders, and views about which issues are worthy of attention find outlets among the media and political leaders.[21] They are not a group with a common point of view, but they can affect how the public and political leaders perceive issues and even the substance of government policy.

19. Nelson W. Polsby, "The Washington Community," in *The New Congress,* ed. Thomas E. Mann and Norman J. Ornstein (Washington, D.C.: American Enterprise Institute, 1981), 8.

20. Ibid., 9.

21. See the account of Washington insider Robert Strauss's activities by Steven V. Roberts, "Out of Texas, the Capital's Leading Wise Man," *New York Times,* Dec. 20, 1987, 10, National edition.

Among the most dramatic changes in the Washington community since the 1950s has been the explosive growth in the number and diversity of interest groups, businesses, consultants, law firms, and think tanks involved in the policy process.[22] Particularly noteworthy has been the proliferation of so-called public interest lobby groups pressing forward on civil rights, the environment, health, women's issues, and poverty issues. Also swelling the ranks of the Washington community have been the representatives of the intergovernmental lobby (agents for states, local governments, and universities), the "hired gun" lobbyists who work on behalf of foreign governments, and representatives of corporations. In the 1960s, as the government's role expanded when President Lyndon Johnson's Great Society programs leapt onto the policy agenda, "firms sprang up designed to hook the bureaucracies into their client groups, to discover needs, to monitor the performance of the public sector in rela-

tion to needs," and to monitor the private sector responses to government interventions.[23]

This proliferating array of interests operating within the Washington community reflects the country's expanded and conflictual issue agenda. During the Eisenhower era of the 1950s, the issue agenda was quite limited and lacking in intense conflict. Foreign policy conflicts subsided with the conclusion of the Korean War, and domestic issues heated up only modestly when dealing with such questions as aid to depressed areas. The 1990s are quite different. With its civil rights revolution, women's and environmental movements, expanded governmental responsibilities, the increased salience of such social issues as abortion, the end of the cold war, instability around the world, and the massive federal budget deficit, Washington's issue agenda has become more crowded and highly conflictual. In turn, decision making has become more complex and difficult for the occupants of formal positions of power within the Congress, White House, bureaucracy, and courts.[24]

22. For an insightful and concise account of how the Washington community changed between the 1950s and 1980s, see Barbara Sinclair, *The Transformation of the U.S. Senate* (Baltimore: Johns Hopkins University Press, 1989), chap. 4. Also see Samuel Kernell, *Going Public: New Strategies of Presidential Leadership* (Washington, D.C.: CQ Press, 1993), chap. 1.

23. Sinclair, *Transformation of the U.S. Senate,* 10.
24. Kernell, *Going Public.*

Working within the Washington Community

It is not possible to come to Washington as president, a presidential assistant, cabinet officer, or member of Congress, and remain aloof from the city's political community. Governing involves more than communicating directly with the American people via television or face-to-face negotiations with senators and representatives. Personnel must be recruited to staff an administration or congressional office, policy initiatives must be developed and meshed with existing policies, and various interests within and outside government must be either accommodated or overcome—all while maintaining public support. In this, the involvement of the Washington political community is inevitable.

The importance of the Washington community has not been lost on foreign governments, which now routinely hire Washington insiders to lobby Congress and the executive branch on their behalf. Even foreign heads of state make it a point to become acquainted with the permanent Washington community during their visits to the United States. A striking example occurred in 1987 during

The Washington area is constantly used by public officials and interest groups as a backdrop for carefully planned events that they hope will be included as film clips on the television networks' evening news programs. President Clinton is shown touring a Washington neighborhood to meet with local business people while seeking to build public support for his economic program.

During her 1987 visit to the United States, Raisa Gorbachev, wife of the Soviet leader, demonstrated a shrewd understanding of the importance of establishing contact with leaders of the Washington community. She is seen here with a prominent Washington insider and Democratic fund raiser, Pamela Harriman. After the 1992 election, President Clinton appointed Harriman to a key diplomatic post, U.S. ambassador to France.

the visit of Soviet leader Mikhail Gorbachev and his wife, Raisa. Schooled by the wily former Soviet ambassador Anatoly Dobrynin before her visit to the United States in 1987, Raisa Gorbachev asked Pamela Harriman, the socially prominent and politically connected widow of governor and ambassador Averell Harriman, to host a small luncheon where she could meet influential women leaders.

Presidential scholar Richard Neustadt, after reviewing five transitions from one president to another, has concluded that future presidents and their administrations will find it harder and harder to adjust to the Washington community. He sees the maze of issues, interests, institutions, and individuals with which presidents must deal growing thicker, more complex, more interactive, more entrenched, and harder to understand.[25] As a result, administrations need more time now than in the past to learn how to cope with the Washington environment. During this learning process, however, presidents are in

danger of the Washington community rendering negative and possibly fatal judgments about their leadership abilities and their administrations' policies. In this, the Washington community's role is similar to that of Broadway's drama critics, who cannot through their reviews guarantee a smash hit but who can guarantee that a show will have a short run. The Washington community's reactions to the nation's political leaders are transmitted to the public via television newscasts, talk shows, and the print media, and their impact on the public can be profound. Indeed, knowledgeable observers have concluded that a major reason President Clinton appointed former Reagan White House aide David Gergen as counselor was a belief that he would be an effective emissary to Washington's permanent community in general and to the members of the media in particular.[26]

Even though some claim that the Washington community is cut off from reality and the rest of America, it is permeated with leadership from throughout the nation and reflects a diversity of views. It is splintered among various interests and specializations, conflicting ideological and partisan loyalties, home state ties, and geological strata. Yet despite its connections to all sectors of society, Washington's political community does share "frames of reference, life styles, media, customs, and language."[27] Where else but in Washington can people, in the jargon of the locals, just "disappear" because they have taken up residence some place in the world out beyond the Beltway?[28] People interested in politics can, of course, live far from Washington, but from one election and from one administration to the next, the Washington political community acts as an ever-present force in the corridors of power affecting the actions of Congress, the presidency, the bureaucracy, and the Supreme Court. Indeed, a now-accepted piece of lore, even among political observers outside the Beltway, is that national political leadership requires an ability "to work with or otherwise win over the Washington community."[29]

25. Richard E. Neustadt, *Presidential Power: The Politics of Leadership from FDR to Carter* (New York: Wiley, 1980), 232.

26. Fred Barnes, "Press Gang," *New Republic,* June 21, 1993, 17.
27. Neustadt, *Presidential Power,* 240.
28. Polsby, "The Washington Community," 13.
29. See Fred I. Greenstein, ed., *Leadership in the Modern Presidency* (Cambridge, Mass.: Harvard University Press, 1988). Also see the comments on this book by David Broder, "The Qualities of a President," *Washington Post,* March 25, 1988, C7.

10. Congress

M OST NATIONS' legislatures are primarily arenas for debate where decisions of the executive or national political parties are ratified and some oversight of the executive is exercised. They are not places where important policy decisions are made. The Congress of the United States, however, is a legislature of a different stripe. It does make important decisions that significantly shape domestic and foreign policy, and the ebb and flow of its business serve as the political heartbeat of the nation.[1] The centrality of Congress in the policy-making process has been aptly summarized by congressional scholar Ralph Huitt: "Whoever tries to weave the seamless web of American policy . . . will find soon enough that all threads lead ultimately to Congress."[2]

This chapter describes the organization and operation of the Congress and explains why Congress has retained a prominent policy-making role, why the institution and its members function and behave as they do, and what the consequences of those behavior patterns have been. The starting point for this exploration of congressional politics is the process through which members of Congress are selected.

The Electoral Connection

A closer look at the Congress quickly reveals the connection between how Congress functions and the processes used to choose its members. The composition of Congress is determined by constitutional and statutory rules that govern eligibility to serve and apportionment of representation among the states, as well as by the processes used to recruit and nominate candidates. The behavior of the legislators themselves also is affected by the general electoral process because it gives individual candidates—not party organizations—the primary responsibility for securing election and reelection. Members of the House and Senate, therefore, enter Congress with a substantial degree of independence and a sense of personal responsibility for winning a seat there.

1. See Kenneth A. Shepsle, "Representation and Governance: The Great Legislative Trade-Off," *Political Science Quarterly* 103 (Fall 1988): 653.

2. Ralph K. Huitt, "Congressional Organization and Operations in the Field of Money and Credit," in *Fiscal and Debt Management Policies,* ed. Commission on Money and Credit (Englewood Cliffs, N.J.: Prentice-Hall, 1963), 408. Also see reporter David Broder's comments on how Congress is the best vantage point from which to cover Washington and national politics in his *Behind the Front Page: A Candid Look at How the News Is Made* (New York: Simon and Schuster, 1987), 208–212.

Eligibility and Length of Terms

The Constitution imposes only minimal requirements for holding congressional office: *age*—twenty-five years for House members and thirty years for senators; *citizenship*—seven years for representatives and nine years for senators; and *residency*—officeholders must reside in the state they represent. Even though the Constitution does not require House candidates to reside in the district they represent, voters expect them to do just that. Residency even occasionally becomes a campaign issue—Americans always seem to be on the move. Sen. Frank Lautenberg (D-N.J.), for example, effectively accused his 1988 opponent, Pete Dawkins (Heisman Trophy winner, Rhodes scholar, army general, and Wall Street banker), of being a celebrity in search of a state in which to run. Well-known candidates, however, can occasionally overcome "carpetbagging" charges as did New York Democratic senators Robert Kennedy (1965–1968) and Daniel Patrick Moynihan (1977–   ), both of whom had out-of-state residences before becoming candidates.

House members serve two-year terms, with the entire House up for election in even-numbered years. When a vacancy occurs through death or retirement, the governor of the state in which the vacancy exists may call a special election to choose a successor to fill out the balance of the unexpired term. Governors may not fill House vacancies through appointments.

Senators too are elected in even-numbered years, but they serve six-year terms; one-third of the Senate stands for election every two years. Senate vacancies can be filled either by gubernatorial appointment or by special election, depending on state law.

Apportionment and Redistricting

Under the Constitution representation in the House is based on each state's population, with every state entitled to at least one representative. Each state is also automatically allotted two senators.

To ensure that apportionment of the 435 House seats reflects shifts in the nation's population, Congress is required to reapportion the seats after every decennial (ten-year) census. When that **reapportionment** occurs, states experiencing population growth gain additional congressional representation at the expense of states with lower rates of growth or population losses. The big gainers from the 1990 census were the Sun Belt states of California, Florida, and Texas; the Middle-Atlantic and midwestern states sustained the greatest seat losses (Figure 10.1).

House members are elected from districts whose boundaries are drawn by the various state legislatures. To ensure that all districts with-

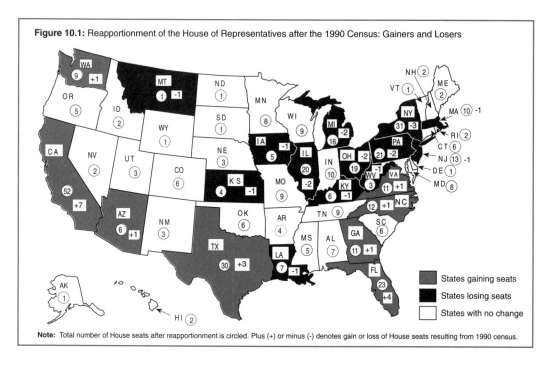

Figure 10.1: Reapportionment of the House of Representatives after the 1990 Census: Gainers and Losers

States gaining seats
States losing seats
States with no change

Note: Total number of House seats after reapportionment is circled. Plus (+) or minus (-) denotes gain or loss of House seats resulting from 1990 census.

in a state are as equal as possible in population, congressional district boundaries are redrawn after each decennial census. The stakes in this *redistricting* process are high. The political careers of incumbents and challengers, party control of congressional seats, and interest group access to representatives can all hinge on how district lines are drawn. Indeed, in most states redistricting is an intensely partisan matter, with both parties trying to create districts that will maximize their control of House seats. With the next election in mind, incumbents and potential challengers look for ways as well to have district lines drawn to their advantage.

Drawing district lines to gain political advantage—known as **gerrymandering**—originated in 1812 when Gov. Elbridge Gerry engineered an unusually blatant manipulation of district lines by the Massachusetts legislature. Gerrymandering for partisan advantage can be achieved by (1) concentrating blocs of opposition party voters in a single or small number of districts while creating safe majorities for one's own party in the remaining districts; or (2) spreading blocs of opposition party voters across a number of districts in a manner that precludes the opposition from gaining district-level majorities. The partisan consequences of redistricting were evident in the redrawing of House district lines in Texas after the 1990 census. The state's population growth between 1980 and 1990 entitled it to three additional House seats. With the Democrats in control of both the Texas legislature and governorship, it was not surprising that the new congressional district map they crafted favored their party's candidates. After redistricting, the Democrats were able in the 1992 elections to protect all of their incumbents, pick up two additional seats, and win 70 percent (twenty-one of thirty) of the state's House seats with 52 percent of the total vote in the state's thirty House races.

Since 1962 the Supreme Court has required that legislative districts within a state be substantially equal in population. In enforcing the Court's "one person, one vote" doctrine, the federal courts have invalidated state redistricting schemes for failing to meet strict standards for equality among a state's districts. The courts also have redrawn district lines themselves when a state legislature either failed to act or passed a plan that did not meet the "one person, one vote" standard. As for the Supreme Court itself, in the future it will review instances of partisan gerrymandering to determine whether voters' constitutional right to the "equal protection of the laws" has been violated.[3]

Redistricting carried out after the 1990 census was dramatically affected by the Voting Rights Act, which was interpreted by the Supreme Court and state legislatures to require the creation of districts in which racial and ethnic minorities were in the majority wherever residential patterns made this possible. This resulted in a substantial increase in minority-majority districts and a corresponding increase in the number of minority members elected to the House (see Chapter 4). In 1992 thirty-eight African American representatives and seventeen Hispanic representatives were elected to the House in contrast to the twenty-five African Americans and eleven Hispanics elected in 1990.

Candidate Recruitment and Nomination

Important influences on the nature of campaigns and their outcomes are the decisions that incumbents make about whether to seek reelection and the decisions that potential challengers and open-seat candidates make about whether to run.[4] In most races the incumbent will seek reelection. If the incumbent is considered electorally secure, meaningful opposition is unlikely to be encountered in either the primary or general election. But when the incumbent is considered vulnerable or there is an open seat (the incumbent is not seeking reelec-

3. *Davis v. Bandemer,* 478 U.S. 109 (1986).

4. For an insightful analysis of the factors influencing candidates' decisions to enter House contests, see Linda Fowler and Robert D. McClure, *Political Ambition: Who Decides to Run for Congress* (New Haven, Conn.: Yale University Press, 1989).

Like many of his colleagues, Rep. David Obey (D-Wis.), chairman of the powerful House Appropriations Committee, began his political career as a state legislator. In 1969, after seven years in the Wisconsin Assembly, he won his House seat in a special election. Obey has now achieved senior member and power broker status, but this is a status that has been possible because he continues to be as attentive to his constituents as he was as a freshman representative.

tion), potentially strong candidates—people with experience in public office or standing in their communities—are likely to emerge. Quality candidates normally can attract the publicity, supporters, and financing essential to a hard-fought, competitive campaign.

Candidates emerge in a variety of ways. Most are self-starters or self-selected. They decide, after weighing their chances and talking with advisers and potential supporters, whether or not the time is right to make a run for the House or Senate. Some candidates are recruited by local and state party leaders. In recent years the national party campaign committees in the House and Senate have played a bigger role in recruiting candidates and seeking to smooth the way to the nomination for these potential candidates by providing financial support and discouraging rival candidates.

It is, however, an unusual party organization that can guarantee a preferred candidate a House or Senate nomination. As was noted in Chapter 6, in nearly every instance congressional candidates are nominated via primary elections by the voters; party organizations have a limited influence over nominations. But in a few areas of the country that is not the case. A prominent example of a party organization that continues to dominate the nomination process is the Nassau County (Long Island, New York) GOP organization. Its leaders select the party's congressional candidates from a pool of party workers who have earned the right to run through lengthy, loyal service to the organization. For most candidates, however, winning a House or Senate nomination through a primary election is a do-it-yourself process, which requires building and financing a personal campaign organization to contest the primary.

Because the recruitment and nomination process is highly fragmented, decentralized, and not controlled by party organizational hierarchies, senators and representatives are able to operate with a substantial measure of independence. The strongest, most experienced candidates tend to emerge from the ranks of state and local officeholders—legislators, district attorneys, governors, mayors. Because Democrats predominate in these lower steppingstones to Congress, the Democratic party has been more successful in recruiting strong candidates than the Republican party. This is one of the factors contributing to continuing Democratic control of the House.[5]

5. L. Sandy Maisel, "Quality Candidates in House and Senate Elections, from 1982 to 1990," in *Atomistic Congress: An Interpretation of Congressional Change,* ed. Allen D. Hertzke and Ronald M. Peters, Jr. (Armonk, N.Y.: M.E. Sharpe, 1992), 141–171. Also see Gary C. Jacobson, *The Politics of Congressional Elections,* 3d ed. (New York: HarperCollins, 1992), chap. 2.

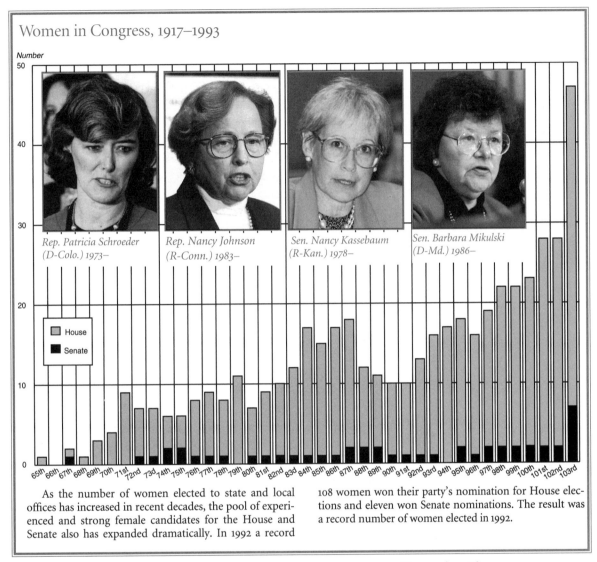

Women in Congress, 1917–1993

Number

Rep. Patricia Schroeder
(D-Colo.) 1973–

Rep. Nancy Johnson
(R-Conn.) 1983–

Sen. Nancy Kassebaum
(R-Kan.) 1978–

Sen. Barbara Mikulski
(D-Md.) 1986–

House
Senate

As the number of women elected to state and local offices has increased in recent decades, the pool of experienced and strong female candidates for the House and Senate also has expanded dramatically. In 1992 a record 108 women won their party's nomination for House elections and eleven won Senate nominations. The result was a record number of women elected in 1992.

Campaign Finance

A critical element of electoral success is having enough money to run a competitive campaign. Costs, however, have been escalating steadily as campaigns have come to rely more heavily on sophisticated technology, television advertising, and professional consultants. Unlike presidential elections, congressional races receive no public funding and have no limits on campaign expenditures. In 1991–1992 the mean expenditure by a Senate incumbent was $3.7 million, and the mean expenditure by a House incumbent was $584,650, with fifty candidates spending more than $1 million. Indeed, the million-dollar House campaign is no longer unusual. In California the 1992 expenditures of eight candidates exceeded $1 million, led by Republican Michael Huffington with $5.4 million.

Campaign finance in congressional races is governed by the 1971 Federal Election Campaign Act (FECA), which was amended significantly in 1974, 1976, and 1979. It provides for the following limits on contributions *per election* (the primary and general elections are considered to be separate): (1) individuals, $1,000; (2) political action committees (PACs), $5,000; and (3) political party committees, $5,000 to House candidates and $17,500 to Senate candidates. Party committees also are authorized to make **coordinated expenditures** (for polling, media advertising, consultants, voter mobilization) to support House and Senate candidates.[6] In the two California Senate races of 1992, party-coordinated expenditures totaled $8.1 million: $4.9 million by the Republican party to support Bruce Herschensohn and John Seymour ($2.45 million for each candidate) and $3.23 million by the Democratic party to assist its winning candidates, Barbara Boxer ($1.74 million) and Dianne Feinstein ($1.49 million). Because the national Republican organizations have been more effective in raising party funds, the GOP plays a more significant role in financing congressional campaigns than the Democratic party.

A major consequence of the 1974 amendments to the FECA has been the formation of political action committees (PACs), an increasingly important source of campaign funds (see Chapter 7). The obvious willingness of PACs to contribute to incumbents (71 percent of PAC funds in 1991–1992 went to incumbents) is a source of incumbent advantage over their challengers.

The two parties' views of campaign finance reform proposals are, as might be expected, heavily influenced by their respective fund-raising abilities. Congressional Democrats are wary of Republican proposals to either severely limit or eliminate PAC contributions because the Democrats raise more money from PACs than Republicans. Democrats also oppose Republican proposals to substantially increase the amount contributed to campaigns by party organizations because of the GOP's advantage in party fund-raising. As the minority party in Congress, the Republicans generally reject any proposals for public funding of campaigns because such proposals also impose ceilings on campaign

6. For a detailed analysis of national party committee involvement in House and Senate elections, see Paul S. Herrnson, *Party Campaigning in the 1980s* (Cambridge, Mass.: Harvard University Press, 1988); and Jacobson, *Politics of Congressional Elections*, 71–77.

expenditures. These limits would work to the disadvantage of challengers, who normally must pull out all the financial stops to have a chance of unseating an incumbent.[7]

House Elections

The normal pattern of outcomes in House elections is easily summed up: "Incumbents win!" In the 1980s House incumbents had a 94.5 percent reelection rate, and in the early 1990s they continued to enjoy reelection rates of over 90 percent, but their victory margins were narrower. In 1992, as Congress's standing with the American people was jolted by the House bank scandal, the Clarence Thomas-Anita Hill controversy, policy gridlock, and worries about the economy, competition for House seats intensified. The average share of the two-party vote won by incumbents in 1992 fell to 63.6 percent, its lowest level since 1966, and the proportion of incumbents (33.4 percent) winning by less than 60 percent of the vote was the highest since 1964 (see Figure 10.2).

Incumbents generally win because they are able to publicize their activities through franked (paid with public funds) mailings to their constituents, press releases and radio tapes and videotapes sent to constituency news outlets, frequent trips back to their districts, and the work of their official staffs. Incumbents also benefit from the tendencies of PACs to give primarily to incumbents. With these publicity and resource advantages, incumbents have been able to build personal followings among their constituents at a time when voters have been paying less attention to partisan considerations in making their election day choices. Finally, strong challengers are increasingly reluctant to enter what often appear to be contests they are sure to lose.

The Democrats have maintained uninterrupted control of the House since 1954 in spite of GOP successes in winning the presidency. This Democratic dominance of the House has been aided not only by incumbency advantages but also by the party's success in winning open-seat contests (those in which the incumbent does not seek reelection). For example, in the ninety-one open-seat contests of 1990 the Democrats won fifty-seven contests (63 percent) to the Republicans' thirty-four (37 percent).

Senate Elections

While most House incumbents coast to relatively lopsided victories,

7. See Jacobson, *Politics of Congressional Elections*, 56–60; and David B. Magleby and Candice Nelson, *The Money Chase: Congressional Campaign Finance Reform* (Washington, D.C.: Brookings, 1990), chap. 9.

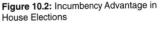

Figure 10.2: Incumbency Advantage in House Elections

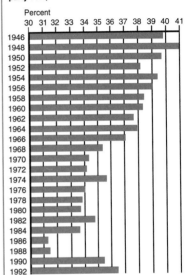

Average House challenger's share of the major party vote, 1946–1992

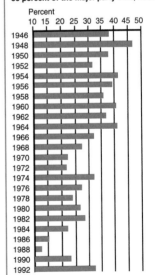

House seats won by incumbents with less than 60 percent of the major party vote, 1946–1992

Sources: Gary C. Jacobson, "Congress: A Singular Continuity," in *The Elections of 1988*, ed. Michael Nelson (Washington, D.C.: CQ Press, 1989), 132–133; Gary C. Jacobson, "Congress: Unusual Year, Unusual Election," in *The Elections of 1992*, ed. Michael Nelson (Washington, D.C.: CQ Press, 1993), 168; and Norman J. Ornstein, Thomas E. Mann, and Michael Malbin, eds., *Vital Statistics on Congress, 1993–1994* (Washington, D.C.: CQ Inc., 1994), 61.

many Senate elections in recent years have been vigorously contested, and control of the Senate has hinged on a small proportion of the total vote cast. Thus, a shift of just 35,000 votes in 1982 would have returned the chamber to Democratic control, and a switch of just 55,000 votes in 1986, properly distributed among various candidates, would have left the Senate in Republican hands.

Senate elections are sharply contested more often than House elections—for example, in fourteen (39 percent) of the thirty-six Senate elections in 1992 the winners received less than 55 percent of the vote, and seven senators were elected with less than 52 percent of the vote. This level of competition occurs because of the attractiveness of the office and the fact that Senate constituencies, which are statewide, tend to be more evenly balanced between Democratic and Republican voters than is the case in most House districts. These factors increase the likelihood that potentially strong candidates will enter Senate contests because they believe they have a credible chance of winning. Although incumbency is an advantage in Senate elections (82 percent of incumbents seeking reelection between 1980 and 1992 were victorious), senators find it more difficult than House members to develop reputations of electoral invincibility that will scare off strong challengers. Senate races, therefore, tend to attract more electable candidates, who in turn are able to attract the resources—money and workers—needed to mount full-scale campaign efforts.

Congressional elections analyst Gary Jacobson has summarized the differences between House and Senate elections:

Competition breeds competition. Senate contests are more often competitive than House elections because Senate challengers are more often experienced, high-quality candidates who are able to raise adequate funds. Superior candidates run because the record shows that Senate challengers have a decent chance of winning. The same dynamic that inhibits competition in House elections encourages it in Senate elections.[8]

Candidate-centered Campaigns

Whether the race is for the House or the Senate, competitive or noncompetitive, congressional elections share certain common characteristics. Candidates are largely on their own and can normally rely on only moderate levels of support from their party organizations. They build their own campaign organizations, collect their own financial contri-

8. Gary C. Jacobson, "Congress: A Singular Continuity," in *The Elections of 1988*, ed. Michael Nelson (Washington, D.C.: CQ Press, 1989), 136.

butions, and stress their own records. Most have been able through highly personalized campaigning to insulate themselves from national swings of electoral sentiment. As a result, presidential coattails (when popular presidential candidates are able to transfer their popularity to their party's House and Senate candidates) have worn extremely thin in recent elections.

The 1992 presidential race among Clinton, Bush, and Perot was no exception. Because it did not produce a landslide victory for Clinton, the effects of presidential coattails were again limited. Broad public concern about the economy and dissatisfaction with divided government in Washington—themes stressed by Clinton—certainly worked to the Democrats' advantage, however, in the House and Senate races. Clinton's campaign strategy of focusing resources on states rich in electoral votes also tended to help Democratic congressional candidates, particularly in such states as New York, California, and Illinois, where Clinton held a wide lead in the polls, spurring the Bush campaign to largely abandon its campaigns there and leave its GOP congressional candidates to fend for themselves against united, energized Democratic organizations.[9]

What kind of legislator emerges from Congress's decentralized and highly personalized electoral environment? Most members of the Senate and House consider themselves loyal party members and generally vote with their party leadership on roll-call votes. But they also recognize that it was their own campaign efforts and the image they conveyed to their constituents—not their party's—that got them elected. They further understand a basic reality of political survival: reelection ultimately depends on their own ability to satisfy constituents and not on loyalty to their party's or president's policy positions. Neither the president nor a party organization is capable of saving a member whose constituents are disenchanted.

The electoral process has profound implications for the way Congress operates. Given the independence encouraged by the electoral process, today's senators and representatives could be described as *independent political entrepreneurs*—free enterprisers in politics. The men and women elected are responsible for sustaining a personal political enterprise and for achieving their personal goals within the legislative arena. Thus, although Americans speak frequently of "the Congress," "the Senate," or "the House," such general images give a false sense of unity to these institutions. Congress is actually 535 separate political

9. Gary C. Jacobson, "Congress: Unusual Year, Unusual Election," in *The Elections of 1992*, ed. Michael Nelson (Washington, D.C.: CQ Press, 1993), 175–178.

The Composition of Congress: 103d Congress, First Session, 1993

Although Congress functions as a representative body for all Americans, its membership is hardly representative of the social and economic characteristics of the population. Like most leadership groups, it is predominantly white, middle-aged, male, and middle to upper middle class. The 1992 elections, however, significantly changed the demographic profile of the Congress. The number of women members of the House and Senate jumped from twenty-nine in 1990 to forty-eight in 1992. African Americans gained fourteen members in the House and their first U.S. senator, Carol Moseley-Braun (D-Ill.). And the Hispanic membership grew from fifteen to nineteen. (These numbers include not only senators and representatives but also delegates from the District of Columbia, Puerto Rico, and U.S. territories.)

	House	Senate
Republicans	167	45[a]
Democrats	267	55
Independents	1	0
Average years of tenure	10.7	11.3
First-term members	110	14[a]
Average age	51.7	58.0
Men	388	93
Women	48[b]	7[a]
Whites	397	97
African Americans	39[b]	1
Hispanics	19[c]	0
Asians and Pacific Islanders	7[d]	2
RELIGION[e]		
Protestants (traditional)[f]	237	58
Catholics	118	23
Jews	32	10
Others[g]	48	9
PRIOR OCCUPATIONS (MAJOR CATEGORIES)		
Law	181	58
Business or banking	131	24
Public service/politics	87	10
Education	66	11
Journalism	24	9
Agriculture	19	8
Engineering	5	0
Medicine	6	0
Professional sports	1	1

Source: *Congressional Quarterly Weekly Report,* November 7, 1992.
   Notes:. a. Includes results of the 1993 special election in Texas won by Republican Kay Bailey Hutchison. b. Includes nonvoting delegate from the District of Columbia. c. Includes nonvoting delegates from Puerto Rico and the Virgin Islands. d. Includes nonvoting delegates from American Samoa and Guam. e. Includes all nonvoting delegates. f. Includes Baptists, Episcopalians, Lutherans, Methodists, Presbyterians, United Church of Christ/Congregational, and unspecified Protestant. g. Includes nontraditional Protestant, Mormon, Unitarian, Seventh-Day Adventist, Greek Orthodox, and unspecified.

enterprises, all being run simultaneously. Not a paradigm of orderliness, to be sure, but that is Congress—a highly individualized and decentralized institution. It is an institution in which individuals with diverse objectives—reelection, power in the chamber, policy leadership, service to constituents, and even presidential aspirations—pursue their goals, sometimes in conflict with colleagues, sometimes with the acquiescence of colleagues, and sometimes with the cooperation and assistance of colleagues.

What Does Congress Do?

Congress is first and foremost a legislative body, but its activities and functions within the political system extend beyond lawmaking and include overseeing the administration, educating the public, and representing its constituents. Congress should not be viewed as some kind of bill and resolution factory, where the members are graded on a piecework basis.[10]

Lawmaking

Lawmaking is the principal legal function of the Congress—a function that has taken on massive proportions as the role of government and the complexity of the issues to be resolved have increased. Approximately ten thousand bills are introduced during the two years between congressional elections, with each senator introducing an average of thirty-eight bills and each House member averaging fifteen bills. Eight thousand committee meetings are held to review these measures, and the House and Senate are normally in session approximately 285 days.[11]

In spite of all this activity only a small share of the bills introduced ever reaches the president's desk for signature. This high mortality rate reflects the difficulties encountered in developing sufficient support for a bill as well as the fact that not all legislation is introduced with the expectation that it will be passed. Often bills are introduced with the objective of beginning a long process of building public, interest group, administration, and congressional support for the measure. For example, many of the New Frontier and Great Society measures of the Kennedy and Johnson administrations—including the Peace Corps and Medicare—had incubated in the Congress in the 1950s until momentum developed for their passage in the early 1960s. Similarly, the Reagan administration's 1981 tax-reduction bill had its roots in proposals

10. See Ralph K. Huitt, "The Outsider in the Senate: An Alternative Role," *American Political Science Review* 55 (September 1961): 566–575.

11. Norman J. Ornstein, Thomas E. Mann, and Michael J. Malbin, eds., *Vital Statistics on Congress, 1989-1990* (Washington, D.C.: CQ Inc., 1990), 155–156.

made in the 1970s by Rep. Jack Kemp (R-N.Y.) and Sen. William Roth, Jr. (R-Del.). Legislation also may be introduced to satisfy the demands of interest groups or to apply pressure to administrators to change the implementation of an existing law.

Since the 1980s the number of bills passed by Congress has declined; as part of a government awash in a huge budget deficit, Congress has found its ability to initiate new or expanded spending programs restricted. The length of the fewer bills enacted, however, has gone up. The cause is the increasing complexity of the problems—drug abuse, health care reform, clean air, tax reform—with which Congress must wrestle and the statutory requirements to pass comprehensive budget legislation (the congressional budget process is described later in this chapter).

In seeking to pass bills, members of Congress stick to one overriding strategy: attract majority support while making as few concessions as possible to opponents. Compromise and accommodation with potential supporters as well as opponents are inevitable, however, because lawmaking requires finding a majority that will support a bill. Not surprisingly, then, few bills emerge from the House and Senate chambers in the same form in which they were introduced. In fashioning legislative compromises that a majority finds satisfactory, Congress plays a major role in resolving and managing the conflicts that exist in American society.

Oversight of Administration

After legislation has been enacted, the responsibility for its implementation falls to the bureaucracy. In carrying out congressional mandates the bureaucracy inevitably has a great deal of discretion. The Environmental Protection Agency, for example, can enforce antipollution laws aggressively or look for more accommodating solutions for those industries and communities threatening the environment. And the Justice Department through litigation can seek to broaden or restrict the reach of affirmative action legislation. Because such actions can have profound policy consequences, Congress actively oversees how its mandates are being carried out by administrators.[12] For their part, administrators are all too conscious of the wary eye of Congress because that body is able to enact legislation altering the structures, budgets, and authority of government agencies.

The focal point for oversight of administration is congressional committees. During committee hearings on proposed bills, administra-

12. See Joel D. Aberbach, *Keeping a Watchful Eye: The Politics of Congressional Oversight* (Washington, D.C.: Brookings, 1990).

tors are asked to account for past decisions and to assess the effectiveness of the programs they administer. Controversial administration actions or scandals—such as the 1987 Iran-contra affair or the influence peddling revealed in 1989 within the Department of Housing and Urban Development—can provoke highly publicized congressional investigations. The pain and unpleasantness administrators must en-dure during lengthy, hostile questioning by senators or representatives at committee hearings often render them quite compliant when pressed for changes in administrative policy. Indeed, just the threat of congressional criticism can cause administrators to adjust their policies to avoid hostile reactions from Capitol Hill.

Oversight occurs not just in committee meetings; individual legislators and their staffs continually check on administrative actions as they assist constituents having difficulties with the bureaucracy (also called casework). Examples include helping the elderly to secure Social Security benefits, helping veterans to obtain medical assistance, or speeding up the processing of a community's application for a grant for new sewer construction. Recognizing Congress's legislative power and access to publicity, the bureaucracy is responsive to congressional intervention in behalf of constituents. Members devote a substantial share of their staff resources to casework because (1) it provides the assistance that ordinary citizens so badly need when confronting a vast federal bureaucracy, and (2) a reputation for responsiveness to constituency interests is definitely an asset at reelection time.[13]

Public Education

The activities of Congress and its members are prime subjects for coverage by both the national and local and regional media. With its ability, then, to generate publicity, Congress has found itself in the public education business of informing citizens about current issues. Debates in the House and Senate chambers, committee hearings, interviews with representatives and senators, and press releases cover virtually every aspect of government activity. Moreover, congressionally generated publicity has often helped to crystallize public opinion on issues and facilitate passage of new legislation and changes in administration policy. During the 1960s and 1970s, for example, persistent criticism of America's Vietnam War policy before the Senate Foreign Relations Committee swayed public opinion and government policy on this divi-

13. For consideration of the electoral benefits of effective casework for members of Congress, see Morris P. Fiorina, *Congress: Keystone of the Washington Establishment* (New Haven, Conn.: Yale University Press, 1977); and Bruce Cain, John Ferejohn, and Morris Fiorina, *The Personal Vote* (Cambridge, Mass.: Harvard University Press, 1988).

sive issue. More recently, in 1991, Congress helped to make clear the stakes and consequences of authorizing military action against Iraq, and in 1994 congressional deliberations helped to focus public attention on the president's health care policies. Members of Congress also have been able to dramatize the problems created by drug abuse, rising medical costs, military procurement fraud, homelessness, and nuclear wastes. Congress is thus more than an object of public opinion; it is also a mover and shaker of public opinion, stimulating public interest in issues and influencing public thinking.

Representation

Legislators go to great lengths to stay in touch with their constituents, making grueling schedules the rule for most members. For representatives and senators a typical week includes three to five days in Washington, each of which often starts with breakfast meetings with administrators, interest group representatives, or constituents, and ends with a series of evening receptions and fund-raisers. After tending to legislative business in Washington, most members board planes and spend the balance of the week back in their districts or states with constituents—holding town meetings and office hours, appearing on local television programs, speaking to community groups, cutting ribbons, and marching in local parades. In the process they develop a **home style**—a way of presenting themselves and explaining their actions to constituents—which helps to build a sense of trust among the "home folks."[14]

Representation is a complex phenomenon. Some legislators view themselves primarily as *delegates* from their constituencies. They carry to Washington the views and interests of the voters who elected them. Legislators who adopt a delegate style of representation do not try to exercise independent judgment in casting their votes on the floor of the House or Senate. Rather, they vote their constituency's viewpoint. The personalized nature of campaigning in the United States and the weakness of the parties in compelling members to vote a party line encourage members to adopt a local or district orientation toward issues.

But even if members of Congress adopt a delegate style of representation, their behavior is also influenced by how they perceive their constituencies and by which interests within their constituencies they feel deserve their representation and support. Democrat Daniel Patrick Moynihan and Republican Alphonse D'Amato, for example, both represent the same geographic area—the state of New York—in the Senate.

14. See Richard F. Fenno, Jr., *Home Style: House Members in Their Districts* (Boston: Little, Brown, 1978), especially 151–169.

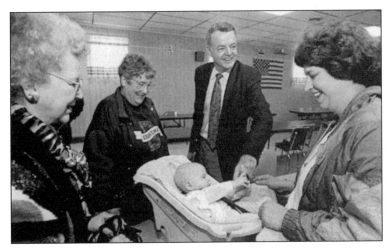

Maintaining close ties with the folks back home is essential to reelection and representation. As a result, most members of Congress spend at least one-third of the year in their districts. Republican representative John Myers listens to the concerns of his constituents in a "Tell John" meeting in Martinsville, Indiana.

Yet they represent their state quite differently. Moynihan has compiled a liberal voting record and D'Amato a conservative one because in part they perceive New York quite differently.

Unlike delegate-type legislators who try to mirror the views of their constituents in making legislative decisions, legislators who adopt a *trustee* style of representation do not feel bound to follow the dictates of their constituents. Rather, when they believe their constituents are wrong they feel free to follow their own judgments about what is or is not wise public policy. Members of Congress often have more freedom from constituency pressures in deciding how to vote than is commonly believed. In his study of members' behavior in their districts, Richard Fenno discovered that a home style that successfully builds a sense of trust among constituents is also one that often frees members to vote as they see fit in Washington. He concluded that voters are seeking more than representation of their policy views in Congress; they are also seeking representation by individuals they consider accessible and trustworthy.[15]

The Committee System

Responsible lawmaking requires specialized knowledge and expertise. Since its earliest days Congress has relied on committees to collect the information needed to make informed decisions and to draft and refine legislative proposals. Initially temporary committees were created to refine each bill developed on the floors of the House and Senate. By 1816, however, Congress had recognized that ad hoc committees were just not up to the task of developing complex legisla-

15. Ibid.

tive proposals. For the Congress to compete for influence with the executive branch and interest groups, it needed permanent committees with subject matter expertise. By the mid-1800s permanent or standing committees with specific subject matter jurisdictions and composed of member specialists were being used to develop and recommend legislation for the full House and Senate.[16] Indeed, the influence of committees on the legislative process had become so dominant by the late 1800s that Woodrow Wilson, in his classic treatise *Congressional Government,* stated that "Congress in session is Congress on display, but Congress in committee is Congress at work."[17]

Today committees continue to play a major role in shaping legislation. Virtually all legislation that reaches the floors of the House and Senate for consideration has first been reviewed and frequently revised by a committee.

Types of Committees

The most important congressional committees are the standing committees—twenty-two in the House and seventeen in the Senate (Tables 10.1 and 10.2). They continue to operate in each succeeding congressional session (hence the term *standing committee*) and have fixed subject matter jurisdictions. The House Ways and Means Committee, for example, has jurisdiction over taxes and trade legislation, while the bailiwick of the House Banking, Finance, and Urban Affairs Committee is housing, community development, financial institutions, and international lending agencies. Standing committees have the power to report bills to the full House and Senate.

Of the four basic types of standing committees, the most numerous are the *authorizing committees.* These bodies develop legislation spelling out the substance or content of policy and empowering the government to act—for example, the House Education and Labor Committee drafts legislation governing education policy and authorizing government agencies to carry out that policy. *Appropriations committees* control the actual appropriation of money from the federal Treasury to pay for programs recommended by the authorizing committees. Jurisdiction over revenue-raising measures is exercised by the *taxing committees*—the Senate Finance Committee and the House Ways and Means Committee. And the *Budget committees* in both chambers coordinate expenditures and revenues.

16. For an insightful account of the development of congressional committees and the consequences of recent changes in the committee system, see Shepsle, "Representation and Governance," 461–484.

17. Woodrow Wilson, *Congressional Government* (Baltimore: Johns Hopkins University Press, 1980), 79 (first published in 1885).

Table 10.1 Standing Committees of the House, 103d Congress (1993–1995)

Standing Committee	Party Ratio	Number of Subcommittees
Agriculture	27D : 18R (60.0% D)	6
Appropriations	37D : 23R (61.7% D)	13
Armed Services	34D : 22R (60.7% D)	6
Banking, Finance, and Urban Affairs	30D : 20R (60.0% D)	8
Budget	26D : 17R (60.5% D)	0
District of Columbia	8D : 4R (66.7% D)	3
Education and Labor	28D : 15R (65.1% D)	6
Energy and Commerce	27D : 17R (61.4% D)	6
Foreign Affairs	27D : 18R (60.0% D)	7
Government Operations	25D : 16R (61.0% D)	6
House Administration	12D : 7R (63.2% D)	6
Judiciary	21D : 14R (60.0% D)	6
Merchant Marine and Fisheries	28D : 18R (60.9% D)	6
Natural Resources	28D : 15R (65.1% D)	5
Post Office and Civil Service	15D : 9R (62.5% D)	7
Public Works and Transportation	39D : 24R (61.9% D)	6
Rules	9D : 4R (69.2% D)	2
Science, Space, and Technology	33D : 22R (60.0% D)	5
Small Business	27D : 18R (60.0% D)	5
Standards of Official Conduct	7D : 7R (50.0% D)	0
Veterans' Affairs	21D : 14R (60.0% D)	5
Ways and Means	24D : 14R (63.1% D)	6

Source: *Congressional Directory, 1993-1994: 103rd Congress* (Washington, D.C.: Government Printing Office, 1993), 419–476.

Table 10.2 Standing Committees of the Senate, 103d Congress (1993–1995)

Standing Committee	Party Ratio	Number of Subcommittees
Agriculture, Nutrition, and Forestry	10D : 8R (55.6% D)	6
Appropriations	16D : 13R (55.2% D)	13
Armed Services	11D : 9R (55.0% D)	6
Banking, Housing, and Urban Affairs	11D : 8R (52.6% D)	4
Budget	12D : 9R (57.1% D)	0
Commerce, Science, and Transportation	11D : 9R (55.0% D)	8
Energy and Natural Resources	11D : 9R (55.0% D)	5
Environment and Public Works	10D : 7R (58.8% D)	5
Finance	11D : 9R (55.0% D)	8
Foreign Relations	11D : 8R (52.6% D)	7
Governmental Affairs	8D : 5R (61.5% D)	5
Indian Affairs	10D : 8R (55.6% D)	0
Judiciary	10D : 8R (55.6% D)	7
Labor and Human Resources	10D : 7R (58.8% D)	6
Rules and Administration	9D : 7R (56.3% D)	0
Small Business	12D : 9R (57.1% D)	6
Veterans' Affairs	7D : 5R (58.3% D)	0

Source: *Congressional Directory, 1993-1994: 103rd Congress* (Washington, D.C.: Government Printing Office, 1993), 385–412.

The size of committees and the ratio of Democrats to Republicans on standing committees are determined through bargaining between the two parties' leaders after each election. These party ratios, which normally reflect party strength in the two chambers, can dramatically affect the outcomes of committee decisions on legislation. To exert maximum party influence on important legislation, the majority party has customarily insisted on extraordinary majorities on such key committees as the tax-writing House Ways and Means Committee (24D : 14R) and the House Rules Committee (9D : 4R), which controls the procedures under which bills are considered on the House floor.[18]

Select committees study and investigate specific problems and issues. Unlike the standing committees, select committees are not generally considered permanent bodies, and they do not have authority to report bills to the full House and Senate for consideration. Select committees have been used to educate the Congress and the public about such problems as drug abuse, hunger, and the elderly, and to make legislative recommendations. These committees also enable members of Congress to become personally identified with a particular issue or cause. The late Claude Pepper (D-Fla.), for example, gained national attention as a champion of the elderly through his work as leader of the House Select Committee on Aging.

Joint committees are composed of both senators and representatives, with committee leaderships rotating between the chambers at the beginning of each newly elected Congress. These committees perform studies, investigations, and administrative tasks, and oversee the executive. The Joint Economic Committee, for example, conducts hearings on and studies of a wide range of economic issues, and the Joint Committee on Printing oversees the Government Printing Office.

Before legislation can be sent to the president, it must pass both the House and Senate in identical form. But since the two chambers often pass different versions of a bill, reconciliation of these differences is a must. This task usually falls to a **conference committee** composed of representatives and senators. Conference committees negotiate compromises between the House and Senate and then report the results of their negotiations back to the full House and Senate, which must approve the compromise bill before it can be sent to the president (for a more detailed discussion of conference committees, see "The Legislative Process: How a Bill Becomes a Law" in this chapter).

18. For a comprehensive consideration of the role of committees, see Steven S. Smith and Christopher J. Deering, *Committees in Congress,* 2d ed. (Washington, D.C.: CQ Press, 1990).

Because committees often play a crucial role in shaping legislation, members wage fierce campaigns to land desirable committee assignments. In both the House and Senate the Republican and Democratic parties have committees on committees which handle the delicate task of members' assignments. Committee assignments are particularly important in the House, where the large membership and procedural rules restrict individual members' opportunities to exert influence when bills are being considered by the full House. Senators, by contrast, are less concerned about their committee assignments because the chamber's rules give individual members ample opportunities to shape bills after they have been reported from committee and are being considered on the Senate floor (see "The Legislative Process: How a Bill Becomes a Law" in this chapter for a look at the differences in House and Senate floor procedures).

The committee assignments sought by members depend on their personal goals. Those interested in wielding power over a wide range of issues often aim for a seat on the money committees such as the House and Senate Appropriations or Budget committees. Other committees serve members' reelection needs by giving them a chance to assist constituents and influential interest groups. Thus, legislators from farm areas often gravitate toward the agriculture committees, big city members toward the banking committees (housing and urban development), and representatives from coastal regions toward the House Merchant Marine and Fisheries Committee. Members also may seek assignments in which they can have a say in policy of special concern to them. Senators with an interest in foreign policy, for example, may seek slots on the Foreign Relations Committee.

The tendency of members to be attracted by committees that will help them to achieve their career goals means that committees are not necessarily representative of their parent chambers. They are apt to be composed of members with the same particular constituency interests or policy orientations. Indeed, the House Agriculture Committee is composed exclusively of members from agricultural constituencies. Consumers in Brooklyn, Chicago, or Los Angeles simply have no voice on this committee.

The makeup of a committee naturally affects its decisions on policy matters. And because members normally retain their committee assignments as a sort of "property right" for the duration of their congressional careers, the impact of committee assignments on policy can be long term. Is it any wonder then that party leaders, senior committee members, and interest groups seek to "stack" committees to favor particular policy outcomes? According to Rep. Henry Waxman (D-Calif.), who has skillfully worked to achieve majorities on the Energy and Commerce Committee favoring tougher environmental protection and expanded health care legislation, "There are enormous policy implications in the committee assignment process. . . . A number of issues on the Energy and Commerce Committee were decided by one or two votes. Millions, if not billions, of dollars are at stake for major industries in this country."[19]

Committee Leadership Selection: A Modified Seniority System

Committee leaders are always members of the majority party. From early in this century until the 1970s these leaders were selected automatically via the seniority system[20] under which the member of the majority party with the longest continuous service on a committee automatically became its chair. Awarding committee leadership on the basis of seniority tended to restrict such positions to members from electorally safe constituencies since they were the members who piled up seniority. Also under the seniority system, committee leaders may have been unrepresentative of their party's regional composition and policy orientation. This was particularly true for the House Democrats in the 1960s and 1970s, when their party's committee heads were disproportionately southern conservatives. Some of these conservative Democrats used their procedural powers to call meetings, appoint subcommittees, and hire staff to stymie liberal legislation. Frustrated with these maneuvers, younger liberal Democrats successfully pressed for a change in the method of selecting committee chairs that would make them more accountable to the members of their party.

As a result of their efforts, since 1975 House Democratic committee leaders have been elected by the party caucus (the full party membership in the House) at the beginning of each new Congress. Although normally the caucus has followed seniority in choosing leaders, between 1975 and 1993 seven elderly committee heads were deposed. In recent years this system of election has reduced the independence of the chairs in leading their committees because reelection by their col-

19. Quoted by Steven V. Roberts, "Committee Selection: Art and Science," *New York Times*, Jan. 13, 1983, 10Y, National edition.

20. The development of the seniority system in the House is described in Nelson W. Polsby, Miriam Gallaher, and Barry S. Rundquist, "The Growth of the Seniority System in the U.S. House of Representatives," *American Political Science Review* 63 (September 1969): 787–807.

leagues, not automatic retention of their posts based on seniority, is the rule. In 1993, for example, every House Democratic committee leader supported President Clinton's budget reconciliation bill, even G.V. ("Sonny") Montgomery (Miss.), a traditional southern conservative who chaired the Veterans' Affairs Committee.

The influence of committee leaders also has been restricted, particularly in the House, by the rise since the 1970s of subcommittee government. Nearly every standing committee now has subcommittees that consider most legislation (see Table 10.1 and Table 10.2). In the past, subcommittees were subject to control by the full committee chairs who appointed subcommittee members, controlled the size of their staffs, and managed their budgets. Through a series of 1970s reforms, however, House subcommittees now function as relatively autonomous power centers within the Congress. They have specific subject matter jurisdictions, elect their own leaders, and control their budgets and staffs.

Dependent on their party colleagues for reelection and seeing subcommittees playing a larger role in congressional policy making, full committee chairs have lost the dominance they exerted in the 1950s and 1960s. Nevertheless, through the sheer force of their personalities and well-honed political skills these leaders still have substantial clout over their committees. For example, House Energy and Commerce Chairman John ("Big John") Dingell (D-Mich.) zealously guards his committee's jurisdiction ("turf"). Among his colleagues he wields great power because he is a shrewd negotiator who stands by his word. He rules his committee with a strong hand—indeed, junior members think twice before voting against him. Federal administrators know him as a stern watchdog with a passion for inquisition.

In the Senate, committee leaders also are subject to election by their party colleagues, but the seniority system in that chamber has engendered much less controversy than that in the House, and the chamber adheres much more strictly to seniority in selecting committee chairs. Committee leaderships, however, are not as important in the Senate because (1) the Senate tends to resolve more issues on its floor rather than rely on its committees to shape legislation, and (2) in the smaller Senate it is possible for every senator of the majority party to serve as a committee or subcommittee chair.

Rep. John Dingell (D-Mich.), chair of the House Energy and Commerce Committee, is one of the chamber's most powerful members. His power has both institutional and personal bases. His committee has jurisdiction over almost 40 percent of all House bills—including those dealing with clean air, securities markets, telecommunications, energy, railroads, toys, and consumer protection—and he has a reputation for being able, tough, aggressive, determined, and hardworking.

Decentralizing Power within Congress

The standing committee system, with its twenty-two House and seventeen Senate committees, as well as its over 140 subcommittees, creates multiple power centers within Congress based on subject matter jurisdiction and expertise. But such fragmented power has its benefits: it is extremely difficult for anyone either inside or outside Congress to dominate that body; there are just too many centers of power and too many influential leaders. This fragmentation of power also contributes to Congress's autonomy from national political parties, presidents, and interest groups, as well as its vitality. In this decentralized environment members of Congress have many outlets for their initiatives.

But for all its contributions toward maintaining the autonomy and vitality of Congress, the committee system does create problems. With policy making scattered among numerous committees and subcommittees, it becomes difficult for Congress to develop consistent, coordinated policies. For example, the following House committees have a significant role in the field of foreign policy, but each operates independently of the others.

Committee	Foreign Policy Jurisdiction
Foreign Affairs	Foreign aid, State Department
Appropriations	Funds for Departments of Defense and State and for other agencies
Armed Services	Defense Department
Banking, Finance, and Urban Affairs	International lending agencies; monetary policy
Budget	Spending for foreign policy and national security
Energy and Commerce	Foreign commerce, aviation, communications
Intelligence (select committee)	Oversight of Central Intelligence Agency
Judiciary	Immigration
Merchant Marine and Fisheries	Merchant marine and fisheries
Science, Space, and Technology	International scientific cooperation
Ways and Means	Trade
Agriculture	Food for Peace; export guarantees

Unsurprisingly, with this array of House committees, as well as a similar collection of Senate committees, decisive, timely, and coordinated foreign policy making is extremely difficult to achieve.

The specific subject matter jurisdictions of congressional committees also can complicate consideration of major and complex legislative proposals. For example, the massive health care reform bills of 1993–1994 fell within the jurisdictions of nine House committees and seven Senate committees.

Congressional Parties and Leadership

Counterbalancing both the individualism of members of Congress who find themselves responsible for their own reelection and the fragmentation of the decision-making process stemming from the committee system are the political parties in Congress. It is the parties that select congressional leaders, organize both the House and Senate, determine the schedule of business, and play a major role in determining the content of legislation.

A Partisan Environment

Almost all representatives and senators gain office by securing party nominations and running as Republicans and Democrats. Then, in the heat of campaigning partisan commitments are forged, and most members enter Congress with a sense of loyalty to their party and a desire to advance its policies. This sense of partisanship is often reinforced by Congress's organizational and social environment.

Congress is organized on a partisan basis. Party leaders are elected by their fellow party members in caucus or in conference. Only members of the majority party hold the powerful positions of Speaker of the House and Senate majority leader and the leaderships of committees and subcommittees. It is the parties that assign members to committees, and in rare instances parties discipline maverick members by removing them from committees. For example, after leading a battle to enact Republican president Ronald Reagan's budget and tax measures, Democratic representative Phil Gramm (Texas) was removed by the Democratic Steering and Policy Committee from the influential Budget Committee for what his colleagues considered political treason. He then resigned his seat and was subsequently elected as a Republican. Domination of chamber leadership positions and committees gives the majority party control over the schedule, policy agenda, and procedures of Congress. This procedural power aids majority party members in passing legislation and often leaves members of the minority party frustrated.

The physical setting and the social life of Congress contribute to the partisanship that pervades the institution as well. The Senate and House chambers each have a center aisle with Republicans on one side and Democrats on the other. A similar seating arrangement is used in committee meetings. As a result, information, political gossip, and pleasantries are shared with fellow partisans. This segregation even extends to the cloakrooms off the House and Senate chambers, where members can relax, chat, make a phone call, or get a cup of coffee.

Party Leadership in the House

The Speaker of the House is the chamber's most influential leader.[21] This post combines the duties of presiding officer with those of leading the majority party. Although modern Speakers lack the formal powers wielded by those legendary Speakers Thomas ("Czar") Reed (R-Maine, 1889–1891 and 1895–1899) and Joseph ("Uncle Joe") Cannon (R-Ill., 1903–1911), they can exert substantial influence over the House's schedule and policy decisions. The Speaker (1) refers bills to committee, (2) influences members' committee assignments, (3) coordinates the work of committees, (4) influences the procedures under which bills will be considered on the House floor, and (5) presides at House sessions. From the presiding officer position the Speaker also recognizes members who wish to speak and applies the chamber's complex and voluminous rules (often in a manner beneficial to the majority party). The Speaker serves as well as the public spokesperson for the majority party. The influence that Speakers can bring to bear on their colleagues depends heavily on their skills in persuasion, negotiation, and bargaining. In fact, each occupant of the office brings to it a different style of leadership. The current Speaker, Thomas Foley (D-Wash.), is noted for his accommodating, collegial, and low-key manner, in contrast to the highly partisan, confrontational, and frequently lone-wolf style of his predecessor, Jim Wright (D-Texas).

The second-ranking leadership position is that of the majority leader, who schedules bills, handles party strategy, and serves as party spokesperson on the House floor. Assisting the majority leader is the whip organization, composed of a majority whip, deputy whips, and a group of at-large and regional whips (the term *whip* originated with the English hunt; it was the job of the whip to keep the dogs together). The whip organization informs members about upcoming key votes, conducts head counts of member sentiment on controversial issues, and attempts to "whip up" support for the party position on important roll-call votes.

The minority leader is the highest-ranking figure in the minority party and acts as its principal spokesperson and strategist. When the minority party controls the White House, as was the case for Republican leader Robert Michel of Illinois from 1981 to 1992, the minority leader serves as the president's principal advocate within the House and carries major responsibility for guiding the president's legislative pro-

21. For a thorough analysis of the Speaker and majority party leadership in the House, see Barbara Sinclair, *Majority Party Leadership in the U.S. House* (Baltimore: Johns Hopkins University Press, 1983).

A Legendary Speaker: Thomas Brackett Reed, Czar of the House

Before 1890 legislative business in the House could be stalled because the rules permitted members to engage in a variety of delaying actions, including use of the "disappearing quorum"—members present in the House chamber would refuse to vote when their names were called, resulting in lack of the quorum needed to conduct business. Frustrated by the House's seeming inability to act, Speaker Thomas B. Reed (R-Maine) led a reform effort in 1890 which put the majority in firm control of House business. He declared that the "object of a parliamentary body is action, and not stoppage of action." And when confronted with a "disappearing quorum," he ordered that the clerk of the House count as present all members who had refused to vote. Under Reed's guidance, the House adopted the so-called Reed Rules, which facilitated the passage of legislation by severely weakening the ability of a minority to delay or prevent House action.

First elected to the House in 1876, Reed served in the chamber for almost a quarter century and as its Speaker from 1889 to 1891 and from 1895 to 1899. He was an intimidating figure, standing over six feet two inches, weighing over 300 pounds, with a drooping mustache and a booming voice. But more intimidating than his size was his formidable intellect. Reed also was renowned for his biting wit.

He exercised power in a bold and often brazen manner that earned him the nickname "Czar." When challenged and asked about the rights of the minority in the House, Reed replied, "The right of the minority is to draw its salaries and its function is to make a quorum." And after having decided on a parliamentary procedure to advance legislation he favored, he would announce with grim sarcasm, "Gentlemen, we have decided to perpetrate the following outrage."

Of two House colleagues he once said, "They never open their mouths without subtracting from the sum of human knowledge." And it was Reed who coined the classic definition of a statesman—"a successful politician who is dead." Reed's retort to a House colleague who said that like Henry Clay he would rather be right than president was, "The gentleman need not be disturbed, he never will be either." And when asked to attend the funeral of a longtime political foe, he declined with the comment, "but that does not mean to say I do not heartily approve of it."

Present-day Speakers do not have the czar-like power exercised by Reed. They must constantly consult, negotiate, and persuade their independent-minded colleagues. Present Speaker Thomas Foley (D-Wash.), noting the limitations on his power over his colleagues, recently observed that "you don't get support for these programs by routine arm twisting. It's mythical to think members can be forced to do something they don't want to do." Even so, the Speaker's positions as majority party leader and arbiter of House procedures, the schedule of business, and committee assignments for party colleagues make the Speakership the crucial power center of the chamber.

---

gram through the chamber. Like the majority party, the minority has a whip organization to assist its leader.

As a large body of 435 members, the House has developed a relatively complicated set of rules that put the majority party firmly in control of its proceedings and impose restrictions on the abilities of individual members to delay and obstruct legislative action. The willingness of the Democratic party's majority to use its procedural powers to dominate the House, the Republicans' frustration at having been in the minority since 1954, and a sharpening of policy differences between the parties caused by the decline of the conservative southern influence within the

Sen. Bob Dole (R-Kan.), the GOP leader in the Senate since 1984, emerged after the 1992 elections as the most prominent Republican voice in Congress. Dole's congressional career, which began in 1961, has been marked by tough partisanship, hard work, legislative skill, acerbic wit, and a midwestern abhorrence of budget deficits combined with a willingness to raise taxes to prevent them.

Democratic party and an increasingly conservative orientation among the Republicans have all combined to create a highly charged, partisan atmosphere within the House of Representatives.[22]

Party Leadership in the Senate

The Senate with its only one hundred members, who expect substantial deference, operates with more relaxed rules and in a more informal manner than the House. Party leaders, therefore, have fewer formal powers under the rules and must rely primarily on their skills of persuasion and negotiation to lead their colleagues.

There is no position comparable to the Speaker of the House in the Senate; the presiding officer there is not an influential leader. The vice president, who is not a member of the Senate, is constitutionally empowered to preside over the chamber but seldom performs this duty. Nor does the **president pro tempore** often preside. This strictly honorific post is given to the member of the majority party with the longest continuous service in the chamber. Rather, the duty of presiding falls to new senators as a way for them to learn the rules and ways of Senate life.

The most important leaders of the Senate are the majority and minority leaders and their assistants, the party whips. The majority leader is responsible for scheduling Senate business, a procedural prerogative that gives this leader some bargaining leverage in dealing with colleagues. The majority leader also serves as the party's chief spokesperson and legislative tactician. Lacking the formal powers of the Speaker of the House, recent majority party floor leaders in the Senate—Republicans Howard Baker (1981–1985) and Robert Dole (1985–1987) and Democrat George Mitchell (1989–1995)—operated in a highly collegial manner, engaging in wide-ranging consultations and consensus-seeking as they sought to lead their party colleagues. With the Democrats in control of the White House, the major responsibility for steering President Clinton's legislative program through the Senate rests with the Democratic majority leader.

The minority leader of the Senate, Robert Dole (Kan.), is the Republicans' principal legislative strategist and spokesperson. In exercising his influence as minority leader, Dole is heavily dependent on the level of unity he can negotiate among GOP senators. By taking advantage of

22. For a concise discussion of the increasingly powerful role played by majority party leaders and the intensified partisanship of the modern House, see Lawrence C. Dodd and Bruce I. Oppenheimer, eds., *Congress Reconsidered*, 5th ed. (Washington, D.C.: CQ Press, 1993), 41–66; and David W. Rohde, *Parties and Leaders in the Post Reform House* (Chicago: University of Chicago Press, 1991).

Senate majority leader Lyndon Johnson (1955–1961) exercises his persuasive powers by giving Sen. Theodore Green (D-R.I.) "the treatment."

Senate rules which enable forty-one of the chamber's one hundred senators to block consideration of legislation, the minority leader, with the unified backing of his party, can defeat even high-priority bills of the majority party (see the discussion of the rules and the filibuster in the section "The Legislative Process: How a Bill Becomes a Law"). Indeed, Dole and his Republican colleagues have employed this tactic frequently against President Clinton's legislative program and were successful in sidetracking his 1993 economic stimulus package and in forcing modifications of the motor voter and national youth service bills.

In his classic analysis of the Senate majority leader, congressional expert Ralph Huitt observed that such leaders, having no patronage and no power to discipline or fire other senators, must rely heavily on their skills of persuasion and their abilities to help individual senators to achieve their personal goals in the Senate. Huitt also noted that Lyndon Johnson, an unusually successful Democratic majority leader (1955–1961), "never forgot the basic skill of politicians, the ability to divide by two and add one . . . and the need to find a ground on which a majority could stand. . . ."[23]

Party Influence on Decision Making

Party unity on roll-call votes in the Senate and House stems not only from the efforts of party leaders but also from the common ideological orientations, similar constituencies, and shared ties to interest groups

23. Ralph K. Huitt, "Democratic Party Leadership in the Senate," *American Political Science Review* 55 (June 1961): 337.

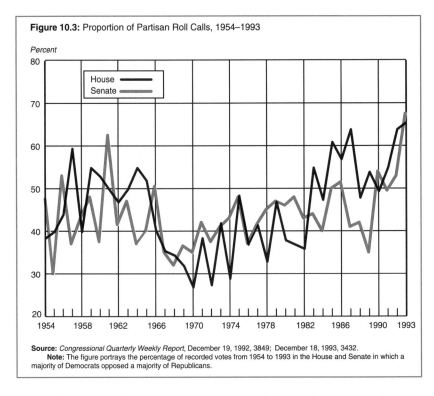

Figure 10.3: Proportion of Partisan Roll Calls, 1954–1993

Source: *Congressional Quarterly Weekly Report*, December 19, 1992, 3849; December 18, 1993, 3432.
Note: The figure portrays the percentage of recorded votes from 1954 to 1993 in the House and Senate in which a majority of Democrats opposed a majority of Republicans.

of party members (see Figure 10.3, which charts for 1954–1993 the percentage of times a majority of Republicans aligned themselves against a majority of Democrats on House and Senate roll-call votes). Although party-line votes only recently once again exceeded 50 percent of total roll calls, the extent of partisanship is impressive, especially when it is remembered that each chamber holds eight hundred to one thousand roll calls during the two-year life of each Congress and that a large number of bills are minor and not controversial.

The sharp increase in party-line votes in the 1980s and 1990s, especially in the House, reflects the divisiveness of such issues as the budget, taxes, defense versus social program spending, affirmative action, and aid to the Nicaraguan contras (Figure 10.3). During the Reagan and Bush administrations these and other issues pitted Democrats in Congress against a Republican president and his congressional partisans. With the shoe now on the other foot, since the 1992 election many of the Clinton administration's legislative proposals have encountered heavy GOP opposition. For example, every Republican member of the House and Senate opposed President Clinton and the Democrats' budget for fiscal year 1994.

Besides the divisiveness of such issues as the extent to which spending cuts or increased taxes should be used to reduce the budget deficit, intensified partisanship in the 1990s mirrors the changing composition of the two parties in Congress. As partisan realignment has occurred among southern voters, Republicans have won an increasingly larger share of the region's House and Senate seats.[24] Thus, the Republican congressional membership has become more southern and more conservative and the Democratic membership has become less southern and less conservative. Further contributing to heightened partisanship is the growing number of Republicans from generally conservative western constituencies and the expanding size and influence of the liberal Black Caucus within the congressional Democratic party.[25] As the two congressional parties, then, have become more internally homogeneous, they also have become more divergent in their policy orientation. Partisan conflict has been the inevitable consequence.

This being said, neither party in Congress is monolithic in its policy orientation. The Republican party includes the far-right senator Jesse Helms (N.C.) and the moderate senator John Chafee (R.I.). Within the Democratic ranks reside the likes of the conservative Alabama senators

24. See Rohde, *Parties and Leaders in the Post Reform House;* and Viveca Novak, "After the Boll Weevils," *National Journal,* June 26, 1993, 1630–1634.

25. Kitty Cunningham, "Black Caucus Flexes Muscle on Budget—and More," *Congressional Quarterly Weekly Report,* July 5, 1993, 1711–1715.

Table 10.3 Congressional Party Unity, 1982–1993 *(percent)*

	House			Senate		
Year	*All Democrats*	*Southern Democrats*	*Republicans*	*All Democrats*	*Southern Democrats*	*Republicans*
1982	77	62	76	76	62	80
1983	82	67	80	76	70	79
1984	81	68	77	75	61	83
1985	86	76	80	79	68	81
1986	86	76	76	74	59	80
1987	88	78	79	85	80	78
1988	88	81	80	85	78	74
1989	86	77	76	79	69	79
1990	86	78	78	82	75	77
1991	85	78	81	82	73	83
1992	87	79	83	81	69	82
1993	88	83	88	87	78	87

Sources: Harold W. Stanley and Richard G. Niemi, eds., *Vital Statistics on American Politics,* 4th ed. (Washington, D.C.: CQ Press, 1994), 214; *Congressional Quarterly Weekly Report,* December 18, 1993, 3479.

Note: The data in each column show the percentage of members voting with a majority of their party members on roll-call votes in which a majority of Democrats voted against a majority of Republicans.

Richard Shelby and Howell Heflin, as well as the staunch liberal Ted Kennedy (Mass.). Despite such internal diversity, the Republicans and Democrats have a relatively high degree of internal unity. During the 102d Congress (1991–1992), for example, Republicans and Democrats in both the House and Senate maintained party unity scores of approximately 80 percent on the roll calls that divided the parties (see Table 10.3). The party unity scores for 1982–1993 reveal a high level of agreement on controversial issues within both the Democratic and Republican parties. Particularly noteworthy are the relatively high party unity scores of southern Democrats, a traditionally dissident conservative contingent of the party which, in its congressional voting, is now resembling the northern wing of the party.

Democrats and Republicans Really Are Different

Congressional Democrats and Republicans have substantial policy and ideological differences. On economic, social, and foreign policy issues, Democrats take a vastly more liberal policy stance than Republicans (Table 10.4). Indeed, even the most conservative element of the Democratic party, southern senators and representatives, are more liberal than the most liberal group in the GOP, the eastern Republicans. Despite the fact, then, that some Democrats are conservative and some Republicans are moderate to liberal, the center of gravity for the Democrats is distinctly on the liberal side of the political spectrum,

Table 10.4 There Really Is a Difference between Democrats and Republicans! Congressional Party Support for Business, Labor, Liberal, and Conservative Interest Groups, 1991

| Interest Group | *Average Support Score, 1991 (%)* | |
	House	Senate
Americans for Democratic Action (liberal)		
Democrats	67	75
Republicans	14	18
American Conservative Union (conservative)		
Democrats	18	22
Republicans	82	76
AFL-CIO (organized labor)		
Democrats	67	75
Republicans	24	29
Chamber of Commerce (business)		
Democrats	32	20
Republicans	83	73

Source: *Congressional Quarterly Weekly Report*, May 2, 1992, 1137.

while the Republicans tend toward the conservative side. The conclusion? Clearly, the frequently laid charge that the Democrats and Republicans are as little different as Tweedledum and Tweedledee has almost no basis in fact.

The Congressional Bureaucracy

When most Americans think of a bureaucracy, piles of paperwork, red tape, and civil servants toiling in anonymity may come to mind. Although Congress is thought to be anything but a bureaucracy, a vast staff bureaucracy has grown up nevertheless—particularly during the 1970s—around its 100 senators and 435 representatives. Numbering approximately 18,000, the House and Senate staffs are large enough to populate a small city. When the entire support staff of the Congress is included, the congressional bureaucracy numbers more than 31,000 employees.

Every senator and representative has a personal staff, divided between personnel working in Washington and those working in the member's state or district. The size of a senator's staff depends on his or her state's population and can be as large as seventy. House members usually have staffs of about seventeen. Much of the staff work involves constituent relations—answering correspondence, doing casework, handling press relations, and arranging meetings with constituents.

The legislative assistants on members' staffs analyze legislation being considered in committee or on the floor, prepare bills and amendments, write speeches, go to meetings that members cannot attend, and represent members in meetings with lobbyists and administration officials.

Each committee and subcommittee also has a professional staff to assist its members in their deliberations on legislation. Much of the staff work is organized along party lines. Committee staffs primarily serve the senior members of committees and subcommittees, although all senators have staff assistance on their major committees. Staff members are strategically placed to advance or hinder the legislative proposals before their committees. During hearings they help to recruit witnesses, plan the order in which the witnesses will appear, and develop the questions that representatives and senators ask. They also assist committee members both when bills are being considered in committee and on the floor of the House and Senate by giving advice, drafting amendments, and helping to negotiate compromises.

To give it specialized advice and information Congress has created a series of support agencies staffed by professionals. These include

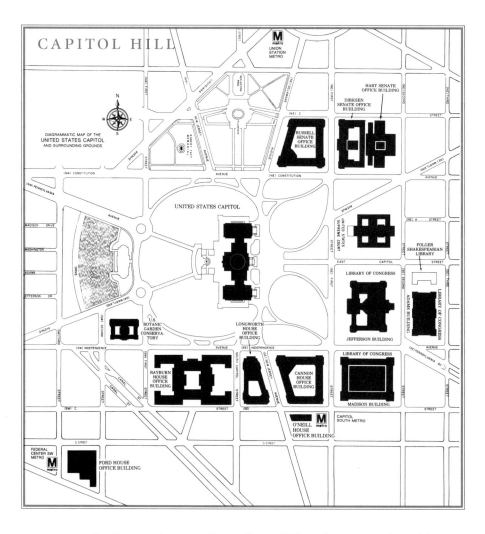

the Congressional Budget Office, which evaluates presidential budget proposals; the General Accounting Office, a congressional watchdog agency that audits and investigates government agencies and programs; the Congressional Research Service, whose specialists respond to requests for research and information; and the Office of Technology Assessment, an agency created to inform Congress about the impacts of scientific and technological advances.

Congress could not function without staff assistance. Many observers, however, worry that these "unelected representatives" are wielding too much power. As the workload of Congress has expanded and members have become busier, they find it increasingly necessary to rely on their staffs for the information needed to make decisions and to

The Explosion in Congressional Staff

The explosion in congressional staff reflects the expanding role of the U.S. government, the increased complexity of public policy issues, and the changing role of the individual legislator. The most dramatic staff growth since World War II has been in the personal staff of House and Senate members, stemming from the increased demands on members for constituency service and members' encouragement of those demands for reelection purposes. Committee staff also have expanded dramatically. As a result, Congress has become increasingly independent of the executive branch (and interest groups) because it has its own sources of expertise on complex issues of public policy.

Source: Norman J. Ornstein, Thomas E. Mann, and Michael J. Malbin, eds., *Vital Statistics on Congress, 1993-1994* (Washington, D.C.: CQ Inc., 1994), 129.

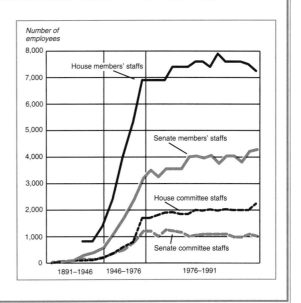

maintain communication with the administration, interest groups, the media, and even other members. This is particularly true in the Senate, where members have more committee assignments, larger constituencies, more interest groups with which to deal, and greater media exposure than is true of representatives. In fact, some key congressional staffers have become almost surrogate senators and representatives.

There is no easy answer to the question of what role staff should play in the congressional process. Most observers believe that representatives and senators, to do their jobs and to maintain a strong and independent Congress, must depend heavily on their staffs. But this does not diminish the need to monitor continually the role of staff, who do not have to face the voters at election time and whose interests may not be quite the same as those of their members.[26]

The Legislative Process: How a Bill Becomes a Law

Passage of a bill is a lengthy, complicated, and frequently conflict-ridden struggle that involves building majorities at each stage of the process (see Figure 10.4). Because of the different systems of election, memberships, and procedural rules in the House and Senate, the

26. For an informed analysis of the role of congressional staff, see Michael J. Malbin, *Unelected Representatives: Congressional Staff and the Future of Representative Government* (New York: Basic Books, 1979).

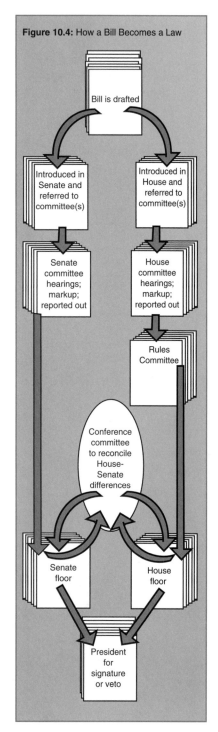

Figure 10.4: How a Bill Becomes a Law

Bill is drafted

Introduced in Senate and referred to committee(s)

Introduced in House and referred to committee(s)

Senate committee hearings; markup; reported out

House committee hearings; markup; reported out

Rules Committee

Conference committee to reconcile House-Senate differences

Senate floor

House floor

President for signature or veto

requirements for building a majority in the House are quite unlike those for passing a bill in the Senate. Then, when all the congressional hurdles to passage have been cleared, a bill must still receive presidential approval or at least acquiescence to become a law.[27]

Introduction and Committee Consideration

Only representatives and senators can introduce bills, although the legislative proposals they introduce may have been developed by the administration, interest groups, concerned citizens, or congressional staff. After a bill has been introduced, it is referred to the standing committee that has jurisdiction over the subject matter of the legislation. Thus, aid-to-education bills fall under the jurisdiction of the House Education and Labor Committee, and measures dealing with the licensing of radio and television stations are within the purview of the House Energy and Commerce Committee.

Strategic considerations enter into the introduction and referral process. Because committees differ in their composition and policy preferences, and because some committees' jurisdictions overlap, proponents of bills try to draft those bills in a way that will land them on the table of a friendly committee. When legislation falls within the jurisdiction of more than one standing committee because it is multifaceted and comprehensive, it may be referred to several standing committees. Indeed, multiple referrals are becoming commonplace for major bills. During the 99th Congress (1985–1987), for example, Superfund legislation designed to clean up toxic waste was referred to three House committees—Ways and Means, Energy and Commerce, and Public Works and Transportation. And the banking reform bill of the 102d Congress (1991–1993) went to the Banking, Finance, and Urban Affairs Committee as well as to the Committees on Agriculture, Judiciary, and Ways and Means.[28]

Another strategic consideration is deciding whether a bill's chances will be enhanced by having the House or the Senate give first approval to the legislation. Proponents normally seek action first in the chamber they believe to be most sympathetic, in the hope that passage in one

27. For a detailed account of the procedures and strategies used in the legislative process in Congress, see Walter J. Oleszek, *Congressional Procedures and the Policy Process,* 3d ed. (Washington, D.C.: CQ Press, 1989); and Edward V. Scheier and Bertram Gross, *Legislative Strategy: Shaping Public Policy* (New York: St. Martin's, 1993).

28. On multiple referrals in the modern House, see Garry Young and Joseph Cooper, "Multiple Referral and the Transformation of House Decision Making," in Dodd and Oppenheimer, *Congress Reconsidered,* chap. 9.

house will create pressure to pass the bill in the more resistant chamber. For example, while the Senate was in Republican hands between 1981 and 1986, the Reagan administration often pressed its advantage there as a way to influence the decisions of the Democratic House.

After a bill has been sent to committee, it is normally referred to the subcommittee specializing in the subject matter of the legislation. Most legislation dies at this stage because of insufficient interest or support from committee members. But those bills that are deemed important or have substantial member support are scheduled for hearings, usually before the subcommittee. At congressional hearings witnesses testify and are questioned by committee members about the consequences of proposed bills. Hearings are usually characterized as fact-gathering operations designed to give members the information they need to develop effective legislation and to aid them in deciding how to vote on a bill. But because Congress is an arena of conflict, hearings involve more than neutral fact-gathering. They also provide an opportunity to generate publicity for and against the bill as each side in a controversy seeks to build a case that will bolster its cause later in the decision process. Thus during the 1989 hearings on President George Bush's proposal to lower the capital gains tax (a tax on the sale of assets that have increased in value), proponents argued that the reduced tax would stimulate investment and create jobs, and opponents claimed the proposal was a tax break for the wealthy.

After the hearings have been completed, the subcommittee schedules *markup* sessions. During markup the subcommittee goes through the bill section by section—amending, deleting, and sometimes engaging in wholesale rewriting. Markup is a critical stage in the process because it determines the form in which the bill will emerge from the subcommittee.

If the subcommittee approves the bill, it is reported to the full committee for consideration. Because the membership of a full committee differs from that of a subcommittee, the full committee may repeat the subcommittee procedures, including hearings and another markup (perhaps introducing substantial changes), or it may simply approve the bill and vote to report it to the full House or Senate.

Committee and subcommittee procedures are similar in both chambers, although in the Senate the markup is usually undertaken by the full committee. But after bills have been reported from committee, the procedures for scheduling and considering legislation in the House and Senate are quite different.

To promote the administration's health reform proposal, which she was in charge of developing, Hillary Rodham Clinton is shown here testifying before the House Ways and Means Committee in 1993. Her appearance before the committee also marked a new era in the role of first ladies and provided a glimpse into her influence within the White House.

Scheduling Bills for Floor Consideration

Because Congress must consider many bills in a limited amount of time, both chambers of Congress have adopted procedures for scheduling floor consideration of legislation. In the House, scheduling is tightly controlled by the majority party leadership, and individual representatives have little influence over the floor schedule. By contrast, in the Senate individual senators have such leverage under the rules.

Most bills reach the House floor after being recommended for scheduling by the House Rules Committee. This committee has special powers, including the right to introduce a resolution—normally called a rule—that brings a bill up for immediate House consideration. The rule also sets the conditions under which the House will consider a bill: (1) the length of time allotted for debate; (2) whether amendments can be considered, which amendments can be considered, and how voting on amendments will be conducted; and (3) whether certain House procedural rules can be waived during consideration of the pending bill. If the rule recommended by the Rules Committee is approved by the full House, the bill is brought before the House for consideration.

Because of its power to control the flow of legislation to the House floor and its ability to influence legislative outcomes by controlling the conditions under which legislation is considered, the Rules Committee is a crucial seat of power in the House. Indeed, the committee is so important to the majority Democratic party in the House that it has allocated itself nine of the thirteen positions on the committee. Selected by the Speaker, the committee's Democratic majority works closely with the Speaker to construct rules that will help the party to achieve its legislative goals.[29] For example, during House consideration of a bill to give nonlethal aid to the Nicaraguan contras in 1988, the rule devised by the Democrats on the Rules Committee in close consultation with the Speaker did not guarantee the Republicans that they would ever get a separate House vote on their contra aid proposal. Under the rule's provisions, the Democratic alternative would be voted on first, and, if passed, no vote would be held on the GOP alternative. This rule virtually assured passage of the Democratic leadership's proposal. In 1993 special rules devised by the Democratic-controlled Rules Committee also significantly restricted Republican attempts to amend President Clinton's budget legislation. With the Democrats utilizing the Rules

29. For a thorough look at the use of special rules to influence the outcome of House decisions, see Stanley Bach and Steven S. Smith, *Managing Uncertainty in the House of Representatives: Adaption and Innovation in Special Rules* (Washington, D.C.: Brookings, 1988).

Committee to assert firm procedural control and to prevent what they consider to be GOP obstructionism, the minority Republicans are disadvantaged and often frustrated. At the same time, through its domination of the Rules Committee and frequent use of restrictive rules when major bills are being considered on the House floor, the Democratic leadership has been able increasingly to centralize power in its own hands.[30]

No Senate committee has scheduling powers comparable to those of the House Rules Committee. In the Senate the majority leader schedules legislation, most of it through a unanimous consent procedure in which the floor leader asks members of the Senate for unanimous consent to bring a bill up for floor action. If there is an objection to this request, a motion to the same effect requiring majority approval is needed. This is harder than it appears because individual senators wishing to block a bill can engage in prolonged debate—a filibuster—to prevent a bill from being considered. Breaking a filibuster is difficult because an extraordinary three-fifths majority of the Senate membership (sixty votes) is required under Senate rules to invoke cloture—or to cut off debate. As a result, individual senators have the power—if they wish to use it—to delay Senate consideration of legislation, to gain assurances that the majority leader's unanimous consent agreement will enable them to offer certain amendments to a bill, or to wring concessions from a bill's proponents by objecting or reserving the right to object to unanimous consent requests. This means that the majority party leadership does not control the Senate's schedule as firmly as is the case in the House. Rather, the leader must contend with senators whose individualism is backed up by Senate rules. As former Senate majority leader George Mitchell observed, "We have 100 equal Senators. I am constantly reminded of the limitations on my authority on a daily basis."[31] While often difficult to implement, Senate unanimous consent agreements are the functional equivalent of a rule from the House Rules Committee in that they can limit time for debate, determine which amendments are in order, and provide for waivers of Senate rules.[32]

30. On the use of restrictive rules to advantage the majority party, see Steven S. Smith, *Call to Order: Floor Politics in the House and Senate* (Washington, D.C.: Brookings, 1989), 74–83, 188–195. See the comments of former representative Dick Cheney (R-Wyo.) in "An Unruly House: A Republican View," *Public Opinion,* January/February 1989, 41–44.

31. Quoted by Robin Toner, "Beset by Critics Hungry for a Dynamic Leader, Dogged Mitchell Lashes Back," *New York Times,* Oct. 17, 1989, 9Y, National edition.

32. On unanimous consent agreements, see Smith, *Call to Order,* 94–119.

Floor Consideration
of Legislation

Floor consideration of legislation in the House proceeds in accordance with the rule proposed by the Rules Committee and adopted by the full House. This means that there is a fixed time limit on debate, and procedures are frequently in place to give an advantage to the majority party leaders.

House rules permit members to speak for only five minutes when debating an amendment, which is apt to be the most important floor action on a bill. Floor amendments give the House an opportunity to work its will on legislation as reported from standing committees. The proposal of amendments also provides even junior members with an opportunity to influence the content of bills not handled by their committees and to gain national visibility. For example, Rep. Henry Hyde (R-Ill.), as a freshman member of the House, began his fight against public funding of abortions by adding his now-famous "Hyde amendments" to a variety of funding bills.

Amendments take many forms. *Sweetener amendments* make legislation more attractive to members by, for example, providing for construction of dams, highways, and airports, and other grants to various congressional districts. *Saving amendments* are compromises that, if adopted, enhance the prospects for passage of a bill. By contrast, *killer amendments* deliberately strengthen a bill too much and turn a majority against it.[33]

As a general rule the House tends to accept committee legislation involving technical issues, minor modifications of existing government programs, and issues without strong partisan and ideological overtones. Any problems with such legislation are usually resolved in committee before the legislation reaches the House floor. But highly visible, partisan, ideological issues—such as military action in the Persian Gulf, savings and loan bailouts, funding of abortions, health care, taxes, minimum wage rates, federal budget priorities—tend to be fought out on the floor.

While the House extends considerable deference to the decisions of its committees when acting on legislation, the Senate is more reluctant to do so, preferring instead to resolve disputes on the floor. Operating under rules that permit wide latitude to individual members, senators freely offer floor amendments to bills that did not originate in committees on which they serve.

33. Oleszek, *Congressional Procedures*, 162.

A further difference between the chambers is the degree to which the majority or minority is advantaged by procedural rules. Under House procedures, which utilize rules proposed by the Rules Committee, the majority is in control and the minority's ability to engage in lengthy delaying tactics is severely limited. In the Senate the situation is just the reverse. As former Democratic leader Robert Byrd (W.Va.) noted, "[Senate rules] were meant to favor the minority and prevent the majority from running over the minority. That is why there is a Senate. That is why this Senate ought to remain a Senate and not become a second House of Representatives."[34]

The principal reason for the minority's strong position in the Senate is the chamber's cloture rule requiring sixty votes to bring speechmaking to an involuntary end. Since it is frequently difficult to muster the votes necessary to invoke cloture, the filibuster can be used to block passage of a bill or to force concessions from a bill's proponents, especially toward the end of a session when little time is available for consideration of bills. Once, filibusters were used primarily by conservative southern Democrats to block civil rights bills. In 1957, for example, Sen. Strom Thurmond (R-S.C.), then a Democrat, set the Senate filibuster record by holding the floor for twenty-four hours and eighteen minutes. Today, filibusters are used by liberals and conservatives alike against a wide range of bills about which they feel strongly. In a chamber in which the two parties have been so closely divided during the 1980s and 1990s, it has been particularly difficult for the majority party leaders to muster the votes necessary to cut off debate. Minority party filibusters or threats of filibusters have then resulted in the majority party making concessions to the minority or the death of legislation.

Resolving House-Senate Differences: The Conference Committee

Normally a bill passes the House and Senate in different forms. For a bill to become law, however, it must pass both chambers in identical form. The task of hammering out a compromise between the House and Senate versions of a bill is usually left to a joint House-Senate conference committee.

Conference committees are composed of representatives and senators appointed by the presiding officers of the House and Senate. Conference committee members are usually selected from among the senior members of the committee in each chamber that had initial

34. Quoted by Oleszek, ibid., 286.

Using Floor Amendments to Build Majorities (AKA Softening Up the Membership)

Time's congressional correspondent Neil MacNeil provided the following account of how the amending process is used to build support for legislation in the House of Representatives.

[In attempting] to pass a farm bill, Harold Cooley of North Carolina, chairman of the Agriculture Committee and floor manager of the bill, desperately and openly bargained for votes for the bill by accepting amendments, and he made no pretense at hiding his intent. ... At one point, William Avery of Kansas challenged Cooley to explain why he was willing to accept a particular amendment. Cooley answered candidly. "The membership probably might be softened up by this amendment," Cooley replied.

Avery was startled. "What was that?" he asked. "Will the gentleman restate that?"

Cooley began to reply. "Do you want me to tell you the truth?" he asked. Cooley, however, did not get the chance to explain. Frank Chelf of Kentucky, one of the Representatives who had demanded the amendment, interrupted him. "It is because he needs fellows like me to vote for the bill," Chelf said bluntly. "That is why. I cannot vote for it unless you adopt this amendment."

"That," said Avery, having made his point, "clears that up."

Source: Neil MacNeil, *Forge of Democracy: The House of Representatives* (New York: David McKay, 1963), 346–347.

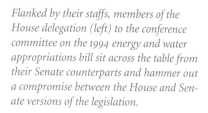

Flanked by their staffs, members of the House delegation (left) to the conference committee on the 1994 energy and water appropriations bill sit across the table from their Senate counterparts and hammer out a compromise between the House and Senate versions of the legislation.

jurisdiction over the legislation. As a result, the impact of the congressional committee system is felt strongly not just in the initial consideration of a bill but also in the critical final stages of the legislative process.

Conference committees are arenas of hard bargaining and negotiations between representatives of the two chambers, perhaps leading to substantial rewriting of the House and Senate versions of a bill. In conference, both the proponents and opponents of legislation have another chance to influence the legislative product. A majority of both House and Senate conferees must agree to any compromises that are worked out in conference.

If a conference committee succeeds in resolving House-Senate differences on a bill, the compromise legislation still needs full House and Senate approval. In both the House and Senate, conference committee reports are considered privileged legislation and are quickly scheduled for floor action. When both chambers have approved the conference committee bill, it is sent to the president for either a signature or veto.

The Congressional Labyrinth

The tortuous path that bills must travel to become law demonstrates that the congressional process is not geared to speedy action. Much more is needed to pass legislation than a majority on the House and Senate floors; majorities are required at each stage in the process—in the subcommittee, full committee, and House Rules Committee; on the floor; and in the conference committee. At each stage a small band of representatives or senators can either delay, severely weaken, or even kill a bill. To muster the votes necessary to move a bill to the next stage in the process, it is normally necessary to bargain, negotiate, and compromise—all of which will probably substantially change the legislation. As a result, the bills that emerge from Congress are seldom as strong as their original supporters had envisioned, nor are they as objectionable as their opponents had initially feared. Enacted legislation reflects the price that had to be paid to gain approval at each stage of the process.

Critics complain that congressional processes make prompt, decisive action difficult. Indeed, because it is so hard to navigate this process, those advocating policy changes normally operate at a disadvantage and the defenders of the status quo happily relish their advantage. Defenders of the congressional policy-making process make no boasts about the system's efficiency. They argue instead that Congress, because of its procedures and fragmented power, effectively compromises competing interests and resolves differences. The products that emerge from Congress may be less bold and decisive than some might wish, but congressional bargaining and compromising usually result in laws that are widely accepted by the public and competing interests in society.

The Congressional Budget Process

Until the mid-1970s Congress dealt with budgetary issues through a series of separate bills—over a dozen measures that appropriated money from the Treasury and several that raised revenues. This fragmentation of budgetary decisions meant that Congress seldom had to confront the overall fiscal consequences of its actions. Indeed, Congress was encouraged to indulge in its preference for spending money over raising taxes, a problem further complicated by the growth of entitlement programs in the 1960s and 1970s. These programs—such as Social Security, food stamps, and Medicare—transfer funds to individuals who qualify for, or are entitled to, federal payments.

As federal budget deficits mounted in the late 1960s and early 1970s, President Richard Nixon criticized Congress for overspending and then *impounded* (refused to spend) congressionally appropriated funds. In response, Congress enacted in 1974 the Budget and Impoundment Control Act. This act created procedures under which Congress could fix overall federal spending and revenue levels and review and rescind presidential impoundments. In addition, two new standing committees were created—the House and Senate Budget committees—together with the Congressional Budget Office, designed to provide technical

Sen. James Sasser's (D-Tenn.) influence and prominence as chair of the Senate Budget Committee, which is responsible for setting spending limits for thousands of programs, made him a contender for the position of Senate Democratic leader when George Mitchell (D-Maine) retired after the 1994 elections.

expertise to Congress as it deliberated on the budget. To keep track of its revenues and expenditures the federal government established a twelve-month period known as a **fiscal year** (FY). Under the 1974 budget act the government's fiscal year begins on October 1.

As federal budget deficits ballooned in the 1980s and early 1990s, budget legislation took center stage and dominated congressional decision making. In 1990, for example, congressional leaders and the president were involved in extended and often intense maneuvering, recriminations, negotiations, and bargaining from spring through October before an agreement on budget legislation was reached. In the process President George Bush was forced to go back on his campaign pledge of "No new taxes" as Congress and the president wrangled over issues of tax rates for the middle class and wealthy and spending priorities for military and domestic programs.

In taking the first step in the budget process, the president submits budget recommendations to Congress in early February for the following fiscal year. The Budget committees in each chamber then draw up their own budget resolutions, specifying overall government spending, revenue, and debt levels. These budget resolutions also break down spending among functional areas of government activity (for example, defense, health, and income security). The full House and Senate are required to pass one agreed-on budget resolution by April 15. Once passed, the budget resolution guides Congress as it acts on separate appropriations and other measures that provide the actual authority for spending on federal programs.

Bargain, Bargain, Bargain . . .

Neither the Democratic nor Republican party in Congress agrees internally on its policy outlook. Efforts to resolve internal differences within the Democratic party, however, have taken on heightened importance since the era of divided party control of the government ended with Bill Clinton's election in 1992. Now that the two parties are more united in opposition to each other than at any time since World War II, the use of cross-party coalitions has almost ceased to be a viable option, particularly on budget issues. Thus, passage of budget legislation in 1993 was accomplished exclusively with Democratic votes. Not one Republican voted for Democratic-sponsored budget resolutions.

With the Democratic leadership entirely dependent on its own members for votes, the bargaining power of various elements of the party has increased. In the House, conservative southern Democrats, organized into the Democratic Forum led by Rep. Charles Stenholm (Tex.), and moderate Democrats of the

Mainstream Forum leveraged their votes to bargain successfully for more spending cuts in the budget bill than President Clinton had proposed. But the Democratic budget could not be passed without the votes of the thirty-eight Democratic members of the liberal Black Caucus, whose bargaining position had been enhanced after thirteen additional African American representatives were elected in 1992. As a price for its support, the caucus insisted on maintaining the social programs important to its constituents.

Rep. Kweisi Mfume (D-Md.), Black Caucus leader

Building majorities has never been easy in Congress. Just ask the Democratic leaders who eventually mediated their fractious party's internal disputes over the budget in 1993. As President Clinton and the Democratic House and Senate leaders have discovered since the 1992 elections, forging legislative majorities is fraught with problems even when one party controls both the presidency and Congress and the complications of 1980s-style divided government are not present.

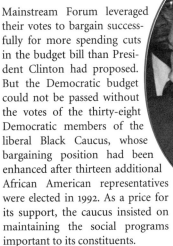

Rep. Charles Stenholm (D-Texas)

To impose tighter fiscal discipline on this process, Congress enacted in 1985 and 1987 the Gramm-Rudman-Hollings laws (usually referred to simply as Gramm-Rudman), sponsored by Senators Phil Gramm (R-Texas), Warren Rudman (R-N.H.), and Ernest Hollings (D-S.C.). These bills were designed to force the president and Congress to arrive at spending and taxing decisions that would steadily reduce the budget deficit to zero by 1991. Gramm-Rudman's most publicized provision specified that if deficit-reduction targets in the law were not met, automatic budget cuts were to go into effect (**sequestration**). Despite its good intentions, however, Gramm-Rudman did not succeed in bringing the budget deficit down to zero because 70 percent of federal expenditures were exempt from its sequester provisions, a number of political difficulties were involved in either reducing spending or raising taxes, and periodic adjustments were required in the laws' provisions. One of the consequences of the prolonged struggle over the budget for FY 1991 was an overhaul of the Gramm-Rudman laws. The FY 1991 budget law called for caps on future spending and for sequestration to go into effect if Congress exceeded those spending limits.[35]

In 1993 President Clinton proposed a massive five-year budget plan calling for a combination of new taxes and spending cuts designed to lower the federal budget deficit. The major elements of the president's plan, as modified by Congress, were incorporated into the budget reconciliation bill, which was the top legislative priority of the administration during its first year in office and the focal point of congressional policy making. But this legislation, as approved by Congress, fell somewhat short of the president's deficit-reduction goal primarily because of congressional opposition to higher energy taxes.

If the failed history of Gramm-Rudman, the prolonged maneuvering over the budget for FY 1991, and the Clinton administration's difficulties in achieving meaningful deficit reduction are any indication, Congress has a way to go to make the budget process work effectively. Delays in meeting deadlines have been common, as have accounting tricks and reliance on unrealistic assumptions about the performance of the economy (sometimes called "smoke and mirrors"). To find money to expand existing programs or to create new ones in a period of huge federal budget deficits, Congress must either cut other existing programs or raise taxes, but it has found neither alternative appealing. Further complicating the partisan maneuvering that accompanies budget deliberations are the inevitably differing priorities and perspectives of the people's elected representatives. In 1993, for example, within the majority Democratic party the thirty-eight members of the Black Caucus in the House opposed cuts in social programs such as Medicare and the earned-income tax credit (a program to assist the working poor) that had been approved by the Senate Democrats. And Democratic lawmakers from the oil-producing western states opposed energy taxes supported by colleagues from other regions. For all its problems, however, the new congressional budget process has forced Congress to deal with fiscal issues in a way that it never did in the past—from a total federal budget perspective.

An additional consequence of the new congressional budget process

35. See James A. Thurber and Samantha L. Durst, "The 1990 Budget Enforcement Act: The Decline of Congressional Accountability," in Dodd and Oppenheimer, *Congress Reconsidered,* chap. 16.

has been the introduction of an element of centralization into congressional decision making. The budget resolutions rank among the most important pieces of legislation passed each year because they affect the levels of spending on virtually all federal programs and activities. As a result, those representatives and senators in a position to have a say on the content of these critical measures have seen their influence enhanced. Among the major beneficiaries have been the members on the Appropriations, tax-writing, and Budget committees. But because budget resolutions impose limits on how much money other standing committees can propose for programs within their jurisdictions, the influence of the other standing committees has been severely restricted. Party leaders have gained influence as well through the new budget process because budget resolutions normally involve major battles on the floors of the House and Senate. At the floor consideration stage of the legislative struggle, party leaders often are in a position to exert substantial influence on the process.

Congress and the Web of American Policy Making

Old Washington hands find Congress one of the best vantage points from which to watch and gain insights into American politics because many of the strands of the political system come together on Capitol Hill. During their tenures there, representatives and senators are sensitive to the shifting tides of public opinion—indeed, their survival depends on being able to spot those shifts. The White House and its occupants are part of the view from the Capitol as well. In fact, information flows continually between "downtown" and "the Hill," where, according to the *Washington Post*'s David Broder, the reputations of presidents, their top aides, and agency heads "are made and broken."[36] There is even a back channel of information that flows between career civil servants in the various executive agencies and members of Congress and their staffs. Anyone tapping into this channel will better understand the workings of the executive agencies.

Congress is at the center of this political universe, but its role has shifted over time. During some periods it has clearly dominated policy making—such as the post-Civil War era when the Radical Republicans were riding high in Congress, the post-World War I period of Normalcy in the 1920s, and Gerald Ford's post-Watergate administration in the mid-1970s. But there also have been times when Congress has been

36. Broder, *Behind the Front Page,* 209.

completely dominated by popular presidents whose agendas coincided with the public's desire for a change of policy—during the first years of Franklin Roosevelt's New Deal in the 1930s, Lyndon Johnson's Great Society days in the mid-1960s, and Ronald Reagan's one-year honeymoon with Congress in 1981. At other times the balance of power between the branches has been shared more evenly—as during the presidencies of Dwight Eisenhower, John Kennedy, George Bush, and Bill Clinton. As these examples suggest, Congress's role in policy making has been one of neither steady decline nor ascendancy.

But whether dominant, dominated, or coequal, Congress brings to the policy-making process a special perspective: that of its constituency. Electoral realities create incentives for members of Congress to look at issues from the perspectives of the voters who sent them to Washington. Members understand that the cloak of statesmanship cannot be worn by those defeated and out of office. Ever mindful of this, politicians have made sure over the years that Congress conducts its business in ways that enhance their chances for reelection. Through their personal staffs, members maintain contact with their constituents; committees permit members to shape the policies important to their constituencies and interest groups active in election campaigns; and the party organizations in Congress are tolerant of their members' needs to deviate periodically from the party position on an issue in order to maintain electoral support back home.

Reelection is never far from the minds of this nation's representatives and senators, especially when they pursue other goals such as advancing the national interest and maintaining a strong, independent Congress. But because excessive attention to reelection can undermine Congress's capacity as an institution to maintain its influence and to make responsible decisions, that body tries to strike a balance between meeting the reelection needs of its members and maintaining the decision-making capacity of the institution.[37] Nevertheless, members' reelection goals have a significant impact on congressional policy making.[38] For example:

37. For insightful consideration of the tension between members' reelection needs and the needs of Congress as an institution, see Jacobson, *Politics of Congressional Elections*, chap. 7.

38. The following list of policy consequences flowing from Congress's electoral connection is taken from David R. Mayhew, *Congress: The Electoral Connection* (New Haven, Conn.: Yale University Press, 1974), chap. 2.

■ Congress tends to shape legislation in a way that distributes its benefits widely among the congressional districts and states. In other words, Congress likes bills in which nearly every member's constituency wins and few folks lose. Wrapping bills up in this kind of package helps, of course, to build congressional majorities for legislation, but it may result in watered-down legislation that fails to target the areas in greatest need of federal action.

■ When issues create clear losers and winners (bills that do not distribute benefits widely), Congress tends to service those interests that are well organized and have electoral clout.

■ When the alternative policies available to Congress all involve unpleasant consequences for constituents (taxes) and interest groups (cuts in services or tighter regulation), Congress tends to delay action for as long as possible. One example of this that stands head and shoulders above others is Congress's difficulty in coming to terms with the huge federal budget deficit.

■ Symbolic action is common because the public frequently responds to righteous position taking, even when it has little practical impact.

These tendencies in congressional policy making have provoked criticism of the institution, yet they are the natural consequences of an electoral and party system with which most Americans feel comfortable. Americans want their senators and representatives to be responsive to and dependent on their constituencies and citizens' concerns. They prefer weak parties incapable of controlling nominations and disciplining dissident legislators. Their admiration normally goes out to those independent-minded politicians who do not follow the party line once elected. Congress's approach to national issues, therefore, is not likely to change unless Americans also change their preferences about the nature of the electoral process and party system.

But is Congress's approach to policy making as harmful as it appears at first blush? The institution's defenders readily admit to the policy-making tendencies just identified. They would argue, however, that Congress also should be judged by such considerations as its capacity to (1) compromise societal conflicts; (2) reflect the concerns of a diverse people; (3) protect the interests of specific persons, communities, and interests; and (4) act as a check on presidential power. Judged by these criteria, Congress's performance is cast in a more favorable light. In addition, representatives and senators are aware of the potential threat their reelection orientation can pose for Congress's capacity to govern itself and the nation. They have, therefore, adopted a variety of institutional structures to cope with these threats and force members to make hard choices. For example, the congressional budget process was instituted in response to the need for greater fiscal discipline in both chambers.[39]

Given its reelection orientation, its often local perspective, and its relatively fragmented power structure, Congress does find it difficult to approach societal problems from a truly national perspective and to develop genuinely comprehensive and coherent policies. To a considerable degree, however, the national orientation and the comprehensive, coherent approach to policy making that Congress finds so difficult to achieve may be found in the presidency and executive branch. Under the American constitutional system, Congress and the executive must share policy-making responsibility. In the process they tend to counterbalance each other's approaches to decision making.

39. On Congress's experiments with self-control, see Jacobson, *Politics of Congressional Elections,* 208–226.

For Review

1. To reflect shifts in population, seats in the House are reapportioned among the states after every decennial census. Since the 1960s this process has caused a major shift of seats from the Northeast and Midwest to the Sun Belt states. Under the Supreme Court's "one person, one vote" rule, every congressional district must be as equal in population as possible. To meet this judicially mandated standard, state legislatures must redraw congressional district lines after every census. The redistricting process inevitably involves maneuvering for partisan advantage.

2. Because senators and representatives are ultimately responsible for their own electoral survival, they develop their own campaign organizations to run their candidate-centered campaigns. A prominent pattern in congressional elections: incumbents win.

3. The functions of Congress within the political system extend beyond lawmaking to include oversight of administration, public education, and representation.

4. Committees are major and specialized power centers within Congress that frame legislation for consideration by the full House and Senate. Committees have the power to block and delay legislation as well as the power to develop and refine bills. The committee and subcommittee systems tend to decentralize power within Congress. Committee chairs are still chosen primarily on the basis of seniority, but they must now be more responsive to their party colleagues because they are elected to their posts.

5. Congress is organized on a partisan basis, and party affiliation is a major predictor of how members will vote. The political parties in Congress exhibit different policy and ideological orientations on roll-call votes. Party leaders in Congress have limited formal powers and must rely heavily on more informal, collegial techniques.

6. The lengthy, complex legislative process of Congress requires building majorities at each stage. As a result, proponents of legislation must often bargain and compromise to secure its passage.

7. Because of the huge federal budget deficit, the budget process has assumed a central position in congressional decision making. The congressional budget process tends to centralize decision making and strengthen the role of party leaders.

For Further Reading

Congressional Directory. An invaluable official directory of Congress containing biographical information, statistical data, and listings of committees, congressional staff, and executive officials.

Congressional Quarterly publishes a series of periodicals and volumes of authoritative and up-to-date information on Congress: *Congressional Quarterly Weekly Report,* a weekly magazine of congressional and national politics; *Congressional Quarterly Almanac,* an annual compendium of data on congressional activities; *Guide to Congress* and *Congress A to Z,* complete reference guides to Congress; and *Politics in America,* a reference guide to the individual members of Congress—their constituencies, backgrounds, electoral histories, and voting records.

Dodd, Lawrence C., and Bruce I. Oppenheimer, eds. *Congress Reconsidered.* 5th ed. Washington, D.C.: CQ Press, 1993. An up-to-date and insightful series of essays on various aspects of congressional life—elections, committees, parties, and policy making—by leading scholars.

Fenno, Richard F., Jr. *Home Style: House Members in Their Districts.* Boston: Little, Brown, 1978. An analysis by the preeminent congressional scholar of House members in their constituencies and how "home style" affects members' behavior in Washington. Fenno also has written a series of masterful narratives of Senate life (published by CQ Press) focusing on the careers of five senators: *The Making of a Senator: Dan Quayle* (1989); *The Presidential Odyssey of John Glenn* (1990); *The Emergence of a Senate Leader: Pete Domenici and the Reagan Budget* (1991); *Learning to Legislate: The Senate Education of Arlen Specter* (1991); and *When Incumbency Fails: The Senate Career of Mark Andrews* (1992).

Jacobson, Gary C. *The Politics of Congressional Elections.* 3d ed. New York: HarperCollins, 1992. The most complete analysis of congressional elections available.

Mayhew, David R. *Congress: The Electoral Connection.* New Haven, Conn.: Yale University Press, 1974. An extremely insightful examination of how legislators' reelection sights affect the organization and functioning of Congress.

Ornstein, Norman J., Thomas E. Mann, and Michael J. Malbin, eds. *Vital Statistics on Congress, 1993-1994.* Washington, D.C.: CQ Inc., 1994. A compendium of statistics on major aspects of Congress (such as elections, staffing, committees, parties, workload, and activities) as well as interpretive essays. This publication is updated every two years.

Sinclair, Barbara. *The Transformation of the U.S. Senate.* Baltimore: Johns Hopkins University Press, 1989. A careful analysis of recent changes in the Senate with attention to the causes and consequences of change.

Smith, Steven S. *Call to Order: Floor Politics in the House and Senate.* Washington, D.C.: Brookings, 1989. The politics of the House and Senate floors is described, with special emphasis on recent changes in procedures and tactics.

Smith, Steven S., and Christopher J. Deering. *Committees in Congress.* 2d ed. Washington, D.C.: CQ Press, 1990. An analysis of the committee system which takes into account the changes of the 1970s.

11. The Presidency

THE WORDS AND DEEDS of the president of the United States, as the nation's most prominent and powerful political leader, can reverberate to the far corners of the nation and the world. Examples abound: Abraham Lincoln's decisions to defend the Union and free the slaves; Franklin Roosevelt's use of federal government resources to combat the depression; Harry Truman's commitment to containment of post-World War II Soviet expansionism; Lyndon Johnson's support of civil rights legislation as well as his escalation of the war in Vietnam; Ronald Reagan's efforts to scale back the role of government; George Bush's decision to use military force against Iraq after its invasion of Kuwait; and Bill Clinton's proposal for massive changes in the health care system.

Unlike members of the House and Senate, the president is known countrywide and is, in fact, a national symbol. This visibility is a potent tool when the president needs the public's support. Preeminence, however, carries risks. Americans have high expectations of their presidents. The chief executive is expected to maintain prosperity, hold inflation in check, and protect American interests around the world. Presidents whose governing performances are found wanting in these areas are apt to be rejected at the polls as were Gerald Ford (1976), Jimmy Carter (1980), and George Bush (1992), and those viewed as relatively successful are reelected—Franklin Roosevelt (three times!), Dwight Eisenhower, and Ronald Reagan found themselves happily in this category.

Because presidents have different goals, party affiliations, personalities, political allies, and styles of leadership, the presidency will always have a highly personal dimension. But the office has an impersonal side to it as well: the many layers of bureaucracy surrounding the occupant of the Oval Office. How well a presidency functions, as well as how presidential greatness is evaluated, are no less affected by what is happening within the country and world before and during a president's tenure. For example, the extent of presidential influence may depend on whether the president was elected on a wave of popular support for policy changes (Franklin Roosevelt) or came to the presidency without having been popularly elected (Gerald Ford); whether the president faces a Congress controlled by his own party (Bill Clinton) or the opposition (George Bush); whether the country is at war (FDR) or at peace (Ronald Reagan); whether the economy is healthy (Lyndon Johnson) or depressed (Herbert Hoover); and whether serious scandals have occurred (Richard Nixon, Warren Harding). This chapter examines the role of the president in American politics, the powers and organizational structure of the office, and the relationships between the president and the White House staff, the public, the media, Congress, and the executive branch.

The President and the Constitution

The nature and powers of the presidency were among the most difficult problems confronting the writers of the Constitution.[1] Most were convinced of the need for stronger executive leadership because of their post-Revolution experiences under the Articles of Confederation with all-powerful legislatures and weak governors at the state level and with a national government that had no chief executive. But at the same time, with the memory of arbitrary rule by colonial governors and the British Crown still fresh in their minds, they did not want to create a monarchical regime or conditions conducive to executive abuse of power. One of the foremost advocates of a strengthened executive was Alexander Hamilton, who believed that "energy in the executive" was a "leading character in the definition of good government" (*Federalist* No. 70). A majority of the delegates to the Constitutional Convention, including James Madison, also favored a strengthened executive to prevent congressional abuses of power, but they wanted the president's power to be circumscribed by checks and balances.

Checks and Balances with an Ambiguous Grant of Power

Convention delegates solved the problem of presidential power by fashioning a constitutional arrangement that both checked presidential power and yet left room for the expansion of presidential power if need be. Under the separation of powers and checks and balances system, presidents are required to share with the Congress power over taxing, spending, war making, and appointments within the executive branch. The president cannot govern without Congress, and governmental action requires executive-legislative cooperation.

A second element in the constitutional arrangement devised by the Founders was the broad and somewhat ambiguous language used to list presidential powers. This language imposed few specific limitations,

1. A concise summary of the constitutional decision making surrounding the presidency is found in Sidney M. Milkis and Michael Nelson, *The American Presidency: Origins and Development (1776-1993)*, 2d ed. (Washington, D.C.: CQ Press, 1994), chaps. 1 and 2.

and it ensured that the executive would have sufficient power to cope with future contingencies. Thus, Article II of the Constitution states that "the executive Power shall be vested in a President. . . . The President shall be Commander in Chief of the Army and the Navy. . . . [H]e shall take Care that the Laws be faithfully executed."

These constitutional phrases have been subjected to sweeping interpretations that have vastly expanded the legal basis for the exercise of presidential power. The president's position as commander in chief of the military, for example, has been used as a constitutional justification for sending American forces into action abroad without a formal declaration of war by Congress. And the president's command of the military, along with the power to execute the laws faithfully, has provided legal authority for the use of federal troops and marshals to enforce the integration of public schools, quell domestic disorders, and maintain such government services as mail delivery.

The Continuing Debate over Presidential Power

The Founders' formula of shared power with the other branches and presidential grants of authority stated in broad, ambiguous language guaranteed that over the years the issue of presidential power would remain the subject of periodic squabbling as future presidents interpreted and tested the limits of their powers and succeeding generations evaluated the office in light of their own experiences. From the 1930s to the 1950s most scholars and commentators believed that the president needed additional power to move the nation out of the depression, win World War II, fight the cold war, and advance social justice at home.[2] By the mid-1960s and early 1970s, however, presidential decisions to intervene in the Vietnam conflict and revelations of abuses of power at home had created fears that a dangerous "imperial presidency" was emerging.[3] The mid-1970s saw the concerns of observers of the presidency come full circle. They asserted that the presidency was "imperiled" and that the nation's well-being was threatened by the weakened circumstances of Presidents Gerald Ford and Jimmy Carter.[4] But those fears eased in the first years of the Reagan administration as the president successfully implemented a series of

2. See Thomas E. Cronin, *The State of the Presidency,* 2d ed. (Boston: Little, Brown, 1980), chap. 3.

3. See Arthur M. Schlesinger, Jr., *The Imperial Presidency* (Boston: Houghton Mifflin, 1989); George Reedy, *The Twilight of the Presidency* (New York: New American Library, 1970); and Cronin, *State of the Presidency.*

4. See Thomas E. Cronin, "The Post Imperial Presidency," in *The Post Imperial Presidency,* ed. Vincent Davis (New Brunswick, N.J.: Transaction Books, 1980).

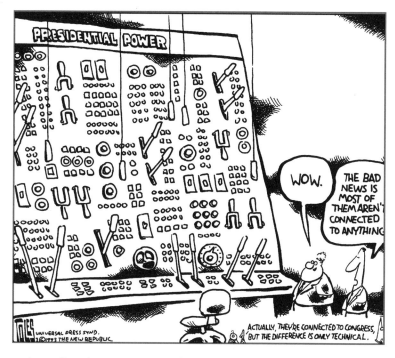

major policy changes—cuts in domestic spending, tax reductions, and a military buildup.

The easing of presidential scholars' worries about the president's capacity for effective leadership, however, was only temporary. The difficulties Reagan and Bush encountered in heading a divided government—difficulties Bill Clinton has had even without this burden— have produced two new concerns about the adequacy of presidential power. The first has stemmed from the problems presidents have had in governing because the coalitions they forged to get themselves elected tended to differ from the governing coalitions they needed to implement their policies.[5] Thus, much of the electoral coalition, particularly organized labor and environmental groups, that helped to put Bill Clinton in the Oval Office opposed him as president in his efforts to implement the North American Free Trade Agreement (NAFTA). Ratification of NAFTA, then, depended on the support of the Republicans and the business interests that had opposed his election. The second concern about the president's leadership capacity has arisen from changes in the international arena. America no longer occupies the position of overwhelming dominance that it did during the immediate post-World War II and cold war eras. This has reduced presidential

5. Lester G. Seligman and Cary R. Covington, *The Coalitional Presidency* (Chicago: Dorsey Press, 1989).

influence and compelled presidents to bargain with foreign governments (as George Bush did in rounding up support for the Persian Gulf War in 1991, and Bill Clinton tried to do against Serbian aggression in Bosnia) at a time when worldwide economic interdependence requires greater presidential involvement to achieve international cooperation.[6]

Who Can Be President?

The Constitution imposes only minimal restrictions on who can serve as president. The president must be thirty-five years of age, a native-born citizen, and a resident of the United States for at least fourteen years. One informal requirement for the office, however, is much more demanding. The president must be capable of winning a Republican or Democratic national convention nomination by contesting primaries and caucuses across the nation. This requirement tends to limit the field of potential presidential candidates to the holders of high elective office—senators, governors, or vice presidents or to people with national prominence such as Gen. Dwight Eisenhower, the commander of Allied Forces in Europe during World War II.

To date, all presidents have been white males, and, with the exception of John Kennedy, all have been Protestants. Most were born into relatively prosperous families and were well educated. Many practiced law before entering politics.[7]

While certain social characteristics do tend to dominate the backgrounds of presidents, such characteristics are not prerequisites for becoming president. Seven presidents—Andrew Johnson, James Garfield, Herbert Hoover, Dwight Eisenhower, Richard Nixon, Ronald Reagan, and Bill Clinton—emerged from working-class families. Hoover was an engineer, Carter a peanut farmer, and Reagan an actor. Truman never attended college. The backgrounds of recent presidents differ from those of their predecessors. For example, of the ten presidents since World War II, only three—Nixon, Ford, and Clinton—have been lawyers. This shift away from presidents with legal backgrounds reflects the increasing numbers of senators and governors—the positions from which presidents are frequently recruited—who come from the ranks of business and education. And, as members of such traditionally disadvantaged groups as blacks, women, and descendants of immigrants from eastern and southern Europe, Latin America, and

6. Richard Rose, *The Postmodern President: George Bush Meets the World,* 2d ed. (Chatham, N.J.: Chatham House, 1991).

7. The social backgrounds of presidents are summarized by Norman C. Thomas, Joseph A. Pika, and Richard A. Watson, in *The Politics of the Presidency,* 3d ed. (Washington, D.C.: CQ Press, 1993), 146–155.

Asia rise through the political ranks, the backgrounds of presidents will change even more.

Presidential Succession and Disability

The Constitution provides that the vice president shall serve as president if the president dies, resigns, is impeached and convicted, or is unable to discharge the duties of the office. The succession of vice presidents to the presidency has gone smoothly in the nine instances that it has occurred because of death or resignation.

A more difficult problem is presidential disability. According to the Twenty-fifth Amendment, the vice president shall become *acting president* if (1) the president informs Congress in writing that he or she is incapable of performing the duties of the office, or (2) the vice president and a majority of the cabinet, or another body created by Congress, decide that the president is unable to discharge his or her duties. The president may resume office by a written declaration to Congress that no inability exists, unless the vice president and a majority of the cabinet or other body believe that the president is still unable to perform the duties of that office. In the latter instance, the vice president

---

Line of Succession

On March 30, 1981, President Ronald Reagan was shot by John Hinckley outside a Washington hotel and rushed to an area hospital for surgery. In the meantime, Vice President George Bush was on a plane returning to Washington from Texas. Presidential aides and cabinet members gathered at the White House, where questions arose among them and the press corps about who was "in charge."[1] Secretary of State Alexander M. Haig, Jr., rushed to the press briefing room and, before an audience of reporters and live television cameras, said, "As of now, I am in control here in the White House, pending the return of the vice president. . . . Constitutionally, gentlemen, you have the president, the vice president, and the secretary of state."

Haig was, as many gleeful critics subsequently pointed out, wrong. The Constitution says nothing about who follows the vice president in the line of succession. The Succession Act of 1947 (later modified to reflect the creation of new departments) established which congressional leaders and heads of the departments (in the order the departments were created) would fill the line of succession that follows the vice president.

The line of succession is:

- vice president
- Speaker of the House of Representatives
- president pro tempore of the Senate
- secretary of state
- secretary of the Treasury
- secretary of defense
- attorney general
- secretary of the interior
- secretary of agriculture
- secretary of commerce
- secretary of labor
- secretary of health and human services
- secretary of housing and urban development
- secretary of transportation
- secretary of energy
- secretary of education
- secretary of veterans affairs

1. "Confusion over Who Was in Charge Arose Following Reagan Shooting," *Wall Street Journal*, April 1, 1981.

On August 9, 1974, Gerald Ford became president when he succeeded Richard M. Nixon, who had resigned in the wake of the Watergate scandal. Ford was also the first person to become vice president under the Twenty-fifth Amendment. With the vice presidency vacant due to the resignation of Spiro Agnew, Nixon nominated Ford, who was then House minority leader, for the post. Ford assumed the vice presidency after his nomination was approved by both houses of Congress.

would continue as acting president if backed by a two-thirds vote of both houses of Congress.

Since the Twenty-fifth Amendment was ratified in 1967, its disability provisions have never been formally invoked, although there were two instances of presidential hospitalization during the Reagan administration. In 1981 President Reagan was wounded in an assassination attempt and was rushed into surgery. White House aides monitored events, and Vice President Bush hurried back to the White House from a speaking engagement. The president, however, recovered quickly, and the amendment was not invoked. In 1985, when Reagan underwent cancer surgery, he transferred power temporarily (for eight hours) to Bush but without invoking the amendment.

The Twenty-fifth Amendment also provides for filling a vacancy in the office of vice president through presidential nomination, confirmed by a majority vote in both houses of Congress. This provision has been invoked twice: first, in 1973 when President Nixon nominated Gerald Ford to replace Vice President Spiro Agnew, who had resigned amid scandal, and again a year later when New York governor Nelson Rockefeller was appointed vice president by Ford, who had moved up to the presidency following Nixon's resignation.

Impeachment

Because of their worries about possible executive abuse of power, the writers of the Constitution included an **impeachment** clause as the ultimate congressional check on the president. For the removal of a president from office to occur through impeachment, he or she must be (1) charged by the House of Representatives with "Treason, Bribery, or other high Crimes and Misdemeanors," (2) then tried before the Senate with the chief justice of the Supreme Court presiding, and (3) convicted by a two-thirds vote of the Senate. No president has ever been removed from office in this manner, but in two instances impeachment proceedings were advanced in Congress. In 1868 impeachment charges were voted against Andrew Johnson by the House, but he was not convicted by the Senate. In 1974, following a 1972 break-in at the Democratic National Committee's Watergate headquarters and subsequent presidential complicity in a coverup of the affair, impeachment proceedings were begun in the House against President Richard Nixon. But before the full House could bring impeachment charges against him, Nixon resigned. He is the only president ever to be forced from office by impeachment proceedings initiated in the House of Representatives.

The Evolution of the Presidency

The modern presidency is the product of an evolutionary process in which the power advantage has shifted periodically between the president and Congress. The long-term trend, however, has been toward a stronger, more influential presidency that seeks to mobilize public support for its policies.

Washington, Jackson, and the Pre-Civil War Presidents

As the nation's first president, George Washington (1789–1797) made a major contribution to the office by establishing the legitimacy of the presidency. He lent his prestige to the position, kept the powers and trappings of the office modest, and sought to stay above the fray of political conflict. Washington cast but two **vetoes** and then only because he believed the legislation to be unconstitutional. His relations with Congress were correct but somewhat distant as Congress asserted its independence. When in 1789 he went to the Senate in person for "advice and consent" on a treaty, he was rebuffed in an embarrassing incident in which the senators made it clear that they preferred to consider treaties in private.

The presidency of Andrew Jackson (1829–1837) shifted the balance of power between the president and Congress toward the president. Jackson took a more expansive view of his powers than did his predecessors, and he did not shrink from open sparring with Congress. His twelve vetoes were more than all those of his predecessors, and he used them not only against bills he considered unconstitutional but also against those he viewed as just bad policy. Because of his personal popularity with the expanding electorate, none of his vetoes was overridden. Jackson provided a glimpse into the future of the presidency by demonstrating the power potential of a president capable of generating broad public support.

After the Jackson administration and through the pre-Civil War period, the government wrestled unsuccessfully with the problems of slavery and sectional rivalries. The pre-Civil War era was a period of congressional dominance and little-known presidents—Zachary Taylor, Millard Fillmore, Franklin Pierce, and James Buchanan. It was not until the crisis of the Civil War that a president acted in a manner that significantly expanded the powers of the office.

President Abraham Lincoln, as commander in chief, was deeply involved in Civil War battlefield strategy and occasionally issued direct orders to his generals about troop movements. Here he confers with Gen. George McClellan after the battle of Antietam.

Lincoln and Congressional Government after the Civil War

After a divisive election campaign in 1860, Abraham Lincoln (1861–1865) assumed office in the midst of a secession crisis. In response, he used the broad language of the Constitution designating him commander in chief and charging him to "take Care that the Laws be faithfully executed" to justify a series of unprecedented actions to suppress the Confederate rebellion. Among other things, Lincoln activated state militia, suspended the writ of *habeas corpus* (a court order directing an official holding a person in custody to show cause for his or her detention) in militarily insecure areas, blockaded southern ports, spent appropriations for unauthorized purposes, and issued the Emancipation Proclamation without congressional approval. The Supreme Court failed to overturn any of these actions and set a precedent for supporting presidential actions in time of war.[8]

Lincoln's post-Civil War successors were dominated by an assertive Congress that imposed Reconstruction on the South and dominated American politics for the balance of the nineteenth century. The basic character of American government in the latter part of the century was captured in Woodrow Wilson's phrase "congressional government."[9] Except for the presidencies of Theodore Roosevelt (1901–1909) and Woodrow Wilson (1913–1921), congressional dominance of the federal government continued into this century. Both Roosevelt and Wilson

8. Ibid., 459.
9. Woodrow Wilson, *Congressional Government* (New York: Meridian Books, 1956), originally published in 1885.

used the high visibility of the presidency to mobilize public support for their policies. They also sought to lead Congress by developing legislative programs and pressing aggressively for their adoption. Congressional government, however, reestablished itself in the 1920s and continued until national emergencies—the depression of the 1930s and the world war that followed—combined with the actions of Franklin Roosevelt to transform and enlarge the powers of the office.

The Modern Presidency

The modern presidency really begins with that of Franklin Roosevelt (1933–1945). His administration formulated and aggressively pressed for congressional approval of massive government programs to cope with the depression and turn the economy around. As the Jacksonian experience had foretold, a president capable of garnering public support can in turn use that support to successfully wring concessions out of a reluctant Congress. As for winning public support, Roosevelt, with his buoyant and optimistic manner, flare for the dramatic, and communications skills (he was the first president to effectively use radio to appeal to the public), was a master.

And like Lincoln before him, Roosevelt freely used his powers as commander in chief and the nation's chief diplomat. For example, in spite of strong isolationist sentiment in Congress, he provided U.S. support for the Allies before America's entry into World War II. In one such instance, through an executive agreement, which did not have to be ratified by the Senate, he traded fifty over-age destroyers to Britain in return for a lease to British bases in the Caribbean, Bermuda, and Newfoundland. After the United States entered the war, Roosevelt continued to use his war powers freely to direct the war effort at home and negotiate strategy and postwar occupation arrangements with the Allies.

Presidential scholar Fred Greenstein has identified four features of the modern presidency that bear a Roosevelt imprint: (1) the president is expected to develop a legislative program and gain its adoption by Congress; (2) the president engages in direct policy making without congressional approval; (3) the presidency has become a large bureaucracy designed to assist the chief executive in policy development and implementation; and (4) presidents have come to symbolize and personify the government to such a degree that the public, who monitors presidential performance through its saturation coverage by the media, holds the president personally responsible for the state of the Union.[10]

10. Fred I. Greenstein, "Change and Continuity in the Modern Presidency," in *The New American Political System,* ed. Anthony King (Washington, D.C.: American Enterprise Institute, 1979), 45–46; and Thomas et al., *Politics of the Presidency,* 33.

These features of the modern presidency have been continued and expanded by Roosevelt's successors. For example, when President Clinton presented and then aggressively lobbied Congress to support his programs for the economy, health care reform, and national service, he was fulfilling what has become an accepted presidential responsibility for leadership of Congress. Roosevelt's successors also have regularly engaged in direct policy making. For example, Reagan signaled a new era in labor policy by firing striking air traffic controllers in 1981, and Clinton changed abortion policy by lifting the so-called gag rule, which had banned health care providers at federally assisted clinics from providing patients with abortion counseling. Recent presidents have taken an expansive view of their war powers and committed American troops to combat without a congressional declaration of war—Truman in Korea, Johnson and Nixon in Vietnam, Carter in Iran (in an attempt to free American hostages), Reagan in Grenada and in an air strike against Libya, and Bush in Panama and the Persian Gulf. Much of the growth of presidential power has been accomplished with congressional support or acquiescence, as during the depression of the 1930s and World War II. Indeed, Congress has periodically delegated to the president the politically difficult decisions such as implementing wage and price controls or rationing petroleum.

The relationship between the president and Congress has not, however, been one of steady presidential aggrandizement. Just as the strong Lincoln presidency was followed by an era of "congressional government," continued assertions of presidential power in the 1960s and 1970s brought a congressional reaction. Johnson's and Nixon's use of their war powers to prosecute the war in Vietnam, Nixon's attempt to restrict or close down social programs by impounding (refusing to spend) congressionally appropriated funds, and the Watergate scandal resulted in Congress asserting its might through a series of measures designed to limit presidential power. One of the most important was the **War Powers Resolution of 1973.** This act requires the president to notify Congress promptly of the use of military forces abroad and to terminate military action if congressional approval is not given within sixty days. Congress also is empowered to pass a resolution directing the president to disengage American armed forces when they are engaged in hostilities without a declaration of war or specific congressional authorization. Presidents have consistently asserted, however, that the War Powers Resolution is unconstitutional. A second important measure was the *Budget and Impoundment Control Act of 1974.* According to this act, congressional approval of presidential impoundments must be obtained within forty-five days or the impoundment is rescinded. If the president tries to defer congressionally approved expenditures, these deferrals can be overruled by Congress. In addition, Congress strengthened its own capacity to handle budget issues by creating specialized budget committees in both chambers and a Congressional Budget Office.

After a period of diminished presidential influence during the Ford and Carter administrations, the Reagan presidency (1981–1989) seemed to signal a shift in the balance of power back toward the president. Reagan engineered a major shift in government policy in 1981 by gaining congressional approval of a program of tax cuts, reduced growth in domestic spending, and a military buildup. Reagan also demonstrated that it was possible for a president to circumvent the provisions of the War Powers Resolution and commit American troops to action without gaining congressional approval. After initial successes, however, Reagan, like his successor, George Bush, was largely stalemated in his efforts to achieve his legislative goals when the Democratic Congress sought to control the nation's policy agenda. Bill Clinton, too, has found that even though fellow Democrats control Congress, his programs must frequently undergo major surgery before gaining House and Senate approval.

The inability of recent presidents to dominate Congress reflects the extent to which Congress has equipped itself to participate broadly in the policy-making process from problem definition through program evaluation. The president and Congress are thus continually engaged in competition for influence in this nation's system of separated governing institutions that share power.[11]

Why Have Presidents Become So Influential?

As this brief historical survey has shown, the broad, general language of the Constitution has permitted presidents, frequently with judicial approval and congressional support or acquiescence, to establish precedents that have expanded the powers of their office. The language of the Constitution by itself, however, does not explain why these grants of authority have been used to parlay the presidency into such a prominent position in the American system. A combination of historical and institutional forces provides at least a partial explanation.[12]

11. See Charles O. Jones, "The Separated Presidency—Making It Work in Contemporary Politics," in *The New American Political System,* 2d ed., ed. Anthony King (Washington, D.C.: American Enterprise Institute, 1990), chap. 1.

12. For a concise and insightful consideration of the historical and institutional bases for the expanded role of the president, see Nelson W. Polsby, *Congress and the*

As America has emerged as an economic, political, and military superpower, the scope of presidential responsibilities and influence has grown. On the international front the president's power to recognize foreign governments by sending and receiving ambassadors, to negotiate treaties and agreements with foreign governments, and to command the army and navy place the chief executive in a preeminent position to determine the nation's foreign policy. The president can, for example, suspend diplomatic relations with a hostile country, as Carter did with Iran after the 1979 seizure of the U.S. embassy, or open relations with a former enemy, as Nixon did in 1972 with China; make agreements with foreign nations, as Roosevelt did with the Allied powers about the occupation of Germany at the end of World War II; negotiate arms control treaties with the Soviet Union, as Reagan did in the 1980s for medium-range missiles; and mobilize and lead an alliance of nations in war, as Bush did in 1991 against Iraq. In a world that has been shrunk by technological advances and economic interdependence, the public expects and constitutional powers provide the means for the president to act to protect the prosperity, tranquillity, and safety of the United States.

The president's potential for influence also has grown as the domestic responsibilities of the federal government have expanded since the New Deal era of the 1930s. The long arm of the federal government has now stretched to managing the economy, protecting the environment, and providing for the public's health, welfare, and safety—all requiring, of course, a bigger, more powerful executive branch with the president at its head. As described later in this chapter, all presidents find it difficult to control the massive bureaucracy of the executive branch. But through presidential appointments of cabinet and subcabinet officers and overall budget and policy decisions, the president can substantially influence executive agency decisions. Whether enforcement of environmental protection, antitrust, or antidiscrimination statutes is vigorous or lax, for example, often depends on the policies adopted by the president.

Yet another basis for increased presidential influence is the relationship that has evolved between the president and the media. In the early days of the Republic the media did not adhere to the professional norms of objectivity now associated with good journalism. The press was openly partisan, and the president was given coverage heavily laced with vituperation and name-calling. Today, however, in a period of

Presidency, 4th ed. (Englewood Cliffs, N.J.: Prentice-Hall, 1986), 15–17. Also see Thomas et al., _Politics of the Presidency,_ chap. 1.

more responsible and objective journalism, the media expect the president to play a less partisan or more impartial role as "a kind of guardian of national morale, a focus for affectionate emotions, an animate symbol of American sovereignty."[13] Presidents have found that by donning this mantle of nonpartisanship fashioned for them by the press, they appear to be above politics. This is of great value when trying to win the support of a public suspicious of political parties and politicians.

Bill Clinton, like Ronald Reagan and George Bush before him, has benefited from media coverage of his every move—from his early morning jogs with Secret Service agents and the odd celebrity in tow to high-level news briefings at the Tokyo summit meeting of the leaders of the world's major industrial (G-7) nations. No one can compete with the president when it comes to news coverage. Presidential news coverage is intense, automatic, and instantaneous. First radio and now television have made it possible to forge direct links between the president and the American people, and by skillful manipulation of this coverage, the president can gain political leverage. Often this involves mixing pictures of the president as family member (frolicking in the surf with a daughter and spouse) and as ceremonial head of state (greeting foreign leaders) with the White House presentation of domestic and foreign policy initiatives.

The Presidential Establishment

The president is expected to play many roles—head of state, commander in chief, manager of the economy, legislative leader, chief diplomat, head administrator, and world leader. Although the presidency combines all these roles in one person, the president is not a factotum—these jobs are too much for just one person. Recognizing this, the Committee on Administrative Management appointed by Franklin Roosevelt concluded in 1936 that "the president needs help." Thus, in 1939 the Executive Office of the President (EOP) was created to supply this help. Originally the EOP was composed of the White House staff (the immediate assistants to the president) and the Bureau of the Budget (now called the Office of Management and Budget—OMB), a budget-making and review agency. Since then, as the responsibilities of the federal government and the president have burgeoned, the EOP has

13. Polsby, *Congress and the President,* 16. Also see Samuel Kernell, *Going Public: New Strategies of Presidential Leadership,* 2d ed. (Washington, D.C.: CQ Press, 1993), chap. 3.

grown into a large bureaucracy with over fifteen hundred employees[14] molded by individual presidents to suit their own particular style of leadership. The flow of influence between the president and EOP, however, is reciprocal. Not only does the president affect the functioning of the EOP, but this bureaucracy exerts a powerful influence on presidential decision making.

The White House Staff

As the president's closest associates, more often than not members of the White House staff have been chosen for their posts because of their loyalty to the president. Former campaign aides and supporters are no exceptions; they frequently occupy White House offices. Bill Clinton's senior counselor and first chief of staff, Thomas ("Mack") McLarty, for example, is a lifelong friend, campaign fund-raiser, and adviser.

Given their proximity, both personally and spatially, to the president, senior White House staff personnel are among the most powerful figures in the government. They are quite literally the president's eyes and ears, arms and legs, providing the information on which presidential decisions will be made, evaluating policy proposals submitted by cabinet secretaries, monitoring the activities of the executive branch, controlling access to the president, and maintaining liaison with Congress, interest groups, party leaders, and the media. Among the most important White House staff members are the chief of staff, national security adviser, counselor, senior advisers, press secretary, communications advisers, and legal counsel. The White House staff also includes domestic and economic policy advisers, as well as special assistants to handle relations with Congress, interest groups, the party organization, and state and local government officials.

In any organization there is an ongoing contest for influence. At the White House this struggle is particularly intense because so much is at stake—billion-dollar policies that affect the lives of millions of people, personal careers, and ideological principles. White House personnel have been described as "young, highly intelligent, . . . unashamedly on the make,"[15] hard driving, and highly skilled in bureaucratic infighting. As Bradley Patterson, a former White House staffer, has observed, "Policy differences, piled on top of personality clashes, multiplied by time pressures, and heated by sometimes vindictive news leaks, can add up to an incandescent plasma of high-voltage conflict."[16]

14. For an account of the development of the Executive Office of the President, see John Hart, *The Presidential Branch* (New York: Pergamon Press, 1987), 1–132.

15. Patrick Anderson, *The President's Men* (New York: Doubleday, 1969), 469.

16. Bradley Patterson, "The Buck Still Stops at 1600 Pennsylvania Avenue," *Washingtonian,* December 1980, 205.

What ultimately matters in the White House is whether one has access to the president or to the people who have that access. Symbols of access and status are particularly important—such as a position high on the organizational chart, an office (however small and windowless) in the West Wing of the White House rather than next door in the Old Executive Office Building, or luncheon privileges in the White House Mess, which is nestled in the West Wing basement. At the White House the struggle for influence and power heralds each new day.

Every president has organized the White House staff somewhat differently to serve his interests as he defined them. Presidents Franklin Roosevelt, John Kennedy, Lyndon Johnson, and Jimmy Carter operated with a relatively loose organizational structure that permitted a number of key aides and cabinet officers to have regular access to the president. In this way these presidents were privy to information from a variety of sources and perspectives when weighing their various policy options. By contrast, Presidents Eisenhower, Nixon, Reagan, and Bush preferred a more hierarchical staff arrangement with a chief of staff in charge of running the White House. Although he has a chief of staff, Bill Clinton, like other Democratic presidents, operates with a substantially looser and more youthful White House organization than did Ronald Reagan or George Bush. Senior aides are linked to the president in a spokes-of-the-wheel structure that places the president at the hub. With a chief of staff, two deputy chiefs of staff, senior advisers, plus at least a dozen others having access to the Oval Office, lines of authority and responsibility in the Clinton White House have been unusually fluid and flexible. In addition, there are circles of authority emanating from the first lady, Hillary Rodham Clinton, and Vice President Al Gore.[17] More than other recent presidents, Clinton utilizes special task forces (for example, the health reform task force headed by Hillary Rodham Clinton) and policy councils (such as the National Economic Council directed by White House aide Robert Rubin and composed of high-ranking officials having responsibility for economic policy). Another feature of the Clinton White House is the periodic creation of a "war room," staffed by an array of tacticians from various White House offices (such as public liaison, communications, congressional relations) assigned to a single office to carry out a single task. A carryover from the 1992 presidential campaign, the war room technique has been used to build support for health care reform, gain congressional approval of the North American Free Trade Agreement, and

The Old Executive Office Building

Once characterized by President Harry Truman as "the greatest monstrosity in America," the Old Executive Office Building, adjacent to the West Wing of the White House, is filled to capacity with aides to the president. It stands today not only as a monument of French Second Empire architecture that was saved from the wrecker's ball by First Lady Jacqueline Kennedy, but also as a monument to the growth of the president's staff. Before World War II this building was called the State, War, and Navy Building and housed the modern-day equivalents of the Departments of Defense and State. Today, however, it is not even large enough to hold all the aides to the president, who constitute the Executive Office of the President.

17. Ann Devroy, "Loops of Power Snarl in the Clinton White House," *Washington Post*, April 3, 1994, A1, A30.

The First Lady: A Demanding Public and Political Role

Hillary Rodham Clinton

When attorney and political activist Hillary Rodham Clinton (1993–) sat down after the 1992 election with other senior Clinton aides to chart the future of the new administration and then was officially appointed head of the task force charged with developing the president's health care reform initiative, the transition of the first lady's role from one of an often highly influential, but behind-the-scenes White House policy insider to that of a professional political leader with specific policy responsibilities was accomplished. While not abandoning such traditional roles of White House manager and hostess, Mrs. Clinton, more than any earlier first lady, has been an active and acknowledged participant in high-level policy and personnel decision making. She is the first presidential spouse to have her own power base in the White House and her own officials throughout the government who owe their positions and loyalty as much to her as to her husband.

The location of Hillary Clinton's office symbolizes the shift in the status of the first lady. Whereas recent first ladies and their principal staff personnel were housed in the East Wing of the White House (at the opposite end of the building from the president's Oval Office), Mrs. Clinton's office is in the prestigious West Wing close to the offices of the president and senior White House staff. This reflects not only Hillary Clinton's position and influence, but also the more general trend among women of her generation toward increased involvement in the professions, business, and politics. It also acknowledges that the spouses of politicians now often have their own professional careers.

The early first ladies were not expected to play any political role at all. Their official responsibilities were restricted to acting as hostesses at White House functions. But, as the nation's attitudes toward women in public life changed and the mass media made presidents' wives celebrities, the public and political dimensions of their jobs expanded.

The increasing attention of the media, changing attitudes toward women's roles, and the development of the first lady's office came together with *Eleanor Roosevelt*, who from 1933 to 1945 redefined the role of the first lady. She was always in motion—visiting the rural poor, miners, soldiers, hospitals, and New Deal social program sites. To an unprecedented degree, she was active politically, openly pushing for an end to racial segregation and equality for women and drawing attention to the plight of the slum dwellers, the unemployed, and World War I veterans without pensions. She scrutinized New Deal programs and offered suggestions when possible. In an effort to push her programs, she frequently pressured the president (sometimes to such an extent that he would leave the room), and her political clout was thought to be extensive. By the time she left the White House, the role of the first lady had changed drastically. Mrs. Roosevelt had established it as something separate from the presidency and, with her outspokenness, activity, and visibility, had made it independent from, although linked to, the Oval Office. Mrs. Roosevelt also had changed public expectations. After her, the public would begin to look for an active woman in the White House. The days of the passive, retiring first lady were gone for good.

Lady Bird Johnson (1963–1969) used her position to press for policy goals about which she cared deeply. She traveled the country supporting her beautification program and personally lobbied Congress in behalf of the Highway Beautification Act of 1965. She also was an active campaigner for her husband and an unofficial presidential aide whom White House staffers frequently used as a channel to influence the president.

The somewhat liberal views of *Betty Ford* (1974–1977) on social issues supplemented the more traditional ones of her moderately conservative spouse, and she was active in a variety of social causes. She became perhaps the most visible spokesperson for women's rights and the Equal Rights Amendment. Among the most candid of the first ladies, Betty Ford was willing to discuss such controversial issues as abortion, premarital sex, and even personal problems including her bout with breast cancer.

Rosalynn Carter (1977–1981) was distinguished by her political involvement. She testified before a congressional committee to promote mental health legislation, sat in on cabinet meetings, met heads of state as her husband's representative, and held regular working luncheons with the president. As essentially an equal partner in her husband's presidency, she functioned effectively as a presidential adviser, and her influence with the president was openly acknowledged by both.

Nancy Reagan (1981–1989) was much less public in her political involvement, but her behind-the-scenes influence was extensive. Reportedly she played a leading role in cashiering Chief of Staff Donald Regan and in pressing the president to move forward on an arms control agreement with the Soviet Union.

Barbara Bush (1989–1993) was also considered an important behind-the-scenes influence in the White House. She campaigned actively for her husband's election and promoted literacy.

handle damage control in the Whitewater affair, a real estate savings-and-loan problem in Arkansas.[18]

Former presidential aides and scholars generally agree that the White House functions best when it has a disciplined chief of staff system. Indeed, no president has successfully run the White House without a chief of staff since 1968, and no one since Jimmy Carter, for a period from 1977 to 1979, has tried. A chief of staff is required to perform at least three essential functions: (1) to impose order on the policy process and prevent the president from being overwhelmed by managerial and policy details; (2) to arbitrate disputes among cabinet secretaries, who are rivals for policy turf and often differ in viewpoints; and (3) to control access to the president and to play the "heavy" in saying no to requests—that is, "to be the 'abominable no man' and serve as a lightning rod by absorbing attacks meant for the president."[19]

In performing these functions, the chief of staff inevitably exercises vast power—much greater than that of most cabinet secretaries. And when an experienced and skilled political operative, such as James Baker during Reagan's first term, is at the helm of the White House organization, the likelihood of a forward moving, successful administration is enhanced. Baker played the role of facilitator, coordinator, and broker within the administration's policy process. But when the position is occupied by a less skillful, domineering person, the chances for presidential embarrassments increase, as the Iran-contra affair, described shortly, demonstrates. An overly domineering chief of staff could shut the president off from diverse points of view thereby preventing a presidential "reality check," shield the president from unwelcome news, and press his or her own policies on the president.

The weighty responsibilities of chiefs of staff and the problems that can arise if they become too dominant were noted by the Tower Commission (named for former senator John Tower, R-Texas), which investigated White House operations during the Iran-contra affair of the mid-1980s. In this affair presidential aides made unauthorized arms sales to Iran in an attempt to gain the release of American hostages in Lebanon. Profits from the sales were then illegally diverted to support the contra rebels fighting the Sandinista government of Nicaragua. In addition to criticizing Reagan for his detached leadership style and noting the errors in judgment of senior administration officials, the com-

18. Jack H. Watson, Jr., "The Clinton White House," *Presidential Studies Quarterly* 23 (Summer 1993): 431; and Burt Solomon, "A Modish Management Style Means Slip-Sliding around the West Wing," *National Journal*, October 30, 1993, 2606–2607.

19. James P. Pfiffner, "The President's Chief of Staff: Lessons Learned," *Presidential Studies Quarterly* 23 (Winter 1993): 78.

mission laid much of the blame for this fiasco on the shoulders of President Reagan's chief of staff, Donald Regan. Regan was faulted for failing to insist that prescribed, orderly policy-making processes be followed in the White House. Reagan's secretary of state, George Shultz, who had argued against the arms-for-hostages deal, was even harsher in his criticism of the White House staff. There was, he said,

a staff con job on the president, playing on his very human desire to get the hostages released. They told the president what they wanted him to know. A responsible staff . . . should have called his attention to the violations of his own policies and warned that the intelligence about Iran was fragile at best and obtained from parties with strong interests and biases of their own.[20]

Although the president requires extensive staff assistance to perform the duties of the office, serious problems have developed as the size and power of the White House staff have grown. Indeed, maintaining control over the large presidential bureaucracy has become a presidential-size headache. Too-solicitous a staff can cut the president off from reality—from hearing unpleasant news and critical assessments of the administration. Overly zealous, inexperienced, or misguided White House aides may act without full presidential approval or in ways that contradict established policy and even violate the law.

The Iran-contra affair is a clear example of White House staff exceeding their authority and acting in ways contrary to established policy. It also illustrates how a president's personal style (in this case, a detached management style) can magnify the difficulties of controlling the White House bureaucracy. The net result of this incident was a major foreign policy embarrassment for the United States and damage to the president's standing at home.

An efficient and politically sensitive White House staff is therefore an essential ingredient in any president's success. But keeping these unelected, often intensely committed, ambitious, and powerful officials under the presidential thumb is one of the continuing problems of the American presidential system.

The Executive Office of the President

The White House staff is but a part of the much larger presidential bureaucracy, the Executive Office of the President (Figure 11.1). The agencies making up EOP provide the president with specialized information and help to coordinate government policy related to the budget, the economy, trade, drug abuse, science and technology, and the environment. The Office of Management and Budget, National Securi-

20. Quoted in the *Economist*, May 29, 1993, 96.

ty Council, Council of Economic Advisers, and Office of Policy Development are the main units of EOP.

The large (approximately six hundred employees), politically sensitive, and highly professional *Office of Management and Budget (OMB)* is primarily responsible for preparing the federal budget. Federal agencies submit their budget requests to OMB, which reviews them—often making substantial cuts—and then in accord with presidential guidelines puts together a composite budget for the entire government. The president reviews the OMB budget before submitting the administration's final budget recommendations to Congress. All requests by federal agencies for money from Congress must go through a central clearance process at OMB. Since the budget constitutes a comprehensive statement of administration policy and a means of exerting control over the far-flung executive branch, OMB is one of the most important power centers in any administration.

The role of OMB has reached new heights in recent years. The omnipresent massive budget deficit has forced Washington decision makers, whether in the executive branch or in Congress, to heed the budgetary implications of their decisions. As the president, cabinet officers, and Congress seek to make decisions while swimming in this sea of budgetary red ink, the director of OMB—most recently former Congressional Budget Office Director Alice Rivlin—has become the key policy maker and administration strategist in negotiations with Congress.

The *National Security Council (NSC)* is a cabinet-like body composed by statute of the president, vice president, and secretaries of state and defense, with the leader of the Joint Chiefs of Staff and director of the Central Intelligence Agency as statutory advisers. This body makes formal decisions about foreign and military affairs—such as the 1991 decision to go to war in the Persian Gulf. The NSC staff of approximately sixty persons is headed by the national security adviser to the president, who is Anthony Lake in the Clinton administration. The staff operates as a kind of miniature State/Defense Department within the White House, providing information to the president and helping to coordinate national security policy. Because of their daily contact with the president, national security advisers have exerted a weighty influence on foreign policy. This was particularly true during the administration of Richard Nixon, who used his NSC adviser, Henry Kissinger, rather than the State Department to conduct foreign policy.

A domestic policy staff assists the president with policy development and evaluating recommendations from cabinet departments much as

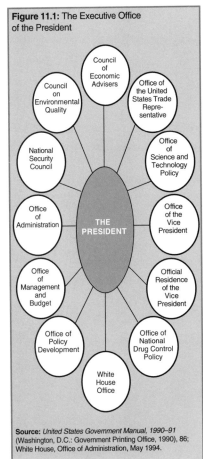

Figure 11.1: The Executive Office of the President

Source: *United States Government Manual, 1990–91* (Washington, D.C.: Government Printing Office, 1990), 86; White House, Office of Administration, May 1994.

the NSC does in national security matters. For example, Clinton's senior adviser for policy development, Ira Magaziner, headed the staff responsible for assisting the president and first lady in devising their health care plan.

Because the actions of the government can affect the economy so profoundly (and because voters tend to hold the president accountable for the state of the economy), the president needs the expert economic advice provided by the *Council of Economic Advisers (CEA),* presently headed by Laura D'Andrea Tyson. The CEA consists of three professional economists and a small staff. Economic advisers are not always popular within the White House because what they consider to be sound economic policies may be viewed as political bombshells.

Supplementing the work of the CEA and OMB and playing a major role in domestic policy is the *National Economic Council (*NEC), created by President Clinton as an advisory body within the Office of Policy Development. NEC director Robert Rubin, a former Wall Street banker, regularly briefs the president and provides a practical business perspective on the economy.

The Cabinet

By tradition the cabinet is composed of the heads of the major departments of the executive branch. Since Dwight Eisenhower's administration, however, presidents, at their discretion, have elevated other senior members of their administrations to cabinet rank. President Clinton, for example, included in his cabinet White House Chief of Staff Leon Panetta, OMB Director Alice Rivlin, Environmental Protection Agency Administrator Carol Browner, and U.S. Trade Representative Mickey Kantor.

Cabinet officers are chosen for a variety of reasons: to provide subject matter expertise and administrative competence, to build support among diverse elements of the president's party and electoral coalition, to win the backing of key interest groups, and to achieve geographic, racial, gender, and religious representation. As a result, a cabinet is unlikely to be composed of people with close personal ties to the president, which means that presidents rarely use cabinet meetings to make important decisions. Also working against use of the cabinet as a decision-making mechanism is the tendency of the White House to view departmental secretaries as representatives of their departments' bureaucracies and clienteles (interests served by the departments) and not necessarily as advocates of the president's priorities (a phenomenon called "going native").

As administrators responsible for government programs in such specific areas as defense, health, education, veterans' affairs, or transportation, cabinet secretaries are not well equipped to give advice outside their agencies' fields of jurisdiction. Presidents, then, tend not to work with the cabinet as a group but with individual department secretaries or groups of cabinet officers responsible for related areas of policy. For example, President Clinton meets each week with the secretary of state, defense secretary, and his national security advisers. The full cabinet, however, does not meet often or on a regular basis.

Both Presidents Bush and Clinton have tended to give their cabinet secretaries considerable leeway in developing policy—such as the efforts of Secretaries of State James Baker and Warren Christopher to induce Israel and its Arab neighbors to negotiate a peace settlement. Over the long term, however, the White House staff has gained influence at the expense of cabinet officers.[21] Members of the cabinet labor under a number of disadvantages: (1) they lack the proximity and relatively easy access to the Oval Office enjoyed by senior White House staff; (2) some had little or no contact with the president before being appointed; and (3) they are subject to the pressures exerted by the departmental bureaucracies, clientele groups, and congressional committees with which they must work. White House staff operate from a uniquely presidential perspective. The emergence of the National Economic Council (NEC) as Clinton's chief domestic policy body illustrates the trend of power flowing into the hands of senior White House staff at the expense of the cabinet. Although the NEC is composed of cabinet members, it is run by one of the president's most trusted aides and campaign advisers, Assistant to the President for Economic Affairs Robert Rubin. And it is Rubin, not cabinet officials in the domestic policy field, who commands ready access to the Oval Office and holds regular briefing sessions with Clinton.

Recent presidents, especially since the Kennedy administration, have expanded the policy advisory and executive branch monitoring responsibilities of their White House staffs. But this expanded role has frequently produced policy conflicts and power rivalries between department heads and presidential aides. The Nixon administration in particular was characterized by friction between the White House staff and the cabinet because Nixon employed his staff to keep an unusually tight rein on cabinet officers (the president's role as chief executive and the president's relations with the executive branch departments and the

21. For a survey of how recent presidents have utilized and sought to control their cabinet officers, see James P. Pfiffner, *The Strategic Presidency: Hitting the Ground Running* (Chicago: Dorsey Press, 1988), 41–67.

federal bureaucracy are considered in more detail in Chapter 12, The Federal Bureaucracy).[22]

The Vice President

Of the forty-one men who have served as president, nine succeeded to the office while serving as vice president (see Table 11.1). Despite the fairly strong odds of a vice president becoming president, the vice presidency has been the object of ridicule since its inception. The nation's first holder of the office, John Adams, described it as "the most in-significant office that ever the invention of man contrived or his imagination conceived." In the 1930s the delightful musical comedy *Of Thee I Sing* had as one of its characters Vice President Throttlebottom, an inept political hack who took tours of the Capitol along with the tourists. Adams's frustration and that of his successors reflect the fact that the role of a vice president in any administration is largely determined by the president.

Since vice-presidential candidates normally have been selected with an eye toward strengthening a party's presidential ticket, vice presidents have seldom been close associates of the president. Indeed, often they have been the president's opponent for the nomination or a member of a different party faction and treated with indifference or largely ignored by the president. As vice president, Harry Truman saw President Franklin Roosevelt mainly at ceremonial affairs. Thus, when he was

22. An informative account of cabinet-White House relations during the Nixon and Reagan administrations is contained in Richard Nathan, *The Administrative Presidency* (New York: Wiley, 1983).

Table 11.1 The Vice Presidency as a Steppingstone to the Presidency, 1789–1992

Total number of presidents		41
Total number of vice presidents		44
Vice presidents who have become president		
Upon death of the president	8	
Upon resignation of the president	1	
Elected after serving as vice president	5	
TOTAL		14
Vice presidents who ran unsuccessfully for president because they		
Failed to gain party nomination	4	
Were nominated by a major party but defeated in general election	3	
Were nominated by a third party but defeated in general election	1	
TOTAL		8

Vice President Al Gore, shown here with President Bill Clinton at a press conference, has emerged as one of the nation's most influential vice presidents. Gore has been assigned responsibilities in the fields of the environment, technology, governmental streamlining, foreign affairs, and congressional relations. Like his predecessors, however, Gore's role and power as vice president are determined by the president.

forced to assume the presidency upon Roosevelt's death, he was not fully informed about the conduct of World War II, including the existence of the atomic bomb and postwar planning.

Because of this experience, Truman and his successors have tried to keep their vice presidents well informed. Recent vice presidents—Walter Mondale, George Bush, and particularly Albert Gore—played more active roles than their predecessors, advising the president, taking on special administrative assignments to develop and coordinate policies, acting as presidential emissaries to foreign governments, and serving as the point men in rebutting administration critics. Even though the vice presidency has grown in stature and achieved unprecedented influence during Gore's tenure, it is still the president who determines the role of the vice president, and it would be an exaggeration to say that any vice president has yet achieved the status of being the number two person in the White House in terms of influence.[23]

The Importance of One Individual

Governmental institutions are affected by the basic beliefs, personalities, and skills of the people who run them. This is particularly true of the executive branch, which is headed by one individual, the president. The chief executive's actions count for more in the federal system than those of anyone else. Since every president is unique, there

23. On Gore as vice president, see Richard L. Berke, "The Good Son," *New York Times Magazine*, February 20, 1994, 29–36, 44, 54, 57, 62.

are as many ways of being president as there are presidents. Each president, therefore, shapes the presidency in accordance with a personal theory of how the office should function. The Washington community in turn adapts to the president's personality and style of operation.

The President's Basic Political Beliefs

Presidential behavior is affected by many different forces, but probably none is more important than the fundamental political beliefs of the person behind the desk in the Oval Office. Herbert Hoover's opposition to relief programs during the Great Depression, for example, was based on his belief that such government programs were inconsistent with a free-enterprise economy and constitutional principles. His successor, Franklin Roosevelt, saw government's responsibilities quite differently and initiated a massive expansion of the federal government's role in regulating the economy and providing social services. In the 1960s domestic social welfare programs were augmented significantly because of the prodding of President Lyndon Johnson, an FDR protegé, who also believed in an activist government. More recently, Ronald Reagan's conservative ideology had a major impact on government policy as he pressed for lower taxes, increased military expenditures, and restraints on domestic spending. George Bush, however, had a less ideological approach; his administration's policy thrust, then, was less focused than that of his predecessor.[24] Bill Clinton's passionate interest in public policy, particularly domestic policy, and the scope of his commitment to policy change and activist government are reflected in his leadership style, White House organization, personnel selections, and policy initiatives.[25] Since presidents' "world views" affect their behavior in office, it behooves voters to listen carefully to presidential candidates for indications of just what their beliefs are.

Presidents' views on how government policy making should be conducted also can profoundly affect their behavior in office.[26] President

24. On the problems Bush had because of an absence of clear policy goals, see Kerry Mullins and Aaron Wildavsky, "The Procedural Presidency of George Bush," *Political Science Quarterly* 107 (Spring 1992): 31–62.

25. Fred I. Greenstein, "The Presidential Leadership Style of Bill Clinton: An Early Appraisal," *Political Science Quarterly* 108 (Winter 1993–94): 589–601.

26. For a discussion of how a president's conception of the president's and Congress's role in policy making affected the presidency of Jimmy Carter, see Charles O. Jones, *The Trusteeship Presidency: Jimmy Carter and the United States Congress* (Baton Rouge: Louisiana State University Press, 1988). Also see his analysis of Carter and Nixon in "Congress and the Presidency," in *The New Congress*, ed. Thomas E. Mann and Norman J. Ornstein (Washington, D.C.: American Enterprise Institute, 1981), 223–249.

The Evolving Presidency of Bill Clinton

As did each of his predecessors, William Jefferson Clinton, the forty-first president, is demonstrating the importance of the personal qualities that the chief executive brings to the office. A "baby boomer" who came of age during the turbulent 1960s, Clinton is the first president born after World War II. And as a man with a passionate interest in public policy, particularly domestic policy, the president is also a political animal with unusual verbal skills, a responsiveness to the mass public, and a relish for the hurly-burly of politics where the arts of persuasion and cajolery are essential.

In an appraisal of Clinton after his first year in office, presidential scholar Fred I. Greenstein noted that Clinton's personal traits include enormous energy, exuberance, intelligence, optimism, and an ingratiating personality. These positive traits are combined with more problematic characteristics: "absence of self-discipline; hubristic confidence in his own views and abilities; and difficulty narrowing his goals, ordering his efforts, and devising strategies for advancing and communicating the ends he seeks to achieve." In addition, the president's predilection to take on large numbers of personal responsibilities makes it difficult for his administration to move on more than one policy front at a time.[1]

These traits combine to produce, in Greenstein's view, two quite different Clinton presidencies. There is the focused and accommodating style that was demonstrated during successful drives for congressional approval of his economic program and the North American Free Trade Agreement. But there also was the troubled and unfocused first one hundred days, which featured a whir of policy proposals, delays and missteps in making appointments, and White House aides preoccupied with damage control.

Because situations change and presidents gain experience while in office, Clinton's leadership style, like those of his predecessors, will evolve over the course of his term. His White House already has undergone several significant changes. For example, although his energy and wide-ranging policy interests seemed to cry out for a well-disciplined management team to keep his administration focused on achieving its high-priority objectives, Clinton apparently gave little thought to White House organization before occupying the Oval Office. And he initially staffed the White House with aides who lacked either Washington experience or the stature to control what Greenstein has called Clinton's "centrifugal tendencies." But when he sensed that his presidency was in trouble, Clinton turned to veteran Washington insiders—former White House aides David Gergen (a Republican), Lloyd Cutler, and former representative and OMB director Leon Panetta—for staff assistance. The president also has tried to strengthen the White House administrative structure by appointing deputy chiefs of staff. But only years after Clinton has left office will it be possible to truly assess his style of leadership and his impact on the office and the nation.

1. Fred I. Greenstein, "The Presidential Leadership Style of Bill Clinton: An Early Appraisal," *Political Science Quarterly* 108 (Winter 1993–94): 594.

Jimmy Carter, who had never served in the federal government before his election, had experiences with the Georgia legislature that left him apprehensive about legislative politics. He believed that presidents had a responsibility to analyze problems carefully and develop policies designed to meet societal needs. Congress should then accept those policies because they had been developed with the best interests of the country in mind. But what he saw up on Capitol Hill—Congress's tendencies to cater to special interests, to make decisions based on electoral considerations, and to compromise—made him reluctant to negotiate and bargain with members of Congress to gain approval of his policies. Not surprisingly, this approach to relations with an institution that thrives on representation and identification with special interests was largely unsuccessful.[27]

27. Charles O. Jones, "Carter and Congress: From the Outside In," *British Journal of Political Science* 15 (July 1985): 271.

Years earlier, President Richard Nixon also had questioned Congress's competence to make major policy decisions. Moreover, he questioned its legitimacy because in his mind the president was the only true representative of all the American people, accountable to the electoral majority, not to Congress. Nixon sought, then, to run the government without Congress by impounding funds, deferring spending, and shifting money from one purpose to another. By contrast, Presidents Johnson and Ford, who had served as party leaders in Congress, as well as President Bush, an experienced Washington insider, readily accepted sharing power with Congress and were comfortable in bargaining directly with its members.

Presidential Character

According to presidential scholar James David Barber, presidential character is of prime importance in explaining the behavior of presidents. In his research Barber analyzed two features of presidential character: (1) whether presidents were "active" or "passive" (invested a lot or a little energy in political activity), and (2) whether they were "positive" or "negative" (enjoyed their activities or engaged in them out of a sense of compulsion and obligation). Barber believes that these character traits develop early in childhood and can be identified before an individual is elected president. Using Nixon and Johnson as examples, Barber warns against "active-negative" politicians taking on the presidency. They are, he believes, driven personalities—"ambitious, striving upward, and power-seeking"—apt to behave too aggressively and to view the world with which they must deal as excessively hostile.[28]

Although few presidential observers would dispute that character has an impact on presidential behavior, many scholars are less confident than Barber that enough is known about political psychology to predict how presidential candidates will act once in office. Indeed, Barber's predictions about the types of presidents that Ford, Carter, and Reagan would become have been shown to be of doubtful validity by students of the presidency. In addition, if Barber's preference for "active-positive" character types had been used as a criterion for determining who was fit to serve as president, the list of eligibles would have not included the often moody and depressed Abraham Lincoln. Nor would Presidents George Washington, John Adams, Woodrow Wilson, and Dwight Eisenhower—all of whom have been ranked in the top ten by historians—have qualified.[29] There is also the possibility that a per-

28. James David Barber, *Presidential Character*, 3d ed. (Englewood Cliffs, N.J.: Prentice-Hall, 1985), 9.

29. See Michael Nelson, "The Psychological Presidency," in *The Presidency and the*

son's character may change while in the White House. Another fundamental criticism of studies like Barber's is that they overemphasize psychological determinants and underemphasize the structures within which presidents must operate—for example, the institutionalized nature of the presidency, the types of problems with which presidents must deal, and the political and public support they enjoy.[30]

Leadership Skills and the Power to Persuade

In his classic study of the presidency Richard Neustadt argued that the president is too often portrayed as a person possessed of great formal authority—the power to command. Presidents, however, do not govern the nation by command;[31] the Constitution requires that they share power, particularly with Congress. Moreover, to achieve their goals presidents have to persuade others to support their policies. Some of the powers presidents do have can act as significant bargaining chips when dealing with other politicians. When played skillfully, these chips can advance presidential causes. Presidents are in a position, for example, to influence the careers and goals of most political leaders in the United States. Presidents draw up the budget, exercise significant (though not complete) control over the vast executive branch, make appointments to the executive and courts, and enjoy special advantages in appealing to the public.

President Lyndon Johnson's hard-nosed approach to bargaining with opponents was legendary. When seeking congressional support for Medicare, he once told a senator that he understood the senator's problems with Medicare but that much worse might befall him if he did not see things the president's way. At White House state dinners, cooperative senators like Republican minority leader Everett Dirksen (Ill.) were seated at the head table with the president and visiting heads of state, but those who opposed the president, including fellow Democrats, were assigned to side tables or were not invited at all. And when vexed by an Idaho senator's opposition to his Vietnam policy, Johnson remarked, "The next time Frank Church wants a dam, let him build it."[32]

Political System, 4th ed., ed. Michael Nelson (Washington, D.C.: CQ Press, 1994), 198–221.

30. Thomas et al., *Politics of the Presidency*, 155–163; and Fred I. Greenstein, *Personality and Politics: Problems of Evidence, Inference, and Conceptualization* (New York: Norton, 1975), 19.

31. See Richard E. Neustadt, *Presidential Power and the Modern Presidents: The Politics of Leadership from Roosevelt to Reagan* (New York: Free Press, 1990).

32. Quoted by George C. Edwards, III, *Presidential Influence in Congress* (San Francisco: Freeman, 1980), 140.

Though less inclined to use some of Johnson's "hardball" techniques, President Clinton has shown a readiness to bargain for congressional support of his policies. *Time* reported that in May 1993, when he was on the verge of having his budget bill go down in defeat in the House of Representatives,

Clinton quickly telephoned Representative Billy Tauzin of Louisiana and promised to tinker with the energy tax. He called Dave McCurdy of Oklahoma, who had been holding out all day; in return for a yes vote, he agreed to make additional spending cuts and shift his policies to the center. . . . Clinton promised to toughen his policy toward Haiti to woo several black lawmakers. . . . [And] as many as 15 lawmakers from peanut-growing states switched when the White House agreed to curb the flow of imported Chinese peanut butter.[33]

A representative painted quite a different picture of President Carter's method of Oval Office persuasion with members of Congress:

I came in with other members to discuss a bill we were working on in committee. We had hardly got seated and Carter started lecturing us about the problems he had with one of the sections of the bill. He knew the details better than most of us, but somehow that caused more resentment than if he had left the specifics to us.[34]

The ability of presidents to persuade other political leaders to back their policies is not exclusively a matter of interpersonal skills or manipulation of presidential favors. Presidents also need a reputation for political competence and for an ability to use their powers skillfully and willingly. Such a reputation will cause representatives, senators, governors, cabinet officers, senior civil servants, and foreign diplomats to sit up and take notice of the advantages of working with the president and the potential adverse consequences of not cooperating. Finally, presidents who can create and sustain popular support will find warmer receptions when they begin courting members of Congress for their votes (a subject covered more thoroughly later in this chapter).

The Impact of the Presidency on the President

Most studies of the presidency have stressed the impact of individual presidents on the presidency and how they have used the office to achieve their goals. But influence can flow in the other direction as well; the presidency can leave its mark on the occupant of the Oval Office.

The problems, crises, powers, responsibilities, and deference that go

33. Michael Duffy, "That Sinking Feeling," *Time*, June 7, 1993, 23, 28.
34. Quoted by Allen Schick, "How the Budget Was Won and Lost," in *The President and Congress: Assessing Reagan's First Year*, ed. Norman J. Ornstein (Washington, D.C.: American Enterprise Institute, 1982), 23–24.

along with the office can transform its occupants in different ways. Harry Truman, for example, changed from a quiet, unassuming senator into a confident, forceful, farsighted executive. Lyndon Johnson and Richard Nixon isolated themselves and adopted a bunker mentality when faced with mounting criticisms of their policies and leadership styles. As president, Gerald Ford, a former House minority leader from Michigan, shed much of his midwestern conservatism, adapted easily to international diplomacy, and demonstrated unusual skill in restoring public confidence in the integrity of the presidency. And George Bush, who was criticized for being excessively passive as vice president, demonstrated forcefulness and determination in seeking to roll back Iraq's 1990 invasion of Kuwait.

Reporters and commentators watch every move a president makes and assess its significance, even to the extent of questioning competence because a president bumps his head on the doorway to *Air Force One* (Ford) or fails to show emotion when commenting on the dismantling of the Berlin Wall (Bush). The psychological strain that this incessant coverage, commentary, and criticism imposes on a president is considerable and helps to explain the defensiveness and obsession with press leaks that frequently characterize the White House when things are not going well for the president.

Close observers of the presidency have expressed fears about the royal court-type environment in which presidents often must operate— deferential aides anxious to please and ease presidential burdens, high levels of public respect for the office, and isolation from ordinary citizens and the political hurly-burly of give-and-take with peers. Indeed, because presidents have no real peers or equals in the American system, some believe they are in danger of losing touch with reality, too enamored with their own importance and power, and apt to make imprudent decisions. Speaker of the House Sam Rayburn (D-Texas), therefore, gave Harry Truman the following admonition when Truman was suddenly thrust into the presidency upon Franklin Roosevelt's death in 1945.

You have got a great many hazards, and one of them is in this White House. I have been watching this thing for a long time. I have seen people in the White House try to build a fence around the White House and keep the very people away from the President that he should see. That is one of your hazards. The special interests and sycophants will stand in the rain a week to see you and treat you like a king. They'll come sliding in and tell you you're the greatest man alive—but you know and I know you ain't.[35]

35. David McCullough, *Truman* (New York: Simon and Schuster, 1992), 357. Also see George Reedy, *The Twilight of the Presidency* (New York: New American Library, 1970), 27.

The heady atmosphere of the White House combined with the almost inevitable isolation that the presidency imposes on all its incumbents not only may result in the pursuit of unwise policies, but also may help to explain the periodic escapades of White House personnel that go beyond the law.

The President and the Public

The ability of presidents to lead the nation depends heavily on their standing with the American public. Indeed, public support is an important ingredient of any president's efforts to entice members of Congress and other political leaders to back administration policies. The public's steady backing, however, is not something on which presidents can rely. Over the course of an administration there are peaks and valleys of public support, and, unfortunately for most presidents, the trend is normally downward. Popular support, which cannot be turned up on command, is affected by international and domestic conditions and events often beyond the president's capacity to control.

The Shifting Tides of Presidential Popularity

Presidential popularity is generally measured in public opinion surveys by asking voters for a job approval rating. The Gallup poll, for example, periodically asks: "Do you approve of the way _____ is handling his job as president?" The percentage of respondents approving of the president's performance is used as a measure of presidential support or popularity.

Most administrations begin with a "honeymoon" period; the public shows its goodwill toward the president and a willingness to give the new leader a chance. In this relatively noncritical environment high public expectations envelop the president. Also early in their terms presidents benefit from not yet having made any controversial decisions that cost them support.

The media generally adopt a similar stance toward the new administration. Reporters refrain from sharp criticism and provide abundant human interest-type coverage of the new White House residents. Thus, Millie, the Bush family dog, generated more television stories in 1989, Bush's first year in office, than did the secretaries of education, agriculture, or veterans affairs.[36] Reporters showed a similar interest in Chelsea Clinton's cat, Socks.

36. Ann Devroy, "Bush Less a TV President than Reagan, Study Shows," *Washington Post*, Dec. 16, 1989, A2.

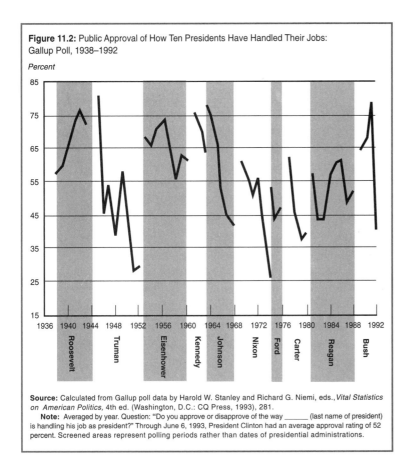

Figure 11.2: Public Approval of How Ten Presidents Have Handled Their Jobs: Gallup Poll, 1938–1992

Source: Calculated from Gallup poll data by Harold W. Stanley and Richard G. Niemi, eds., *Vital Statistics on American Politics*, 4th ed. (Washington, D.C.: CQ Press, 1993), 281.

Note: Averaged by year. Question: "Do you approve or disapprove of the way _____ (last name of president) is handling his job as president?" Through June 6, 1993, President Clinton had an average approval rating of 52 percent. Screened areas represent polling periods rather than dates of presidential administrations.

But this honeymoon atmosphere is usually short-lived.[37] Presidents Truman, Johnson, Nixon, Ford, Carter, and Bush all left office substantially less popular than when they entered. But Reagan did not suffer as dramatic a fall in public support as his predecessors; indeed, he showed remarkable recuperative powers from adverse economic conditions and foreign policy setbacks. Nevertheless, his administration experienced an overall downward trend in public support. For George Bush the drop in approval ratings was particularly precipitous after the record heights he had achieved in the wake of his leadership during the Persian Gulf War in 1991 (see Figure 11.2). He found that worries about the economy quickly erased the public's temporary, war-inspired euphoria. President Clinton sustained a downward slide in his public approval ratings at an unusually early point in his first term amid a storm of

37. For an analysis of trends in presidential approval, see Paul Brace and Barbara Hinckley, *Follow the Leader: Opinion Polls and the Modern Presidents* (New York: Basic Books, 1992).

adverse publicity about, among other things, foul-ups in handling presidential appointments. At the traditional first one hundred-day benchmark, his approval level was lower than that of eight of nine of his immediate predecessors.[38] Clinton, however, ended 1993 with his popularity on the rise following congressional victories on the budget and NAFTA, announcement of a health care proposal, and several rounds of meetings with foreign leaders.

The problems with which the president must deal—budget and trade deficits, job growth, drug abuse, terrorism, uncooperative foreign governments—are not ones that will show improvement overnight. Most, in fact, have proven to be relatively intractable. When solutions to such problems are not forthcoming, high public expectations go unfulfilled, and some voters are alienated by the controversial decisions that presidents inevitably must make. President Gerald Ford, for example, took office in 1974 with substantial public support after the prolonged period of divisiveness and the Watergate scandal that had caused President Nixon's job rating to plummet (see Figure 11.2). But after his pardon of former president Nixon, Ford saw his popular support nose dive, and an extended period of presidential-congressional wrangling ensued.

The news media are likely to file a higher proportion of critical stories as an administration ages. Although news organizations have tended to produce more favorable than unfavorable stories about presidents, a content analysis of media coverage between 1953 and 1978 showed that favorable stories declined overall by more than 20 percent from the first to last years of the Truman, Eisenhower, and Nixon administrations. At the same time the percentage of unfavorable stories increased nearly 10 percent for Eisenhower and Johnson and 30 percent for Nixon.[39] For President Clinton the barrage of critical commentary began early. A survey of all references to the president by network reporters and people interviewed during his first four months in office found 61 percent of comments to be negative.[40]

Because people usually hold the president responsible for the state of the Union, presidential popularity is closely linked with the well-being of the economy. America's economic problems in the late 1970s eroded President Jimmy Carter's popularity and played a critical role in his reelection defeat in 1980. After defeating Carter, Ronald Reagan saw his

38. Greenstein, "The Presidential Leadership Style of Bill Clinton," 591.

39. Michael Baruch Grossman and Martha Joynt Kumar, *Portraying the President* (Baltimore: Johns Hopkins University Press, 1981), 262, figs. 4 and 5.

40. Center for Media and Public Affairs survey, reported in the *New York Times,* June 17, 1993, A11, National edition.

public support also fall victim to a sagging economy between 1981 and 1983. By the midterm elections of 1982, his approval rating for that point in an administration stood lower than that of any other president since Truman. Later, when the economy improved, so did the president's popularity. Indeed, by 1984 the Gallup poll reported that voters cited his handling of the economy as their main reason for voting for him.[41] Although George Bush's public approval rating soared to a record-breaking 89 percent as the U.S.-led alliance defeated Iraq with minimal casualties during the Persian Gulf War of 1991, public concern about the state of the economy caused his public support to plummet to an August 1992 level of 33 percent. This dissatisfaction with presidential performance was a precursor of his electoral defeat in November.

Presidential popularity also reflects the state of America's foreign relations. In times of international tension—when the peace or American interests are threatened—Americans tend to rally around the president, who is the symbol of the nation. In fact, they respond with support whether the president's policy was a success or less than successful (see box "Rallying 'Round the President"). Thus, the Gallup poll showed President Kennedy's popularity moving from 73 percent before the disastrous 1961 Bay of Pigs invasion of Cuba to 83 percent after the crisis, and from 61 percent before the Cuba missile crisis to 73 percent after the Soviets backed down on placing missiles within ninety miles of Florida.[42]

The public's assessment of the president's persona or character is yet another factor in determining presidential support. When presidents meet public expectations for integrity, strength, and competence, their public standings are enhanced. For example, analyses of Reagan's popularity indicate that he benefited from an image of decisiveness and toughness as a leader, a dedication to his basic political convictions, and a "common touch"—openness, likability, and absence of pomposity.[43] But public assessments of Reagan's character declined and with them his popularity when the Iran-contra affair was publicized in 1986–1987. For the first time in his presidency questions were raised about his honesty. Had he really not known about the illegal transfer of profits from arms sales to the contra rebels in Nicaragua? And he looked weak and

41. James W. Ceaser, "The Reagan Presidency and Public Opinion," in *The Reagan Legacy: Promise and Performance*, ed. Charles O. Jones (Chatham, N.J.: Chatham House, 1988, 1990). Ceaser provides an in-depth analysis of Reagan's changing levels of public approval.

42. Evidence of the American people rallying to support the president in times of international crisis has been compiled in the *Gallup Poll Monthly*, June 1991, 18–22.

43. Ceaser, "The Reagan Presidency," 183, 197.

Rallying 'Round the President

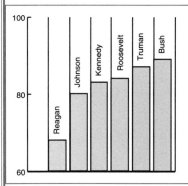

M ajor military events, glorious or ignominious, have often propelled presidents to their peaks in popular approval. The Persian Gulf victory lifted George Bush to an 89 percent approval rating in the Gallup poll released March 5, 1991, the highest rating since Gallup began measuring presidential approval in 1938. Shown here are the personal highs in the Gallup survey for presidents who reached 80 percent approval, as well as the high mark for Bush's predecessor, Ronald Reagan.

George Bush (89%), March 1991. After liberation of Kuwait in Persian Gulf War.

Harry Truman (87%), May–June 1945. After surrender of Nazi Germany.

Franklin Roosevelt (84%), January 1942. After Japanese attack on Pearl Harbor.

John Kennedy (83%), April–May 1961. After abortive Bay of Pigs invasion.

Lyndon Johnson (80%), January 1964. In aftermath of the Kennedy assassination.

Ronald Reagan (68%), May 1981. After assassination attempt. Reagan duplicated this peak in May 1986.

Source: *Congressional Quarterly Weekly Report*, March 9, 1991, 585.

unaware of what was going on in his administration. The greatest asset of the Reagan persona—his strength as a leader, his "Rambo" image—was challenged. When public interest in the Iran-contra affair faded in late 1987 during a period of improved relations with the Soviet Union and continued economic expansion at home, Reagan's popularity partially recovered. "Real world" conditions and the president's record in office thus do color the public's assessments of a president's character.

Going Public

In the American constitutional system of shared powers, presidents must inevitably win the support of other political leaders to achieve their policy goals. The Washington political community, however, is complex and highly fragmented. It is populated by independent-minded representatives and senators, proliferating interest group representatives, issue specialists, insiders, aggressive journalists, and senior bureaucrats. As a result, presidents have found it more and more difficult to persuade and bargain with the leaders whose support they need. In their dealings with Congress, for example, modern presidents have found that party leaders and committee chairs often have insufficient clout to deliver their colleagues' votes in support of a deal they might cut with the president. But members of the Washington political community are hesitant about opposing a president backed by the weight of public opinion. Indeed, congressional support for the president's legislative program is related to the president's public approval rating.[44] Faced with all these difficulties, presidents have increasingly "gone public" in an attempt to achieve administration objectives.[45] Going public takes a variety of forms—televised speeches from the Oval Office, ceremonial functions in the White House Rose Garden, media events abroad or outside Washington, informal talks with visiting interest group leaders, off-the-cuff comments to reporters, and leaks of inside information by White House staff. The informal techniques are impossible to quantify, but the more formal methods of sending messages to the public—such as public addresses and public appearances—can be analyzed quantitatively. These measures of going public reveal that modern presidents are much more into public relations than were their predecessors thirty or forty years ago.[46]

Sophisticated attempts to manage the news go back at least to Eisenhower's press secretary, James Hagerty. According to *Washington Post*

44. See George C. Edwards, III, *At the Margins: Presidential Leadership of Congress* (New Haven, Conn.: Yale University Press, 1989), chap. 6.

45. Samuel Kernell, *Going Public,* chaps. 2–4.

46. For data on the trends in going public by presidents, see ibid., chap. 4.

political reporter David Broder, the Reagan administration built on the techniques developed by Hagerty and his successors. It explicitly recognized that "managing the news and public opinion . . . is such a central part of running the presidency" that it constitutes "a major part of the work day of senior policy aides."[47] In the Reagan White House presidential assistants met regularly to plan a communications strategy. With a general strategy in place, a daily 8:15 A.M. senior staff meeting was held to finalize each day's White House program with an eye toward dominating that night's network news programs and the next morning's newspaper headlines. The Bush administration was much less explicit and programmed in its approach. It tended to rely more on impromptu news conferences, although it too tried to stage presidential events that provide good visuals and sound bites for television. In an attempt to go around the national news media in getting its message to the public, the Clinton administration has supplemented the techniques of its predecessors with televised town hall meetings, talk show interviews, and press conferences via satellite with local reporters.

The President and the Media:
An Adversarial Relationship

As presidents and their staffs have sought to manage the news and, in the case of news conferences, to use the press as "one of the props,"[48] the relationship between the president and the media has become increasingly adversarial. White House reporters tend to seek out and pounce on the facts behind a president's statement or press release and take pleasure in uncovering mistakes and highlighting what they perceive to be failures and contradictions in administration policy. For example, reporters took copies of Clinton's campaign manifesto, *Putting People First,* to White House news briefings so that they could compare campaign promises with Clinton's actual governing policies. According to one senior Washington journalist, "The White House reporter has one accepted role—to report the news—and several self-appointed roles. . . . I feel I'm there, in part, to compel the government to explain and justify what it's doing. A lot of people don't like that, but I feel we're the permanent in-house critics of the government."[49] White House reporters are also sensitive to the charge that they are giving the president a free ride. All this adds up to a future in which adversarial relations between the White House and media are apt to be the norm.

47. David S. Broder, *Behind the Front Page: A Candid Look at How the News Is Made* (New York: Simon and Schuster, 1987), 180.

48. Reporter Peter Lisagor quoted by Kernell, *Going Public,* 78.

49. James Deakin quoted by Kernell, ibid.

The President as Chief Legislator

The Constitution thrusts presidents into the legislative process by giving them the power to recommend legislation, call Congress into special session, and veto laws passed by Congress. Their own interest in having a say in the direction of American policy pushes them into the legislative arena as well. And not to be forgotten, the public and the media now expect the president to lead the Congress. Although presidents have no power to introduce bills, speak during debate, or vote on the floor, they leave a deep imprint on congressional decision making.

Setting the Legislative Policy Agenda

With their high public visibility, national constituency, and unrivaled political resources, presidents are able to play a major role in determining which issues come up on the government's agenda for action. Among other things, presidential speeches and messages to Congress help to determine exactly which of the many issues fighting for space on the policy agenda will receive top priority. Charles Jones, a close observer of White House-congressional relations, has described the president's role in setting the government's policy agenda as a "certifying function."[50] By giving an issue priority (certifying its place on the policy agenda), the president normally triggers the development of policy proposals that become the focus of public and congressional attention. After his election in 1992, for example, President Clinton had a clear policy agenda—deficit reduction, economic stimulus, a national youth service program, health care reform, and a family leave program. His agenda then became the central concern of Congress.

But as much as they would like to be, presidents are not in complete control of the government's policy agenda; events in the "real world" impinge on the president's agenda-setting power. Ethnic strife in the former Yugoslavia and U.S. interests in the world's many trouble spots, such as Russia, the Middle East, Haiti, and Somalia, as well as the Whitewater controversy, have periodically diverted the Clinton administration from the domestic economic issues that have been its stated priority. Moreover, large budget deficits have severely limited Clinton, who believes in activist government, in his ability to propose new domestic programs.

50. Charles O. Jones, "Presidents and Agenda Politics: Sustaining the Power of the Office" (Paper delivered at the annual meeting of the American Political Science Association, Atlanta, August 30–September 3, 1989), 13.

The president's agenda-setting power is strengthened by Congress's decentralized power structure and its members' proclivities toward political independence. Congress needs a presidential agenda for action. The president's budget, for example, is the usual starting point for congressional deliberations on fiscal policy, even though Congress may elect to set aside much of what the president has recommended.

Sources of Conflict between the President and Congress

As the Founders envisioned, the separation of powers system has resulted in recurrent sparring matches between presidents and members of the Congress. The complaints are unending. About this situation Abraham Lincoln reportedly said, "I have been told I was on the road to Hell, but I had no idea that it was just a mile down the road with a dome on it." Lincoln also probably was aware that presidential-congressional conflicts have deep electoral and institutional roots.

The principal basis for executive-legislative conflict is that the president and members of Congress have different constituencies—states or districts for senators and representatives, a national constituency for the president. It is not surprising, then, that the president and members of Congress bring to their offices quite different perspectives. Members of Congress worry about how proposed policies will affect the folks back home, while the president looks at issues from a more national perspective. Thus, when President Clinton proposed a broad-based energy (Btu) tax as a major revenue raiser in his 1993 economic program, he was immediately confronted with determined opposition from within his own party, as oil state senators John Breaux (La.) and David Boren (Okla.) led a successful fight to kill the tax in the Finance Committee.

Differences between the White House and Congress are further exacerbated by the presidential, Senate, and House election schedules—no two the same. With the entire House up for reelection midway through a president's term and two-thirds of the Senate elected at a different time than the president, legislators and the president are likely to see their electoral mandates quite disparately.

As noted in Chapter 7, different constituencies and staggered terms allow different parties to control the presidency and the Congress. Indeed, this has been commonplace in the post-World War II era. But divided party control of the presidency and Congress leads inevitably to conflict, maneuvering for partisan advantage, and difficulties for presidents in securing passage of their legislative programs.

As for institutional sources of conflict between the president and

The president's role as a policy agenda setter for the nation and Congress was amply illustrated in September 1993 when President Clinton in a nationally televised address before a joint session of Congress called upon members to enact his plan to overhaul the nation's health care system. To dramatize this call for action, the president displayed a sample health security card, a symbol of his health reform plan.

Congress, the Constitution interweaves executive and legislative functions, giving the president such legislative powers as the veto and Congress the authority to confirm major presidential appointments and ratify treaties. Under such conditions, struggles for influence between these two coequal branches of government are bound to erupt.

The president and members of Congress also approach their work from different time perspectives. Members of Congress view their congressional careers as open-ended and potentially lifetime. Among their main concerns, then, are achieving power within the chamber, getting reelected, helping out constituents, and enacting their own policy goals. Serving presidential ends is not their first priority. Presidents, by contrast, have only a fixed period of time in which to achieve their objectives and establish their niches in history.

Sources of Presidential
Influence and Support

Although presidential conflicts with the Congress are inevitable, presidents are able to claim victory on a relatively high percentage of congressional roll-call votes. Thus, cooperation between the two branches is possible as well.

The most important basis for cooperation between the president and Congress is partisan loyalty. Studies of congressional roll-call votes have shown consistently that presidents can expect at least two-thirds of their party's members to support their legislative proposals, and frequently 80 percent or more. Because no Republican president since Eisenhower has served with a Congress controlled by his party (1953–1955), recent Democratic presidents (Johnson, Kennedy, and Carter) have generally fared better with Congress than GOP presidents (Figure 11.3).

The importance of partisanship in securing congressional support was dramatically demonstrated during the August 1993 roll-call votes on President Clinton's budget reconciliation bill. This bill, which was the president's top legislative priority, passed by the narrowest of margins in both chambers with exclusively Democratic votes. Democratic lawmakers, many reluctant supporters of the bill, reportedly were heavily influenced in their decisions by the belief that the viability of their party's president was riding on this measure.

When party unity in Congress breaks down, as it does frequently, the president cannot necessarily depend on party loyalty to prevail in the end. It is just in such situations that the benefits of keeping the lines of communication open to members of the opposition party become apparent. But cutting deals with the opposition party to achieve legisla-

Facing stiff opposition among congressional Democrats, President Clinton sought in 1993 to rally bipartisan support for the North American Free Trade Agreement (NAFTA) by bringing former presidents Ford (left), Carter (center), and Bush (to the left of Vice President Gore) to stand shoulder to shoulder behind him at a signing ceremony for NAFTA side agreements. Joining the former presidents are (from left) Speaker of the House Thomas Foley, Senate Majority Leader George Mitchell, Senate Minority Leader Bob Dole, and House Minority Leader Robert Michel.

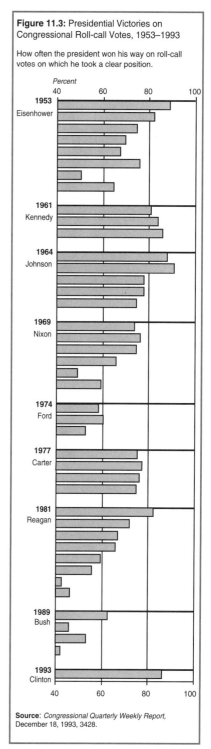

Figure 11.3: Presidential Victories on Congressional Roll-call Votes, 1953–1993

How often the president won his way on roll-call votes on which he took a clear position.

Source: *Congressional Quarterly Weekly Report,* December 18, 1993, 3428.

tive victories has its risks, including resentment among members of the president's party. Presidents must, therefore, seek to balance the interests of their own party's members against their needs for bipartisan support to achieve their policy goals.

The ability of the White House to win victories in Congress has varied substantially during presidential terms, as well as among presidents (Figure 11.3). Presidential support in Congress is thus affected by factors other than party control of the chamber. One such factor is the tie between a president's victories in Congress and high public approval ratings (Figure 11.4). That relationship is not always direct and immediate, but it certainly appears to be one of the reasons that two Democratic presidents, Kennedy and Johnson (especially early in his administration), had greater success than fellow Democrat Jimmy Carter with Democratic-controlled Congresses.

Because both the president and members of Congress have an interest in maintaining government programs and initiating new ones to meet social problems—neither achievable if a policy deadlock occurs because of presidential-congressional conflicts—they do cooperate to make certain that basic services and programs are maintained. At the end of the 1990 session of Congress, for example, Republican President Bush and Democratic congressional leaders achieved a compromise on the FY 1991 budget and spending levels for the next five years after

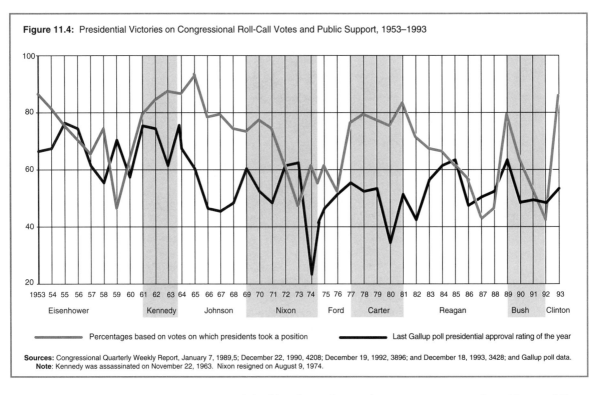

Figure 11.4: Presidential Victories on Congressional Roll-Call Votes and Public Support, 1953–1993

Percentages based on votes on which presidents took a position

Last Gallup poll presidential approval rating of the year

Sources: Congressional Quarterly Weekly Report, January 7, 1989,5; December 22, 1990, 4208; December 19, 1992, 3896; and December 18, 1993, 3428; and Gallup poll data.
Note: Kennedy was assassinated on November 22, 1963. Nixon resigned on August 9, 1974.

much highly televised wrangling. It was not popular with Republicans or Democrats, but neither side was prepared to permit the government to shut its doors because of a stalemate over funding.

Influencing Congress

All presidents have a variety of resources at their disposal to influence Congress. In this work they are assisted by the White House congressional relations office (their personal lobbyists), the congressional relations personnel of the various executive departments, and the White House interest group liaison staff (Office of Public Liaison).

Every member of the Congress needs *administration assistance* at some point. Perhaps it is a promise of presidential campaign assistance, support for a public works project for the member's constituency, appointment of a supporter to a federal position, public endorsement of a member's policy proposal, adjustment of an administration decision affecting a member's constituents, or an invitation to a White House state dinner. Because presidents head the vast executive branch and have more influence than any other American politician, they are in a position to advance the interests of members of Congress. Skillful presidents have used this bargaining position to build support for their legislative proposals. Thus, in an unusually candid moment Sen. John

Breaux (D-La.) once remarked, after striking a deal with the White House, that his vote could not be bought but that "it could be rented."

Members of Congress want to make rational decisions that will advance their policy and political goals, but to do this they must have *sound information*. In the nation's capital information is power, and those with the best and most up-to-date information are at an advantage. With its ability to draw on the entire executive branch, the administration frequently has an information edge over Congress. This is particularly the case in national security matters where the president is able to call on the resources of the Departments of State and Defense, the Central Intelligence Agency, and the National Security Council.

When President Lyndon Johnson once told members of Congress, "I'm the only president you've got," he was reminding them of the importance of maintaining the *prestige of the office of president* even though the incumbent might not be held in high regard. The respect that legislators, like other Americans, have for the office is another basis for presidential influence. Appeals for support made in a one-on-one conversation with the president in the White House are difficult to resist. In the Oval Office the president is surrounded by the trappings of the office—the presidential flag, the massive desk, and the military aide nearby with the "presidential emergency satchel" containing the authentication codes to be used in the event of war. A presidential appeal for support in this setting can be compelling, even for hardened congressional veterans.

The veto and the threat of a veto is another source of presidential clout over Congress. When a bill has been passed by Congress, the president has four options:

1. Sign the bill into law.

2. Allow the bill to become law without a signature by holding the bill for more than ten days (a little-used procedure reserved for bills the president dislikes but prefers not to veto).

3. Veto the bill. It becomes law only if the veto is overridden by a two-thirds vote of both the House and Senate.

4. Veto the bill by failing to sign it within ten days (pocket veto). This is possible only when Congress has adjourned, and the president is therefore unable to return the bill to that body for a possible veto override.

The veto is the president's ultimate weapon. And rarely is one overridden because to defeat an override attempt, the president needs the sup-

Table 11.2 Presidential Vetoes, 1945–1993

Years	President (Party)	Party Control of Congress	Regular Vetoes	Overridden Number	Overridden %	Pocket Vetoes	Total Vetoes
1945–1953	Truman (Dem.)	Dem. 1945–1946 Rep. 1947–1948 Dem. 1949–1953	180	12	6.7	70	250
1953–1961	Eisenhower (Rep.)	Rep. 1953–1954 Dem. 1955–1961	73	2	2.7	108	181
1961–1963	Kennedy (Dem.)	Dem.	12	0	0.0	9	21
1963–1969	Johnson (Dem.)	Dem.	16	0	0.0	14	30
1969–1974	Nixon (Rep.)	Dem.	26	7	26.9	17	43
1974–1977	Ford (Rep.)	Dem.	48	12	25.0	18	66
1977–1981	Carter (Dem.)	Dem.	13	2	15.4	18	31
1981–1989	Reagan (Rep.)	House: Dem. Senate: Rep. 1981–1986 Dem. 1987–1989	39	9	23.1	39	78
1989–1993	Bush (Rep.)	Dem.	29	1	0.3	17	46
1993	Clinton (Dem.)	Dem.	0	0	0	0	0
TOTAL			436	45	10.3	310	746

Source: Harold W. Stanley and Richard G. Niemi, eds., *Vital Statistics on American Politics*, 4th ed. (Washington, D.C.: CQ Press, 1993), 278.

port of only one-third plus one of the members of either the House or Senate. By relying on party loyalty, the chief executive can usually muster the votes needed to sustain a veto (see Table 11.2).

Because it is so difficult to override presidential vetoes, the threat of a veto can have a substantial impact on congressional decision making. When faced with such a threat, senators and representatives often seek compromises with the White House rather than risk total defeat of their legislative proposals.

When the White House and Congress are controlled by different parties, vetoes and override attempts tend to occur more frequently. Presidential popularity also affects veto politics. When the president's popularity is low, Congress is likely emboldened to pass bills over the president's objections. This provokes presidential vetoes and ensuing override attempts. But when the president's popularity is high, Congress is less likely to pass bills to which the president objects, thereby reducing the number of presidential vetoes and congressional override attempts.[51]

51. For an analysis of the circumstances that produce vetoes, override attempts, and successful overrides, see David W. Rohde and Dennis M. Simon, "Presidential

The White House may even resort to *appeals to interest groups and the public* to gain support in Congress. Because senators and representatives must stand periodically for reelection, White House staff often work in harness with supportive interest groups to exert pressure on wavering members of Congress. Presidents also may make dramatic television appeals for public support. Several popular presidents have used this technique effectively. In the 1950s, for example, President Eisenhower appealed to voters in a television address to support his call for labor reform legislation. The result was an outpouring of public support that caused a reluctant Congress to pass the Landrum-Griffin Act. But public appeals should not be made too frequently lest they lose their unique character and effectiveness. And there is also a risk in presidential appeals to the public over the head of Congress. Should such an appeal fail to arouse public support as Reagan's appeal for support of contra aid did in the 1980s, Congress then finds it much easier to oppose the president.

The president's ongoing quest for congressional support, the ups and downs of presidential influence with Congress, and the seemingly never-ending controversies between the branches are a reminder of the wisdom of Edwin Corwin, a constitutional scholar, who observed that "the Constitution is an invitation to struggle for the privilege of directing American . . . policy."[52]

The President as Commander in Chief and Chief Diplomat

In the foreign policy arena, as in other policy fields, the president must share power with Congress. Even so, the Constitution gives the president an impressive array of powers: to act as commander in chief of the military, to bestow (and withdraw) formal diplomatic recognition on foreign governments, and to negotiate treaties.

Because Congress is not equipped to undertake comprehensive strategic military planning, make timely foreign or national security decisions (including decisions about the deployment of troops and the use of nuclear weapons), or conduct relations with other governments

---

Vetoes and Congressional Response," *American Journal of Political Science* 29 (1985): 397–427. There is evidence that recent presidents have found it necessary to use the veto power more frequently on major bills than their predecessors. See David McKay, "Presidential Strategy and the Veto Power: A Reappraisal," *Political Science Quarterly* 104 (Fall 1989): 447–461.

52. Edwin S. Corwin, *The President: Office and Powers,* 4th ed. (New York: New York University Press, 1957), 171.

After Iraq invaded and occupied Kuwait in 1990, President George Bush, as commander in chief, sent American troops to the Persian Gulf to defend other Gulf nations. Later, following congressional approval of military action against Iraq, Bush gave the order for the American military to attack Iraq. The president and first lady Barbara Bush are shown here expressing their appreciation to the men and women who fought in the Persian Gulf.

on a day-to-day basis, foreign policy leadership tends to reside with the president. The president's preeminent role in foreign policy was demonstrated dramatically in December 1989. In that one month President Bush held a mini-summit/get-acquainted meeting at Malta with President Mikhail Gorbachev of the Soviet Union; met with the heads of the member states of the North Atlantic Treaty Organization (NATO); authorized American military jets to fly over Manila during a coup attempt to demonstrate support for Philippine president Corazon Aquino; sent a high-level secret diplomatic delegation to China; recognized new governments in Eastern Europe and granted them some special trade concessions; and ordered an American invasion of Panama to remove President Manuel Noriega from power. All of this was accomplished without any formal action on the part of the Congress, which had adjourned until January 1990.

The President's War Powers

As several of these examples indicate, an important source of the president's foreign policy authority is derived from the war powers that go with the office—the constitutional designation of commander in chief of the military. Although this constitutional provision was designed to ensure civilian supremacy over the military, the president's war powers extend beyond purely military operations. Abraham Lincoln, for example, issued the Emancipation Proclamation as a war measure, and at the beginning of World War II President Franklin Roosevelt authorized the army to create "defense zones" on the West Coast and by executive order, supported by an act of Congress, forcibly moved people of Japanese ancestry to relocation centers.

The president shares authority over the military with Congress, which must vote the money to support the armed forces and can enact regulations governing the military. Although Congress has the power to declare war, presidential conduct of foreign relations and orders to the military may lead to hostilities. Many examples of this situation are found throughout American history: in 1846 President James K. Polk sent troops into disputed territory in Texas, thereby precipitating the Mexican War; President Harry Truman ordered American troops to resist the 1950 invasion of South Korea by North Korea; and in 1965 President Lyndon Johnson used American troops to intervene in the Dominican Republic. Presidents Eisenhower, Kennedy, and Johnson ordered troops into Vietnam before Johnson secured congressional support in 1964 for escalating American involvement. And in more recent years, in the Mideast, President Reagan used the navy to escort oil tankers through the Persian Gulf during the last two years of the Iran-Iraq War (1980–1988), President Bush ordered American forces to the Persian Gulf after Iraq invaded Kuwait in 1990, and in 1994 President Clinton authorized U.S. forces to participate through NATO in United Nations peacekeeping operations in Bosnia.

Congress has the authority to resist such actions by refusing to grant funds for military uses or putting conditions on the use of the funds it does grant. But it has rarely used these powers to limit presidential war powers in a significant way. The problems faced by Congress when the president has sent American armed forces abroad had a humorous outcome in 1907 when President Theodore Roosevelt sent the U.S. Navy halfway around the world to demonstrate that the United States had become a major world power. Congress threatened to withhold the money for this adventure but was then faced with the choice of either providing the funds to get the fleet back to the United States or leaving it stranded in the Pacific. It voted the money.

More recently, however, Congress has taken actions to curb presidential discretion in military matters. In 1970 Congress reacted to growing domestic opposition to the Vietnam War by imposing an unprecedented restraint on the president's discretion as commander in chief: it stipulated that no funds could be used to send ground troops into Laos or Cambodia. When opposition to presidential policies in Vietnam continued, Congress passed in 1973 the War Powers Resolution over President Nixon's veto. The act required the president to notify Congress within forty-eight hours of the commitment of American troops abroad and provided that the troop commitment would be terminated within sixty days if Congress did not give its approval. An additional thirty days was allowed if the president certified to Congress that an unavoidable military necessity required continued use of American troops. Congress also was authorized to terminate a deployment of troops at any time.

Although the War Powers Resolution was designed by Congress to limit the president's war powers, it has in fact imposed few limits on the president and has been implemented only twice (in 1975 when marines were sent to rescue a U.S. merchant vessel captured by Cambodia, and in 1982 when marines were sent to Lebanon). Since the War Powers Resolution was enacted, presidents have opposed it as an unwise and undue restriction on presidential foreign policy prerogatives. And not only have presidents opposed it, but they also have not implemented it. Without invoking the War Powers Resolution, President Reagan invaded Grenada in 1983 and bombed Libya in 1986, and President Bush invaded Panama in 1989 and sent troops to the Persian Gulf in 1990. Some members of Congress have complained, but Congress itself has been reluctant to implement the resolution for fear of endangering military missions and causing the United States to appear less than resolute in its dealing with hostile governments.[53]

Probably more important than the War Powers Resolution are the political constraints on the president. The American experiences in the Korean and Vietnam wars show that presidential popularity can quickly erode and cause electoral defeat if military actions lead to high U.S. casualty counts, drag on without victory, and evoke extensive public and congressional opposition. Thus, before ordering American troops into battle to drive Iraq from Kuwait in 1991, President Bush sought and secured advance congressional approval.

Chief Diplomat

The president is responsible for conducting day-to-day relations with foreign governments. As chief diplomat, the president is assisted by the Department of State, which maintains embassies around the globe, as well as by a large bureaucracy in Washington. Included in the

53. On the implementation and difficulties with the War Powers Resolution, see Robert A. Katzman, "War Powers: Toward Accommodation," in *A Question of Balance: The President, the Congress and Foreign Policy,* ed. Thomas E. Mann (Washington, D.C.: Brookings, 1990), chap. 2.

In a moment of high drama and significance for the future of the Middle East, Israeli Prime Minister Yitzhak Rabin, left, and PLO leader Yasir Arafat shake hands under the approving gaze of President Clinton after having signed a historical peace agreement on the White House lawn in September 1993.

president's responsibilities are the sending and receiving of ambassadors, through which the United States extends official diplomatic recognition to foreign governments. Disapproval of a foreign government is expressed by withdrawing the U.S. ambassador as was the case for Cuba's Castro government. Presidents also convey their views of foreign governments and events through public statements—for example, President Clinton's statements of support for President Boris Yeltsin and his pledge of financial aid during their 1993 summit meeting in Vancouver.

In addition to public and formal actions, presidents also maintain informal contact with foreign heads of state. Presidents Bush and Clinton, for example, have chatted periodically by phone with European heads of state.

Traditionally treaty negotiations have been an important part of American foreign policy making. Treaty-signing ceremonies, like that held in 1988 when Presidents Reagan and Mikhail Gorbachev of the Soviet Union signed the Intermediate Nuclear Forces (INF) Treaty, are preceded by extensive negotiations between presidential envoys and representatives of foreign governments. Treaties must be ratified by a two-thirds vote of the Senate before they become part of the "law of the land," but they do not become operative until the president takes steps to implement them, often requiring congressional appropriations or legislation.

In addition to their treaty-making powers, presidents have the power to enter into executive agreements with foreign governments. Executive agreements are much like treaties except that they do not require Senate ratification to go into effect. Unless countermanded by Congress, executive agreements, like treaties, become law. They are even used frequently in major negotiations. For example, the Yalta (1944) and the Potsdam (1945) agreements among the World War II Allies provided for the occupation of Germany and the future of Europe. In most years five times more executive agreements have been negotiated than formal treaties ratified.[54] Congress has periodically expressed disapproval of executive agreements and under the Case Act of 1972 it has required presidents to notify Congress of all such agreements. Congress, however, has found no effective way to limit the president's power to make executive agreements.

Other foreign policy tools are economic and military aid to foreign governments. In 1989 the new, democratically elected government of Poland received economic aid as a show of U.S. support. Similarly, a key element of American policy in the Middle East has been steady support for Israel through high levels of economic and military aid. But just as foreign aid can be used as a sign of support, its withdrawal can be used to signal American disapproval of a foreign government's actions. Thus, the Bush administration reduced aid to Jordan after it tilted toward Iraq in the Persian Gulf conflict of 1991.

Control over foreign aid policy is shared by the president, who administers the aid, and the Congress, which provides the funds and spells out general guidelines for their distribution. In their efforts to use aid to gain maximum influence with foreign governments, presidents naturally seek wide discretionary authority in administering foreign aid. In recent years, however, Congress has sought to play a more active role in foreign policy making by attaching restrictions to the granting of American aid. For example, aid to El Salvador is conditional on the president's certifying that the Salvadoran government is making progress in protecting human rights. Such attempts by Congress to influence policy by imposing restrictions on how the president administers foreign aid have been a source of friction between the White House and Congress since the 1970s.

54. J. W. Peltason, *Understanding the Constitution*, 11th ed. (New York: Holt, Rinehart, and Winston, 1988), 95.

The Presidency: A Continuing American Dilemma

The presidency brings to American government qualities not found in either the Congress or the judiciary. Unlike Congress, the president provides a national rather than local perspective for national and international problems as well as a capacity to develop comprehensive and consistent policy proposals. The presidency is a symbol around whom all Americans can rally when the nation faces a crisis. And unlike the judiciary, which is an appointed institution lacking the democratic legitimacy derived from a popular election, the president is selected by the voters.

As America has become a world power over this century and the government's role has grown, the power of the office of president has expanded tremendously. Yet for all this presidential power, there are times when presidents appear hemmed in and incapable of decisive action. Presidential scholar Fred Greenstein believes that the modern presidency has developed a "double-edged" quality. Presidents may have greater formal and informal powers than ever in history, but they are subject as well to a greater potential for backlash. Presidents, he observed,

serve as the chief agenda setters for the nation, but in the process they create expectations that they can rarely fulfill; preside over a huge White House bureaucracy, which is necessary to achieve presidential goals, but which can also become a liability by distorting information and abusing power in the president's name; and are the most visible actors in American politics, which carries the danger of being made scapegoats for national disappointments.[55]

Presidents also must labor under the limitations imposed by deadlines, conduct routine business, and share power with Congress and the courts. They have to deal with difficult allies and cope with hostile foreign and domestic opponents while trying to resolve thorny, seemingly unsolvable problems. Often decisions must be made when the correct course of action is by no means clear.

Under these circumstances, does the president have too much power? Compared to other participants in the political system, the president has enormous powers. But when presidential powers are

55. Greenstein's notion of a "double-edged" presidency is summarized by Dom Bonafede in "Presidential Focus: What's a Leader?" *National Journal,* April 18, 1987, 972.

stacked up against the problems to be solved, they appear less substantial. The presidency is now, as it was for the Founders, a dilemma. How can it be made strong enough to serve the nation's leadership needs without becoming too powerful and a threat to democracy itself?

For Review

1. The Constitution both grants power to and limits the power of the president, who must share power with the other branches of government. Because the constitutional powers of the president are stated in broad terms, it has been possible to interpret them in ways that have permitted a vast expansion of presidential influence.

2. A combination of historical and institutional forces provides at least a partial explanation for the increased prominence and power of the president in the twentieth century. These include America's expanded role in world affairs, the widening of government responsibilities in domestic affairs and the accompanying growth of the executive branch, and the changed relationship between the president and the public stemming from the rise of the electronic media.

3. The presidency itself encompasses a sizable bureaucracy—the Executive Office of the President. Presidents mold this bureaucracy to fit their particular leadership styles and objectives. The presidential bureaucracy, particularly the White House staff, exercises great influence over administration policy making, but two major problems have confronted modern presidents: how to effectively utilize and control this presidential bureaucracy. Indeed, the White House staff is frequently the center of intense power and policy struggles.

4. Presidential power depends heavily on public support—a fragile commodity that is subject to sharp fluctuations depending on economic and world conditions. After an early "honeymoon" period, most presidents see their public approval ratings fall, although the public normally rallies to support the president in international crises.

5. The president plays a major role in establishing the congressional policy agenda. But presidential success with Congress is strongly affected by whether or not the president's party controls Congress and by the president's level of public support.

6. Presidents exert preeminent influence on foreign policy, but even in this area they must share power with Congress, which can restrict presidential initiatives through its legislative and funding powers.

For Further Reading

Edwards, George C., III. *At the Margins: Presidential Leadership of Congress.* New Haven, Conn.: Yale University Press, 1989. An analysis of the sources and conditions for presidential leadership of Congress.

Jones, Charles O. *The Presidency in a Separated System.* Washington, D.C.: Brookings, 1994. An explanation of how the president's role within a separated system of government depends on his resources, advantages, and strategic position.

Kernell, Samuel. *Going Public: New Strategies of Presidential Leadership.* 2d ed. Washington, D.C.: CQ Press, 1993. A consideration of how presidents increasingly rely on public relations to build support for their programs in Washington.

Mann, Thomas E., ed. *A Question of Balance: The President, the Congress and Foreign Policy.* Washington, D.C.: Brookings, 1990. A collection of essays on the problem of balancing presidential and congressional prerogatives and power in the making of foreign policy.

Mayhew, David R. *Divided We Govern: Party Control, Lawmaking, and Investigations, 1946-1990.* New Haven, Conn.: Yale University Press, 1991. An analysis that challenges the conventional wisdom about the adverse consequences of divided party control of government.

Milkis, Sidney. *The President and the Parties: The Transformation of the American Party System since the New Deal.* New York: Oxford University Press, 1993. An account of how the Roosevelt presidency and New Deal have transformed American politics from a system focused on patronage and local government into one attuned to national politics and programmatic concerns.

Nelson, Michael, ed. *The Presidency and the Political System.* 4th ed. Washington, D.C.: CQ Press, 1994. An excellent collection of essays analyzing such topics as presidential power; presidential relations with the press, interest groups, Congress, the bureaucracy, and the judiciary; and domestic and foreign policy leadership.

Neustadt, Richard E. *Presidential Power and the Modern Presidents: The Politics of Leadership from Roosevelt to Reagan.* New York: Free Press, 1990. A classic analysis of how presidents acquire and maintain power.

Peterson, Mark A. *Legislating Together: The White House and Capitol Hill from Eisenhower to Reagan.* Cambridge, Mass.: Harvard University Press, 1990. An analysis of presidential-congressional decision making.

Polsby, Nelson W. *Congress and the Presidency.* 4th ed. Englewood Cliffs, N.J.: Prentice-Hall, 1986. Contains lively and concise accounts of presidential leadership styles, insightful evaluations of modern presidents, and an analysis of congressional-presidential relations.

Rose, Richard, *The Postmodern President: George Bush Meets the World.* 2d ed. Chatham, N.J.: Chatham House, 1991. A perceptive look at the presidency emphasizing the impact of global forces over which the president has limited influence.

Safire, William. *Full Disclosure.* Garden City, N.Y.: Doubleday, 1977. A Washington insider and former presidential speech writer provides a fictionalized but highly insightful glimpse of life within the White House and the Beltway.

Thomas, Norman C., Joseph A. Pika, and Richard A. Watson. *The Politics of the Presidency.* Rev. 3d ed. Washington, D.C.: CQ Press, 1994. A comprehensive text on the modern presidency.

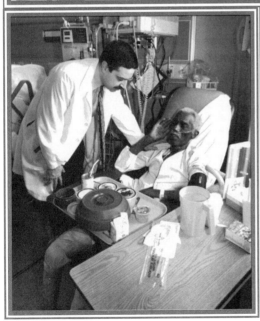

12. The Federal Bureaucracy

P RESIDENT Jimmy Carter probably voiced the thoughts of many Americans when he once said, "Before I became president, I realized and was warned that dealing with the federal bureaucracy would be one of the worst problems I would have to face. It has been worse than anticipated." Indeed, for better or worse the tentacles of the massive federal **bureaucracy** reach into Americans' lives in many ways. Among other things, the Internal Revenue Service (IRS) collects their taxes, federal air traffic controllers oversee their otherwise hazardous skyways, government-paid health care professionals tend to their military veterans, Federal Bureau of Investigation (FBI) agents chase their lawbreakers, and Social Security Administration employees provide their retirement checks and Medicare benefits when they get older. Because without all these government employees Congress and the president would be unable to carry out the policies they have authorized, the bureaucracy is an essential element of the governing process.

The term *bureaucracy* refers to the complex of agencies that administers government programs and policies. The men and women who work for these government agencies are often called **bureaucrats.** Most bureaucracies are structured hierarchically with clear lines of authority running from the department or agency head to subordinates. Within each organization there is a substantial division of labor based on specialized subunits. Bureaucracy is not just a governmental phenomenon. Massive bureaucracies also flourish within the private sector, especially in large corporations. Moreover, bureaucracies run unions, churches, universities, foundations, and health care institutions.

As the government's role in providing services and regulating the economy has expanded over the last sixty years, the bureaucracy has expanded as well. In fact, each new government function spawns a new bureaucracy. In the 1970s, for example, the energy bureaucracy ballooned in the wake of the Arab oil embargo as the government became a bigger player in the energy field and concerns surfaced about the effects of nuclear energy on the environment. Initially the responsibility for energy matters was given to the existing Office of Emergency Preparedness. But when this small agency, which had been operating in the backwaters of government policy making, proved inadequate to the task, two new agencies were created in 1974—the Federal Energy Office (FEA) in the Executive Office of the President and the Energy Research

Included among the millions of federal bureaucrats are the air traffic controllers, a highly skilled and trained group who perform an essential public service.

and Development Administration (ERDA). In 1977 FEA and ERDA became components of the present-day cabinet-level Department of Energy.

Most government bureaucracies develop a survival instinct along with powerful allies who enable them to resist dismantlement. For example, although created only in 1977, the Department of Energy was able to resist President Ronald Reagan's 1980 campaign pledge to oversee its demise because Congress and interest groups rallied to its defense. Today the department is firmly established with seventeen thousand employees and annual expenditures of over $15 billion.

The growth of the bureaucracy is more than simply a matter of expanding agencies, staffs, and budgets. Its impact on people's daily lives has grown by leaps and bounds as well. The food on the breakfast table is certified by the U.S. Department of Agriculture; labor-management relations are regulated by the National Labor Relations Board; exhaust emissions on cars are controlled by catalytic converters required by the Environmental Protection Agency; all the advertisements heard on car radios are subject to Federal Trade Commission (FTC) regulations, while the radio stations themselves are licensed by the Federal Communications Commission; workplaces are subject to standards imposed by the Occupational Safety and Health Administration; and universities must meet the nondiscrimination standards of the Departments of Education and Labor.[1]

The recent history of the Federal Trade Commission is a good

1. On the growth and impact of the bureaucracy, see Kenneth J. Meier, *Politics and Bureaucracy: Policymaking in the Fourth Branch of Government,* 3d ed. (Pacific Grove, Calif.: Brooks/Cole, 1993), 1–3.

The Federal Trade Commission assumed a more activist role on consumer protection issues under the leadership of Janet Steiger, a Bush administration appointee to the five-member, bipartisan, independent regulatory commission.

example of just how broad the implications of such government agency activities and policy making are for citizens everywhere. For much of its existence the FTC was a rather quiescent agency, but after congressional criticism and a critical exposé by consumer advocate Ralph Nader in 1969, President Richard Nixon appointed Casper Weinberger to chair the commission and change its image. Weinberger reorganized the FTC, fired one-third of its employees, and recruited young, aggressive, consumer-oriented lawyers for its staff. The result was heightened regulatory activity through the 1970s, which included antitrust suits filed against major oil companies and cereal makers; attacks on doctors, accountants, and lawyers for prohibiting advertising and other forms of competition; rules to prevent anticompetitive practices in the eyeglass industry; and investigations of the insurance industry, children's television shows, used-car marketing, and funeral homes. Although Congress initially encouraged these activities, the FTC developed its own policies.

Not surprisingly, the FTC's aggressive consumer protection activities provoked howls of protest from many of the industries and professions affected, who demanded that Congress pass legislation to restrict the FTC. But in spite of threats from some in Congress to either restrict or even abolish the agency, the commission continued its aggressive, consumer-oriented policies during the Carter administration. When President Reagan appointed a new FTC chair after the 1980 election, its policies finally changed: the commission shifted its focus from the consumer to the market and became a strong advocate of market-oriented solutions to consumer problems. With the appointment, however, of Janet Steiger as FTC chair by the Bush administration, the commission resumed its activist role in consumer protection, antitrust, and misleading advertising issues.[2]

The knowledge and expertise that bureaucrats develop in the course of carrying out their duties produce the essential information needed for congressional and presidential decision making. When developing tax policies, for example, both the president and Congress must depend heavily on the IRS to provide data on the impacts of existing tax laws and proposed changes. In truth, without the bureaucracy the government could not enforce the law or provide the services its citi-

2. For an account of FTC politics by a former commission chairman, see Michael Pertschuk, *Revolt against Regulation* (Berkeley: University of California Press, 1982). Also see Barry Weingast and Mark J. Moran, "Bureaucratic Discretion or Congressional Control? Regulatory Policymaking by the Federal Trade Commission," *Journal of Political Economy* 91 (May 1983): 765–800; Meier, *Politics and Bureaucracy,* 12–13; and W. John Moore, "Stoking the FTC," *National Journal,* May 19, 1990, 1217–1221.

zens have come to expect. Even so, for many Americans the term *bureaucracy* implies endless delays, arbitrary decisions, confusion, inefficiency, and inflexibility. Its critics charge as well that the bureaucracy is not sufficiently accountable to elected officials, as the controversy over FTC policy illustrates. Indeed, the bureaucracy is sometimes called the "fourth branch" of government—a vast army of nonelected administrators whose power to make administrative decisions threatens to usurp the policy-making powers of the Congress and the president. It is thus ironic that while the knowledge and skills bureaucrats bring to policy development and implementation are indispensable, many Americans tend to view the bureaucracy as somewhat illegitimate.[3] By a large majority (70 percent), they believe that when something is run by the government it is usually inefficient and wasteful.[4] This chapter reviews the constitutional position of the bureaucracy, gives an account of its growth and structure, and, most important, analyzes the bureaucracy's participation in the policy-making process.

The Constitutional Setting for the Bureaucracy

Because the writers of the Constitution were more concerned about the balance of power among the legislative, executive, and judicial branches than about the administration of government policies, the Constitution gives the structure of the executive branch only indirect attention. Yet this inattention to administration is hardly surprising given the few functions the government carried out in the late eighteenth century. It was expected to defend the shores, maintain order, deliver the mail, assist with a few public works projects, and little else.

The Founders did envision that Congress would create executive departments and delegate to them the power to carry out national policies (departments are mentioned in Article I). Moreover, in Article II Congress was empowered to give the president, courts, and department heads the authority to appoint government officials. This article also invested in the president the right to require written opinions from the "principal Officer in each of the executive Departments."

But what the Constitution did not spell out clearly was who was responsible for the exercise of administrative power—the Congress or the president? As a result, the years have seen a tug of war between the two branches to control the bureaucracy. A recent example of this

3. Francis E. Rourke, "Bureaucracy in the American Constitutional Order," *Political Science Quarterly* 102 (Summer 1987): 232.

4. Press release, *Times Mirror* Center for the People and the Press, Washington, D.C., May 28–June 10, 1992.

struggle occurred in 1994 when the House of Representatives, led by the head of its Veterans' Affairs Committee, G. V. ("Sonny") Montgomery (D-Miss.), overwhelmingly passed a bill prohibiting the president and secretary of the Department of Veterans Affairs from eliminating workers at veterans hospitals for five years. This legislation was a serious setback for President Clinton's goal of eliminating 272,900 federal workers over six years.

Whatever the ambiguities of the Constitution on who would control the administration of policy, two points were made clear by the nation's Founders. First, in Article I, section 6, of the Constitution, members of Congress were explicitly forbidden to hold concurrently a federal executive office. This reflected the Constitution writers' aversion to the practice in the British parliamentary system of appointing cabinet and lesser executive officers from the ranks of Parliament. Second, the president's power to remove executive branch officials whose original appointments had been confirmed by the Senate was recognized in the 1789 statute that created the first executive department. Presidents can therefore hold administrators accountable for their actions and prevent them from becoming independent of the chief executive.

The Constitution has left its mark on the American bureaucracy in other ways as well. Under its separation of powers principle, both the president and Congress exercise authority over the bureaucracy. Congressional statutes create government agencies, determine their powers and functions, set their organizational structures, and provide for their funding. Committees of the Congress can use their investigative authority to review administrative performance and exert pressure on administrators. In addition, the Senate confirms presidential appointments to major policy-making posts within agencies. But, at the same time, executive power is "vested in a President," who is charged with seeing that the laws are "faithfully executed." Bureaucrats in America thus serve two masters—the Congress and the president. In the process they often play one off against the other to gain a measure of independence. In countries with parliamentary systems, by contrast, the lines of authority are more clearly drawn, and the prime minister and the cabinet exercise greater control over the bureaucracy.

The constitutional principle of federalism, which assures the states of a prominent role in the governmental system, also has had profound effects on the administration of government programs. Many major government programs and policies are administered jointly by federal government agencies and state and local governments—for example, Aid to Families with Dependent Children (welfare), food stamps, unemployment compensation, mass transit, housing, and educational programs (see Chapter 3, Federalism). Unlike in governments organized on a unitary (nonfederal) basis, only a limited number of U.S. federal government agencies—such as the IRS, FBI, Postal Service, National Park Service, Social Security Administration, and Bureau of Indian Affairs—deal directly with the American people.

The Development of the Bureaucratic State

The bureaucratic state, with its sprawling organizational structure, complex procedures, service and regulatory activities, and millions of civilian employees, is a twentieth-century phenomenon in America. This vast administrative apparatus, however, had modest beginnings.[5]

The Executive Branch in Its Infancy: 1789 to the Civil War

In 1789, the first year of the government under the Constitution, Congress authorized three executive departments—State, War, and Treasury—and the offices of the attorney general and the postmaster general. The U.S. Post Office was actually created in 1792 and the Department of the Navy in 1798. By the time the Federalists left office after the election of 1800, the government had three thousand civilian employees. The State Department had a staff of nine plus a messenger boy, and the attorney general was expected to earn his living in private practice. The Jeffersonians retained the administrative structure inherited from the Federalists and did not add substantially to the federal bureaucracy. From 1830 until the Civil War, only one new department—Interior—was created, and the government's administrative apparatus remained "small, unpretentious and limited to a few essential functions."[6] Much of the increase in employment during this period was accounted for by the growth of the Post Office.

Growth of the Bureaucracy, 1861–1930

With the onset of the Civil War the ranks of the federal government began to swell significantly. After the war economic and social changes—industrialization, development of an urban working class, the emergence of corporations and monopolistic trusts, the building of

5. For concise accounts of the development of the American administrative state, see Lawrence C. Dodd and Richard L. Schott, *Congress and the Administrative State* (New York: Wiley, 1979), 16–57; and James Q. Wilson, "The Rise of the Bureaucratic State," *Public Interest* 41 (Fall 1975): 77–103.

6. Dodd and Schott, *Congress and the Administrative State*, 20.

transcontinental railroads, farm recessions, waves of immigration, and the rise of large, impersonal cities—created new pressures for government services and for economic regulatory activity to protect the consumer. Between 1881 and 1910 the number of civilians working for the federal government increased fourfold—from 100,000 to 400,000. The Departments of Agriculture and of Labor and Commerce were created to provide services to important sectors of the economy. In addition, the government embarked on its first serious steps toward regulating the economy with the creation of the Interstate Commerce Commission in 1887 to regulate the railroads, passage of the Sherman Anti-Trust Act in 1890 (enforced by the Justice Department), and establishment of the Federal Reserve System (1913), the Federal Trade Commission (1914), and the Federal Power Commission (1920). The Pure Food and Drug and Meat Inspection acts of 1906 created agencies to protect the food supply. World War I further spurred the development of the federal bureaucracy as new agencies were created to coordinate the war effort.

After World War I most of the wartime agencies were abolished and the number of government employees shrank, but not back to prewar levels. The 1920s saw only modest growth in government programs—regulation of some farm products and radio stations, additions to the national park and forest systems, and credit assistance to farmers.

Replacing the Spoils System with a Merit System

Although the government was small during the early years of the Republic, the struggles over who would be appointed to government posts were often bitter and intense. Beginning with the administration of Andrew Jackson (1829–1837), the practice of awarding jobs in the federal executive branch to presidential supporters and friends became entrenched. Under this practice, known as the **spoils system** (taken from the expression "to the victor belong the spoils"), winning presidential candidates and parties dismissed many of the government employees of the previous administration and installed their own loyalists instead. By the time the Civil War had begun, the system was a way of life in Washington—so much so, in fact, that on assuming the presidency Abraham Lincoln turned 90 percent of federal employees out of office and replaced them with loyal party supporters. He even reportedly wrote a letter dunning a patronage employee for his failure to pay the usual assessment on his salary to the party.[7]

7. Paul Van Riper, *History of the U.S. Civil Service* (New York: Harper and Row, 1958), 43–47.

Charles Guiteau, a disgruntled federal job seeker, was arrested on July 2, 1881, after shooting President James Garfield. Guiteau's bullet killed Garfield and gave birth to a reform movement that helped to eliminate the federal spoils system.

One rationale for this system was that government would remain responsive to the people by circulating ordinary citizens through its ranks. Furthermore, it was claimed that the patronage system assured the president that subordinates would be reasonably supportive of his policies. Finally, the spoils system was justified as a means of nurturing political party organizations by providing their supporters with government employment.

Although the spoils system had its benefits, it brought in its wake substantial graft and corruption. The sale of government jobs and kickbacks to party officials were commonplace. Instead of keeping government close to the people, the unsavory aspects of the spoils system undermined public trust in the government, and civil service reform became a prominent issue after the Civil War. The spoils system also imposed overwhelming burdens on newly elected presidents who were besieged by federal job seekers. President James Garfield, for example, complained, "The stream of callers . . . became a torrent and swept away my day. . . . I felt like crying out in the agony of my soul against the greed for office and its consumption of my time."[8] The final, but tragic, impetus for civil service reform was Garfield's assassination in 1881, just a few months after he took office, at the hand of a disappointed job seeker.

The Pendleton Act of 1883 created a Civil Service Commission and introduced hiring based on competence (not political connections),

8. Leonard D. White, *The Republican Era* (New York: Macmillan, 1958), 94.

normally determined by open, competitive examinations. The basic principles of the civil service system are (1) selection of subordinate government officials on the basis of merit—the ability to perform the work—rather than partisan or personal favoritism; (2) job tenure for those hired regardless of any political changes at the top of the government organization; and (3) "willing responsiveness to political leaders of the day" on the part of government employees in return for guarantees of job security.[9]

Passage of the Pendleton Act coincided with a steady rise in the number of federal employees as the government expanded its functions. The act thus began a process of transforming a group of executive branch personnel from patronage appointees closely tied to elected politicians into an independent career civil service. Particularly important in this process were the efforts of two Progressive era presidents, Theodore Roosevelt (1901–1909) and Woodrow Wilson (1913–1921). Roosevelt was instrumental in creating the Commerce and Labor departments, the Forest Service, and the Food and Drug Administration. In keeping with the Progressive philosophy, he insisted that these agencies be professionally staffed. Wilson led the movement for a nonpartisan Federal Reserve System to regulate the currency and banks and for an independent Federal Trade Commission to enforce antitrust legislation.

Gradually the merit system was extended so that by 1930, 80 percent of federal employees were covered. A further effort to depoliticize the bureaucracy came with the 1939 passage of the Hatch Act, which severely restricted the extent to which government employees could participate in partisan politics. These restrictions were eased in 1993 when Congress amended the Hatch Act to permit federal civil service and postal employees to engage (on their own time) in such political activities as registering voters, making telephone calls, stuffing envelopes, holding office in a political party, and speaking at political gatherings. Bans on federal employees soliciting campaign funds from the general public and running for partisan office continue in effect under the 1993 Hatch Act amendments.

A major effect of the introduction of the merit system was the creation of a governmental work force separate from both the Congress and president. With its emphasis on merit as the basis for appointment, expertise, and permanence in office, the federal civil service has become fairly insulated from direct control by the president or Congress. Yet

9. Hugh Heclo, *A Government of Strangers: Executive Politics in Washington* (Washington, D.C.: Brookings, 1977), 20.

because it leads an existence balanced between the president and Congress, it also must be sensitive to the political forces operating within both institutions.

The Impact of the New Deal and World War II

The bureaucratic state of today is largely the product of the depression of the 1930s and World War II. These crises changed public attitudes about the role of government in American society. The public accepted an activist government staffed by technical experts as a means of coping with the depression and the external threat posed by Nazi Germany and Imperial Japan. President Franklin Roosevelt's New Deal policies to combat the depression led to an explosion in the size of the federal bureaucracy as existing government programs were expanded, additional economic regulations were imposed, and new social services were provided. Among the welter of new agencies created were the Tennessee Valley Authority, Securities and Exchange Commission, Social Security Administration, Export-Import Bank, Federal Deposit Insurance Corporation, and the National Labor Relations Board. In mobilizing for World War II, the government became involved in the economy to unprecedented levels as the War Production Board marshalled the resources of industry and the Office of Price Administration regulated prices and rationed scarce consumer goods. To fund the war effort and the government's domestic programs, the federal government dramatically increased individual and corporate income taxes. With this lucrative source of revenue, the federal government was able to support its expanded role.

During the war years scientific and technological advances caused the bureaucracy to grow in ways unimaginable earlier. The development of atomic energy prompted creation of a government bureaucracy to regulate its use for military and peaceful purposes. Advances in rocket technology underlay the establishment of the National Aeronautics and Space Administration (NASA) after the war. And the growth of the airline industry, which had benefited from military research and development, spawned a system of federal regulation currently administered by the Federal Aviation Administration.

"There is no idea so uplifting as the ideal of the service of humanity."
—Woodrow Wilson

Further Expansion of Government Activity since World War II

The 1950s through the 1970s brought forth new government initiatives in health, civil rights, education, housing, income maintenance, transportation, and urban development. Particularly notable for their contributions to the growth of the federal government in the 1960s were President Lyndon Johnson's Great Society programs aimed at eliminating the causes of poverty. Among the additional federal departments and agencies created from the 1950s through the 1970s were the Departments of Health and Human Services (originally named Health, Education, and Welfare), Housing and Urban Development, Transportation, Education, and Energy, as well as the Environmental Protection Agency, Occupational Safety and Health Administration, Consumer Product Safety Commission, Equal Employment Opportunity Commission, and the Peace Corps.

Unlike previous periods of growth in government activity, the era since the 1950s has not been accompanied by significant increases in federal government employment. The growth in federal government spending from 1960 into the 1980s was dramatic (see Figure 3.1 in Chapter 3, Federalism), but, interestingly, during this expansion in government activity federal employment remained relatively stable. This paradox reflected higher costs for such existing programs as Social Security as well as increases in federal payments to state and local governments and to government contractors and consultants. Although the number of federal employees has remained relatively stable since the 1960s, employment in state and local governments implementing federal policies with grants-in-aid has increased substantially. Under the federal system, growing federal government budgets and activities do not necessarily translate into a corresponding surge in the number of federal employees. The employment impact of increased federal spending is often at the state and local levels where the programs are administered.

The executive branch presently has over 3 million civilian employees, but only about 358,000 work in the Washington, D.C., area. The rest work in the fifty states, the territories, and around the world. To provide work space for these employees, the federal government owns 446,000 buildings with 2.8 billion square feet of floor space. It also leases an additional 234 million square feet of building space (see Figure 12.1, an organization chart of the sprawling executive establishment, for a more complete indication of the size of the bureaucracy and the scope of its activities). In civilian employees, the Department of Defense ranks first with over a million workers (33 percent of the federal civilian work force), followed by the U.S. Postal Service (26 percent), the Department of Veterans Affairs (8 percent), and the Department of Health and Human Services (4 percent).

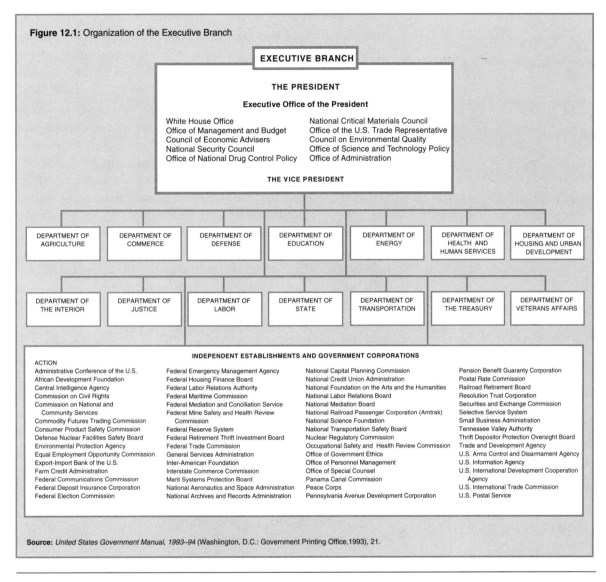

Figure 12.1: Organization of the Executive Branch

EXECUTIVE BRANCH

THE PRESIDENT

Executive Office of the President

White House Office
Office of Management and Budget
Council of Economic Advisers
National Security Council
Office of National Drug Control Policy

National Critical Materials Council
Office of the U.S. Trade Representative
Council on Environmental Quality
Office of Science and Technology Policy
Office of Administration

THE VICE PRESIDENT

| DEPARTMENT OF AGRICULTURE | DEPARTMENT OF COMMERCE | DEPARTMENT OF DEFENSE | DEPARTMENT OF EDUCATION | DEPARTMENT OF ENERGY | DEPARTMENT OF HEALTH AND HUMAN SERVICES | DEPARTMENT OF HOUSING AND URBAN DEVELOPMENT |

| DEPARTMENT OF THE INTERIOR | DEPARTMENT OF JUSTICE | DEPARTMENT OF LABOR | DEPARTMENT OF STATE | DEPARTMENT OF TRANSPORTATION | DEPARTMENT OF THE TREASURY | DEPARTMENT OF VETERANS AFFAIRS |

INDEPENDENT ESTABLISHMENTS AND GOVERNMENT CORPORATIONS

ACTION
Administrative Conference of the U.S.
African Development Foundation
Central Intelligence Agency
Commission on Civil Rights
Commission on National and
   Community Services
Commodity Futures Trading Commission
Consumer Product Safety Commission
Defense Nuclear Facilities Safety Board
Environmental Protection Agency
Equal Employment Opportunity Commission
Export-Import Bank of the U.S.
Farm Credit Administration
Federal Communications Commission
Federal Deposit Insurance Corporation
Federal Election Commission

Federal Emergency Management Agency
Federal Housing Finance Board
Federal Labor Relations Authority
Federal Maritime Commission
Federal Mediation and Conciliation Service
Federal Mine Safety and Health Review
   Commission
Federal Reserve System
Federal Retirement Thrift Investment Board
Federal Trade Commission
General Services Administration
Inter-American Foundation
Interstate Commerce Commission
Merit Systems Protection Board
National Aeronautics and Space Administration
National Archives and Records Administration

National Capital Planning Commission
National Credit Union Administration
National Foundation on the Arts and the Humanities
National Labor Relations Board
National Mediation Board
National Railroad Passenger Corporation (Amtrak)
National Science Foundation
National Transportation Safety Board
Nuclear Regulatory Commission
Occupational Safety and Health Review Commission
Office of Government Ethics
Office of Personnel Management
Office of Special Counsel
Panama Canal Commission
Peace Corps
Pennsylvania Avenue Development Corporation

Pension Benefit Guaranty Corporation
Postal Rate Commission
Railroad Retirement Board
Resolution Trust Corporation
Securities and Exchange Commission
Selective Service System
Small Business Administration
Tennessee Valley Authority
Thrift Depositor Protection Oversight Board
Trade and Development Agency
U.S. Arms Control and Disarmament Agency
U.S. Information Agency
U.S. International Development Cooperation
   Agency
U.S. International Trade Commission
U.S. Postal Service

Source: *United States Government Manual, 1993–94* (Washiington, D.C.: Government Printing Office, 1993), 21.

The Organization of the Federal Bureaucracy

The federal government is composed of a bewildering array of agencies with diverse histories, statutory authorities, activities, and bases of political support. Government organization charts convey something of the scope of the bureaucracy (see Figure 12.1) but not the power struggles involved in creating an agency, ensuring its survival, determining where it will be located within the executive branch, or deciding on its budgets and policies.

The rise and fall of the Office of Economic Opportunity (OEO), the centerpiece of President Lyndon Johnson's War on Poverty, demonstrate the importance of organizational structure and political support in the functioning of a government agency and its programs. OEO was created by the Economic Opportunity Act of 1964 to serve as the lead agency in coordinating the government-wide War on Poverty. In addition, OEO was to administer the most innovative and controversial aspect of the act: a program of direct grants to community action agencies in which the poor were to take an active part in developing and carrying out antipoverty initiatives. To give his War on Poverty visibility and White House backing, President Johnson lodged OEO in the Executive Office of the President, where, with his active support, the agency thrived during the mid-1960s. But the succeeding Nixon and Ford administrations were not OEO backers, and the agency was downgraded administratively. The agency was then dismantled, and what remained of its programs was transferred to a new independent agency, the Community Services Administration (CSA), and to existing departments such as Health, Education, and Welfare. In its new form as CSA the agency lacked its former prestige and political muscle as a presidential agency in the Executive Office of the President. The administrative downgrading of the agency continued under President Ronald Reagan. In 1981 CSA was abolished and its functions transferred to the Office of Community Services within the massive Department of Health and Human Services (HHS). Whereas OEO had once been a prestigious and influential agency with programs receiving vigorous presidential support, it was now a bureau almost lost within the sprawling HHS bureaucracy. Most agencies are able to defend themselves more successfully than OEO, but all face recurring efforts to either expand or restrict their effectiveness, prominence, and power through changes in organizational structure.

Cabinet-level Departments

The fourteen departments of the federal executive branch are headed by a secretary or by the attorney general in the case of the Department of Justice (see Table 12.1). The heads of these departments make up the president's cabinet.[10] Because an agency's importance within the executive branch is affirmed when it receives departmental or cabinet status, supporters of programs administered by agencies lacking cabi-

10. The president may designate other officials to be members of the cabinet. Frequently included are the White House chief of staff, the director of the Office of Management and Budget, the U.S. trade representative, and the ambassador to the United Nations. President Clinton also has made the director of the Environmental Protection Agency a cabinet member.

Table 12.1 Cabinet-level Departments of the Federal Government

Department	Year Established	Historical Development
State	1789	Originally named Department of Foreign Affairs but redesignated Department of State in 1789
Treasury	1789	Expanded through a subsequent series of statutes
Interior	1849	Created by the merger of the General Land Office, Bureau of Indian Affairs, Pension Office, and Patent Office
Agriculture	1862	Originally administered by a commissioner, the department saw its powers expand in 1889.
Justice	1870	Before 1870 the attorney general was a cabinet officer but not head of a department
Labor	1913	Originally a bureau within the Department of Interior, it became an independent department in 1913.
Commerce	1913	Designated a department when the Department of Commerce and Labor, created in 1903, was reorganized
Defense	1949	After several reorganizations, the original Departments of War (1789) and Navy (1798) were merged into the Department of Defense.
Health and Human Services	1953	Established as the Department of Health, Education, and Welfare but redesignated Health and Human Services when Education was made a separate department in 1979
Housing and Urban Development	1965	Created by combining agencies responsible for housing, including the Housing and Home Finance Agency, with those involved in urban development
Transportation	1966	Created out of eight existing agencies
Energy	1977	Created by transferring existing energy agencies and bureaus to the new department
Education	1979	Originally the Office of Education in the Department of Health, Education, and Welfare
Veterans Affairs	1988	Created by elevating the Veterans Administration to cabinet-level status

Source: *United States Government Manual, 1993-94* (Washington, D.C.: Government Printing Office, 1993).

net rank lobby from time to time for their pet agencies to become departments as a means of raising their visibility and budgets. In 1988, for example, veterans organizations and their administrative and congressional allies succeeded in having the Veterans Administration elevated to cabinet status for these reasons. Likewise, some members of Congress have sought to raise the Environmental Protection Agency to cabinet status so that its voice will be heard more forcefully on major policy issues.

Within each department a chain of command runs from the secretary to the various units of the organization, normally designated as bureaus, administrations, offices, or divisions. Each is responsible for carrying out a congressionally mandated function of the department. The secretary is responsible for the entire agency. Under secretaries and assistant secretaries, who report to the secretary, control various segments of the department's activities. In the Department of Commerce,

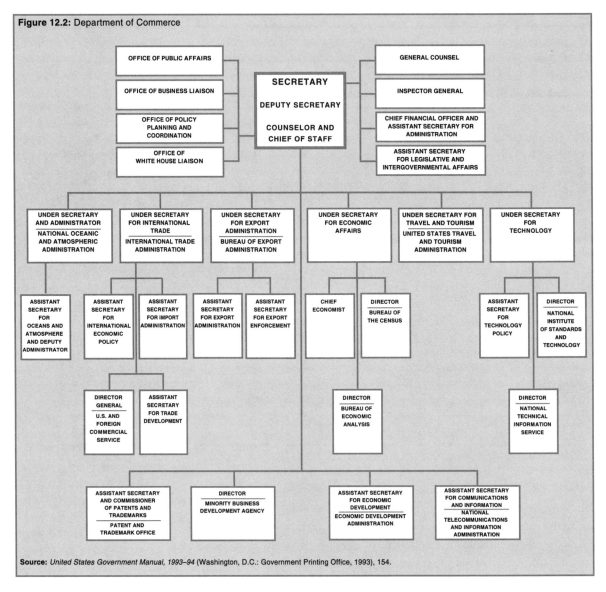

Figure 12.2: Department of Commerce

Source: *United States Government Manual, 1993–94* (Washington, D.C.: Government Printing Office, 1993), 154.

for example, the under secretary for economic affairs is responsible for the Bureau of the Census, Bureau of Economic Analysis, and Office of the Chief Economist (Figure 12.2). Although the secretary sets general policy, the actual implementation of policy occurs at the bureau level, where the permanent civil service personnel have a major influence over the program's operation. For example, a major responsibility of the Commerce Department is conducting the decennial census, an extremely technical operation designed and implemented by the professional staff of the Bureau of the Census. But even so technical an

THE FEDERAL BUREAUCRACY 499

activity as the census has major policy implications. In conducting the 1990 census, for example, the bureau became embroiled in a controversy over the extent to which people living in the nation's largest cities had been undercounted. This issue was of critical importance because population determines the apportionment of congressional representation among the states and figures in the amount of federal aid states and cities receive.

Independent Agencies

Independent agencies are headed by presidential appointees, but they operate outside the jurisdiction of departments. In spite of their lack of cabinet status, independent agencies can have major policy-making roles. Examples of such agencies are the Central Intelligence Agency (CIA), Environmental Protection Agency (EPA), and NASA.

The extent of independent agencies' autonomy from presidential direction varies from agency to agency, depending on the statute that created them. Such agencies as the CIA, EPA, NASA, United States Information Agency, and Small Business Administration are subordinate to the president just as any department would be. The U.S. Postal Service, however, operates quite independently of the president. It is governed by an eleven-member board appointed by the president for overlapping terms. The board appoints the postmaster general, who is responsible to the board, not to the president.

Independent Regulatory Commissions

A special category of independent agency is the independent regulatory commission. These commissions regulate major sectors of the economy and are empowered to hold hearings, investigate business practices, and make rulings that affect both individual firms and whole industries. Members of regulatory commissions are appointed by the president with the consent of the Senate. But unlike departments, commissions are headed by several commissioners (often five) instead of a single administrator. To insulate them from partisan and presidential pressures, commissioners are required by statute to be from both parties and are appointed for fixed, overlapping terms of at least five years. In addition, commission members may not be removed by the White House because the president disagrees with their policies.

Examples of major independent regulatory agencies include the Interstate Commerce Commission (ICC), which regulates railroads, bus lines, water carriers, trucking companies, and coal slurry pipelines, and the Federal Trade Commission (FTC), created to promote competition and prevent restraints on trade, prevent false advertising and discriminatory pricing, and ensure truthful labeling of products and disclosure of credit charges. The Federal Communications Commission (FCC) was created in 1934 to regulate radio and television broadcasting, as well as telephone, telegraph, cable television, and satellite communications. And the National Labor Relations Board (NLRB), established in 1935, is responsible for preventing and remedying unfair labor practices by employers and unions and conducting collective bargaining elections.

Although the regulatory commissions were designed to be insulated from political pressures, they are not, in reality, immune from such influences. Regulatory commission decisions have far-reaching consequences for both the regulated industries and the public. For example, the ICC can rule against railroad mergers; the FCC can either grant or deny the renewal of a television station's license which is worth millions of dollars; and the FTC can rule that a cereal company is guilty of false and misleading advertising for its leading product. These kinds of impacts spur the affected interests, particularly regulated industries and more recently public interest groups, to seek influence over commission policy.

The potential for interest group influence is enhanced by the organizational structures of the independent regulatory agencies, which limit direct presidential and congressional control of agency policy. This lack of control can increase agencies' dependence on the interests they regulate for support, leading in some instances to their "capture" by regulated interests. Indeed, after the initial reform fervor favoring regulation has subsided, agencies may find that the expertise, interest, and dependable political support they need to sustain themselves rest mainly in the regulated industry. The regulator and regulated, therefore, tend to develop a relationship of mutual support, the kind found, for example, between the ICC and the railroads or the Federal Energy Regulatory Commission and the natural gas producers.[11] Not all regulatory agencies are "captured," however. The Environmental Protection Agency and the Occupational Safety and Health Administration, for example, have been less vulnerable to "capture" because, among other things, the statutes they administer contain strict guidelines and, in the case of EPA, the timetables for compliance leave limited discretion to administrators. They also regulate an array of industries and do not

11. For a discussion of "capture," see Carl Van Horn, Donald C. Baumer, and William T. Gormley, Jr., *Politics and Public Policy*, 2d ed. (Washington, D.C.: CQ Press, 1991), 107–109. For an alternate view, see Paul J. Quirk, *Industry Influence in Federal Regulatory Agencies* (Princeton, N.J.: Princeton University Press, 1981).

have to confront a single, united opposition. Finally, these agencies have been supported by activist public interest groups and the media.

Although their direct influence is limited, neither the president nor Congress is without weapons to influence regulatory commissions. A president can affect agency policy through commission appointments. Presidents Nixon and Carter, for example, appointed consumer-oriented chairs to the FTC; Reagan, in contrast, appointed nonactivist commissioners. Congress can influence policy by changing the regulatory statutes the agencies enforce, passing legislation to reorganize the agencies, reducing or increasing agency budgets, and lobbying the White House on appointments. But the critics of such measures point out that things can quickly get out of hand. They charge, for example, that Congress bears some responsibility for the massive savings and loan association collapse of the 1980s that cost taxpayers billions because it relaxed regulatory statutes, limited funds available to the Federal Savings and Loan Insurance Corporation, and intervened in the regulatory process to assist constituents.[12]

Government Institutes and Foundations

To promote science, scholarship, and the arts, Congress created a series of independent institutes and foundations, each with its own board of directors responsible for its operations. The oldest is the Smithsonian Institution, which operates museums, art galleries, the John F. Kennedy Center for the Performing Arts, and a zoo in the District of Columbia. Medical research institutes include the National Institutes of Health, National Cancer Institute, and the National Heart Institute. Among the foundations established to promote scholarship and the arts are the National Science Foundation, a major funding source for scientific research, and the National Foundation on the Arts and the Humanities.

Government Corporations

Government corporations, which are chartered by congressional statute, operate much like private corporations except that the president, not stockholders, selects the board of directors. Some of these corporations provide consumer services, such as the National Railroad Passenger Corporation (Amtrak, the intercity passenger train service) and COMSAT, the communications satellite system. Other government corporations provide insurance; the Federal Deposit Insurance Corpo-

12. Thomas Romer and Barry R. Weingast, "Political Foundations of the Thrift Debacle," in *Politics and Economics of the 1980s*, ed. Alberto Alesina and Geoffrey Carliner (Chicago: University of Chicago Press, 1991).

ration, which insures bank depositors' savings, and the Federal Crop Insurance Corporation for farmers are two examples. Some government corporations function as a unit within a regular department—for example, the Department of Agriculture's Commodity Credit Corporation. Others, like the Export-Import Bank and Pension Benefit Guaranty Corporation, operate as independent agencies.

Advisory Committees, Minor Boards, and Commissions

Federal programs and agencies frequently have advisory committees to provide expert advice on a variety of topics—for example, intelligence gathering, census data, and educational programs. These committees also provide a link between agencies and the clientele with whom they deal, as well as an opportunity for prestigious presidential patronage. In addition, over one hundred minor boards, committees, and commissions have been established by Congress or the president to perform specific functions, provide advice, or operate small programs. Examples are the White House Commission on Presidential Scholars, National Council on Disability, American Battle Monuments Commission, and Migratory Bird Commission.

The Federal Service

The men and women who staff the federal government are a diverse lot. They range from the presidential appointees who handle delicate relations with other nations, to the doctors in the U.S. Public Health Service, to the forest rangers, astronauts, nurses, painters, secretaries, lawyers, accountants, and cooks who labor in the other far corners of the government. They work in sharply contrasting bureaucratic cultures—the rather staid, tradition-bound professionalism of the Bureau of the Census or Department of the Treasury; the protocol-laden, cautious, procedure-conscious atmosphere of the State Department; the socially activist milieu of the Department of Housing and Urban Development; the pressure-packed environment of the Federal Aviation Administration's air-traffic controllers.

The federal service is not composed of people cut from the same cloth. Because of the wide variety of jobs within the federal government, the federal work force is quite representative of the American population for such social characteristics as region of origin, occupation, education, income, social background, and race.[13] Although women (50.7 percent of total civilian employment in 1991) and minori-

13. Kenneth J. Meier and Lloyd G. Nigro, "Representative Bureaucracy and Policy Preferences," *Public Administration Review* 36 (July/August 1976): 458–469; and Meier, *Politics and Bureaucracy,* 205–210.

Women and Minorities in the Federal Work Force (1992)

As more women and minorities enter the ranks of the federal government's civilian work force, its demographic profile is changing. Between 1982 and 1992 the percentage of women employees increased by 20 percent and minorities by 25 percent. In 1992, however, women held only 13 percent of the top jobs and minorities 8 percent. Wide variation exists among the cabinet-level departments in the proportions and levels of jobs held by women and minorities.

Percent of Total Employees

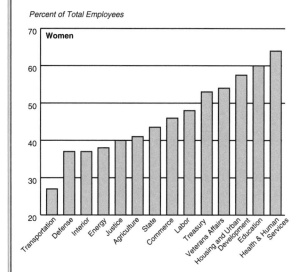

Percent of Employees in High-Level Positions

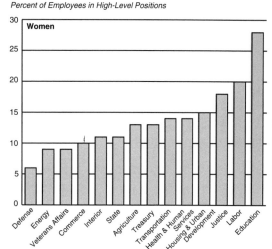

Percent of Total Employees

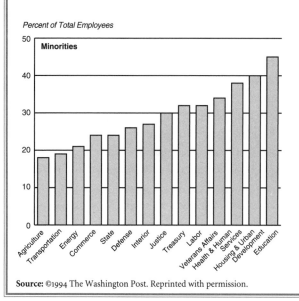

Percent of Employees in High-Level Positions

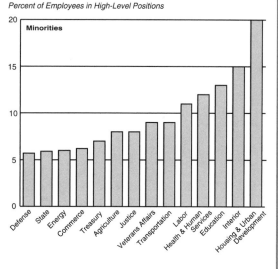

Source: ©1994 The Washington Post. Reprinted with permission.

Table 12.2 Composition of the Federal Service by Salary Level, Racial/Ethnic Group, and Sex: 1991

The lower ranks of the federal service are filled by a substantial proportion of minority and female employees. Even with government affirmative action programs, the upper levels of the federal service are composed predominantly of white males.

Government Service (GS) Salary Level		Total Number	Percent Black	Percent Hispanic	Percent Female
GS-01	$11,903–14,891	4,655	38.9	11.1	75.8
GS-02	$13,382–16,843	10,928	35.0	11.2	71.0
GS-03	$14,603–18,986	56,907	29.5	7.8	71.3
GS-04	$16,393–21,307	151,274	27.7	6.7	74.9
GS-05	$18,340–23,839	208,905	23.6	6.4	73.8
GS-06	$20,443–26,572	113,999	24.8	5.6	77.1
GS-07	$22,717–29,530	162,356	20.5	5.9	68.7
GS-08	$25,159–32,710	35,730	24.3	4.5	60.9
GS-09	$27,789–36,123	186,134	14.2	6.2	52.8
GS-10	$30,603–39,783	32,031	13.3	6.2	53.4
GS-11	$33,623–43,712	208,770	11.5	5.0	38.1
GS-12	$40,298–52,385	233,909	10.0	3.8	30.8
GS-13	$47,920–62,293	154,057	7.9	3.1	23.1
GS-14	$56,627–73,619	87,135	5.9	2.4	18.1
GS-15	$66,609–86,598	48,096	4.3	2.3	14.2
TOTAL, all pay plans		2,183,403	16.7	5.4	43.6
TOTAL, GS and equivalent		1,694,886	16.6	5.2	50.7

Source: Office of Personnel Management data compiled by Harold W. Stanley and Richard G. Niemi, eds., *Vital Statistics on American Politics,* 4th ed. (Washington, D.C.: CQ Press, 1993), 406.
    Note: Amounts in current dollars. Pay schedules effective January 1993.

ties (African Americans, 16.6 percent, and Hispanics, 5.2 percent) are substantially represented, they tend to be concentrated in the lower pay grades (Table 12.2). The upper levels of the civil service are composed mainly of highly educated, white, male, urban-dwelling professionals from middle-class backgrounds.[14] But individual government agencies show wide variation in their employment records for women and minorities. For example, the Department of Education has the highest percentage of women in high-level positions (28 percent) and 60 percent of its employees are female. By contrast, in the Department of Defense, with a work force that is 37 percent female, only 6 percent of its top jobs are held by women. The Department of Housing and Urban Development has the highest proportion of minorities in high-level jobs (20 percent), while at the Departments of Defense and State

14. Harold W. Stanley and Richard G. Niemi, *Vital Statistics on American Politics,* 4th ed. (Washington, D.C.: CQ Press, 1993), 406.

minorities hold less than 6 percent of these positions (see box Women and Minorities in the Federal Work Force).[15]

Merit System Employees

Ninety percent of federal civilian employees are selected through a merit system. In addition, some professional and managerial personnel are appointed on the basis of their job qualifications (much like in the private sector), as specified by the Office of Personnel Management (OPM). Several agencies have their own merit hiring systems, which operate outside the jurisdiction of OPM. These include the State Department (for its Foreign Service employees), CIA, FBI, U.S. Postal Service, Department of Veterans Affairs, and Public Health Service (for its physicians).

Merit System Employees

Political Appointees

Also exempt from the civil service merit system are the approximately 3,900 presidential appointees who serve at the pleasure of the chief executive. Through these appointments presidents are able to install their own people in policy-making positions and in slots that involve confidential relationships with policy makers. With this system of hiring, however, a substantial turnover in the federal service occurs whenever a new administration takes office. By contrast, in Britain only a small number of senior civil service positions change hands when a new prime minister is chosen. All remaining personnel are expected to assist the new cabinet and implement its policies.

Among the top-level policy-making positions subject to presidential control in the U.S. government are the over six hundred cabinet secretaries and subcabinet officers (including under, deputy, and assistant secretaries; top-level independent agency personnel; ambassadors; U.S. attorneys; and members of various commissions and boards). In addition, the so-called Schedule C appointees (1,794 in 1993) are entrusted with policy-determining responsibilities or have a confidential relationship with key decision makers. Since 1977, as presidents have sought to exert more influence over the executive branch, the number of high-level political appointees has increased dramatically.

Surgeon General Joycelyn Elders, an outspoken and often controversial advocate of measures to prevent the spread of communicable diseases, helps to direct the work of thousands of health care professionals in the massive Department of Health and Human Services.

The Senior Executive Service (SES)

The Civil Service Reform Act of 1978, by creating a Senior Executive Service, gave presidents and their appointees even more flexibility in managing the federal bureaucracy. The reformers behind this act recognized that career civil service executives had important policy-making

15. "A Snapshot of Women and Minorities in Federal Jobs," *Washington Post*, Jan. 3, 1994, A17.

responsibilities but that their primary loyalty was normally to their agency, not necessarily to the administration's objectives. In fact, according to the reformers these career bureaucrats were excessively insulated from the legitimate control of their politically appointed superiors. To rectify this situation, the act created an 8,500-member Senior Executive Service, 10 percent of whom can be political appointees. Unlike regular civil service personnel, SES members can be transferred from one agency to another and to different positions within an agency. They also can be dismissed for ineffectiveness more readily than regular members of the civil service. Both President Jimmy Carter, who had pressed for enactment of the Civil Service Reform Act, and President Ronald Reagan took advantage of the flexibility the act provided to restructure the senior bureaucracy. Indeed, by taking advantage of the 1978 act's provisions permitting political appointments and employee transfers from one agency to another, the Reagan administration successfully used the act to achieve substantial control over bureaucratic decision making.[16] George Bush thus inherited and worked with a senior-level bureaucracy that was more conservative in its outlook than was the case when Reagan became president in 1981. The 1992 election gave the Clinton administration an opportunity to use the Civil Service Reform Act to again restructure the higher levels of the federal service so that it better fits the goals of a president who believes in activist government.

The Political Outlook of the Bureaucracy

Because the bureaucracy is in a position to influence the direction of departmental and agency policy, political activists and scholars worry about how well the bureaucracy represents the public's political outlook. A related issue is the extent to which the personnel of various agencies differ in their policy orientations and what impact those differences may have.

Representativeness and Interagency Differences

Surveys show that when upper-level civil servants are viewed in the aggregate, they appear to have policy views quite similar to those of the total U.S. population. Though somewhat more liberal than the public

16. Joel D. Aberbach, "The President and the Executive Branch," in *The Bush Administration: First Appraisals,* ed. Colin Campbell and Bert A. Rockman (Chatham, N.J.: Chatham House, 1991), 231. Also see William T. Gormley, Jr., *Taming Bureaucracy: Muscles, Prayers, and Other Strategies* (Princeton, N.J.: Princeton University Press, 1989), 131.

as a whole, the bureaucracy is not a hotbed of radicalism as some con-servative critics have charged.[17] Indeed, government employees' views on whether the government should spend more on such activities as a war on crime, education, and foreign aid have been shown to be virtu-ally the same as those of the public as a whole. And, ironically, bureau-crats are no more likely to have confidence in the people running gov-ernmental institutions than the public at large.[18] Nor are bureaucrats disaffected by American values. In fact, their views are more supportive of American society than those of the leading journalists, public in-terest group activists, or Hollywood elites (TV writers, producers, and directors).[19] The civil service and the public do differ somewhat in their partisanship, however. Government employment is more likely to appeal to Democrats than to Republicans, whose commitment to smaller government makes private sector employment more attrac-tive.[20]

The roughly representative nature of upper-level civil servants' poli-cy views should not obscure the fact that employees' political outlooks vary from agency to agency. Certain types of agencies tend to attract people with particular policy orientations; indeed, departments and bureaus often recruit employees from among the clienteles they serve. Thus, the Department of Agriculture recruits heavily from farm inter-ests and state land-grant universities, and the Department of Housing and Urban Development recruits from urban dwellers and minorities. In addition, bureaus within departments are quite successful in social-izing their personnel to the values and roles prescribed by the agency.[21]

The relationship between the type of agency a bureaucrat works for and his or her political viewpoint is evident in a comparison of the attitudes of employees in activist and traditional agencies (Table 12.3). Employees of such activist agencies as the Environmental Protection

17. Meier, *Politics and Bureaucracy,* 208.

18. Gregory Lewis, "In Search of the Machiavellian Milquetoasts: Comparing Atti-tudes of Bureaucrats and Ordinary People," *Public Administration Review* 50 (March 1990): 220–227.

19. Stanley Rothman and S. Robert Lichter, "How Liberal Are Bureaucrats?" *Regu-lation* 7 (December 1983): 17–18.

20. Meier, *Politics and Bureaucracy,* 36; James C. Garand, Catherine T. Parkhurst, and Rusanne Jourdan Seoud, "Bureaucrats, Policy Attitudes, and Political Behavior: Extensions of the Bureau Voting Model of Government Growth," *Journal of Public Administration Research and Theory* 1 (April 1991): 177–212.

21. For a discussion of the impact of agency socialization processes and social backgrounds on top-level administrators' political attitudes, see Meier and Nigro, "Representative Bureaucracy and Policy Preferences"; and Joel D. Aberbach and Bert A. Rockman, "Clashing Beliefs within the Executive Branch: The Nixon Administra-tion," *American Political Science Review* 70 (June 1976): 456–468.

Table 12.3 Political Orientation of Senior Bureaucrats

Attitude/Behavior	Percent of Bureaucrats Agreeing from		
	Traditional Agencies[a]	Activist Agencies[b]	Combined
Liberal	48	63	56
Voted for Carter (1980)	34	55	45
Voted for Reagan (1980)	48	27	36
Government should substantially redistribute income.	49	55	52
Government should guarantee a good standard of living.	41	46	43
A woman has a right to an abortion.	80	82	81
U.S. institutions need complete overhaul.	25	16	20
U.S. should move toward socialism.	14	14	14
CIA overthrows are sometimes necessary.	57	63	60
Adultery is wrong.	69	65	67
Homosexuality is wrong.	54	40	47
In America hard work leads to financial security.	72	63	67

Source: Stanley Rothman and S. Robert Lichter, "How Liberal Are Bureaucrats?" *Regulation* 7 (December 1983): 18. Reprinted with the permission of the American Enterprise Institute for Public Policy Research, Washington, D.C.

Notes: a. Traditional agency administrators consisted of a sample of ninety-eight persons in the Departments of Agriculture, Commerce, and Treasury, and the Bureau of Prisons in the Department of Justice. b. Activist agency administrators consisted of a sample of 102 persons in the Environmental Protection Agency, Federal Trade Commission, Consumer Product Safety Commission, Equal Employment Opportunity Commission, Food and Drug Administration of the Department of Health and Human Services, Department of Housing and Urban Development, and Justice Department's civil rights division.

Agency, Federal Trade Commission, Consumer Product Safety Commission, Equal Employment Opportunity Commission, and the civil rights division of the Justice Department are more apt to be liberals than members of such traditional departments as Agriculture, Commerce, and Treasury, or the Bureau of Prisons in the Department of Justice.[22]

But the extent to which personal ideology actually affects bureaucratic behavior is complicated by a variety of other forces impinging upon government workers. Civil servants must carry out the policies contained in the federal statutes, some of which may be categorized as liberal and others as conservative. Government employees also must be sensitive to the wishes of influential members of Congress, their politically appointed superiors, the clienteles that they serve, and their co-workers. Finally, most senior bureaucrats are professionally trained as, for example, lawyers, doctors, engineers, administrators, accountants, or economists—and they are therefore affected by the norms and ways of thinking that characterize their professions.

22. Rothman and Lichter, "How Liberal Are Bureaucrats?" 21.

Bureaucratic Conflict

Bureaucratic power struggles and conflicts among agencies over policy are an enduring feature of the governmental process. Each department and agency was created by its own statutes, has its own programs to administer, serves a particular clientele, and, of course, has its own permanent staff. As a result, distinctive traditions, ways of thinking, policy orientations, and modes of operation are found within government agencies. Such differences can lead to interagency conflicts.

Because almost all bureaucratic personnel are highly protective of their particular missions and programs, they usually try to prevent other agencies from encroaching on their activities. Thus, "turf" battles over control of programs, policy, budgets, and personnel are an additional source of interagency conflict. For example, a proposal within the Clinton administration to consolidate the nation's fight against drugs by merging the Drug Enforcement Administration (DEA) into the Federal Bureau of Investigation (FBI) touched off a ferocious bureaucratic battle as the DEA and its supporters fought to maintain the agency's autonomy. As part of this effort DEA distributed memoranda throughout the government claiming that the proposed merger would cripple the fight against illegal drugs.[23]

One of the most prominent examples of the continuing pattern of interagency maneuvering and conflict has been the relationship among the Department of State, Department of Defense, and the National Security Council (NSC) staff at the White House. Each agency has a different mission and orientation. The State Department's mission is to seek diplomatic accommodation, sometimes through the selective use of military force. The Pentagon is interested in maintaining force levels and improving its technology. It is reluctant to commit American forces to further diplomatic objectives and supports such actions only when the military objectives of the engagement are clearly spelled out and there is a high probability of achieving the stated objectives because the United States has an overwhelming military advantage over the adversary. The NSC staff at the White House is concerned with presidential policy priorities as well as with the president's political standing.

Conflicts among these foreign policy institutions frequently dominate Washington's bureaucratic landscape. During the Reagan presidency, for example, State and Defense clashed over such arms control issues as whether to abide by the provisions of the unratified SALT II agreement with the Soviets. There were also differences over sending

23. Neil A. Lewis, "White House Seeks to Combine FBI with Drug Agency," *New York Times,* Aug. 19, 1993, A1, A12, National edition.

marines on a peace-keeping mission to Lebanon. State favored deployment; Defense opposed it. A related incident in November 1983 proved to be a dramatic example of the State-Defense conflict. Following the October 1983 terrorist bombing that killed 241 marines and 59 French paratroopers in Beirut, Lebanon, the United States planned a joint air strike with the French against the Shiite militia believed by the CIA to be responsible for the bombing. At the appointed hour, however, the French jets took off alone; the final go-ahead order had not been given by the Pentagon. The Defense Department had opposed the operation, which was championed by the State Department and the National Security Council staff, who had secured the president's approval. Secretary of Defense Caspar Weinberger explained the Pentagon's failure to order the planes into action by saying that the navy needed more time to plan and execute the mission.[24]

The military and the State Department also differed on how to deal with Panamanian dictator Manuel Noriega, who had been accused of running drugs in the United States. In 1988 and 1989 the military indicated its substantial reluctance to confront Noriega, despite being urged to do so by the Department of State. Thus, the December 1989 invasion of Panama occurred only after the White House asserted its authority.[25] Since that time, however, the institutional rivalries that were so prominent during the Reagan administration seem to have subsided. For example, during the Bush administration apparently no major interdepartmental conflicts arose over America's response to Iraq's invasion of Kuwait in 1990. Nevertheless, as the foreign policy disputes within the Reagan administration illustrate, interagency conflicts are likely to surface again, confirming that they are a recurring feature of the governing process.

The Political Environment of Bureaucratic Policy Making

When administering the laws passed by Congress, the bureaucracy must apply the laws to specific circumstances in a manner consistent with the intent and statutory guidelines set by Congress. Congress, however, is often vague about both the intent of a new law and how it should operate—usually a side effect of the delicate negotiations and compromises needed to muster congressional majorities for pas-

24. Hedrick Smith, *The Power Game: How Washington Works* (New York: Random House, 1988), 583.

25. Joe Pichirallo and Patrick E. Tyler, "Long Road to the Invasion of Panama," *Washington Post*, Jan. 14, 1990, A1, A20.

sage of a bill and the inability of Congress to anticipate all the circumstances administrators will face in implementing the law. To offset this ambiguity, the bureaucracy is given substantial administrative discretion in implementing statutes. For example, after Congress in 1993 repealed the tax deduction for lobbying expenses, the task of making certain that the new policy was actually put into effect fell to the Department of the Treasury. The department's bureaucrats first had to develop a workable definition of lobbying that would guide the behavior of interest groups and corporations (and their accountants) as well as enforcement personnel in the Internal Revenue Service. This complicated process consumed eight months and produced a thirty-page definition of lobbying.[26] Similarly, the Environmental Protection Agency is responsible for implementing the 1990 Clean Air Act by developing administrative policies designed to limit the amount of pollutants released into the air by autos, power plants, and factories.

Rule Making and Regulations

In exercising administrative discretion, the bureaucracy engages in rule making, aimed at developing a set of regulations (rules) to govern the functioning of a government program. The procedures for rule making are set forth in the Administrative Procedures Act of 1946, which was designed to ensure that rule making occurs openly and systematically so that all the interested parties can be heard. Proposed regulations are published in the *Federal Register,* an official document that also publishes finalized government regulations. The public is then given an opportunity to comment on the proposed regulations (which may include public hearings) before administrators decide on their final form. Administrative regulations have the force of law because they are authorized by congressional statutes.

In exercising administrative discretion and its rule-making powers, the bureaucracy is an integral part of the political or policy-making process. Indeed, administrative processes are in no way separate and distinct from politics—interests who lost in the policy-making struggles in the Congress frequently try to recoup some of their losses by influencing the administrative process, while those who were successful in Congress find that they must protect victories at the implementation stage of policy making.

Iron Triangles: Mutual Support Environments

The Washington political environment is highly charged, competitive, and combative. And making things worse, the leadership on Capi-

26. Robert D. Hershey, Jr., "Everyone Knows a Lobbyist: Now the U.S. Defines One," *New York Times,* May 11, 1994, A1, A11, National edition.

TO CARE FOR HIM WHO SHALL
HAVE BORNE THE BATTLE AND
FOR HIS WIDOW. AND HIS ORPHAN

The mission of the massive and far-flung Department of Veterans Affairs (over 200,000 employees, 171 hospitals and 362 clinics, 128 nursing home units) is emblazoned on a plaque at the entrance of the Department's headquarters in downtown Washington. The department's programs and budget benefit from the political muscle provided by their interest groups and congressional allies. Among these allies are organized veterans organizations, such as the disabled American Veterans (shown testifying at a congressional hearing), and the leaders of the House and Senate Veterans Affairs Committees, Rep. Sonny Montgomery (D-Miss.) (left) and Sen. Jay Rockefeller (D-W.Va.).

tol Hill and at 1600 Pennsylvania Avenue is subject to change with each election; when this happens the thrust of government policy can shift as well. In this uncertain atmosphere and because inevitably their actions arouse controversy and opposition, agency bureaucracies seek the constancy of stable, long-term relationships with both their supporters in government and their clientele groups outside government. In addition, agencies must fight for a share of the government's limited budgetary resources, defend their "turf" (policy jurisdictions and missions) from poachers in other agencies, and fend off critics seeking agency dismantlement.

One possible source of support is the White House, but presidents and their staffs come and go. Moreover, presidents may not be particularly supportive of an agency's activities, as President Richard Nixon's policies toward the Office of Economic Opportunity demonstrated. Some agencies, however, are able to develop relationships of mutual

support with members of the congressional committees having jurisdiction over them and with the interest groups they serve. As noted
in Chapter 8, these mutually advantageous and durable three-sided
alliances of the bureaucracy, congressional committees, and clientele
groups have been described as *iron triangles* or *subgovernments*.[27] Such
alliances permit agency personnel to gain support for their programs,
interested senators and representatives to promote policies in which
they believe (and in the process pick up electoral backing from interest
groups and constituents), and clientele groups to derive benefits from
agency programs. Although this description makes iron triangles appear self-serving for their members, most participants sincerely believe
in the merits of the government programs in which they are involved.
For members of the bureaucracy, their agency and its programs are
their life's work; for members of Congress, agency programs can be a
way of promoting their conception of the public interest and their constituents' interests (legislators frequently see them as one and the
same); and for an agency's clientele, the agency programs from which
they benefit are sound policy.

One stable and powerful subgovernment is composed of the Department of Veterans Affairs, the Veterans' Affairs committees of the
House and Senate, and veterans organizations. All these groups cooperate to maintain and expand the programs of the department. Another
example of a subgovernment is the alliance of the Federal Maritime
Commission, the House Merchant Marine and Fisheries Committee,
and the maritime industry and its unions. This subgovernment promotes Maritime Commission programs, which subsidize shipbuilding
and ocean-going transportation. In promoting these interests, the maritime industry and unions have been particularly aggressive in lobbying
and making campaign contributions to their congressional allies.

With alliances such as these it is often difficult to alter agency policies substantially or to eliminate government agencies. Once in operation, most government domestic programs build a cadre of supporters
within Congress, among benefiting groups and individuals, and, of
course, among the agency's staff. Although Ronald Reagan retained a
high level of popularity throughout most of his presidency, he was consistently thwarted by these three-way alliances in his efforts to eliminate
what he considered unnecessary agencies and programs. In fact, he
failed to ax forty-three of the forty-five programs on his hit list. For

27. For a discussion of iron triangles or subgovernments, see Douglas Cater,
Power in Washington (New York: Random House, 1964), 26–50; and Roger Davidson,
"Breaking Up Those 'Cozy Triangles': An Impossible Dream," in *Legislative Reform
and Public Policy,* ed. Susan Welch and J. G. Peters (New York: Praeger, 1977).

In its efforts to protect the northern spotted owl, mandated by the Endangered Species Act, the Environmental Protection Agency has been buffeted by conflicting political pressures. Environmental groups demand that EPA impose tough limits on logging in old-growth forests, while lumber interests, forestry workers, and local businesses claim that logging restrictions threaten the region's economy.

example, when he proposed abolishing the Small Business Administration (SBA) on the grounds that it was wasteful and subject to undue political influence, small business organizations and the SBA's allies on the House and Senate Small Business committees effectively blocked the president's proposal.

Iron triangles tend to occur in policy fields that are not highly visible or conflictual. For example, neither the media nor the public pays much attention to veterans, the Small Business Administration, or maritime policy, and none of the areas produce much controversy. Not every agency, however, operates in such a cozy, calm environment.

For an iron triangle to exist, an agency normally must have clientele groups that do not have conflicting goals. The Environmental Protection Agency, for example, finds itself being praised or attacked almost daily by such diverse interests as industry, public health interest groups, and environmentalists as it implements controversial clean air and water statutes. Even members of Congress, acting for one of these interests, may exert pressure on the agency—all of which, of course, makes the life of the top EPA administrator unenviable. He or she cannot benefit from a tight, supportive alliance composed of the agency, the appropriate congressional committees, and clientele groups.

Issue Networks: Open, Conflictual Environments

Many agencies, like EPA, operate in environments inhabited by interests with different goals and levels of political activity and clout. Called *issue networks,* these diverse and often conflicting configurations of interests can be composed of interest groups, members of Congress and their staffs, bureaucrats, experts from academe and think tanks, concerned individuals, Washington insiders, and journalists.[28] Whereas iron triangles and subgovernments suggest a stable set of participants who coalesce to control a narrow area of policy from which they derive benefits, issue networks convey a strikingly different image. These are characterized by fluid, ever-changing participation by individuals or groups with often sharp differences of opinion and the absence of a tight agency-congressional committee-clientele group controlling policy.

The emergence of issue networks stems from the proliferation of interest groups (described in Chapter 8) and the expanded role of gov-

28. The concept of issue networks has been developed by Hugh Heclo, "Issue Networks and the Executive Establishment," in *The New American Political System,* ed. Anthony King (Washington, D.C.: American Enterprise Institute, 1978), 87–124.

ernment in providing services and regulating the economy.[29] In the current political environment of Washington, some policy areas once dominated by iron triangles are now multidimensional: the number of participants has increased along with the frequency of conflict. Perhaps nowhere is this more evident than in the rivers and harbors improvement program of the U.S. Army Corps of Engineers—once a textbook example of an iron triangle. In those days the corps built dams, levees, and harbors for the benefit of local business interests in representatives' and senators' constituencies in accordance with legislation drafted by the congressional Public Works committees. But what was once a small, close-knit policy community controlling operations stemming from **pork-barrel legislation** (pet projects of less critical need for legislators' constituencies) had to cave in to today's major environmental concerns. Abandoned by its iron triangle which operated in relative anonymity and without open conflict, rivers and harbors policy is now made within the context of a larger, less stable, and conflictual issue network.

With the proliferation of issue networks, a broader array of concerns and interests is being brought to bear on the decisions of the executive branch and the Congress. But policy making within such an issue network environment is extremely complex and time-consuming.

Coping with the Bureaucracy: Presidential, Congressional, and Judicial Strategies

In spite of people's dependence on it for cradle-to-the-grave services, the bureaucracy finds few champions in America. Indeed, hostility to the bureaucracy has been bipartisan. "Bureaucracy-bashing" was a common and compelling theme of the presidential campaigns of Republican Richard Nixon and American Independent George Wallace in 1968 (Wallace complained of "pointy headed bureaucrats that couldn't park their bicycles straight"), Democrat Jimmy Carter in 1976, Republican Ronald Reagan in 1980, and Democrat Bill Clinton in 1992 who vowed to cut the number of government employees. As the bureaucracy has grown, some observers fret that it poses a threat to the nation's constitutional order and to its institutions—the presidency, the Congress, and the courts.

29. For a description of how an expanded issue agenda, the growth of and change in interest groups, and an increased role for the media have transformed the Washington political community, see Barbara Sinclair, *The Transformation of the U.S. Senate* (Baltimore: Johns Hopkins University Press, 1989), chap. 4.

"Think of it! Presidents come and go, but we go on forever!"

The President and the Executive Branch

Although the Constitution charges the president with the responsibility for taking "Care that the Laws be faithfully executed," presidents cannot, of course, personally supervise the vast federal executive apparatus. But they do have the means to significantly influence administrative decision making. Presidents have the power to appoint high-level administrators, draw up the federal budget, and give policy direction to administrators.

Ronald Reagan, for example, had a profound impact on federal regulatory policy. Whereas his predecessor, Jimmy Carter, had appointed pro-regulation officials to head up the federal regulatory agencies, Reagan advocated a policy of deregulation and appointed individuals who were not strong advocates of regulation to such agencies as the National Highway Traffic Safety Administration (NHTSA), Occupational Safety and Health Administration (OSHA), Environmental Protection Agency, Federal Trade Commission, and Consumer Product Safety Commission (CPSC). The Reagan appointees were supported by a White House order that subjected all regulations to an exacting cost-benefit analysis. The impact of the administration's policies and appointees was substantial: to assist the auto industry NHTSA repealed twenty-four rules; OSHA emphasized voluntary compliance instead of agency enforcement; EPA became a battleground between political appointees and civil service employees over environmental policy; the FTC became a free-market advocate; and CPSC became an inactive industry regulator.[30] The 1992 elections, which brought the Clinton administration to Washington, prompted a new cycle of policy shifts as Democrats replaced Reagan-Bush appointees. For example, at the Department of Labor, Secretary Robert Reich stepped up enforcement of workplace safety regulations by OSHA, and at the Justice Department, Assistant Attorney General Anne Bingaman pursued a more aggressive antitrust policy than her predecessors.[31]

The Problem of Presidential Control. Although presidential influence over government policy stems from the president's position as head of the executive branch, over the years presidents have had their hands full in trying to control the massive executive establishment. In theory, the nonelected personnel of the executive branch are accountable to and take their marching orders from the president, who is ultimately

30. Meier, *Politics and Bureaucracy,* 169.

31. Barbara Presley Noble, "Breathing New Life into OSHA," *New York Times,* Jan. 23, 1994, F25, National edition; and Stephen Labaton, "Rousing Antitrust Law from Its 12 Year Nap," *New York Times,* July 25, 1993, F8, National edition.

responsible to the American people. But because the president has limited time and energy and is able to participate personally in only a small fraction of the government's activities, it is up to the president's appointees to carry forward administration policies.

The problem of maintaining presidential control over the executive branch is further complicated by the multiple constituencies that the heads of federal agencies must serve. Presidents fear that the people they have appointed to high-level executive positions will "go native"— that is, they will adopt the orientations of their agency's career employees, of the clientele groups served by the agency, and of the congressional committees with which the agency must deal. To do their jobs, cabinet and subcabinet appointees of the president must work with staffs of all these groups. But the need to accommodate these constituencies often causes department heads to see issues from a perspective different from that of the occupant of the Oval Office. It is hard to imagine, for example, a secretary of agriculture being effective without cordial relations with at least some of the major farm interest groups and key members of the Agriculture committees on Capitol Hill.

This tendency for cabinet officers to see the president as only one of several constituencies they must serve led Charles Dawes, Calvin Coolidge's vice president and holder of a variety of high executive posts, to remark that "the members of the Cabinet are the President's natural enemies."[32] Although Dawes's use of the word "enemies" may have been a bit strong, his comment does convey presidents' recurring worries about the extent of cabinet commitment to presidential priorities. President Lyndon Johnson lamented,

When I looked out at the heads of the departments, I realized that while all had been appointed by me, not a single one was really mine. I could never fully depend on them to put my priorities first. All too often, they responded to their constituencies instead of mine.[33]

After the 1980 election the transition team of Reagan loyalists planning for his administration were so concerned about this problem that they seriously considered housing the cabinet secretaries in the Old Executive Office Building next door to the White House instead of in the various departmental office buildings.[34]

Presidential elections bring in their wake changes in the leadership and policies of executive agencies. Thus Carol Browner, President Clinton's administrator of the Environmental Protection Agency, has sought to overturn controversial concessions made by the Bush administration to industries that enabled them to expand their operations even if the expansion resulted in higher levels of emissions than allowed by the permits they had obtained.

32. Quoted by Richard E. Neustadt, *Presidential Power: The Politics of Leadership* (New York: Wiley, 1960), 39.

33. Doris Kerns, *Lyndon Johnson and the American Dream* (New York: Harper and Row, 1976), 253.

34. Hugh Heclo, "One Executive Branch or Many?" in *Both Ends of the Avenue*, ed. Anthony King (Washington, D.C.: American Enterprise Institute, 1983), 46.

But the president's difficulties in controlling the executive departments stem not just from problems with department heads. The permanent bureaucracy may seek to thwart presidential policies because of genuine policy disagreements with the president or in an effort to protect the budget, personnel, and programs of their agencies. Presidential appointees within departments and agencies serve on average only about two years, but key committee and subcommittee chairs in Congress are apt to be around for a long time. Thus, according to David Broder of the *Washington Post,* senior civil servants give their formal

allegiance to their executive superiors and their knowledge to their old pals on Capitol Hill. The bureaucrat can say "Yes, sir," when an assistant secretary directs him to do something [with which he disagrees] . . . , and then make certain that the memorandum he had written protesting the order falls into the hands of the right congressman or staff member. It happens everyday. And the congressman or staff member, instead of confronting the assistant secretary, often leaks the memorandum to a Capitol Hill reporter and, when the story is published, declares solemnly that the issue deserves investigation.[35]

Bureaucratic sabotage such as this again demonstrates that administration and politics are inseparable.[36]

Presidential Strategies to Achieve Control. Faced with a massive bureaucracy beyond the scope of one person to supervise personally and the tendency of department heads to have multiple loyalties, presidents have tended to rely on their White House staffs to assess policy recommendations coming from the departments and to supervise departmental activities. In contrast to agency personnel, White House staff have only one constituency—the president—and their influence depends on their relationship with the occupant of the Oval Office.

The rise of the White House staff, however, has created its own problems. It has caused tension and conflict between department heads and the White House and has given the president a new control problem: how to supervise the large and sometimes overly active White House staff.

While all modern presidents have worried about gaining control over the executive branch, probably no president has gone to the lengths that Richard Nixon did to corral what he considered to be a hostile executive establishment. In 1971 he proposed the creation of a "supercabinet," which would have merged the eight existing domestic

35. David S. Broder, *Behind the Front Page: A Candid Look at How the News Is Made* (New York: Simon and Schuster, 1987), 210.

36. For a discussion of bureaucratic sabotage and political executives' responses, see Heclo, *Government of Strangers,* 224–232.

departments into four new superagencies: natural resources, human resources, economic affairs, and community development. Congress, however, rejected the idea. Nixon also sought to appoint emissaries—some have called them "spies"—within each department to work with the White House staff in controlling the departments. But his attempt to gain presidential control over the executive branch was cut short by the Watergate scandal and his forced resignation from the presidency. Like his predecessors and his successors, then, Nixon left office dissatisfied with his ability to direct the executive branch.[37]

President Reagan's approach to the problem of presidential control over the executive branch was quite different than Nixon's. He entered office with clearly defined policy goals that departmental appointees were expected to implement. Heavy emphasis was placed on appointing people loyal to the president and his positions on issues. But where Presidents Nixon and Carter had given their cabinet officers a relatively free hand in appointing subordinates, the Reagan White House scrutinized and cleared appointees for compatibility with the Reagan philosophy. The Reagan administration also took full advantage of the flexibility afforded by the Civil Service Reform Act of 1978 to shift Senior Executive Service personnel about so that Republican civil servants moved into top-level career service positions while Democratic SES personnel were shifted to slightly lower positions. In addition, the development of legislative strategy was centralized in the White House so that departmental officials had little power to negotiate with Congress on their own. Centralized policy planning was encouraged as well by the use of cabinet councils—cabinet subgroups with responsibility for developing coordinated policies in various areas of governmental activity such as economic policy. These cabinet councils were kept on a short leash by having their work coordinated and reviewed by White House staff.[38]

In spite of the Reagan administration's intensive efforts to control the bureaucracy, its actual success in gaining the support and cooperation of career civil servants varied, depending on the nature of an agency's mission and the ideological orientation of its career civil servants. In the conservative Department of Defense the Reagan administration encountered minimal resistance to its policies. That was not the case, however, in social service agencies like Health and Human Services,

37. For an account of the Nixon strategy for controlling the executive branch, see Richard P. Nathan, *The Administrative Presidency* (New York: Wiley, 1983), chaps. 3 and 4.

38. Peter M. Benda and Charles H. Levine, "Reagan and the Bureaucracy," in *The Reagan Legacy: Promise and Performance,* ed. Charles O. Jones (Chatham, N.J.: Chatham House, 1988), chap. 4; and Aberbach, "The President and the Executive Branch," 224–235.

President Clinton and Vice President Gore announced their plan to "reinvent government" by making it leaner and more user-friendly while surrounded on the White House lawn by forklifts loaded with government manuals and regulations.

which were staffed by personnel who were of a generally liberal persuasion.[39]

The Clinton administration, too, has sought to use the appointment process to achieve control over the executive branch. For the "tier one" jobs—deputy secretaries, under secretaries, and general counsels—the White House personnel office submits the names of possible appointees to cabinet officers, and if one of the people on the list is not chosen by the cabinet officer, the selection must be justified to the White House. The Clinton White House also has had a team "to take care of Clinton political supporters, . . . to find and root out Bush holdovers, and to put pressure on department heads to prove that they are considering Clinton recommendations [on appointees]." In addition to these policy and loyalty concerns, the Clinton administration has placed a heavy emphasis on achieving ethnic, racial, and gender diversity in its appointments. Thus, when Clinton's first secretary of defense, Les Aspin's, initial selections were found to be insufficiently diverse, he was forced to renegotiate his selections with the White House.[40]

Responsible Government or a "Fourth Branch"? Democratic theory would seem to dictate that since presidents are constitutionally responsible for the actions of the executive branch and are held politically

39. Robert Maranto, "Still Clashing after All These Years: Ideological Conflict in the Reagan Executive," *American Journal of Political Science* 37 (August 1993): 681–698.

40. Ann Devroy, "Late Appointments: Presidential Hiring Process Slower Than Ever," *Washington Post,* March 3, 1993, A1, A9.

accountable for them, presidents also should have the power needed to control the executive agencies. It is, after all, the president who is elected, not the personnel staffing the agencies. Acting on this theory, reformers have traditionally advocated giving presidents more authority and staff to carry out their administrative responsibilities.

An alternative argument, however, is that the bureaucracy should be an independent force within the government—that is, a "fourth branch of government" to check on potential abuses of power by any president bent on centralizing power in the White House. This perspective sees the executive establishment as a representative institution, reflecting the concerns of a wide variety of societal interests, some of which lack the normal bases for political power such as large formal memberships, lobbyists, and money. The bureaucracy also has been viewed as a source of rationality in decision making—a place where decisions are based on analyses of the relevant information to achieve identifiable objectives.[41] In addition, some argue that attempts to centralize power in the White House tend to create cumbersome and inflexible decisional structures that inhibit effective management.

These alternative theories of presidential responsibility and representative bureaucracy reflect a continuing dilemma of American democracy: how to achieve a government staffed by competent, professional civil servants who are responsive and accountable to the public through elected officials, while preventing any one of those officials from becoming too powerful.

Congress and the Bureaucracy

Not just the president is concerned with controlling the bureaucracy; Congress also has a stake in how the bureaucracy performs (see Chapter 10). After all, the bureaucracy administers the laws that Congress passes, and those administrative actions can affect the general direction of public policy, powerful interest groups, and legislators' constituents. But as Congress has delegated more and more authority to the bureaucracy, it has sought to maintain its policy influence by engaging in *oversight of administration.*

Most oversight is conducted by the congressional committees and subcommittees that have jurisdiction over executive departments and agencies. During hearings on proposed legislation, for example, bureaucrats and other witnesses are called before committees to discuss, explain, and defend past administrative decisions and justify budget requests.

41. See Norton E. Long, "Bureaucracy and Constitutionalism," *American Political Science Review* 46 (September 1952): 808. Also see Peter Woll, *The American Bureaucracy* (New York: Norton, 1963), 3.

The Separation of Powers: A Victim of Congressional Micromanagement of the Executive

There is nothing "New Age" about Congress's tendency to wade into the details of administration in order to achieve policy goals and gain benefits for constituents and personal publicity for members. In fact, Woodrow Wilson recognized this trait over a century ago in his classic treatise *Congressional Government*. Today the political incentives to become involved in administrative details remain overwhelming—to the point that they have successfully blurred the line between executive and legislative activities in America's separation of powers system.

Divided party control of the government in the years following World War II and the distrust it engendered between the executive and legislative branches provided a powerful impetus for expanded congressional micromanagement of the executive. This process was encouraged by the explosion in congressional staff during the 1970s and 1980s. In response to the often open warfare of the 1980s between Reagan-Bush appointees in the executive branch and Democrats on Capitol Hill, members of Congress found hundreds of ways to "bridge the separation of powers and deal themselves in on the day to day running of government." These included fine-tuning legislation to severely restrict the administration's discretion and flexibility in administering programs authorized by law, holding up the confirmation of presidential appointees, conducting congressional hearings and investigations, and informally interjecting senators, representatives, and congressional staff into administrative decision making.

President Bush's secretary of Veterans Affairs, Edward Derwinski, himself a twenty-four-year veteran of the House, testified to having been summoned before the entire Texas congressional delegation to explain his decision to eliminate thirty-eight jobs in that state. He also reported that a senator once held up the confirmation of two Veterans Affairs appointees for four months over a dispute about losing ten jobs in his state.

Unsurprisingly, then, when they took office in 1993 the Clinton administration's cabinet secretaries found "Capitol Hill loom[ing] high as an alp in their daily lives." Secretary of Interior Bruce Babbitt is no exception. He spends 30 percent of his time in Washington on Capitol Hill because he has learned that members of Congress and their staffs can often exert more influence over his subordinates in the Department of Interior than he can by issuing directives. As for more evidence of the ingrained patterns of congressional involvement in administrative decision making, because of congressional mandates the secretary must maintain twenty-three positions in the Wilkes-Barre, Pennsylvania, field office of the anthracite reclamation program. Moreover, in FY 1993 he spent $100,000 in Hawaii "to sniff out brown tree snakes."

Secretary Babbitt's experience is not unique. Congressional micromanagement is rife in all departments and agencies. Vice President Albert Gore, who has been charged by President Clinton with making recommendations for improving the efficiency of the executive branch, considers micromanagement "a very serious problem" even though he readily admits to having engaged in the practice while a member of the Senate. As Secretary of Housing and Urban Development Henry Cisneros has commented, "The tension between the executive and Congress is natural and embedded in the Constitution. . . . I understand the necessity for oversight, but it's very difficult to follow the directives of 535 members of Congress."

Source: David S. Broder and Stephen Barr, "Hill's Micromanagement of Cabinet Blurs Separation of Powers," *Washington Post*, July 7, 1993, A1, A16, A17.

But much of the responsibility for oversight rests with the committee staff who monitor agency performance, delve into the backgrounds of presidential appointees seeking Senate confirmation, and do the background work for committee hearings. Congressional staff members also maintain informal information networks within the bureaucracy and among interest group representatives.

The ultimate source of congressional committee influence over bureaucrats is Congress's lawmaking power. Using this power, Congress can alter, expand, or reduce the functions of an agency; reorganize an agency; or cut its budget and the size of its staff. Is it any wonder then that bureaucrats tend to develop a strategic sensitivity to a committee leader's concerns?

Although in recent years Congress has increased its oversight activities, the oversight process by congressional committees is rarely systematic and ongoing. Rather, it tends to be episodic and irregular, usually occurring when members of Congress realize that oversight may produce some political benefits. The political incentives for legislators to invest their scarce time, energy, and staff resources in oversight activities may surface when a powerful interest group is complaining about the adverse effects of bureaucratic decisions; partisan advantage can be gained from a critical investigation into the opposition party's administration of an agency; or a legislator may gain extensive media coverage by holding hearings on a controversial administrative decision.[42]

In addition to committees, congressional oversight is carried out by those individual representatives and senators trying to help out constituents who are having problems with the bureaucracy (casework).

The Judiciary and the Bureaucracy

The judiciary's role in the political system, like those of the presidency and Congress, also has been affected by the growth of the bureaucracy. The statutes creating a vast regulatory bureaucracy contain provisions that give private parties opportunities to challenge the decisions of executive agencies. With the proliferation of these lawsuits, the courts have found themselves thrust into the process of bureaucratic decision making. The judiciary generally applies two standards when considering the legality of bureaucratic actions. The first is whether an agency's action is consistent with congressional intent. When it can be demonstrated that an agency has overstepped congressional intent, the courts may overrule the agency's decision. In reviewing an agency's implementation of congressional legislation, the courts also may prod agencies into more aggressive regulatory activity. For example, the judiciary pushed the EPA into requiring tougher clean air standards than it had originally planned and helped to persuade the Equal Employment Opportunity Commission to take stronger action to protect women in the workplace.[43] It is, however, often difficult to clearly identify con-

A dramatic instance of congressional oversight occurred in 1987 when a special House-Senate investigating committee called former White House aide Lt. Col. Oliver North to testify about his role in the Iran-contra affair. This scandal involved the secret sale of weapons by the United States to Iran and the use of profits from the sale to support contra rebels fighting the Sandinista government of Nicaragua.

42. On congressional oversight, see Matthew D. McCubbins and Thomas Schwartz, "Congressional Oversight Overlooked: Police Patrols versus Fire Alarms," *American Journal of Political Science* 28 (February 1984): 165–179; and Joel D. Aberbach, *Keeping a Watchful Eye: The Politics of Congressional Oversight* (Washington, D.C.: Brookings, 1990).

43. Rourke, "Bureaucracy," 227.

gressional intent. Advocates of a bill frequently have conflicting goals, and the efforts to build congressional majorities may have required drafting a bill filled with compromise and ambiguous language capable of various interpretations.

The second standard used by the courts in overruling an executive agency is agency adherence to proper procedures. Environmental groups, for example, have instituted hundreds of court challenges to government construction projects on the grounds that the agencies involved failed to file environmental impact statements as required by the National Environmental Policy Act of 1969. Using such suits, environmental groups have been able to delay a number of federal construction projects. Lawsuits can be used as well to force government agencies to meet congressionally mandated timetables for implementation of legislation.

Although the courts periodically impose significant restraints on the bureaucracy, judicially imposed controls have limited effectiveness. As a general rule, the courts have been quite willing to permit Congress to delegate to the bureaucracy wide discretion in implementing statutes. Furthermore, the costs of litigation are high and beyond the resources of many would-be challengers of administrative decisions, and judicial remedies for alleged bureaucratic injustices are time-consuming and often characterized by lengthy delays. Thus, while the courts provide one avenue for influencing bureaucratic decisions, those who choose this route are by no means assured of success.[44]

The Essential but Ambiguous Place of the Bureaucracy in the American System

Although nearly all government policies depend on some kind of bureaucratic organization for their implementation and enforcement—in fact, the modern, Western-style democracy with its many citizen services and regulatory functions could not function without such organizations—the bureaucracy lacks legitimacy in the American political culture. Indeed, since the 1960s campaigning against bureaucracy has been a winning presidential campaign strategy. And members of Congress, through their extensive casework activities, have exploited the inefficiencies and red tape of the bureaucracy for electoral gain.[45]

44. Meier, *Politics and Bureaucracy,* 162–167.

45. See Morris P. Fiorina, *Congress: Keystone of the Washington Establishment* (New Haven, Conn.: Yale University Press, 1977). Also see Rourke, "Bureaucracy," 226–227.

Unlike the presidency, the Congress, and the judiciary, the bureaucracy has a rather ambiguous constitutional status. The Constitution does not speak directly about the administrative aspects of the state. The legitimacy of the bureaucracy is further diminished by its appointed character; unlike the president and the Congress, it is not chosen by the people, making its responsiveness to elected officials an ongoing concern. At the same time, however, too much presidential or congressional control over the bureaucracy could cause excessive concentrations of power and damage to the professionalism and integrity of bureaucratic decision making. Contributing further to the legitimacy problems of the bureaucracy is its lack of the dignity and honored traditions characteristic of the judiciary. Thus, as distinguished scholar of the bureaucracy Francis Rourke has pointed out, one of the paradoxes of American government is that the bureaucracy is "at one and the same time altogether indispensable, and, at least in the eyes of many citizens, somewhat illegitimate."[46]

Although the bureaucracy may be suspect in many quarters and a ready target for government's critics, one fact stands out: the bureaucracy is a major player in the policy-making process—a coparticipant and competitor for influence with the White House, Congress, and interest groups.

46. Rourke, "Bureaucracy," 232.

For Review

1. The bureaucracy is the complex of agencies that administers government programs and policies. It is an essential part of the governmental system, but it lacks the legitimacy accorded the presidency, the Congress, and the courts.

2. The process of interpreting and implementing the laws passed by Congress and the executive orders of the president is inevitably political in character because these administrative acts of the bureaucracy have consequences for individuals and groups in society.

3. The organizational elements of the federal bureaucracy include departments, independent agencies, independent regulatory agencies, and government institutes, foundations, and corporations. The vast majority of bureaucrats are selected on the basis of merit, with only a small percentage appointed at the discretion of the president.

4. Each government agency operates in a separate political environment affected by its statutory base, unique subject matter and functions, clientele groups, departmental traditions and norms, White House relations, and ties to Congress.

5. One of the unresolved issues of the bureaucracy is how to achieve accountability to elected officials without giving those officials excessive power or causing the bureaucracy to become so overly politicized that it loses its professionalism and integrity.

For Further Reading

Garand, James C. *Are Bureaucrats Different? A Study of Political Attitudes and Political Behavior*. Armonk, N.Y.: M.E. Sharpe, 1994. An exploration of the attitudinal and behavioral differences between bureaucrats and other citizens that challenges conventional wisdom about government employees.

Goodsell, Charles T. *The Case for Bureaucracy: A Public Administration Polemic*. 3d ed. Chatham, N.J.: Chatham House, 1994. A vigorous defense of the bureaucracy and its essential role in the government system.

Gormley, William T., Jr. *Taming the Bureaucracy: Muscles, Prayers, and Other Strategies*. Princeton, N.J.: Princeton University Press, 1989. An analysis of strategies to control the bureaucracy and their consequences.

Heclo, Hugh. *A Government of Strangers: Executive Politics in Washington*. Washington, D.C.: Brookings, 1977. An examination of the relationship between the career federal service and political appointees.

Kettl, Donald F. *Government by Proxy: (Mis?)Managing Federal Programs*. Washington, D.C.: CQ Press, 1988. An analysis of the consequences of using private companies, individuals, and state and local governments to carry out federal policy.

Meier, Kenneth J. *Politics and Bureaucracy: Policymaking in the Fourth Branch of Government*. 3d ed. Pacific Grove, Calif.: Brooks/Cole, 1993. A text stressing and critically examining the policy-making role of the bureaucracy.

Nathan, Richard P. *The Administrative Presidency*. New York: Wiley, 1983. A fascinating and instructive account of Nixon's attempts to control the executive branch.

Seidman, Harold, and Robert Gilmour. *Politics, Position, and Power: From Positive to Regulatory State*. 4th ed. New York: Oxford University Press, 1986. A perceptive account of bureaucratic politics by a former Washington insider.

Shultz, George P. *Turmoil and Triumph: My Years as Secretary of State*. New York: Macmillan, 1993. Contains intriguing accounts of interagency conflicts and White House-department relations during the Reagan presidency.

Wilson, James Q. *Bureaucracy: What Government Agencies Do and Why They Do It*. New York: Basic Books, 1989. A comprehensive review of bureaucratic behavior in the United States.

Wood, B. Dan, and Richard W. Waterman, *Bureaucratic Dynamics: The Role of Bureaucracy in a Democracy*. Boulder, Colo.: Westview Press, 1994. An analysis which seeks to dispel the notion that bureaucracy is unresponsive and instead portray it as dynamic and democratic.

13. The Judiciary

M OST AMERICANS look upon the courts as institutions that are, or at least should be, nonpolitical. But it is impossible to take the judiciary out of politics. An integral part of government, the courts are, by their very nature, political institutions. Most federal judges, in fact, were active in party politics before their appointment to the bench, and their personal values, experiences, and perceptions of the political climate in the country at large and within the Congress and White House affect their judgments while on the bench.

Although the judiciary, like the Congress and presidency, is a political institution that makes important policy decisions, it is also quite different from the legislative or executive branches: judges must make their decisions within the framework of the existing law. Court decisions are matters of legal interpretation, and judges are restricted to interpreting the meaning of the Constitution and laws (statutes) enacted by Congress. Thus, whereas legislators are free to advocate publicly and propose new laws, judges are confined to interpreting laws. Presidents, too, may campaign for changes in the law and seek public and congressional support for constitutional and statutory changes.

Judges also are expected to adhere to the norms of the legal profession; they are not free to decide cases based exclusively on their personal views of what constitutes sound policy. One of the most important of these norms is the doctrine of **stare decisis** ("let the decision stand")— abiding by the principles of law set forth in prior decisions of one's own court or of higher courts. Under *stare decisis,* citizens know before entering court their rights and obligations because this norm encourages consistent, predictable application of legal rules. But the doctrine of *stare decisis* is not as restrictive as it first appears. Conflicting precedents in some areas of the law can provide a judge with substantial discretion in making a decision. In the field of constitutional law the Supreme Court has periodically reversed past decisions when it thought those decisions were in error or no longer appropriate. It was a reversal of precedent, for example, that enabled the Court to declare segregated school systems unconstitutional in 1954.

Public expectations that the courts will operate in a nonpolitical manner also provide judges with a bit of cover from the more routine political pressures. It is, for example, considered improper for a judge to engage in partisan activity—such as endorsing a presidential or congressional candidate—or for interest groups to informally discuss a pending case with a judge over lunch or cocktails. Interest groups can, however, use more formal means of trying to influence judicial decisions such as filing legal briefs and making formal arguments before the courts.

Although as legal institutions the courts operate in a political atmosphere different from those of the other branches of government, their policy-making role is no less important. Early in the history of the Republic, French observer Alexis de Tocqueville noted, "Scarcely any political question arises in the United States that is not resolved, sooner or later, into a judicial question."[1] De Tocqueville's observation remains valid in the 1990s. This chapter, therefore, analyzes the judiciary as a policy-making institution deeply enmeshed in today's political process.[2]

Judicial Policy Making

Courts make policy in the course of deciding legal conflicts brought before them as cases—disputes between two or more litigants (individuals, organizations, or governments) who are asserting their rights under the law. The millions of cases that are filed each year fall into two broad categories. **Civil cases** are disputes between individuals, groups, or governments about rights and responsibilities. Disputes over contracts, business relations, domestic relations, and personal injuries fall into this category. If involved in a civil suit, the government may be either the **defendant** (the party being sued) or the **plaintiff** (the party bringing suit).

Criminal cases concern violations of state or federal law that are punishable by fines or imprisonment. A defendant in a state criminal case might be charged with a theft or drug offense (the most common) or with a felony such as murder, rape, armed robbery, assault and battery, or manslaughter. Congress has specified that certain crimes are federal offenses—for example, attempting to murder the president, transporting stolen property across state lines, and kidnapping. In criminal cases either the state or federal government is always the prosecutor (plaintiff).

1. Alexis de Tocqueville, *Democracy in America* (New York: Knopf, 1945), 280.
2. For an overview of the Supreme Court in American politics, see Lawrence Baum, *The Supreme Court,* 4th ed. (Washington, D.C.: CQ Press, 1991), 2–7.

Policy Making by Interpreting
the Constitution and the Laws

In the course of deciding both civil and criminal cases by interpreting the Constitution and laws passed by Congress, courts influence the law as surely as do legislatures (see Chapter 2, The Constitution). This has been true since the early days of the Republic when Chief Justice John Marshall (1801–1835) led the Supreme Court in establishing the principle of judicial review (*Marbury v. Madison,* 1803), stating the doctrine of implied powers for the national government (*McCulloch v. Maryland,* 1819), and upholding federal supremacy over interstate commerce in the face of state government intrusions (*Gibbons v. Ogden,* 1824).[3] No less significant were the decisions made in the early 1930s by conservative justices who declared New Deal legislation recommended by a popular president and endorsed by Congress to be unconstitutional. Nevertheless, the Court's narrow view of the government's power to regulate the economy and to take steps to lift the nation out of the Great Depression was reversed in 1938 when two justices changed their interpretation of the Constitution to form a Court majority in support of the federal government exercising broad powers over the economy.

Just as the so-called Judicial Revolution of 1938 changed the direction of government policy in the 1930s, the Court since the 1950s has created new legal doctrines that have been both far-reaching in their implications and controversial. For example, it was the Supreme Court, particularly in *Brown v. Board of Education of Topeka* (1954), that initiated a government policy designed to achieve *racial equality* (see Chapter 4, Civil Liberties and Civil Rights). In recent years one of the most controversial racial issues the Court has been asked to decide is the constitutionality of affirmative action programs designed to assure minorities access to jobs, government contracts, and admission to universities. In 1989 the Court sided with those who charged that these programs can constitute reverse discrimination when it declared unconstitutional a Richmond, Virginia, ordinance requiring that 33 percent of city contracts be set aside for minorities.

In addressing the *reapportionment* issue, the Supreme Court announced in 1962 (*Baker v. Carr*) that henceforth the judiciary would interject itself into the process of drawing legislative district lines to ensure that districts were equal in size and followed the "one person, one vote" principle (see Chapter 10, Congress). This decision dramatically changed how Americans were represented in their state legisla-

3. *Marbury v. Madison,* 1 Cr. 137 (1803); *McCulloch v. Maryland,* 4 Wheat. 316 (1819); and *Gibbons v. Ogden,* 9 Wheat. 1 (1824).

WORDS THAT LIVE

Many Supreme Court decisions are historic because of what they did. A few contain lines that are remembered more than the decision itself. Some examples:

The power to tax involves the power to destroy.
—Chief Justice John Marshall in *McCulloch v. Maryland,* 1819

The most stringent protection of free speech would not protect a man in falsely shouting fire in a theatre and causing a panic. . . . The question in every case is whether the words used are used in such circumstances and are of such a nature as to create a clear and present danger that they will bring about the substantive evils that Congress has a right to prevent. It is a question of proximity and degree.
—Justice Oliver Wendell Holmes in *Schenck v. United States, Baer v. United States,* 1919

The power to tax is not the power to destroy while this Court sits.
—Justice Oliver Wendell Holmes dissenting, in *Panhandle Oil Co. v. Mississippi,* 1928

One who belongs to the most vilified and persecuted minority in history is not likely to be inensible to the freedoms guaranteed by our Constitution. . . . But as judges we are neither Jew nor Gentile, neither Catholic nor agnostic. . . .
—Justice Felix Frankfurter in a rare reference to his Jewish heritage, dissenting from the Court's ban on mandatory flag salutes, in *West Virginia State Board of Education v. Barnette,* 1943

[The states should proceed on school desegregation] with all deliberate speed.
—Chief Justice Earl Warren in *Brown v. Board of Education of Topeka,* 1955

But implicit in the history of the First Amendment is the rejection of obscenity as utterly without redeeming social importance.
—Justice William J. Brennan, Jr., in *Roth v. United States,* 1957

The conception of political equality from the Declaration of Independence, to Lincoln's Gettysburg Address, to the Fifteenth, Seventeenth, and Nineteenth Amendments can mean only one thing—one person, one vote.
—Justice William O. Douglas in *Gray v. Sanders,* 1963

[Before a suspect is questioned] the person must be warned that he has a right to remain silent, that any statement he does make may be used against him, and that he has the right to the presence of an attorney, either retained or appointed.
—Chief Justice Earl Warren in *Miranda v. Arizona,* 1966

tures and Congress. In 1986 the Court took a step further into this politically charged area when it stated that in the future it would review instances of partisan gerrymandering in legislative redistricting to determine whether a political minority had been caused substantial and longstanding harm in violation of the Fourteenth Amendment's equal protection clause. The Court's controversial role in redistricting policy was expanded again in 1993 when it ruled in *Shaw v. Reno* that it would consider whether majority-minority congressional districts created under the Voting Rights Act could deprive white voters of the equal protection of the laws.

Through a series of decisions beginning in the 1920s, which have resulted in *nationalization of the Bill of Rights,* the Court has protected people's basic First Amendment rights from infringement by the states as well as by the federal government. In the 1960s and 1970s it took dramatic steps to extend the Bill of Rights protections afforded defendants in federal courts to the people accused of crimes in state courts. These actions caused wholesale changes in state criminal justice systems: the provision of attorneys for the poor, requirements that people in custody be advised of their constitutional rights, and the exclusion from trials of evidence taken illegally by the police (see Chapter 4).

In taking on the highly volatile issue of *abortion,* the Supreme Court declared in *Roe v. Wade* (1973) that states may not interfere with a woman's right to an abortion during the first three months of pregnancy. This decision, as well as subsequent decisions that indicated that the Court would permit greater state regulation of abortions (*Webster v. Reproductive Health Services,* 1989, and *Planned Parenthood v. Casey,* 1992), ignited a controversy that continues to swirl around all three branches of government at the national and state levels as pro-choice groups battle to protect the *Roe* decision and pro-life groups fight to overturn it (see Chapter 4 for more on these decisions).

Judicial Activism versus Judicial Restraint

When the Supreme Court demonstrates a willingness to make significant changes in public policy—in particular, policies established by the legislative and executive branches—it is said to be engaged in **judicial activism.** An activist judiciary inevitably spawns debate not just about the substance of the judicial decisions but also about the proper role of the judiciary. An independent judiciary is the keystone of a free society and a key feature of the American constitutional system. But, unlike the president and the Congress, the federal judiciary is not popularly elected. Its members are nominated by the president and confirmed by the Senate. Moreover, they have life tenure and cannot be removed except in extraordinary circumstances through impeachment.

Supporters of judicial activism believe it is legitimate for appointed judges to act as a check on the unwise and arbitrary acts of elected legislatures and executives. They particularly endorse judicial activism and court leadership when the elected branches of government have failed, in their view, to protect vigorously civil rights and civil liberties. But advocates of **judicial restraint** argue that it is not proper for nonelected officials to take over from elected officials the responsibility for major policy decisions. According to these observers of the judicial system, the courts should defer to the decisions of elected executives and legislators and not impose their own views of what is desirable government policy on the public.[4]

Of course, whether people stand with the advocates of judicial activism or those of judicial restraint depends to some degree on whether they support or disagree with the content of Court decisions. Activists on the Court, it must be remembered, hail from either the liberal or conservative schools of political thinking. For example, in the early 1930s liberal Court watchers argued for judicial restraint when a conservative Court attacked government regulation of the economy. But in the 1960s they became supporters of the Warren Court's activism, particularly its emphasis on civil rights and civil liberties. By contrast, conservatives defended the activist Court in the early 1930s. Yet during the 1960s and 1970s they argued for judicial restraint and frequently urged justices to confine themselves to determining the true intent of the drafters of the Constitution.

In 1986 Associate Justice William Rehnquist, an articulate conservative, was elevated to the position of chief justice when Chief Justice Warren Burger retired. The Rehnquist promotion, as well as the appointment by President Ronald Reagan of two conservative justices, Antonin Scalia (1986) and Anthony Kennedy (1988), created expectations (hope among conservatives and fear among liberals) that the Rehnquist Court would pursue an activist conservative policy. But to date the highest hopes of conservatives and greatest fears of liberals have not been realized. The Rehnquist Court has tended, however, toward conservative policies—for example, its ruling against the Richmond affirmative action program; its approval of drug testing for selected types of transportation and federal employees; its allowance of exceptions to the exclusionary rule, which bars the use of evidence gathered illegally in criminal trials; its restrictions of appeals by prisoners on death row; and its willingness to permit state restrictions on a woman's right to an abortion.

4. See the discussion of judicial activism and judicial restraint in David F. Forte, ed., *The Supreme Court in American Politics: Judicial Activism versus Judicial Restraint* (Lexington, Mass.: D.C. Heath, 1972); and Stephen C. Halpern and Charles M. Lamb, eds., *Supreme Court Activism and Restraint* (Lexington, Mass.: Lexington Books, 1982), especially chapter 15 by Bradley C. Canon, which analyzes the six dimensions of judicial activism.

The debate over the role of an appointed judiciary in a democracy deals with fundamental issues of governance. It is unlikely, however, that the controversy over judicial activism versus judicial restraint will ever be finally resolved. In a free society with an independent judiciary, individuals and groups will continue to use litigation as a means of achieving their policy goals. The courts, therefore, will be no stranger to the political arena, where they will be forced to decide vital issues of public policy.

A Dual Judicial System: Federal Courts and State Courts Side by Side

The Constitution created a federal system of government in which both the national and state governments exercise significant powers (see Chapter 3, Federalism). Thus, in the United States fifty state judicial systems operate side by side with the federal court system. Each system has its own personnel and jurisdiction, and each interprets and enforces its own constitution and laws. But while the two court systems are separate and distinct, they do overlap: the constitutional principle of federal supremacy enables the federal courts to throw out state actions that they deem to be in violation of the U.S. Constitution or acts of Congress.

Both the federal and state systems have trial courts and appellate courts. Trial courts are the tribunals in which a case is first heard—that is, they are courts of original jurisdiction. Cases in trial courts may be heard before a jury, or a judge may render the verdict. Appellate courts hear cases on appeal from lower courts. But appellate courts have no juries; all cases are decided by a panel of judges. These courts are concerned primarily with whether the lower courts correctly interpreted the applicable laws and followed the proper judicial procedures in deciding a case. Appellate courts normally do not consider new factual evidence since the record of the lower court constitutes the basis for judgment.

Whether a case is tried in federal or state court depends on which court has jurisdiction—the authority to hear the case. The rules of federal court jurisdiction are contained in the Constitution and federal statutes, and only if a case meets specific jurisdictional tests can it be heard in a federal court (it is not enough to believe that one has a "federal case"). Access to the federal court system is determined by (1) the nature of the legal conflict and (2) the nature of the parties or litigants in the suit. Conflicts that fall within the jurisdiction of the federal courts are those arising under the Constitution, federal laws, or treaties, and admiralty and maritime law. In addition, federal courts can exercise jurisdiction over cases in which the United States is a party to the dispute, or in which there are conflicts between states or between citizens of different states and the amount at issue is more than $50,000.

The U.S. Supreme Court is the only federal court with the authority to review the decisions of state courts. The Supreme Court, therefore, acts as umpire of the federal system by enforcing the federal supremacy clause of the Constitution, which requires that state laws conform to the Constitution, federal laws, and treaties. If the Court did not have the power to review state laws, chaos would reign as fifty different state courts determined whether their laws conformed to the U.S. Constitution and laws. Thus, the Supreme Court is the final arbiter of the federal system.

The Structure of the Federal Judiciary

The judicial article of the Constitution, Article III, calls for the creation of only one court—the Supreme Court—and empowers Congress to establish inferior federal courts. The First Congress, then, was faced with the task of creating a federal judicial system. But it was not to be an easy task. Disagreements immediately broke out between the Antifederalists and Federalists in the Congress over the power and extent of the federal judiciary. Fearful that a strong federal judiciary would impinge upon the power of the states, the Antifederalists tried to derail the creation of lower federal courts. The majority prevailed, however, and in passing the Judiciary Act of 1789 Congress set up the Supreme Court (then composed of a chief justice and five associate justices) and a series of lower federal district courts in each of the states and in the territories of Maine and Kentucky.[5]

Courts created by Congress under its authority in Article III are called constitutional courts. These courts handle the bulk of the caseload within the federal judicial system. Congress also used the legislative powers granted to it in Article I to create a series of legislative courts. These courts, which handle specialized and technical types of cases, relieve the caseload burden on the regular constitutional courts. For example, the U.S. Court of Military Appeals was created under

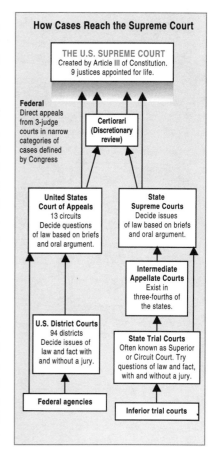

How Cases Reach the Supreme Court

THE U.S. SUPREME COURT
Created by Article III of Constitution.
9 justices appointed for life.

Federal
Direct appeals from 3-judge courts in narrow categories of cases defined by Congress

Certiorari
(Discretionary review)

United States
Court of Appeals
13 circuits
Decide questions of law based on briefs and oral argument.

State
Supreme Courts
Decide issues of law based on briefs and oral argument.

Intermediate
Appellate Courts
Exist in three-fourths of the states.

U.S. District Courts
94 districts
Decide issues of law and fact with and without a jury.

State Trial Courts
Often known as Superior or Circuit Court. Try questions of law and fact, with and without a jury.

Federal agencies

Inferior trial courts

5. For a brief account of the creation of the federal judiciary, see Carl B. Swisher, *American Constitutional Development,* 2d ed. (Boston: Houghton Mifflin, 1954), 56–61. Also see Charles Warren, "History of the Judiciary Act of 1789," *Harvard Law Review* 37 (November 1923): 49–123.

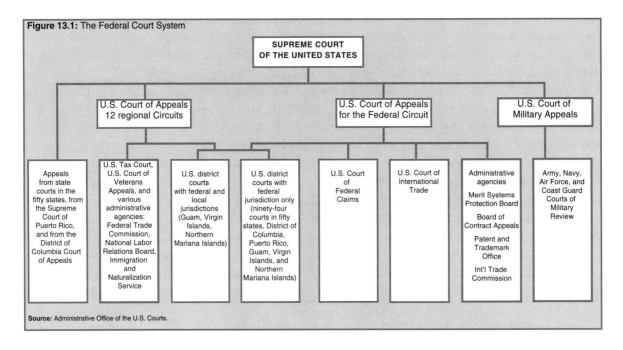

Figure 13.1: The Federal Court System

SUPREME COURT OF THE UNITED STATES

U.S. Court of Appeals 12 regional Circuits

U.S. Court of Appeals for the Federal Circuit

U.S. Court of Military Appeals

Appeals from state courts in the fifty states, from the Supreme Court of Puerto Rico, and from the District of Columbia Court of Appeals

U.S. Tax Court, U.S. Court of Veterans Appeals, and various administrative agencies: Federal Trade Commission, National Labor Relations Board, Immigration and Naturalization Service

U.S. district courts with federal and local jurisdictions (Guam, Virgin Islands, Northern Mariana Islands)

U.S. district courts with federal jurisdiction only (ninety-four courts in fifty states, District of Columbia, Puerto Rico, Guam, Virgin Islands, and Northern Mariana Islands)

U.S. Court of Federal Claims

U.S. Court of International Trade

Administrative agencies

Merit Systems Protection Board

Board of Contract Appeals

Patent and Trademark Office

Int'l Trade Commission

Army, Navy, Air Force, and Coast Guard Courts of Military Review

Source: Administrative Office of the U.S. Courts.

Congress's Article I authority "to make rules for the government and regulation of the land and naval forces." Other legislative courts include the U.S. Tax Court, a court that decides disputes between taxpayers and the Internal Revenue Service, and the U.S. Court of Federal Claims, which hears cases in which claims are brought against the U.S. government.

The federal court system, then, is a three-tiered structure of constitutional courts: federal district courts, courts of appeals, and the Supreme Court. In addition, there are several legislative courts with limited jurisdictions (see Figure 13.1).

U.S. District Courts

U.S. district courts are the principal trial courts—courts of original jurisdiction—of the federal judiciary. They are the busiest of the federal courts, handling over 275,000 civil and criminal cases a year, plus over 857,000 (1992) bankruptcy proceedings. Most federal cases begin and end in these courts. There is at least one federal district court in each state, but some states have as many as four. In California, for example, there are federal district courts for the northern, southern, central, and eastern regions (see Figure 13.2, which shows the boundaries of federal district courts). Altogether the fifty states have eighty-nine district courts, and there is one each for the District of Columbia, Puerto Rico, Guam, the Northern Mariana Islands, and the Virgin Islands.

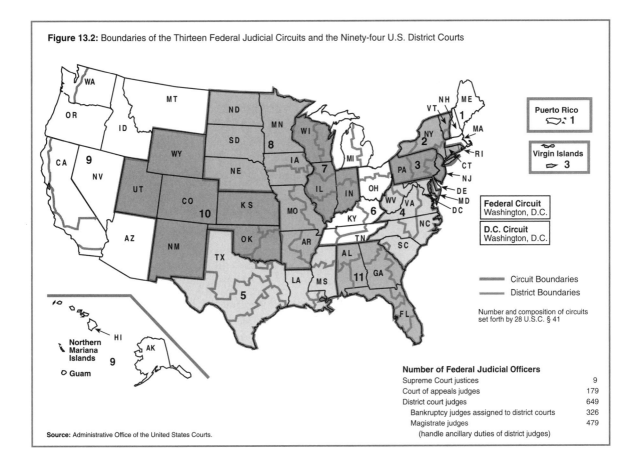

Figure 13.2: Boundaries of the Thirteen Federal Judicial Circuits and the Ninety-four U.S. District Courts

Federal Circuit
Washington, D.C.

D.C. Circuit
Washington, D.C.

Puerto Rico 1

Virgin Islands 3

Circuit Boundaries
District Boundaries

Number and composition of circuits
set forth by 28 U.S.C. § 41

Number of Federal Judicial Officers

Supreme Court justices	9
Court of appeals judges	179
District court judges	649
Bankruptcy judges assigned to district courts	326
Magistrate judges	479
(handle ancillary duties of district judges)	

Source: Administrative Office of the United States Courts.

The number of judges assigned to a district court varies from two to twenty-eight (in the Southern District of New York), depending on the caseload in the district. Most cases are heard with a single judge presiding, but for certain kinds of cases a panel of three judges may decide.

U.S. Courts of Appeals

The U.S. courts of appeals, which are exclusively appellate in jurisdiction, hear appeals from the decisions of the federal district courts, the Tax Court, some District of Columbia courts, and some federal regulatory agencies such as the Federal Trade Commission. Cases being appealed from the highest state courts bypass both the district courts and the U.S. courts of appeals. Rather, these cases go directly to the Supreme Court, provided it agrees to accept jurisdiction.

Because they are appellate courts, the courts of appeals do not conduct jury trials. Rather, all cases are heard before a panel of normally three judges. Cases are decided by a majority vote of the judges participating. Each court of appeals is headed technically by a Supreme Court justice, who, while not actively involved in court business, can act upon petitions for extraordinary procedures such as pleas for a stay of execution in death sentence cases. Most of the over forty thousand cases heard annually on appeal are finally adjudicated by the U.S. courts of appeals. In selected instances, however, cases decided by the courts of appeals and highest state courts are appealed to the U.S. Supreme Court, the nation's highest body.

The nation is divided geographically into eleven judicial circuits, each of which has a court of appeals (also known as circuit courts); each state and territory is assigned to a circuit. The District of Columbia also has a court of appeals, a particularly important court because it is located in the seat of the government (see Figure 13.2). The Court of Appeals for the Federal Circuit, located in Washington as well, hears only cases dealing with specific subject matter (for example, appeals from the U.S. Court of Federal Claims, the U.S. Court of International Trade, U.S. Court of Veterans Appeals, regulatory agencies, and trademark, patent, and copyright cases from federal district courts).

The 179 court of appeals judges are assigned to a particular court according to the volume of judicial business in the circuit. For example, the Ninth Circuit (which includes California) has twenty-eight judges, while only six are assigned to the First Circuit in New England.

The U.S. Supreme Court: How Cases Reach the Court

The nation's highest tribunal, the Supreme Court, is composed of a chief justice and eight associate justices, each of whom is appointed by the president and confirmed by the Senate. Justices "hold their Offices during good Behavior" (Article III, section 1). The Supreme Court has both original jurisdiction and appellate jurisdiction but acts almost exclusively as an appellate court.

The Court's original jurisdiction includes some cases in which a state is a party (for example, disputes between states or between a state and the federal government) and cases involving foreign diplomatic personnel. Cases heard in the Court's original jurisdiction, such as a dispute between California and Arizona over water rights,[6] are rare—only 1 out of 130 cases disposed of by the Court in 1991 (less than 1 percent).

In its appellate jurisdiction the Court hears cases brought by parties dissatisfied with the decisions of U.S. courts of appeals and specialized federal appellate courts. The Court also hears cases appealed from spe-

6. *Arizona v. California*, 373 U.S. 546 (1963).

cial three-judge federal district courts that Congress has created to adjudicate a narrow category of cases. For example, because questions were raised about the constitutionality of the 1985 Gramm-Rudman-Hollings budget-deficit control act, Congress included in the law a provision calling for challenges to the law to be heard before a special three-judge federal district court with the appeal process to be expedited by permitting direct appeal to the Supreme Court.

The Supreme Court also hears cases appealing the decisions of the highest state courts when issues of federal or constitutional law are involved. An issue of federal law could be raised in state court proceedings when, for example, an individual charged with violating a state murder statute claims that during the course of his arrest and trial in the state courts his constitutional rights were violated (such as through an illegal search or interrogation). In such a circumstance a constitutional issue is raised, and the case could be brought to the Supreme Court. If the Supreme Court heard such a case, it would confine itself to determining whether the defendant's constitutional rights had been violated and would not seek to decide questions of state law or whether the defendant actually committed a crime.

Although disappointed litigants may say that they are going to appeal their cases "all the way to the Supreme Court," there is only the remotest likelihood of their succeeding in this threat. The Constitution gives Congress the power to determine the appellate jurisdiction of the Supreme Court, and in exercising this power Congress has granted the Court wide discretion in determining which cases it wishes to consider. Congress requires that the Court hear only two types of cases on appeal: cases arising from special three-judge district courts (usually voting rights cases), and those that Congress has specifically ordered the Court to decide (for example, in enacting the 1989 Flag Protection Act, Congress ordered the Court to hear challenges to the act's constitutionality).

As a result, practically all cases considered by the Supreme Court are heard under the Court's discretionary jurisdiction—that is, the Court exercises its discretion over its review of cases primarily through a **writ of certiorari** ("to make more certain")—an order from a higher court to a lower court to deliver up the records of a case so that the higher court may review the lower-court decision.

People seeking to have the Supreme Court review their cases in its appellate jurisdiction must request or petition for such a review. If four justices (one less than a majority—the so-called rule of four) vote to grant the petition, the Court will review the decision of the lower court.

Solicitor General Drew Days holds the number three position in the Department of Justice where he must delicately balance his roles of representative of the Clinton administration and its politics, defender of executive power, and informal adviser to the Supreme Court.

This, however, is more easily said than done: only 5 percent of the more than 4,000 annual requests for certiorari are granted,[7] and, on average, the Court hears oral arguments on about 150 cases each year.

A particularly important figure in determining which cases that involve the U.S. government reach the Supreme Court is the **solicitor general.** As the third-ranking official in the Justice Department, the solicitor general is responsible for (1) deciding which cases the government will try to have reviewed by the Supreme Court, (2) reviewing briefs filed by the government, and (3) presenting oral arguments before the Court (wearing, by the way, the traditional tails and striped trousers). This is an extremely sensitive post because it influences the extent to which an administration engages in litigation to advance its policy goals. Traditionally the solicitor general has functioned with a moderate amount of independence from the normal political pressures within an administration. Because of this tradition and his position as the government's lawyer, the solicitor's arguments have had special significance before the Court. For example, the solicitor general is more successful than most private attorneys in getting the Court to accept petitions for certiorari, doing so at a rate of over 70 percent.[8]

In determining which cases it will review, the Court is doing more than just managing a heavy caseload; its choice of cases sets the substantive policy agenda of the Court as well. For example, in the 1950s and 1960s a Court majority led by Chief Justice Earl Warren (1953–1969) used its discretionary power over the Court agenda to advance liberal policies. Thus, the Warren Court heard a large number of cases involving the rights of persons accused of crimes and used these cases to extend the guarantees of the Bill of Rights to the accused in the state as well as federal courts. The composition of the Court, however, became more conservative under Chief Justice, Warren Burger (1969–1986) and William Rehnquist (1986–) in the 1970s through the early 1990s when new justices were appointed by Presidents Nixon, Reagan, and Bush. Unlike the Warren Court, the Burger and Rehnquist Courts have been generally hostile to considering cases brought by indigent defendants challenging government actions. Indeed, through their selection of cases the Burger and Rehnquist Courts have adjusted somewhat the direction of constitutional law espoused by the Warren Court. For example,

7. Thomas G. Walker and Lee Epstein, *The Supreme Court of the United States: An Introduction.* (New York: St. Martin's Press, 1993), 70.

8. Baum, *Supreme Court,* 94–96, 108; Also see Lincoln Caplan, *Tenth Justice: The Solicitor General and the Rule of Law* (New York: Knopf, 1987). On the role of the solicitor general in the Clinton administration, see W. John Moore, "Middle Man," *National Journal,* April 9, 1994, 824–828.

the requirement that police act only on the basis of search and arrest warrants has been limited, and government affirmative action programs that provide for automatic or quota-like educational, employment, and contracting opportunities for minorities have been thrown out.[9] Because of the "rule of four," the bloc of generally conservative justices (Chief Justice Rehnquist and Justices Sandra Day O'Connor, Antonin Scalia, Anthony Kennedy, and Clarence Thomas) is currently in a position to influence substantially the agenda of the Court.

How the Supreme Court Does Its Work

With the words "Equal Justice Under Law" carved above the massive bronze doors at its entrance, the Supreme Court's five-story, white marble building is an imposing monument to the law. It occupies a square block across from the East Front of the Capitol. On days when the Court is in open session, the justices, led by the chief justice, enter from behind purple drapes. The audience rises, and a marshal makes the traditional announcement: "Oyez, Oyez, Oyez! All persons having business before the Honorable, the Supreme Court of the United States, are admonished to draw near and give their attention, for the Court is now sitting. God save the United States and this Honorable Court." The black-robed justices then take their seats behind the high judicial bench, with the chief justice in the center and the associate justices seated to his right and left alternately in declining order of seniority. The atmosphere is one of legal ritual, dignity, solemnity, and respect for the law.

Near the courtroom are the conference room, where the Court meets to decide cases, and the chambers that contain the offices of the justices and their staffs. The chief justice has five law clerks and each associate justice has four to assist them in researching cases and preparing opinions. The justices' law clerks are recent graduates of the nation's most prestigious law schools who ranked at the top of their classes.

The Court is normally in session for thirty-six weeks annually from the first Monday in October through June. A Court term is divided into *sittings*—about two weeks in length—during which the Court meets in open session and holds private conferences. The Court then goes into

9. For discussions of the different policy orientations of the Supreme Court since the 1950s, see David M. O'Brien, *Storm Center: The Supreme Court in American Politics*, 3d ed. (New York: Norton, 1993), chap. 4; and Martin Shapiro, "The Supreme Court from Burger to Rehnquist," in *The New American Political System*, 2d ed., ed. Anthony King (Washington, D.C.: AEI Press, 1990), 47–86.

recess so that the justices can work behind closed doors to consider cases and write decisions.

*Filing Briefs
and Oral Arguments*

For the approximately 150 cases that receive detailed review each year, the process begins with the filing of printed briefs (detailed legal arguments and supporting material) prepared by the attorneys in the cases. Amicus curiae ("friend of the court") briefs also may be filed by individuals, interest groups, and governments seeking to influence the Court's decision. Department of Justice amicus curiae briefs are particularly important because through them the government can express a point of view on a case even though it is not a party to the lawsuit. The briefs of the litigants and the friends of the court are reviewed by the justices and their clerks before oral arguments are presented to the entire Court.

During oral arguments, which are conducted on Mondays through Wednesdays during sittings, attorneys for both sides have the opportunity to supplement the material in their briefs. Often attorneys are subjected to interruptions and sharp questioning from justices seeking to influence their colleagues' perceptions of the case. Justices Rehnquist, O'Connor, Ruth Bader Ginsburg, and John Paul Stevens are particularly aggressive in their questioning, and Justice Scalia frequently consumes large segments of the strict time allotments made to attorneys with his questions.

*The Conference and
Opinion Writing*

On Wednesday afternoons and Fridays the justices discuss cases behind locked doors in the conference room. The chief justice presides during conferences, speaks first, and is followed by the other justices in order of seniority. As each justice speaks he or she indicates his or her vote on the case. The justices keep informal track of the voting.

During the conference justices use a variety of strategies to influence the outcome of a case. Chief Justice Earl Warren, determined to have a unanimous Court strike down school segregation as unconstitutional in the landmark case of *Brown v. Board of Education of Topeka*,[10] postponed the voting until he could persuade the entire Court to support his position. At times a justice will vote with the others if they appear to have a majority even though he or she may disagree with the majority's decision. That justice will then bargain with other members of the majority in order to influence the content of the majority's written

10. *Brown v. Board of Education of Topeka*, 347 U.S. 483 (1954).

Members of the U.S. Supreme Court, 1994

Justice	Year Appointed	Law School	Appointing President	Prior Party Affiliation	Age When Appointed	Prior Government/ Judicial Position
William H. Rehnquist [a]	1971	Stanford	Nixon	Republican	48	Ass't U.S. Attorney General
John Paul Stevens	1975	Chicago	Ford	Republican	55	U.S. Appeals Court Judge
Sandra Day O'Connor	1981	Stanford	Reagan	Republican	50	State Court Judge
Antonin Scalia	1986	Harvard	Reagan	Republican	50	U.S. Appeals Court Judge
Anthony M. Kennedy	1988	Harvard	Reagan	Republican	51	U.S. Appeals Court Judge
David H. Souter	1990	Harvard	Bush	Republican	50	U.S. Appeals Court Judge
Clarence Thomas	1991	Yale	Bush	Republican	43	U.S. Appeals Court Judge
Ruth Bader Ginsburg	1993	Columbia	Clinton	Democrat	60	U.S. Appeals Court Judge
Stephen G. Breyer	1994	Harvard	Clinton	Democrat	55	U.S. Appeals Court Judge

a. Became chief justice on September 26, 1986, after being nominated by President Reagan.

opinion and thereby limit what he or she perceives as the damage of the Court's decision. To further influence the final decision, justices may even threaten to file a **dissenting opinion** stating why they disagree with the outcome of the case.[11]

The assignment of opinion-writing responsibility is particularly important because skillful drafting of an opinion may be required to maintain a Court majority. Moreover, the written opinion formally expresses the Court's interpretation of federal law and sets a precedent that will be followed in the future. The impact of a decision is thus likely to be affected by how the opinion is drafted. If the chief justice has voted with the majority of the Court, he assigns responsibility for writing the opinion to either himself or another justice. When the chief justice is in the minority, the most senior justice in the majority makes the assignment. While Warren Burger was chief justice, opinion-writing assignments were extremely contentious. At times Burger would switch his vote to the majority side in an effort to prevent such liberal justices as William Brennan and William O. Douglas from controlling opinion assignments.[12]

A written opinion states the facts of the case, the legal issues at stake, the decision of the Court, and, most important, the reasoning of the Court in making its decision. In this way the Court advises lower-court judges on how to decide similar cases in the future.

The justice finally assigned responsibility for writing an opinion cir-

11. O'Brien, *Storm Center,* 303–304.

12. Bob Woodward and Scott Armstrong, *The Brethren: Inside the Supreme Court* (New York: Simon and Schuster, 1979), 210–213.

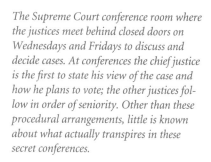

The Supreme Court conference room where the justices meet behind closed doors on Wednesdays and Fridays to discuss and decide cases. At conferences the chief justice is the first to state his view of the case and how he plans to vote; the other justices follow in order of seniority. Other than these procedural arrangements, little is known about what actually transpires in these secret conferences.

culates a draft to his or her colleagues. The drafter of an opinion normally tries to maintain the support of the majority and win over justices who initially voted in the minority. Negotiations among the justices occur, and wording may be changed to gain support for the opinion.

In most cases a majority of the Court will support a single opinion—the **majority opinion.** But justices who disagree with the outcome of the case may file dissenting opinions. Sometimes a justice will agree with the decision of the Court but will disagree with the rationale used in reaching the decision. In these circumstances justices may file a **concurring opinion** to explain the legal reasoning they followed in arriving at a decision. Concurring opinions do not count as a vote against the opinion of the majority, but they may introduce an element of ambiguity into the rule of law being enunciated by the decision.

Judicial Decision Making

A variety of forces influence and constrain judicial decision making. These include the constraints of the legal system and governmental structure, the personal values and ideologies of the justices, the group life of the Court, and the forces within the larger political system such as public opinion and interest groups.

Legal and Governmental Constraints. The constraints of the legal system and the governmental structure are many. For example, justices are limited to ruling on just those cases that fall within the Court's jurisdiction and for which litigants have legal standing to enter the judicial process. The discretion of justices in deciding cases is restricted by the expectation that they will follow recognized modes of legal interpretation. They are normally expected, as noted previously, to follow past precedents of the Court in making decisions.

There are also practical limits on the Court's decision-making powers stemming from the nature of the governmental structure. The Court must rely on the executive branch to enforce its decisions since it has no police force or army of its own. Indeed, in the end the Court must depend on the other branches of government and the American people to obey its rulings. And, as revealed later in this chapter, the Court also is limited by the fact that the other branches of government have powers they can use against it. Congress controls the Court's budget and can regulate its jurisdiction, and the president can refuse to enforce Court decisions, can rally public opinion against Court decisions, and can even pardon people convicted of violating Court rulings.

Values and Ideology. In 1971 the role of values and ideology in judicial decision making was addressed by William Rehnquist during his confirmation hearing before the Senate Judiciary Committee: "My fundamental commitment, if I am confirmed, will be to totally disregard my own personal belief."[13] This assertion that a justice's personal policy preferences are not relevant to the judicial decision-making process does not appear to be consistent with the actual behavior of judges. Granted, there are legal and practical constraints on judges in making their decisions, but there are also ample opportunities for personal attitudes and values to influence decisions.[14]

13. Quoted by Baum, *Supreme Court,* 144.

14. On the impact of legal and extralegal factors on Court decision making, see Tracey E. George and Lee Epstein, "On the Nature of Supreme Court Decision-Making," *American Political Science Review* 86 (June 1992): 323–337.

President Bill Clinton poses with members of the Supreme Court, October 1, 1993, the day his appointee, Ruth Bader Ginsburg, signed her judicial oath. From left, Justices Antonin Scalia, Ginsburg, Anthony M. Kennedy, John Paul Stevens, Chief Justice William H. Rehnquist, the president, Justices Harry A. Blackmun, Sandra Day O'Connor, David H. Souter, and Clarence Thomas.

Indeed, at times the Court has adopted major legal doctrines that appeared to have little basis in recognized modes of legal interpretation and instead seemed to have been dictated by the personal views of the justices. For example, in *Griswold v. Connecticut* (1965)[15] the Court, while striking down a state statute limiting the availability of contraceptives, declared that people have the constitutional right to privacy. The inability of the seven justices who adopted this view to agree on the constitutional provisions that provided the basis for this liberty led judicial scholar Lawrence Baum to conclude that the justices "reached their conclusion first and then searched for a supporting rationale."[16]

Justices' personal attitudes stem from their life experiences—political socialization by their families, educations, and careers. The influence of gender is suggested by Justice Sandra Day O'Connor's dissent against the Court's failure to hear a sex discrimination case (at the time she was the Court's only female member) and by Justice Lewis Powell's statements about how his experience as a college trustee influenced his decision on an affirmative action admissions case. The link between background and judicial attitude, however, is complex. In fact, justices with similar backgrounds often vote differently.[17] Chief Justice Warren Burger and Justice Harry Blackmun went to the same Minnesota high school, for example, but frequently opposed each other on the Court.

This being said, students of judicial behavior have demonstrated that most justices establish quite consistent positions on an ideological spectrum that spans a broad range of issues. This is particularly true of the justices at the ends of the liberal-conservative spectrum. For example, Court watchers have had no trouble identifying Chief Justice Rehnquist and Justice Scalia as conservatives and former justice Marshall as a liberal. In recent years, however, even the Court's most consistent conservatives—Chief Justice Rehnquist and Justices O'Connor, Scalia, Kennedy, and Thomas—have broken ranks on occasion. At times, Justices O'Connor and Kennedy have split from their conservative colleagues on selected issues because of a more cautious approach to deciding cases and a reluctance to overturn established precedents of the Court. Until his retirement in 1991 the Court's most liberal member, Justice Thurgood Marshall, frequently had been joined by Justices Blackmun and Stevens. President Clinton's appointees, Justices Ginsburg and Stephen Breyer, are expected by Court watchers to follow a liberal line on social issues and civil rights and take a moderate to conservative position on business and crime issues.

15. *Griswold v. Connecticut*, 381 U.S. 479 (1965).
16. Baum, *Supreme Court*, 134.   17. Ibid., 146.

Group Life of the Court. Although the group life of the Supreme Court is very much evident, members of the Court work for the most part as individuals or as nine separate law firms staffed with bright, young clerks who assist the justices in researching legal issues, developing positions, and writing opinions. The decisional process of the Court, however, is affected by the group setting of oral arguments and the conference. To secure a majority decision on each case, the justices must interact, often leading to competition among them to persuade colleagues to accept their viewpoints and to win votes in cases in which the Court is narrowly divided.

Lawrence Baum has described the Court as a "quasi-collegial body, one in which group interaction plays a limited but significant role in the decisionmaking process."[18] Because decisions are shaped by negotiations between the justice assigned to write an opinion and other members of the Court, these negotiations may result in a final opinion that is quite different than the one initially drafted by the assigned justice. While these negotiations are under way, justices demonstrate considerable "fluidity of judicial choice" and may shift their votes in response to arguments presented by their colleagues.[19]

While the small-group atmosphere of the Court does affect decisions, the impact of these interactions should not be overstated. After justices have developed a position on a case, or on an issue that runs through a series of cases over time, a colleague is apt to find it difficult to dislodge them from their positions, and many votes are quite predictable.

Influence of Public Opinion and Interest Groups. Although justices, unlike the president and members of Congress, do not stand for election, the Supreme Court does not operate in a political vacuum. Indeed, even the "High Nine" are not immune from the influence of public opinion and interest groups. The Court's decisions affect people and organized interests prepared to use their political resources to influence judicial decisions. The Court also is subject to pressures from the elected branches of government—the executive, which often is responsible for enforcing Court orders, and the legislature, which through legislation can affect the size, jurisdiction, and budget of the Court. It should not be surprising, then, that Court decisions reflect a sensitivity to public opinion. For example, by throwing out state laws that mandated segregated schools, banned interracial marriage, restricted women's rights, and prohibited abortions, the Court acted in a

18. Ibid., 160.

19. J. Woodward Howard, "On the Fluidity of Judicial Choice," *American Political Science Review* 62 (March 1968): 43–56.

manner consistent with trends in public opinion. These examples of Court sensitivity to public opinion are not meant to suggest that justices slavishly follow the Gallup poll when making their decisions. In fact, because of a series of conservative appointments by Presidents Nixon, Reagan, and Bush, the Court's policies have been less in line with public opinion since 1981 than over the period 1956–1980. Nevertheless, the overall pattern of decision making is one of responsiveness to public opinion, indicating that the oft-cited notion that the Court is an antimajoritarian institution is an overstatement.[20]

The Court's sensitivity to external political forces is also seen in its decisions to grant writs of certiorari, thereby bringing specific cases before the Court for consideration. Researchers have found that the Court is more likely to grant certiorari when organized interests, including the government, file amicus curiae briefs either favoring or opposing a grant of certiorari.[21]

The Power of Judicial Review

Using the power of judicial review, the courts are able to declare acts of Congress, orders of the executive branch, or state laws unconstitutional—that is, they cannot be put into effect. As the ultimate authority on interpretation of the Constitution, the Supreme Court is a crucial power center in the American political system. Court decisions about the meaning of the Constitution can be changed only through a later reinterpretation of the Constitution by the Court or through the difficult and time-consuming process of amending the Constitution.

Incorporating Judicial Review into the Constitution

Judicial review is one of the basic principles of the American constitutional system, but, surprisingly, this power is not mentioned in the Constitution. Rather, the power of judicial review was asserted by the Court in the case of *Marbury v. Madison* (1803).

The case arose on the heels of the election of 1800. After losing the election, President John Adams late in the same year appointed a series

20. See William Mishler and Reginald J. Weber, "The Supreme Court as a Countermajoritarian Institution? The Impact of Public Opinion on Court Decisions," *American Political Science Review* 87 (March 1993): 87–101; and David G. Barnum, "The Supreme Court and Public Opinion: Decision Making in the Post-New Deal Era," *Journal of Politics* 47 (May 1985): 652–666.

21. Gregory A. Caldeira and John R. Wright, "Organized Interests and Agenda Setting in the U.S. Supreme Court," *American Political Science Review* 82 (December 1988): 1109–1127.

of federal judges in an effort to control the judiciary after his successor, Thomas Jefferson, took office. One of these appointees, William Marbury, was designated justice of the peace for the District of Columbia, a minor judicial post. Before leaving office, however, the Adams administration neglected to give Marbury his commission to office, and the new secretary of state, James Madison, refused to do so. Marbury then brought suit in the Supreme Court in its *original jurisdiction* asking that Madison be required to give him his commission. Suits such as Marbury's in the original jurisdiction of the Supreme Court were permitted under the Judiciary Act of 1789.

Chief Justice John Marshall, a former official in the Federalist administration of John Adams, was confronted with a delicate problem in deciding the case. If the Court ordered Madison to give Marbury his commission, Madison, with the backing of President Jefferson, was expected to ignore the Court order. The prestige and power of the fledgling Court would then suffer a heavy blow. But if Madison was not ordered to give Marbury the commission, the Jeffersonians would achieve a political triumph over the Federalists, the party of John Marshall.

To solve this dilemma, Marshall's opinion for the Court stated that Marbury was indeed entitled to his commission and that Madison had been in error in denying it to him. The Court ruled, however, that it lacked the power to order Madison to give Marbury his commission because the Court did not have jurisdiction over the case. According to Marshall, the provisions in the Judiciary Act of 1789 giving the Supreme Court jurisdiction over cases such as Marbury's were an unconstitutional extension by Congress of the Court's original jurisdiction, which had already been provided for in Article III, section 2. In asserting its power of judicial review, Marshall wrote that

the particular phraseology of the constitution of the United States confirmed and strengthens the principle, supposed to be essential to all written constitutions, that a law repugnant to the constitution is void; and that *courts,* as well as other departments [branches of government] are bound by that instrument.[22]

As noted earlier, the Court's power of judicial review also extends to interpretations of the U.S. Constitution by state governments. In such instances the principle of federal supremacy governs and enables the Court to strike down state actions that it deems to be violations of the Constitution, federal laws, or treaties. Thus, in a dramatic confrontation between Arkansas and the federal courts over integration of Cen-

22. *Marbury v. Madison,* 1 Cr. 137 (1803).

Exercising the Power of
Judicial Review

tral High School in Little Rock in 1959, the Supreme Court upheld the power of the federal district courts to supervise the integration of the school over the state's objections.[23]

Judicial review is not a power that the Court has used frequently. Indeed, after *Marbury v. Madison* it was fifty-four years before another act of Congress was declared unconstitutional. This occurred in the case of *Dred Scott v. Sandford* (1857) in which a slave claimed to be free when his master took him to a territory where slavery was banned.[24] The Court, however, ruled that the Missouri Compromise of 1820, which outlawed slavery in the northern territories, was unconstitutional because it took the slaveowner's property without due process of law. In declaring that free Negroes were not citizens and without constitutional rights, the Court in the *Dred Scott* case created a public furor and helped to precipitate the Civil War.

Since it asserted its power of judicial review, the Supreme Court has declared state laws or provisions of state constitutions unconstitutional over a thousand times. But out of a total of over 95,000 laws passed through 1992, only 141 were declared unconstitutional in whole or in part.[25] The most conflictual period between the Court and Congress was from 1933 to 1936 when the Court struck down important New Deal legislation in a frontal attack on the policies of the Franklin Roosevelt administration. Since the late 1930s, when the Court retreated from its opposition to the New Deal, the most frequent instances of declaring federal laws unconstitutional have involved findings that laws violated the personal rights and liberties guaranteed by the Constitution.

When judicial review is viewed in historical perspective, it is clear that by striking down a number of important government decisions, the Supreme Court has established itself as a major participant in the policy-making process. The Court, however, has been selective in exercising its power, and the great majority of government policies—particularly in the case of foreign policy—have operated without Court interference. Thus, while judicial review has helped the Court to play a major role in the policy process, it has not made the Court the dominant participant.[26]

23. *Cooper v. Aaron,* 358 U.S. 1 (1958).

24. *Dred Scott v. Sandford,* 19 How. 393 (1857).

25. Henry J. Abraham, *The Judicial Process,* 6th ed. (New York: Oxford University Press, 1993), 272.

26. Baum, *Supreme Court,* 188.

Judicial Selection

Federal judges are nominated by the president and confirmed by a majority vote of the Senate. Judgeships are lifetime appointments, although judges, like all other civil officers of the government, can be removed for "high Crimes and Misdemeanors" through impeachment procedures in which the House of Representatives brings impeachment charges against a judge and the Senate then votes to impeach. With the prospects of a lengthy tenure in office, federal judges, particularly Supreme Court justices, can have a long-term impact on judicial policy making. It is not greatly surprising, then, that Supreme Court appointments often engender intense controversy as members of Congress, interest groups, and others jockey to influence judicial policy making by determining the composition of the Court.

In contrast to the federal government where all judges are appointed by the president, the states use a variety of selection procedures, depending on state constitutions and statutes. Both appointment and election are used. Almost half the states follow a mixed appointment and election process, such as the Missouri plan, in which the governor appoints judges from a list of candidates approved by a judicial commission, and a referendum is held on each appointee's performance at the next general election.

U.S. District Court and Court of Appeals Judges

In appointing federal district and court of appeals judges, presidents are forced to share power with their party's senators. The practice of senatorial courtesy enables the senior senators of the president's party to block federal appointments within their own states when they disapprove of a nominee. As a result, these senators do much of the screening of lower-federal court judges. Many, in fact, have set up judicial selection committees in their states to assist them in picking well-qualified judicial nominees to propose to the Department of Justice and the president for nomination. For appointments within states where there is no senator of the president's party, the president usually consults with state party leaders. During the Kennedy and Johnson administrations, for example, the legendary leader of the Cook County Democratic organization, Chicago mayor Richard Daley, personally approved every federal judge appointed to the Northern District of Illinois.[27]

Also involved in the selection process is the American Bar Associa-

27. Robert A. Carp and Ronald Stidham, *Judicial Process in America,* 2d ed. (Washington, D.C.: CQ Press, 1993), 234.

tion (ABA), which evaluates the qualifications of judicial nominees. Because a "not qualified" rating by the ABA can quickly kill Senate confirmation of a nominee, presidents rarely nominate people whom they believe cannot pass muster with the ABA screening panel.

Federal judicial appointments, then, have a significant policy-making impact and are among the most prized patronage plums at the disposal of the president and the Senate. Although there is a great deal of jockeying for influence among home state senators of the president's party, White House staff, the Department of Justice, and interest groups, the ultimate decision on which name will be submitted to the Senate for confirmation is a presidential one. During the Reagan and Bush administrations, periodic clashes between the Justice Department and GOP senators over federal district court nominations prompted delays in the president's submission of judicial nominees to the Senate for confirmation. The Clinton White House has told Democratic senators that they are expected to include women and minorities on the lists of potential judicial appointees they submit to the administration.

The impact of the appointments process on the federal judiciary can be profound (see box Imprints on the Bench). Approximately 90 percent of judicial appointees come from the ranks of the president's own party (see Table 13.1), and the president and Department of Justice commonly seek appointees who share the president's political and judicial philosophies. During his eight years in office, Ronald Reagan was able to transform the federal bench from a predominantly Democratic institution into one with a Republican majority. Because of the unusually high level of concern shown by the Reagan and Bush administrations for appointing judges who shared their ideology, it is likely that one of their administrations' more lasting legacies will be a federal judiciary with a sizable proportion of conservative Republican judges.[28] Of course, President Clinton too will leave his mark on the judiciary as he appoints Democrats of a more liberal ideological bent to the courts.

Both Democratic and Republican court appointees have tended to be white males educated at a top university, with prior judicial experience or membership in a medium-sized to large law firm. The percentage of appointees drawn from the ranks of women and minorities increased significantly during the Carter administration, declined under Reagan, and rose again during the Bush presidency (see Figure

28. For an account of the Reagan administration's judicial selection practices and their impact, see David M. O'Brien, "The Reagan Judges: His Most Enduring Legacy?" in *The Reagan Legacy: Promise and Performance*, ed. Charles O. Jones (Chatham, N.J.: Chatham House, 1988), 60–101.

Imprints on the Bench

By the end of his presidency Franklin Roosevelt had appointed an estimated 75 percent of the judgeships authorized at that time for the federal courts. As of 1992 Presidents Ronald Reagan and George Bush together had appointed 60 percent of total federal judges (including 70 percent of appellate court judges).

This chart shows the impacts of Presidents Roosevelt to Bush on the federal bench. But these figures do not present a precise picture. The total number of life-tenured judgeships reflects all appointments made during a term, including those to replace deceased, retiring, or elevated judges who the same president had appointed earlier. No numbers are readily available for all ten presidents that would eliminate those duplications, which are generally believed to be proportionately few. For example, although Reagan appointed 51 percent of all positions available over the eight years of his term, his legacy of the entire judiciary in 1989 generally has been calculated at 47 percent. (The longer presidents are in office, the more likely they are to fill the same spot twice, thus slightly inflating the percentage.)

Through his power to appoint federal judges, President Bill Clinton will have an opportunity to unmake the Reagan-Bush legacy of generally conservative appointments to the courts. When Clinton took office there were nearly 130 vacancies in the federal judiciary. His initial appointments indicated that he was likely to appoint liberals and a higher percentage of women and minorities than his Republican predecessors. He also pledged during the 1992 campaign to appoint judges who accepted abortion as a constitutional right.

In the table at right, "total judgeships" represents the number of positions authorized in a president's last year in office. Appeals court judges include members of all twelve regional circuits. The appeals court for the Federal Circuit, created in 1982, is not included because, unlike the other circuits, it has limited jurisdiction. The district courts include those in each state and in each of the four territories.

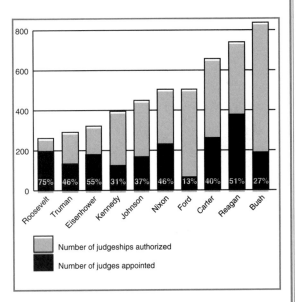

Number of Federal Judges Appointed, 1933–1993

President	Supreme Court	Courts of Appeals	District Courts	Total Judges Appointed	Total Judgeships Authorized
Roosevelt (1933–45)	9	52	136	197	262
Truman (1945–53)	4	27	102	133	292
Eisenhower (1953–61)	5	45	127	177	322
Kennedy (1961–63)	2	20	102	124	395
Johnson (1963–69)	2	41	125	168	449
Nixon (1969–74)	4	45	182	231	504
Ford (1974–77)	1	12	52	65	504
Carter (1977–81)	0	56	206	262	657
Reagan (1981–89)	3	83	292	378	740
Bush (1989–93)	2	37	150	189	837

Source: Administrative Office of the United States Courts.

Table 13.1 Political Party Backgrounds of Federal District Court and Appellate Court Appointees, Presidents Johnson to Bush *(percent)*

| | Nominees of Presidents | | | | | |
	Johnson	Nixon	Ford	Carter	Reagan	Bush
DISTRICT COURTS						
Democrat	94.3	7.3	21.2	92.6	4.8	5.4
Republican	5.7	92.7	78.8	4.4	93.4	88.5
Independent	0.0	0.0	0.0	2.9	1.7	6.1
Active in party politics	49.2	48.6	50.0	60.9	58.6	60.8
COURTS OF APPEALS						
Democrat	95.0	6.7	8.3	82.1	0.0	5.4
Republican	5.0	93.3	91.7	7.1	97.4	89.2
Independent	0.0	0.0	0.0	10.7	1.3	5.4
Other	0.0	0.0	0.0	0.0	1.3	0.0
Active in party politics	57.5	60.0	58.3	73.2	69.2	70.3

Source: Harold W. Stanley and Richard G. Niemi, eds., *Vital Statistics on American Politics,* 4th ed. (Washington, D.C.: CQ Press, 1994), 290–291.

13.3). The pattern of President Clinton's appointments during his first year in office indicated that he would increase the proportion of women and minorities in the federal judiciary. Of the eighty-four appointments made from 1993 to mid-1994, 39 percent were minorities (twenty-three African Americans and ten Hispanics) and 35 percent (twenty-nine) were women.[29]

U.S. Supreme Court Justices

Between 1789 and 1994 only 106 men and 2 women served on the nation's highest tribunal, the Supreme Court. Because this select group has tremendous power to influence the direction of public policy, the resignation, death, or infirmity of a justice is an immediate cause for speculation and maneuvering about a successor.

In making Supreme Court nominations, presidents consider professional competence and integrity, party affiliation and service, political ideology and judicial philosophy, and matters of race, gender, ethnic background, religion, and geography. President Lyndon Johnson, for example, appointed longtime adviser, friend, and liberal Jewish Democrat Abe Fortas. He also appointed Thurgood Marshall to be the Court's first black justice, an act that the president recognized had great symbolic significance and political benefits for his party.[30] President

29. Al Kaman, "In the Loop . . . and of Judicial Appointments," *Washington Post,* April 29, 1994, A25.

30. O'Brien, *Storm Center,* 87–89.

The first woman to be appointed to the Supreme Court was Sandra Day O'Connor, who ironically had difficulty landing a job as an attorney after she graduated from Stanford University Law School in 1952 (in the same class as Chief Justice William Rehnquist) because of discrimination against female attorneys. She is shown here with President Ronald Reagan at the time of her appointment in 1981.

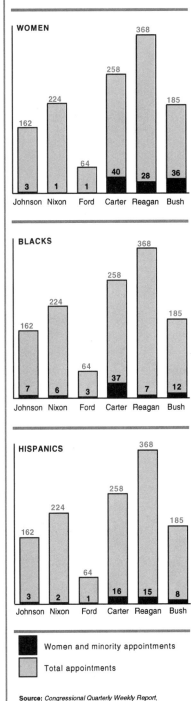

Figure 13.3: Female and Minority Appointments to Federal Judgeships, 1963–1993

WOMEN

	Johnson	Nixon	Ford	Carter	Reagan	Bush
Total	162	224	64	258	368	185
Women/minority	3	1	1	40	28	36

BLACKS

	Johnson	Nixon	Ford	Carter	Reagan	Bush
Total	162	224	64	258	368	185
Women/minority	7	6	3	37	7	12

HISPANICS

	Johnson	Nixon	Ford	Carter	Reagan	Bush
Total	162	224	64	258	368	185
Women/minority	3	2	1	16	15	8

■ Women and minority appointments

▨ Total appointments

Source: *Congressional Quarterly Weekly Report,* February 13, 1993, 318.

Reagan's appointees shared his conservative ideology: William Rehnquist, the Court's most conservative justice, was elevated to the position of chief justice; conservative Sandra Day O'Connor, who had served as GOP leader in the Arizona State Senate, was the fulfillment of a 1980 campaign promise to appoint a woman to the Court; and Antonin Scalia (the Court's first Italian American justice) and Anthony Kennedy strengthened the Court's conservative bloc and served as recognition of the importance of Catholics in Reagan's electoral coalition. In selecting Ruth Bader Ginsburg and Stephen Breyer, President Clinton picked persons who reflected his own liberal views of social issues and whom he believed could move the Court toward the political center.

Most presidential choices for the federal judiciary are confirmed easily by the Senate. For example, in 1993 the Senate confirmed Ruth Bader Ginsburg by a vote of 96–3. But because appointments to the Supreme Court can change the direction of judicial policy over a long period, major controversies arise periodically over presidential nominees. Intense confirmation battles tend to occur when (1) the Court is closely divided between Republican and Democratic appointees; (2) the nominee is perceived as not being moderate in ideology; (3) questions are raised about the qualifications of the nominee; (4) the president is politically weak; or (5) different parties control the presidency and Sen-

In nominating Stephen Breyer, a federal court of appeals judge, to replace retiring justice Harry Blackmun, President Clinton in 1994 avoided the intense ideological and policy battles that had characterized Supreme Court nominations during the Reagan and Bush administrations. With his reputation as a moderate consensus-builder, Breyer breezed through the Senate confirmation process while picking up plaudits from senators of both parties. Breyer (center) is shown conferring with members of the Senate Judiciary Committee at his confirmation hearing, from left: Senators Orrin Hatch (R-Utah), Alan Simpson (R-Wyo.), Patrick Leahy (D-Vt.), Howell Heflin (D-Ala.), and Paul Simon (D-Ill.).

ate.[31] Some or all of these conditions were present from the 1970s through the early 1990s as a divided Court wrestled such divisive issues as criminal defendants' rights, abortion, and affirmative action. Since 1789, 29 of 145 nominations to the Supreme Court have failed to gain Senate confirmation, including 6 since 1968 (see Table 13.2). Twelve were rejected outright by the Senate, and the others were either withdrawn or allowed to lapse in the face of opposition.

The public policy implications of Supreme Court appointments were dramatically displayed in 1987 when the Senate rejected President Reagan's nomination of U.S. Court of Appeals Judge Robert Bork to replace retiring justice Lewis Powell. Bork was an outspoken conservative intellectual, who as a Yale law professor had harshly criticized liberal Court decisions of the 1960s and 1970s. With the Court narrowly divided between its liberal and conservative wings, the Bork nomination became an all-out battle over the future of judicial policy. On one side were the Reagan administration and its allies and on the other a Democratic-controlled Senate and such liberal interest groups as Planned Parenthood, organized labor, and civil rights organizations. Although Bork was rejected by a 42–58 Senate vote, President Reagan was able to strengthen the Court's conservative bloc when he later nominated and gained confirmation for Judge Anthony Kennedy, a less

31. See Charles M. Cameron, Albert D. Cover, and Jeffrey A. Segal, "Senate Voting on Supreme Court Nominees: A Neoinstitutional Model," *American Political Science Review* 84 (June 1990): 525–534; and, by the same authors, "A Spatial Model of Roll Call Voting: Senators, Constituents, Presidents, and Interest Groups in Supreme Court Confirmations," *American Journal of Political Science* 36 (February 1992): 96–121.

Table 13.2 Supreme Court Nominations That Failed to Gain Senate Confirmation

Nominee	Year	President	Action
William Paterson	1793	Washington	Withdrawn
John Rutledge	1795	Washington	Rejected, 10–14
Alexander Wolcott	1811	Madison	Rejected, 9–24
John Crittenden	1828	J. Q. Adams	Postponed[d]
Roger B. Taney[a]	1835	Jackson	Postponed[d]
John Spencer	1844	Tyler	Rejected, 21–26
R. Walworth	1844	Tyler	Withdrawn
Edward King	1844	Tyler	Withdrawn
Edward King	1844	Tyler	Withdrawn
John Read	1845	Tyler	Postponed[d]
G. Woodward	1846	Polk	Rejected, 20–29
Edward Bradford	1852	Fillmore	Postponed[d]
George Badger	1853	Fillmore	Postponed[d]
William Micou	1853	Fillmore	Postponed[d]
Jeremiah Black	1861	Buchanan	Rejected, 25–26
Henry Stanbery	1866	A. Johnson	Postponed[d]
Ebenezer Hoar	1870	Grant	Rejected, 24–33
George Williams	1874	Grant	Withdrawn
Caleb Cushing	1874	Grant	Withdrawn
Stanley Matthews[b]	1881	Hayes	Postponed[d]
W. B. Hornblower	1894	Cleveland	Rejected, 24–30
Wheeler H. Peckham	1894	Cleveland	Rejected, 32–41
John J. Parker	1930	Hoover	Rejected, 39–41
Abe Fortas[c]	1968	L. Johnson	Withdrawn
Homer Thornberry	1968	L. Johnson	Withdrawn
C. Haynsworth	1969	Nixon	Rejected, 45–55
G. H. Carswell	1970	Nixon	Rejected, 45–51
Robert Bork	1987	Reagan	Rejected, 42–58
Douglas Ginsburg	1987	Reagan	Not submitted[e]

Source: Harold W. Stanley and Richard G. Niemi, eds., *Vital Statistics on American Politics*, 2d ed. (Washington, D.C.: CQ Press, 1990), 269.

Note: Twenty-nine of 145 presidential nominations to the Court have failed to obtain Senate confirmation. Five nominees, however, declined appointment after having been nominated (Harrison, 1789; W. Cushing, 1796; Jay, 1800; Lincoln, 1811; Adams, 1811) and two withdrew after being confirmed (W. Smith, 1837; Conkling, 1882). a. Later nominated for chief justice and confirmed. b. Later nominated and confirmed. c. In 1968 Fortas, an associate justice, was nominated chief justice. d. Senate either postponed or failed to act on nomination. e. Publicly announced but withdrawn before the president formally submitted his nomination to the Senate.

well-known and less politically vulnerable conservative, as a replacement for Powell.

In 1990 Justice William Brennan (1956–1990), the leader of the Court's liberal wing, resigned, giving President Bush an opportunity to strengthen the bloc of conservative justices. His nominee to replace Brennan was David Souter, a New Hampshire Supreme Court justice whom the president described as a conservative who would not "legislate from the bench." This nomination reflected the president's desire to avoid the type of ideological and partisan controversy that had torpedoed the Bork nomination three years earlier. Unlike Bork, Souter had left no extensive "paper trail" of court decisions or scholarly writings outlining his views on contentious legal issues. This lack of a written record of his views made him a difficult target for liberal senators and interest groups. His quiet New England manner, seemingly moderate philosophy, and deft responses to senators' inquiries at the confirmation hearings also helped him to secure Senate approval. On the Court, Souter has become a member of the body's moderate wing.

The relative calm that characterized the Souter confirmation process was breached in 1991 when President Bush nominated a controversial and outspoken black conservative, U.S. Court of Appeals Judge Clarence Thomas, to replace Justice Thurgood Marshall. Thomas's conservative views aroused both fervent support and opposition. But when accusations were leaked to the media that he had sexually harassed former coworker Anita Hill while serving as chairman of the Equal Employment Opportunity Commission, an extraordinary political drama unfolded. The Senate postponed its scheduled confirmation vote, and the Senate Judiciary Committee conducted hearings into Hill's accusations that mesmerized massive television audiences over an October weekend. While the hearings were often tense and dramatic, they were also inconclusive. And when they were over, a handful of mainly southern Democratic senators joined with Republicans to provide Thomas with a narrow confirmation victory that strengthened the conservative bloc on the Court.

In selecting U.S. Court of Appeals Judges Ruth Bader Ginsburg and Stephen Breyer, President Clinton found a way to cool the superheated atmosphere that had surrounded Supreme Court nominations during the Reagan-Bush years. His formula involved selecting a nominee with "distinguished legal credentials, a wide-ranging and accessible record, and no hard ideological edges."[32] Judge Ginsburg's and Judge Breyer's quick and easy confirmation by the Senate also were facilitated by the compatibility of their judicial philosophies with those of the Democratic majority on the Senate Judiciary Committee, and by the fact that an era of divided party control of the presidency and Congress had come to at least a temporary end with Clinton's election in 1992.

32. Linda Greenhouse, "The Ginsburg Hearings: An Absence of Suspense Welcomed," *New York Times*, July 25, 1993, E3.

The policy implications of Supreme Court appointments were clearly evident when President George Bush nominated Judge Clarence Thomas, an outspoken conservative, in 1991. The heat of controversy became white hot when in televised hearings before the Senate Judiciary Committee Anita Hill accused Thomas, her former boss at the Equal Employment Opportunity Commission, of sexual harassment.

Influencing Judicial Policy Making

The politics of influencing judicial decisions is different than that of influencing Congress or the executive branch. Judges and justices cannot be buttonholed in the corridors, nor is it deemed ethical to meet privately with them in their chambers or take them to lunch to discuss a pending case. Grass-roots lobbying—such as mass letter-writing campaigns orchestrated by interest groups—which can be so effective in dealing with Congress are not thought to be appropriate in the case of the judiciary. The tactics of influence must, therefore, be more indirect and sometimes subtle. One tactic is to influence the composition of the federal judiciary. Other techniques include shaping opinion in the legal community, sponsoring litigation or test cases, and filing amicus curiae briefs.[33]

Court Packing: Influencing Policy through Appointments

Presidential appointments do affect judicial policy making. Indeed, presidents have largely succeeded in gaining supportive Supreme Court decisions on the issues most important to them from the justices they appointed. Scholarly studies, moreover, have shown that judges ap-

33. The following discussion of techniques for influencing the judiciary relies heavily on Kay Lehman Schlozman and John T. Tierney, *Organized Interests and American Democracy* (New York: Harper and Row, 1986), chap. 14.

pointed by Nixon, Ford, and Reagan, for example, have decided cases in a more conservative manner than Kennedy, Johnson, and Carter appointees. Furthermore, Reagan appointees have been more likely to render conservative decisions than either Nixon- or Ford-appointed judges.[34] Based on this, judicial selection expert Sheldon Goldman concluded, "When we elect a president, we're electing a judiciary."[35]

Although presidents often consciously pack the Supreme Court with ideological soul mates and longtime political associates, they have at times been disappointed by their appointees. For example, after two justices he had appointed voted to strike down his assertion of broad executive authority to seize steel mills during the Korean War, President Harry Truman lamented that "packing the Supreme Court simply can't be done. I've tried it and it won't work."[36] Truman's successor, Dwight Eisenhower, suffered from similar misgivings. He called his appointment of Earl Warren as chief justice "the biggest damn-fooled mistake"[37] he ever made. Once justices are on the Court, their perspective on controversial issues may change. In addition, new issues arise. Chief Justice Rehnquist has observed,

History teaches us . . . that even a "strong" president determined to leave his mark on the Court, like Lincoln or Franklin Roosevelt, is apt to be only partly successful. . . . Neither the President nor his appointees can foresee what issues will come before the Court during the tenure of the appointees, and it may be that none had thought very much about these issues. Even though they agree as to the proper resolution of current issues, they may well disagree as to future cases involving other questions.[38]

Presidents also have been frustrated when elderly justices have stayed on the Court rather than retire and let a president with whom they disagreed appoint their successor. Thus, in 1987 seventy-nine-year-old liberal justice Thurgood Marshall, whose health was declining, vowed to stay on the Court until after conservative Ronald Reagan left office, saying, "Don't worry, I'm going to outlive those bastards."[39]

34. For a summary of studies assessing the impact of presidential appointees on judicial policy, see Sheldon Goldman, "Reagan's Second Term Judicial Appointments: The Battle at Midway," *Judicature* 70 (April-May 1987): 335–338.

35. Quoted by Howard Kurtz, "Reagan Transforms the Federal Judiciary," *Washington Post*, March 31, 1985, A4.

36. Quoted by Henry J. Abraham, *Justices and Presidents* (New York: Oxford University Press, 1985), 70.

37. O'Brien, *Storm Center*, 106.

38. Quoted by Stuart Taylor, Jr., "Re: Shaping the Court," *New York Times*, July 2, 1988, 1, 9, National edition.

39. Stephen Labaton, "Justice Marshall Tells Critics He Is Going to Outlive Them," *New York Times*, Oct. 18, 1987, Y17, National edition.

President Franklin Roosevelt's proposal to "pack" the Supreme Court became a favorite with cartoonists. Though his Court-packing plan failed, Roosevelt and recent presidents Ronald Reagan and George Bush have succeeded in influencing Court policy though their appointments.

Perhaps the most blatant attempt at "Court packing" was Franklin Roosevelt's attempt to expand the size of the Court in 1937. Roosevelt was confronted with a Court that blocked his New Deal policies by regularly declaring major legislative enactments unconstitutional, usually by narrow 5–4 votes. It was Roosevelt's further misfortune that during his first term no vacancies developed, and he was denied the opportunity to make a Court appointment. To cope with a hostile Court the president proposed that the maximum size of the Court be set at fifteen and that when a justice reached age seventy the president be authorized to appoint an additional justice. This proposal to pack the Court sparked a huge controversy. With the Court's independence apparently threatened, one of the conservative justices announced his retirement, and two other justices changed their views on the meaning of the Constitution and voted to sustain New Deal legislation. With this "switch in time that saved nine," the Court-packing plan became unnecessary, and it was allowed to lapse in Congress.[40]

The extent to which presidents can actually exercise their appointive powers and shape Court policy varies greatly from president to president. But the fact is, a president can only make appointments when there is a vacancy. Luck, therefore, counts. Some presidents—like Jimmy Carter—never get a chance to make a Supreme Court appointment.

40. See Michael Nelson, "The President and the Court: Reinterpreting the Court-packing Episode of 1937," *Political Science Quarterly* 103 (Summer, 1988): 267–294.

Table 13.3 Shaping the Supreme Court through Appointments: Presidential Opportunities Vary Greatly

President	Party	Period in Office	Number of Nominees Confirmed	Number of Nominees Not Confirmed or Withdrawn
Hoover	Rep.	1929–1933	3	1
Roosevelt	Dem.	1933–1945	9	0
Truman	Dem.	1945–1953	4	0
Eisenhower	Rep.	1953–1961	5	0
Kennedy	Dem.	1961–1963	2	0
Johnson	Dem.	1963–1969	2	2
Nixon	Rep.	1969–1974	4	2
Ford	Rep.	1974–1977	1	0
Carter	Dem.	1977–1981	0	0
Reagan	Rep.	1981–1989	4	2
Bush	Rep.	1989–1993	2	0
Clinton	Dem.	1993–	2	0

But others can reshape the Court—for example, Roosevelt appointed nine justices in his over twelve years in office, and Nixon and Reagan each made four appointments (see Table 13.3).

Changing the Judicial Structure and Jurisdiction

Congress can exert influence over judicial decision making through its powers to control the organizational structure, size, and jurisdiction of the federal courts. For example, after Woodrow Wilson's election in 1912 Democrats and progressive Republicans in Congress passed a bill abolishing the Commerce Court, which they believed had treated the railroads too favorably.

Even the Supreme Court's jurisdiction has been the object of congressional tampering. The most famous instance occurred in 1869 when Congress passed a law removing from the Court's jurisdiction a case that involved the constitutionality of post-Civil War Reconstruction legislation. More recently, opponents of Court policies on abortion, school prayer, and school busing have introduced bills to withdraw these kinds of cases from the Court's jurisdiction. These efforts, however, have gained little support in Congress.

Shaping Opinion in the Legal Community

Organized interests may seek to influence the thinking of judges, lawyers, and legal scholars by preparing articles supporting a particular point of view for law reviews and other professional journals read by members of the legal fraternity—so-called law review lobbying. Well-placed articles advocating a particular line of judicial reasoning written by experts can change the opinions of judges, their clerks, and attorneys on key issues in the legal community and can be used by lawyers in preparing their briefs and cited by judges in their written opinions. The National Association for the Advancement of Colored People (NAACP) has used this technique effectively to alter legal opinion about government policies that the NAACP believed discriminated unconstitutionally against blacks. Women's rights groups also have sought to advance their goals by shaping the opinions of members of the legal community.

Engaging in Litigation

The NAACP and women's rights groups—as well as environmentalists, consumer groups, corporations, and, recently, conservative legal foundations—also have used lawsuits to advance policy objectives. Although the benefits of winning an important lawsuit can be awesome—for example, the NAACP's victory in the famous school desegregation case of *Brown v. Board of Education of Topeka* (1954)—the consequences of losing a major case can be no less so. Litigation carries big risks because losing a case means that an adverse legal precedent for the future has been created.

When organized interests bring test cases that seek to overturn existing court policy, they carefully choose the strongest case possible for their purposes. For example, in 1935 the National Association of Manufacturers used the case of a small kosher butcher in Brooklyn, New York, to challenge the constitutionality of a major and controversial piece of New Deal legislation, the National Recovery Act (NRA). As a result, the NRA was debated before the courts in terms of its impact on a small merchant who claimed to be involved merely in intrastate commerce rather than in interstate commerce where the federal government would have regulatory power.[41] Under these circumstances, the anti-NRA forces, who succeeded in getting the Court to declare the NRA unconstitutional, had a much more persuasive case than they would have had if such giant interstate enterprises as railroads or auto makers had been parties to the suit.

Filing Amicus Curiae Briefs

Through amicus curiae, or "friend of the court," briefs, organized groups that are not parties to a suit can present their organizations' views on an issue to the Court. These briefs present information and arguments favoring a group's point of view. For example, in the *Webster v. Reproductive Health Services* case, which upheld state-imposed re-

41. *Schechter Poultry Corporation v. United States*, 295 U.S. 485 (1935).

strictions on a woman's right to an abortion,[42] amicus briefs were filed by such pro-choice organizations as the American Nurses Association, the National Organization for Women (NOW), and the American Public Health Association. Among right-to-life groups filing amicus briefs were the U.S. Catholic Conference, National Right to Life, and the Knights of Columbus.

The federal government also seeks to advance its policy agenda by filing amicus briefs in cases in which the United States is not a party to the suit. Such briefs, which are filed by the Department of Justice on behalf of the administration, are particularly important because they advise the Court of the government's position on important issues.

Role of Other Government Institutions in the Implementation of Federal Court Decisions

Supreme Court decisions are not self-enforcing. The Court, which has no enforcement machinery of its own, must rely on others to implement its decisions. Compliance with Court decisions depends on the clarity, quality, and unanimity of the Court's decision; the kind of issue at stake; and the number of institutions, groups, and individuals affected by the decision. When the issue is clear-cut and only one person is ordered by the Court to act in a prescribed manner, compliance is prompt. This was the case in 1974 when President Nixon was ordered to turn over taped Oval Office conversations about the Watergate coverup to a lower federal court. But when the issue is complicated and many people and government units are affected, implementation is more difficult and drawn out. For example, the Court's 1963 decision in *Gideon v. Wainwright* that the states must provide attorneys for poor defendants in felony trials affected state governments, lower courts, attorneys, and taxpayers.[43] As a result, implementation was slow and complicated. Likewise, the Court's earlier decision, in 1962, declaring prayer in public schools unconstitutional did not result in immediate compliance across the country.[44] Prayers continued to be recited in school districts where people supported school prayer and where no one brought suit to prevent the practice. Noncompliance with Court decisions is, however, not the norm, and eventually the existence of

42. *Webster v. Reproductive Health Services*, 492 U.S. 490 (1989).
43. *Gideon v. Wainwright*, 372 U.S. 335 (1963).
44. *Engel v. Vitale*, 370 U.S. 421 (1962).

legally enforceable Court rulings tends to bring individuals, private organizations, and government units into compliance with the law.

Chief Justice Charles Evans Hughes once commented that the "Constitution is what the Supreme Court says it is." Certainly the Court plays a critical role in constitutional as well as statutory interpretation, but as this brief look at the implementation of court decisions will indicate, the policy struggle does not end with the announcement of a Court decision. Contending forces seek to influence how the decision will be implemented, and those who are dissatisfied with the decision, especially Congress and the president, may even seek to overturn the action of the Court.

The Lower Federal Courts

Lower-court federal judges are particularly important in carrying out Supreme Court decisions. In performing this function, they demonstrate considerable independence and discretion; they do not function as mere bureaucratic arms of the Supreme Court. Their independence is encouraged by life tenure, traditions of running their courts as they see fit, an absence of disciplinary measures, and virtually no fear of impeachment.[45] The discretion of lower-court judges also may be the product of the language of the Supreme Court's decision. For example, in its landmark school desegregation decision, the Supreme Court required public school systems to make a prompt and reasonable start toward desegregation and to proceed with "all deliberate speed" to bring about desegregation. But the Court did not specify what constituted promptness, reasonableness, or all deliberate speed. As a consequence, lower-district court judges used substantial discretion when confronted with community opinion opposed to desegregation and with school districts that were dragging their feet on integration while claiming that they were proceeding with all deliberate speed.

The Congress

After the judiciary has made a decision, Congress can respond in ways that either facilitate implementation of the decision or hinder it. Where Congress disapproves of a judicial decision, it has a variety of legislative weapons available to it for use against the courts. For example, the courts are regularly required to engage in *statutory interpretation*—interpreting the meaning of laws passed by Congress and applying them to specific cases. But when a court interprets a congressional statute in a manner in which Congress disapproves, Congress can pass a new statute that in effect overturns the Court's decision. A notable

45. Carp and Stidham, *Judicial Process in America*, 352.

example occurred in 1988 when Congress overturned the Supreme Court's 1984 decision in *Grove City College v. Bell,* a case involving a small Pennsylvania college.[46] The Court interpreted Title IX of the 1972 Education Act amendments, which forbids sex discrimination, to apply only to the specific program receiving federal funds. As a result, the college's financial aid office alone was affected by the law instead of the entire college. Congress responded to this decision by passing the Civil Rights Restoration Act of 1988, which stated that if one part of a college receives federal funds, the entire institution is covered by the Title IX antidiscrimination provisions. Such actions by Congress, however, are relatively rare, and the vast majority of federal judicial decisions are not challenged by Congress.[47]

In addition to interpreting statutes, the Supreme Court also interprets the Constitution. Here, too, Congress may act legislatively either to reverse a decision or to alter its effects. For example, after the Court in 1973 struck down government prohibitions on abortions as unconstitutional, Congress responded in 1976 with the Hyde Amendment and other statutes restricting the use of federal funds for elective or therapeutic abortions. These congressional actions were upheld by the Court.[48] Or Congress can take another avenue if it disapproves of—and wants to reverse—a Court decision: a constitutional amendment. For example, the Thirteenth Amendment (1865) reversed a decision dealing with the legality of slavery, and the Sixteenth Amendment (1913) overturned a Court decision invalidating a federal income tax. Amending the Constitution is, of course, a difficult and time-consuming process. It requires a two-thirds vote of both houses of Congress and ratification by three-fourths of the states.

Other legislative weapons available to Congress for use against the courts are the previously noted "Court packing" in which Congress attempts to change the composition of the Supreme Court by expanding its size; altering the Supreme Court's appellate jurisdiction; or exercising budgetary control over the federal courts, although the Constitution prohibits reducing judges' salaries. While individual members of Congress have occasionally tried to pressure the Supreme Court through budgetary measures, the Congress itself has refrained from engaging in such actions.

More informal congressional or individual member responses to disfavored Supreme Court decisions may take the form of an attack,

---

46. *Grove City College v. Bell,* 465 U.S. 555 (1984).

47. Carp and Stidham, *Judicial Process in America,* 359–360; and Baum, *Supreme Court,* 230.

48. *Harris v. McRae,* 448 U.S. 297 (1980).

usually verbal, on the Court or specific justices. One representative in 1956, for example, even asserted that the Court was a "greater threat to this Union than the entire confines of Soviet Russia."[49] While such attacks may weaken the Court by undermining public confidence in the institution, the actual impact is difficult to assess.

The ultimate weapon against all federal judges that Congress has at its disposal is its power to impeach and remove them from office. Although this power is seldom used, its use against three lower-federal court judges in the 1980s is a reminder that Congress does have this weapon in its arsenal.

The reluctance of Congress to use its powers to pressure the Court reflects the influence of several factors. First, a substantial number of members of Congress usually agree with Court decisions and will resist attempts to undermine those decisions. Second, legislative assaults on the Court are frequently perceived by the public as lacking in legitimacy. The public tends to believe that the Court should be independent from the other branches of government. And, third, the Court has often retreated from positions that would provide the impetus for congressional intervention.[50]

The President

Presidents, too, can affect the implementation of judicial decisions. For example, when a Supreme Court decision meets open opposition, the president must decide whether and with what degree of force the power of the federal government will be used to support that decision. In these matters the president has considerable discretion. President Andrew Jackson purportedly said, after the Marshall Court rendered a decision of which he heartily disapproved, "John Marshall has made his decision; now let him enforce it." This oft-quoted statement aptly captures the Court's dependence on the executive branch for assistance in enforcing its decisions.

At times presidents have used the most coercive powers of the government to gain compliance with Court decisions. In 1957, for example, federal troops under the command of President Dwight Eisenhower ultimately forced the governor of Arkansas to comply with the Court-ordered integration of Little Rock Central High School. And in 1963 federal marshals under the command of the Kennedy administration's Justice Department compelled Gov. George Wallace of Alabama to admit blacks to the University of Alabama.

Through their public statements or failure to speak out in support

49. Quoted by Lawrence Baum, *The Supreme Court,* 3d ed. (Washington, D.C.: CQ Press, 1989).

50. Baum, *Supreme Court,* 4th ed., 235.

of Court decisions, presidents are thought to be able to affect the level of compliance as well. Some observers, for example, believe that had President Eisenhower spoken more forcefully in support of the 1954 school desegregation decision, southern officials would have made fewer attempts to circumvent the Supreme Court decision banning segregated public school systems.

Because public expectations for compliance with Court decisions are so strong, presidents normally respond promptly to Supreme Court decisions even when the Court has ruled against a presidential action. Presidents are not, however, without retaliatory weapons. They may, for example, propose legislation or constitutional amendments aimed at retaliating against the Court—Franklin Roosevelt's "Court-packing" plan was a dramatic example. President Ronald Reagan sought to use the constitutional amendment approach. He vigorously, though unsuccessfully, supported amendments designed to overturn the Court's ban on school prayer.

Where Does the Judiciary Fit in the American Political Process?

Although the popular image of the federal courts is one of an apolitical third branch of government, it is clear from this look at the courts that this image does not conform to reality. The members of the judiciary gain their positions through a highly politicized process of presidential appointment and Senate confirmation. Most were active in partisan politics before their appointments, and they do not suddenly shed attitudes and approaches to issues the moment they put on judicial robes. Once on the bench, judges are confronted with some of the most controversial issues facing society: abortion, the rights of the accused, the powers of the president to use military force, and affirmative action. In shaping public policy on such issues, the courts are not immune from political pressures from litigants, interest groups, public opinion, political parties, Congress, and the executive branch.

As it decides cases and resolves societal conflicts, the Supreme Court gains strength and independence from the discretion it exercises over its caseload and the types of cases that it will consider. The Court's stature with the public has meant that other political leaders, even the president, are expected to comply with Court orders. The Supreme Court also benefits from public expectations that it will be independent of the Congress and the president and insulated from such direct pressures as lobbying. These public expectations constrain the Congress and the president from aggressively using their full array of powers to attack the actions of the Supreme Court.

The Court, too, operates under constraints. As a legal institution it is required to follow legal procedures in making its decisions. Thus, there is the expectation that normally it will follow past precedents in making its rulings. Then too, the Court can deal only with those issues that arise from the cases that are brought before it. Unlike the president and Congress, justices are limited in their ability to initiate government action; they must wait for a case to come before them before making policy. Supreme Court justices also are heavily dependent on the willingness of the American people to comply with their decisions. Moreover, the Court is dependent on the executive branch to enforce its policies if those policies meet with open opposition.

The position of the federal courts in the American political system is a unique one. They operate in an environment that provides them with a degree of independence and insulation not enjoyed by the other branches. The judiciary, however, is not immune from attempts to exert influence on its decision-making processes because the courts are major policy makers in the American system.

For Review

1. Although commonly considered apolitical, the federal judiciary plays a central and prominent policy-making role along with the president and Congress. Many of the most important issues facing Americans eventually find their way to the courts.

2. The United States has a dual judicial system in which federal and state courts operate with their own personnel and jurisdictions and interpret and enforce their own constitutions and laws. But overlap exists between the two as well: the federal judiciary is able to declare state actions unconstitutional.

3. The federal judicial system is composed of federal district courts (trial courts), courts of appeals (intermediate appellate courts), and the Supreme Court (which has discretion over the cases it chooses to hear and decide). A series of legislative courts hears specialized types of cases.

4. In the case of *Marbury v. Madison* the Supreme Court read into the Constitution the power of the federal courts to declare acts of Congress unconstitutional. The federal judiciary has used its power of judicial review sparingly against acts of Congress but has frequently asserted this power to strike down state laws.

5. Federal judges are appointed by the president, must be confirmed by the Senate, and have lifetime appointments. Presidents normally appoint members of their own parties to the federal bench and, particularly in the case of the Supreme Court, seek to appoint individuals who share their

views on important matters of public policy. The policy orientation of the Court can be altered by presidential appointments.

6. Although the Supreme Court with its appointed justices is often considered an antimajoritarian institution, Court decisions tend to be in accord with trends in public opinion.

7. Among the techniques used to influence judicial decisions are: changing the composition and size of the judiciary, seeking to shape public opinion within the legal community, bringing test cases to the courts, and filing "friend of the court" briefs.

For Further Reading

Abraham, Henry J. *The Judiciary.* 7th ed. Boston: Allyn and Bacon, 1987. A description of the operation of the American judiciary, with special emphasis on the Supreme Court as policy maker in the area of fundamental freedoms.

___. *The Judicial Process.* 6th ed. New York: Oxford University Press, 1993. A comprehensive description of the functioning of the American judicial system with comparisons to the judicial processes in other countries.

Baum, Lawrence. *The Supreme Court.* 4th ed. Washington, D.C.: CQ Press, 1991. An account of how the Supreme Court functions, forces that influence judicial decisions, and the Court's policy impact.

Carp, Robert A., and Ronald Stidham. *Judicial Process in America.* 2d ed. Washington, D.C.: CQ Press, 1993. A description of the federal court system and its decision-making process and impact.

Gates, John B., and Charles A. Johnson, eds. *The American Courts: A Critical Assessment.* Washington, D.C.: CQ Press, 1991. A collection of essays by leading scholars analyzing the role of the courts in America.

O'Brien, David M. *Storm Center: The Supreme Court in American Politics.* 3d ed. New York: Norton, 1993. Both a scholarly and a readable account of the Court's role in politics.

O'Connor, Karen. *Women's Organizations' Use of the Courts.* Lexington, Mass.: Lexington Books, 1980. An account of how women's organizations have used the courts to achieve policy goals.

Walker, Thomas G., and Lee Epstein. *The Supreme Court of the United States: An Introduction.* New York: St. Martin's Press, 1993. A concise description of the operations and politics of the Court.

Woodward, Bob, and Scott Armstrong. *The Brethren: Inside the Supreme Court.* New York: Simon and Schuster, 1979. A behind-the-scenes look at Supreme Court decision making.

PART IV

Politics and Public Policy

14. Public Policy, Politics, and Democracy in America

T HE CONGRESS, the presidency, the bureaucracy, and the courts—what ultimately makes these institutions so important? The answer: their *policy* decisions affect people both in the United States and around the world. It follows, then, that students of American politics would be concerned about the inner workings of *public policy,* which is whatever the government chooses to do or not to do about perceived problems, and *policy making,* which is how the government decides what will and will not be done about perceived problems.[1]

These definitions of public policy and policy making recognize that government inaction can have just as great an impact on society as government action. The failure of the government earlier in this century to rid the public schools of racial segregation and to prevent denials of the right to vote to all voting-age people had momentous consequences for America, just as government steps in these same areas since the 1950s have dramatically changed American society.

For most government officials the overarching goals of public policy are to defend the nation from external enemies and to keep inevitable internal conflicts from becoming so bitter and intense that they lead to secession or civil war. The second of these tasks involves satisfying many of society's needs by sifting through the deluge of demands made on the government, blending those demands into public policies, and carrying out those policies in such a manner that no group feels compelled to engage in secession, violence, or insurrection.[2]

American public policy is, of course, affected by the constitutional framework, societal characteristics, political processes, and governmental institutions discussed in previous chapters. A combination of these forces constitutes the unique context for American policy making.

1. These definitions are derived from Thomas R. Dye, *Understanding Public Policy,* 6th ed. (Englewood Cliffs, N.J.: Prentice-Hall, 1987), 3; and Randall B. Ripley and Grace A. Franklin, *Congress, the Bureaucracy, and Public Policy,* 5th ed. (Pacific Grove, Calif.: Brooks/Cole, 1991), 1.

2. On the basic tasks of policy makers, see Austin Ranney, *Governing: An Introduction to Political Science,* 6th ed. (Englewood Cliffs, N.J.: Prentice-Hall, 1993), 9.

Policy Making in the American Context

The early Americans who crafted the Constitution primarily were concerned about how to create a government able to maintain public order and yet at the same time able to protect personal liberty. In their efforts to restrain government, they sought to fragment the government's power by separating powers at the national level and creating a federal system. Three separate branches of government were created, each with the power to check the other two. In this way the national government was strengthened, but it still had to share power with the states. These features of the Constitution have had a lasting effect on the policy-making process. Indeed, the Constitution writers devised a system that makes it difficult to adopt new policies or change existing policies. Legislation, for example, must be approved by the House, Senate, and president; implemented by the bureaucracy; and accepted by the courts.

The Constitution, however, is an incomplete guide to American policy making because America has more than just the three formal branches of government specified in that document. There also are the hybrid government organizations that have significant policy-making authority such as the independent regulatory agencies, government corporations, and foundations. Some, like the regulatory commissions, even combine judicial, administrative, and legislative functions. The actions of government decision makers also are swayed by interested citizens, public opinion, elections, political parties, interest groups, and the media. In fact, some informed observers have found nongovernmental organizations such as interest groups to be so prominent and permanent a feature of government decision making that they have called these organizations the fourth branch of government—a title others reserve for the bureaucracy. But, in reality, many different political interests, processes, and institutions join together to make policy. Moreover, as revealed later in this chapter, the kinds of decisional processes used and the types of institutions playing the chief roles will depend on the nature of the issue being considered.

Although the constitutional order often makes government action more easily talked about than done, the federal government has become quite active in the twentieth century. This is in contrast to its relative passivity in the early days of the Republic when it simply delivered the mail, defended the shores, levied tariffs and regulated foreign commerce, and built a few public works projects. The government was not involved in the lives of its citizens to any significant degree. But even if it had wanted to, the Constitution and restrictive Supreme Court definitions of the national government's authority would have severely limited its activities. Moreover, there was little in the way of public demand for services from the national government, and those citizens who sought them often lacked the political clout needed to get them. The government's policy agenda was, therefore, limited.

In the depression of the 1930s and during World War II the government saw its role expand tremendously. The Supreme Court stopped adhering to restrictive definitions of the federal government's power, people began to demand government services and regulation of the economy, and even those who before had lacked the political resources needed to obtain services developed them through such organizations as labor unions.

The 1960s and 1970s were a particularly turbulent period in the nation's history. Blacks and women demanded equality; young people, in particular, protested America's military involvement in Vietnam; and environmental, consumer, health care, poverty, and energy concerns took on new urgency. To accommodate these public concerns, the number and variety of interest groups operating in Washington exploded between the 1960s and 1980s. In response to these pressures, the government's role in society again expanded.

The issues on the policy agenda of the 1990s are almost endless. The range is suggested by the major categories of policy on the government's front burner. *Economic policy* includes government taxing and spending, job creation, regulation and promotion of business, monetary (money supply) policy, and agriculture. Under *social policy* fall income security (Social Security, Aid to Families with Dependent Children, food stamps), housing, health care, and education. *Civil rights and civil liberties policy* is geared toward safeguarding basic liberties, preventing discrimination, addressing affirmative action and abortion issues, protecting the rights of the accused, and ensuring voting rights. *Natural resources and environmental policy,* which has come of age in this century, revolves around clean air and water, preservation of wilderness areas, wildlife protection, national parks, public lands, and water resources. Finally, *foreign and national security policy* covers such wide-ranging areas as weapons systems, troop levels, military alliances, intelligence activities, treaties, foreign aid, trade, immigration, relations with foreign governments, and the United Nations.

Given the wide-ranging, complicated nature of these policy areas, analysis and understanding of policy making can appear staggering to even the most sophisticated analyst. But the job is made easier and the policy process more comprehensible by examining the stages of the policy-making process and the different types of public policy.

Stages in the Policy-making Process

The government's policies are contained in its official statements of goals and projected activities. The most important of these policy statements are found in the laws passed by Congress and in the executive orders of the president. Government policies also arise from bureaucratic regulations designed to implement congressional and presidential actions and from court decisions. But if these policies are to have any real impact, they must be implemented through concrete actions. Thus, when Congress passed the landmark Clean Air Act of 1990, mandating cleaner air for America, the actual impact of the act depended on the effectiveness of the Environmental Protection Agency's enforcement actions.[3]

The actual process of making public policy can be broken down into four main stages: (1) setting the agenda, (2) formulating and legitimating a policy, (3) implementing a policy, and (4) evaluating policy implementation, performance, and impact (see Figure 14.1).[4]

Stage One: Agenda Setting

Agenda setting is a process in which decision makers perceive that a problem exists, leading them to adopt broad goals to cope with the problem. In the current era of government activism, the government's agenda is full—controlling the federal budget deficit, dealing with instability and conflict in the Middle East, improving health care, eliminating the trade deficit, adapting to the collapse of communism in the former Soviet Union and Eastern Europe, coping with the spread of AIDS, combating terrorism, and dealing with the problems of crime, environmental pollution, airline safety, housing, family farmers,

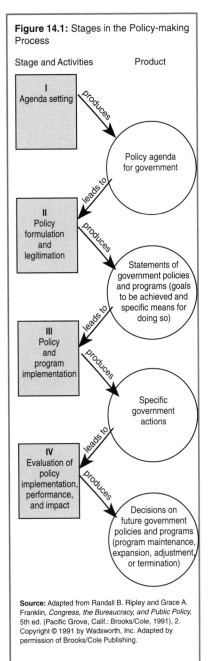

Figure 14.1: Stages in the Policy-making Process

Stage and Activities   Product

I Agenda setting — *produces* → Policy agenda for government

leads to

II Policy formulation and legitimation — *produces* → Statements of government policies and programs (goals to be achieved and specific means for doing so)

leads to

III Policy and program implementation — *produces* → Specific government actions

leads to

IV Evaluation of policy implementation, performance, and impact — *produces* → Decisions on future government policies and programs (program maintenance, expansion, adjustment, or termination)

Source: Adapted from Randall B. Ripley and Grace A. Franklin, *Congress, the Bureaucracy, and Public Policy,* 5th ed. (Pacific Grove, Calif.: Brooks-Cole, 1991), 2. Copyright © 1991 by Wadsworth, Inc. Adapted by permission of Brooks/Cole Publishing.

3. On the impact of the implementation process, see Gary C. Bryner, *Blue Skies, Green Politics: The Clean Air Act of 1990* (Washington, D.C.: CQ Press, 1993), 170–178.

4. The stages discussed are derived from the conceptual framework developed by Randall B. Ripley, *Policy Analysis in Political Science* (Chicago: Nelson-Hall, 1985); and Ripley and Franklin, *Congress, the Bureaucracy, and Public Policy.*

gender and racial discrimination, and the list goes on. Agenda space is limited because government decision makers can pay attention only to so many things.

The greater the number of people who perceive that a problem exists, the greater is the likelihood that it will move onto the government's policy agenda. For example, foreign trade is an extremely complicated subject to which few Americans or members of Congress have paid much attention. But that changed when America's trade deficit with foreign nations reached unprecedented levels in the 1980s and manufacturing industries closed their factories and laid off workers because they found it difficult to compete in the world market. In that atmosphere, with some communities ravaged by unemployment and even employed people frightened about their future, trade became a highly salient issue in terms of media attention, interest group agitation, and congressional and administration maneuvering. The result was congressional passage of a major revision of American trade policy in 1988. And continuing concern about the need to expand America's markets among its neighbors in this hemisphere, Canada and Mexico, while preventing the export of American jobs south of the border, made the North American Free Trade Agreement (NAFTA) a contentious issue during both the Bush and Clinton administrations.

Even a specific event can push an issue onto the public policy agenda. The Iraqi invasion of Kuwait in August 1990, for example, prompted the dispatch of a massive U.S. military force to the Persian Gulf to defend Saudi Arabia, as well as the formation of a U.S.-led alliance,

The tide of Japanese products flooding the U.S. marketplace, like these Nissan automobiles, has helped to put foreign trade policy on the public agenda.

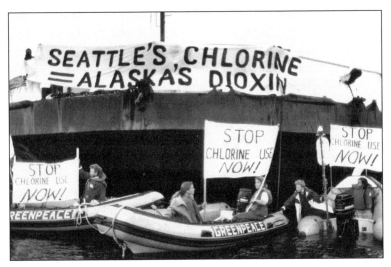

Activists from Greenpeace use unconventional and aggressive tactics to pressure the government into strengthening environmental protection regulations.

which launched a war that removed Iraq from Kuwait. Earlier, in 1957, the Soviet launching of the first satellite, *Sputnik,* spurred the United States to activate its space program.

Many interest groups are no less effective in grabbing the attention of government officials and helping to push issues onto the government's policy agenda. They soon learn, however, that agenda setting is a competitive process because the government's policy agenda is crowded and any shift in policy is likely to engender opposition from those who would bear the burdens of a policy change. For example, business organizations have pressed for congressional action to limit their vulnerability to costly product liability lawsuits, but in the process they have encountered stiff opposition from trial lawyers. Environmentalists have demanded protection for old-growth timber and the habitats of such endangered species as the spotted owl in the Pacific Northwest, but as a consequence they have stirred fierce resistance from the lumber industry and its workers. And organized labor has exerted pressure on Congress for legislation dealing with health care reform, family leave, plant closings, the minimum wage, and limits on companies hiring replacement workers during strikes—measures that have faced varying degrees of opposition from the business community.

Political leadership is another important factor in the agenda-setting process. The preeminent agenda setter in the government is the president. Thus, when Ronald Reagan became president in 1981 the major items on the government's agenda were also those foremost on Reagan's—lower taxes, cuts in domestic spending, and higher expenditures on defense. Similarly, the post-1992 governmental agenda bears the stamp of President Clinton, who during his first year in office provided Congress with a broad array of proposals including a major deficit-reduction package, economic stimulus legislation, a complex health care reform measure, a national service program, a family leave bill, the North American Free Trade Agreement, and revision of aid to education. Political scientist Paul Light has found that in selecting major domestic issues on which to advocate action, presidents have been motivated by three primary considerations: electoral benefits, concern about their places in history, and a desire for good policy.[5] Activist members of the House and Senate also serve as agenda setters.

The mass media also have a say in the agenda-setting process. Through their reporting, the media highlight issues that might otherwise not find their way onto the policy agenda. For example, media publicity raised the visibility of rampant starvation and lawlessness in Somalia; ethnic cleansing in the former Yugoslavia; the safety of nuclear power plants, automobiles, and coal mines; sexual harassment in the workplace; and violent crime.

Stage Two: Formulating and Legitimating Policies

Once it has been acknowledged that a problem deserves the government's attention, the government must decide what to do about the problem and what goals must be met to achieve the solution. As the discussion in Chapter 10 on lawmaking in Congress demonstrated, this can be a long, tortuous process. *Policy formulation* involves developing alternative proposals and collecting, analyzing, and disseminating the information needed to assess the alternatives and persuade people to support one proposal or another. Next, specific policies have to be adopted, but in a way that uses procedures widely accepted by society. This is the *legitimation process*—adopting government policies in a manner that conforms to the public's expectations about what is the proper and correct way to do things. A common method of legitimation is passage of a law by Congress, but Supreme Court decisions and White House executive orders also give legitimacy to government policies. Legitimation is extremely important because without it public acceptance of a policy is easily undermined.

Policy formulation normally has its strategic implications—that is, information is assembled, arguments developed, and alternatives shaped with an eye toward winning the approval of official decision makers. When Congress is the legitimating agent, the rule of the day is

5. Paul Light, *The President's Agenda* (Baltimore: Johns Hopkins University Press, 1982), chap. 3.

coalition building—shaping policy in such a way that it will attract a majority. In the House of Representatives, for example, passage of legislation is facilitated when a proposed program will distribute benefits widely among a large number of congressional districts.[6] Thus, legislation dealing with federal highways, rivers and harbors, and water reclamation projects is usually a shoo-in. Knitting together a congressional majority normally involves extensive negotiation, bargaining, and compromise.

Although the formal decisions on public policy are made by government officials, they are not the only participants in policy making. As revealed in Chapter 7, interest groups can have a profound impact on that process, as well as ordinary citizens when they are mobilized. In 1988, for example, Congress responded to pressure from the multimillion-member American Association of Retired Persons and passed the Medicare Catastrophic Coverage Act, which provided the elderly with catastrophic illness benefits but also imposed an increase in Medicare taxes. Only seventeen months after passage of the law, it was repealed by a Congress that was feeling the heat from its elderly constituents. Outraged senior citizens, objecting to increased Medicare taxes ($800 per person in 1989 and a projected $1,050 in 1993) formed grass-roots organizations and deluged their senators and representatives with angry demands for the law's repeal. Congress responded.

Not all policy decisions take the form of positive government action. Government decision makers also may decline to act, and that too is a policy decision. Strongly organized opposition within and outside the government, for example, blocked legislation on key elements of President Reagan's social agenda—permitting prayer in the public schools and banning abortions—and in 1993 a Republican filibuster killed President Clinton's $16.3 billion economic stimulus program.

Stage Three:
Policy Implementation

Few government policies are self-implementing. Once a policy has been proclaimed officially through the passage of legislation, issuance of an executive order by the president, or the announcement of a court decision, it must be implemented. Even the most brilliantly conceived policy will fail to achieve its designers' goals if it is poorly implemented.[7]

6. See David R. Mayhew, *Congress: The Electoral Connection* (New Haven, Conn.: Yale University Press, 1974), 127–130.

7. George C. Edwards, III, *Implementing Public Policy* (Washington, D.C.: CQ Press, 1980), 1.

Implementation is those activities directed toward putting a program into effect. It is "getting the job done."[8] One of the three major activities required for implementation is *interpretation*—translation of the program language into acceptable and feasible administrative directives.[9]

Administrators must be able to discern Congress's intent when it passes a law creating a new government program. Legislation often sets lofty goals—achieving clean air or declaring war on poverty and drugs—but it is left to the administrators to fill in the details about how the goals will be accomplished. Frequently laws purposely are left vague to avoid offending key lawmakers whose votes are needed to enact a bill. When this happens, the implementers of the legislation have a great deal of leeway in determining how the new program will actually operate. The Occupational Safety and Health Act of 1970, for example, was designed to promote workplace safety and health, yet the act contained no substantive safety and health standards. Instead it authorized the Department of Labor to set such standards and then enforce them. Thus within the framework of legislation passed by Congress, the Occupational Safety and Health Administration (OSHA) both makes and implements policy on safety and health in the workplace.[10]

The second major activity needed for implementation is *organization*—establishing administrative units and methods for putting a program into effect. Resources, in the form of money, buildings, equipment, and information, must be acquired and a staff hired and trained.

For the third activity, *application*, services and benefits are routinely provided (for example, mailing out Social Security checks, providing health care for veterans) and sanctions and regulations are imposed (for example, enforcing OSHA regulations and criminal statutes).

As described here, interpretation, organization, and application may appear rather dull and routine. But, in fact, the manner in which these activities are carried out can dramatically affect the extent to which policy goals are achieved. A striking example is the National Health Service Corps, a program designed by Congress in 1970 to encourage doctors to practice in areas lacking adequate health care. The brief four-page law gave the Health Services Administration (HSA) (designated the Health Resources and Services Administration in a 1982 reorganization) little in the way of guidance about implementation. But the

---

8. Charles O. Jones, *An Introduction to the Study of Public Policy,* 3d ed. (Monterey, Calif.: Brooks/Cole, 1984), 165.

9. See Jones's consideration of implementation activities, ibid., chap. 8.

10. James E. Anderson, *Public Policymaking: An Introduction,* 2d ed. (Boston: Houghton Mifflin, 1994), 196.

intent of the law was clear: to place physicians in areas that could support them economically. In implementing the law, HSA administrators defined an area lacking physicians loosely and allowed exceptions to the "shortage"-of-doctors requirement if an area had low utilization of health services. They then placed physicians in urban sites where HSA-sponsored group practices were already operating. Thus, rather than providing doctors for rural areas, the implementation process funneled many physicians into inner-city areas, and rather than fighting the geographic barriers inhibiting health care availability, the HSA sought to fight the economic barriers. In other words, the HSA used its administrative discretion to implement the program in a way that was consistent with the agency's traditional emphasis on delivering health care to the poor rather than, as Congress had intended, to establish physicians in private practice. By 1990, budget cuts had reduced the number of doctors participating in the program and had forced administrators to alter their implementation policy. In an effort to cover as many areas of the country as possible, the agency shifted family practitioners out of urban areas into poverty-stricken rural ones. As might be expected, this policy shift stimulated complaints from urban clients and members of Congress.[11]

Stage Four: Evaluation of Policy Implementation, Performance, and Impact

After a government policy has been put into effect, it is evaluated to determine how well it was implemented, whether its goals were achieved, and what its impact was. The results of these assessments can result in a program being maintained, expanded, changed, or even terminated. In effect, after the results of the evaluation stage are in, an existing policy may go back on the government's policy agenda.

Some government programs do achieve their desired goals. The Voting Rights Act of 1965, for example, substantially increased the percentage of eligible blacks exercising their right to vote. Other programs, however, fall short of their objectives. In the 1960s, for example, President Lyndon Johnson's War on Poverty did not end poverty, although such programs as Head Start (preschool education for disadvantaged children) won widespread praise. And the Safe Streets Act of 1968 did

11. For a more detailed account, see Frank J. Thompson, "Bureaucratic Discretion and the National Health Service Corps," *Political Science Quarterly* 97 (Fall 1982): 427–445; and Josh Barbanel, "U.S. Orders Family Doctors from Cities to Country," *New York Times*, June 24, 1990, 1Y, 17Y, National edition.

Head Start, a federally funded preschool program for poor children, has been unusual in the high level of public and bipartisan congressional support it has achieved and maintained since it was instituted in 1965.

not cause people to feel safe in the nation's cities. Indeed, Washington's great, and at times exaggerated, expectations of the programs it has conceived can be dashed because of implementation problems out in the field. There, a variety of factors may impede or prevent full attainment of policy goals. Among them,[12]

■ Inadequate resources may be provided to implement a policy. The federal government, for example, has been sharply criticized for failing to commit adequate resources to coping with AIDS, hazardous wastes, crime, and drug abuse. Moreover, the costs of really solving a problem may be beyond what people are willing to accept—such as the hundreds of billions of dollars it would cost to totally eliminate water pollution.

■ Programs may be administered in a manner that lessens their potential impact. In the 1965 Elementary and Secondary Education Act, for example, disadvantaged children were clearly specified as the focus for assistance. The Office of Education (now the Department of Education), however, initially did not direct federal funds toward aiding such children because of its reluctance to regulate and police local school agencies and thereby to ensure that the funds were expended in the way intended.

■ People may respond or adapt to public policies in ways that negate some of the policies' impacts. For example, policies designed to

12. The factors listed are derived from the analysis of Anderson, *Public Policymaking*, 263–265.

reduce surplus farm commodities by imposing acreage allotments on farmers (rather than by limiting the quantity of commodities they produce) have been largely negated by the scientific revolution in agriculture which enables farmers to increase their crop yields through improved plant varieties, pesticides, and chemical fertilizers.

■ Government policies may have conflicting or incompatible goals. For example, the government's tobacco price support program seems inconsistent with the goals of the National Cancer Institute and the antismoking campaign of the Department of Health and Human Services.

One major difficulty in achieving federal program objectives is the use of third parties—instead of the federal government—to implement a large share of government programs. This occurs when (1) the federal government contracts with the private sector for a wide array of goods and services (for example, weapons for the Department of Defense or concession stands for national parks); (2) through federal grants, state and local governments build highways, construct public housing, administer welfare programs, or operate mass transit systems (see Chapter 3); (3) tax incentives (sometimes called tax breaks or loopholes) encourage selected types of behavior in taxpayers, such as taking tax deductions for home ownership and charitable contributions; (4) the federal government extends or assists with billions of dollars in loans to make credit available where private money markets might not—for example, for student loans, home mortgages, and small business investments; and (5) federal government rules and regulations determine the cost and availability of many private sector goods and services such as interest rates and the availability of bank loans and govern the safety of such consumer products as food, drugs, and cars. Political scientist Donald Kettl has described these practices as "government by proxy." He also has noted that when implementation of federal programs is turned over to third parties, the government loses control of the programs because the goals of third-party administrators are apt to differ from those of the federal government.[13]

Some government policies, such as the amendments to the 1974 Federal Election Campaign Act (FECA), have unintended consequences. Intended to restrict the role of money in campaigns by strictly limiting contributions by individuals, interest groups, and parties, the amendments also facilitated the formation of political action committees

13. See Donald F. Kettl, *Government by Proxy: (Mis?)Managing Federal Programs* (Washington, D.C.: CQ Press, 1988).

(PACs), thereby stimulating the almost immediate creation of thousands of primarily business-oriented PACs. Contrary to the hopes of the campaign finance reformers, then, money did not lose its significance for elections. Indeed, campaign funds from organized interests increased substantially. And even more dismaying for the liberal advocates of campaign finance reform was the realization that they had helped to create the conditions that encouraged the development of business-oriented PACs, to the detriment of their supporters in politically active labor unions.

Because the verdicts rendered on a program's implementation, performance, and impact can influence whether that program is continued, expanded, changed, or terminated, the policy evaluation process can be highly controversial. When most people think of policy evaluation, they tend to think in terms of objective social science analyses. This may be part of the process, but, in truth, in the world of practical politics policy evaluation has a much broader meaning. For that world, it is a process in which many different types of people—bureaucrats, members of Congress, interest group representatives, academicians, White House staffers, and ordinary citizens—assess a policy based on their own unique sets of criteria and experiences with government programs. It is not surprising, then, that their evaluations are apt to differ. For example, Republican and Democratic members of Congress have entirely different ideas about the problems associated with the Federal Election Campaign Act and thus divergent reform agendas. According to Republicans, FECA-encouraged PACs are giving large and disproportionate shares of their contributions to incumbent Democrats. GOP lawmakers believe that electoral reform should make it possible to channel more money to congressional challengers, thereby overcoming the advantages of incumbents (who are mostly Democrats). The Republican reform agenda, then, calls for tight restrictions or even bans on PAC contributions, higher contribution limits for parties, and opposition to expenditure limits on candidates.

The Democrats, however, define the problem as too much money being spent on elections and too much time being spent by members of Congress on chasing campaign contributions. Their reform proposals place limits on expenditures and call for some form of public funding for elections. Since the two parties define the problems with the existing law so differently, it is small wonder that campaign finance reform has been such a contentious issue.

Another example of the controversy that can surround the implementation and impact of government policy is the effects of government transfer payments under the Aid to Families with Dependent Children (AFDC) program. Some argue that this welfare program, which gives aid to families headed by single mothers, has deprived recipients of incentives for self-improvement and self-sufficiency. It is further charged that AFDC has encouraged fathers to be absent from their families because aid goes only to households headed by a single woman. Others hotly dispute these contentions and see the program primarily as an essential safety net for the nation's most disadvantaged citizens.

As these examples demonstrate, policy making is a difficult, often controversial process. But a look at only the stages in this process does not constitute a well-rounded view of public policy in America. That requires a review of the different types of policies on the national agenda.

Types of Public Policies

The nature of the policy-making process varies tremendously from one issue area to another. Decisions in 1991 about whether to go to war with Iraq and how the war would be conducted, for example, were made by the president and his national security and foreign policy advisers. Once it had authorized the president to take military action, Congress was not a major policy maker, nor were interest groups highly visible or influential. By contrast, the major participants in the enactment and subsequent repeal of the 1988 Medicare Catastrophic Coverage Act were, as noted earlier, the Congress and interest groups representing the elderly. Health care reform in 1993–1994 has involved an even wider array of participants—Hillary Rodham Clinton's White House task force, executive branch agencies, Congress, a myriad of aggressive interest groups, and experts drawn from academe, business, and think tanks. Other less visible policy issues—such as those involving the protection of copyrights and patents—may be left to the bureaucracy or committees of the Congress to resolve.

To understand the policy-making process in a way that moves beyond examining such isolated examples, it is helpful to think in terms of types of government policies (see Figure 14.2). Using these types, it is then possible to identify the different patterns of government decision making that occur across a range of government policies.[14]

14. The following consideration of different types of public policy relies heavily on the conceptualization and analysis in Ripley, *Policy Analysis in Political Science*, and in Ripley and Franklin, *Congress, the Bureaucracy, and Public Policy*.

With health care constituting approximately one-seventh of the U.S. economy, President Clinton's plan to overhaul the system stimulated intense lobbying by a broad array of interests and the involvement of high-level leaders in the administration and Congress. Hillary Rodham Clinton, whose task force drafted the president's plan, is shown at the Capitol briefing reporters after a strategy session with supportive Democratic senators: (from left) Thomas Daschle (S.D.), Paul Wellstone (Minn.), Harris Wofford (Pa.), Edward Kennedy (Mass.), and Majority Leader George Mitchell (Maine).

Domestic Policies

Four types of policies reside within the domestic policy sphere: distributive, redistributive, protective regulatory, and competitive regulatory. Each has its own particular pattern of decision making.

Distributive policies promote desirable private activities by providing government subsidies (not necessarily in the form of cash). The examples of government subsidy programs are legion and include (1) loans and loan guarantees to home buyers, college students, owners of small and some large businesses, and farmers; (2) grants to farmers in the form of price supports, to universities for scientific research, and to state and local governments for housing, community development, education, mass transit, airports, highways, environmental protection, libraries, and health care; (3) income tax deductions for interest paid on home mortgages, local property taxes, and charitable contributions; (4) permits to encourage utilization of public resources for cutting timber, mining, and grazing on public lands at rates below those determined on the open market; and (5) tariffs to protect American products from foreign competition.

Typically, distributive policies are enacted with a minimum of controversy because for such policies there appear to be only winners, no losers. It is a matter of distributing benefits widely while not inflicting any readily apparent harm on others. Thus, when the federal government provides the states with highway grants, all the states (as well as car owners and manufacturers, road contractors, and concrete suppliers) benefit, and the costs are hardly noticeable to the individual taxpayers who ultimately foot the bill.

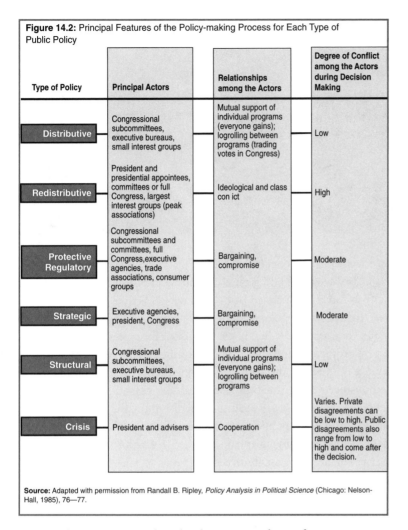

Figure 14.2: Principal Features of the Policy-making Process for Each Type of Public Policy

Type of Policy	Principal Actors	Relationships among the Actors	Degree of Conflict among the Actors during Decision Making
Distributive	Congressional subcommittees, executive bureaus, small interest groups	Mutual support of individual programs (everyone gains); logrolling between programs (trading votes in Congress)	Low
Redistributive	President and presidential appointees, committees or full Congress, largest interest groups (peak associations)	Ideological and class con ict	High
Protective Regulatory	Congressional subcommittees and committees, full Congress, executive agencies, trade associations, consumer groups	Bargaining, compromise	Moderate
Strategic	Executive agencies, president, Congress	Bargaining, compromise	Moderate
Structural	Congressional subcommittees, executive bureaus, small interest groups	Mutual support of individual programs (everyone gains); logrolling between programs	Low
Crisis	President and advisers	Cooperation	Varies. Private disagreements can be low to high. Public disagreements also range from low to high and come after the decision.

Source: Adapted with permission from Randall B. Ripley, *Policy Analysis in Political Science* (Chicago: Nelson-Hall, 1985), 76—77.

Subsidy programs tend to develop a strong base of support among their beneficiaries, program administrators, and interested members of Congress. These mutually beneficial, three-sided alliances have been dubbed "iron triangles" or "subgovernments" (see Chapter 12, The Bureaucracy). One powerful subgovernment dominating veterans policy includes veterans groups (American Legion and Veterans of Foreign Wars), the Department of Veterans Affairs, and the members of the House and Senate Veterans' Affairs Committees. Subgovernments tend to dominate policy making for each subsidy program, as major issues are normally resolved among the interested parties at the congressional subcommittee level. The president and the full House and Senate do not usually play an active role in distributive issues.

Redistributive policies are designed to shift wealth, property rights,

Public housing projects, such as Chicago's Robert Taylor Homes, are examples of a controversial redistributive policy designed to provide decent housing for America's disadvantaged. Robert Taylor Homes is the nation's largest public housing project—a four-mile stretch of high-rise buildings on 95 acres of land and home to 23,000 Chicagoans—mostly African-American families who are very poor, dependent on welfare, and headed by unmarried women.

or other values (access to education, jobs, and government services) among social classes and groups (including racial) in society, and especially to those perceived to be disadvantaged. Unlike distributive policies, redistributive policies have clear winners and losers, and, as a result, they tend to be highly controversial. Examples of these policies are (1) progressive income taxes (where the wealthy pay a higher percentage of their incomes in taxes than the poor); (2) food stamps, public housing, welfare, medical care, legal services, and job training for the poor; (3) prohibitions against racial discrimination in voting, housing, education, and public accommodation, and requirements for affirmative action in employment; and (4) health care for the elderly.

The debate on redistributive issues tends to take on an ideological and class conflict cast, with liberals generally supportive of such programs and conservatives either opposed or giving reluctant assent. Whereas distributive policies are likely to arouse only low-level conflicts that can be resolved in congressional subcommittees, redistributive policies tend to be highly visible, ideological, and partisan. As a result, strong presidential leadership is usually needed to resolve such issues (for example, President Johnson's enthusiastic support for a war on poverty and medical care for the elderly). Redistributive issues also normally receive the attention of the full House and Senate, the executive agencies, and the major interest groups in society.

Since the 1930s and the administration of Franklin Roosevelt, presidents have tended to take the lead in pressing for the redistribution of resources to aid the relatively disadvantaged. But, after the explosion of often controversial redistributive programs in the 1960s and early 1970s, interest in and support for such programs ebbed. In the 1980s the Reagan administration, especially in its tax and budget policies, pursued a

course designed to limit and in some instances curtail previously enacted redistributive programs.[15]

Although the tax, health care, and national service proposals of the
Clinton administration show a redistributive bent, it is useful to remember that American public policy overall has not been strongly
redistributive in character. This reflects the absence of a genuine working-class party in the United States, a relative lack of economic-class
consciousness and militancy among Americans, and a continuing public belief in progress, self-reliance, free enterprise, and limited government. Moreover, because most Americans are not poor, redistributive
policies require, then, the support of middle-class voters.

Once enacted, redistributive policies are difficult to retain as demonstrated by the passage of the Tax Reform Act of 1986. Before enactment
of the 1986 law, the federal income tax was relatively progressive (and
therefore redistributive)—that is, those with higher incomes paid taxes
at a higher rate than those with lower incomes. Tax rates ranged from
14 to 50 percent. The 1986 act reduced the upper rates by providing for
two tax brackets of 15 and 28 percent (with some paying 33 percent).
Although President Clinton forced through Congress a modest increase
for high-income earners in 1993, the income tax no longer is as redistributive in character as it was in 1980. Another significant feature of redistributive policy making in the United States is the tendency, once
programs are enacted, to extend their benefits to people who are not
deprived. President Johnson's Model Cities program, for example, was
designed to target for federal aid the most deprived neighborhoods in a
limited number of cities. Congress, however, altered the program to
permit aid to less-deprived neighborhoods in 150 cities, including small
ones.

Regulatory policies fall into two categories: protective and competitive. *Protective regulatory policies* are designed to protect the public by
specifying the conditions under which various private as well as government activities can take place. When it follows its normal pattern,
Congress legislates broad policy goals (protecting patient rights in
nursing homes, bans on unfair methods of competition or on false and
misleading advertising) but gives few details. It then establishes a regulatory commission or designates some other agency in the bureaucracy
to develop and administer the necessary details. Thus, the Department
of Health and Human Services is responsible for enforcing the 1987 law
setting requirements to improve patient care in nursing homes, and the

15. Ripley and Franklin, *Congress, the Bureaucracy, and Public Policy,* 122–123.

Protective regulatory policies, such as the warning label on cigarette packages, are usually enacted only after intense efforts to exert political influence by the advocates of regulation and their opponents in the affected industry, in this instance, the cigarette manufacturers.

Federal Trade Commission polices business trade and advertising practices. Examples of protective regulatory policy are requirements that banks, savings and loans, credit card companies, and department stores disclose their interest rate charges; high "sin" taxes on such goods as tobacco and alcohol; prohibitions against unfair labor and business practices; penalties for auto manufacturers whose cars do not meet clean air standards; inspection of food processing; safety standards for pharmaceuticals; minimum wage and occupational safety standards; and requirements that government agencies comply with Freedom of Information rules and publish proposed administrative rule changes in advance.

Conflicts over protective regulatory policies are frequent and often bitter because regulations can impose costs on the regulated businesses and restrict their activities. The tobacco industry, for example, has consistently fought against a series of protective regulations, including warning messages on cigarette packages and bans on smoking on domestic airline flights. Not to be outdone, coal strip-mine operators have sought to prevent regulation of their operations and requirements that they restore land after mining it.

Protective regulatory conflicts are rarely resolved at the congressional subcommittee and agency bureau levels; negotiations and bargaining are normally required higher up in the chain of command. Passage of clean air legislation in 1990, for example, required extensive, high-level negotiations among the White House, executive agencies, congressional party and committee leaders, and organized interests.

Competitive regulatory policies limit the number of people or organizations within the economy that can supply a particular good or service. More specifically such policies set the framework within which the government determines who will have the right to provide a good or service. Competitive regulatory policies often allocate scarce resources when it has been determined that free access to the marketplace would be impossible or unworkable. To prevent chaos in the broadcasting industry, for example, the Federal Communications Commission (FCC) allocates the limited number of highly valued radio frequencies and television channels. But in return for obtaining their broadcast licenses, radio and television stations are required to meet standards of public service. In the transportation sector, before the deregulation movement of the 1970s and 1980s, such regulatory agencies as the Interstate Commerce Commission (ICC) and the Civil Aeronautics Board (CAB) were heavily involved in determining which transportation companies would and would not have access to the marketplace. This effort to ensure approved standards of service was carried out by allocating routes to airlines, railroads, barge lines, and truckers.

Because of its technical, complicated nature, decision making in competitive regulatory policy tends to be delegated to such independent regulatory agencies as the FCC. Representatives and senators, however, sometimes intervene to influence individual decisions, and interest groups representing regulated industries are extremely active in this field.

After regulatory policies that substantially restricted access and competition, particularly in transportation and telecommunications, were criticized for hiking prices, distorting the marketplace, and being cumbersome and ineffective, a movement for deregulation took hold in the late 1970s and 1980s. The amount of regulation in the transportation field was then reduced, most notably for the airlines. With the abolition of the CAB and the deregulation of routes and prices, airlines now wage fierce price wars and provide other incentives (such as frequent flyer programs) to win passengers. Deregulation in most modes of transportation and some aspects of communications has meant that positive policy formulation in these areas has diminished in recent years.

The distinction between competitive and protective regulatory policies often becomes blurred in public discussions because agencies playing heavy roles in competitive regulation also are engaged in protective regulation. For example, the FCC not only allocates radio frequencies and television channels but also enforces the "equal time" rules requiring stations that sell time to one candidate to sell it as well to other candidates for the same office. And the ICC has rules to protect consumers who hire moving companies.

Foreign and National Security Policies

The tragedy of the former Yugoslavia with its wars of ethnic cleansing is a painful reminder: there is as yet no international police force waiting in the wings to offer protection when a nation's interests or very existence are threatened. Nations must look after their own security and interests in the international system. American foreign policy, then, provides for this nation's security and protects American interests around the globe. It also advances causes to which the United States is committed such as human rights, remedies for disease and poverty, environmental protection, and economic development. Like domestic policy, foreign and national security policies can be broken down into different types, each with its own distinctive policy-making process.

Strategic policies and programs assert and provide for the implemen-

U.S. troops move out of Somalia in March 1994 after President Clinton ordered their withdrawal when the public and Congress ceased to be willing to pay the price of American lives for maintaining a humanitarian and peacekeeping mission. The Somalia operation thus illustrated the difficult task policy makers face in a world racked by ethnic strife and where the United States is expected to assert leadership in its status as the world's only superpower.

tation of the basic foreign and military stances of the United States toward other nations. Strategic policies deal with, among other things, arms control (the mix of weapons systems and forces to be deployed at home and around the world); alliances (for example, the United States-led alliance to enforce U.N. resolutions calling for an end to Iraq's invasion of Kuwait, or America's role in the North Atlantic Treaty Organization in the aftermath of the cold war); America's position toward countries with records of human rights abuses (such as Haiti and the People's Republic of China); foreign trade (tariffs, import quotas, and export policy); immigration; and foreign aid—who will receive how much of what kind of aid (foreign and military).

Decisions on strategic policy tend to be dominated by the president and the executive agencies, especially the Departments of Defense and State. When dealing with strategic issues, Congress has either supported the administration's requests—such as that by President Bush to use military means to remove Iraq from Kuwait in 1991 and that by President Clinton for technical and economic assistance for the former Soviet Union in 1993—or sought to register a competing point of view without completely depriving the administration of its flexibility—such as the nonbinding resolutions passed by the Senate in the spring of 1994 calling on the president to work through the United Nations to limit the arms embargo against Bosnia so that it could better defend itself from Serbian attacks (the Senate also passed a resolution calling on the United States to lift the arms embargo unilaterally).[16] While usually

16. For an informed series of analyses of presidential-congressional relations in foreign policy making, see Thomas E. Mann, ed., *A Question of Balance: The President, the Congress, and Foreign Policy* (Washington, D.C.: Brookings, 1990).

Military procurement policies, such as production of the F-18 fighter, have a major impact on employment and local economies and, therefore, are the subject of intense lobbying within the executive branch and Congress.

willing to give at least grudging support to most administration strategic policy recommendations, Congress can attach conditions to its support, which can have a substantial impact. In 1974, for example, through the Jackson-Vanik amendment Congress tied expansion of American trade with the Soviet Union to freer emigration policies for Russian Jews. As the cold war thawed in the late 1980s and President Bush looked for ways in 1989 to integrate the Soviet Union into the world economy, this law delayed granting the Soviet Union most-favored-nation trade status.

On occasion, Congress has come into direct conflict with the administration on strategic issues. One dramatic example was the Boland amendments of the 1980s banning military aid to the anti-Sandinista insurgents (contras) in Nicaragua. Attempts by the White House staff during the Reagan administration to circumvent the Boland amendments led to a major administration embarrassment—the Iran-contra affair—and to the criminal conviction (later overturned on appeal) of the president's national security adviser, John Poindexter, for lying to Congress.

Structural policies are concerned primarily with the procurement, deployment, and organization of military personnel and materiel, as well as the organization and maintenance of civilian foreign affairs operations such as the State Department, Agency for International

Development, and the U.S. Information Agency. Structural policies cover such matters as defense procurement of weapons systems and supplies, as well as the specific suppliers to be used; the creation (including their location and size) and closing of military installations; the size, composition, and location of reserve forces; the staffing and compensation for the Departments of Defense and State; and programs to distribute surplus American agricultural products.

Structural policies clearly affect important economic interests within the United States—major defense industry corporations and their unions, localities dependent on defense contracts and military installations for jobs, and farmers whose incomes are affected by whether surplus farm products are distributed abroad.[17] Such policies have their distributive aspects and often call for subsidies. And like domestic distributive policies, structural defense policies are heavily influenced by subgovernments. Defense procurement decisions, for example, tend to be dominated by policy subgovernments composed of Pentagon procurement officials, private sector contractors, subcommittees of the congressional Armed Services and Appropriations committees, and senators and representatives whose states and districts benefit from defense contracts. Reserve forces policy is heavily influenced by the close relationship that exists among the Reserve Officers Association, congressional Armed Services committees, members of Congress who are themselves members of the reserves or have an interest in them, and interested members of the executive branch. This subgovernment has been largely successful in attaining its goals of retaining a large reserve force, generous pay and retirement income, and other benefits.[18]

Crisis policies are made in response to immediate problems that are viewed as serious and demand prompt action. Examples of such policies are the U.S. government's responses to the Japanese attack on Pearl Harbor in 1941, the Soviet imposition of the Berlin blockade in 1949, the erection of the Berlin Wall in 1961, the placement of Soviet offensive missiles in Cuba in 1962, the Iranian seizure of the U.S. embassy in Tehran in 1979, terrorists' seizure of the cruise ship *Achille Lauro* and a TWA airliner in the Middle East in 1985, and Iraq's 1990 invasion of Kuwait. In such crises the principal decision makers are the president and high-level officials of the executive branch, who function with a minimum of publicized conflict. Congressional involvement, in most cases, is limited to briefings by officers of the executive branch and gestures of symbolic support for administration policies.

17. Ripley, *Policy Analysis in Political Science*, 72–73.
18. Ripley and Franklin, *Congress, the Bureaucracy, and Public Policy*, 163–164.

Policy Types and Patterns of Policy Making

The types of public policy just described are not airtight compartments; a government policy can contain elements of more than one type. Military procurement, for example, not only is a structural foreign policy but also has its domestic distributive policy dimensions. These policy types are of value, however, when trying to understand the various policy-making patterns that exist within the political system.

Key to these patterns, of course, are the people who are influential in shaping a policy and who vary from one policy type to another. As mentioned earlier, close-knit subgovernments—congressional subcommittees, agency bureaus, and program beneficiaries—dominate most domestic distributive and structural foreign policy decisions, which are made in an atmosphere largely free of ideological conflict. Because the benefits of governmental largess are distributed widely, there are no apparent losers in these policy processes.

By contrast, redistributive policies are made in an atmosphere charged with intense ideological and partisan conflicts—conflicts that cannot be resolved at the subcommittee level in Congress but must be fought out at a higher level by the president, the full Congress, the heads of executive departments, and the major interest groups.

Protective regulatory policy making is characterized by high levels of conflict and requires the involvement of congressional and executive branch leaders, along with interest groups, whereas competitive regulatory policy, which is highly technical and complicated, tends to be delegated to regulatory agencies, which are subject to pressure from affected interest groups. In strategic, and particularly crisis, foreign policy making, the president and executive branch leaders are the dominant participants.

Assessing the American Political System

Any assessment of the American political system depends in part on which evaluative criteria are being used. Should the American system be judged in terms of how "democratic" it is? In other words, does it permit relatively open participation? Is it responsive to societal concerns? Do citizens have a relatively high degree of control over their leaders? Or should the main concern be whether the policy-making process effectively manages conflict within society and maintains political stability—change without violence? Another basis for evaluation relates to the adequacy of the public policies the system produces—do they adequately provide for freedom, national security, educational opportunities, and economic well-being?

Salient Features of the American Policy-making Process

Before considering these issues, it is useful to recall the features of the political process identified in previous chapters. The American system is characterized by fragmented power. The Constitution's principles of separation of powers and federalism have created numerous power centers within the government. Thus, to formulate, enact, and implement policies, the various branches and levels of government must share power. This fragmentation of power is further encouraged by weak political parties, the procedures and practices of the House and Senate, and the proliferation of organized interest groups. As a result, policy making in the American system is an exercise in coalition politics—building coalitions within and across party lines to pass legislation, building coalitions among interest groups to exert influence on decision makers, and building coalitions between members of the executive and legislative branches of government. Coalition building, of course, takes time and inevitably involves bargaining, negotiation, and compromise before a majority can be created for a new policy. It was, for example, only after months of tortuous and delicate negotiations among a Republican president, senior administration officials, Democratic and Republican congressional party leaders, and influential congressional committee members, that it was possible for the Congress to pass budget legislation for fiscal year 1991. It was no less difficult to enact budget legislation after the problems created by divided party control of the government were eliminated by the 1992 election. President Clinton and his Democratic colleagues in the Congress still had to engage in months of negotiation and bargaining before the budget bill of 1993 could pass both the House and Senate by the narrowest of margins and only with Democratic votes.

With power so fragmented it is possible for interests in control of a critical juncture in the policy process (such as a congressional committee or an agency bureau responsible for carrying out a policy) to virtually veto policy changes until their concerns have been at least partially satisfied. The policies that then emerge from this process, because they are generally compromises forged through coalition building, rarely constitute dramatic changes of direction. Rather, policy change in the United States is usually incremental in character. And because so many officials and interests must either agree or acquiesce before a policy change can occur, delay is commonplace.

The federal budget, which affects virtually every facet of domestic and foreign policy making, is produced through negotiation and bargaining among the leaders of the executive and legislative branches. Shown negotiating a budget deal in August 1993 are Senate Finance Committee Chairman Daniel Patrick Moynihan (D-N.Y.) in the bow tie, and, to his left, House Ways and Means Committee Chairman Daniel Rostenkowski (D-Ill.), House Speaker Thomas Foley (D-Wash.), Senate Majority Leader George Mitchell (D-Maine), and Secretary of the Treasury Lloyd Bentsen.

The Issue of Public Policy Adequacy

The major governance problem of the United States is creating "policies of sufficient coherence, consistency, foresight, and stability that the national welfare is not sacrificed for narrow or temporary gains."[19] Achieving such policies within the American system, however, is extremely difficult because they must be fashioned by four substantially autonomous institutions—the Congress, the presidency, the bureaucracy, and the judiciary—that represent different interests and views of effective government. It is, then, no small wonder that critics of the adequacy of American public policies abound.

Some critics stress the apparent inability of the government to confront and cope with today's problems and injustices. This is a serious matter because certain major problems stand out like festering sores on the body politic. Liberal and conservative critics alike have complained about the steps being taken to deal with the massive federal budget deficit and the government's seeming inability to cope with a wave of violent crime that is terrorizing many neighborhoods. Liberals, especially, have criticized the political process for not developing the social programs needed to deal with homelessness, inadequate housing and education, high rates of unemployment among minority youth, and a health care system characterized by spiraling costs and millions of Americans without access to care. Many conservatives also complain about the inadequacy of government responses to what they see as the salient problems and have advocated stepped-up government activity to limit abortions, curb obscenity, permit prayer in public schools, maintain law and order, and protect traditional values.

19. John E. Chubb and Paul E. Peterson, *Can Government Govern?* (Washington, D.C.: Brookings, 1989), 4.

But while some critics fault the political system for its failure to act and would favor steps making it easier for government to act more decisively, others criticize the government for trying to do too much, interfering unduly in the economic marketplace, and providing services and benefits to virtually every group in society—students, farmers, educators, veterans, the elderly, the poor, industry, homeowners, and environmentalists. It is claimed that the result is "Big Government" and a heavy burden on the taxpayer. Big government, they assert, is virtually impossible to manage; it does little well and is thus ineffective, burdensome, and expensive. These generally conservative critics support measures that they believe would restrain politicians' tendencies to provide benefits to key constituency groups. Among these measures are constitutional amendments to require a balanced federal budget each year and to grant the president a line-item veto—the power to veto specific items in a bill instead of having to either accept or veto the entire bill.

These two evaluations of American policy making—one pointing to the government's lack of responsiveness to major societal problems and the other citing the government's overextension—reflect these two groups' different philosophies about the role of government and their distinctly different views about the government's capacity to deal with societal problems. These philosophies and viewpoints are not easily reconciled.

The issue of public policy adequacy also can be approached from a less philosophical perspective. The delays inevitably involved in the coalition building needed to enact government programs, it is argued, are costly. Indeed, the delays encountered in enacting programs to provide improved and less expensive health care or to rebuild America's aging infrastructure of roads, bridges, and water and sewer systems prevent the nation from profiting from these investments. Even worse, these delays, which are inherent in the system, may cause such problems as urban decay to worsen and therefore become more expensive to remedy.

There is the danger as well that the policies and programs that do emerge from the system of bargaining and compromise will end up being "too little, too late." Yet the patchwork of policies that manage to survive the American process of bargaining, negotiation, and compromise stands a good chance of remaining in force and being accepted by the public because of the broad coalitions required to adopt such policies in the first place. The American process—even with its delays and patchwork character—does seem to contribute to policy stability. Contrast the stability of policies in the United States with that of policies in Great Britain where dramatic policy reversals occur regularly, depending on whether the Conservative party or the Labour party controls the government.[20] For example, the steel industry was nationalized by a Labour government after World War II, denationalized by a Conservative government in 1953, nationalized again by Labour in 1963, and substantially denationalized and restructured by the Conservative government of former prime minister Margaret Thatcher which took office in 1977. Under Thatcher, the Conservatives transformed government policy related to taxation, local government, education, and organized labor. Should Labour replace the Conservatives as the ruling party in the near future, it is expected to modify much that Thatcher's Conservatives did in these areas. By contrast, the American policy process is characterized by greater policy stability. The Republican administration of Dwight Eisenhower (1953–1961), for example, did not repeal the New Deal of the Roosevelt era, nor did the Reagan administration (1981–1989) repeal—although it did modify and in some instances cut back—the major programs of Lyndon Johnson's Great Society. Once a program is enacted in the United States, it tends to become part of a national consensus.

Another possible benefit of the American policy-making process is its ability to manage conflict. With the major exception of the Civil War, political conflict in the United States has been kept within tolerable levels. It is essential, then, that government policies not only respond to society's problems but also be made in a way that does not tear the political system apart. The American governmental system, with its many power centers that together shape policy, does this by allowing competing interests to find supporters within the government, resulting in policies borne of bargaining and compromise. Those policies that do emerge are rarely all that their sponsors sought, nor are they as threatening as their opponents originally feared. Both sides usually can live with the outcome even though they are not satisfied. And both sides have the option of seeking to change the policy at a later date.

Thus, the American policy process is seldom speedy, and its products are rarely clear-cut, final solutions to problems. Rather, as laws passed by Congress illustrate, today's policies are verbal formulae that a majority of the members of Congress "find adequate as a basis for their continuing policy struggle."[21] In the 1990s policy-making processes will

20. Fred I. Greenstein and Frank B. Feigert, *The American Party System and the American People,* 3d ed. (Englewood Cliffs, N.J.: Prentice-Hall, 1985), 155–156.

21. Raymond A. Bauer, Ithiel de Sola Pool, and Lewis Anthony Dexter, *American Business and Public Policy* (New York: Atherton, 1963), 426.

be put to severe tests because of problems created by America's growing vulnerability to economic developments in the rest of the world. Until now, the president and Congress have on the whole managed the major problems of the country with a reasonable degree of effectiveness. But in a world of intensified interdependence, the government will find it a challenge of daunting dimensions to fashion policy-making processes that protect the national interest.

Is the Process Democratic?

Most Americans would probably accept the notion that they live under a democratic political order. But there are also those who believe that to say America is a democracy implies a sort of smug satisfaction with the status quo that does not take into account the government's apparent incapacity to cope with serious problems and injustices. Certainly the overview in this chapter of different types of policies has suggested that redistributive policies, designed to shift wealth and opportunity to the relatively disadvantaged in society, are much more difficult to enact than distributive policies, which bestow government subsidies and largess widely within the country. Indeed, there is even a tendency for the redistributive policies that are in effect to be gradually converted into distributive programs. While acknowledging that injustices do exist and public policies are not necessarily responsive to societal needs, one could still make a strong argument that the American political process is more democratic than many political systems because, in political scientist Nelson Polsby's words, it (1) permits "relatively (but not perfectly) open participation by those possessing requisite skills and interests," (2) it is "relatively (but not perfectly) responsive to the demands of a variety of participants," and (3) it is "run (but not flawlessly) according to a relatively stable and equitable set of rules."[22]

Application of these relativist standards, however, still leaves open the question of the extent to which the system actually meets such standards as the ideal of majority rule. As the chapters dealing with the Constitution, public opinion, interest groups, and Congress have shown, it would be inaccurate to suggest that the majority always decides issues of policy in the United States. But would Americans really want pure majority rule if it resulted in the majority being able to permanently disenfranchise a minority? Or if the winning party in an election rolled up huge majorities but no opposition was tolerated? Or if a majority, which did not really care about an issue, still voted down a proposal that a minority supported fervently? Such a majoritarian sys-

22. Nelson W. Polsby, *Congress and the Presidency,* 4th ed. (Englewood Cliffs, N.J.: Prentice-Hall, 1986), 6–7. This discussion relies heavily on Polsby's insights.

tem would be viewed as "less open, less responsive, less stable, less equitable, and therefore less democratic" than most Americans would find acceptable.[23]

The American federal government, then, does operate in ways that can thwart majority rule.

■ The electoral college system for electing presidents does not give equal weight to each person's vote. Because state electoral votes are allocated among candidates on a winner-take-all basis, a vote in California is worth more than a vote in Wyoming (a vote in California helps to determine the disposition of fifty-four electoral votes, but a vote in Wyoming affects only three electoral votes).

■ Equal representation of the states in the Senate also works to thwart majority rule. Because each state, regardless of the size of its population, has two senators, the senators from the nine least populous states (containing less than 3 percent of the nation's population) can cancel out the votes of the senators from the nine most populous states (containing over 50 percent of the nation's people).

■ Congressional procedures also may prevent the majority from exercising its will. In the Senate a determined minority using the filibuster can prevent the majority from working its will on legislation. And in both chambers committees unrepresentative of the total membership may bottle up legislation and prevent it from reaching the floor for a vote. Furthermore, the modified seniority system used to select committee chairs can elevate to positions of power people who are out of step with both a majority of their party and congressional colleagues.

■ An unelected Supreme Court whose members are appointed for life has the power to interpret the laws passed by Congress and even declare the actions of an elected Congress and president unconstitutional.

■ Unelected bureaucrats engage in major policy making as they implement laws enacted by the people's representatives in Congress sometimes in ways that are at odds with congressional intent.

These majority-thwarting institutions are at least in part responsible for the openness, responsiveness, and stability of the American political system and, therefore, may actually contribute to democracy. But what makes the American system democratic is more complicated than having a few majority-thwarting devices built into the Constitution and government practices. The American system's fragmented power also stems from federalism, separation of powers, a far-flung bureaucracy,

23. Ibid., 7.

multiple centers of congressional power, thousands of organized interests, and decentralized political parties. Fragmented political power has contributed to democracy because "each center of special power is for various reasons responsive to different segments of society."[24] Thus, because many power centers must share in the making of policy, public policies are likely to reflect a variety of societal interests and to constitute compromises among competing power centers that must share in decision making.

What ultimately makes these power centers responsive to various interests, as well as willing to make alliances and admit new participants, are the uncertainties introduced by frequent elections. Although most incumbents win reelection, elections conducted within the context of a competitive party system mean that politicians cannot take their tenure in office for granted. They must be concerned about developing and maintaining an electoral base of support. This requires sensitivity to shifting tides of opinion, the activities of other politicians, and changes in the makeup of one's constituency. Elections may not say precisely what the voters want in terms of public policy, but by electing politicians responsive to different segments of society, the voters do contribute to democracy by keeping the system open and responsive.

Reform the System?

Some political observers recognize the contributions that a policy-making system characterized by extensive negotiation, bargaining, and compromise makes to managing societal conflict, political stability, and democracy, yet they continue to believe that major institutional reforms are required. A group of distinguished and experienced Washington hands, led by President Jimmy Carter's senior White House aide Lloyd Cutler and former undersecretary of state and secretary of the Treasury Douglas Dillon, has come to the conclusion that power in the American system is too fragmented and that the government, especially the president, cannot assemble enough power to carry out the policies needed in these difficult times.[25] This concern was particularly strong in the last days of the Carter administration because of the president's inability to secure congressional approval of his energy program and the SALT II treaty with the Soviets. Their solution to what they see to be insufficient presidential power is the adoption of some version of a parliamentary system so that presidents can muster automatic congressional majorities for what they consider to be desirable, albeit controversial, policies. Of course, constitutional change so far-reaching in character is not like-

24. Ibid., 9.
25. Lloyd N. Cutler, "To Form a Government," *Foreign Affairs* (Fall 1980): 126–130.

ly to occur in the foreseeable future. The issue of whether decision makers can aggregate sufficient power to lead the government and shape its policies is, however, a serious and legitimate question that deserves thoughtful consideration, especially in an era when the thrust of many reform proposals has been to weaken the institutional power bases of party leaders, presidents, and congressional leaders by making the government and party processes more open and participatory.

Maintenance of a democratic government requires an ongoing reassessment of how the system is functioning. But each assessment must be an informed one. It must reflect an understanding of how the governmental system actually operates, attention to its evolving nature, and clarity about the criteria being used for evaluation. In observing the world of politics, one must probe deeply. Indeed, in doing so one might do well to remember the lines from Gilbert and Sullivan's *H.M.S. Pinafore,*

> Things are seldom what they seem,
> Skim milk masquerades as cream.

For Review

---

1. *Public policy* is whatever the government chooses to do or not to do about perceived problems, and *policy making* is how the government decides what will be done about perceived problems.

2. The policy-making process involves a series of stages: agenda setting, formulation and legitimation of policies, policy implementation, and evaluation of policy implementation, performance, and impact.

3. For analytic purposes, public policies can be classified by types. Domestic policies are either distributive, redistributive, protective regulatory, or competitive regulatory, and foreign and national security policies are either strategic, structural, or crisis.

4. Each type of policy is characterized by a particular set of principal participants, distinctive relationships among the participants, and certain levels of conflict during decision making.

5. Because power within the American political system is fragmented, policy making normally is an exercise in coalition building, which involves negotiation, bargaining, and compromise. As a result, in the United States public policy is relatively stable, and policy change is normally incremental.

For Further Reading

Anderson, James E. *Public Policymaking: An Introduction.* 2d ed. Boston: Houghton Mifflin, 1994. An informative overview of the policy-making process.

Birnbaum, Jeffrey H., and Alan S. Murray. *Showdown at Gucci Gulch*. New York: Random House, 1987. A lively, fascinating account of the passage of the Tax Reform Act of 1986 by two reporters who covered the action.

Jones, Charles O. *An Introduction to the Study of Public Policy*. 3d ed. Monterey, Calif.: Brooks/Cole, 1984. A concise, insightful consideration of the forces shaping the development of public policy.

Kennedy, Robert F. *Thirteen Days: A Memoir of the Cuban Missile Crisis*. New York: Norton, 1969. An insider's account of a dramatic instance of foreign policy making in a crisis.

Kettl, Donald F. *Government by Proxy: (Mis?)Managing Federal Programs*. Washington, D.C.: CQ Press, 1988. A probing analysis of the consequences of using third parties to implement federal programs.

Kingdon, John W. *Agendas, Alternatives, and Public Policies*. Boston: Little, Brown, 1984. An analysis of how issues find their way onto the public agenda.

Mann, Thomas E., ed. *A Question of Balance: The President, the Congress, and Foreign Policy*. Washington, D.C.: Brookings, 1990. A series of analyses focusing on balancing presidential and congressional influence in foreign policy making.

Meier, Kenneth J. *Politics and the Bureaucracy: Policymaking in the Fourth Branch of Government*. Pacific Grove, Calif.: Brooks/Cole, 1993. An insightful analysis of the role of the bureaucracy in policy making.

Mezey, Michael L. *Congress, the President, and Public Policy*. Boulder, Colo.: Westview Press, 1989. An analysis of the capacity of Congress and the president to produce sound public policy.

Polsby, Nelson W. *Political Innovation in America*. New Haven: Yale University Press, 1984. An explanation of how the government instituted eight major policy innovations.

Ripley, Randall B., and Grace A. Franklin. *Congress, the Bureaucracy, and Public Policy*. 5th ed. Pacific Grove, Calif.: Brooks/Cole, 1991. An analysis of how public policy is made in different policy arenas.

Schick, Allen. *The Federal Budget, 1994-95: Politics, Policy, Process*. Washington, D.C.: Brookings, 1994. A guide to the federal budget process dealing with three elements of budget strategy: political tactics and relationships, policy objectives pursued through the budget, and the rules governing congressional and presidential action.

Spanier, John W. *American Foreign Policy since World War II*. 12th ed. rev. Washington, D.C.: CQ Press, 1992. A historical survey of American foreign policy making since 1945.

Appendix

Glossary

Index

Photo Credits

Declaration of Independence

In Congress, July 4, 1776

The Unanimous Declaration of the Thirteen United States of America

When in the Course of human events, it becomes necessary for one people to dissolve the political bands which have connected them with another, and to assume among the Powers of the earth, the separate and equal station to which the Laws of Nature and of Nature's God entitle them, a decent respect to the opinions of mankind requires that they should declare the causes which impel them to the separation. We hold these truths to be self-evident, that all men are created equal, that they are endowed by their Creator with certain unalienable Rights, that among these are Life, Liberty and the pursuit of Happiness. That to secure these rights, Governments are instituted among Men, deriving their just powers from the consent of the governed. That whenever any form of Government becomes destructive of these ends, it is the Right of the People to alter or to abolish it, and to institute new Government, laying its foundation on such principles and organizing its powers in such form, as to them shall seem most likely to effect their Safety and Happiness. Prudence, indeed, will dictate that Government long established should not be changed for light and transient causes; and accordingly all experience hath shown, that mankind are more disposed to suffer, while evils are sufferable, than to right themselves by abolishing the forms to which they are accustomed. But when a long train of abuses and usurpations, pursuing invariably the same Object evinces a design to reduce them under absolute Despotism, it is their right, it is their duty, to throw off such Government, and to provide new Guards for their future security.—Such has been the patient sufferance of these Colonies; and such is now the necessity which constrains them to alter their former Systems of Government. The history of the present King of Great Britain is a history of repeated injuries and usurpations, all having in direct object the establishment of an absolute Tyranny over these States. To prove this, let Facts be submitted to a candid world. He has refused his Assent to Laws, the most wholesome and necessary for the public good. He has forbidden his Governors to pass Laws of immediate and pressing importance, unless suspended in their operation till his Assent should be obtained; and when so suspended, he has utterly neglected to attend to them.

He has refused to pass other Laws for the accommodation of large districts of people, unless those people would relinquish the right of Representation in the Legislature, a right inestimable to them and formidable to tyrants only.

He has called together legislative bodies at places unusual, uncomfortable, and distant from the depository of their Public Records, for the sole purpose of fatiguing them into compliance with his measures.

He has dissolved Representative Houses repeatedly, for opposing with manly firmness his invasions on the rights of the people.

He has refused for a long time, after such dissolutions, to cause others to be elected; whereby the Legislative Powers, incapable of Annihilation, have returned to the People at large for their exercise; the State remaining in the mean time exposed to all the dangers of invasion from without, and convulsions within.

He has endeavored to prevent the population of these States; for that purpose obstructing the Laws of Naturalization of Foreigners; refusing to pass others to encourage their migration hither, and raising the conditions of new Appropriations of Lands.

He has obstructed the Administration of Justice, by refusing his Assent to Laws for establishing Judiciary Powers.

He has made Judges dependent on his Will alone, for the tenure of their offices, and the amount and payment of their salaries.

He has erected a multitude of New Offices, and sent hither swarms of Officers to harass our People, and eat out their substance.

He has kept among us, in times of peace, Standing Armies without the Consent of our legislature.

He has affected to render the Military independent of and superior to the Civil Power.

He has combined with others to subject us to a jurisdiction foreign to our constitution, and unacknowledged by our laws; giving his Assent to their acts of pretended legislation:

For quartering large bodies of armed troops among us:

For protecting them, by a mock Trial, from Punishment for any Murders which they should commit on the Inhabitants of these States:

For cutting off our Trade with all parts of the world:

For imposing taxes on us without our Consent:

For depriving us in many cases, of the benefits of Trial by Jury:

For transporting us beyond Seas to be tried for pretended offences:

For abolishing the free System of English Laws in a neighbouring Province, establishing therein an Arbitrary government, and enlarging its Boundaries so as to render it at once an example and fit instrument for introducing the same absolute rule into these Colonies:

For taking away our Charters, abolishing our most valuable Laws, and altering fundamentally the Forms of our Governments:

For suspending our own Legislature, and declaring themselves invested with Power to legislate for us in all cases whatsoever.

He has abdicated Government here, by declaring us out of his Protection and waging War against us.

He has plundered our seas, ravaged our Coasts, burnt our towns, and destroyed the lives of our people.

He is at this time transporting large armies of foreign mercenaries to compleat the works of death, desolation and tyranny, already begun with circumstances of Cruelty & perfidy scarcely paralleled in the most barbarous ages, and totally unworthy the Head of a civilized nation.

He has constrained our fellow Citizens taken Captive on the high Seas to bear Arms against their Country, to become the executioners of their friends and Brethren, or to fall themselves by their Hands.

He has excited domestic insurrections amongst us, and has endeavoured to bring on the inhabitants of our frontiers, the merciless Indian Savages, whose known rule of warfare, is an undistinguished destruction of all ages, sexes and conditions.

In every stage of these Oppressions We have Petitioned for Redress in the most humble terms: Our repeated Petitions have been answered only by repeated injury. A Prince, whose character is thus marked by every act which may define a Tyrant, is unfit to be the ruler of a free People.

Nor have We been wanting in attention to our British brethren. We have warned them from time to time of attempts by their legislature to extend an unwarrantable jurisdiction over us. We have reminded them of the circumstances of our emigration and settlement here. We have appealed to their native justice and magnanimity, and we have conjured them by the ties of our common kindred to disavow these usurpations, which would inevitably interrupt our connections and correspondence. They too have been deaf to the voice of justice and of consanguinity. We must, therefore, acquiesce in the necessity, which denounces our Separation, and hold them, as we hold the rest of mankind, Enemies in War, in Peace Friends.

We, therefore, the Representatives of the United States of America, in General Congress, Assembled, appealing to the Supreme Judge of the world for the declaration of independence rectitude of our intentions, do, in the Name, and by Authority of the good People of these Colonies, solemnly publish and declare, That these United Colonies are, and of Right ought to be Free and Independent States; that they are Absolved from all Allegiance to the British Crown, and that all political connection between them and the State of Great Britain, is and ought to be totally dissolved; and that as Free and Independent States, they have full Power to levy War, conclude Peace, contract Alliances, establish Commerce, and to do all other Acts and Things which Independent States may of right do. And for the support of this Declaration, with a firm reliance on the Protection of Divine Providence, we mutually pledge to each other our Lives, our Fortunes and our sacred Honor.

John Hancock

New Hampshire:
Josiah Bartlett,
William Whipple,
Matthew Thornton.

Massachusetts-Bay:
Samuel Adams,
John Adams,
Robert Treat Paine,
Elbridge Gerry.

Rhode Island:
Stephen Hopkins,
William Ellery.

Connecticut:
Roger Sherman,
Samuel Huntington,
William Williams,
Oliver Wolcott.

New York:
William Floyd,
Philip Livingston,
Francis Lewis,
Lewis Morris.

Pennsylvania:
Robert Morris,
Benjamin Harris,
Benjamin Franklin,
John Morton,
George Clymer,
James Smith,
George Taylor,
James Wilson,
George Ross.

Delaware:
Caesar Rodney,
George Read,
Thomas McKean.

Georgia:
Button Gwinnett,
Lyman Hall,
George Walton.

Maryland:
Samuel Chase,
William Paca,
Thomas Stone,
Charles Carroll
  of Carrollton.

Virginia:
George Wythe,
Richard Henry Lee,
Thomas Jefferson,
Benjamin Harrison,
Thomas Nelson Jr.,
Francis Lightfoot Lee,
Carter Braxton.

North Carolina:
William Hooper,
Joseph Hewes,
John Penn.

South Carolina:
Edward Rutledge,
Thomas Heyward Jr.,
Thomas Lynch Jr.,
Arthur Middleton.

New Jersey:
Richard Stockton,
John Witherspoon,
Francis Hopkinson,
John Hart,
Abraham Clark.

Federalist No. 10

Among the numerous advantages promised by a well-constructed Union, none deserves to be more accurately developed than its tendency to break and control the violence of faction. The friend of popular governments never finds himself so much alarmed for their character and fate, as when he contemplates their propensity to this dangerous vice. He will not fail, therefore, to set a due value on any plan which, without violating the principles to which he is attached, provides a proper cure for it. The instability, injustice, and confusion introduced into the public councils, have, in truth, been the mortal diseases under which popular governments have everywhere perished; as they continue to be the favorite and fruitful topics from which the adversaries to liberty derive their most specious declamations. The valuable improvements made by the American constitutions on the popular models, both ancient and modern, cannot certainly be too much admired; but it would be an unwarrantable partiality, to contend that they have as effectually obviated the danger on this side, as was wished and expected. Complaints are everywhere heard from our most considerate and virtuous citizens, equally the friends of public and private faith, and of public and personal liberty, that our governments are too unstable, that the public good is disregarded in the conflicts of rival parties, and that measures are too often decided, not according to the rules of justice and the rights of the minor party, but by the superior force of an interested and overbearing majority. However anxiously we may wish that these complaints had no foundation, the evidence of known facts will not permit us to deny that they are in some degree true. It will be found, indeed, on a candid review of our situation, that some of the distresses under which we labor have been erroneously charged on the operation of our governments; but it will be found, at the same time, that other causes will not alone account for many of our heaviest misfortunes; and, particularly, for that prevailing and increasing distrust of public engagements, and alarm for private rights, which are echoed from one end of the continent to the other. These must be chiefly, if not wholly, effects of the unsteadiness and injustice with which a factious spirit has tainted our public administrations. By a faction, I understand a number of citizens,

whether amounting to a majority or minority of the whole, who are united and actuated by some common impulse of passion, or of interest, adverse to the rights of other citizens, or to the permanent and aggregate interests of the community. There are two methods of curing the mischiefs of faction: the one, by removing its causes; the other, by controlling its effects. There are again two methods of removing the causes of faction: the one, by destroying the liberty which is essential to its existence; the other, by giving to every citizen the same opinions, the same passions, and the same interests. It could never be more truly said than of the first remedy, that it was worse than the disease. Liberty is to faction what air is to fire, an aliment without which it instantly expires. But it could not be less folly to abolish liberty, which is essential to political life, because it nourishes faction, than it would be to wish the annihilation of air, which is essential to animal life, because it imparts to fire its destructive agency.

The second expedient is as impracticable as the first would be unwise. As long as the reason of man continues fallible, and he is at liberty to exercise it, different opinions will be formed. As long as the connection subsists between his reason and his self-love, his opinions and his passions will have a reciprocal influence on each other; and the former will be objects to which the latter will attach themselves. The diversity in the faculties of men, from which the rights of property originate, is not less an insuperable obstacle to a uniformity of interests. The protection of these faculties is the first object of government. From the protection of different and unequal faculties of acquiring property, the possession of different degrees and kinds of property immediately results; and from the influence of these on the sentiments and views of the respective proprietors, ensues a division of the society into different interests and parties.

The latent causes of faction are thus sown in the nature of man; and we see them everywhere brought into different degrees of activity, according to the different circumstances of civil society. A zeal for different opinions concerning religion, concerning government, and many other points, as well of speculation as of practice; an attachment to different leaders ambitiously contending for pre-eminence and power; or to persons of other descriptions whose fortunes have been interesting to the human passions, have, in turn, divided mankind into parties, inflamed them with mutual animosity, and rendered them much more disposed to vex and oppress each other than to co-operate for their common good. So strong is this propensity of mankind to fall into mutual animosities, that where no substantial occasion presents itself, the most frivolous and fanciful distinctions have been sufficient to kindle their unfriendly passions and excite their most violent conflicts. But the most common and durable source of factions has been the various and unequal distribution of property. Those who hold and those who are without property have ever formed distinct interests in society. Those who are creditors, and those who are debtors, fall under a like discrimination. A landed interest, a manufacturing interest, a mercantile interest, a moneyed interest, and many lesser interests, grow up of necessity in civilized nations, and divide them into different classes, actuated by different sentiments and views. The regulation of these various and interfering interests forms the principal task of modern legislation, and involves the spirit of party and faction in the necessary and ordinary operations of the government.

No man is allowed to be a judge in his own cause, because his interest would certainly bias his judgment, and, not improbably, corrupt his integrity. With equal, nay with greater reason, a body of men are unfit to be both judges and parties at the same time; yet what are many of the most important acts of legislation, but so many judicial determinations, not indeed concerning the rights of single persons, but concerning the rights of large bodies of citizens? And what are the different classes of legislators but advocates and parties to the causes which they determine? Is a law proposed concerning private debts? It is a question to which the creditors are parties on one side and the debtors on the other. Justice ought to hold the balance between them. Yet the parties are, and must be themselves the judges; and the most numerous party, or, in other words, the most powerful faction must be expected to prevail. Shall domestic manufactures be encouraged, and in what degree, by restrictions on foreign manufactures? are questions which would be differently decided by the landed and the manufacturing classes, and probably by neither with a sole regard to justice and the public good. The apportionment of taxes on the various descriptions of property is an act which seems to require the most exact impartiality; yet there is, perhaps, no legislative act in which greater opportunity and temptation are given to a predominant party to trample on the rules of justice. Every shilling with which they overburden the inferior number, is a shilling saved to their own pockets.

It is in vain to say that enlightened statesmen will be able to adjust these clashing interests, and render them all subservient to the public good. Enlightened statesmen will not always be at the helm. Nor, in many cases, can such an adjustment be made at all without taking into view indirect and remote considerations, which will rarely prevail over the immediate interest which one party may find in disregarding the rights of another or the good of the whole.

The inference to which we are brought is, that the *causes* of faction cannot be removed, and that relief is only to be sought in the means of controlling its *effects*.

If a faction consists of less than a majority, relief is supplied by the republican principle, which enables the majority to defeat its sinister views by regular vote. It may clog the administration, it may convulse the society; but it will be unable to execute and mask its violence under the forms of the Constitution. When a majority is included in a faction, the form of popular government, on the other hand, enables it to sacrifice to its ruling passion or interest both the public good and the rights of other citizens. To secure the public good and private rights against the danger of such a faction, and at the same time to preserve the spirit and the form of popular government, is then the great object to which our inquiries are directed. Let me add that it is the great desideratum by which this form of government can be rescued from the opprobrium under which it has so long labored, and be recommended to the esteem and adoption of mankind.

By what means is this object attainable? Evidently by one of two only. Either the existence of the same passion or interest in a majority at the same time must be prevented, or the majority, having such coexistent passion or interest, must be rendered, by their number and local situation, unable to concert and carry into effect schemes of oppression. If the impulse and the opportunity be suffered to coincide, we well know that neither moral nor religious motives can be relied on as an adequate control. They are not found to be such on the injustice and violence of individuals, and lose their efficacy in proportion to the number combined together, that is, in proportion as their efficacy becomes needful.

From this view of the subject it may be concluded that a pure democracy, by which I mean a society consisting of a small number of citizens, who assemble and administer the government in person, can admit of no cure for the mischiefs of faction. A common passion or interest will, in almost every case, be felt by a majority of the whole; a communication and concert result from the form of government itself; and there is nothing to check the inducements to sacrifice the weaker party or an obnoxious individual. Hence it is that such democracies have ever been spectacles of turbulence and contention; have ever been found incompatible with personal security or the rights of property; and have in general been as short in their lives as they have been violent in their deaths. Theoretic politicians, who have patronized this species of government, have erroneously supposed that by reducing mankind to a perfect equality in their political rights, they would, at the same time, be perfectly equalized and assimilated in their possessions, their opinions, and their passions.

A republic, by which I mean a government in which the scheme of representation takes place, opens a different prospect, and promises the cure for which we are seeking. Let us examine the points in which it varies from pure democracy, and we shall comprehend both the nature of the cure and the efficacy which it must derive from the Union.

The two great points of difference between a democracy and a republic are: first, the delegation of the government, in the latter, to a small number of citizens elected by the rest; secondly, the greater number of citizens, and greater sphere of country, over which the latter may be extended.

The effect of the first difference is, on the one hand, to refine and enlarge the public views, by passing them through the medium of a chosen body of citizens, whose wisdom may best discern the true interest of their country, and whose patriotism and love of justice will be least likely to sacrifice it to temporary or partial considerations. Under such a regulation, it may well happen that the public voice, pronounced by the representatives of the people, will be more consonant to the public good than if pronounced by the people themselves, convened for the purpose. On the other hand, the effect may be inverted. Men of fractious tempers, of local prejudices, or of sinister designs, may, by intrigue, by corruption, or by other means, first obtain the suffrages, and then betray the interests, of the people. The question resulting is, whether small or extensive republics are more favorable to the election of proper guardians of the public weal; and it is clearly decided in favor of the latter by two obvious considerations:

In the first place, it is to be remarked that, however small the republic may be, the representatives must be raised to a certain number, in order to guard against the cabals of a few; and that, however large it may be, they must be limited to a certain number, in order to guard against the confusion of a multitude. Hence, the number of representatives in the two cases not being in proportion to that of the two constituents, and being proportionally greater in the small republic, it follows that, if the proportion of fit characters be not less in the large than in the small republic, the former will present a greater option, and consequently a greater probability of a fit choice.

In the next place, as each representative will be chosen by a greater number of citizens in the large than in the small republic, it will be more difficult for unworthy candidates to practise with success the vicious arts by which elections are too often carried; and the suffrages of the people being more free, will be more likely to centre in men who possess the most attractive merit and the most diffusive and established characters.

It must be confessed that in this, as in most other cases, there is a mean, on both sides of which inconveniences will be found to lie. By enlarging too much the number of electors, you render the representatives too little acquainted with all their local circumstances and lesser interests; as by reducing it too much, you render him unduly attached to these, and too little fit to comprehend and pursue great and national objects. This federal Constitution forms a happy combination in this respect; the great and aggregate interests being referred to the national, the local and particular to the State legislatures.

The other point of difference is, the greater number of citizens and extent of territory which may be brought within the compass of republican than of democratic government; and it is this circumstance principally which renders factious combinations less to be dreaded in the former than in the latter. The smaller the society, the fewer probably will be the distinct parties and interests composing it; the fewer the distinct parties and interests, the more frequently will a majority be found of the same party; and the smaller the number of individuals composing a majority, and the smaller the compass within which they are placed, the more easily will they concert and execute their plans of oppression. Extend the sphere, and you take in a greater variety of parties and interests; you make it less probable that a majority of the whole will have a common motive to invade the rights of other citizens; or if such a common motive exists, it will be more difficult for all who feel it to discover their own strength, and to act in unison with each other. Besides other impediments, it may be remarked that, where there is a consciousness of unjust or dishonorable purposes, communication is always checked by distrust in proportion to the number whose concurrence is necessary.

Hence, it clearly appears, that the same advantage which a republic has over a democracy, in controlling the effects of faction, is enjoyed by a large over a small republic,—is enjoyed by the Union over the States composing it. Does the advantage consist in the substitution of representatives whose enlightened views and virtuous sentiments render them superior to local prejudices and to schemes of injustice? It will not be denied that the representation of the Union will be most likely to possess these requisite endowments. Does it consist in the greater security afforded by a greater variety of parties, against the event of any one party being able to outnumber and oppress the rest? In an equal degree does the increased variety of parties comprised within the Union, increase this security. Does it, in fine, consist in the greater obstacles opposed to the concert and accomplishment of the secret wishes of an unjust and interested majority? Here, again, the extent of the Union gives it the most palpable advantage.

The influence of factious leaders may kindle a flame within their particular States, but will be unable to spread a general conflagration through the other States. A religious sect may degenerate into a political faction in a part of the Confederacy; but the variety of sects dispersed over the entire face of it must secure the national councils against any danger from that source. A rage for paper money, for an abolition of debts, for an equal division of property, or for any other improper or wicked project, will be less apt to pervade the whole body of the Union than a particular member of it; in the same proportion as such a malady is more likely to taint a particular country or district, than an entire State.

In the extent and proper structure of the Union, therefore, we behold a republican remedy for the disease most incident to republican government. And according to the degree of pleasure and pride we feel in being republicans, ought to be our zeal in cherishing the spirit and supporting the character of Federalists.

Federalist No. 51

To what expedient, then, shall we finally resort, for maintaining in practice the necessary partition of power among the several departments, as laid down in the Constitution? The only answer that can be given is, that as all these exterior provisions are found to be inadequate, the defect must be supplied, by so contriving the interior structure of the government as that its several constituent parts may, by their mutual relations, be the means of keeping each other in their proper places. Without presuming to undertake a full development of this important idea, I will hazard a few general observations, which may perhaps place it in a clearer light, and enable us to form a more correct judgment of the principles and structure of the government planned by the convention. In order to lay a due foundation for that separate and distinct exercise of the different powers of government, which to a certain extent is admitted on all hands to be essential to the preservation of liberty, it is evident that each department should have a will of its own; and consequently should be so constituted that the members of each should have as little agency as possible in the appointment of the members of the others. Were this principle rigorously adhered to, it would require that all the appointments for the supreme executive, legislative, and judiciary magistracies should be drawn from the same fountain of authority, the people, through channels having no communication whatever with one another. Perhaps such a plan of constructing the several departments would be less difficult in practice than it may in contemplation appear. Some difficulties, however, and some additional expense would attend the execution of it. Some deviations, therefore, from the principle must be admitted. In the constitution of the judiciary department in particular, it might be inexpedient to insist rigorously on the principle: first, because peculiar qualifications being essential in the members, the primary consideration ought to be to select that mode of choice which best secures these qualifications; secondly, because the permanent tenure by which the appointments are held in that department, must soon destroy all sense of dependence on the authority conferring them. It is equally evident, that the members of each department should be as little dependent as possible on those of the others, for the emoluments

annexed to their offices. Were the executive magistrate, or the judges, not independent of the legislature in this particular, their independence in every other would be merely nominal. But the great security against a gradual concentration of the several powers in the same department, consists in giving to those who administer each department the necessary constitutional means and personal motives to resist encroachments of the others. The provision for defence must in this, as in all other cases, be made commensurate to the danger of attack. Ambition must be made to counteract ambition. The interest of the man must be connected with the constitutional rights of the place. It may be a reflection on human nature, that such devices should be necessary to control the abuses of government. But what is government itself, but the greatest of all reflections on human nature? If men were angels, no government would be necessary. If angels were to govern men, neither external nor internal controls on government would be necessary. In framing a government which is to be administered by men over men, the great difficulty lies in this: you must first enable the government to control the governed; and in the next place oblige it to control itself. A dependence on the people is, no doubt, the primary control on the government; but experience has taught mankind the necessity of auxiliary precautions.

This policy of supplying, by opposite and rival interests, the defect of better motives, might be traced through the whole system of human affairs, private as well as public. We see it particularly displayed in all the subordinate distributions of power, where the constant aim is to divide and arrange the several offices in such a manner as that each may be a check on the other—that the private interest of every individual may be a sentinel over the public rights. These inventions of prudence cannot be less requisite in the distribution of the supreme powers of the State.

But it is not possible to give to each department an equal power of self-defence. In republican government, the legislative authority necessarily predominates. The remedy for this inconveniency is to divide the legislature into different branches; and to render them, by different modes of election and different principles of action, as little connected with each other as the nature of their common functions and their common dependence on the society will admit. It may even be necessary to guard against dangerous encroachments by still further precautions. As the weight of the legislative authority requires that it should be thus divided, the weakness of the executive may require, on the other hand, that it should be fortified. An absolute negative on the legislature appears, at first view, to be the natural defence with which the executive magistrate should be armed. But perhaps it would be neither altogether safe nor alone sufficient. On ordinary occasions it might not be exerted with the requisite firmness, and on extraordinary occasions it might be perfidiously abused. May not this defect of an absolute negative be supplied by some qualified connection between this weaker department and the weaker branch of the stronger department, by which the latter may be led to support the constitutional rights of the former, without being too much detached from the rights of its own department?

If the principles on which these observations are founded be just, as I persuade myself they are, and they be applied as a criterion to the several State constitutions, and to the federal Constitution, it will be found that if the latter does not perfectly correspond with them, the former are infinitely less able to bear such a test.

There are, moreover, two considerations particularly applicable to the federal system of America, which place that system in a very interesting point of view.

First. In a single republic, all the power surrendered by the people is submitted to the administration of a single government; and the usurpations are guarded against by a division of the government into distinct and separate departments. In the compound republic of America, the power surrendered by the people is first divided between two distinct governments, and then the portion allotted to each subdivided among distinct and separate departments. Hence a double security arises to the rights of the people. The different governments will control each other, at the same time that each will be controlled by itself.

Second. It is of great importance in a republic not only to guard the society against the oppression of its rulers, but to guard one part of the society against the injustice of the other part. Different interests necessarily exist in different classes of citizens. If a majority be united by a common interest, the rights of the minority will be insecure. There are but two methods of providing against this evil: the one by creating a will in the community independent of the majority—that is, of the society itself; the other, by comprehending in the society so many separate descriptions of citizens as will render an unjust combination of a majority of the whole very improbable, if not impracticable. The first method prevails in all governments possessing an hereditary or self-appointed authori-

ty. This, at best, is but a precarious security; because a power independent of the society may as well espouse the unjust views of the major, as the rightful interests of the minor party, and may possibly be turned against both parties. The second method will be exemplified in the federal republic of the United States. Whilst all authority in it will be derived from and dependent on the society, the society itself will be broken into so many parts, interests and classes of citizens, that the rights of individuals, or of the minority, will be in little danger from interested combinations of the majority. In a free government the security for civil rights must be the same as that for religious rights. It consists in the one case in the multiplicity of interests, and in the other in the multiplicity of sects. The degree of security in both cases will depend on the number of interests and sects; and this may be presumed to depend on the extent of country and number of people comprehended under the same government. This view of the subject must particularly recommend a proper federal system to all the sincere and considerate friends of republican government, since it shows that in exact proportion as the territory of the Union may be formed into more circumscribed Confederacies, or States, oppressive combinations of a majority will be facilitated; the best security, under the republican forms, for the rights of every class of citizens, will be diminished; and consequently the stability and independence of some member of the government, the only other security, must be proportionally increased. Justice is the end of government. It is the end of civil society. It ever has been and ever will be pursued until it be obtained, or until liberty be lost in the pursuit. In a society under the forms of which the stronger faction can readily unite and oppress the weaker, anarchy may as truly be said to reign as in a state of nature, where the weaker individual is not secured against the violence of the stronger; and as, in the latter state, even the stronger individuals are prompted, by the uncertainty of their condition, to submit to a government which may protect the weak as well as themselves; so, in the former state, will the more powerful factions or parties be gradually induced, by a like motive, to wish for a government which will protect all parties, the weaker as well as the more powerful. It can be little doubted that if the State of Rhode Island was separated from the Confederacy and left to itself, the insecurity of rights under the popular form of government within such narrow limits would be displayed by such reiterated oppressions of factious majorities that some power altogether independent of the people would soon be called for by the voice of the very factions whose misrule had proved the necessity of it. In the extended republic of the United States, and among the great variety of interests, parties, and sects which it embraces, a coalition of a majority of the whole society could seldom take place on any other principles than those of justice and the general good; whilst there being thus less danger to a minor from the will of a major party, there must be less pretext, also, to provide for the security of the former, by introducing into the government a will not dependent on the latter, or, in other words, a will independent of the society itself. It is no less certain than it is important, notwithstanding the contrary opinions which have been entertained, that the larger the society, provided it lie within a practical sphere, the more duly capable it will be of self-government. And happily for the *republican cause,* the practicable sphere may be carried to a very great extent, by a judicious modification and mixture of the *federal principle.*

Constitution of the United States

We the People of the United States, in Order to form a more perfect Union, establish Justice, insure domestic Tranquility, provide for the common defence, promote the general Welfare, and secure the Blessings of Liberty to ourselves and our Posterity, do ordain and establish this Constitution for the United States of America.

Article I

SECTION 1. All legislative Powers herein granted shall be vested in a Congress of the United States, which shall consist of a Senate and House of Representatives.

SECTION 2. The House of Representatives shall be composed of Members chosen every second Year by the People of the several States, and the Electors in each State shall have the Qualifications requisite for Electors of the most numerous Branch of the State Legislature. No Person shall be a Representative who shall not have attained to the age of twenty five Years, and been seven Years a Citizen of the United States, and who shall not, when elected, be an Inhabitant of that State in which he shall be chosen. [Representatives and direct Taxes shall be apportioned among the several States which may be included within this Union, according to their respective Numbers, which shall be determined by adding to the whole Number of free Persons, including those bound to Service for a Term of Years, and excluding Indians not taxed, three fifths of all other Persons.][1] The actual Enumeration shall be made within three Years after the first Meeting of the Congress of the United States, and within every subsequent Term of ten Years, in such Manner as they shall by Law direct. The Number of Representatives shall not exceed one for every thirty Thousand, but each State shall have at Least one Representative; and until such enumeration shall be made, the State of New Hampshire shall be entitled to chuse three, Massachusetts eight, Rhode-Island and Providence Plantations one, Connecticut five, New-York six, New Jersey four, Pennsylvania eight, Delaware one, Maryland six, Virginia ten, North Carolina five, South Carolina five, and Georgia three. When vacancies happen in the Representation from any State, the Executive Authority thereof shall issue Writs of Election to fill such Vacancies. The House of Representatives shall chuse their Speaker and other Officers; and shall have the sole Power of Impeachment.

SECTION 3. The Senate of the United States shall be composed of two Senators from each State, [chosen by the Legislature thereof,][2] for six Years; and each Senator shall have one Vote.

Immediately after they shall be assembled in Consequence of the first Election, they shall be divided as equally as may be into three Classes. The Seats of the Senators of the first Class shall be vacated at the Expiration of the second Year, of the second Class at the Expiration of the fourth Year, and of the third Class at the Expiration of the sixth Year, so that one third may be chosen every second Year; [and if Vacancies happen by Resignation, or otherwise, during the Recess of the Legislature of any State, the Executive thereof may make temporary Appointments until the next Meeting of the Legislature, which shall then fill such Vacancies.][3]

No Person shall be a Senator who shall not have attained to the Age of thirty Years, and been nine Years a Citizen of the United States, and who shall not, when elected, be an Inhabitant of that State for which he shall be chosen.

The Vice President of the United States shall be President of the Senate, but shall have no Vote, unless they be equally divided.

The Senate shall chuse their other Officers, and also a President pro tempore, in the Absence of the Vice President, or when he shall exercise the Office of President of the United States.

The Senate shall have the sole Power to try all Impeachments. When sitting for that Purpose, they shall be on Oath or Affirmation. When the President of the United States is tried the Chief Justice shall preside: And no Person shall be convicted without the Concurrence of two thirds of the Members present.

Judgment in Cases of Impeachment shall not extend further than to removal from Office, and disqualification to hold and enjoy any Office of honor, Trust or Profit under the United States: but the Party convicted shall nevertheless be liable and subject to Indictment, Trial, Judgment and Punishment, according to Law.

SECTION 4. The Times, Places and Manner of holding Elections for Senators and Representatives, shall be prescribed in each State by the Legislature thereof; but the Congress may at any time by Law make or alter such Regulations, except as to the Places of chusing Senators.

The Congress shall assemble at least once in every Year, and such Meeting shall [be on the first Monday in December],[4] unless they shall by Law appoint a different Day.

SECTION 5. Each House shall be the Judge of the Elections, Returns and Qualifications of its own Members, and a Majority of each shall constitute a Quorum to do Business; but a smaller Number may adjourn from day to day, and may be authorized to compel the Attendance of absent Members, in such Manner, and under such Penalties as each House may provide.

Each House may determine the Rules of its Proceedings, punish its Members for disorderly Behaviour, and, with the Concurrence of two thirds, expel a Member.

Each House shall keep a Journal of its Proceedings, and from time to time publish the same, excepting such Parts as may in their Judgment require Secrecy; and the Yeas and Nays of the Members of either House on any question shall, at the Desire of one fifth of those Present, be entered on the Journal.

Neither House, during the Session of Congress, shall, without the Consent of the other, adjourn for more than three days, nor to any other Place than that in which the two Houses shall be sitting.

SECTION 6. The Senators and Representatives shall receive a Compensation for their Services, to be ascertained by Law, and paid out of the Treasury of the United States. They shall in all Cases, except Treason, Felony and Breach of the Peace, be privileged from Arrest during their Attendance at the Session of their respective Houses, and in going to and returning from the same; and for any Speech or Debate in either House, they shall not be questioned in any other Place.

No Senator or Representative shall, during the Time for which he was elected, be appointed to any civil Office under the Authority of the United States, which shall have been created, or the Emoluments whereof shall have been encreased during such time; and no Person holding any Office under the United States, shall be a Member of either House during his Continuance in Office.

SECTION 7. All Bills for raising Revenue shall originate in the House of Representatives; but the Senate may propose or concur with amendments as on other Bills.

Every Bill which shall have passed the House of Representatives and the Senate, shall, before it become a Law, be presented to the President of the United States; If he approve he shall sign it, but if not he shall return it, with his Objections to that House in which it shall have originated, who shall enter the Objections at large on their Journal, and proceed to reconsider it. If after such Reconsideration two thirds of that House shall agree to pass the Bill, it shall be sent, together with the Objections, to the other House, by which it shall likewise be reconsidered, and if approved by two thirds of that House, it shall become a Law. But in all such Cases the Votes of both Houses shall be determined by yeas and Nays, and the Names of the Persons voting for and against the Bill shall be entered on the Journal of each House respectively. If any Bill shall not be returned by the President within ten Days (Sundays excepted) after it shall have been presented to him, the Same shall be a Law, in like Manner as if he had signed it, unless the Congress by their Adjournment prevent its Return, in which Case it shall not be a Law.

Every Order, Resolution, or Vote to which the Concurrence of the Senate and House of Representatives may be necessary (except on a question of Adjournment) shall be presented to the President of the United States; and before the Same shall take Effect, shall be approved by him, or being disapproved by him, shall be repassed by two thirds of the Senate and House of Representatives, according to the Rules and Limitations prescribed in the Case of a Bill.

SECTION 8. The Congress shall have Power To lay and collect Taxes, Duties, Imposts and Excises, to pay the Debts and provide for the common Defence and general Welfare of the United States; but all Duties, Imposts and Excises shall be uniform throughout the United States;

To borrow Money on the credit of the United States;

To regulate Commerce with foreign Nations, and among the several States, and with the Indian Tribes;

To establish an uniform Rule of Naturalization, and uniform Laws on the subject of Bankruptcies throughout the United States;

To coin Money, regulate the Value thereof, and of foreign Coin, and fix the Standard of Weights and Measures;

To provide for the Punishment of counterfeiting the Securities and current Coin of the United States;

To establish Post Offices and post Roads;

To promote the Progress of Science and useful Arts, by securing for limited Times to Authors and Inventors the exclusive Right to their respective Writings and Discoveries;

To constitute Tribunals inferior to the supreme Court;

To define and punish Piracies and Felonies commited on the high Seas, and Offences against the Law of Nations;

To declare War, grant Letters of Marque and Reprisal,

and make Rules concerning Captures on Land and Water;

To raise and support Armies, but no Appropriation of Money to that Use shall be for a longer Term than two Years;

To provide and maintain a Navy;

To make Rules for the Government and Regulation of the land and naval Forces;

To provide for calling forth the Militia to execute the Laws of the Union, suppress Insurrections and repel Invasions;

To provide for organizing, arming, and disciplining, the Militia, and for governing such Part of them as may be employed in the Service of the United States, reserving to the States respectively, the Appointment of the Officers, and the Authority of training the Militia according to the discipline prescribed by Congress;

To exercise exclusive Legislation in all Cases whatsoever, over such District (not exceeding ten Miles square) as may, by Cession of Particular States, and the Acceptance of Congress, become the Seat of the Government of the United States, and to exercise like Authority over all Places purchased by the Consent of the Legislature of the State in which the Same shall be, for the Erection of Forts, Magazines, Arsenals, dock-Yards, and other needful Buildings;—And

To make all Laws which shall be necessary and proper for carrying into Execution the foregoing Powers, and all other Powers vested by this Constitution in the Government of the United States, or in any Department or Officer thereof.

SECTION 9. The Migration or Importation of such Persons as any of the States now existing shall think proper to admit, shall not be prohibited by the Congress prior to the Year one thousand eight hundred and eight, but a Tax or duty may be imposed on such Importation, not exceeding ten dollars for each Person.

The Privilege of the Writ of Habeas Corpus shall not be suspended, unless when in Cases of Rebellion or Invasion the public Safety may require it.

No Bill of Attainder or ex post facto Law shall be passed.

No capitation, or other direct, Tax shall be laid, unless in Proportion to the Census of Enumeration herein before directed to be taken.[5]

No Tax or Duty shall be laid on Articles exported from any State.

No Preference shall be given by any Regulation of Commerce or Revenue to the Ports of one State over those of another; nor shall Vessels bound to, or from, one State, be obliged to enter, clear or pay Duties in another.

No Money shall be drawn from the Treasury, but in Consequence of Appropriations made by Law; and a regular Statement and Account of the Receipts and Expenditures of all public Money shall be published from time to time.

No Title of Nobility shall be granted by the United States: And no Person holding any Office of Profit or Trust under them, shall, without the Consent of the Congress, accept of any present, Emolument, Office, or Title, of any kind whatever, from any King, Prince or foreign State.

SECTION 10. No State shall enter into any Treaty, Alliance, or Confederation; grant Letters of Marque and Reprisal; coin Money; emit Bills of Credit; make any Thing but gold and silver Coin a Tender in Payment of Debts; pass any Bill of Attainder, ex post facto Law, or Law impairing the Obligation of Contracts, or grant any Title of Nobility.

No State shall, without the Consent of the Congress, lay any Imposts or Duties on Imports or Exports, except what may be absolutely necessary for executing its inspection Laws: and the net Produce of all Duties and Imposts, laid by any State on Imports or Exports, shall be for the Use of the Treasury of the United States; and all such Laws shall be subject to the Revision and Controul of the Congress.

No State shall, without the Consent of Congress, lay any Duty of Tonnage, keep Troops, or Ships of War in time of Peace, enter into any Agreement or Compact with another State, or with a foreign Power, or engage in War, unless actually invaded, or in such imminent Danger as will not admit of delay.

Article II

SECTION 1. The executive Power shall be vested in a President of the United States of America. He shall hold his Office during the Term of four Years, and, together with the Vice President, chosen for the same Term, be elected, as follows.

Each State shall appoint, in such Manner as the Legislature thereof may direct, a Number of Electors, equal to the whole Number of Senators and Representatives to which the State may be entitled in the Congress: but no Senator or Representative, or Person holding an Office of Trust or Profit under the United States, shall be appointed an Elector.

[The Electors shall meet in their respective States, and vote by Ballot for two Persons, of whom one at least shall not be an Inhabitant of the same State with themselves. And they shall make a List of all the Persons voted for, and of the Number of Votes for each; which List they shall sign and certify, and transmit sealed to the Seat of the Government of the United States, directed to the President of the Senate. The President of the Senate shall, in the Presence of the Senate and House of Representatives, open all the Certificates, and the Votes shall then be counted. The Person having the greatest Number of Votes shall be the President, if such Number be a Majority of the whole Number of Electors appointed; and if there be more than one who have such Majority, and have an equal Number of Votes, then the House of Representatives shall immediately chuse by Ballot one of them for President; and if no Person have a Majority, then from the five highest on the list the said House shall in like Manner chuse the President. But in chusing the President, the Votes shall be taken by States, the Representation from each State having one Vote; a quorum for this Purpose shall consist of a Member or Members from two thirds of the States, and a Majority of all the States shall be necessary to a Choice. In every Case, after the Choice of the President, the Person having the greatest Number of Votes of the Electors shall be the Vice President. But if there should remain two or more who have equal Votes, the Senate shall chuse from them by Ballot the Vice President.][6]

The Congress may determine the Time of chusing the Electors, and the Day on which they shall give their Votes; which Day shall be the same throughout the United States.

No Person except a natural born Citizen, or a Citizen of the United States, at the time of the Adoption of this Constitution, shall be eligible to the Office of President; neither shall any Person be eligible to that Office who shall not have attained to the Age of thirty five Years, and been fourteen Years a Resident within the United States.

In Case of the Removal of the President from Office, or of his Death, Resignation, or Inability to discharge the Powers and Duties of the said Office,[7] the Same shall devolve on the Vice President, and the Congress may by Law provide for the Case of Removal, Death, Resignation or Inability, both of the President and Vice President, declaring what Officer shall then act as President, and such Officer shall act accordingly, until the Disability be removed, or a President shall be elected.

The President shall, at stated Times, receive for his Services, a Compensation, which shall neither be encreased nor diminished during the Period for which he shall have been elected, and he shall not receive within that Period any other Emolument from the United States, or any of them.

Before he enter on the Execution of his Office, he shall take the following Oath or Affirmation:—"I do solemnly swear (or affirm) that I will faithfully execute the Office of President of the United States, and will to the best of my Ability, preserve, protect and defend the Constitution of the United States."

SECTION 2. The President shall be Commander in Chief of the Army and Navy of the United States, and of the Militia of the several States, when called into the actual Service of the United States; he may require the Opinion, in writing, of the principal Officer in each of the executive Departments, upon any Subject relating to the Duties of their respective Offices, and he shall have Power to grant Reprieves and Pardons for Offenses against the United States, except in Cases of Impeachment.

He shall have Power, by and with the Advice and Consent of the Senate, to make Treaties, provided two thirds of the Senators present concur; and he shall nominate, and by and with the Advice and Consent of the Senate, shall appoint Ambassadors, other public Ministers and Consuls, Judges of the supreme Court, and all other Officers of the United States, whose Appointments are not herein otherwise provided for, and which shall be established by Law: but the Congress may by Law vest the Appointment of such inferior Officers, as they think proper, in the President alone, in the Courts of Law, or in the Heads of Departments.

The President shall have Power to fill up all Vacancies that may happen during the Recess of the Senate, by granting Commissions which shall expire at the End of their next Session.

SECTION 3. He shall from time to time give to the Congress Information of the State of the Union, and recommend to their Consideration such Measures as he shall judge necessary and expedient; he may, on extraordinary Occasions, convene both Houses, or either of them, and in Case of Disagreement between them, with Respect to the Time of Adjournment, he may adjourn them to such Time as he shall think proper; he shall receive Ambassadors and other public Ministers; he shall take Care that the Laws be faithfully executed, and shall Commission all the Officers of the United States.

SECTION 4. The President, Vice President and all Civil Officers of the United States, shall be removed from office on Impeachment for, and Conviction of, Treason, Bribery, or other high Crimes and Misdemeanors.

Article III

SECTION 1. The judicial Power of the United States, shall be vested in one supreme Court, and in such inferior Courts as the Congress may from time to time ordain and establish. The Judges, both of the supreme and inferior Courts, shall hold their Offices during good Behaviour, and shall, at stated Times, receive for their Services, a Compensation, which shall not be diminished during their Continuance in Office.

SECTION 2. The judicial Power shall extend to all Cases, in Law and Equity, arising under this Constitution, the Laws of the United States, and Treaties made, or which shall be made, under their Authority;—to all Cases affecting Ambassadors, other public Ministers and Consuls;—to all Cases of admiralty and maritime Jurisdiction;—to Controversies to which the United States shall be a Party;—to Controversies between two or more States;—between a State and Citizens of another State;[8]—between Citizens of different States;—between Citizens of the same State claiming Lands under Grants of different States, and between a State, or the Citizens thereof, and foreign States, Citizens or Subjects.[8]

In all Cases affecting Ambassadors, other public Ministers and Consuls, and those in which a State shall be Party, the supreme Court shall have original Jurisdiction. In all the other Cases before mentioned, the supreme Court shall have appellate Jurisdiction, both as to Law and Fact, with such Exceptions, and under such Regulations as the Congress shall make.

The Trial of all Crimes, except in cases of Impeachment, shall be by Jury; and such Trial shall be held in the State where the said Crimes shall have been committed; but when not committed within any State, the Trial shall be at such Place or Places as the Congress may by Law have directed.

SECTION 3. Treason against the United States, shall consist only in levying War against them, or in adhering to their Enemies, giving them Aid and Comfort. No Person shall be convicted of Treason unless on the Testimony of two Witnesses to the same overt Act, or on Confession in open Court.

The Congress shall have Power to declare the Punishment of Treason, but no Attainder of Treason shall work Corruption of Blood, or Forfeiture except during the Life of the Person attainted.

Article IV

SECTION 1. Full Faith and Credit shall be given in each State to the public Acts, Records, and judicial Proceedings of every other State. And the Congress may by general Laws prescribe the Manner in which such Acts, Records and Proceedings shall be proved, and the Effect thereof.

SECTION 2. The Citizens of each State shall be entitled to all Privileges and Immunities of Citizens in the several States.

A Person charged in any State with Treason, Felony, or other Crime, who shall flee from Justice, and be found in another State, shall on Demand of the executive Authority of the State from which he fled, be delivered up, to be removed to the State having Jurisdiction of the Crime.

[No Person held to Service or Labour in one State, under the Laws thereof, escaping into another, shall, in Consequence of any Law or Regulation therein, be discharged from such Service or Labour, but shall be delivered up on Claim of the Party to whom such Service or Labour may be due.][9]

SECTION 3. New States may be admitted by the Congress into this Union; but no new State shall be formed or erected within the Jurisdiction of any other State; nor any State be formed by the Junction of two or more States, or Parts of States, without the Consent of the Legislatures of the States concerned as well as of the Congress.

The Congress shall have Power to dispose of and make all needful Rules and Regulations respecting the Territory or other Property belonging to the United States; and nothing in this Constitution shall be so construed as to Prejudice any Claims of the United States, or of any particular State.

SECTION 4. The United States shall guarantee to every State in this Union a Republican Form of Government, and shall protect each of them against Invasion; and on Application of the Legislature, or of the Executive (when the Legislature cannot be convened) against domestic Violence.

Article V

The Congress, whenever two thirds of both Houses shall deem it necessary, shall propose Amendments to this Constitution, or, on the Application of the Legislatures of two thirds of the several States, shall call a Convention for proposing Amendments, which, in either Case, shall be valid to all Intents and Purposes, as Part of this Constitution, when ratified by the Legislatures of three fourths of the several States, or by Conventions in three fourths thereof, as the one or the other Mode of Ratification may be proposed by the Congress; Provided [that no Amendment which may be made prior to the Year One thousand eight hundred and eight shall in any Manner affect the first and fourth Clauses in the Ninth Section of the first Article; and][10] that no State, without its Consent, shall be deprived of its equal Suffrage in the Senate.

Article VI

All Debts contracted and Engagements entered into, before the Adoption of this Constitution, shall be as valid against the United States under this Constitution, as under the Confederation.

This Constitution, and the Laws of the United States which shall be made in Pursuance thereof; and all Treaties made, or which shall be made, under the Authority of the United States, shall be the supreme Law of the Land; and the Judges in every State shall be bound thereby, any Thing in the Constitution or Laws of any State to the Contrary notwithstanding.

The Senators and Representatives before mentioned, and the Members of the several State Legislatures, and all executive and judicial Officers, both of the United States and of the several States, shall be bound by Oath or Affirmation, to support this Constitution; but no religious Test shall ever be required as a Qualification to any Office or public Trust under the United States.

Article VII

The Ratification of the Conventions of nine States, shall be sufficient for the Establishment of this Constitution between the States so ratifying the Same. Done in Convention by the Unanimous Consent of the States present the-Seventeenth Day of September in the Year of our Lord one thousand seven hundred and Eighty seven and of the Independence of the United States of America the Twelfth. In witness whereof We have hereunto subscribed our Names, George Washington, President and deputy from Virginia.

New Hampshire:
John Langdon,
Nicholas Gilman.

Massachusetts:
Nathaniel Gorham,
Rufus King.

Connecticut:
William Samuel Johnson,
Roger Sherman.

New York:
Alexander Hamilton.

New Jersey:
William Livingston,
David Brearley,
William Paterson,
Jonathan Dayton.

Pennsylvania:
Benjamin Franklin,
Thomas Mifflin,
Robert Morris,
George Clymer,
Thomas FitzSimons,
Jared Ingersoll,
James Wilson,
Gouverneur Morris.

Delaware:
George Read,
Gunning Bedford Jr.,
John Dickinson,
Richard Bassett,
Jacob Broom.

Maryland:
James McHenry,
Daniel of St. Thomas
Jenifer,
Daniel Carroll.

Virginia:
John Blair,
James Madison Jr.

North Carolina:
William Blount,
Richard Dobbs Spaight,
Hugh Williamson.

South Carolina:
John Rutledge,
Charles Cotesworth
Pinckney,
Charles Pinckney,
Pierce Butler.

Georgia:
William Few,
Abraham Baldwin.

[The language of the original Constitution, not including the Amendments, was adopted by a convention of the states on Sept. 17, 1787, and was subsequently ratified by the states on the following dates: Delaware, Dec. 7, 1787; Pennsylvania, Dec. 12, 1787; New Jersey, Dec. 18, 1787; Georgia, Jan. 2, 1788; Connecticut, Jan. 9, 1788; Massachusetts, Feb. 6, 1788; Maryland, April 28, 1788; South Carolina, May 23, 1788; New Hampshire, June 21, 1788.

Ratification was completed on June 21, 1788.

The Constitution subsequently was ratified by Virginia, June 25, 1788; New York, July 26, 1788; North Carolina, Nov. 21, 1789; Rhode Island, May 29, 1790; and Vermont, Jan. 10, 1791.]

Amendments

Amendment I

(First ten amendments ratified December 15, 1791.)

Congress shall make no law respecting an establishment of religion, or prohibiting the free exercise thereof; or abridging the freedom of speech, or of the press; or the right of the people peaceably to assemble, and to petition the Government for a redress of grievances.

Amendment II

A well regulated Militia, being necessary to the security of a free State, the right of the people to keep and bear Arms, shall not be infringed.

Amendment III

No Soldier shall, in time of peace be quartered in any house, without the consent of the Owner, nor in time of war, but in a manner to be prescribed by law.

Amendment IV

The right of the people to be secure in their persons, houses, papers, and effects, against unreasonable searches and seizures, shall not be violated, and no Warrants shall issue, but upon probable cause, supported by Oath or affirmation, and particularly describing the place to be searched, and the persons or things to be seized.

Amendment V

No person shall be held to answer for a capital, or otherwise infamous crime, unless on a presentment or indictment of a Grand Jury, except in cases arising in the land or naval forces, or in the Militia, when in actual service in time of War or public danger; nor shall any person be subject for the same offence to be twice put in jeopardy of life or limb; nor shall be compelled in any criminal case to be a witness against himself, nor be deprived of life, liberty, or property, without due process of law; nor shall private property be taken for public use, without just compensation.

Amendment VI

In all criminal prosecutions, the accused shall enjoy the right to a speedy and public trial, by an impartial jury of the State and district wherein the crime shall have been committed, which district shall have been previously ascertained by law, and to be informed of the nature and cause of the accusation; to be confronted with the witnesses against him; to have compulsory process for obtaining witnesses in his favor, and to have the Assistance of Counsel for his defence.

Amendment VII

In Suits at common law, where the value in controversy shall exceed twenty dollars, the right of trial by jury shall be preserved, and no fact tried by a jury, shall be otherwise re-examined in any Court of the United States, than according to the rules of the common law.

Amendment VIII

Excessive bail shall not be required, nor excessive fines imposed, nor cruel and unusual punishments inflicted.

Amendment IX

The enumeration in the Constitution, of certain rights, shall not be construed to deny or disparage others retained by the people.

Amendment X

The powers not delegated to the United States by the Constitution, nor prohibited by it to the States, are reserved to the States respectively, or to the people.

Amendment XI *(Ratified February 7, 1795)*

The Judicial power of the United States shall not be construed to extend to any suit in law or equity, commenced or prosecuted against one of the United States by Citizens of another State, or by Citizens or Subjects of any Foreign State.

Amendment XII- *(Ratified June 15, 1804)*

The Electors shall meet in their respective states and vote by ballot for President and Vice-President, one of whom, at least, shall not be an inhabitant of the same state with themselves; they shall name in their ballots the person voted for as President, and in distinct ballots the person voted for as Vice-President, and they shall make distinct lists of all persons voted for as President, and of all persons voted for as Vice-President, and of the number of votes for each, which lists they shall sign and certify, and transmit sealed to the seat of the government of the United States, directed to the President of the Senate;—The President of the Senate shall, in the presence of the Senate and House of Representatives, open all the certificates and the votes shall then be counted;—The person having the greatest number of votes for President, shall be the President, if such number be a majority of the whole number of Electors appointed; and if no person have such majority, then from the persons having the highest numbers not exceeding three on the list of those voted for as President, the House of Representatives shall choose immediately, by ballot, the President. But in choosing the President, the votes shall be taken by states, the representation from each state having one vote; a quorum for this purpose shall consist of a member or members from two-thirds of the states, and a majority of all the states shall be necessary to a choice. [And if the House of Representatives shall not choose a President whenever the right of choice shall devolve upon them, before the fourth day of March next following, then the Vice-President shall act as President, as in the case of the death or other constitutional disability of the President—][11] The person having the greatest number of votes as Vice-President, shall be the Vice-President, if such number be a majority of the whole number of Electors appointed, and if no person have a majority, then from the two highest numbers on the list, the Senate shall choose the Vice-President; a quorum for the purpose shall consist of two-thirds of the whole number of Senators, and a majority of the whole number shall be necessary to a choice. But no person constitutionally ineligible to the office of President shall be eligible to that of Vice-President of the United States.

Amendment XIII *(Ratified December 6, 1865)*

SECTION I. Neither slavery nor involuntary servitude, except as a punishment for crime whereof the party shall have been duly convicted, shall exist within the United States, or any place subject to their jurisdiction.

SECTION 2. Congress shall have power to enforce this article by appropriate legislation.

Amendment XIV *(Ratified July 9, 1868)*

SECTION 1. All persons born or naturalized in the United States and subject to the jurisdiction thereof, are citizens of the United States and of the State wherein they reside. No State shall make or enforce any law which shall abridge the privileges or immunities of citizens of the United States; nor shall any State deprive any person of life, liberty, or property, without due process of law; nor deny to any person within its jurisdiction the equal protection of the laws.

SECTION 2. Representatives shall be apportioned among the several States according to their respective numbers, counting the whole number of persons in each State, excluding Indians not taxed. But when the right to vote at any election for the choice of electors for President and Vice President of the United States, Representatives in Congress, the Executive and Judicial officers of a State, or the members of the Legislature thereof, is denied to any of the male inhabitants of such State, being twenty-one years of age,[12] and citizens of the United States, or in any way abridged, except for participation in rebellion, or other crime, the basis of representation therein shall be reduced in the proportion which the number of such male citizens shall bear to the whole number of male citizens twenty-one years of age in such State.

SECTION 3. No person shall be a Senator or Representative in Congress, or elector of President and Vice President, or hold any office, civil or military, under the United States, or under any State, who, having previously taken an oath, as a member of Congress, or as an officer of the United States, or as a member of any State legislature, or as an executive or judicial officer of any State, to support the Constitution of the United States, shall have engaged in insurrection or rebellion against the same, or given aid or comfort to the enemies thereof. But Congress may by a vote of two-thirds of each House, remove such disability.

SECTION 4. The validity of the public debt of the United States, authorized by law, including debts incurred for payment of pensions and bounties for services in suppressing insurrection or rebellion, shall not be questioned. But neither the United States nor any State shall assume or pay any debt or obligation incurred in aid of insurrection or rebellion against the United States, or any claim for the loss or emancipation of any slave; but all such debts, obligations and claims shall be held illegal and void.

SECTION 5. The Congress shall have power to enforce, by appropriate legislation, the provisions of this article.

Amendment XV (Ratified February 3, 1870)

SECTION 1. The right of citizens of the United States to vote shall not be denied or abridged by the United States or by any State on account of race, color, or previous condition of servitude.

SECTION 2. The Congress shall have power to enforce this article by appropriate legislation.

Amendment XVI (Ratified February 3, 1913)

The Congress shall have power to lay and collect taxes on incomes, from whatever source derived, without apportionment among the several States, and without regard to any census or enumeration.

Amendment XVII (Ratified April 8, 1913)

The Senate of the United States shall be composed of two Senators from each State, elected by the people thereof, for six years; and each Senator shall have one vote. The electors in each State shall have the qualifications requisite for electors of the most numerous branch of the State legislatures.

When vacancies happen in the representation of any State in the Senate, the executive authority of such State shall issue writs of election to fill such vacancies: Provided, That the legislature of any State may empower the executive thereof to make temporary appointments until the people fill the vacancies by election as the legislature may direct.

This amendment shall not be so construed as to affect the election or term of any Senator chosen before it becomes valid as part of the Constitution.

Amendment XVIII (Ratified January 16, 1919)

SECTION 1. After one year from the ratification of this article the manufacture, sale, or transportation of intoxicating liquors within, the importation thereof into, or the exportation thereof from the United States and all territory subject to the jurisdiction thereof for beverage purposes is hereby prohibited.

SECTION 2. The Congress and the several States shall have concurrent power to enforce this article by appropriate legislation.

SECTION 3. This article shall be inoperative unless it shall have been ratified as an amendment to the Constitution by the legislatures of the several States, as provided in the Constitution, within seven years from the date of the submission hereof to the States by the Congress.[13]

Amendment XIX (Ratified August 18, 1920)

The right of citizens of the United States to vote shall not be denied or abridged by the United States or by any State on account of sex.

Congress shall have power to enforce this article by appropriate legislation.

Amendment XX (Ratified January 23, 1933)

SECTION 1. The terms of the President and Vice President shall end at noon on the 20th day of January, and the terms of Senators and Representatives at noon on the 3d day of January, of the years in which such terms would have ended if this article had not been ratified; and the terms of their successors shall then begin.

SECTION 2. The Congress shall assemble at least once in every year, and such meeting shall begin at noon on the 3d day of January, unless they shall by law appoint a different day.

SECTION 3.[14] If, at the time fixed for the beginning of the term of the President, the President elect shall have died, the Vice President elect shall become President. If a President shall not have been chosen before the time fixed for the beginning of his term, or if the President elect shall have failed to qualify, then the Vice President elect shall act as President until a President shall have qualified; and the Congress may by law provide for the case wherein neither a President elect nor a Vice President elect shall have qualified, declaring who shall then act as President, or the manner in which one who is to act shall be selected, and such person shall act accordingly until a President or Vice President shall have qualified.

SECTION 4. The Congress may by law provide for the case of the death of any of the persons from whom the House of Representatives may choose a President whenever the right of choice shall have devolved upon them, and for the case of the death of any of the persons from whom the Senate may choose a Vice President whenever the right of choice shall have devolved upon them.

SECTION 5. Sections 1 and 2 shall take effect on the 15th day of October following the ratification of this article.

SECTION 6. This article shall be inoperative unless it shall have been ratified as an amendment to the Constitution by the legislatures of three-fourths of the several States within seven years from the date of its submission.

Amendment XXI (Ratified December 5, 1933)

SECTION 1. The eighteenth article of amendment to the Constitution of the United States is hereby repealed.

SECTION 2. The transportation or importation into any State, Territory or possession of the United States for delivery or use therein of intoxicating liquors, in violation of the laws thereof, is hereby prohibited.

SECTION 3. This article shall be inoperative unless it shall have been ratified as an amendment to the Constitution by conventions in the several States, as provided in the Constitution, within seven years from the date of the submission hereof to the States by the Congress.

Amendment XXII (Ratified February 27, 1951)

SECTION 1. No person shall be elected to the office of the President more than twice, and no person who has held the office of President, or acted as President, for more than two years of a term to which some other person was elected President shall be elected to the office of the President more than once. But this Article shall not apply to any person holding the office of President when this Article was proposed by the Congress, and shall not prevent any person who may be holding the office of President, or acting as President, during the term within which this Article becomes operative from holding the office of President or acting as President during the remainder of such term.

SECTION 2. This Article shall be inoperative unless it shall have been ratified as an amendment to the Constitution by the legislatures of three-fourths of the several States within seven years from the date of its submission to the States by the Congress.

Amendment XXIII (Ratified March 29, 1961)

SECTION 1. The District constituting the seat of Government of the United States shall appoint in such manner as the Congress may direct:

A number of electors of President and Vice President equal to the whole number of Senators and Representatives in Congress to which the District would be entitled if it were a State, but in no event more than the least populous State; they shall be in addition to those appointed by the States, but they shall be considered, for the purposes of the election of President and Vice President, to be electors appointed by a State; and they shall meet in the District and perform such duties as provided by the twelfth article of amendment.

SECTION 2. The Congress shall have power to enforce this article by appropriate legislation.

Amendment XXIV (Ratified January 23, 1964)

SECTION 1. The right of citizens of the United States to vote in any primary or other election for President or Vice President, for electors for President or Vice President, or for Senator or Representative in Congress, shall not be denied or abridged by the United States or any State by reason of failure to pay any poll tax or other tax.

SECTION 2. The Congress shall have power to enforce this article by appropriate legislation.

Amendment XXV (Ratified February 10, 1967)

SECTION 1. In case of the removal of the President from office or of his death or resignation, the Vice President shall become President.

SECTION 2. Whenever there is a vacancy in the office of the Vice President, the President shall nominate a Vice President who shall take office upon confirmation by a majority vote of both Houses of Congress.

SECTION 3. Whenever the President transmits to the President pro tempore of the Senate and the Speaker of the House of Representatives his written declaration that he is unable to discharge the powers and duties of his office, and until he transmits to them a written declaration to the contrary, such powers and duties shall be discharged by the Vice President as Acting President.

SECTION 4. Whenever the Vice President and a majority of either the principal officers of the executive departments or of such other body as Congress may by law provide, transmit to the President pro tempore of the Senate and the Speaker of the House of Representatives their written declaration that the President is unable to discharge the powers and duties of his office, the Vice President shall immediately assume the powers and duties of the office as Acting President.

Thereafter, when the President transmits to the President pro tempore of the Senate and the Speaker of the House of Representatives his written declaration that no inability exists, he shall resume the powers and duties of his office unless the Vice President and a majority of either the principal officers of the executive department or of such other body as Congress may by law provide, transmit within four days to the President pro tempore of the Senate and the Speaker of the House of Representatives their written declaration that the President is unable to discharge the powers and duties of his office. Thereupon Congress shall decide the issue, assembling within forty-eight hours for that purpose if not in session. If the Congress, within twenty-one days after receipt of the latter written declaration, or, if Congress is not in session, within twenty-one days after Congress is required to assemble, determines by two-thirds vote of both houses that the President is unable to discharge the powers and duties of his office, the Vice President shall continue to discharge the same as Acting President; otherwise, the President shall resume the powers and duties of his office.

Amendment XXVI (Ratified July 1, 1971)
SECTION 1 The right of citizens of the United States, who are eighteen years of age or older, to vote shall not be denied or abridged by the United States or by any State on account of age.

SECTION 2. The Congress shall have power to enforce this article by appropriate legislation.

Amendment XXVII (Ratified May 7, 1992)
No law varying the compensation for the services of the Senators and Representatives shall take effect, until an election of Representatives shall have intervened.

Notes

1. The part in brackets was changed by section 2 of the Fourteenth Amendment.

2. The part in brackets was changed by section 1 of the Seventeenth Amendment.

3. The part in brackets was changed by the second paragraph of the Seventeenth amendment.

4. The part in brackets was changed by section 2 of the Twentieth Amendment.

5. The Sixteenth Amendment gave Congress the power to tax incomes.

6. The material in brackets has been superseded by the Twelfth Amendment.

7. This provision has been affected by the Twenty-fifth Amendment.

8. These clauses were affected by the Eleventh Amendment.

9. This paragraph has been superseded by the Thirteenth Amendment.

10. Obsolete.

11. The part in brackets has been superseded by section 3 of the Twentieth Amendment.

12. See the Twenty-sixth Amendment.

13. This Amendment was repealed by section 1 of the Twenty-first Amendment.

14. See the Twenty-fifth Amendment.

SOURCE: *United States Government Manual, 1993–94* (Washington, D.C.: Government Printing Office, 1993), 5–20.

Tables

Table A-1 Summary of Presidential Elections, 1952–1992

Year	No. of states	Candidates Dem.	Candidates Rep.	Electoral vote Dem.	Electoral vote Rep.	Popular vote Dem.	Popular vote Rep.
1952	48	Adlai E. Stevenson II John J. Sparkman	Dwight D. Eisenhower Richard M. Nixon	89	442	27,314,649 44.4%	33,936,137 55.1%
1956[a]	48	Adlai E. Stevenson II Estes Kefauver	Dwight D. Eisenhower Richard M. Nixon	73	457	26,030,172 42.0%	35,585,245 57.4%
1960[b]	50	John F. Kennedy Lyndon B. Johnson	Richard M. Nixon Henry Cabot Lodge	303	219	34,221,344 49.7%	34,106,671 49.5%
1964	50*	Lyndon B. Johnson Hubert H. Humphrey	Barry Goldwater William E. Miller	486	52	43,126,584 61.1%	27,177,838 38.5%
1968[c]	50*	Hubert H. Humphrey Edmund S. Muskie	Richard M. Nixon Spiro T. Agnew	191	301	31,274,503 42.7%	31,785,148 43.4%
1972[d]	50*	George McGovern Sargent Shriver	Richard M. Nixon Spiro T. Agnew	17	520	29,171,791 37.5%	47,170,179 60.7%
1976[e]	50*	Jimmy Carter Walter F. Mondale	Gerald R. Ford Robert Dole	297	240	40,830,763 50.1%	39,147,793 48.0%
1980	50*	Jimmy Carter Walter F. Mondale	Ronald Reagan George Bush	49	489	35,483,883 41.0%	43,904,153 50.7%
1984	50*	Walter F. Mondale Geraldine Ferraro	Ronald Reagan George Bush	13	525	37,577,185 40.6%	54,455,075 58.8%
1988[f]	50*	Michael S. Dukakis Lloyd Bentsen	George Bush Dan Quayle	111	426	41,809,083 45.6%	48,886,097 53.4%
1992	50*	Bill Clinton Al Gore, Jr.	George Bush Dan Quayle	370	168	43,728,275 43.2%	38,167,416 37.7%

Sources: Harold W. Stanley and Richard G. Niemi, *Vital Statistics on American Politics,* 2d ed. (Washington, D.C.: CQ Press, 1990), 102–106; *Guide to U.S. Elections,* 2d ed. (Washington, D.C.: Congressional Quarterly, 1985), 329–366; Federal Election Commission; *Congressional Quarterly Weekly Report,* Nov. 7, 1992, 3549, 3552.

Notes: Dem.—Democratic; Rep.—Republican. a. 1956: Walter B. Jones, Democrat, received 1 electoral vote. b. 1960: Harry Flood Byrd, Democrat, received 15 electoral votes. c. 1968: George C. Wallace, American Independent Party, received 46 electoral votes. d. 1972: John Hospers, Libertarian Party, received 1 electoral vote. e. 1976: Ronald Reagan, Republican, received 1 electoral vote. f. 1988: Lloyd Bentsen, the Democratic vice-presidential nominee, received 1 electoral vote for president. * Fifty states plus District of Columbia.

Table A-2 Political Party Affiliations in Congress and the Presidency, 1951–1993

Year	Congress	House			Senate			President
		Majority party	Principal minority party	Other (except vacancies)	Majority party	Principal minority party	Other (except vacancies)	
1993–1995	103rd	D-258	R-176	1	D-57	R-43	—	(D) Clinton
1991–1993	102nd	D-267	R-167	1	D-56	R-44	—	R (Bush)
1989–1991	101st	D-259	R-174	—	D-55	R-45	—	R (Bush)
1987–1989	100th	D-258	R-177	—	D-55	R-45	—	R (Reagan)
1985–1987	99th	D-252	R-182	—	R-53	D-47	—	R (Reagan)
1983–1985	98th	D-268	R-166	—	R-55	D-45	—	R (Reagan)
1981–1983	97th	D-243	R-192	—	R-53	D-46	1	R (Reagan)
1979–1981	96th	D-276	R-157	—	D-58	R-41	1	D (Carter)
1977–1979	95th	D-292	R-143	—	D-61	R-38	1	D (Carter)
1975–1977	94th	D-291	R-144	—	D-60	R-37	2	R (Ford)
1973–1975	93rd	D-239	R-192	1	D-56	R-42	2	R (Nixon-Ford)
1971–1973	92nd	D-254	R-180	—	D-54	R-44	2	R (Nixon)
1969–1971	91st	D-243	R-192	—	D-57	R-43	—	R (Nixon)
1967–1969	90th	D-247	R-187	—	D-64	R-36	—	D (L. Johnson)
1965–1967	89th	D-295	R-140	—	D-68	R-32	—	D (L. Johnson)
1963–1965	88th	D-258	R-177	—	D-67	R-33	—	D (L. Johnson)
								D (Kennedy)
1961–1963	87th	D-263	R-174	—	D-65	R-35	—	D (Kennedy)
1959–1961	86th	D-283	R-153	—	D-64	R-34	—	R (Eisenhower)
1957–1959	85th	D-233	R-200	—	D-49	R-47	—	R (Eisenhower)
1955–1957	84th	D-232	R-203	—	D-48	R-47	1	R (Eisenhower)
1953–1955	83rd	R-221	D-211	1	R-48	D-47	1	R (Eisenhower)
1951–1953	82nd	D-234	R-199	1	D-49	R-47	—	D (Truman)

Sources: U.S. Bureau of the Census, *Historical Statistics of the United States, Colonial Times to 1970* (Washington, D.C.: Government Printing Office), 1975; *Congressional Quarterly Weekly Report,* various issues.

Note: Figures are for the first session of each Congress. D—Democratic; R—Republican.

Table A-3 U.S. Presidents and Vice Presidents

President and political party	Born	Died	President's term of service	Vice president	Vice president's term of service
George Washington (F)	1732	1799	April 30, 1789–March 4, 1793	John Adams	April 30, 1789–March 4, 1793
George Washington (F)			March 4, 1793–March 4, 1797	John Adams	March 4, 1793–March 4, 1797
John Adams (F)	1735	1826	March 4, 1797–March 4, 1801	Thomas Jefferson	March 4, 1797–March 4, 1801
Thomas Jefferson (DR)	1743	1826	March 4, 1801–March 4, 1805	Aaron Burr	March 4, 1801–March 4, 1805
Thomas Jefferson (DR)			March 4, 1805–March 4, 1809	George Clinton	March 4, 1805–March 4, 1809
James Madison (DR)	1751	1836	March 4, 1809–March 4, 1813	George Clinton[a]	March 4, 1809–April 12, 1812
James Madison (DR)			March 4, 1813–March 4, 1817	Elbridge Gerry[a]	March 4, 1813–Nov. 23, 1814
James Monroe (DR)	1758	1831	March 4, 1817–March 4, 1821	Daniel D. Tompkins	March 4, 1817–March 4, 1821
James Monroe (DR)			March 4, 1821–March 4, 1825	Daniel D. Tompkins	March 4, 1821–March 4, 1825
John Q. Adams (DR)	1767	1848	March 4, 1825–March 4, 1829	John C. Calhoun	March 4, 1825–March 4, 1829
Andrew Jackson (DR)	1767	1845	March 4, 1829–March 4, 1833	John C. Calhoun[b]	March 4, 1829–Dec. 28, 1832
Andrew Jackson (D)			March 4, 1833–March 4, 1837	Martin Van Buren	March 4, 1833–March 4, 1837
Martin Van Buren (D)	1782	1862	March 4, 1837–March 4, 1841	Richard M. Johnson	March 4, 1837–March 4, 1841
W. H. Harrison[a] (W)	1773	1841	March 4, 1841–April 4, 1841	John Tyler[c]	March 4, 1841–April 6, 1841
John Tyler (W)	1790	1862	April 6, 1841–March 4, 1845		
James K. Polk (D)	1795	1849	March 4, 1845–March 4, 1849	George M. Dallas	March 4, 1845–March 4, 1849
Zachary Taylor[a] (W)	1784	1850	March 4, 1849–July 9, 1850	Millard Fillmore[c]	March 4, 1849–July 10, 1850
Millard Fillmore (W)	1800	1874	July 10, 1850–March 4, 1853		
Franklin Pierce (D)	1804	1869	March 4, 1853–March 4, 1857	William R. King[a]	March 24, 1853–April 18, 1853
James Buchanan (D)	1791	1868	March 4, 1857–March 4, 1861	John C. Breckinridge	March 4, 1857–March 4, 1861
Abraham Lincoln (R)	1809	1865	March 4, 1861–March 4, 1865	Hannibal Hamlin	March 4, 1861–March 4, 1865
Abraham Lincoln[a] (R)			March 4, 1865–April 15, 1865	Andrew Johnson[c]	March 4, 1865–April 15, 1865
Andrew Johnson (R)	1808	1875	April 15, 1865–March 4, 1869		
Ulysses S. Grant (R)	1822	1885	March 4, 1869–March 4, 1873	Schuyler Colfax	March 4, 1869–March 4, 1873
Ulysses S. Grant (R)			March 4, 1873–March 4, 1877	Henry Wilson[a]	March 4, 1873–Nov. 22, 1875
Rutherford B. Hayes (R)	1822	1893	March 4, 1877–March 4, 1881	William A. Wheeler	March 4, 1877–March 4, 1881
James A. Garfield[a] (R)	1831	1881	March 4, 1881–Sept. 19, 1881	Chester A. Arthur[c]	March 4, 1881–Sept. 20, 1881
Chester A. Arthur (R)	1830	1886	Sept. 20, 1881–March 4, 1885		
Grover Cleveland (D)	1837	1908	March 4, 1885–March 4, 1889	Thomas A. Hendricks[a]	March 4, 1885–Nov. 25, 1885
Benjamin Harrison (R)	1833	1901	March 4, 1889–March 4, 1893	Levi P. Morton	March 4, 1889–March 4, 1893
Grover Cleveland (D)	1837	1908	March 4, 1893–March 4, 1897	Adlai E. Stevenson	March 4, 1893–March 4, 1897
William McKinley (R)	1843	1901	March 4, 1897–March 4, 1901	Garret A. Hobart[a]	March 4, 1897–Nov. 21, 1899
William McKinley[a] (R)			March 4, 1901–Sept. 14, 1901	Theodore Roosevelt[c]	March 4, 1901–Sept. 14, 1901
Theodore Roosevelt (R)	1858	1919	Sept. 14, 1901–March 4, 1905		
Theodore Roosevelt (R)			March 4, 1905–March 4, 1909	Charles W. Fairbanks	March 4, 1905–March 4, 1909
William H. Taft (R)	1857	1930	March 4, 1909–March 4, 1913	James S. Sherman[a]	March 4, 1909–Oct. 30, 1912
Woodrow Wilson (D)	1856	1924	March 4, 1913–March 4, 1917	Thomas R. Marshall	March 4, 1913–March 4, 1917
Woodrow Wilson (D)			March 4, 1917–March 4, 1921	Thomas R. Marshall	March 4, 1917–March 4, 1921
Warren G. Harding[a] (R)	1865	1923	March 4, 1921–Aug. 2, 1923	Calvin Coolidge[c]	March 4, 1921–Aug. 3, 1923
Calvin Coolidge (R)	1872	1933	Aug. 3, 1923–March 4, 1925		
Calvin Coolidge (R)			March 4, 1925–March 4, 1929	Charles G. Dawes	March 4, 1925–March 4, 1929
Herbert Hoover (R)	1874	1964	March 4, 1929–March 4, 1933	Charles Curtis	March 4, 1929–March 4, 1933
Franklin D. Roosevelt (D)	1882	1945	March 4, 1933–Jan. 20, 1937	John N. Garner	March 4, 1933–Jan. 20, 1937
Franklin D. Roosevelt (D)			Jan. 20, 1937–Jan. 20, 1941	John N. Garner	Jan. 20, 1937–Jan. 20, 1941
Franklin D. Roosevelt (D)			Jan. 20, 1941–Jan. 20, 1945	Henry A. Wallace	Jan. 20, 1941–Jan. 20, 1945
Franklin D. Roosevelt[a] (D)			Jan. 20, 1945–April 12, 1945	Harry S. Truman[c]	Jan. 20, 1945–April 12, 1945
Harry S. Truman (D)	1884	1972	April 12, 1945–Jan. 20, 1949		
Harry S. Truman (D)			Jan. 20, 1949–Jan. 20, 1953	Alben W. Barkley	Jan. 20, 1949–Jan. 20, 1953
Dwight D. Eisenhower (R)	1890	1969	Jan. 20, 1953–Jan. 20, 1957	Richard Nixon	Jan. 20, 1953–Jan. 20, 1957
Dwight D. Eisenhower (R)			Jan. 20, 1957–Jan. 20, 1961	Richard Nixon	Jan. 20, 1957–Jan. 20, 1961

Table A-3 U.S. Presidents and Vice Presidents *(Continued)*

President and political party	Born	Died	President's term of service	Vice president	Vice president's term of service
John F. Kennedy [a] (D)	1917	1963	Jan. 20, 1961–Nov. 22, 1963	Lyndon B. Johnson[c]	Jan. 20, 1961–Nov. 22, 1963
Lyndon B. Johnson (D)	1908	1973	Nov. 22, 1963–Jan. 20, 1965		
Lyndon B. Johnson (D)			Jan. 20, 1965–Jan. 20, 1969	Hubert H. Humphrey	Jan. 20, 1965–Jan. 20, 1969
Richard Nixon (R)	1913	1994	Jan. 20, 1969–Jan. 20, 1973	Spiro T. Agnew	Jan. 20, 1969–Jan. 20, 1973
Richard Nixon[b] (R)			Jan. 20, 1973–Aug. 9, 1974	Spiro T. Agnew[b]	Jan. 20, 1973–Oct. 10, 1973
				Gerald R. Ford[c]	Dec. 6, 1973–Aug. 9, 1974
Gerald R. Ford (R)	1913		Aug. 9, 1974–Jan. 20, 1977	Nelson A. Rockefeller	Dec. 19, 1974–Jan. 20, 1977
Jimmy Carter (D)	1924		Jan. 20, 1977–Jan. 20, 1981	Walter F. Mondale	Jan. 20, 1977–Jan. 20, 1981
Ronald Reagan (R)	1911		Jan. 20, 1981–Jan. 20, 1985	George Bush	Jan. 20, 1981–Jan. 20, 1985
Ronald Reagan (R)			Jan. 20, 1985–Jan. 20, 1989	George Bush	Jan. 20, 1985–Jan. 20, 1989
George Bush (R)	1924		Jan. 20, 1989–Jan. 20, 1993	Dan Quayle	Jan. 20, 1989–Jan. 20, 1993
Bill Clinton (D)	1946		Jan. 20, 1993–	Al Gore, Jr.	Jan. 20, 1993–

Sources: *Presidential Elections Since 1789*, 4th ed. (Washington, D.C.: Congressional Quarterly, 1987), 4.; Daniel C. Diller, "Biographies of the Vice Presidents," in *Guide to the Presidency*, ed. Michael Nelson (Washington, D.C.: Congressional Quarterly, 1989), 1319–1346.

Note: D—Democrat; DR—Democratic-Republican; F—Federalist; R—Republican; W—Whig. a. Died in office. b. Resigned. c. Succeeded to the presidency.

Table A-4 Chief Justices of the United States

Chief Justice	Nominated by President	Date sworn in as Chief Justice	End of term as Chief Justice
John Jay	George Washington	October 19, 1789	June 29, 1795
John Rutledge	George Washington	August 12, 1795	December 15, 1795
Oliver Ellsworth	George Washington	March 8, 1796	December 15, 1800
John Marshall	John Adams	February 4, 1801	July 6, 1835
Roger Brooke Taney	Andrew Jackson	March 28, 1836	October 12, 1864
Salmon Portland Chase	Abraham Lincoln	December 15, 1864	May 7, 1873
Morrison Remick Waite	Ulysses S. Grant	March 4, 1874	March 23, 1888
Melville Weston Fuller	Grover Cleveland	October 8, 1888	July 4, 1910
Edward Douglass White	William Howard Taft	December 19, 1910	May 19, 1921
William Howard Taft	Warren G. Harding	July 11, 1921	February 3, 1930
Charles Evans Hughes	Herbert Hoover	February 24, 1930	July 1, 1941
Harlan Fiske Stone	Franklin D. Roosevelt	July 3, 1941	April 22, 1946
Frederick Moore Vinson	Harry S. Truman	June 24, 1946	September 8, 1953
Earl Warren	Dwight D. Eisenhower	October 5, 1953	June 23, 1969
Warren Earl Burger	Richard Nixon	June 23, 1969	September 26, 1986
William Hubbs Rehnquist	Ronald Reagan	September 26, 1986	

Glossary

access The ability of individuals and groups to gain a hearing for their positions on policy issues before officeholders. *(Ch. 8)*

affirmative action The term applied to programs of hiring and education designed to remedy past acts of discrimination on the basis of race or gender. Such programs may call for either voluntary or mandatory actions to provide equality of opportunity or equality of outcomes. *(Ch. 4)*

amicus curiae brief A "friend of the court" brief submitted by government officials or private groups who are not parties to a lawsuit. *(Ch. 13)*

Antifederalists Opponents of a strong national government and adoption of the U.S. Constitution. *(Ch. 2)*

appellate courts Courts that hear cases on appeal from lower courts. *(Ch. 13)*

Articles of Confederation The first constitution of the United States which took effect in 1781. It created a weak national government and was replaced in 1789 by the Constitution of the United States. *(Ch. 2)*

automatic (super) delegate A delegate to the Democratic national convention who gains delegate status by virtue of holding a party or public office—for example, members of Congress, governors, state party chairs and vice chairs, and members of the Democratic National Committee. *(Ch. 6)*

"bad tendency" test A test no longer used by the Supreme Court to determine the constitutionality of restrictions on speech. It permitted restrictions if the speech was deemed to have a tendency to lead to illegal acts. *(Ch. 4)*

bicameral legislature A legislature that consists of two houses (such as the U.S. Congress); a unicameral legislature has only one house (such as the Continental Congress under the Articles of Confederation). *(Ch. 2)*

bill of attainder A legislative act declaring an individual guilty of a crime and imposing punishment without a judicial trial. Bills of attainder are banned by Article I of the Constitution. *(Ch. 2)*

Bill of Rights The first ten amendments to the Constitution. Ratified in 1791, these amendments limit governmental power and protect the basic rights and liberties of individuals. *(Ch. 2)*

blanket primary A primary election procedure used in Washington State that permits a voter to vote in the primaries of more than one party but for only one candidate per office. *(Ch. 6)*

block grant Grant-in-aid awarded by the federal government to a state for a general area of governmental activity such as crime control, job training, or community development (also see *categorical grant*). *(Ch. 3)*

bureaucracy The organizations that implement government policies. *(Ch. 12)*

bureaucrat An individual who works within the bureaucracy. *(Ch. 12)*

candidate image A voter's perception of the personal attributes of a candidate. *(Ch. 7)*

casework Assistance given by members of Congress to constituents experiencing problems dealing with the federal bureaucracy. *(Ch. 10)*

categorical grant A federal grant-in-aid awarded to a state and certain localities for a specific purpose, normally requiring matching funds and adherence to federal guidelines in spending the funds (also see *block grant*). *(Ch. 3)*

caucus A meeting of political party members to select delegates to national nominating conventions. A meeting of the Democratic membership of the House of Representatives is also called a caucus. *(Chs. 6, 10)*

checks and balances Constitutional mechanisms that authorize each branch of government to share powers with the other branches and thereby check their activities. For example, the president may veto legislation passed by Congress, the Senate must confirm major executive appointments, and the courts may declare acts of Congress unconstitutional. *(Ch. 2)*

civil (law) cases Court cases that involve disputes among individuals, groups, or governments. *(Ch. 13)*

civil liberties Constitutional and legal protections from governmental interference. Civil liberties include the basic freedoms of speech, the press, assembly, and religion, as well as guarantees of procedural due process and fairness, such as protection from unreasonable searches and seizures. *(Ch. 4)*

civil rights The government's responsibilities and policies to protect people from arbitrary and discriminatory acts by the government and individuals—for example, removing barriers to equality created by discrimination based on race, gender, religion, ethnicity, and disability. *(Ch. 4)*

"clear and present danger" test A judicial test devised by the Supreme Court to determine whether the government may restrict speech. To be restricted under this test, speech must constitute a "clear and present danger" of bringing about substantive evils which the government has a right to prevent. *(Ch. 4)*

closed primary A type of primary election that restricts voter participation to those who are registered political party members or who publicly declare in which party's primary they wish to vote. *(Ch. 6)*

cloture The process by which a filibuster can be ended in the Senate, other than by unanimous consent. The invocation of cloture in the Senate requires the consent of three-fifths of the Senate membership. *(Ch. 10)*

Commerce and Slave Trade Compromise An agreement reached at the Constitutional Convention of 1787 that granted the national government the power to regulate foreign and interstate commerce, prohibited taxes on U.S. exports, specified that all treaties were to be ratified by a two-thirds vote of the Senate, and prohibited Congress from banning the importation of slaves before 1808. *(Ch. 2)*

concurrent powers Powers that may be exercised by both the federal government and the state governments—for example, levying taxes, borrowing money, and spending for the general welfare. *(Ch. 3)*

concurring opinion An opinion of a Supreme Court justice who agrees with the decision of a majority of the justices but disagrees with their reasons for the decision. *(Ch. 13)*

confederation A league of independent states in which the central government may not make laws applicable to individuals without the approval of the member states. *(Ch. 2)*

conference committee A congressional committee composed of representatives of the House and Senate that reconciles differences between the two houses on provisions of a bill passed by both chambers. *(Ch. 10)*

conservatism A political philosophy favoring limited government involvement in the economy, a strong military, and government action to protect traditional moral values. *(Ch. 5)*

constitutional courts Courts created by Congress by virtue of the powers granted to it in Article III of the Constitution. *(Ch. 13)*

constitutional government A government based on the principle of limited governmental power as specified in a constitution drawn up by the people. *(Ch. 2)*

cooperative federalism A sharing of responsibilities among the federal government and the states and localities. The relationship is encouraged and typified by federal grants-in-aid to states and localities. *(Ch. 3)*

coordinated expenditures Expenditures made by party organizations in support of their candidates for federal office. The Federal Election Campaign Act strictly limits the amount of coordinated expenditures that party organizations can make in any given election cycle. *(Ch. 10)*

criminal (law) cases Court cases that involve violations of the law punishable by fines or imprisonment. *(Ch. 13)*

crossover voting Voting in the primary election of the party with which one does not identify or belong. This occurs in states that use the open primary procedure (see *open primary*). *(Ch. 6)*

dealignment The tendency of voters not to identify with either of the major parties and to view themselves as independents. *(Ch. 6)*

Declaration of Independence The document adopted by the Second Continental Congress on July 4, 1776, declaring the independence of the American colonies from Great Britain and justifying the Revolution. It draws heavily on the natural rights philosophy of John Locke (see *natural rights*). *(Ch. 2)*

de facto segregation Racial segregation that "in fact" exists but is not required by law. *(Ch. 4)*

defendant The party being sued or accused in a court of law. *(Ch. 13)*

de jure segregation Racial segregation that is required by law. *(Ch. 4)*

delegated powers Powers granted to the national government under the Constitution, as enumerated in Articles I, II, and III. *(Ch. 3)*

democracy A system of government in which citizens have a relatively high degree of control over their leaders. *(Ch. 1)*

direct democracy A system of government in which citizens participate directly in making decisions. *(Ch. 1)*

direct primary A popular election in which voters select the nominees who will run for public office in the general election. *(Ch. 6)*

dissenting opinion An opinion of a Supreme Court

justice stating the reasons for disagreeing with the decision of a majority of the justices in a case. *(Ch. 13)*

divine right of kings   A theory supporting the right of a king or queen to rule with absolute power because he or she was believed to have been appointed to rule by a supreme being. *(Ch. 1)*

dual federalism   A federal system of government in which the functions of the national and regional *(state)* governments are separate and distinct. *(Ch. 3)*

due process clause   A Fourteenth Amendment provision protecting people's basic liberties and rights from infringement (denials of life, liberty, or property without due process of law) by the states. *(Ch. 4)*

electoral college   The assembly that formally elects the president and vice president of the United States. Each state's number of electoral votes equals its representation in Congress and the District of Columbia has three electoral votes. An absolute majority of the total electoral votes is required to elect a president and vice president. *(Ch. 2)*

entitlements   Benefits provided by government programs to individuals or organizations based on eligibility criteria defined by law (for example, Social Security and civil service retirement benefits). *(Ch. 1)*

equal protection clause   A Fourteenth Amendment provision prohibiting the states from denying people the equal protection of the laws—that is, discriminating against individuals in an arbitrary manner such as on the basis of race. *(Ch. 1)*

equal time rule   A federal rule requiring a radio or television station that gives or sells time to one candidate for a specific office to make the same opportunity available to other candidates for the same office. *(Ch. 9)*

establishment of religion clause   The First Amendment clause stating that "Congress shall make no law respecting an establishment of religion." *(Ch. 4)*

exclusionary rule   The judicial doctrine based on the Fourth Amendment's protection against illegal searches and seizures, which provides that evidence obtained illegally may not be used in a trial. *(Ch. 4)*

executive agreement   An agreement between the president, on behalf of the United States, and another country that does not require the advice and consent of the Senate. *(Ch. 11)*

ex post facto law   A retroactive criminal law making actions that were not criminal at the time they were committed criminal offenses after the fact. Ex post facto laws are banned by Article I of the Constitution. *(Ch. 2)*

expressive (purposive) incentives   Incentives to participate in or join an organization in the form of such intangible rewards as working for a just cause. *(Ch. 8)*

extradition   The responsibility of the states to apprehend fugitives who flee across state lines and return them to the state having jurisdiction over the crime. *(Ch. 3)*

fairness doctrine   A Federal Communications Commission policy, abandoned in 1987, requiring radio and television stations to give reasonable time for opposing views on controversial issues discussed on the air. *(Ch. 9)*

federalism (federal system)   A constitutional division of the powers of government between the national government and the regional (state) governments in which both exercise significant powers. *(Chs. 2, 3)*

Federalists   Advocates of a strong national government and supporters of adoption of the U.S. Constitution. *(Ch. 2)*

federal matching funds   Federal money given to candidates seeking presidential nominations. To qualify for these funds, candidates must meet the requirements of the Federal Election Campaign Act. *(Ch. 6)*

federal supremacy clause   Article VI of the Constitution providing that the Constitution and all federal laws and treaties shall be the "supreme Law of the Land." Therefore, all federal laws take precedence over state and local laws. *(Ch. 2)*

filibuster   A congressional delaying tactic used by a minority to prevent a vote on a bill that probably would pass if voted on directly. The most common method of delay is to take advantage of the Senate's rule permitting unlimited debate. *(Ch. 10)*

fiscal year   The twelve-month period, October 1–September 30, during which the financial operations of the government are carried out. The fiscal year carries the date of the calendar year in which it ends. *(Ch. 10)*

franchise   The right to vote (also see *suffrage*). *(Ch. 6)*

free exercise of religion clause   The First Amendment clause prohibiting Congress from interfering with the free exercise of religion. *(Ch. 4)*

free-rider problem   A problem arising when the benefits of interest group activity (for example, cleaner air, Social Security benefits) are available to both group members and nonmembers—that is, nonmembers can receive the benefits of group efforts without paying the costs of membership. *(Ch. 8)*

front loading   The scheduling of a large number of presidential primaries and state party caucuses during February and March of presidential election years. As a result, the bulk of the national convention delegates are chosen early in the delegate selection process. *(Ch. 6)*

full faith and credit clause   A constitutional provision requiring the states to honor the civil acts, judgments, and public documents of every other state. *(Ch. 3)*

gerrymandering   The drawing of legislative district lines in a manner that gives advantage to one political party over another. *(Ch. 4)*

government   The institution and processes through which values are allocated and a society is ruled. *(Ch. 1)*

grants-in-aid   Grants of funds from the federal government to states and local units of government to carry out federal policies. States also make grants-in-aid to localities. *(Ch. 3)*

Great Compromise   (also known as the Connecticut Compromise) A proposal submitted by the Connecticut representatives to the Constitutional Convention of 1787 that broke the deadlock between the large and small states over representation in Congress. It provided for a popularly elected House of Representatives with representation based on a state's population and a Senate composed of two senators from each state elected by their respective state legislatures. *(Ch. 2)*

home style   The manner in which a member of Congress presents himself or herself to constituents. *(Ch. 10)*

impeachment   The power of Congress to remove the president, vice president, federal judges, and other federal officers from office. *(Ch. 11)*

implied powers   Powers that Congress may exercise in carrying out its delegated or enumerated powers listed in Article I of the Constitution (derived from the necessary and proper—elastic—clause). The doctrine of implied powers was established in the 1819 case of *McCulloch v. Maryland.* *(Ch. 3)*

incumbency   Holding public office. Incumbency normally carries with it an electoral advantage. *(Ch. 6)*

independent   An individual who does not identify with a political party. *(Ch. 7)*

inherent powers   Powers that the federal government may exercise in foreign affairs, which do not derive from a specific grant of authority in the Constitution. These are the powers that the United States has by virtue of its status as a national government. *(Ch. 3)*

interest group   An organized body of individuals who share some goals and try to influence public policy to meet those goals. *(Ch. 8)*

iron triangle   (also known as a subgovernment) A close-knit alliance of interest groups, congressional committee members, and executive agency personnel capable of exerting a powerful influence over an aspect of public policy. *(Ch. 8)*

issue network   A loose, flexible collection of groups, individuals, and public officials concerned about an aspect of public policy. *(Ch. 8)*

issue publics   Those members of the public affected by and aware of a particular issue. *(Ch. 5)*

joint committee   A congressional committee composed of a specified number of members from both the House and Senate that normally has investigative, research, or housekeeping functions. *(Ch. 10)*

judicial activism   A term used to describe judicial actions that expand the policy-making role of the courts by striking down or modifying the policies of the executive and legislative branches. *(Ch. 13)*

judicial restraint   The belief and practice that judges should restrict the policy-making role of the courts and show reluctance to set aside the judgments of the executive and legislative branches. *(Ch. 13)*

judicial review   A doctrine that permits the federal courts to declare unconstitutional, and thus null and void, acts of the Congress, the executive, and the states. The precedent for judicial review was established in the 1803 case of *Marbury v. Madison.* *(Ch. 2)*

jurisdiction   The authority of a court to try a case. *(Ch. 13)*

legislative courts   Courts created by Congress under the legislative authority granted to it by Article I of the Constitution. *(Ch. 13)*

libel   The creation and dissemination of written material that falsely and maliciously damages another person's reputation. *(Ch. 4)*

liberalism   Since the 1930s, a political philosophy favoring active government involvement in regulating the economy, providing social services, and assisting minorities and the disadvantaged. *(Ch. 5)*

limited government   The constitutional principle that governmental power is limited through restrictions imposed by the Constitution. *(Ch. 2)*

lobbying   Activities designed to influence the policy decisions of public officials. *(Ch. 8)*

lobbyist   An individual who seeks to influence legislative or administrative decision making. *(Ch. 8)*

majority leader   The chief strategist and floor spokesperson for the majority party in the House and in the Senate, elected by his or her party colleagues in the chamber. *(Ch. 10)*

majority opinion   The decision of a majority of Supreme Court justices, which states the reasons they reached the decision they did in a particular case. *(Ch. 13)*

material incentives   Incentives to participate in or join an organization in the form of tangible economic benefits. *(Ch. 8)*

minority leader   The chief strategist and floor spokesperson for the minority party in the House and in the Senate, elected by his or her party colleagues in the chamber. *(Ch. 11)*

muckraking Investigative journalism that, early in the twentieth century, revealed wrongdoing in government and industry. (*Ch. 9*)

narrowcasting Technological advances that enable radio and cable television outlets to target specific audiences—for example, sports fans, religious fundamentalists, rock music enthusiasts, or public affairs followers. By contrast, major television broadcasts are designed to reach a diverse audience. (*Ch. 9*)

national (presidential) nominating convention A political party convention composed of delegates from the states, the District of Columbia, and the territories that nominates candidates for president and vice president, drafts a party platform, and makes rules to govern the party. (*Ch. 6*)

natural rights A belief that individuals are naturally endowed with basic human rights. The Declaration of Independence states that these natural rights include the rights to "Life, Liberty and the pursuit of Happiness." (*Ch. 2*)

necessary and proper (elastic) clause Article I, section 8, of the Constitution which provides that Congress shall have the power to make all laws "necessary and proper" for carrying out its delegated or enumerated powers. (*Ch. 3*)

New Deal The programs and policies of the Franklin Roosevelt administration designed to combat the depression of the 1930s. New Deal programs vastly expanded the regulatory and social service role of the federal government. (*Ch. 3*)

New Deal Democratic coalition The electoral coalition forged by Franklin Roosevelt in the 1930s that provided the basis for the Democratic party's electoral successes. It was composed of white southerners, Catholics, Jews, blue-collar workers, union members, and blacks. (*Ch. 6*)

New Jersey Plan A proposal submitted to the Constitutional Convention of 1787 by William Paterson of New Jersey. It provided for a unicameral national legislature in which each state would have equal representation, a plural executive appointed by Congress, and a judiciary appointed by the executive. (*Ch. 2*)

news media The diverse array of outlets from which the public derives news, including national and local newspapers, weekly and monthly news magazines, television networks and stations, and radio stations. (*Ch. 9*)

nomination The official designation of an individual as a candidate for public office—for example, the selection of a Democratic or Republican candidate for president or senator. (*Ch. 6*)

open primary A type of primary election in which voters decide in the secrecy of the polling booth in which party's primary they will vote. Voters are permitted to vote in only one party's primary. (*Ch. 6*)

original jurisdiction The authority of a court to try a case in the first instance, in contrast to hearing a case on appeal. (*Ch. 13*)

oversight (congressional) Congressional surveillance and supervision of how executive agencies implement laws passed by Congress. (*Ch. 10*)

PAC See *political action committee.*

pack journalism The tendency of journalists to watch the way high-status media outlets such as the *New York Times* present and interpret a news event and then to adjust their own presentations accordingly. (*Ch. 9*)

parliamentary system A system of government in which governmental authority is vested in the legislature, which chooses from among its members a cabinet headed by a prime minister or premier. The cabinet stays in office as long as it commands a majority in the legislature. (*Ch. 6*)

party identification A feeling of attachment or loyalty to a political party. (*Ch. 5*)

party system The form and character of political parties operating within a particular governmental order. (*Ch. 6*)

plaintiff The person or party bringing suit in a court of law. (*Ch. 13*)

pocket veto An act in which the president withholds approval of a bill after Congress has adjourned. It is a method of killing a bill without formally vetoing it. (*Ch. 11*)

political action committee An organization authorized by law to collect money and make campaign contributions to candidates. (*Ch. 8*)

political culture The fundamental beliefs and assumptions of a people about how government and politics should operate. (*Ch. 1*)

political efficacy A belief that one can be effective and have an impact on public affairs. (*Ch. 5*)

political ideology An organized, coherent set of attitudes about government and public policy. (*Ch. 5*)

political party Any group, however loosely organized, that seeks to elect government officials under a given label. (*Ch. 6*)

political socialization The process through which people acquire political attitudes. (*Ch. 5*)

politics The process through which a society manages and resolves conflicts. Alternative perspectives include the acquisition, retention, and exercise of power, and the process of deciding "who gets what, when, how." (*Ch. 1*)

popular sovereignty The principle that government derives its power from the people. The Preamble to the Constitution, for example, states: "We the People of the United States . . . do ordain and establish this Constitution for the United States of America." (*Ch. 2*)

pork-barrel legislation Bills authorizing expenditures in the constituencies of members of Congress for projects that may not be needed but that enhance the reelection prospects of the members. *(Ch. 12)*

preferred position doctrine   A doctrine used by the Supreme Court to determine the constitutionality of restrictions on speech. It holds that because free expression is essential for democracy, any restriction is unconstitutional unless the government can show that the speech constitutes an immediate and serious threat to society. *(Ch. 4)*

presidential coattails   The ability of a presidential candidate to attract votes to other candidates of his or her party. *(Ch. 10)*

presidential primary   An election held within a state to select delegates to the presidential nominating conventions. *(Ch. 6)*

presidential system   A system of government in which the president, who is head of the executive branch, is elected separately from the members of the national legislature for a fixed term of office. The president is not a member of the national legislature. *(Ch. 1)*

president pro tempore   The chief officer of the Senate in the absence of the vice president, elected by the Senate. Recent practice has been to choose the senator of the majority party who has the longest period of continual service. *(Ch. 10)*

prior restraint   Censoring written material or broadcasts before their publication or presentation. *(Ch. 4)*

privileges and immunities clause   A provision in Article IV, section 2, of the Constitution designed to prevent states from discriminating against out-of-state residents. It provides that "[t]he Citizens of each State shall be entitled to all Privileges and Immunities of Citizens in the several States." *(Ch. 3)*

probability sampling   A procedure for selecting a sample of respondents for public opinion surveys in which every individual in the population being surveyed has the same chance of being chosen as everyone else. *(Ch. 5)*

procedural due process   Protection from arbitrary deprivation of life, liberty, or property. The Fifth and Fourteenth amendments prohibit the states from denying people life, liberty, or property without due process of law. *(Ch. 4)*

proportional representation   A system for electing legislators in which each party proposes a slate of candidates and legislative seats are awarded to the parties on the basis of their shares of the popular vote. *(Ch. 6)*

public agenda   Issues that command the attention of public officials. *(Ch. 9)*

public interest groups   A name given to interest groups that claim to advocate a broad public good rather than economic self-interest. *(Ch. 8)*

public opinion   People's attitudes about an issue or question. *(Ch. 5)*

realignment   A major change in the partisan identification of the voters. *(Ch. 6)*

reapportionment   The allocation of seats in the House of Representatives among the states on the basis of population after each decennial census. *(Ch. 10)*

redistricting   The redrawing of congressional district boundaries within the states to reflect shifts in population. *(Ch. 10)*

representative democracy   A system of government in which elected representatives of the people make decisions. *(Ch. 1)*

reserved powers   Powers not delegated to the national government by the Constitution and thus reserved or left to the states (the constitutional basis for the states' reserved powers is the Tenth Amendment). Although not specifically defined in the Constitution, reserved powers normally include states' police powers to protect the health, welfare, and morals of their citizens. *(Ch. 3)*

retrospective voting   Voting based on an evaluation of the performance of a political party, officeholder, or administration. *(Ch. 7)*

revenue sharing   The sharing of federal government tax revenues with the states and localities under which only minimal restrictions are imposed on the states and localities for the expenditure of such funds. Such a program was initiated in 1972 and discontinued in 1984 *(Ch. 8)*

rule making   The development of rules and regulations by the bureaucracy for the implementation of government policies. *(Ch. 12)*

runoff (second) primary   A nominating procedure used in some southern and border states when no candidate receives a majority of the votes in a primary election. A runoff or second primary is then held between the two highest vote-getters in the first primary to determine the nominee. *(Ch. 6)*

sampling error   The error caused in public opinion surveys by using a sample of a population to generalize about the attitudes or behavior of the entire population. *(Ch. 5)*

select committee   A congressional committee set up for a special purpose, and generally for a limited time, by a resolution of either the House or Senate. Most special committees are investigative, rather than legislative, in nature. *(Ch. 10)*

selective incorporation   The process through which the judiciary has incorporated almost all of the protections of the Bill of Rights into the due process clause of the Fourteenth Amendment. As a result, most rights guaranteed against infringement by the federal government are also protected from state infringement. *(Ch. 4)*

senatorial courtesy   A general practice of the Senate in which it only confirms judicial and executive branch nominations from a state approved by the senators of the president's party from that state. *(Ch. 13)*

seniority system The practice of designating as chair of a congressional committee the member of the majority party with the longest continual service on the committee. *(Ch. 10)*

separate but equal doctrine A Supreme Court-adopted doctrine in the 1896 case of *Plessy v. Ferguson* holding that government-enforced segregation of the races was constitutional as long as the facilities for blacks and whites were equal. *(Ch. 4)*

separation of powers The constitutional division of government powers among three branches of government: the legislature, the executive, and the judiciary. *(Ch. 2)*

sequestration A procedure initially specified in the Gramm-Rudman-Hollings law of 1985 requiring automatic budget cuts (funds would be sequestered) if Congress failed to meet specified reductions in the federal budget deficit. *(Ch. 10)*

single-member district A legislative district in which only one person is elected—for example, all members of the House of Representatives are elected from single-member districts. *(Ch. 6)*

social compact A theory regarding the origins of government in which people, through a contract or compact, create a government. The compact specifies the rights and obligations of the government and its citizens. *(Ch. 2)*

solicitor general The third-ranking official of the Department of Justice responsible for deciding which cases the government will seek to have reviewed by the Supreme Court, reviewing legal briefs led by the government, and presenting oral arguments for the government before the Court. *(Ch. 13)*

solidary incentives Incentives to participate in or join an organization in the form of such social rewards as companionship, status, and pleasure. *(Ch. 8)*

Speaker of the House The presiding officer of the House of Representatives, selected by the caucus of the party to which he or she belongs and formally elected by the entire House. *(Ch. 10)*

splinter parties Political parties that break away from one of the major political parties. *(Ch. 6)*

spoils system A pejorative term derived from the expression "to the victor belong the spoils" and used to describe the patronage system of making appointments to government jobs. *(Ch. 12)*

standing committee A congressional committee permanently authorized by the House and Senate. *(Ch. 10)*

stare decisis The judicial practice of following precedents of previous court decisions. *(Ch. 13)*

subcommittee government A term used to characterize the major role played by congressional subcommittees in the House of Representatives since a series of committee reforms was initiated in the 1970s. *(Ch. 10)*

suffrage The right to vote (also see *franchise*). *(Ch. 7)*

third party A political party composed of dissidents from the two major parties and independents. *(Ch. 6)*

Three-fifths Compromise A compromise reached between northern and southern factions at the Constitutional Convention of 1787 under which each slave would be counted as three-fifths of a person in apportioning congressional seats among the states. *(Ch. 2)*

ticket splitting When a voter casts his or her ballot for candidates of more than one party—for example, voting Republican for president and Democratic for senator. *(Ch. 6)*

trial courts Courts that hear or try cases in the first instance—that is, courts of original jurisdiction (see *original jurisdiction*). *(Ch. 13)*

turnout The percentage of the eligible electorate that actually goes to the polls and votes. *(Ch. 7)*

two-party competition Electoral competition between two major political parties, as between the Republicans and Democrats. *(Ch. 6)*

unanimous consent agreement A device used in the Senate to expedite business. An agreement may list the order in which bills will be considered and specify the length of time for debate on bills and contested amendments and when they will be voted on. *(Ch. 10)*

unitary government A government system in which all governmental authority is vested in a central government from which regional and local governments derive their powers. Examples are Great Britain and France, as well as the American states within their spheres of authority. *(Ch. 3)*

veto Disapproval by the president of a bill passed by Congress. When Congress is in session, the president must veto a bill within ten days, excluding Sundays, after its receipt; otherwise, it becomes law with or without the president's signature. *(Ch. 11)*

Virginia Plan A major proposal submitted by Virginia representatives to the Constitutional Convention of 1787 calling for a bicameral national legislature, with the lower house chosen by the voters and the upper house chosen by the lower house from among nominees submitted by the states. Representation in both houses was to be based on each state's population and wealth. *(Ch. 2)*

War Powers Resolution of 1973 A law that seeks to limit the president's ability to commit military forces abroad for unspecified time periods without the consent of Congress. Under this act the president must report to Congress within forty-eight hours of the commitment of forces, and Congress must decide within sixty days whether to approve or disapprove of the president's action. *(Ch. 11)*

whip   The assistant majority and minority leaders in both the House and the Senate, who are responsible for marshalling their party's members to support party strategy and legislation. *(Ch. 10)*

whistle-blower   A person who calls public or official attention to bureaucratic mismanagement, waste, or wrongdoing. *(Ch. 8)*

white primary   A technique used to disenfranchise African Americans in the South by banning them from voting in Democratic primaries. The white primary was declared unconstitutional in *Smith v. Allwright* in 1944. *(Ch. 4)*

winner-take-all (electoral) system   Method of electing candidates to public office in which there can be only one winner—for example, as in the presidential, House, and Senate elections. *(Ch. 6)*

writ of certiorari   An order issued by the Supreme Court, upon the approval of four justices, to bring up a case for review. *(Ch. 13)*

yellow journalism   A type of journalism practiced in the late nineteenth century and characterized by sensationalism, partisanship, and often distortion. *(Ch. 9)*

Index

Italicized page numbers refer to photographs.

Photo Credits

Chapter 1: 3 WETA/James D. Scherlis. 9 Reuters. 15 Library of Congress. 21 (clockwise from top right) Department of Housing and Urban Development, American Health Care Association, Jim Hubbard, Connecticut Yankee Atomic Power Company, R. Michael Jenkins.

Chapter 2: 31, 37, 40, 43 Library of Congress.

Chapter 3: 65 courtesy of the John F. Kennedy Center for the Performing Arts. 68, 70, 77 Library of Congress. 84, 86 R. Michael Jenkins.

Chapter 4: 97 collection of the Supreme Court of the United States. 99 (left) Bill Pierce, (right) R. Michael Jenkins. 100 (left) Tommy Giles, (right) *Washington Post*, Washingtoniana Division, D.C. Public Library. 105 R. Michael Jenkins. 109 (left) Thomas Ondrey, (right) Andy Starnes. 114 R. Michael Jenkins. 119 Flip Schulke, *Life Magazine* © 1964 Time Warner Inc. 123 Library of Congress. 125 NAACP. 131 U.S. Air Force. 133 R. Michael Jenkins.

Chapter 5: 141 Associated Press/Washingtoniana Division, D.C. Public Library. 145 Washington Post Writers Group. Reprinted with permission. 149 R. Michael Jenkins. 153 MTV. 171 R. Michael Jenkins.

Chapter 6: 181 R. Michael Jenkins. 186 Reuters. 192 Theodore Roosevelt Collection, Harvard College Library. 219 Reuters. 221, 225 R. Michael Jenkins.

Chapter 7: 231 Fred Sons. 234 Library of Congress. 243 (left) Smithsonian Institution, (right) courtesy of 1988 Bush/Quayle campaign. 245 (left) Cable News Network, (right) Bush Presidential Materials Project. 248 Reuters.

Chapter 8: 275 R. Michael Jenkins. 277 Jerry Orvedahl. 286 Washington Post. 288 Children's Defense Fund/Lynn Diederich. 292 Citizens for Congressional Reform. 295 (top) R. Michael Jenkins, (bottom) Library of Congress. 298 American Trucking Associations. 307 R. Michael Jenkins. 309 Department of Agriculture/Kachergis Book Design.

Chapter 9: 315 David Valdez/Bush Presidential Materials Project. 317 Reagan Presidential Library. 319 Library of Congress. 322 U.S. Information Agency in the National Archives. 325 C-SPAN. 337 USA Today. 351 Reuters. 352 Agence France-Presse. 355 Republican National Committee. 356 National Public Radio/Michael Geissinger.

Chapter 10: 377 Air Photographics, Inc. 382 R. Michael Jenkins. 383 (Schroeder, Johnson, Mikulski) R. Michael Jenkins, (Kassebaum) John Blodgett. 393 Barry Baron. 399 R. Michael Jenkins. 403 Library of Congress. 404 R. Michael Jenkins. 405 George Tames. 413, 418, 420, 421 R. Michael Jenkins.

Politics Along the Potomac: 362 R. Michael Jenkins. 363 (top and middle) Library of Congress, (bottom) John L. Moore. 364 Jerry Orvedahl. 365 (from top left) courtesy of Washington, D.C., Convention and Visitors Association, Jerry Orvedahl, courtesy of Washington, D.C., Convention and Visitors Association, Reuters. 366 Library of Congress. 367 (top) John L. Moore, (bottom) Jerry A. Orvedahl. 368 (cemetery) Jerry A. Orvedahl, (parking sign) R. Michael Jenkins, (boarded-up housing) R. Michael Jenkins. 369 (top) Carter Presidential Library, (bottom) R. Michael Jenkins. 371 (top) courtesy of the Austrian Embassy, (bottom) courtesy of the Canadian Embassy. 372 (top) Meet the Press, (bottom) Jerry Orvedahl. 373 R. Michael Jenkins. 374 Reuters. 375 R. Michael Jenkins. 376 AP/Wide World Photos.

Chapter 11: 429 National Park Service. 433 TOLES copyright 1993 The Buffalo News. Reprinted with permission of Universal Press Syndicate. All rights reserved. 438 National Portrait Gallery. 445 White House. 446, 453, 467, 469 Reuters. 474 Bush Presidential Materials Project. 477 Reuters.

Chapter 12: 483 (mail) U.S. Postal Service, (park ranger) National Park Service, (health care worker) R. Michael Jenkins. 486 Federal Trade Commission. 491, 493 Library of Congress. 505 Reuters. 512 (left and right) R. Michael Jenkins. 514 U.S. Forest Service. 516 Jim Berry. 517 R. Michael Jenkins. 520 Reuters. 523 AP/Wide World Photos.

Chapter 13: 531 (left and middle) Library of Congress, (right) collection of the Supreme Court of the United States. 540 R. Michael Jenkins. 544 collection of the Supreme Court of the United States. 545 Ken Heinen for the Supreme Court. 555 AP/Wide World Photos. 556, 559 R. Michael Jenkins. 561 Library of Congress.

Chapter 14: 573 courtesy of the Statue of Liberty National Monument. 578 Bob Thomas and Associates, Inc. 579 Greenpeace. 584, 588 R. Michael Jenkins. 590 AP/Wide World Photos. 594 Reuters. 595 Northrop Corporation. 599 R. Michael Jenkins.